The Illustrated Price Guide of
ANTIQUE BOTTLES

Left to right: *A medicine bottle, two milk glass barber bottles, snuff jar, drop bottle, pickle jar and fire extinguisher (#7156).*

Left to right: *An igloo ink (#6530), a medicine bottle (#1432), a bitters bottle (#383),
a soap bottle (#7267), a medicine bottle (#2146), and a square ink (#6535).*

The Illustrated Price Guide of
ANTIQUE BOTTLES

By Carlo and Dot Sellari
and the Editors of Country Beautiful

Country Beautiful
Waukesha, Wisconsin

Left to right: A medicine bottle, a spirits bottle (#5060), an ink bottle (#6425), two whiskey bottles (#5129 and #4506), and a miniature case bottle (#3630).

This cigar-shaped whiskey container (#4440), carried in the shirt pocket, insured a gentleman a nip or two without his wife's knowledge.

Publisher and Editorial Director: Michael P. Dineen; *Vice President, Editorial:* Robert L. Polley; *Vice President, Operations:* Donna Griesemer; *Managing Editor:* John M. Nuhn; *Senior Editors:* Kenneth L. Schmitz, James H. Robb, Stewart L. Udall; *Art Director:* Buford Nixon; *House Editors:* Jeanie Holzwart, D'Arlyn Marks; *Associate Editor:* Kay Kundinger; *Promotion and Sales Director:* Sally K. Repa; *Production Manager:* Fran Gregg.

Chapter introductions by Nancy Backes

Country Beautiful Corporation is a wholly owned subsidiary of Flick-Reedy Corporation: *President:* Frank Flick; *Vice President and General Manager:* Michael P. Dineen; *Treasurer and Secretary:* August Caamano.

PHOTO CREDITS: Anheuser-Busch, Inc., 35, 241; Bennington Museum Collections, Forward's Color Productions, Manchester, Vt., 9; Bon Ton Beverages, Inc., by Photographics, 185; Clement Photographers, 22, 29, 32, 215, 219, 220; The Coca-Cola Company, 183; The Corning Museum of Glass, Corning, NY, 12 (bottom), 25, 253, 410-1; Durkee Famous Foods, SCM Corporation, 303; The Henry Ford Museum, Dearborn, Mi., 301, 409; H. J. Heinz Company, 415; Jimmie Jamieson, 238; National Gallery of Art, Washington, D.C., 39, 212, 259, 261 (both), 343, 356-7, 377 (left), 389, 416; Old Sturbridge Village, 133, 325, 407, 413-4; Photographics, 341, all color except where otherwise noted; Smithsonian Institution, 197 (bottom), 391, 406, 412 (top); Ronald Rutherford Collection, Wheaton Museum of Glass, 59, 67, 141, 145, 327, 359, 375, 408 (bottom), 412 (bottom), 418 ; The Henry Francis du Pont Winterthur Museum, 197 (top), 377 (right), 408 (top).

Acknowledgements

The Authors and Editors wish to thank the following dealers, collectors and editors for their suggestions in compiling this price guide: Special thanks to Mary Lou Pferffer, Huntsville, Alabama, for her photos and suggestions on crocks; thanks to the editors of *Bottle News, Old Bottle Magazine, Bottle Trader, The Illustrated Guide to Collecting Bottles, Antique Trader, Western Collector* and *The Pontil,* and to these individuals: Bill Agee, Waco, Texas; Carl Benson, Orlando, Florida; Edgar and Louise Curtis, New Port Richey, Florida; Harbor Bottle Shop, Venice, Florida; Robert Hinely, Decatur, Georgia; Tom and Eileen Jevcak, Tampa, Florida; May Jones, Nara Visa, New Mexico; Mangrove Antique Bottle Shop, Miami, Florida; Bob and Beka Mebane, San Antonio, Texas; Neil Prietz, Tampa, Florida; Jo Pyne, Orlando, Florida; Don Robinson, Memphis, Tennessee; Watson and Mildred Shannon, Savannah, Georgia; Wayne and Beth Shulter, Brandon, Florida; Art and Jewel Umberger, Tyler, Texas; Roy Webb, Fairhope, Alabama; Carl and Bess Withrow, St. Petersburg, Florida; B. W. Yarbrough, Miami, Florida, and many more who have assisted the authors at shows.

CONTENTS

Pricing Guidelines

Most bottle collectors do not have any idea as to the value of their finds. It is with this in mind that this price guide has been compiled. All bottle prices in this price guide have been derived from trade papers, collectors' shows, auctions and antique stores all over the U.S.A. Bottles differ in price in different areas, which makes it difficult to arrive at a fair average. Certain bottles may be high in one area and lower in price in others. That is why a price range is used in this guide. *This book is not intended to be the last word in pricing bottles—just a guide.*

A Hobby

All work and no play may make Jack, but getting the most out of life isn't spelled with dollar signs only. Someone without a hobby hasn't really *lived* until he wakes up and claims one of his own.

A hobby will allow one to ride the rough edges off of life—in short, make a new man of him. A hobby will become a safety-valve to release pent-up everyday cares and troubles. The fellow who walks down the street with a glint in his eye, a smile on his face, and his chin up is usually the one we envy. This fellow is getting the most out of life; he has more than one interest—he has a hobby.

PREFATORY NOTE

We mean to acquaint all ages with the fascinating hobby of bottle collecting.

The mystery and many pleasures derived from bottle collecting and digging is that you may always come home with some rare bottles—a very good profit for certain collectors. That is what this book is all about.

Readers are reminded that all bottles and prices in this book are gathered from trade papers, collectors, shows, auctions and antique stores all over the U.S.A.

This book will enable the collector to determine the value of a particular bottle and, with a little study, the value of certain categories of bottles. It must be kept in mind, though, that the price of a particular bottle will vary depending on (1) the condition of the bottle—is it cracked?, how did it "clean up"?, and so forth; and (2) following the law of supply and demand, a bottle may have more value in one section of the country than the other.

Opposite, left to right: A case bottle (#3781), a Chinese pottery jug (#6172), a coffin-type pottery flask (#4489), a jug (#4796) and a medicine bottle (#693). Below: Stoneware vases, crocks and cider jugs.

Beauty and Legend on Your Windowsill

*Due to the variety of their shapes, sizes and colors,
and the fascinating tales behind antique bottles,
Americans delight in having them in their homes*

Back row: goofus glass pickle jar, soda or beer,
patent medicine, pottery beer, fire grenade, case
gin, poison (skull); front row: snuff, chemical,
ale or gin, soda, ink, ale, nursing bottle.

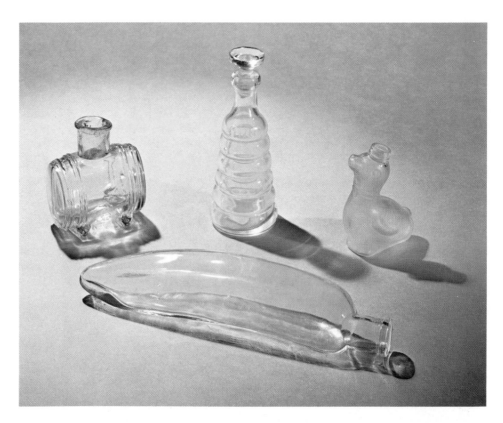

Above: This assortment includes a barrel ink container (#6382), a rum decanter (#4873), a figural scent bottle and a figural whiskey bottle. Opposite: This scroll flask (#4203–#4215) dates back to the mid-19th-century. Below: These early to mid-19th-century flasks, identified by their motifs, are a sailing vessel (#4201), a scroll or violin, a Union flask with clasped hands (#4252), a sunburst (#4239) and an Andrew Jackson (#4258).

Above: These two ornately patterned bottles are a
whiskbroom-shaped whiskey flask (#4268) and a late
19th-century peppersauce container (#5425) with the
familiar gothic arches. Right: This spirits
container in the shape of a ham (#4615) is said to
be figural because, by definition, the bottle
is shaped in the form of a common object.

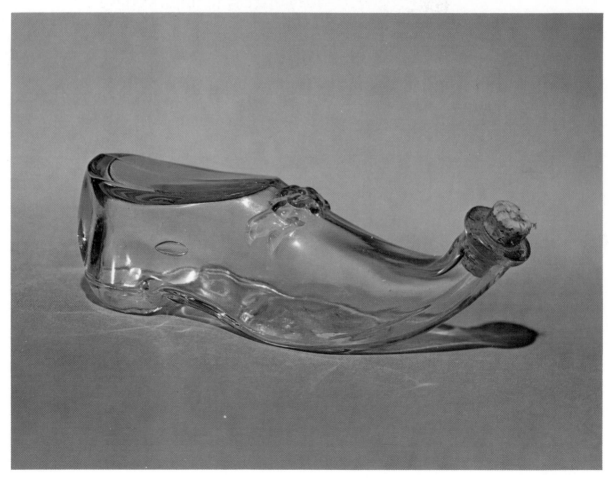

Opposite, above: *Miniature containers such as this medicine
bottle (#2025–2027) and this pottery jug were given away as free
samples in the 19th century and are in high demand today.* Above: *This
17th-century free-blown container (#3660) is commonly known as a
Dutch squat wine bottle as evidenced by the severe kick-up.* Opposite, below:
An unusual desk ink container (#6694) is this shoe figural.

Above: A barrel-shaped whiskey bottle (similar to #4269) and a patterned whiskey flask, both late 19th-century, were sealed with cork. Right: This setting includes a jug claiming the contents to be an "eye opener," three whiskey bottles, an ink crock and a remarkably realistic pretzel flask.

Above: The first jar (#5914) is topped by a zinc lid perfected by John Landis Mason, while the second jar has a Lightning stopper. Right: Most fruit jars had ground lips and were light green in color like these Mason jars (similar to #5897 and #5898), circa 1880–1904.

Opposite: This unique milk-glass medicine bottle
(#1659) is embossed "Odoj" on the bottom. Above: Made by
the Whitney Glass Works, Glassboro, New Jersey, circa
1860–1870, this figural whiskey container (#4343–4345) was
one of the first to be embossed with a brand name.

Overleaf: These bottles held bitters,
a mixture of gin and herbs marketed as a
medicinal liquor. For a detailed description
of these 19th-century bottles see #157,
#207, #109, #55 and #345.

Opposite: *Imported from Germany in the late 19th-century,
this ornately enameled bottle (#6854) contained perfume or
cologne.* Above: *Perhaps the most distinguished of all
food containers were those manufactured by Planters Peanuts
(#5487) with their familiar peanut nobs.*

At one time these bottles, including a sample bitters (#207), a Carter's Ink (#6397), a beer and a poison bottle, were everyday items, not the curiosity-provoking objects they are for Americans today.

BOTTLE TERMS AND DETERMINING BOTTLE AGE

These miniature beverage bottles were found buried near an old abandoned homestead and include a beer bottle, two case or gin bottles (#3630), and two soda or mineral water bottles.

BOTTLE TERMS

Amethyst colored glass: clear glass that has been exposed to the sun or a very bright light for a period of time and has turned a light purple color.

Note: Only glass containing manganese will turn purple.

Blob Top: thick rounded lip, on most soda and mineral water bottles.

Blowpipe: a long tube used by the blower to pick up the molten glass which is then either blown into a mold or free-blown outside a mold to create unlimited varieties of shapes.

Mold: either one-part, two-part, three-part, etc. made of wood, iron or steel; used to shape the bottle as it is being made.

Pontil and Mark: The pontil is a long rod used to hold a bottle when it is being made in order to give the glass blower a chance to apply or finish the top. When finished this pontil is broken or ground off. This process leaves a scar on the bottom of the bottle.

Glass is usually made of silicate of lime, soda and sand. First glassmaking in America started in Jamestown, Virginia, around 1608, and the first major glasshouse was established in 1739 by Caspar Wistar in New Jersey.

First bottle machines developed by Michael J. Owens around 1899-1906.

BOTTLE AGE

Free-Blown Bottles: B.C. to 1860—some are still free-blown today.

Pontil: 1618-1866; also some modern hand-blown bottles.

Raised Letters: 1750 to date.

Three-Part Mold: 1806-1889.

Amethyst or Sun-Colored Glass: 1800 to 1930.

Sheared Lip: 1800-1840 (the top has been sheared off).

Machine Made Bottles: 1903 to date (mold line runs from base through the top).

Black or Dark Olive Green Glass: 1700-1880 approximately.

Crown Cap or Top: 1894-1904.

Applied Lip: a handmade top. The lip and mouth of the bottle were handmade and applied after the bottle was freed from the mold. May be identified by the crude lip and neck, the mold line stops somewhere in the neck—to 1912. Some modern machine made bottles may appear to have an applied lip.

BOTTLE AGE AS DETERMINED BY MOLD LINE

to 1800+
blob top

to 1880+
tapered blob top

to 1890+
wide collar
under it a ring

to 1895+
crown top

1910 to date
crown top
machine made

TRADEMARKS AND OTHER IDENTIFICATION

The words and letters in bold are only a representation or brief description of the trademark as it appeared on a bottle. This is followed by the complete name and location of the company and the approximate period of time in which the trademark was in use.

A—John Agnew & Son, Pittsburgh, PA, 1854-1866

A in a circle—American Glass Works, Richmond, VA and Paden City, WV, circa 1909 to 1936

A in a circle—Armstrong Cork Co., Glass Division, Lancaster, PA, 1938-1968

A & B together (AB)—Adolphus Busch Glass Manufacturing Co., Bellville, IL and St. Louis, MO, circa 1904 to 1907

A B Co.—American Bottle Co., Chicago, IL, 1905-1930

A B G M Co.—Adolphus Busch Glass Manufacturing Co., Bellville, IL and St. Louis, MO, circa 1886 to 1928

A & Co.—John Agnew & Co., Pittsburgh, PA, Indian Queen, Ear of Corn and other flasks, circa 1854 to 1892

A C M E—Acme Glass Co., Olean, NY, circa 1920 to 1930

A & D H C—A. & D.H. Chambers, Pittsburgh, PA, Union flasks, circa 1842 to 1886

A G B Co.—Albion Glass Bottle Co., England, trademark is found under Lea & Perrins, circa 1880 to 1900

AGEE and Agee in script—Hazel Atlas Glass Co., Wheeling, WV, circa 1921 to 1925

Anchor figure with H in center—Anchor Hocking Glass Corp., Lancaster, OH, circa 1955

A.R.S.—A.R. Samuels Glass Co., Philadelphia, PA, circa 1855 to 1872

A S F W W Va.—A.S. Frank Glass Co., Wellsburg, WV, circa 1859

ATLAS—Atlas Glass Co., Washington, PA and later Hazel Atlas Glass Co., 1896-1965

AVH—A. Van Hoboken & Co., Rotterdam, The Netherlands, 1800-1898

BALL and Ball in script—Ball Bros. Glass Manufacturing Co., Muncie, IN and later Ball Corp., 1887-1973

BEAVER—Beaver Flint Glass Co., Toronto, Ontario, Canada, circa 1897 to 1920

Bernardin in script—W.J. Latchford Glass Co., Los Angeles, CA, circa 1932 to 1938

THE BEST—Gillender & Sons, Philadelphia, PA, circa 1867 to 1870

B F B Co.—Bell Fruit Bottle Co., Fairmount, IN, circa 1910

BISHOP'S—Bishop & Co., San Diego and Los Angeles, CA, circa 1890 to 1920

B K—Benedict Kimber, Bridgeport and Brownsville, PA, circa 1822 to 1840

Boyds in script—Illinois Glass Co., Alton, IL, circa 1900 to 1930

Brelle (in script) JAR—Brelle Fruit Jar Manufacturing Co., San Jose, CA, circa 1912 to 1916

BRILLIANTINE—Jefferis Glass Co., Fairton, NJ and Rochester, PA, circa 1900 to 1905

C in a circle—Chattanooga Bottle & Glass Co. and later Chattanooga Glass Co., since 1927

C in a square—Crystal Glass Co., Los Angeles, CA, circa 1921 to 1929

C in a star—Star City Glass Co., Star City, WV, since 1949

CANTON DOMESTIC FRUIT JAR—Canton Glass Co., Canton, OH, circa 1890 to 1904

C & Co. or C Co.—Cunninghams & Co., Pittsburgh, PA, 1880-1907

C C Co.—Carl Conrad & Co., St. Louis, MO, 1876-1883

C C G Co.—Cream City Glass Co., Milwaukee, WI, 1888-1893

C.F.C.A.—California Fruit Canners Association, Sacramento, CA, circa 1899 to 1916

C G M Co—Campbell Glass Manufacturing Co., West Berkeley, CA, 1885

C G W—Campbell Glass Works, West Berkeley, CA, 1884-1885

C & H—Coffin & Hay, Winslow, NJ, circa 1838 to 1842

C L G Co.—Carr-Lowrey Glass Co., Baltimore, MD, circa 1889 to 1920

CLYDE, N.Y.—Clyde Glass Works, Clyde, NY, circa 1870 to 1882

The Clyde in script—Clyde Glass Works, Clyde, NY, circa 1895

C MILW—Chase Valley Glass Co., Milwaukee, WI, circa 1880

COHANSEY—Cohansey Glass Manufacturing Co., Philadelphia, PA, 1870-1900

CROWN with figure of a crown—Excelsior Glass Co., St. Johns, Quebec and later Diamond Glass Co., Montreal, Quebec, Canada, circa 1879 to 1913

CS & Co.—Cannington, Shaw & Co., St. Helens, England, circa 1872 to 1916

DB—Du Bois Brewing Co., Pittsburgh, PA, circa 1918

DEXTER—Franklin Flint Glass Works, Philadelphia, PA, circa 1861 to 1880

THE DICTATOR—William McCully & Co., Pittsburgh, PA, circa 1855 to 1869

DICTATOR—same as above only circa 1869 to 1885

D & Ö—Cumberland Glass Mfg. Co., Bridgeton, NJ, circa 1890 to 1900

D O C—D.O. Cunningham Glass Co., Pittsburgh, PA, circa 1883 to 1937

D S G Co.—De Steiger Glass Co., LaSalle, IL, circa 1867 to 1896

DUFFIELD—Duffield, Parke & Co., Detroit, MI, 1866-1875

DYOTTSVILLE—Dyottsville Glass Works, Philadelphia, PA, 1833-1923

Economy (in script) TRADE MARK—Kerr Glass Manufacturing Co., Portland, OR, 1903-1912

Electric Trade Mark in script—Gayner Glass Works, Salem, NJ, circa 1910

ELECTRIC TRADE MARK—same as above only circa 1900 to 1910

ERD & CO., E R DURKEE—E.R. Durkee & Co., New York, NY, post-1874

E R DURKEE & CO—same as above only circa 1850 to 1860

EUREKA 17—Eurkee Jar Co., Dunbar, WV, circa 1864

Eureka in script—same as above only 1900-1910

Everlasting (in script) JAR—Illinois Pacific Glass Co., San Francisco, CA, circa 1904

EXCELSIOR—Excelsior Glass Co., St. John, Quebec, Canada, 1878-1883

F inside of a jar outline—C.L. Flaccus Glass Co., Pittsburgh, PA, circa 1900 to 1928

F & A—Fahnstock & Albree, Pittsburgh, PA, 1860-1862

FL or FL & Co.—Frederick Lorenz & Co., Pittsburgh, PA, circa 1819 to 1841

G E M—Hero Glass Works, Philadelphia, PA, circa 1884 to 1909

G & H—Gray & Hemingray, Cincinnati, OH, circa 1848 to 1864

GILBERDS—Gilberds Butter Tub Co., Jamestown, NY, circa 1883 to 1890

GREENFIELD—Greenfield Fruit Jar & Bottle Co., Greenfield, IN, circa 1888 to 1912

H (with varying numerals)—Holt Glass Works, West Berkeley, CA, circa 1893 to 1906

HAMILTON—Hamilton Glass Works, Hamilton, Ontario, Canada, 1865-1872

HAZEL—Hazel Glass Co., Wellsburg, WV, 1886-1902

HELME—Geo. W. Helme Co., Jersey City, NJ, circa 1870 to 1895

HEMINGRAY—Hemingray Brothers & Co. and later Hemingray Glass Co., Covington, KY, since 1864

H.J. HEINZ—H.J. Heinz Co., Pittsburgh, PA, circa 1860 to 1869

HEINZ & NOBLE—same as above only circa 1869 to 1872

F. & J. HEINZ—same as above only circa 1876 to 1888

H.J. HEINZ CO.—same as above only since 1888

HS in a circle—Twitchell & Schoolcraft, Keene, NH, 1815-1816

HUNYADI JANOS—Andreas Saxlehner, Buda-Pesth, Austria-Hungary, circa 1863 to 1900

I G Co.—Ihmsen Glass Co., Pittsburgh, PA, circa 1870 to 1898

I G—Illinois Glass Co., Alton, IL, before 1890

IG Co. in a diamond—same as above only circa 1900 to 1916

IMPROVED G E M—Hero Glass Works, Philadelphia, PA, circa 1868

I P G—Illinois Pacific Glass Co., San Francisco, CA, 1902-1932

JAF & Co., PIONEER AND FOLGER—J. A. Folger & Co., San Francisco, CA, since 1850

J D 26 S—John Duncan & Sons, New York, NY, circa 1880 to 1900

J R—Stourbridge Flint Glass Works, Pittsburgh, PA, circa 1823 to 1828

JSB monogram—Joseph Schlitz Brewing Co., Milwaukee, WI, circa 1900

J T—Mantua Glass Works and later Mantua Glass Co., Mantua, OH, circa 1824

J T & Co—Brownsville Glass Works, Brownsville, PA, circa 1824 to 1828

KENSINGTON GLASS WORKS—Kensington Glass Works, Philadelphia, PA, circa 1822 to 1932

Kerr in script—Kerr Glass Manufacturing Co. and later Alexander H. Kerr Glass Co., Portland, OR, Sand Spring, OK, Chicago, IL, Los Angeles, CA, since 1912

K H & G—Kearns, Herdman & Gorsuch, Zanesville, OH, 1876-1884

K & M—Knox & McKee, Wheeling, WV, 1824-1829

K Y G W and KYGW Co—Kentucky Glass Works Co., Louisville, KY, 1849-1855

LAMB—Lamb Glass Co., Mt. Vernon, OH, 1855-1964

L G Co—Louisville Glass Works, Louisville, KY, circa 1880

LIGHTNING—Henry W. Putnam, Bennington, VT, 1875-1890

L I P—Lea & Perrins, London, England, 1880-1900

L K Y G W—Louisville Kentucky Glass Works, Louisville, KY, circa 1873 to 1890

"MASCOT," "MASON" and M F G Co—Mason Fruit Jar Co., Philadelphia, PA, all circa 1885 to 1900

MASTADON—Thomas A. Evans Mastadon Works, and later Wm. McCully & Co., Pittsburgh, PA, 1855-1887

McC & Co and Mc & Co—Wm. McCully & Co., Pittsburgh, PA, circa 1841 to 1886

McKEE & CO.—S. McKee & Co., Pittsburgh, PA, circa 1860 to 1890

M G Co—Millgrove Glass Co., Millgrove, IN, 1897-1912

M. G. & M. Co.—Millville Glass & Manufacturing Co., Millville, NJ, circa 1869 to 1900

MOORE BROS.—Moore Bros., Clayton, NJ, 1864-1880

N A G C—North American Glass Co., Montreal, Quebec, Canada, 1883-1890

N B B G Co—North Baltimore Bottle Glass Co., North Baltimore, OH, 1885-1930

P G W—Pacific Glass Works, San Francisco, CA, 1862-1876

PREMIUM—Premium Glass Co., Coffeyville, KS, circa 1908 to 1914

PUTNAM GLASS WORKS in a circle—Putnam Flint Glass Works, Putnam, OH, circa 1852 to 1871

P & W—Perry & Wood and later Perry & Wheeler, Keene, NH, circa 1822 to 1830

Queen (in script) TRADE MARK all in a shield—Smalley, Kivlan & Onthank, Boston, MA, 1906-1919

R—Louit Frères & Co., France, circa 1870 to 1890

RAU'S—Fairmount Glass Works, Fairmount, IN, circa 1898 to 1908

R & Co—Roth & Co., San Francisco, CA, 1879-1888

RED with a key through it—Safe Glass Co., Upland, IN, circa 1892 to 1898

R G Co—Renton Glass Co., Renton, WA, 1911

ROOT—Root Glass Co., Terre Haute, IN, 1901-1932

S & C—Stebbins & Chamberlain or Coventry Glass Works, Coventry, CT, circa 1825 to 1830

S F G W—San Francisco Glass Works, San Francisco, CA, 1869-1876

S & M—Sykes & Macvey, Castleford, England, 1860-1888

SQUIBB—E.R. Squibb, M.D., Brooklyn, NY, 1858-1895

Standard (in script) MASON—Standard Coop. Glass Co. and later Standard Glass Co., Marion, IN, circa 1894 to 1932

STAR GLASS Co—Star Glass Co., New Albany, IN, circa 1860 to 1900

SWAYZEE—Swayzee Glass Co., Swayzee, IN, 1894-1906

T C W—T.C. Wheaton Co., Millville, NJ, since 1888

T S—Coventry Glass Works, Coventry, CT, 1820-1824

W & CO—Thomas Wightman & Co., Pittsburgh, PA, circa 1880 to 1889

W C G Co—West Coast Glass Co., Los Angeles, CA, 1908-1930

WF & S MILW—William Franzen & Son, Milwaukee, WI, 1900-1929

W G W—Woodbury Glass Works, Woodbury, NJ, 1882-1900

W T & Co—Whitall-Tatum & Co., Millville, NJ, 1857-1935

It is interesting to note on the label of this beer bottle, circa 1880-1890, that the product had already reached such far-off places as Asia, Africa and Australia.

BOTTLE SHAPES
AND COLLARS

lady's leg neck
plain top
with narrow band

wide mouth
case bottle
flared top

medicine or bitters,
label
long tapered top
with ring beneath

old pop
blob tapered top

new pop
crown top
machine made

Hutchinson
blob top

eight-sided conical
ring top

conical
ring top

cylindrical
ring top

round bottom
blob top

tear drop
blob top

sheared lip (1800's)
screw top

old beer
tapered top
under it ring

new beer
crown top
machine made

36

old whiskey
double top

new whiskey
screw top
machine made

18 "Seal"

graphite pontil

broken pontil

shoe polish
flared top

glue
sheared mouth

cone ink
sheared mouth

fire extinguisher
tapered top
with ring

scroll
sheared top

squat or onion
laid-on ring or
sheared top

two-part mold
tapered top

three-part mold
short collar with
ring beneath

side mold
tapered collar
with ring

free-blown bottle
ring top

ten pin bottle
ring top

old medicine
double collar

new medicine
screw top
machine made

Bitters

In the days when Americans were attempting to cure their ailments by consuming the contents of patent (or non-prescription) medicine bottles, bitters were agreed to be the most potent of such cures. Though it is not known if bitters ever actually cured anything, they were indeed potent—one bitters product was calculated to be nearly 120 proof liquor. Unique bottles were designed to catch the eye and launch effective bitters marketing: In addition to the round, triangular and rectangular shapes, bitters bottles were also made in figural shapes of pigs, fish, cannons, drums, ears of corn and cabins.

Bitters manufacturing began when England's George II (reigned 1727-1760) tried to control overindulgence in the evils of gin through a heavy liquor tax. The gin sellers would not acquiesce: They added herbs to their commodity and called it medicine. American colonists began to drink the "medicine" to avoid the tax. Following an article published in 1785 by Dr. Benjamin Rush of Philadelphia entitled "Inquiry into the Effects of Ardent Spirits on the Human Mind and Body," it became socially acceptable to drink the patent medicine and leave the nastiness of gin and brandy alone. The Revenue Act of 1862 further stimulated bitters consumption by taxing liquor more than medicine. Bitters, of course, were taxed as medicine—strong medicine, to be sure, most with more than fifty percent alcohol, not to mention the strychnine and belladonna also contained.

Many Americans actually believed in the medicinal value of bitters. After all, nearly all of the manufacturers or endorsers were medical doctors, though their qualifications were rarely verified. Jacob Hostetter of Lancaster County, Pennsylvania, used his own bitters formula in his private practice. Upon his retirement in 1853 he granted his son, David, permission to manufacture it, and David established a partnership with George W. Smith. Their advertising budget was huge, but it paid off. "Hostetter's California Almanac of 1861" advertised Hostetter's Celebrated Stomach Bitters on every other page. The ads warned that the bitters was not a panacea. All it would cure is "dyspepsia, diarrhea, dysentery, general debility, chills and fever, liver complaint, bilious remittent fevers, and the pains and weaknesses which creep upon us in old age." The ad's dramatic conclusion adds:

It lives, and continues to thrive and increase in popularity, with marvelous rapidity, simply because the world wants it, will have it, cannot do without it.... Furnished with this pre-

Forced by a heavy tax, gin sellers simply added herbs to their product and changed its name. This is evidenced here by the first and third (#383) of these bottles which greatly resemble gin containers. The milk glass bottle (#3628) is most likely a German product. Drakes Plantation Bitters (#157), circa 1865-1875, was supposedly 38.24 percent alcohol. The fourth bottle (#109) is known as a lady's leg neck.

ventative, the pioneer of California may fearlessly prosecute his search for gold and silver. . . . He may sleep wrapped in his blanket or buffalo robe on the damp ground by night, and brave the hot beams of the sun by day without incurring the usual penalties . . . provided he reinforces his constitution, his appetite and his strength by moderate and regular use of the Hostetter's Bitters.

David Hostetter always had an eye open for new markets. During the Civil War, he managed to convince the Federal Government to purchase the bitters as a before-battle invigorant. Following the war, one historian wrote, ". . . Many a frightened Yankee at Gettysburg knew he faced Pickett's charge as bravely as he did because of a swig of Hostetter's under his belt." Though Hostetter's Bitters practically guaranteed victory in battle and gold to California prospectors, it could not cure Hostetter's own kidney ailment from which he died in 1888.

There are over one thousand types of bitters bottles known, most of the collectables having been produced between 1860 and 1900.

2   3   8   9   14   21

25   48   50   53   54   57

Editors' Note: Words, letters and numbers embossed on the bottle or appearing on the label are indicated by capital letters and italic typeface. Photographs of bottles are not shown to a consistent scale. For exact dimensions of bottles refer to individual entries. The height of the bottle is given in inches. Any other dimensions, such as diameter or length of neck, are so indicated. The original spellings or misspellings on the bottles have been kept and sometimes especially noted. Prices are for 1974 dollars and may be adjusted for inflation or deflation as needed.

1 C. W. ABBOTT & CO., BALTIMORE around shoulder; 8½''; amber; *C. W. Abbott & Co., Baltimore* on base $4.00-6.00

2 ABBOTT'S BITTERS on base; *C. W. Abbott & Co., Baltimore* on shoulder; machine made; 8''; amber 4.00-6.00

3 ABBOTT'S BITTERS; 6½''; machine made 8.00-10.00

4 DR. ABELL'S SPICE BITTERS, label; pontil; aqua; 7½'' 30.00-50.00

5 ACORN BITTERS; amber; tapered lip; 9'' 60.00-70.00

6 AFRICAN STOMACH BITTERS in three lines near shoulder; 9½''; amber . . . . 30.00+

7 AFRICAN STOMACH BITTERS in three lines near shoulder; 9½''; amber; round; under Bitters small letters *Spruance Stanley & Co.* . . . 30.00+

8 AIMAR'S SARRACENIA BITTERS; on back *Charleston S. C.*; aqua; 7½'' . . . . 25.00+

9 AIMAR'S SARRACENIA FLY TRAP BITTERS, label; on back embossed *A. S. B. Charleston S. C.*; aqua; 7¼" .... 100.00+

10 ALEX VON HUMBOLDT'S; on back *Stomach Bitters*; tapered neck; ring top; amber; 9¾" 50.00-85.00

11 ALPINE HERB BITTERS in two lines in front; in back in a shield *TT&CO.*; amber; 9¾" 40.00+

12 ALPINE HERB BITTERS, label; *TT & CO.* in a shield on one side; other two sides plain; tapered top; square; 8½" 35.00-55.00

13 DR. ALTHER'S BITTERS; lady's leg shape; clear; 5" 20.00-40.00

14 AMAZON BITTERS; reverse side *Peter Mc-Quade N.Y.*; 9¼"; amber .... 70.00+

15 AMERICAN CELEBRATED STOMACH BITTERS; amber; 9¼" 40.00-50.00

16 AMERICAN LIFE BITTERS; back same; *P. Eiler Mfg. Tiffin Ohio*; log effect; cabin type bottle; tapered lip; light amber to amber 135.00-155.00

17 AMERICAN LIFE BITTERS; same as above except *Omaha, Neb.* .... 135.00+

18 AMERICAN STOMACH BITTERS; amber; 8½" 40.00-65.00

19 DR. ANDREW MUNSO BITTERS; lady's leg shape; 11¼"; amber 50.00-100.00

20 DAVID ANDREW'S VEG. JAUNDICE BITTERS; open pontil; aqua 60.00-90.00

21 ANGOSTURA; *Bitters* on back, *Rheinstorom Bros, N.Y. & Cin.* on bottom; amber 15.00-30.00

22 ANGOSTURA BARK BITTERS; 9½"; clear or aqua 25.00-40.00

23 ANGOSTURA BITTERS on base; 7¾"; green 20.00-30.00

24 APPETINE BITTERS, GEO. BENZ & SONS, ST. PAUL, MINN. MFG., label; 7¼"; amber 10.00-20.00

25 ARGYLE BITTERS, E. B. WHEELOCK N.O.; tapered lip; 9¾"; amber .... 100.00+

26 ARPS STOMACH BITTERS; *Ernest L. Arp & Kiel*, label; round; 11¼"; aqua 20.00-30.00

27 ASPARAGIN BITTERS CO.; 11"; clear to aqua .... 50.00+

28 ATHERTON'S DEW DROP BITTERS; on base *1866 Lowell Mass.*; ringed shoulder; short tapered top; 10"; amber 40.00-50.00

29 ATWOOD GENUINE PHYS. JAUNDICE BITTERS, GEORGTOWN, MASS.; 12-sided; 6½"; aqua 10.00-20.00

30 ATWOOD JAUNDICE BITTER; *by Moses Atwood* on panels; 6"; clear or aqua ... 6.00-8.00

31 same except pontil .... 12.00+

32 ATWOOD JAUNDICE BITTER; *formerly made by Moses Atwood*; 6"; clear or aqua 4.00-6.00

33 ATWOOD JAUNDICE BITTER; machine made; 6"; clear or aqua 2.00-3.00

34 ATWOOD JAUNDICE BITTER; *formerly made by Moses Atwood*; 6"; clear or aqua; screw top 1.00-2.00

35 ATWOOD'S QUININE TONIC BITTERS; 8½"; aqua 40.00-50.00

36 ATWOOD'S QUININE TONIC BITTERS, GILMAN BROS. BOSTON, label; 9"; aqua 40.00-60.00

37 ATWOOD'S VEG. DYSPEPTIC BITTERS; pontil; short tapered top; 6½"; aqua 40.00-60.00

38 AUGAUER BITTERS; 8¼"; green 50.00-70.00

39 AUNT CHARITYS BITTERS, label; *Geo. A. Jameson Druggist, Bridgeport, Conn.*; 8½"; clear and amber 20.00-30.00

40 DR. AURENT IXL STOMACH BITTERS; BARKERS, MOORE & MEIN; *Mfg. Wholesale Merch. Phila.*; 8½"; clear........ 20.00-30.00

41 AYALA MEXICAN BITTERS; on back *M. Rothenberg & Co. San Francisco, Cal.*; long collar with ring; 9½"; amber 25.00-40.00

42 DR. M. C. AYERS RESTORATIVE BITTERS; 8½"; aqua .... 50.00+

43 E. L. BAILEY'S KIDNEY AND LIVER BITTERS; on back *Best Blood Purifier*; 7¾"; amber .... 50.00+

44 BAKER'S HIGH LIFE BITTERS; *The Great Nerve Tonic* embossed on back; tapered top; machine made; pint 18.00-20.00

45 BAKERS ORANGE GROVE; on back *Bitters*; roped corners; tapered top; 9½"; amber 80.00-90.00

46 same as above except yellow .... 100.00+

47 BAKERS STOMACH BITTERS, label; lady's leg shape; 11¼"; amber 40.00-60.00

48 E. BAKERS PREMIUM BITTERS; *Richmond, Va.*; aqua; 6¾"...................... 40.00-50.00

49 DR. BALLS VEG. STOM. BITTERS; pontil; 7"; aqua .... 60.00+

50 BALSDONS GOLDEN BITTERS; *1856 N.Y.* other side; amber; 10½" .... 85.00+

51 BARBER'S INDIAN VEG. JAUNDICE BITTERS; 12-sided; 6¼"; aqua .... 50.00+

52 BARTLETT'S EXCELSIOR BITTERS; on bottom *BARTLETT BROS. N. Y.*; 8-sided; 7¾"; aqua and amber .... 100.00+

53 BARTO'S GREAT GUN BITTERS; in circle in center *Reading, Pa.*; cannon shop bottles; amber, olive amber; 11" x 3¼" 600.00-1,000.00

54 BAVARIAN BITTERS; *Hoffheimer Brothers* other side; amber; 9½"......... 75.00-100.00

55 BAXTERS MANDRAKE BITTERS; *Lord Bros. Prop. Burlington, Vt.* on vertical panels; 6½"; amethyst 12.00-25.00

56 BEECHAM BITTERS; *Woodward Drug Co. Portland, Org.*, label; 8¼"; amber 10.00-15.00

57 BEGGS DANDELION BITTERS; *Chicago, Ill* other side; amber; 9".......... 50.00-60.00

58 BELLE OF ANDERSON BITTERS; 7"; amber 40.00-60.00

59   66   71   76   80   82   87

91   94   95   98   100   102   103

106   107   108   109   111   112   113

59 DR. BELLS BLOOD PURIFYING BITTERS; 9¼"; amber.................... 30.00-60.00

60 BELLS COCKTAIL BITTERS; lady's leg shape; 10¾"; amber 60.00-100.00

61 BELMONTS TONIC HERB BITTERS; 9½"; amber......................... 100.00+

62 BENDERS BITTERS; 10½"; aqua.... 50.00+

63 BENGAL BITTERS; 8½"; amber..... 40.00+

64 BENNETTS CELEBRATED STOMACH BITTERS; 9¼"; amber............. 40.00-60.00

65 BENNETTS WILD CHERRY STOMACH BITTERS; 9¼"; amber 50.00-100.00

66 BERKSHIRE • BITTERS, AMANN & CO., CINCINNATI, O.; ground top; dark amber; 10½"..................... 1,000.00+

67 BERLINER MAGEN BITTERS; *S. B. Rothenberg sole agents S. F.*, label; 9½"; green 100.00+

68 BERLINER MAGEN BITTERS; 9½"; amber 40.00-60.00

69 DR. L. Y. BERTRAMS LONG LIFE AROMATIC STOMACH BITTERS; 9"; aqua 30.00-60.00

70 THE BEST BITTERS OF AMERICA; cabin shape; 9¾"; amber .... 80.00+

71 BIG BILL BEST BITTERS; amber; 12" 60.00-100.00

72 BIRD BITTERS; *Phila. Proprietor;* 4¾"; clear .... 40.00+

73 DR. BIRMINGHAM ANTI BILIOUS BLOOD PURIFYING BITTERS; 9¼"; round; green 60.00-90.00

74 DR. BISHOPS WAHOO BITTERS; 10¼"; amber.......................... 100.00+

75 BISMARCK BITTERS; ½ pint; amber 20.00-30.00

76 THE BITTERS PHARMACY, label; 4½"; clear 3.00-4.00

77 DR. BLAKE'S AROMATIC BITTERS N.Y.; 7¼"; aqua; pontil .... 80.00+

78 BLAKE'S TONIC & DUERETIC BITTERS; round; 10¼"; aqua.............. 20.00-30.00

79 DR. BOERHAAVES STOMACH BITTERS; 9¼"; olive amber.................. 45.00+

80 BOERHAVES HOLLAND BITTERS; one side *B. Page Jr.*; other side *Pittsburg Pa.*; 8"; aqua 40.00-60.00

81 BOSTON MALT BITTERS; round; 9½"; green 20.00-40.00

82 BOTANIC STOMACH BITTERS; same on reverse; paper label; 9"; amber... 40.00-80.00

83 same as above except back reads *BACH MEESE & CO. S.F.*; 9"; amber 20.00-40.00

84 BOURBON WHISKEY BITTERS; barrel; 9"; bright puce .... 100.00+

85 BOURBON WHISKEY BITTERS; barrel; 9"; claret..................... 100.00-150.00

86 BOWES CASCARA BITTERS; *Has No Equal, P. F. BOWES, Waterbury, Conn. U.S.A.;* 9¼"; clear 40.00-60.00

87 DR. BOYCE'S TONIC BITTERS; *Francis Fenn Prop. Rutland Vt.* on panels; bottle has twelve panels; 7¼"; aqua blue 30.00-40.00

88 DR. BOYCE'S TONIC BITTERS, label; sample size; twelve panels; 4½"; aqua 8.00-15.00

89 BOYER'S STOMACH BITTERS; bottle in shape of an arch; fancy bottle; round; 11"; clear 50.00-85.00

90 BOYER'S STOMACH BITTERS CINCINNATI; whiskey shape bottle; fluted shoulder and round base; clear.......... 90.00-125.00

91 BRADY'S FAMILY BITTER on three sunken panels; amber; 9½".............. 40.00-60.00

92 BROPHYS BITTERS; 7"; aqua .. 40.00-60.00

93 BROWN & LYONS BLOOD BITTERS; 8"; amber 80.00-90.00

94 BROWN CHEMICAL CO.; *Brown Iron Bitters* on other side; 8"; amber 10.00-15.00

95 F. BROWN BOSTON SARSAPARILLA STOMACH BITTERS; pontil; 9¼"; aqua 50.00-70.00

96 DR. BROWN'S BERRY BITTERS; 8¼"; aqua or clear..................... 30.00-40.00

97 BROWN'S CASTILIA BITTERS; round; tapered; 10"; amber 40.00-80.00

98 BROWN'S CELEBRATED INDIAN HERB BITTERS; amber; 12½" 175.00-250.00

99 BROWNS INDIAN QUEEN BITTERS; 12½"; reddish amber 150.00-200.00

100 BRYANT'S; *Stomach Bitters* on three panels; green; small kick-up with dot .... 200.00+

101 BRYANTS STOMACH BITTERS on two panels; 8-sided; pontil; 11¾"; olive .... 85.00+

102 H. E. BUCKLEN & CO.; *Electric Brand Bitter* on each side; amber; 9".......... 10.00-20.00

103 same except no *Electric* 10.00-20.00

104 BURDOCK BLOOD BITTERS; Canadian type; early ABM; 8½"; clear........... 8.00-15.00

105 BURDOCK BLOOD BITTERS; *T. Milburn & Co., Toronto, Ont.* on back; tapered neck; 8½"; aqua blue 20.00-30.00

106 BURDOCK BLOOD BITTERS; *Foster Milburn Co.* one side; other side *Buffalo N.Y.*; clear; 8" .... 25.00+

107 PROFESSOR GEO. J. BYRNE NEW YORK; *The Great Universal Compound Stomach Bitters Patd 1870;* fancy ware bottle; amber or clear; 10"........................... 50.00-150.00

108 Bitters, label; *McC* on bottom; gold; 9½" 4.00-6.00

109 Bitters, label; amber; lady's leg neck; 12" .... 35.00+

110 Bitters, label under glass in circle; bar bottle; 12¼"; clear.................... 10.00-25.00

111 Bitters, label; crock; light olive, brown trim; 10¼". 25.00-30.00

112 Bitters, label; different colors and sizes; reproductions................... 4.00-10.00

113 Bitters or whiskey, label; green ...... 45.00+

118   125   132   134   135   137   139

141   142   143   145   147   148   151

152   153   154   156   157   158   160

114 CALIFORNIA FIG. BITTERS; 9¼"; amber 50.00-60.00

115 CALDWELLS HERB BITTERS; 12¼"; pontil; amber 100.00-200.00

116 CALIFORNIA HERB & FIG. BITTERS; 9¾"; amber 60.00-80.00

117 CALIFORNIA WINE BITTERS; M KELLER, L.A. in shield on shoulder; *M. K.* around bottle; 12¼"; olive green .... 85.00+

118 CANTON (★) BITTERS (★), all around the shoulder; long bulged lady's leg neck; round; amber; 12" tall, 3½" round 75.00-150.00

119 CAPITAL BITTERS one side; *Dr. M. M. Fenner's Fredonia, N.Y.* on reverse side; 10½"; aqua 20.00-40.00

120 CARACAS BITTERS; 8¼"; amber to emerald green.......................... 25.00+

121 same as above in dark green...... 25.00-50.00

122 CARMELITE BITTERS; *for the Kidney and Liver Complaints* on one side; on back, *Carmelite, Frank R. Leonori & Co. Proprietors, New York*; square; 10½"; amber, olive ..... 40.00+

123 CARONI BITTERS; pint; amber .. 8.00-12.00

124 CARONI BITTERS; ½ pint; green. 8.00-12.00

125 CARPATHIAN HERB BITTERS; *Hollander Drug Co. Braddock P.* other side; amber; 8½" 15.00-20.00

126 CASSINS GRAPE BRANDY BITTERS; triple ringed top; 10"; dark olive green 85.00-125.00

127 CATAWBA WINE BITTERS; cluster of grapes on front and back; 9";green 40.00-80.00

128 CELEBRATED CROWN BITTERS; *F. Chevalier & Co. Sole Agents*; 9¼"; amber 60.00-80.00

129 CELEBRATED HEALTH RESTORING BITTERS; *Dr. Stephen Jewetts*; pontil; 9½"; aqua 20.00-40.00

130 CELERY & CHAMOMILE BITTERS, label; square; 10"; amber............ 10.00-20.00

131 CHRISTIAN XANDER'S STOMACH BITTERS, label; *Washington, D.C.*; 12"; amber .... 20.00+

132 DR. E. CHYDER STOMACH BITTERS, N.O.; 9"; amber 25.00-50.00

133 CINTORIA BITTER WINE on shoulder; 11"; amber 10.00-20.00

134 CLARKES SHERRY WINE BITTERS; 8"; clear 10.00-20.00

135 CLARKES SHERRY WINE BITTERS; *Only 25¢*; pontil; 8"; blue green 50.00-60.00

136 CLARKS VEG. BITTERS; *only 75¢*; 8"; pontil; aqua.......................... 80.00-100.00

137 CLAW BITTERS, label; 4¾"; light amber 20.00-30.00

138 CLIMAX BITTERS; on back *S. F. Cal.*; 9½"; golden amber.................. 40.00-60.00

139 CLOTWORTHY'S; *Oriental Tonic Bitter* on back; amber; 10".................. 65.00 +

140 COCA BITTERS ANDES MTS.; trademark: picture of Indian carrying man across stream; also *THE BEST TONIC*............ 100.00 +

141 COCKTAIL BITTERS; *Cribbs Davidson & Co* other side; 9¼".................... 75.00 +

142 DR. A. W. COLEMAN'S ANTIDYSPEPTIC TONIC BITTERS; pontil; ground pontil; green .... 75.00 +

143 COLLETON BITTERS; pontil; aqua; 6½" .... 50.00 +

144 same as above without pontil .... 25.00 +

145 COLUMBO PEPTIC BITTERS; on back *L. E. Junc, New Orleans, La.*; square bottle; under bottom *SB&CO*; 8¾"; amber.......... 35.00+

146 CONSTITUTION BITTERS 1880; *Bodeker Bros Prop. Rich. Va.*; 7"; amber .. 50.00-75.00

147 CORN JUICE BITTERS; flask-shaped bottle; quart; aqua 40.00-80.00

148 CORWITZ STOMACH BITTERS; 7½"; amber 25.00-50.00

149 CUNDERANGO BITTERS; same on back side; greenish amber; 7¾"............ 40.00-60.00

150 CURTIS CORDIAL CALISAYA, THE GREAT STOMACH BITTERS; tapered neck; 11½"; amber.................. 100.00-150.00

151 DAMIANA BITTERS; *Baja, Calif.* on back; 8-pointed star under bottom; *Lewis Hess Manufr.* on shoulder; aqua; 11½"......... 30.00-40.00

152 DANDELION BITTERS; 7"; aqua or clear .... 60.00+

153 DeWITTS STOMACH BITTERS; *Chicago*; 8"; amber 50.00-75.00

154 DeWITTS STOMACH BITTERS; *Chicago*; 9¾"; amber...................... 40.00-50.00

155 DOC DUNNING OLD HOME BITTERS; *Greensboro, N. Carolina*; 13"; dark red amber 40.00-60.00

156 DOYLE'S HOP BITTERS; cabin shape; *1872* on roof; 9¼"; several shades of amber and many variants of colors 40.00-80.00

157 S.T. DRAKES on top of roof panel; *1860 plantation* on next panel; *Bitters* on next; reverse center panel *Patented 1862* with six logs; front plain for label, other covered with logs; some have five logs and the earliest have four logs; 10"; amber the most common; others: citron, pale yellow, green, scarce in olive green 50.00-75.00

158 ENGLISH FEMALE BITTERS; on reverse *Dromgoole, Louisville, Ky.*; 8½"; clear or amber 50.00-70.00

159 EXCELCIOR; on back *Bitters*; 9"; tapered top; amber .... 50.00+

160 FAVORITE BITTERS; *Powell & Stutenroth*; 9¼"; barrel shape with swirl ribbing; amber .... 60.00+

161 FEINSTER STUTTGARIES MAGEN BITTERS; *Brand Bros. Co.*, label; 3-sided bottle; long neck and ring top; 10"; amber ... 60.00+

166 167 168 170 174 176 179

182 183 185 186 187 188 189

190 191 198 199 201 202 204

162 DR. M.M. FENNER'S CAPITOL BITTERS; 10½"; aqua 20.00-30.00
same as above; green 30.00-40.00

163 FER-KINA GALENO (Bitters) on shoulder; beer type bottle; 10⅛"; brown; machine made 8.00-16.00

164 FERNET GIGLIANI BITTERS; *San Francisco*, label; wine type bottle; kick-up bottom; green 20.00-25.00

165 FERRO QUINA STOMACH BITTERS BLOOD MAKER; *Dogliani Italia, D.P. Rossi, 1400 Dupont St. S.E. sole agents, U.S.A. & Canada;* 9¼"; lady's leg type neck; amber 40.00-80.00

166 THE FISHBITTERS on side of eye; on reverse *W.H. Ware Patented 1866;* on base *W.H. Ware Patented 1866;* plain rolled top; 11½"; 3½" x 2½"; amber; rare in other color . . . . 100.00+

167 same as above except clear. . . . . 85.00+

168 FITZPATRICK & CO.; shape of stubby ear of corn; 10"; amber 150.00-250.00

169 A.H. FLANDERS M.D. RUSH'S BITTERS; 9"; clear, amethest, amber 30.00-40.00

170 DR. FLINTS QUAKER BITTERS; *Providence R.I.;* 9½"; aqua 40.00-70.00

171 DR. FORMANECK'S BITTER WINE; 10½"; amber; round 4.00-8.00

172 GARRY, OWEN STRENGTHENING BITTERS; on one side *Sole Proprietor's;* on other side *Ball & Lyon's, New Orleans La.;* front plain; under bottom *W.McC & Co. Pitts.;* 9"; amber . . . . 50.00+

173 GERMAN BALSAM BITTERS, W. M. WATSON & CO.; *sole agents for U.S.;* 9"; milk glass 60.00-85.00

174 GLOBE BITTERS; *Manufactured only by Byrne Bros. & Co. New York;* fluted tapered neck; 11"; amber 90.00-110.00

175 GLOBE BITTERS; *Manufactured only by John W. Perkins & Co., Sole Proprietors, Portland Me.;* 10"; amber 100.00-150.00

176 GODFREYS CELEBRATED CORDIAL BITTERS; 10"; iron pontil; aqua 25.00-50.00

177 GEO. C. GODWINS; reverse *Indian Vegetable Sarsaparilla;* each side reads *Bitters;* all lettering reads vertically; 8¼"; pontil; aqua 60.00-100.00

178 GOFF'S BITTERS, label; *Camden, N.H.;* aqua . . . . 10.00+

179 GOFF'S BITTERS; *H* on bottom; machine made; 5¾"; clear and amber 20.00-30.00

180 ST. GOTTHARD HERB BITTERS; *Mette & Kanne Pros. St. Louis, Mo.* in vertical line on front; tapered top; 8¾" 40.00-50.00

181 W.H.GREEG LORIMER'S JUNIPER TAR BITTERS; *Elmira N.Y.;* 9½"; blue green 40.00-80.00

182 GREELEY'S BOURBON BITTERS; amber, olive; 9½" . . . . 100.00+

183 GREER'S ECLIPSE BITTERS; *Louisville Ky* on side; amber; 9" . . . . 85.00+

184 same as above except puce 100.00-150.00

185 J. GROSSMAN; *Old Hickory Celebrated Stomach Bitters* on back; amber; 4½". . 35.00+

186 J. GROSSMAN; *Old Hickory Celebrated Stomach Bitters* on other side; amber; 8¾" 30.00-50.00

187 DR. GRUESSIE ALTHER'S KRAUTER BITTERS, label; *B* under bottom; 10½"; amber 60.00-80.00

188 HAGANS BITTERS; amber; 9½". 30.00-40.00

189 E. E. HALL, NEW HAVEN; *Established 1842* on base; amber; 10¼" . . . . 80.00+

190 HALL'S BITTERS; *E.E. Hall, New Haven, Established 1852* on back; amber; 9¼" 100.00-125.00

191 HANSARDS HOP BITTERS; crock; 8"; tan and green 40.00-60.00

192 DR. MANLEY HARDY'S GENUINE JAUNDICE BITTERS, BOSTON MASS.; long tapered neck; 7½"; aqua 60.00-100.00

193 same as above except BANGOR, MAINE 60.00-100.00

194 same as above except 6½" 40.00-90.00

195 same as above except no pontil. . . . 15.00-30.00

196 DR. HARTER'S WILD CHERRY BITTERS; *St. Louis or Dayton, O.;* rectangular; 7¾"; amber 10.00-20.00

197 same except miniature 10.00-20.00

198 DR. HARTER'S WILD CHERRY BITTER; *Dayton, O.;* four sunken panels; rectangular; 4¾" 12.00-20.00

199 HARTS STAR BITTERS; *Philadelphia Pa.;* 9¼"; aqua 55.00-100.00

200 HARTWIG KANTOROWICZ; *Posen Germany;* 4"; case type bottle; milk glass. 45.00+

201 same as above except 9½" . . . . 40.00+

202 HARZER KRANTER BITTERS; reverse *Herman C. Asendorf, Brooklyn N.Y.;* 9½"; amber 15.00-25.00

203 H.H. HAY CO.; *Selling Agents Portland Me.* on back; on bottom *L.F. Atwood;* in center *L.F.;* 6¾"; aqua . . . . 25.00+

204 DR. HENLEY'S CALIFORNIA IXL (in oval) BITTERS; *W. Frank & Sons. Pitt.* reverse side; sky blue 40.00-60.00

207

208

210

214

216

217

219

220

221

222

229

230

234

242

248

251

252

205 DR. HENLEY'S SPICED WINE; *OK* in a circle; *Bitters* label; reverse *OK Bitters*; round bottle; ring top; 12"; bluish aqua .... 25.00+

206 DR. HENLEY'S WILD GRAPE ROOT; reverse IXL in an oval, *Bitters* under it; tapered and ring top; square bottle; under bottom *W. F. G. Sons*; 12"; amber .... 50.00+

207 HENTZ'S CURATIVE BITTERS; *Phila.*, label; embossed; 9½"; clear 40.00-60.00

208 H. P. HERB WILD CHERRY BITTERS; *Reading Pa.*; in back wild cherry and tree; *Bitter* on all four sides of the roof; 10"; amber .. 50.00+

209 same as above except green .... 75.00+

210 DR. I. HESTER'S STOMACH BITTERS; 8¾"; amber .... 60.00+

211 HIERAPICRA BITTERS; reverse side *Extract of Fig, Botanical Society*; other side *California*; 6½"; aqua .... 50.00+

212 HIGHLAND BITTERS & SCOTCH TONIC; barrel-shaped bottle; ring top; 9½"; amber .... 100.00+

213 same as above except olive .... 125.00+

214 HI HI BITTER CO.; triangular shape; amber; 9½" 50.00-75.00

215 HOBOKEN AVAN BITTERS; 9¼"; olive 20.00-40.00

216 HOFFHEIMER BROS.; reverse *BAVARIAN BITTERS*; 9½"; amber .... 25.00+

217 DR. HOFFMAN'S GOLDEN BITTERS, label; *ACW* under bottom; amber; 9" ... 10.00-15.00

218 HOLTZERMANN'S PATENT STOMACH BITTERS on the roof of cabin-shaped bottle; shingle roof; tapered top; 9¾"; amber 100.00-160.00

219 HOLTZERMANN'S PATENT STOMACH BITTERS, label; 4¼"; amber .... 100.00+

220 same as above except 9¾" .... 100.00+

221 HOME BITTERS COMPANY; *Home Stomach Bitters* one side; *Proprietors St. Louis, Mo.* other side; amber; 8¾" .... 50.00+

222 DR. HOOFLAND'S GERMAN BITTERS LIVER COMPLAINT, DYSPEPSIA; *C.M. Jackson, Philadelphia* in sunken panels; double ring top; pontil; 8"; aqua 30.00-50.00

223 same as above except light blue ... 30.00-60.00

224 DR. VON HOPFS CURACO BITTERS; in back *Chamberlain & Co. Des Moines Iowa*; 9¼"; tapered top; amber 80.00-90.00

225 same as above in a flask type bottle 80.00-90.00

226 DR. J. HOSTETTER'S STOMACH BITTERS; square; 9"; light amber, amber 6.00-12.00

227 same except yellow green 12.00-25.00

228 same except machine made 4.00-6.00

229 DR. J. HOTSETTER'S [sic]; amber; 8¾" 15.00-30.00

230 DR. J. HOSTETTER'S; amber; 8¾" 10.00-18.00

231 DR. HOSTETTER'S STOMACH BITTERS; on base *I.G.L.*; square; amber; 9" 6.00-12.00

232 same as above except on back *18 Fluid oz.*; 8¾" 6.00-12.00

233 same as above, machine made....... 3.00-5.00

234 DR. J. HOSTETTER'S STOMACH BITTERS (J is backwards); 8½"; amber .... 65.00+

235 DR. J. HOSTETTER'S STOMACH BITTERS; *L & W 10* on base; 9½"; yellow amber 10.00-20.00

236 same as above except dark amber . 10.00-20.00

237 same as above except S. McKEE & CO.; *2* on base 10.00-20.00

238 same as above except #2 on base.. 10.00-20.00

239 H. U. A. monogram on bottom; bitters label; lady's leg shape; 10½"; amber .... 25.00+

240 GEO. C. HUBBEL & CO. on each side; blank front and back; 10½"; tapered top; aqua 40.00-50.00

241 HUTCHINS on side; DYSPEPSIA BITTERS on front; *New York* on other side; tapered top; aqua; 8½"; pontil 80.00-125.00

242 J.W. HUTCHINSON'S; reverse *Tonic Bitters, Mobile Ala.*; 8¾"; aqua 85.00-125.00

243 IMPERIAL RUSSIAN TONIC BITTERS; rope design on sides; 9¼"; clear or aqua.... 50.00+

244 INDIAN VEGETABLE SARSAPARILLA; reverse *Bitters, Boston*; all vertical lettering; pontil; 8¼"; aqua............... 60.00-100.00

245 JEWEL BITTERS; reverse *John S. Bowman & Co.*; 9"; amber.................... 50.00+

246 JEWEL BITTERS on side; *John S. Bowman & Co., California* on back; tapered top; quart; amber .... 25.00+

247 JOCKEY CLUB HOUSE BITTERS; *J. H. Dudley & Co.*; 9½"; green 50.00-100.00

248 DR. HERBERT JOHN'S INDIAN BITTERS; *Great Indian Discoveries*; 8½"; amber . 65.00+

249 JOHNSON'S CALISAYA BITTERS; reverse *Burlington Vt.*; tapered top; 10"; amber 20.00-40.00

250 KAISER WILHELM BITTERS CO.; *Sandusky O.*; bulged neck; ringed top; round bottle; 10"; amber .... 100.00+

251 KELLY'S OLD CABIN BITTERS; *Patd March 1870* on one side; olive; 10" .... 300.00+

252 KELLY'S OLD CABIN BITTERS; *Patented 1868* on each side of roof; amber; 9¼" 300.00+

253 KENNEDY'S EAST INDIA BITTERS; 6½"; clear 40.00-60.00

254 KEYSTONE BITTERS; barrel-shaped bottle; ringed top; 10"; amber .... 50.00+

255 KIMBALL'S (has backward S) JAUNDICE BITTERS; *Troy N.H.* on side; tapered top; pontil; 6¾"; dark amber.......... 100.00-200.00

256 KLAS'S OREGON PEACH BITTERS in large letters on shoulder; round; 11½"; aqua 30.00-50.00

257 KOEHLER & HENRICH RED STAR STOMACH BITTERS, *St. Paul Minn.* in a circle; label in red, black and white circle; *1908*; 11½"...................... 100.00-200.00

262   266   269   271   272   275   279

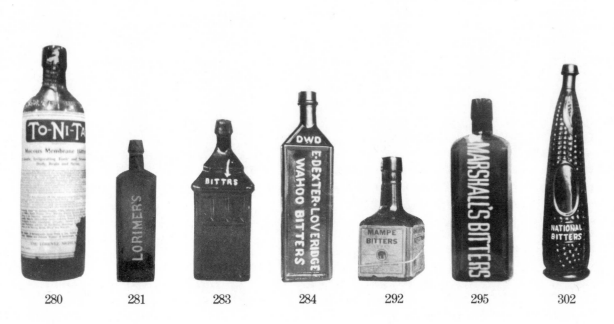

280   281   283   284   292   295   302

258 KOEHLERS STOMACH BITTERS CO.; 12½"; amber 20.00-30.00

259 DR. LANGLEY'S ROOT & HERB BITTERS, *76 Union St. Boston* on front; round; ringed top; 6¾; light green 20.00-40.00

260 DR. LANGLEY'S ROOT & HERB BITTERS, *99 Union St. Boston* on front; ringed top; 8½"; amber 25.00-50.00

261 same as above, but embossing in indented panel 25.00-50.00

262 LASH'S BITTERS CO.; *N.Y., Chicago, San Francisco*; round; clear, dark amber, amethyst; 10¾" and 11" x 3" 5.00-10.00

263 also with label *Cordol Bitter* 2.00-8.00

264 LASH'S BITTERS, with circle between words KIDNEY and LIVER; on back in two lines, *The Best Cathartic and Blood Purifier;* 2¾" x 2¾"; amber; 9½" 10.00-15.00

265 same except 1" x 1" x 3" 4.00-8.00

266 LASH'S LIVER BITTERS; *Nature's Tonic Laxative* on back; machine made; amber; 7½" 4.00-10.00

267 LEAK KIDNEY & LIVER BITTERS; reverse side *The Best Blood Purifier and Cathartec;* 9"; amber 50.00-60.00

268 LEDIARDS; on side *Celebrated Stomach*; on back *Bitters*; tapered top; 10"; sea green .... 80.00+

269 DR. LERIEMONDIE'S SOUTHERN BITTERS; 10"; dark green 35.00-65.00

270 LEWIS RED JACKET BITTERS around bottom; three-piece mold; 11"; amber 30.00-60.00

271 LIFE EVERLASTING BITTERS, ATLANTA GA.; 10"; amber .... 85.00+

272 LIPPMAN'S GREAT GERMAN BITTERS; other side *N.Y. & Savannah, Geo.*; 9¾"; amber .... 125.00+

273 LITTHAUER STOMACH BITTERS; in center *Invented 1884 by Josef Lowenthal, Berlin* in vertical lines; tapered top; 9¾"; milk glass 80.00-100.00

274 same as above except *Berlin* omitted 40.00-80.00

275 DR. LOEW'S CELEBRATED STOMACH BITTERS & NERVE TONIC; 3½"; amber .... 50.00+

276 DR. LOEW'S CELEBRATED STOMACH BITTERS & NERVE TONIC; reverse *The Loew & Son Co.*; tapered top and swirled ribbed neck; fancy bottle; 9½"; apple green 100.00-125.00

277 LORD BROS., DR. MANDRAKE BAXTO'S BITTERS; 12"; amber.......... 10.00-30.00

278 same as above except clear or amber 8.00-15.00

279 LORENTZ MED CO. TRADE MARK around shoulder; bitters label; 9¾"; amber 10.00-20.00

280 LORENTZ MED CO. on bitters label; *Trade To-Ni-Ta Mark* around shoulder; amber; 10" 10.00-15.00

281 LORIMER'S JUNIPER BITTERS; blue green; 9½"; 2¼" square 30.00-40.00

282 DR. XX LOVEGOODS FAMILY BITTERS on roof of cabin-shaped bottle; tapered neck; 10½"; amber 60.00-100.00

283 DR. LOVEGOODS FAMILY BITTRS (E left out of BITTERS); 9½"; amber ...... 300.00+

284 E. DEXTER LOVERIDGE WAHOO BITTERS DWD; *1863 XXX* on roof; tapered top; eagle faces down and left with one arrow; 10"; dark amber 50.00-100.00

285 same except eagle faces up to right; light yellow 50.00-100.00

286 DR. LYFORD'S BITTERS; *C.D. Herrick, Tilton, N.H.*; on bottom *W.T. & Co. C*; ringed top; 8"; aqua 30.00-60.00

287 E. G. LYONS & CO., MFG. SAN. F. CA. (n in SAN is backward); tapered top; 9"; amber .... 50.00+

288 MACK'S SARSAPARILLA BITTERS; in back *Mack & Co. Prop's S. F.*; 8½"; amber .. 25.00+

289 MAGIC BITTERS; *prepared by Minetree & Jackson, Petersburg Va.*; two panels and rounded sides; tapered top; 14½"; olive 55.00-75.00

290 MALARION BITTERS; *Snyder Gue & Condell, St. Louis, Mo.*; 8½"; amber.......... 55.00+

291 MALT BITTERS CO.; *Boston U.S.A.* under bottom; round; 8½; emerald green ... 20.00-30.00

292 MAMPE BITTERS, label; back embossed same with *Carl Mampe, Berlin*; 6"; dark green 50.00-80.00

293 PROFESSOR B.E. MANNS ORIENTAL STOMACH BITTERS; 10¼"; amber 40.00-60.00

294 MARIANI COCO BITTERS; 7½"; green 10.00-15.00

295 MARSHALL'S BITTERS; *The Best Laxative and Blood Purifier* on back; amber; 8¾" 25.00-40.00

296 McKEEVER'S ARMY BITTERS on shoulder; drum-shaped bottom; cannonballs stacked on top; tapered top; 10¼"; amber....... 400.00+

297 MILLS BITTERS; *A. M. Gilman, sole prop.*; lady's leg shape; ringed top; 6 ounce; amber .... 40.00+

298 same except sample size; 2 ounce ..... 40.00+

299 MISHLER'S HERB BITTERS; *S. B. Hartman & Co.* in back; under bottom *Stoeckels Grad Pat. Feb. 6, 66*; tapered top; 8¾"; amber 40.00-60.00

300 same as above except back reads *Wm. McC & Co.* .... 40.00+

301 MOHICA BITTERS; on back *Roth & Co. S. F.*; ringed top; 9"; amber........... 30.00-40.00

302 NATIONAL BITTERS; *Patent 1867* under bottom; amber; 12¼" .... 150.00+

303 NEW YORK HOP BITTERS CO.; tapered top; 9"; aqua 40.00-80.00

304 NORMAN BITTERS; in back *Dr. Bohlins*; 8¾"; clear .... 30.00+

306   307   320   322   325   328   331

332   333   334   335   336   337   339

340   341   345   348   352   353

305 WM. G. OESTING, GERMANIA BITTERS; 9¼"; amber 40.00-60.00

306 O.K. PLANTATION; triangular shape; amber; 11" .... 200.00+

307 OLD HICKORY CELEBRATED STOMACH BITTERS; on other side *J. Grossman, N.O. LA.;* 4½"; amber .... 25.00+

308 OLD HOMESTEAD CABIN BITTERS; 9½"; amber 100.00-125.00

309 OLD HOMESTEAD WILD CHERRY BITTERS; cabin shape; 10"; amber. 100.00-150.00

310 same except PATENT on roof; clapboards not logs and shingled roof; 10"; amber 60.00-100.00

311 same except cobalt blue .... 100.00+

312 same except inside thread; marked on top PAT. 1861 .... 100.00+

313 OLD SACHEM BITTERS & WIGHAM TONIC; barrel type bottle; ringed top; 9¾"; puce, amber, yellow amber 90.00-150.00

314 same except green 90.00-100.00

315 same except with label MERRICK & MOORS OLD SACHEM BITTERS & WIGWAM TONIC, NEW HAVEN CONN. . 90.00-100.00

316 O'LEARY'S 20th CENTURY BITTERS in vertical line; tapered top; 8½"; light amber 75.00+

317 OREGON GRAPE ROOT BITTERS; round; 9¾"; clear 40.00-50.00

318 ORIGINAL POCAHONTAS BITTERS; *Y. Ferguson;* barrel shape; 9½"; aqua 90.00-100.00

319 ORIZABA BITTERS; on back *J. Maristany Jr.;* round bottle; tapered top; 9½"; amber .. 45.00

320 OSWEGO BITTERS; 7¼"; amber. 35.00-45.00

321 OXYGENATED BITTERS; pontil; 6¾"; aqua .... 50.00+

322 PANKNIN'S; *Hepatic Bitters N.Y.* on back; amber; 9" .... 85.00+

323 PAWNEE BITTERS; *Indian Medicine Co. S.F.;* 11¼"; amber 40.00-60.00

324 PENNS BITTERS FOR THE LIVER on front panel; square; beveled edge; 6½"; amber .... 40.00+

325 PEPSIN BITTERS on one side; with *R. W. Davis Drug Co., Chicago, U.S.A.* in two lines on other side; shoulder and neck are raised, but not on ends; sunken panels on front and back; yellow green; 8¼" tall, 4¼" x 2⅛ .... 65.00+

326 PEPSIN CALISAYA BITTERS in two lines; opposite side *Dr. Russell Med. Co.;* rectangular; green, olive green; beveled corners with three vertical ribs; 7½" tall, 4¼" x 2¼" ... 15.00-20.00

327 PERRINS APPLE GINGER, PHILA.; embossed apple on front; cabin type bottle; 10¼"; amber 50.00-100.00

328 DR. D.S. PERRY & CO.; on other side *New York, Excelsior Aromatic Bitters;* roofed shoulder; tapered top; 10½"; amber 90.00-100.00

329 JOHN A. PERRY'S, DR. WARREN'S BILIOUS BITTERS; *Boston Mass.;* 10"; aqua 80.00-100.00

330 DR. PETZOLDS CABIN BITTERS; 11"; amber 80.00-100.00

331 PEYCHAUD'S AMERICAN AROMATIC BITTERS CORDIAL L.E. JUNG, SOLE PROP. N.O.; round tapered top; 10½"; amber 20.00-30.00

332 PHOENIX BITTERS; on back *J. N^o Moffat;* on one side *Price $1.^00;* other side *N.Y.;* pontil; 5"; dark olive .... 40.00+

333 DR. GEO. PIERCES INDIAN RESTORATIVE BITTERS; on side *Lowell, Mass.;* tapered top; 7½"; aqua 40.00-60.00

334 PINEAPPLE BOTTLE; bitters label; 9¼"; light amber 90.00-100.00

335 same except yellow green .... 400.00+

336 DR. PLANETTS BITTERS; iron pontil; aqua; 9¾" 40.00-50.00

337 PLOW'S SHERRY BITTERS; a large leaf on back for label; amber; 7¾" 400.00-600.00

338 POMLO BITTERS CO.; *N.Y.* on back; tapered top and ring; 11½"; light green ... 40.00-70.00

339 POND'S BITTERS CO. CHICAGO, label; *Ponds Genuine Ginger Brandy* on back; clear; 11½" 15.00-25.00

340 POND'S BITTERS; reverse side *Unexcelled Laxative;* on base *76;* 9¾"; amber . 25.00-50.00

341 same except machine made 10.00-20.00

342 POOR MAN'S FAMILY BITTERS; ringed top; 6½"; aqua 30.00-40.00

343 same except label reads POOR MAN'S BITTERS CO.,OSWEGO N.Y., *Entered according to the Act of Congress in 1870* 30.00-50.00

344 R.W. POWERS & CO. AROMATIC PERUVIAN BITTERS; *Rich. Va. 1881;* 10½"; amber 60.00-80.00

345 PRICKLEY ASH BITTER CO. in two lines in sunken panel; other sides are flat for labels; beveled corners; 10"; 2¾" x 2¾"... 25.00-35.00

346 PRUSSIAN BITTERS; tapered top; 9½"; amber 35.00-60.00

347 THE QUININE BITTER CO.; *184-196 Congress St. Chicago, Ill. U.S.A.;* diamond shape; concave sides; 8½"; clear .... 40.00+

348 RAMSEY'S TRINIDAD BITTER on shoulder; *(Bitters* misspelled on bottom); dark olive; 8¼" 70.00-80.00

349 RAMSEY'S TRINIDAD BITTERS; round; dark olive; body 5"; 3¼" neck on a shoulder; under bottom, *Ramsey Trinidad Bitter;* (no date) .... 45.00+

350 DR. MILLER'S RATAFIA, (Sphinx); under it, *Damiana Silbe Bros. Jr. Plagemann, S.F. sole agents, Pacific Coast;* round bottle; tapered and ringed top; 12"; amber 35.00-60.00

351 DR. RENZ'S HERB BITTERS; tapered and ring top; 9"; light green 30.00-65.00

352 REX BITTERS CO.,CHICAGO; whiskey shape; amber, clear; 10¼" 20.00-40.00

353 S.O. RICHARDSON vertically on front; *Bitters So. Reading* on side; other side *Mass.;* flared top; pontil; 6½"; light green 30.00-50.00

354   355   356   357   358   359   366   367

368   369   370   371   375   376   379   381

383   384   385   389   390   393   395   397

354 R.C. RIDGWAY & PHILA.; big *3* under bottom; 11"; amber 85.00-110.00

355 RIVAUD'S (reverse apostrophe) IMPERIAL BITTERS; *Victor Rivaud* on side; *Louisville Ky* on other side; amber; 10½"....... 75.00-85.00

356 DR. C.W. ROBACKS; *Cincinnati, O;* in small circle in center, *Stomach Bitters;* 9¾"; dark brown; barrel shape; ten ribs on top, ten ribs on base.................................... 85.00+

357 ROHRER'S; on one side *Lancaster Pa.;* on the other side *Expectoral-Wild Cherry Tonic;* 10½"; amber .... 100.00+

358 E.J. ROSE'S; *Superior Tonic; Cathartic and Blood Purifier* on back; amber; 9" ...: 60.00+

359 ROYAL PEPSIN STOMACH BITTERS; 8½"; amber 50.00-60.00

360 DR. RUSSELL'S ANGOSTURA BITTERS; round tapered top; 7¾"; amber, medium green, clear 40.00-60.00

361 same except olive green (rare) .... 60.00+

362 SAIDSCHITSER-FURSTLICH-LOBKO-WITZ BITTER WASSER in circle; tan crock; four panels; round bottom; 9½"..... 100.00+

363 SAINSEVINS WINE BITTERS, label; ringed top; 12"; aqua 10.00-20.00

364 SALMON'S PERFECT STOMACH BITTERS; tapered top; square beveled corners; 9½"; amber .... 85.00+

365 SANBORN'S KIDNEY & LIVER VEGETABLE LAXATIVE BITTERS; on bottom *B;* tapered bottle to paneled shoulder with fluted neck; 10"; amber .... 100.00+

366 SAN JOAQUIN WINE BITTERS; on back at bottom *B. F. C. Co.;* deep kick-up in base; 9¾"; amber 25.00-45.00

367 SARSAPARILLA BITTERS; on side *E. M. Rusha;* back side *Dr. De Andrews;* 10"; amber .... 30.00+

368 SAZERAC AROMATIC BITTERS; in a circle on shoulder in monogram *DPH & Co.;* 12½"; milk glass; also in blue, green........... 100.00+

369 SAZERAC AROMATIC BITTERS, D.P.H. in seal; lady's leg shape; 10¼"; light amber .... 200.00+

370 DR. S.B. & CO. ML under bottom; clear or amethyst; 7¼" 4.00-6.00

371 SCHRODER'S BITTERS; three-part mold; *Ky CWC* under bottom; amber; 12". 100.00-150.00

372 SEGRESTAT BITTERS in seal; kick-up on bottom; 11¾"; dark olive .... 50.00+

373 SEGUR'S GOLDEN SEAL BITTERS, SPRINGFIELD, MASS.; pontil; 8"; aqua 60.00-90.00

374 W. F. SEVERA; on back *Stomach Bitters;* tapered top; 10"; red amber 20.00-40.00

375 SHERMAN BITTERS; *Myer Bros. Drug. Co. St. Louis,* label; 7¾"; amber 8.00-10.00

376 DR. B.F. SHERMAN'S PRICKLY ASH BITTERS; machine made; 10"; amber .. 4.00-8.00

377 SIMONS AROMATIC STOMACH BITTERS; 7¼"; clear or amber 50.00-75.00

378 SIMONS CENTENNIAL BITTERS TRADE MARK; bust shape bottle; double ring top; 10¼"; amber, clear or aqua .... 200.00+

379 DR. SIMS ANTI-CONSTIPATION BITTERS; 6½"; amber..................... 50.00-65.00

380 DR. SKINNER'S CELEBRATED 25 CENT BITTERS; *So. Reading, Mass.;* pontil; 9½"; aqua.................................... 20.00-40.00

381 DR. SMITHS COLUMBO BITTERS, label and embossed; 9¾"; amber 30.00-60.00

382 SNYDER BITTERS; *Jonesboro, Ark.;* tapered top; 9½"; amber 40.00-60.00

383 SOLOMON'S STRENGTHENING & INVIGORATING BITTER on one sunken panel; on other *Savannah Ga.;* on other side, sunken panels; back flat; roofed shoulders; 2¾" x 2¾"; 9½" tall; beveled corners; cobalt .. 75.00-86.00

384 DR. SPERRY'S FEMALE STRENGTHENING BITTERS; *Waterbury, Conn.,* label and embossed; 10" 75.00-90.00

385 STAAKE'S ORIGINAL VITAL-TONE BITTERS around shoulder; ringed top; 8¼"; clear 35.00-55.00

386 S. STANLEY & CO. AFRICAN STOMACH BITTERS; 9½"; amber 20.00-30.00

387 STAR KIDNEY & LIVER BITTERS; tapered top; 9½"; amber 20.00-35.00

388 same as above with label........ 15.00-20.00

389 STEKETEES BLOOD PURIFYING BITTERS; 9½"; amber.............. 20.00-40.00

390 DR. STEWARTS TONIC BITTERS; *Columbus Ohio* under bottom; amber; 8"........ 50.00+

391 ST. GOTTHARDS BITTERS; 8½"; amber .... 75.00+

392 ST. GOTTHARDS HERB BITTERS; 8½"; amber 60.00-70.00

393 STONGHTON BITTERS; 7"; clear 10.00-20.00

394 SUFFOLK BITTERS; other side *Philbrook & Tucker, Boston;* 9½" tall, 3½" wide; shape of a pig; ground lip; light amber........ 500.00+

395 SUMTER BITTERS; on front and back *Charleston S.C.;* on back *Dowie Moise & Davis Wholesale Druggist;* 9½"; amber ...... 20.00+

396 DR. SWEET STRENGTHENING BITTER; long tapered top; 8¼"; aqua 20.00-35.00

397 TIPPECANOE; amber, clear, aqua; 9" 50.00+

398   399   400   401   406   412   414

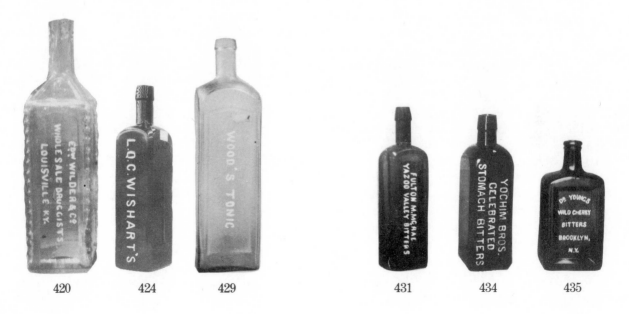

420   424   429   431   434   435

398 TIPPECANOE; misspelled *Rochester* under bottom; 9″; amber .... 60.00+

399 TODD'S BITTERS; machine made; clear; 8¼″ 8.00-10.00

400 TONECO BITTERS; clear; under bottom a diamond shape with number 15.00-25.00

401 OLD DR. TOWNSEND CELEBRATED STOMACH BITTERS in six lines; handled jug; amber; plain band; pontil; 8¾″.... 60.00-75.00

402 TUFTS ANGOSTURA BITTERS, label; 9¾″; green 10.00-15.00

403 TURNER BROTHERS N.Y.; *Buffalo N.Y.,San Francisco Calif.*; tapered top; pontil; 9½″; amber 50.00-85.00

404 ULMAR MT. ASH BITTERS; 7″; aqua 90.00-125.00

405 UNIVERSAL BITTERS; pontil; aqua 100.00+

406 UNIVERSAL BITTERS; *Mfg. by Aug. Horstmann Sole Agent F.J. Schaefer, 231 Market St. Louisville, Ky*; 12″; lady's leg shape; emerald green .... 100.00+

407 UNKA within a ball on front, picture of an eagle on top of the ball, *Army & Navy* around all this, *Unka Bitters 1895* under all this, label; tapered and ringed top; amber; 8½″ 18.00-25.00

408 USAACSON SEIXAS & CO.; other side reads *66 & 68 Common St., C.O. Witheye*; bitters monogram under it; bulged neck; tapered and ring top; kick-up 80.00-160.00

409 VAN OPSAL & CO. MORNING DEW BITTERS, N.Y.; 10½″; amber...... 80.00-100.00

410 VEGETABLE STOMACH BITTERS; reverse side *Dr. Ball's, Northboro, Mass.*; 7¼″; aqua 30.00-60.00

411 VERMO STOMACH BITTERS; reverse side *Tonic & Appetizer*; tapered top; machine made; 9½″........................... 10.00-20.00

412 DR. VON HOPF'S CURACO BITTERS; *Chamberlain & Co. Des Moines, Iowa* on back; amber; 9¼″...................... 40.00-60.00

413 J. WALKER VINEGAR BITTERS; 8½″; aqua 8.00-10.00

414 WARNERS SAFE BITTERS; figure of a safe in center; on base *Rochester N.Y.*; oval shape; round collar; 9¾″; amber .... 65.00+

415 DR. WARREN'S OLD QUAKER BITTERS; *Old Dr. Warren's* on one side; *Quaker Bitters* on other; aqua; 9½″; rectangular 10.00-25.00

416 DR. WHEELER'S TONIC SHERRY WINE BITTERS; round; pontil; 8¼″; plain or aqua .... 100.00+

417 WHITEWELL'S TEMPERENCE BITTERS; *Boston*; pontil; 7″; aqua 80.00-90.00

418 J. T. WIGGINS GENTION BITTERS; ribbed sides; 11″; amber .... 50.00+

419 WILD CHERRY BITTERS; *Mfg. by C.C. Richards & Co. Yarmouth N. S. L. & Co.*; 6¼″; aqua 40.00-60.00

420 EDW. WILDER & CO.; *Edw. Wilder Stomach Bitters* on back; *Patented 5* on one roof; very light green; 10½″ 80.00-90.00

421 WILMERDING & CO.; *Sole agents for Peruvian Bitters,214 & 216 Front St. S.F. in a circle*; flask shape bottle; 6″; amber 40.00-60.00

422 DR. WILSON'S HERBINE BITTERS; *Bragley Sons & Co., Montreal*; oval shape; 8½″; aqua 40.00-80.00

423 same as above except 6″ 40.00-80.00

424 L.Q.C. WISHART'S; pine tree trademark on one side; *Pine Tree Tar Cordial Phila* on other side; different sizes and colors 25.00-50.00

425 DR. WISTERS OXYGENATED BITTERS FOR DYSPEPSIA & GENERAL DEBILITY; pontil; 6″; aqua 50.00-100.00

426 DR. WONSER'S U.S. INDIAN ROOT BITTERS; fancy round type bottle; tapered top; 10½″; amber................... 40.00-60.00

427 same as above except aqua 40.00-60.00

428 WOODBURY'S BITTERS; *Steinhardt Bros. & Co.,N.Y.*; round bottle; tapered top; 8″; amber 40.00-60.00

429 WOOD'S TONIC; *Wine Bitter* on side; *Cincinnati,Ohio* other side; aqua .... 100.00+

430 WRYGHTE'S BITTERS appears on all four sides; *London* also appears on four sides; ringed top; pontil; 5¾″; dark olive .... 100.00+

431 YAZOO VALLEY BITTERS, FULTON M. McRAE; 8¾″; amber 10.00-20.00

432 YERBA BUENA BITTERS,S.F. CAL. on each side; coffin-shaped flask; 8½″; amber 40.00-60.00

433 same as above in quart size with *no. 2* on shoulder front and back 40.00-60.00

434 YOCHIM BROS. CELEBRATED STOMACH BITTERS; 8¾″; amber 40.00-75.00

435 DR. YOUNG'S WILD CHERRY BITTERS; 8¾″; amber.................... 40.00-60.00

436 ZINGARI BITTERS; *F. Rahter* on reverse side; lady's leg type bottle; ringed top; 11½″; amber 150.00-200.00

437 ZOELER'S STOMACH BITTERS; on one side *Zoeler Medical Co;Pittsburgh Pa.*; deep V-like grooves on other side; long graduated top; amber, golden amber; 9½″; rounded corners 40.00-60.00

438 ZU ZU BITTERS appears on all sides; medicine type bottle; ringed top; 8¼″; amber 40.00-60.00

Cure

With undaunted determination medieval alchemists added varying proportions of a substance called elixir to metal in the hope that valuable gold would result. They were unsuccessful and elixir became known as a drug capable of prolonging life, presumably the next best thing to turning metal to gold. Thus Elixir was the name that Richard Stoughton chose for his patented medicinal concoction first produced in England in 1712.

In the age of patent medicines some compounds were known as cures, and the people put their wholehearted faith in them. At the height of the nineteenth-century patent medicine fad, drugstores in the United States sold about 365 million bottles of the wondrous formulas a year. The reasons for the people's stubborn belief in self-prescribed remedies had much to do with the quality of medical care available.

Prior to 1730 most doctors in the New World were trained by apprenticeship. Though European training for doctors began to gain in popularity in the years that followed and medical colleges—however of inferior quality—began to be established, life expectancy in the United States in 1800 was only thirty-five years. Many medical advancements were made in this country during the first decades of the nineteenth century and the profession of physician became a favorite. By 1850, practically any man could become a doctor after a mere year's training. Understandably, confidence in doctors was slight; trusting one's health to the contents of a patent medicine bottle made reasonable sense.

When American romanticists began to idolize the Indian as a symbol of strength and health, it was a simple step for the medicine hawkers to employ Indian names in the promotion of their products. Ka-Ton-Ka Cure was soon available, as was the Kickapoo Indian Cough Cure. To convince the public of their authenticity, many of these were endorsed by assumedly healthy Indians.

The intrigue of the Orient captivated the American people in the mid-1800's. Patent medicine soon stressed the wonders of Far Eastern health secrets with such products as Carey's Chinese Catarrh Cure, a remedy designed to eliminate the discomforts of the common cold.

Cures for diseases that puzzle scientists today could be found lining drugstore shelves in apothecary containers. W. Stoy of Lebanon, Pennsylvania, bottled his cure for hydrophobia in 1809 and J. Andrus of Hillsborough, New Hampshire, began selling his cancer cure in 1816.

Many collectable cure bottles are embossed with an owl and the traditional druggist tools of mortar and pestle. The Owl Drug Store, established in San Francisco in 1892, became associated with Rexall in 1919. Owl Drug sold its rights to the parent firm of Rexall, the United Drug Company, in 1933, and the chain was known as Owl-Rexall Drug Company.

Interest in cures began to decline as higher standards in the practice of medicine were implemented. By the last decade of the nineteenth century it was modern medicine that was promising cures. Following the passage of the Pure Food and Drug Act in 1907, which forced the disclosure of many worthless ingredients, many drug manufacturers supplanted the word "cure" with the less utopian word "remedy."

Opposite: *Peddled in the late 1800's, these proprietary medicines (#496 and #617) ironically contained a high percentage of alcohol, an ingredient that diabetics and those suffering from kidney disease should have shunned.*

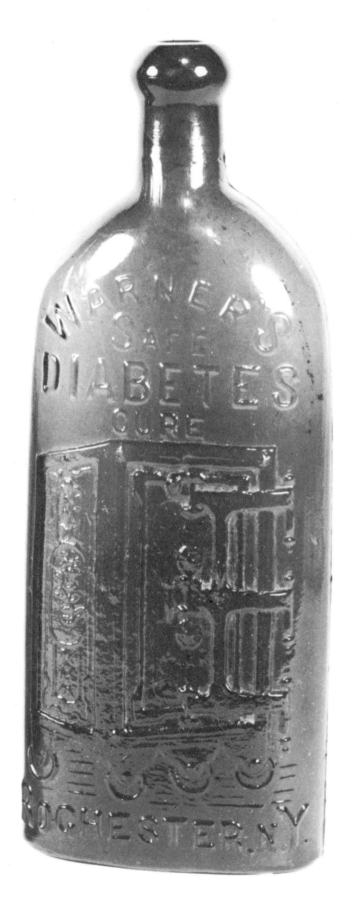

461

491

496

506

439 ACID CURE SOLUTION, EMPIRE MFG. CO., AKRON, OHIO in a circle; crock; 4¾"; white 8.00-10.00

440 DR. AGNEWS CURE FOR THE HEART; ring top; 8½"; clear.................. 8.00-10.00

441 ALEXANDER'S SURE CURE FOR MALARIA, AKRON OHIO; on side *Alexanders Liver & Kidney Tonic*; ring top; 8"; amber 8.00-10.00

442 ALEXANDER'S SURE CURE FOR MALARIA; ring top; 6½"; amber.. 8.00-10.00

443 ANCHOR WEAKNESS CURE; 8¼"; amber 6.00-10.00

444 ANTIMIGRAINE CURE EVERY VARIETY OF HEADACHE; 5¼"; clear or amethyst 4.00-8.00

445 ATLAS KIDNEY & LIVER CURE, ATLAS MEDICINE CO., HENDERSON, N.C. U.S.A. with fancy monogram; AM CO. in sunken panel; 9"; honey amber 6.00-10.00

446 AYERS in sunken panel; on side AGUE; other side LOWELL, MASS.; double ring collar; 7"; aqua.......................... 4.00-8.00

447 B.H. BACON, ROCHESTER N.Y., OTTO'S CURE; 2½"; clear................ 4.00-8.00

448 BAKER'S BLOOD & LIVER CURE; large crown with a flag; 9½"; amber.... 40.00-65.00

449 BAKERS SOUTH AMERICAN FEVER AND AGUE CURE; ring top; 9¾''; amber 25.00-50.00

450 BAUER'S COUGH CURE on front; 2⅞; clear 4.00-6.00

451 BAUER'S INSTANT COUGH CURE; 7"; aqua 6.00-10.00

452 BISHOP'S GRANULAR CITRATE OF MAGNESIA, SAN FRANCISCO, COUGH CURE; 6½"; blue........................ 4.00-8.00

453 BLISS LIVER & KIDNEY CURE; 9¼"; aqua or clear 4.00-10.00

454 BLISS LIVER & KIDNEY CURE; 7"; clear 8.00-12.00

455 THE BLISS REMEDY CO., BLISS LIVER & KIDNEY CURE, STOCKTON, CAL.; 9¼"; aqua.......................... 8.00-10.00

456 BOERIKE & RUNYON, S.F. & PORTLAND; 5½"; clear or amethyst 3.00-6.00

457 DR. BOSAKO'S RHEUMATIC CURE; 5¾"; aqua.......................... 4.00-8.00

458 BREEDENS RHEUMATIC CURE, label; BREEDEN MEDICINE CO., CHATTANOOGA, TENN. on front; 6½"; aqua 8.00-10.00

459 BRIGGS TONIC PILLS, NEVER FAIL TO CURE; *M.A. Briggs, Valdosta, Ga.*; 3"; clear 3.00-6.00

460 BRIGHTSBANE, THE GREAT KIDNEY AND LIVER CURE vertical on front; square beveled corners; 8⅞"; light amber... 8.00-12.00

461 BROWN'S BLOOD CURE, PHILADELPHIA; 6½"; green 10.00-20.00

462 BROWNS HOUSEHOLD PANACEA AND FAMILY LINIMENT vertical on front panels; *Curtis & Brown* on side; *Mfg. Col'd. New York* on opposite side; rectangular; square collar; 5⅛"; aqua.......................... 4.00-8.00

463 BUCHAN'S HUNGARIAN *Balsam of Life, London*; vertical lines *Kidney Cure*; 5¾"; round short neck; green................ 3.00-5.00

464 BUXTON'S RHEUMATIC CURE; 8½"; aqua
.... 4.00-10.00

465 THE DR. D. M. BYE OIL CURE CO.; reverse side, *316 N. Illinois St.*; side *Indianapolis Ind.*; ring top; 6½"; clear 4.00-8.00

466 CANADIAN BOASTER HAIR TONIC; reverse side *Dandruff Cure*; 8¼"; clear   4.00-6.00

467 CAPUDINE HEADACHE CURE; oval; 3⅜; aqua........................ 4.00-6.00

468 CERTAIN CURE FOR RHEUMATISM vertical on front in sunken panel; *Chas. Dennin* on side; *Brooklyn* on opposite side; 6¾"; aqua 8.00-15.00

469 CHAMBERLAINS CURE FOR CONSUMPTION; 5"; aqua 4.00-8.00

470 CILL'S CATARRH CURE vertical on front; sheared top; round bottom; 3¼"; clear 8.00-10.00

471 DR. J.W. COBLENTZ CURE, FT. WAYNE, IND, label; 7¾"; cobalt 4.00-8.00

472 COE'S DYSPEPSIA CURE OR STOMACH BITTERS, THE C. G CLARK CO., NEW HAVEN, CONN. U.S.A.; 7½"; clear or aqua .... 15.00+

473 COKE DANDRUFF CURE on bottom; large ring top; 6½"; clear 8.00-15.00

474 MRS. M.E. CONVERSE'S SURE CURE FOR EPILEPSY; ring top; 6¼"; clear .... 8.00+

475 C.C.C. (CORN CURE) BY MENDENHELL CO., EVANSVILLE IND.; ring top; 4½"; clear or aqua 10.00-15.00

476 also C.C.C. (Certain Cough Cure) .. 10.00-15.00

477 DR. COSTA'S RADICAL CURE FOR DYSPEPSIA in sunken panels; double ring top; 5½"; aqua 4.00-8.00

478 CRISWELL'S BROMO-PEPSIN CURES HEADACHE vertical; round; ring top; 2½"; amber 8.00-12.00

479 CRISWELL'S BROMO-PEPSIN CURES HEADACHE AND DIGESTION vertical on front; 4¾"; amber 8.00-12.00

480 J.M. CURTIS CURE FOR THE BALDNESS; *Providence, R.I.*; flared top; ½ pint; aqua 8.00-10.00

481 THE CUTICURA SYSTEM OF CURING CONSTIPATIONAL HUMORS on front of panel; *Potter Drug and Chemical Corp. Boston, Mass. U.S.A.* on reverse of panel; rectangular; 9¼"; aqua 8.00-10.00

482 DR. DANIEL'S COLIC CURE; ring top; 3¾"; clear or amethyst.............. 4.00-6.00

483 DR. DANIEL'S COLIC CURE NO. 1 on front; square; 3½"; clear 4.00-8.00

484 DR. DANIEL'S COLIC CURE NO. 2; same as above..................... 4.00-8.00

485 DR. DANIEL'S VETERINARY COLIC CURE NO. 1 on front; square; 3½"; clear.... 4.00-8.00

486 DR. DANIEL'S VETERINARY COLIC CURE NO. 2; same as above............. 4.00-8.00

487 DeWITTS COLIC & CHOLERA CURE; 4½"; green.................... 4.00-6.00

488 DR. DeWITT'S LIVER, BLOOD, & KIDNEY CURE; 8½"; amber............. 25.00-30.00

489 DR. DeWITT'S; *Electric Cure, W.J. Parker & Co. Baltimore Md.*; tapered top; aqua; 6½" 8.00-12.00

490 E. C. DeWITT & CO., CHICAGO U.S.A., ONE MINUTE COUGH CURE; tapered top; 4½"; aqua........................ 4.00-8.00

491 E.G. DeWITTS & CO., CHICAGO, label; side mold; *Dyspepsia Cure* on back; clear; 9¼" 8.00-12.00

492 W. H. DOLFS SURE CURE FOR COLIC; flat ring top; *T.C.W. & Co.* under bottom; 3½"; aqua 8.00-12.00

493 DUFFY'S TOWER MINT CURE (TRADE-MARK EST 1842); 6½"; tapered bottle; wide ring top; embossed tower & flag; amber 75.00-100.00

494 ELEPIZONE, A CERTAIN CURE FOR FITS AND EPILEPSY, ELEPIZONE, H.G. ROOT M.C., *183 Pearl St., New York* on front; ring top; 8½"; aqua 25.00-35.00

495 FALEY'S [sic] KIDNEY & BLADDER CURE on front; *Foley's & Co.* on one side; *Chicago, U.S.A.* on reverse; 9½"; amber...... 4.00-8.00

496 DR. M.M. FENNER'S; amber; 10¼" 12.00-15.00

497 DR. M.M. FENNER'S PEOPLES REMEDIES, N.Y., U.S.A., KIDNEY & BACKACHE CURE 1872-1898 all on front horizontally; 10¼"; amber 25.00-45.00

498 FITCH'S DANDRUFF CURE, IDEAL DANDRUFF CURE CO.; ring top; 6¼" 4.00-6.00

499 FITZGERALD'S MEMBRANE CURE vertical on front in sunken panel; aqua.... 10.00-15.00

500 FOLEY'S KIDNEY & BLADDER CURE on front; on one side *Foley & Co.*; reverse *Chicago U.S.A.*; double ring top; 7½"; amber   8.00-10.00

501 SAMPLE BOTTLE FOLEY'S KIDNEY CURE, FOLEY & CO., CHICAGO, U.S.A. vertical around bottle; 4¼"; aqua 4.00-8.00

502 FOLEY'S SAFE DIARRHEA & COLIC CURE, CHICAGO; panels; 5½"; aqua   4.00-8.00

503 H.D. FOWLE, BOSTON in back, label; *Fowle's Pile & Humor Cure*; ring top; 5½"; aqua 8.00-10.00

504 DR. FRANK, TURKEY FEBRIFUGE FOR THE CURE OF FEVER AND AGUE; pontil; 6"; aqua 10.00-20.00

505 FREE SAMPLE CRAMERS KIDNEY CURE; *Albany* and *N.Y.* are reversed; 4¼"; aqua 10.00-12.00

506 FROG POND CHILL & FEVER CURE; flat ring top; 7"; amber .... 25.00+

507 GARGET CURE, C.T. WHIPPLE PROP., PORTLAND, ME.; ring top; 5¾"; aqua 4.00-6.00

| 508 | 510 | 520 | 521 | 522 |

| 529 | 531 | 545 | 555 | 557 | 563 | 567 |

508 DR. A.F. GEOGHEGAN, LOUISVILLE KY., CURE FOR SCROFULA; graphite pontil; 9¼"; aqua .... 45.00+

509 GLOVER'S IMPERIAL DISTEMPER CURE, H. CLAY GLOVER, NEW YORK vertical on front; 5"; amber 4.00-8.00

510 GLOVERS IMPERIAL MANGE CURE; *H. Clay Glover DU'S* on one side; *New York* on other side; amber; 7" 4.00-6.00

511 GOLD DANDRUFF CURE vertical on center front; ring top; 7½"; clear........ 8.00-12.00

512 GOLDEN ROD LOTION, A SAFE AND CERTAIN CURE; 6"; amber........ 10.00-15.00

513 GRAHAM'S DYSPEPSIA CURE; *S. Grover Graham Co., Newburgh, N.Y.*; 8½"; clear 4.00-8.00

514 S. GROVER GRAHAM'S DYSPEPSIA CURE, NEWBURG, N.Y. vertical on front in large letters; 8¼"; amethyst 12.00-15.00

515 DR. GRAVES HEART REGULATOR, CURES HEART DISEASE; ring top; 5¾"; aqua 4.00-8.00

516 THE GREAT DR. KILMER SWAMP ROOT KIDNEY LIVER & BLADDER CURE SPECIFIC; 8¼"; aqua or clear 8.00-12.00

517 same except THE GREAT & SPECIFIC 8.00-12.00

518 GREGORY'S INSTANT CURE; pontil; 4" and 6"; aqua .... 10.00+

519 DR. B.W. HAIRS ASTHMA CURE; 8"; aqua 10.00-12.00

520 HALLS CATARRH CURE; aqua; 4½" 6.00-8.00

521 HALL'S CATARRH CURE; aqua; 4½" 3.00-5.00

522 HALL'S CATARRH CURE; aqua; 4½" 3.00-4.00

523 HART'S SWEDISH ASTHMA CURE; *Buffalo N.Y.* on side; rectangular; beveled corners; 6⅝"; light amber...................... 4.00-8.00

524 same as above except by INDIAN MED. CO., CLINTONVILLE, CONN.......... 4.00-6.00

525 HEALY & BIGELOWS KICKAPOO INDIAN COUGH CURE on panels; ring top; 6¼"; aqua 4.00-6.00

526 DR. J.B. HEMOUS; reverse side *Sure Cure For Malaria*; 6¼"; cobalt............ 8.00-10.00

527 HILLEMANS AMERICAN CHICKEN CHOLERA CURE, ARLINGTON, MINN.; flared top; 6½"; cobalt.......... 30.00-50.00

528 DR. HILLER'S COUGH CURE; tapered top; 7½"; aqua 8.00-10.00

529 HILLS with block *H* letters and arrow; under it DYS-PEP-CU-CURES CHRONIC DYSPEPSIA, INDIAN DRUG SPECIALTY CO.; St. Louis, Indianapolis on front; tapered top; 8½"; amber 15.00-25.00

530 HIMALAYA, THE KOLA COMPOUND, NATURES CURE FOR ASTHMA, NEW YORK, CINCINNATI embossed horizontally on indented front panels; square; 7½"; amber 10.00-15.00

531 HIRES; *Cough Cure, Phila, Pa.* on sides; aqua; 4½" 8.00-10.00

532 HOWARD BROS. on front; on one side *Cough Cure*; other side *Pettit's American*; tapered top; 7"; aqua 6.00-10.00

533 DR. S.D. HOWE'S ARABIAN MILK CURE FOR CONSUMPTION; 6"; clear .. 8.00-10.00

534 same as above except 7½" 15.00-20.00

535 HUNNICUTT'S; reverse side *Rheumatic Cure*; ring top; 8"; aqua 4.00-10.00

536 INDIAN MED. CO., CLINTONVILLE CONN., KICKAPOO INDIAN COUGH CURE; 5¾"; aqua.................... 4.00-8.00

537 W. M. JOHNSON'S PURE HERB TONIC, SURE CURE FOR ALL MALARIAL DISEASES; vertical lettering; 6"; clear 8.00-12.00

538 K.K.K., KAY'S KENTUCKY KURE OR LINIMENT vertical around bottle; 3¾"; aqua 15.00-25.00

539 DR. J. KAUFFMAN'S ANGELINE, INTERNAL RHEUMATISM CURE, HAMILTON, OHIO vertical in three lines on front; flared top; 7⅞"; clear.................... 10.00-18.00

540 DR. L. E. KEELEY, KEELEY'S CURE FOR DRUNKNESS etc.; *Dwight, Ill.*; ring top; 5½"; clear or amethyst.................... 8.00-10.00

541 KEESLING CHICKEN CHOLERA CURE C.C.C.; *Package 25 cents, B. F. Keeslings, Logansport, Ind.* 8.00-10.00

542 KENDALL'S SPAVIN CURE FOR HUMAN FLESH vertical on two panels; ten vertical panels; 5¼"; aqua.................... 4.00-8.00

543 KENDALL'S SPAVIN CURE around shoulders; *Enosburgh Falls, Vt.* on bottom; twelve vertical panels; 5½"; amber ... 4.00-8.00

544 KICKAPOO COUGH CURE vertical on indented panel; round; 6¼"; aqua 8.00-12.00

545 E. J. KIEFFER; amber; 8" 8.00-12.00

546 DR. KILMER'S SURE HEADACHE CURE; *25 doses in a box*; 5¼"; clear....... 8.00-10.00

547 DR. KILMER'S SWAMP ROOT KIDNEY CURE, BINGHAMTON, N.Y.; 1½"; aqua 4.00-6.00

548 KILMERS, THE GREAT *Swamp-Root Kidney Liver and Bladder Cure Specific* on front; *Binghamton, N.Y.* on left; *Dr. Kilmer & Co.* on right; aqua; 8¼"; rectangular 5.00-10.00

549 DR. KING'S NEW CURE FOR CONSUMPTION; 6"; clear or aqua 4.00-6.00

550 KODOL DYSPEPSIA CURE on side; *E. C. DeWitt & Co., Chicago* on opposite side; rectangular; 6⅞"; aqua 6.00-10.00

551 LANGERBACH'S DYSENTARY CURE vertical on front; *San Francisco, Cal.*; round; blob type; 6"; amber 15.00-25.00

552 LASH'S KIDNEY & LIVER CURE; 9"; amber 20.00-30.00

553 JARABE DE LEONARDI, *Para La Tos Creostodado, Leonardi Cough Cure Creosoted, New York and Tampa, Fla.* in four lines in sunken panel; plain back; plain sunken side panels; 5¼"; aqua; under bottom *W. T. Co 4, U.S.A.*; 2.00-4.00

554 LEONARDI'S COUGH CURE, CREOSOTED; *N.Y. & Tampa*; 5½"; aqua........ 4.00-6.00

555 LEONARDI'S TASTELESS; clear or amethyst; 6¼" 2.00-4.00

556 LIGHTNING KIDNEY & LIVER CURE, NO RELIEF, NO PAY, HERB MED CO.; *Weston, West Va.*; 9½"; aqua............. 30.00-40.00

557 LOOKOUT MOUNTAIN MEDICINE CO.; amber; 10½" .... 25.00+

558 J.J. MACK & CO., S.F. CAL., CURTIS COUGH CURE, C.C.C. on both sides; 7" 8.00-10.00

559 MAGIC MOSQUITO BITE CURE & INSECT EXTERMINATOR, SALLADE & CO. N.Y. on front; oval; tapered collar; 7⅞"; aqua 6.00-10.00

560 MALOY OIL H.F.M. in leaf; *Instant Relief Cure Rheumatism*; 4¾"; clear.................... 4.00-8.00

561 MARVINIS CHERRY COUGH CURE, label; tapered top; 9½"; amber.......... 10.00-20.00

562 MERTOL DANDRUFF CURE; 5½"; clear 4.00-6.00

563 DR. MILES NEW HEART CURE vertical on front in sunken panel; double band collar; 8½"; aqua.................... 6.00-10.00

564 same as above; 4¼"; free sample size 8.00-15.00

565 MINER'S DAMIANA NERVE DISEASE CURE; embossed woman; 8¼"; amber 40.00-80.00

566 MUNYON'S INHALER, CURES COLDS, CATARRH AND ALL THROAT & LUNG DISEASES on front; *Patented, Fill to the Line* on back; round; 4⅛"; olive green 10.00-20.00

567 NAU'S DYSPEPSIA CURE; amber; 5" 6.00-8.00

568 NO. 1 LABOREE'S COLIC CURE; 3½"; clear 6.00-8.00

572   584   586   603   604   610   613

615   617   618

619   627   631

569 ONE MINUTE COUGH CURE vertical on front in sunken panel; *E.C. DeWitt & Co.* on side; *Chicago, U.S.A.* on opposite side; rectangular; 5½"; aqua 8.00-12.00

570 same as above except 5" 4.00-8.00

571 ONE MINUTE COUGH CURE vertical on front; *E.C. DeWitt & Co. Chicago, U.S.A.* vertical on back; rectangular; 4¼"; aqua .. 4.00-6.00

572 THE ORIGINAL COPPER CURE; oval; flared lip; 7¾"; amber .... 55.00+

573 OTTO'S CURE FOR THE THROAT & LUNGS on front indented panel; *B.H. Bacon* on right panel; *Rochester, N.Y.* on reverse side; 6"; aqua 4.00-8.00

574 OTTO'S CURE FOR THE THROAT & LUNGS vertical on front indented panel; oval; 2¾"; aqua 4.00-6.00

575 PARIS MED. CO., ST. LOUIS, GROVE'S CHRONIC CHILL CURE; 2¾"; aqua 4.00-8.00

576 PARK'S SURE CURE (KIDNEY CURE); 6½"; aqua........................... 8.00-10.00

577 DR. PARKER'S COUGH CURE; ring top; 6"; aqua........................... 4.00-10.00

578 PISO'S CURE on side; FOR CONSUMPTION on front; other side HAZELTONE & CO.; 5"; emerald green 4.00-6.00

579 same as above except clear 4.00-8.00

580 POLAR STAR COUGH CURE with embossed star in center, vertical on front in sunken panels; rectangular; 5¾"; aqua 4.00-8.00

581 same as above except 4" 4.00-8.00

582 PORTER'S CURE OF PAIN, CLEVELAND, OHIO; 6½"; clear 4.00-8.00

583 PRATTS DISTEMPER & PINK EYE CURE; 7"; amber 4.00-6.00

584 PRATTS DISTEMPER CURE, PRATT FOOD CO.; *Phila. U.S.A.*; ring top; 7"; amber 25.00+

585 QUICK HEADACHE CURE, B.F. KEESLING, LOGANSPORT, IND. 8.00-10.00

586 WM. RADAMIS; amber; 10½" .... 35.00+

587 RAY'S GERMICIDE CURES MANY DISEASES on front in gold paint; hand painted flowers on top half; top half is white, lower half is brown pottery somewhat glazed; sheared type; handle; jug shape; 8½" 10.00-20.00

588 RED STAR COUGH CURE on one side; other side THE CHARLES A. VOGELER CO.; *Baltimore; U.S.A.* on base; tapered top; 7½"; aqua........................ 3.00-6.00

589 REEVE'S COMP. TEREBENE COUGH CURE; 4"; clear 4.00-8.00

590 same as above except 6" 4.00-10.00

591 RHODES FEVER & AGUE CURE; 8½"; aqua 4.00-8.00

592 RIVER SWAMP CHILL AND FEVER CURE; embossed alligator; ring top; 10¼"; amber or clear 10.00-25.00

593 ROCK'S COUGH & COLD CURE, CHAS. A. DARBY, N.Y. vertical on front in sunken panel; rectangular; 5⅝"; aqua........... 8.00-12.00

594 ROLL'S SYRUP WILD CHERRY WHITE PINE AND TAR, CURE COUGHS AND COLDS; flared top; clear.......... 4.00-8.00

595 H. G. ROOT M.C., 183 PEARL ST. N.Y., ELEPIZONE, A CERTAIN CURE FOR FITS AND EPILEPSY; ring top; 8½"; amber 15.00-25.00

596 ROSEWOOD DANDRUFF CURE, PREPARED BY J.R. REEVES CO., ANDERSON, IND. vertical on front; rectangular; paneling on collar; 6½"; amethyst 8.00-15.00

597 SAMPLE SHILOH'S CURE vertical on front; rectangular; 4¼"; aqua 4.00-8.00

598 SANFORD'S on side; RADICAL CURE on opposite side; rectangular; 7¾"; cobalt blue 10.00-25.00

599 SAVE-THE-HORSE, REGISTERED TRADE MARK, SPAVIN CURE, TROY CHEMICAL CO., BINGHAMTON N.Y. on front; ring top; 6½"; aqua...................... 4.00-8.00

600 same as above except TROY N.J. ... 8.00-16.00

601 SHILOH'S CONSUMPTION CURE on front; *S.C. Wells* on side; *Leroy, N.Y.* on opposite side; rectangular; 6"; aqua............ 8.00-12.00

602 same as above except *S.C. Wells & Co.* 8.00-12.00

603 DR. SHOOP'S COUGH CURE; clear; 6½" 2.00-4.00

604 SLOANS SURE COLIC CURE; ring top; 4¾"; clear or amber.................... 4.00-6.00

605 SPARKS KIDNEY & LIVER CURE; ring top; 9¾"; amber.................... 40.00-80.00

606 THE SPECIFIC A NO. 1, A SELF CURE, TRADE MARK on front and bottom; 5½"; aqua 4.00-6.00

607 SPEEDY CURE FOR COUGHS AND COLDS; on one side *Jones & Primley Co.*; other side *Elkhart, Ind.*; ring top; 8"; clear... 8.00-10.00

608 SPOHN'S DISTEMPER CURE, SPOHN MEDICAL COMPANY, GOSHEN, INDIANA U.S.A. vertical on front in sunken panel; 5"; aqua........................ 4.00-8.00

609 DR. SYKES SURE CURE FOR CATARRH in four lines; aqua; 6½" 2.00-4.00

610 DR. SYKES SURE CURE FOR CATARRH in front; four-part mold; aqua; 6¾"; round; short neck................ 6.00-10.00

611 TAMALON SAFE ANIMAL CURE; 11¼"; amber .... 45.00+

612 TAYLOR'S HOSPITAL CURE FOR CATARRH; *N.Y. WT Co. U.S.A.* under bottom; 6¼"; clear or amethyst.......... 10.00-20.00

613 DR. W. TOWNS EPILEPSY CURE, FOND DU LAC, WISCONSIN, U.S.A.; 7½"; amber 8.00-12.00

614 UPHAM'S FRESH MEAT CURE; *Pat. Feb. 12, 1867 Phila.*; flared top; 6¾"; aqua.. 8.00-15.00

615 WADSWORTH LINIMENT; *Rheumatism* on one side; *Cure* on other side; side mold; aqua; 5½"........................ 20.00-30.00

616 WARNER'S SAFE ANIMAL CURE; 11¼"; amber .... 45.00+

617 WARNER'S SAFE CURE embossed; sample; amber .... 20.00+

618 WARNERS SAFE CURE; *London England* on side; *Toronto Canada* other side; amber; 9½" .... 50.00+

619 WARNER'S SAFE KIDNEY & LIVER CURE; in center a safe; under it, *Rochester N.Y.*; various numbers under bottom; 9½"; oval; amber 6.00-10.00

620 same except RHEUMATIC CURE; amber 8.00-12.00

621 same except 6½"; amber 6.00-10.00

622 same except NERVINE; 6½"; clear . 2.00-6.00

623 WARNER'S WHITE WIND OF TAR SYRUP CONSUMPTION CURE, C.D. WARNER M.D; *Coldwater Mich.*; 4½" and 6¼"; aqua 8.00-10.00

624 THE WEST ELECTRIC CURE CO., ELECTRICITY IN A BOTTLE; ring top; cobalt........................ 10.00-20.00

625 C.T. WHIPPLE PROP., PORTLAND ME. GARGET CURE; 6"; aqua........ 4.00-6.00

626 A.J. WHITE CURATIVE SYRUP on sides in sunken panels; rectangular; 5⅛"; aqua 8.00-10.00

627 WHITE'S QUICK HEALING CURE; amber; 6¼"........................ 2.00-6.00

628 WINANS BROS., INDIAN CURE FOR BLOOD; *Price $1*; 9¼"; aqua......... 25.00+

629 WINTERGREEN GREAT RHEUMATIC CURE, J.L. FILKINS; 6"; aqua..... 3.00-6.00

630 WOOD GREAT PEPPERMINT CURE FOR COUGHS & COLDS; 6½"; clear..... 4.00-6.00

631 WOOLDRIDGE WONDERFUL CURE CO.; *Columbus Ga.*; amber; 8½"........ 8.00-12.00

632 WYKOOP'S FEVER & AGUE CURE; tapered top; pontil; 6½"; cobalt............. 75.00+

633 ZEMO CURES ECZEMEE; *E.W. Rose Med. Co. St. Louis* on one side; reverse side *Zemo Cures Pimples and all Diseases of the Skin and Scalp*; fancy bottle; ring top; 6½"; clear.... 7.00-10.00

Medicine

Medicine is as old as history, but patent medicine was first made in England and shipped to America in 1723. By mid-eighteenth century, Americans treated themselves freely with ready-made cures for their physical ailments.

All medicines were not patented; at first only a few in America were. The U.S. Patent Office opened in 1790, but the first patent for medicine was not issued until 1796. Only a few kinds were patented because the maker would have had to disclose the alcoholic or opiate components.

The well-known medicine salesman of the 1880's in America was the show man, who, with his troupe in a covered wagon, hawked his medicinal concoctions from town to town. After passage of the Pure Food and Drug Act in 1907, most patent medicine firms went out of business. Because of the act, shocked Americans learned that the nostrums they had been downing over the last century—T.W. Dyott's, Swaim's Panacea, Kickapoo Medicines, Perry Davis' Pain-Killer, Lydia E. Pinkham's Vegetable Compound, to name a few—were largely liquor and opiates.

One of the oldest types of medicine bottles came out of England embossed *Turlington's Balsam of Life* between the years 1723 and 1900. The earliest truly American medicines came in plain bottles made in this country, and the first embossed bottles in the U.S. are dated around 1810. Medicine bottlemaking grew to an $80-million-a-year industry by 1906.

Embossed "Schenck's Pulmonic Syrups," the contents were guaranteed to combat lung disease, while "Dalby's Carminative" was a general preventative. "Carter's Spanish Mixture" would purify the blood if directions were followed closely. All three were marketed during the first half of the 19th century.

634　　637　　638　　640　　641　　642　　643　　644

645　　646　　647　　648　　649　　651　　655　　657

658　　660　　662　　667　　669　　670　　672　　674

634 THE P.L. ABBEY CO.; 8¾"; clear   8.00-12.00

635 THE ABBOTT AIKAL CO. CHICAGO in vertical lines; ring top; 2⅝"; clear 3.00-6.00

636 THE ABBOTT AIKLORD CO., CHICAGO; 2⅝"; clear or aqua 2.00-4.00

637 ABBOTT BROS., CHICAGO; reverse side *Rheumatic Remedy;* 6½"; amber . . .   10.00-12.00

638 THE ABNER ROYCE CO.; 5½"; clear or amethyst 2.00-4.00

639 ABRAMS & CORROLLS ESSENCE OF JAMAICA GINGER, SAN FRANCISCO; 5¼"; aqua 6.00-10.00

640 ABSORBINE; *Springfield, Mass. U.S.A.;* 7½"; amber 4.00-6.00

641 A & CO. under bottom; label; amber; 5¼" 4.00-8.00

642 A.C. CO. COMFORT, JACKSONVILLE, FLA. under bottom; clear; 5½" 2.00-4.00

643 ACEITE ORIENTAL RESSERT in back; cobalt; 3½" 8.00-10.00

644 ACEITE ORIENTAL RESSERT; moon and star on back; 3½"; amber 6.00-8.00

645 ACID IRON EARTH; reverse side *Mobile, Ala.;* 6¾"; amber 6.00-8.00

646 DR. ACKER'S TU-BER-KU; *Catarrh Of The Head* other side; clear; 8" 4.00-6.00

647 ACKER'S ELIXIR, THE GREAT HEALTH RESTORER, label; 6½"; amber. 2.00-6.00

648 AFFLECKS DRUG STORE, WASHINGTON, D.C.; 3¼"; clear or amethyst 2.00-6.00

649 AFRICANA in script; 8"; amber . .   10.00-15.00

650 AGUA PERUBINAT CONDAL, label; round; 10½" 6.00-8.00

651 AIMARS; reverse side *Charleston S.C.;* reverse *Sarsaparilla & Queens Delight;* 9⅝"; amber . . . .   35.00+

652 ALBANY CO. PHARMACY, LARAMIE, WYO.; aqua 4.00-6.00

653 DR. ALEXANDER on side; *Lung Healer* on opposite side; rectangular; square collar; 6½"; aqua blue. 4.00-6.00

654 DR. W. H. ALEXANDERS WONDERFULL HEALING OIL, label; aqua 4.00-6.00

655 ALLAIRE WOODWARD & CO., PEORIA, ILL; reverse side *Elixir & Nutrans;* 10"; amber 8.00-10.00

656 ALLAN ANTIFAT BOTANIC MED CO., BUFFALO N.Y., 1895; 7½"; aqua . . .   4.00-6.00

657 MRS. A. ALLEN'S; *Worlds Hair Restorer* one side; *New York* other side; amber; 7½" 4.00-6.00

658 MRS. S.A. ALLEN'S; *Worlds Hair Restorer, 355 Produce St. N.Y.* on two panels; dark purple; 7" 10.00-20.00

659 ALLEN'S ESSENCE OF JAMAICA GINGER; 5½"; aqua 8.00-12.00

660 ALLEN'S NERVE & BONE LINIMENT vertical around bottle; square collar; round; 3⅞"; aqua. 4.00-6.00

661 ALLEN'S SARSAPARILLA vertical on front; oval shape; narrow square; 8⅛"; aqua 4.00-10.00

662 ALLE-RHUME REMEDY CO.; machine made; clear; 7¾" 8.00-10.00

663 T. C. CAULK ALLOY on bottom; sunken panel; 2¼"; clear 3.00-4.00

664 AMERICAN DRUG STORE N.O. in center; tapered top; 9¼"; amber. . . . .   50.00+

665 same except sample size; 4¼" . . . .   60.00+

666 AMER'S in vertical writing; clear or amethyst; 1¾" 2.00-4.00

667 SP. AMMON AR; 9¼"; clear 6.00-10.00

668 AMMONIA; flask; all sizes; aqua 1.00-4.00

669 AMMONIA, label; aqua; 10½" 2.00-6.00

670 SPIRITUS AMMONIAE, label; machine made; 6½"; amber. 2.00-4.00

671 DR. H. ANDERS & CO.; on each side, picture of face of sun, under it *Hauriexhal Fontevitale;* ground top; pontil; 9"; aqua 25.00-40.00

672 ANGIERS EMULSION; aqua; 7". . .   2.00-4.00

673 ANGIERS PETROLEUM EMULSION, under bottom in three lines; sunken panel in front; back side is rounded; 7"; aqua. 2.00-4.00

674 ANGIERS PETROLEUM EMULSION; aqua; 7" 2.00-6.00

675 ANODYNE FOR INFANTS vertical on front in sunken arch panel; *Dr. Groves* on side; *Philada* on opposite side; rectangular; 5⅜"; clear 3.00-6.00

676 ANTHONY, 501 BROADWAY N.Y. on front; *Flint Varnish for Negatives* on label on back; round; 5½"; clear 3.00-4.00

677 E. ANTHONY, NEW YORK, vertical on front; oval; 6"; cobalt blue. 4.00-8.00

678 APOTHECARY JARS; open pontil; round; ground stopper; 8½" and 10"; aqua . . .   4.00-6.00

679 APOTHECARY (drug store); different sizes; 2" and up; clear 2.00-8.00

680 APOTHECARY (drug store); different sizes; 2" and up; green, amber, light amber, blue, etc. . . . .   4.00+

681 APOTHECARY (drug store); different sizes; 2" and up; pontil . . . .   6.00+

682 APOTHECARY, label; *100* under bottom; quart size; amber. 8.00-10.00

683 ARMOUR & CO.; 4"; amber 2.00-4.00

682   684   693

695   699   700

704   708   709

711   715   717

721   724   726   728   729   730

684 ARMOUR AND COMPANY, CHICAGO in four lines on cathedral type panels; round corner; lady's leg type neck; taller than 5¼"; milk glass 10.00-14.00

685 ARMOUR LABORATORIES, CHICAGO in egg shape circle in center; 7¾"; amber 1.00-2.00

686 ARMOUR LABORATORIES, CHICAGO on fancy oval panel; rectangular; 5"; amber 2.00-4.00

687 ARMOUR'S VIGORALS CHICAGO; squat body; amber 2.00-4.00

688 ARNICA LINIMENT, J.R. BURDSALL'S, NEW YORK, on front and sides; flask; 5⅝"; aqua 4.00-6.00

689 ARNICA & OIL LINIMENT vertical on two panels; eight vertical panels; 6½"; aqua 4.00-6.00

690 DR. SETH ARNOLD'S BALSAM, GILMAN BROS., BOSTON on front and sides; rectangular; 3¾"; amethyst................. 4.00-8.00

691 DR. SETH ARNOLD'S BALSAM, GILMAN BROS., BOSTON; 7"; aqua 8.00-12.00

692 DR. SETH ARNOLD'S; on side *Cough Killer*; sunken panels; rectangular; banded collar; 5½"; aqua...................... 4.00-6.00

693 AROMATIC SCHNAPPS (S is backwards); 8"; dark olive .... 35.00+

694 ASTER, in script running up; *The Puritan Drug Co. Columbus O.* on base; 8¾"; aqua .. 4.00-8.00

695 ASTYPTODYAE CHEMICAL CO.; clear or amethyst; 4½" 2.00-4.00

696 ASTYPTODYNE CHEMICAL CO., in two lines; 3¾" body, 1" round, 1" neck; clear or amethyst...................... 2.00-4.00

697 ATHIEU'S COUGH SYRUP 4.00-6.00

698 DR. A. ATKINSON, N.Y.; pontil; 8¼"; aqua 8.00-12.00

699 THE ATLANTA CHEMICAL CO., ATLANTA, GA. U.S.A. on side; amber; 8½".. 4.00-6.00

700 ATLAS MEDICINE CO.; *Henderson N.C., U.S.A. 1898*; 9¼"; amber .... 12.00+

701 ATRASK OINTMENT; square bottle; 2½"; aqua......................... 1.00-2.00

702 C. W. ATWELL, PORTLAND, ME. vertical on front in large letters; oval; 8"; light aqua 3.00-6.00

703 C. W. ATWELL; long tapered lip; vertical *C. W. Atwell Portland Me*; oval shape; open pontil; 7½"; aqua 10.00-12.00

704 ATWOODS JANNAICE LAXATIVE; machine made; 6"; clear 4.00-6.00

705 AYER'S AGUE CURE, LOWELL MASS; 5¾"; aqua......................... 4.00-8.00

706 AYER'S CHERRY PECTORAL, LOWELL MASS.; 7¼"; aqua 4.00-8.00

707 AYER'S CONCENTRATED SARSAPARILLA; pontil; aqua....... 10.00-20.00

708 AYER'S HAIR VIGOR, label; aqua; 7½" 8.00-12.00
without label 2.00-6.00

709 AYER'S; *Lowell Mass U.S.A.* on back; 8½" 3.00-6.00

710 AYER'S HAIR VIGOR; square; 7¼"; peacock 6.00-8.00

711 AYER'S PILLS; square; 2⅜"; clear 1.00-2.00

712 AYER'S PILLS, LOWELL MASS.; rectangular; 2"; aqua 4.00-6.00

713 AYER'S in sunken panel; 6¼"; aqua.. 1.00-3.00

714 AYER'S SARSAPARILLA; *Lowell, Mass., U.S.A., Compound Ext.*; 8½"; aqua ... 1.00-3.00

715 AYER'S; reverse side, *Lowell, Mass.*; on side *Pectoral*; other side *Cherry*, 7¼"; aqua 6.00-8.00

716 ELIXIR BABEK FOR MALARIA CHILLS FEVERS, WASHINGTON, D.C. vertical on front in sunken panel; rectangular; 6"; clear 4.00-6.00

717 BABY EASE; aqua; 5½" 2.00-4.00

718 WM. A. BACON, LUDLOW, VT.; pontil; 5½"; aqua............................... 10.00-15.00

719 DR. BAKER'S PAIN PANACEA 1855; pontil; aqua; 5".................... 12.00-20.00

720 DR. IRA BAKER'S HONDURAS SARSAPARILLA; 10½"; aqua or clear 12.00-18.00

721 JOHN C. BAKER & CO., COD LIVER OIL; 9½"........................... 4.00-6.00

722 JN. C. BAKER & CO.; on one side *100 N. 3rd. St.*; on other side *Phild.*; pontil; 4¾"; aqua 8.00-10.00

723 S. F. BAKER & CO., KEOKUK, IOWA; 8½"; aqua............................... 4.00-6.00

724 BALLARD SNOW LINIMENT CO.; clear or amethyst; 4½" 2.00-6.00

725 BALL BALSAM OF HONEY; ringed top; pontil; 3½"; aqua 10.00-20.00

726 BALM-ELIXIR REMEDIES, OSSIPEE, N.H.; 5¾"; clear 2.00-6.00

727 BALSAM OF HONEY; pontil; 3¼"; aqua 6.00-10.00

728 BALSAM VEGETABLE PULMONARY around bottle; aqua; 5" 2.00-6.00

729 JNO. T. BARBEE & CO.; 6"; clear or amethyst; 4.00-6.00

730 JNO. T. BARBEE & CO.; 6"; clear or amethyst; machine made.................. 3.00-4.00

731 BARBER MEDICINE CO., KANSAS CITY, MO., label; 7½"; aqua 10.00-20.00

732 BARKER MOORE & MEIN MEDICINE CO., PHILADELPHIA on front and side; rectangular; 6⅜"; aqua 3.00-4.00

733 BARKER MOORE & MEIN vertical on front; *Druggist* on side; *Philadelphia* on opposite side; 5¼"; aqua 3.00-4.00

734 WM. JAY BARKER, HIRSUTUS, NEW YORK, vertical on front in sunken panel; pewter stopper; square collar; ABM; 6⅝"; clear 8.00-10.00

735 same as above except aqua; 5¼"..... 8.00-10.00

736 DR. BARKMAN'S NEVER FAILING LINIMENT on front; 6¼"; light green 4.00-6.00

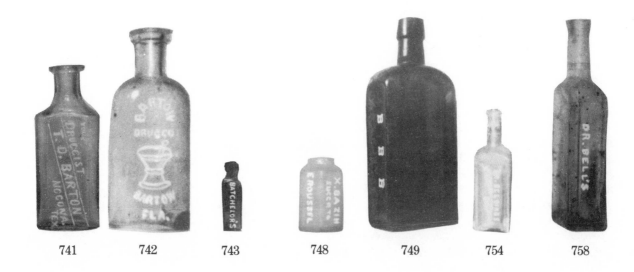

741   742   743   748   749   754   758

761   765   766   767   768   769   771   778

780   782   785   786   792   794   799

737 BARNES & PARKE, N.Y., BALSAM OF WILD CHERRY & TAR; 7½".... 8.00-10.00

738 same as above except 6¼"......... 8.00-10.00

739 BARRY'S TRICOPHEROUS FOR THE SKIN & HAIR, N.Y.; pontil; 5¼"........ 4.00-18.00

740 same as above except five other different sizes 4.00-18.00

741 T.B. BARTON; clear or amethyst; 4½" 2.00-4.00

742 BARTOW DRUG CO.; clear or amethyst; 3½" 2.00-4.00

743 BATCHELOR'S; clear or amethyst; 3" 4.00-6.00

744 BATEMANS DROPS vertical; cylindrical; 5¼"; amethyst...................... 2.00-4.00

745 GEO. H. BATTIER DRUGGIST, 120 BEALE ST.; 5¼" 4.00-8.00

746 J. A. BAUER, S. F. CAL.; 8¼"; lime green 8.00-15.00

747 BAYER ASPIRIN in circles; *Bayer Aspirin* run up and down as cross sign; screw top; machine made; clear, bubble type bottle; 2½" 2.00-3.00

748 X-BAZIN SUCCRTO, E. ROUSSEL; *Philadelphia*; six panels; sheared top; 2¾"; clear 4.00-6.00

749 B.B.B., ATLANTA, GA.; amber; 3¾" x 2¼" 6.00-10.00

750 BEASON'S VEGO SYRUP COMPOUND, *Smith Chemical Corp. Johnson City, Tenn.*, label; 8½"; clear 2.00-4.00

751 BEE-DEE MEDICINE CO., CHATTANOOGA TENN.; on one side *Bee Dee Liniment*; double ring top; 5½"; clear 4.00-6.00

752 BEGGS CHERRY COUGH SYRUP; rectangular; 5¾"; aqua 3.00-4.00

753 BEGGS DIARRHOEA BALSAM; 5½"; aqua 4.00-6.00

754 DR. BELDING'S MEDICINE CO. on one side of sunken panel; other side *Minneapolis, Minn.*; side sizes 1¾"; 3" wide panel; one side plain for label; other in script, *Dr. Belding's Wild Cherry, Sarsaparilla*; body 6", neck 3"; aqua 10.00-25.00

755 DR. BELDING'S WILD CHERRY SARSAPARILLA in sunken panel in front; back plain; *Dr. Belding Medicine Co.* on one side in sunken panel; other side *Minneapolis, Minn.*; aqua; 10" 8.00-12.00

756 BELL ANS on both sides; round; ABM; 3¾"; amber 2.00-3.00

757 BELL, PA PAY ANS BELL & CO. INC., ORANGEBURG, NEW YORK, USA on opposite sides; rectangular; ABM; 2¾"; amber 2.00-3.00

758 DR. BELL'S; *The E.E. Sutherland Medicine Co. Paducah, Ky., Pine Tar Honey*; aqua; 5½" 2.00-3.00

759 BELT & SON, SALEM, ORE.; 5½"; aqua 3.00-6.00

760 BERRY BROS., 323 E. 38TH ST. N.Y. in circle in front; aqua; 11¼" 2.00-4.00

761 THE BETTES PHARMACY, label; clear; 4½" 3.00-4.00

762 EL BIEN PUBLICO DRUG STORE, WEST TAMPA, FLA.; 3¼"; clear 4.00-8.00

763 BIOKRENE HUTCHINGS & HILLYER, N.Y.; 7½"; aqua 2.00-4.00

764 DR. BIRNEY'S CATARRAH ALL POWER; 2¼"; clear..................... 2.00-4.00

765 BISM SUBNITR; clear; 5¼" 8.00-10.00

766 B-L TONIC, THE B-L-CO. ATLANTA, GA., label; *B-L Made in U.S.A.* embossed in back; 10"; amber 4.00-6.00

767 H.C. BLAIR; *8th & Walnut Philada* on side of bottom; clear or amethyst; 6½" 4.00-8.00

768 E. BLOCH & CO.; *W.B.* under bottom; clear; 3½" 4.00-6.00

769 BLOOD BALM CO., label; amber; 9" 4.00-12.00

770 DR. E. BLRICKERS TONIC MIXTURE FOR FEVER AND CHILLS; small tapered top; 6"; aqua 25.00-46.00

771 BLUD-LIFE; clear or amethyst; machine made; 8½" 2.00-4.00

772 DR. A. BOCHIE'S, GERMAN SYRUP in two vertical lines; 6¾"; square; aqua 2.00-3.00

773 BOERICKE & RUNYON COMPANY in script on front; 7¾"; clear 2.00-3.00

774 BOERICKE & RUNYON CO. in large letters vertical on one panel; square; beveled corners; 8⅝"; amethyst 2.00-4.00

775 same as above except sample size; 2½"; amber 2.00-6.00

776 BOLDWIN CHERRY PEPSIN & DANDELION TONIC; 8"; amber 10.00-20.00

777 W. H. BONE CO. C.C. LINIMENT, S.F. CAL. U.S.A.; 6½"; aqua 2.00-4.00

778 BON-OPTO FOR THE EYES; clear or amethyst; 3¼" 2.00-4.00

779 BOOTH'S HYOMEI; *Buffalo N.Y., Rorterie, Canada*; 3"; black 4.00-8.00

780 BORAX; clear; 5¼".............. 8.00-10.00

781 DR. BOSANKO'S PILE REMEDY; *Phila. Pa.*; 2½"; aqua 2.00-4.00

782 DR. BOSANKO'S; *Trial Size* on one side; aqua; 4" 2.00-4.00

783 DR. A. BOSCHEES GERMAN SYRUP in vertical lines; long neck; 6¾"; aqua...... 2.00-3.00

784 BOSTON, MASS on front panel; *Egyptian Chemical Co.*; square; clear; 7½"; screw top; measured 2.00-3.00

785 DR. C. BOUVIER'S; clear; 4½" 4.00-8.00

786 BRADFIELD'S, ATLANTA, GA; 8¼"; aqua 3.00-6.00

787 BRANDRIFFS FOR AGUE on front; *Piqua, Ohio*; ring top; 8"; aqua or green..... 6.00-8.00

788 BRANDRIFFS VEGETABLE ANTIDOTE, PIQUA, O.; 8"; aqua.............. 4.00-8.00

800   802   805   808   811   812   813   814

819   820   825   829   834   835   841   843

789 BRANT'S INDIAN PULMONARY BALSAM, MT. WALLACE PROPRIETOR vertical on three panels; 8″ wide vertical panels; 6¾″; aqua 50.00-75.00

790 BREIG & SHAFER on bottom; on top of it a fish; green 1.00-3.00

791 G.O. BRISTO BACKWAR, BUFFALO; six panels; pontil; 4¾″ 20.00-40.00

792 BRISTOL'S on one side in sunken panel; other side, *New York;* front panel plain for label; on back in sunken panel *Genuine Sarsaparilla;* under bottom in circle panel *#18;* 10¼″ tall; 2¼″ neck; 3¾″ wide; 2¼″ thick; aqua 4.00-6.00

793 BRISTOL'S SARSAPARILLA; pontil; green 20.00-30.00

794 B & P; amber; *Lyons Powder* on shoulder of opposite side; 4¼″ 2.00-6.00

795 B.P. CO. on front, also BP back to back with circle around it; cobalt; 3″; oval...... 8.00-12.00

796 B.P. CO. on front, also BP back to back with circle around it; cobalt; 1½″; oval ... 12.00-15.00

797 BROMATED PEPSIN, HUMPHREY'S CHEMICAL CO., NEW YORK vertical on front; square; 3¾″; cobalt blue...... 4.00-6.00

798 BROMO CAFFEINE; 3¼″; light blue 2.00-4.00

799 BROMO LITHIA CHEMICAL CO.; amber; 4¼" 3.00-4.00

800 BROMO LITHIA CHEMICAL CO.; amber; 3¼" 2.00-3.00

801 BROMO-SELTZER on shoulder; round; machine made; cobalt; under bottom *M1* in a circle; 5" 1.00-2.00

802 BROMO-SELTZER EMERSON DRUG, BALTIMORE, MD. on front; round; cobalt; 5" 2.00-4.00

803 BROMO-SELTZER EMERSON DRUG, BALTIMORE, MD. on front; round; cobalt; machine made; 5" 1.00-2.00

804 BROMO-SELTZER EMERSON DRUG, BALTIMORE, MD. on front; round; cobalt; machine made; 4" 1.00-2.00

805 BROMO-SELTZER EMERSON DRUG, BALTIMORE, MD. on front; round; cobalt; 5" 3.00-5.00

806 BROMO-SELTZER EMERSON DRUG, BALTIMORE, MD. on front; round; cobalt; machine made; 6½" 1.00-3.00

807 BROMO-SELTZER EMERSON DRUG, BALTIMORE, MD. on front; round; cobalt; machine made; 8" 2.00-4.00

808 BROMO-SELTZER EMERSON DRUG, BALTIMORE, MD. on front; round; cobalt; machine made; 2½" 1.00-2.00

809 BROMO-SELTZER EMERSON DRUG, BALTIMORE, MD. on front; round; cobalt; machine made; screw top; 4¾" 1.00-2.00

810 BROMO-SELTZER around shoulder; machine made; screw top; cobalt 1.00-3.00

811 THE BROOKS DRUG CO., BATTLE CREEK, MICH., label; *887* under bottom; clear; 8" 2.00-4.00

812 BROOKS & POTTER DRUGGISTS, SENATOBIA, MISS.; 7¼"; clear or amber 2.00-6.00

813 BROWN CO., W.T. & CO.; 8"; cobalt 8.00-10.00

814 DR. BROWN'S RUTERBA; side mold; amber; 8" 6.00-8.00

815 DR. C.F. BROWN, YOUNG AMERICAN LINIMENT, NEW YORK; ring top; 4"; aqua 6.00-10.00

816 F. BROWNS ESSENCE OF JAMAICA GINGER, PHILADA.; tapered top; pontil; 5½"; aqua 8.00-10.00

817 same except no pontil 4.00-8.00

818 same except no pontil and has ringed top 4.00-8.00

819 F. BROWN'S; aqua; 5½" 3.00-6.00

820 BROWN-FORMAN CO.; clear or amethyst; 4½" 2.00-4.00

821 BROWN HOUSEHOLD PANACEA AND FAMILY LINIMENT vertical on front in sunken panel; *Curtis & Brown* on side; *Mfg. Co. L. D. New York* on opposite side; rectangular; 5⅛"; aqua 3.00-6.00

822 J. T. BROWN, 292 WASHINGTON ST., BOSTON, PREPARATION; pontil; 6"; aqua 8.00-10.00

823 DR. O. PHELPS BROWN; 3½"; aqua 2.00-4.00

824 DR. O. PHELPS BROWN; on side *Jersey City N.J.*; ring top; 2½"; aqua 2.00-4.00

825 BROWN SARSAPARILLA; aqua; 3x1¾x9½" 4.00-6.00

826 W. E. BROWN DRUGGIST, MANCHESTER, IOWA; clear 6.00-8.00

827 W. E. BROWN DRUGGIST, MANCHESTER, IOWA; mixing jar and an eagle over it; 5½"; clear 3.00-6.00

828 BROWN'S INSTANT RELIEF FOR PAIN; aqua; 5¼"; embossed 3.00-4.00

829 B. S. #30 under bottom; drop bottle; 3½"; clear 6.00-8.00

830 BUCHAN'S HUNGARIAN BALSAM OF LIFE, LONDON; vertical lines *Kidney Cure*; 5¾"; round short neck; green 3.00-5.00

831 BUCKINGHAM on one side; *Whisker Dye* on other side; 4¾"; brown 2.00-4.00

832 DR. BULL'S HERBS & IRON; *Pat. Oct. 13, 85* on base; 9½" 15.00-20.00

833 DR. J.W. BULL'S VEG. BABY SYRUP, trade mark; round; 5¼"; aqua 2.00-6.00

834 W.H. BULL MEDICINE CO.; 9½"; amber 4.00-6.00

835 W.H. BULL'S MEDICINE BOTTLE; *Pat Oct 1885* under bottom; clear; 5¼" 2.00-4.00

836 DR. BULLOCKS NEPHRETICURN; *Providence R.I.*; 7"; aqua 10.00-20.00

837 BUMSTEADS WORM SYRUP; *Philada*; 4½"; aqua 8.00-10.00

838 BUMSTEAD WORM SYRUP; *Philada*; #3 under bottom; ring top; aqua 4.00-6.00

839 A. L. BURDOCK LIQUID FOOD, BOSTON, 12½ PERCENT SOLUBLE ALBUMEN on four consecutive panels; twelve vertical panels on bottle; square collar; 6"; amber 4.00-6.00

840 J.A. BURGON, ALLEGHENY CITY, PA., label on back; *Dr. J.A. Burgon* standing and holding a bottle and table; 8¼"; clear 10.00-15.00

841 BURKE & JAMES; *W.T. CO. A.A. U.S.A.* under bottom; clear or amethyst; 6¼".. 4.00-6.00

842 E.A. BURKHOUT'S DUTCH LINIMENT, PREP. AT MECHANICVILLE, SARATOGA CO., N.Y.; pontil; 5¼"; aqua 100.00-150.00

843 BURLINGTON DRUG CO., BURLINGTON VT., label; 5½"; clear 5.00-10.00

845   846   853   856   857   858   860   871

872   875   876   878   885   886   891   896

844   BURNAM'S BEEF WINE E.J.B. & IRON on front; thumb print on back; oval; 9¼"; aqua 3.00-6.00

845   BURNETT; clear; 6¾" 2.00-4.00

846   BURNETT; *Boston* on other side; clear; 4¼" 2.00-4.00

847   BURNETT on side; *Boston* on opposite side; beveled corners; square collar; oval shape; 6½"; aqua............................ 3.00-4.00

848   BURNETTS COCAINE vertical on front; *Burnetts* on side; *Boston* on opposite side; large beveled corners; tapered shoulders; aqua; 7⅜" 4.00-6.00

849   BURNETTS COCOAINE, BOSTON; ringed top; 7¼"; aqua 4.00-6.00

850   BURNETTS COCOAINE, 1864-1900; ringed top; clear........................ 8.00-12.00

851   BURNHAMS BEEF WINE & IRON; 9½"; aqua 2.00-4.00

852 BURNHAM'S CLAM BOUILLON, E.S. BURNHAM CO., NEW YORK, five lines; machine made; 4½" 2.00-3.00

853 BURNHAM'S; aqua; 4¾" 2.00-4.00

854 BURRINGTONS VEGETABLE GROUP SYRUP, PROVIDENCE, R.I. vertical around bottle; ring collar; cylindrical; 5½"; clear 3.00-6.00

855 same as above except aqua 3.00-6.00

856 BURT SMITH CO.; aqua; 7" 6.00-12.00

857 BURTON'S MALTHOP TONIQUE, label; three-part mold; dark olive; 7½" 4.00-6.00

858 BURWELL-DUNN; *R.S.J.; 969* under bottom; clear or amethyst; 3¾" 2.00-4.00

859 BUTLER'S BALSAM OF LIVERWORT; pontil; 4¼"; aqua 10.00-20.00

860 CABOT'S SULPHO NAPTHOL, vertical on front; oval back; beveled corners; square collar; 6½" and 4¾"; amber 3.00-6.00

861 CABOT'S SULPHO NAPTHOL written fancily; large beveled corners; oval back; square collar; 5⅛"; aqua 4.00-6.00

862 CALDWELLS SYRUP PEPSIN; *Mfd by Pepsin Syrup Co., Monticello, Ill.*; aqua; 3"; rectangular 3.00-4.00

863 CALDWELLS SYRUP PEPSIN; *Mfd by Pepsin Syrup Co. Monticello, Ill.*; aqua; rectangular; machine made; screw top; all sizes . . . 1.00-2.00

864 CALIFORNIA FIG SYRUP CO. on front panel; *Louisville, Ky.* on left side; *San Francisco, Calif.* on right side; rectangular; amethyst; 7¼" 3.00-4.00

865 CALIFORNIA FIG. SYRUP CO., SAN FRANCISCO, CAL vertical on front; *Syrup of Figs* on both sides; rectangular; square collar; 6½"; amethyst 4.00-6.00

866 CALIFORNIA FIG SYRUP CO., *Califig, Sterling Products (inc) Successor* on front; rectangular; clear; 6¾" 1.00-2.00

867 CALIFORNIA FIG SYRUP CO., *Califig, Sterling Products (inc) Successor* on front; rectangular; machine made; screw top; all sizes and colors 1.00-2.00

868 CALIFORNIA FIG. SYRUP CO., S.F., CAL.; *Syrup of Fig*; 6¾"; clear or amber 2.00-4.00

869 PROF. CALLAN'S WORLD RENOWNED BRAZILIAN GUM, vertical on one panel; square collar; 4⅛"; aqua 3.00-4.00

870 DR. CALLAN'S WORLD RENOWNED BRAZILIAN GUM; 4½"; clear 3.00-4.00

871 EXT. CALUMB. FL.; cobalt; 9½" 10.00-20.00

872 CALVERT'S; clear or amethyst; 8" 8.00-12.00

873 THE CAMPBELL DRUG CO., THE GENERAL STORE, FOSTORIA, OHIO; on back *Camdrugo*; 5¼"; green 4.00-8.00

874 CAMPBELL V. V.; in script, *the genuine always bears this signature* in the front panel; diamond shaped base; 5⅛"; clear 2.00-4.00

875 CAPLION, label; clear; 5"; *TCWCO. U.S.A.* on bottom 2.00-6.00

876 CAPUDINE CHEMICAL CO. RALEIGH, N.C. in center; *G* under bottom; label; amber; machine made; 7½" 2.00-3.00

877 CAPUDINE FOR HEADACHE on front panel; amber; 3¼"; oval 1.00-2.00

878 DR. M. CARABALLO; *Vermicida* in back; aqua; 4¼" 3.00-6.00

879 CARBONA on the base; paneled; 5½" and 6"; aqua 2.00-5.00

880 CARBONA, CARBONA PRODUCTS CO.; *Carbona* in three lines; hair oil; 6"; aqua 1.00-2.00

881 CARBONA, CARBONA PRODUCTS CO.; *Carbona* in three lines running vertically; round; 6"; aqua; hair dressing 2.00-3.00

882 CARBONA & CARBONA PRODUCTS CO.; *Carbona* on three vertical panels; twelve panels; square collar; 5⅛"; aqua 3.00-4.00

883 CARLO ERBA MIANO, OLEO PICINO; 3¾"; clear or amber 8.00-10.00

884 CARLSBAD; 5½"; clear 4.00-6.00

885 CARLSBAD AH under bottom; sheared top; clear; 4" 2.00-4.00

886 CARLSBAD RA under bottom; sheared top; clear; 4" 4.00-6.00

887 CARPENTER & WOOD, INC.; *Est. 1883 Providence, R.I.* with eagle & shield on center front; glass stopper; round; 2¼"; clear or amethyst 2.00-4.00

888 CARTER'S SPANISH MIX; pontil; 8"; green 10.00-20.00

889 CARY GUM TREE COUGH SYRUP; *S. Fran. U.S.A.*; 7½"; aqua blue 8.00-10.00

890 same as above except lime green . . . 10.00-15.00

891 CASSEBEER; reverse side *N.Y.*; 7½"; amber 8.00-10.00

892 CASTOR OIL, PURE; *2 fl. oz., The Frank Tea & Co*; cintion front; clear; 5¼"; flask . . 4.00-8.00

893 also machine made and screw top; all sizes and colors 1.00-2.00

894 CASTOR OIL; 4" body; 3" neck; 1¼" round bottle; cobalt blue 8.00-12.00

895 same, except smaller, some in different sizes 8.00-12.00

896 Castor oil label; *W.C. 30z* under bottom; cobalt; 8¼" 8.00-10.00

897 C.B. 6B on bottom; green; 7¼" 4.00-6.00

898 C & C inside two concentric circles; sides fluted; amethyst; rectangular; 4½" 2.00-4.00

899 C.C.C. TONIC, BOERICKE & RUNYON NEW YORK vertical on front in large letters; beveled corners; rectangular; large flared square collar; 8"; clear 20.00-30.00

900 C & Co., 3½"; clear or amber 2.00-4.00

897   900   901   912   920   921   923

931 932 933 934 936 938 939 940

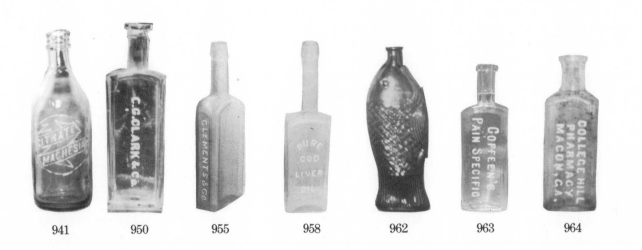

941 950 955 958 962 963 964

901 CELERY MEDICINE CO.; bitters label; clear or amethyst; 9".................. 8.00-15.00

902 CELERY-VESCE, CENTURY CHEMICAL CO; *Indianapolis, Ind. U.S.A.*; 4"; amber 4.00-6.00

903 CELRO-KOLA, PHIL BLUMAUER & CO., PORTLAND, OR.; 10"; clear...... 4.00-6.00

904 CENTOUR LINIMENT; ringed top; 5¼"; aqua 2.00-4.00

905 CENTOUR LINIMENT on shoulder; 3½"; aqua 1.00-2.00

906 CENTOUR LINIMENT on shoulder; aqua; round; 5" 2.00-3.00

907 CENTOUR LINIMENT on shoulder; round bottle; machine made; 5"; aqua........ 1.00-2.00

908 CENTRAL DRUG CO.; *Laramie Wyo.*; clear 4.00-6.00

909 CERTAIN GROUP REMEDY vertical on front in sunken panel; *Dr. Hoxsie's* on side; *Buffalo, N.Y.* on opposite side; rectangular; 4½"; clear 4.00-6.00

910 CHAMBERLAIN'S COLIC CHOLERA AND DIARRHEA REMEDY; *Chamberlain Med. Co. Des Moines, Ia. USA* on front and sides; rectangular; 4½"; aqua 4.00-6.00

911 same as above except 6" 4.00-6.00

912 CHAMBERLAIN'S COUGH REMEDY; on other side *Chamberlains Med. Co.*; 5½"; aqua 4.00-6.00

913 CHAMBERLAIN'S on side panel; *Bottle Made in America* on opposite side; rectangular; 4½"; aqua........................... 2.00-3.00

914 CHAMBERLAIN'S COLIC CHOLERA AND DIARRHEA REMEDY on front; *Des Moines, Iowa U.S.A.* on side panel; *Chamberlain Med. Co.* on opposite; aqua; 5¼"; rectangular . 2.00-4.00

915 CHAMBERLAIN's COUGH REMEDY on front; *Des Moines, Ia. U.S.A.* on left side; *Chamberlain Med. Co.* on right side; 6¾"; rectangular; aqua or clear 2.00-4.00

916 CHAMBERLAIN'S PAIN-BALM on front; *Des Moines, Ia. U.S.A.* on left side; *Chamberlain Med. Co.* on right side; aqua; 7"; rectangular 2.00-4.00

917 CHAMPLIN'S LIQUID PEARL on front; rectangular; square collar; 5"; milk glass 4.00-8.00

918 same as above except 6" 3.00-6.00

919 DR. P. H. CHAPELLE, N.Y., label; flask; 6¾"; clear 8.00-15.00

920 CHELF CHEM. CO.; cobalt; machine made; 4" 2.00-3.00

921 CHEMICAL BOTTLE, label; crystal glass; 6½"; clear...................... 6.00-10.00

922 CHEMICAL CO. D.D. N.Y. SAMPLE on the front panel; amber; 5"; square..... 1.00-2.00

923 CHESEBROUGH; clear or amethyst; 3½" 2.00-3.00

924 CHESEBROUGH MFG. CO. in horseshoe letters; under it *Vaseline*; 2⅞"; clear ... 1.00-2.00

925 CHESEBROUGH VASELINE; 2¾"; clear 3.00-4.00

926 same except 3¾"................. 3.00-6.00

927 same except ABM; amethyst; thread top; 3¼" and 2½" 2.00-3.00

928 same as above except ABM; amber... 2.00-3.00

929 same as above; ABM; clear 2.00-3.00

930 CHESEBROUGH VASELINE TRADE MARK, NEW YORK on front; mold threads; pint size; amethyst................. 2.00-3.00

931 PROF CHEVALIER; clear; 4¼".... 2.00-4.00

932 Chinese bottle; clear; 2½" 2.00-4.00

933 CHINIDIN; clear; 5¼" 8.00-12.00

934 CHLORATE POTASSIQUE; pontil; 6½"; clear glass painted brown 10.00-20.00

935 CHRISTIES MAGNETIC FLUID; flared top; 4¾"; aqua 8.00-10.00

936 T.R. CIMICIFUG; clear; 7¾"....... 4.00-6.00

937 CIRCASSIAN BLOOM; 5"; clear or amber 2.00-6.00

938 THE CITIZENS WHOLESALE SUPPLY CO., label; clear; 7½" 2.00-4.00

939 THE CITIZENS WHOLESALE SUPPLY CO.; *Columbus O. Camphorated Oil* on label; clear; 7½".................................. 4.00-6.00

940 CITRATE MAGNESIA; clear or amethyst; 8" 4.00-6.00

941 CITRATE MAGNESIA; clear or amethyst; three-ring top; 8¾".................. 4.00-6.00

942 CITRATE MAGNESIA in script around bottom; Sanitas bottle; 8"; clear or amethyst 2.00-3.00

943 CITRATE MAGNESIA in script on bottom; Sanitas bottle; 8"; clear or amethyst 1.00-2.00

944 CITRATE MAGNESIA; *National Magnesia Co. Inc.*; clear; 7"; round.......... 2.00-4.00

945 CITRATE MAGNESIA, in a sunken circle; in center *O Dot*, *4T* around it; double-ring top; aqua; 7" 4.00-6.00

946 CITRATE MAGNESIA, embossed in indented curved bands; blob top; 8"; green .. 8.00-10.00

947 CITY DRUG COMPANY; *103 Main St., Anaconda Mont.*; 4¼"; clear............ 2.00-4.00

948 CITY DRUG STORE; *Meridian, Tex.*; 3¼"; amethyst; rectangular 1.00-2.00

949 OTIS CLAPP & SONS MALT & COD LIVER OIL COMPOUND vertical on front in fancy lettering; large square collar; 7¼"; amber 4.00-6.00

950 C. G. CLARK & CO.; *Restorative* other side; 7¾"; aqua 6.00-10.00

951 THE C. G. CLARK CO. vertical on one panel; *New Haven, Ct.* on third panel; twelve vertical panels; square collar; 5½"; aqua 3.00-4.00

952 CLARK'S CORDIAL on front in diamond shape panel; (note: you can see where the words *Clark's Calif. Cherry Cordial* were slugged out of the mold); 8¼"; amber........ 20.00-30.00

953 DR. J. S. CLARK'S, THROAT & LUNGS; reverse side *Balsam For The*; 8½"; aqua 8.00-12.00

965   967   968   973   974   975   976   977

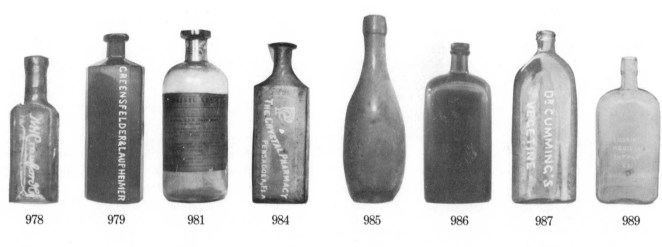

978   979   981   984   985   986   987   989

992   995   998   999   1000   1001   1002   1003

954 W. W. CLARK, 16 N. 5TH. ST. PHILA.; pontil; 5⅜"; aqua 8.00-15.00

955 CLEMENTS & CO.; *Rosadalis* other side; aqua; 8½" 4.00-6.00

956 CREME DE CAMELIA FOR THE COMPLEXION on side; *The Boradent Co. Inc., San Francisco* on opposite side; beveled corners; rectangular; flared collar; *New York* in slug plate; 5⅛"; cobalt blue 4.00-8.00

957 same as above except *San Francisco & New York* embossed 4.00-8.00

958 COD LIVER OIL; aqua; 9¾" 2.00-6.00

959 COD LIVER OIL, with fish in center; screw top; machine made; two sizes; amber; round 2.00-4.00

960 COD LIVER OIL, in front with a fish in sunken panel; square; 9"; amber; screw top; machine made 2.00-4.00

961 COD LIVER OIL, in front with a fish in sunken panel; square; 6"; amber; screw top; machine made 2.00-4.00

962 COD LIVER OIL-FISH; different sizes and many different colors; some made in Italy 8.00-16.00

963 COFFEEN'S PAIN SPECIFIC; clear; 7¼" 6.00-8.00

964 COLLEGE HILL PHARMACY; clear or amethyst; 4½" 2.00-4.00

965 N.A. COLLINGS; *WT Co. U.S.A.* under bottom; clear; 6¼" 2.00-4.00

966 COLY TOOTH WASH, backward S in WASH; 4½"; clear 10.00-15.00

967 COMPOUND ELIXIR; aqua; 8¾" 6.00-10.00

968 W. H. COMSTOCK; on back *Moses Indian Root Pills;* on side *Dose 1 to 3;* 2½"; amber 2.00-6.00

969 CONE ASTHMA CONQUEROR CO.; *Cinncinnati, O.;* 8"; clear 4.00-6.00

970 CONNELL'S BRAHMNICAL MOON PLANT EAST INDIAN REMEDIES; on base in back ten stars around a pair of feet; under it trade mark; 7"; amber .... 25.00+

971 CONNELL'S BRAHMNICAL EAST INDIAN REMEDIES; amber 5.00-10.00

972 COOPE'S NEW DISCOVERY, tonic; 8¾"; label; aqua 1.00-2.00

973 COOPER'S NEW DISCOVERY; 9"; aqua 8.00-10.00

974 COSTAR'S; very light blue; 4" 3.00-6.00

975 COSTAR'S, N.Y. on shoulder; 4"; amber 8.00-10.00

976 GEORGE COSTER; side mold; aqua; 5½" 2.00-6.00

977 CRARY & CO.; aqua; 4¼" 2.00-3.00

978 W. H. CRAWFORD CO.; clear; 4¼" 2.00-3.00

979 CREENSFELDER & LAUPHEIMER DRUGGISTS, BALTIMORE, MD. on three panels; twelve panels; on shoulder *A.R.B.;* 8½"; amber 10.00-20.00

980 CREOMULSION FOR COUGHS DUE TO COLDS; amethyst or clear; 8¼"; rectangular 2.00-4.00

981 CRESOL U.S.P., label; clear; 7¼" ... 2.00-4.00

982 DR. CROSSMANS SPECIFIC MIXTURE vertical around bottle; square collar; 3¾"; aqua 4.00-8.00

983 CROWN CORDIAL & EXTRACT CO. N.Y.; amethyst; 10¼"; round 2.00-6.00

984 THE CRYSTAL PHARMACY; clear or amethyst; 7" 2.00-4.00

985 C.S. & CO. LD 6054 on bottom; 8¾"; aqua 3.00-4.00

986 C.S. & CO. LD 10296 on bottom; 9¾"; dark green 4.00-8.00

987 DR. CUMMING'S VEGETINE; aqua; 9¾" 4.00-6.00

988 CURLINGS CITRATE OF MAGNESIA vertical on front; large beveled corners; crude ring collar; 6⅛"; cobalt blue 3.00-6.00

989 CUSHING MEDICAL SUPPLY CO., N.Y. & BOSTON, FULL QT.; aqua; 10" 4.00-8.00

990 CUTICURA TREATMENT FOR AFFECTATIONS OF THE SKIN; 9⅛"; aqua ... 3.00-4.00

991 DAD CHEMICAL CO. on the shoulders; amber; 6"; round 1.00-2.00

992 DALBYS; *Carminative* on back; *3751* under bottom; clear; 3¾" 2.00-3.00

993 DALBYS CARMINATIVE; pontil; 3½"; clear or aqua 10.00-15.00

994 DALTON'S SARSAPARILLA AND NERVE TONIC; *Belfast, Maine USA* on opposite sides; rectangular; 9¼"; aqua 8.00-10.00

995 C. DAMSCHINSKY; aqua; 3¼" 3.00-4.00

996 DAMSCHINSKY LIQUID HAIR DYE, N.Y.; 3½"; aqua 4.00-6.00

997 C. DAMSCHINSKY LIQUID HAIR DYE, NEW YORK in sunken panels; 3½"; aqua 4.00-6.00

998 same as above except 2¾" 4.00-6.00

999 DANA'S; 9"; aqua 4.00-6.00

1000 DANA'S SARSAPARILLA in two lines in a sunken panel; side and back are plain sunken panels; aqua; 9" 8.00-12.00

1001 DANIEL'S, front side; other sides *Atlanta Ga.;* 4½"; aqua 2.00-6.00

1002 DR. DANIEL'S CARBO-NECUS *Disinfectant Deodorizer Purifier & Insecticide;* clear; 6½" 2.00-4.00

1003 DR. DANIEL'S VETERINARY; clear; 3½" 3.00-4.00

1004 DR. DANIEL'S VETERINARY COLIC DROPS NO. 1; square; 3½"; amethyst 6.00-8.00

1005 DR. A.G. DANIEL'S LINIMENT, OSTER COCUS OIL, BOSTON, MASS. USA vertical on front; oval back; beveled corners; 6¾"; clear 4.00-8.00

1006   1017   1022   1023   1025   1026   1033

1034   1035   1036   1037   1041   1046   1047   1049

1050   1051   1052   1053   1054   1055   1056

1006 DARBY'S PROPHYLACTIC FLUID; *J.H. Zeilen & Co. Phila.;* 7½"; aqua...... 4.00-8.00

1007 CHAS F. DARE MENTHA PEPSIN; *Bridge-town, N.J.*................ 4.00-10.00

1008 DAVIS in an upper sunken panel; bottom of it flat; back full sunken panel; on one side *Geoetable;* other side *Pain Killer;* 6"; aqua or light blue 2.00-4.00

1009 DAVIS in sunken panel in front; medical; 6⅝"; aqua.................... 2.00-3.00

1010 DAVIS in sunken panel in front; medical; 6½"; blue.................... 2.00-4.00

1011 DAVIS VEGETABLE PAIN KILLER on front and sides; rectangular; sunken panels; 6"; aqua 2.00-4.00

1012 D.D. CHEMICAL Co. N.Y. SAMPLE on front of panel; amber; 5"; square 1.00-2.00

1013 D.D.D. on front of panel; amethyst; square; 3½" and 5½" 3.00-6.00

1014 DEAD SHOT VERMIFUGE; pontil; amber or clear .... 10.00+

1015 PROF. DEAN'S BARBED WIRE REMEDY; 5½"; amber.................... 2.00-4.00

1016 DELAVAN'S SYRUP WHOPPING COUGH CROUP, PHILADELPHIA vertical on front; rectangular; square collar; 6¼"; aqua. 4.00-8.00

1017 DELAVAN'S WHOOPING COUGH REMEDY; *Phila.;* 6¼"; aqua....... 2.00-4.00

1018 DR. J. DENNIS GEORGIA SARSAPARILLA; *Augusta, Ga.,* graphite pontil; tapered top; 10½"; aqua .... 75.00+

1019 DERMA-ROYALE FOR THE SKIN AND COMPLEXION; vertical *The Derma Royale Comp'y Cincinnati, O.* also on front, inside of circle; flared lip; square; 6⅛"; clear .. 4.00-6.00

1020 PAUL DEVERED & CO., GENUINE C.V.E.; *Geo. Raphael & Co. sole proprietor;* pontil; flared top; 3½"; clear or amber.......... 8.00-12.00

1021 DEWITT'S SOOTHING SYRUP, CHICAGO; amethyst; round; 5" 3.00-6.00

1022 DEWITTS; aqua; 9".......... 25.00+

1023 E.C. DEWITT & CO.; aqua; 9¼"..... 4.00-8.00

1024 DIAMOND OIL on two sides of panel; aqua; 5½"; rectangular 2.00-4.00

1025 DIAMOND & ONYX; *Phila. U.S.A.;* 4¾"; aqua 2.00-4.00

1026 MAXIMO M. DIAZ; aqua; 7" 2.00-4.00

1027 DICKEY CHEMIST, S.F.; in center *Pioneer 1850;* 5¾"; blue.......... 10.00-15.00

1028 JOHN R. DICKEY'S, *Old Reliable Eye Water, Mfg. by Dickey Drug Co., Bristol, Va.;* aqua; 3¾"; round 2.00-4.00

1029 DILL'S BALM OF LIFE vertical on front; rectangular; ABM; 6"; clear 2.00-4.00

1030 DILL'S COUGH SYRUP vertical on front; *Dill Medicine Co.* on side; *Norristown, Pa.* on opposite side; sunken panels; rectangular; 5⅞"; clear 3.00-6.00

1031 A.M. DINIMOR & CO., BINNINGERS OLD DOMINIAN WHEAT TONIC; tapered top; 9½"; amber.................... 10.00-20.00

1032 MRS. DINMORE'S COUGH & CROUP BALSAM vertical on front in oval end of sunken panel; rectangular; 6"; aqua 4.00-8.00

1033 DIOXOGEN; amber; 4" 2.00-3.00

1034 DIOXOGEN; *The Oakland Chem Co.* on back; amber; 7¾".................... 2.00-4.00

1035 DIPPER DANDY on neck; sheared bottom; 10 to 60 cc grad scale; metal shaker bottom; 6"; clear 4.00-6.00

1036 DR. E. E. DIXON; clear or amethyst; 6½" 2.00-4.00

1037 DODGE & OLCOTT CO, NEW YORK, OIL ERIGERON, label; cobalt; machine made; *D & O* under bottom; 7" 4.00-6.00

1038 DODSON'S on one side of panel; *Livertone* on other side; aqua or amethyst; 7"; rectangular 3.00-4.00

1039 DODSON & HILS, ST. LOUIS U.S.A.; amethyst; 8¼"; round 2.00-4.00

1040 DOLTON'S SARSP. & NERVE TONIC; 9"; aqua.................... 8.00-15.00

1041 DONALD KENNEDY & CO., ROXBURY MASS, label; aqua; 6½" 4.00-8.00

1042 DONNELL'S RHEUMATIC LINIMENT vertical on front; *J.T. Donnell & Co., St. Louis, Mo.* on opposite sides; rectangular; 7¼"; aqua blue 3.00-6.00

1043 C. K. DONNELL, M.D./809 SABATTUS ST., LEWISTON, ME. vertical on front in sunken panel; square collar; rectangular; 6¼"; amethyst 2.00-3.00

1044 GEORGE DOWDEN CHEMIST & DRUGGIST; *No. 175 Broad St. Rich. Va.;* pontil; 4½"; aqua .... 25.00+

1045 REV. N. H. DOWN'S, VEGETABLE BALSAMIC ELIXIR vertical on four panels; twelve vertical panels in all; 5½"; aqua..... 3.00-6.00

1046 DR. DOYEN STAPHYLASE DU; clear or amethyst; 8".................... 3.00-6.00

1047 D.P.S. Co.; amber; 3½"........... 2.00-3.00

1048 DR. DRAKES GERMAN CROUP REMEDY vertical on front in sunken panel; *The Glessner Med. Co.* on side; *Findlay, Ohio* on opposite side; square collar; rectangular; 6⅜"; aqua 4.00-8.00

1049 DREXEL'S; clear; 4½" 3.00-6.00

1050 DROP BOTTLE; *#45* under bottom; 4"; aqua 8.00-10.00

1051 THE DRUGGISTS LINDSEY RUFFIN & CO.; *Senatobia, Miss.;* 6¼"; clear or amber 2.00-6.00

1052 J. DUBOIS; on other panels around bottle; *Great pain Specific and Healing Balm, Kingston, N.Y.;* aqua; 2¼" 2.00-4.00

1053 DUCH POISON, ZUM K. VERSCHLUSS under bottom; 8¼"; clear or amber .. 8.00-10.00

1054 DR. DUFLOT; clear or amethyst; 4¼" 3.00-6.00

1055 S. O. DUNBAR, TAUNTON, MASS.; 6"; aqua 4.00-8.00

1057   1058   1059   1060   1062   1066   1069   1070

1071   1072   1073   1076   1081   1082   1085   1086

1087   1088   1089   1091   1093   1096   1097   1099

1100   1101   1102   1103

1056   T. J. DUNBAR & CO.; on side *Cordial Schnapps;* other side *Schiedam;* 10″; green   20.00-30.00

1057   DUTTON'S VEGETABLE; other side *Discovery;* 6″; aqua 2.00-4.00

1058   E in square; very light green; 4″ 3.00-4.00

1059   THE EASOM MEDICINE CO.; on back a house in center of trade mark; aqua; 2¼″ . . 4.00-8.00

1060   EASTMAN, ROCHESTER, N.Y.; 6½″; clear or amber 2.00-4.00

1061   A.W. ECKEL & CO. APOTHECARIES; *Charleston, S.C.;* 4″; clear 2.00-4.00

1062   EDDY & EDDY; clear; 5″; 1″ x 1¾″   2.00-4.00

1063   EDDY & EDDY CHEMIST, ST. LOUIS; round; 5″; amethyst 3.00-5.00

1064   same as above except 6½″; clear 4.00-6.00

1065   EDDY'S; round; 5¼″; green 2.00-4.00

1066   W. EDWARDS & SON; clear; 5″ . . . 2.00-4.00

1067   W. EDWARDS & SON, ROCHE EMBROCATION FOR WHOOPING COUGH; 5″; clear 4.00-10.00

1068   FRANK H. E. EGGLESTON; *Pharm., Laramie Wy.;* clear or amber 4.00-6.00

1069   THE E.G.L. CO.; aqua; 5¾″; sheared top 5.00-10.00

1070   E. H. CO. MO COCKTAILS; same on reverse side; three-sided bottle; 10″; dark olive   85.00+

1071   EHRLICHER BROS .PHARMACISTS, PEKIN, ILL; clear; 4¼″ 4.00-6.00

1072   E.L. & CO. under bottom; amber; 7¼″   2.00-3.00

1073   ELECTRIC BRAND LAXATIVE, label; 9¾″; amber 8.00-10.00

1074   ELIXIR ALIMENTARE on side; *Ducro A. Paris* on opposite side; beveled corners; large square collar; rectangular; 8¼″; light green 3.00-4.00

1075   COMPOUND ELIXIR OF PHOSPHATES & CALISAYA; 8¾″; aqua 6.00-10.00

1076   ELLEMAN'S ROYAL EMBROCATION FOR HORSE; aqua; 7½″ 8.00-12.00

1077   CHARLES ELLIS, SON & CO., PHILADA. vertical around bottle; round double band; 7″; light green 3.00-4.00

1078   ELY'S CREAM BALM; *Ely Bros. New York, Hay Fever Catarrh* on front and sides; sheared lip; rectangular; 2⅝″; amber 2.00-4.00

1079   same as above except 3¼″ 3.00-4.00

1080   ELYS CREAM BALM on front panel; rectangular; amber; 2½″ 2.00-4.00

1081   C.S. EMERSONS AMERICAN HAIR RESTORATIVE, CLEVELAND, O.; pontil; 6½″; clear or amber . . . . 25.00+

1082   EMPIRE STATE DRUG CO. LABORATORIES; aqua; 6½″ 3.00-5.00

1083   THE EMPIRE MED CO., ROCHESTER N.Y.; blob-top; 8¼″; aqua 8.00-10.00

1084   EMPRESS written on front; round; flared lip; 3¾″; amber 2.00-3.00

1085   E.R.S. & S. 3 under bottom; label; amber; 7½″ 2.00-4.00

1086   E.R.S. & S. under bottom; amber; 4½″   2.00-4.00

1087   ESCHERING; clear or amethyst; 5¼″ 2.00-4.00

1088   ESPEY'S; clear; 4½″ 2.00-4.00

1089   C. ESTANTON; *Sing Sing, N.Y.* other side; *Prepared by Block Hunt's;* aqua; pontil; 5″ 20.00-40.00

1090   EUREKA HAIR RESTORATIVE; *P. J. Reilly, San. Fran.;* dome-type bottle; 7″; aqua 8.00-10.00

1091   EUTIMEN; clear or amethyst; 5¼″ . . 2.00-4.00

1092   D. EVANS CAMOMILE PILLS; pontil; 3¾″; aqua 15.00-25.00

1093   THE EVANS CHEMICAL CO.; clear or amethyst; round back; 6¼″ 3.00-4.00

1094   THE EVANS CHEMICAL CO. PROPRIETORS, CINCINNATI, O. U.S.A. on front with big *G*; oval; 5″; clear 2.00-3.00

1095   DR. W. EVANS TEETHING SYRUP; flared lip; pontil; 2½″; aqua 10.00-20.00

1096   EWBANKS TOPAZ CINCHONA CORDIAL; 9½″; amber 8.00-10.00

1097   Eye Cup; *S* under bottom; clear or amethyst; 2″ 3.00-4.00

1098   EYE-SE, around shoulder twice; on bottom *Gilmer Texas;* decorated; round; aqua; 9¼″ 2.00-4.00

1099   G. FACCELLA on bottom; aqua; 6″   2.00-6.00

1100   B. A. FAHNESTOCKS; in back *Vermifuge;* pontil; aqua; 4″ 6.00-8.00

1101   DR. FAHRNEY'S; *Uterine* other side; clear or amethyst; 8½″ 2.00-4.00

1102   DR. PETER FAHRNEY; *71* under bottom; clear; 6″ 3.00-6.00

1103   FARBENFABRIKEN OF ELBERFELD CO., N.Y.C., label; *90* under bottom; amber; 4¼″ 4.00-6.00

1104   FARR'S GRAY HAIR RESTORER, BOSTON, MASS. 6 OZ. all on front at a slant; beveled corners; ABM; 5⅝″; amber 2.00-4.00

1109   1110   1117   1118   1128   1129

1130   1131   1132   1133   1148   1149

1150   1151   1152   1154   1155   1157

1105 H.G. FARRELLS ARABIAN LINIMENT; pontil; 4¼"; aqua 8.00-12.00

1106 FATHER JOHNS MEDICINE; *Lowell Mass.;* ring top; wide mouth; 12"; dark amber 4.00-10.00

1107 same as above except 8¾" 5.00-10.00

1108 FEBRILENE TRADE MARK on front; aqua; 4½"; rectangular 1.00-2.00

1109 FELLOWS & CO.; aqua; 7¾" 3.00-4.00

1110 FELLOWS & CO. CHEMISTS ST. JOHN. N.B. vertical on front; flask; 8" 3.00-4.00

1111 same as above except ABM 3.00-4.00

1112 FELLOW'S LAXATIVE TABLETS; 2½"; clear or amber 4.00-6.00

1113 FELLOW'S SYRUP OF HYPOPHOSPHITS; deep indentation on lower trunk on face of bottle; oval; 7¾"; aqua.................... 4.00-6.00

1114 DR. M. M. FENNER, FREDONIA, N.Y., ST. VITUS DANCE SPECIFIC; ringed top; 4½"; aqua.......................... 10.00-15.00

1115 DR. M. M. FENNERS PEOPLES REMEDIES vertical on front; *U.S.A. 1872-1898* on side; *Fredonia, N.Y.* on opposite side; graduated collar; rectangular; 6"; amethyst 3.00-6.00

1116 FERRO CHINA MELARO TONICO; lion embossed on three-sided bottle; tapered top with ring; green....................... 25.00+

1117 FERROL THE IRON OIL FOOD; one side *Iron & Phosphorus;* other side *Cod Liver Oil;* 9¼"; amber 8.00-10.00

1118 B. W. FETTERS DRUGGIST; *Phila. Pat. Aug. 1, 1876;* beer bottle shape; 8¾"; blue green 10.00-12.00

1119 B. F. FISH, SAN FRANCISCO, FISH HAIR RESTORATIVE; 7¾"; aqua 4.00-10.00

1120 DR. S. S. FITCH & CO., 714 BROADWAY N.Y.; pontil; 3¼"; aqua 10.00-20.00

1121 DR. S. S. FITCH on side; *707 Broadway N.Y.* on opposite side; sheared collar; rectangular; beveled corners; pontil; 3¾"; aqua . 25.00-30.00

1122 DR. S.S. FITCH, 701 BROADWAY N.Y.; pontil; 1¾"; aqua 8.00-20.00

1123 same as above except 6½" 16.00-22.00

1124 same as above except tapered top; oval 16.00-22.00

1125 DR. S.S. FITCH, 714 BROADWAY N.Y. vertical on front; oval; 6½"; aqua....... 25.00-30.00

1126 FIVE DROPS on side; *Chicago USA* on opposite side; rectangular; 5½"; aqua 2.00-4.00

1127 FLAGG'S GOOD SAMARITANS IMMEDIATE RELIEF, CINCINNATI, O.; pontil; five panels; aqua; 3¾" .... 10.00+

1128 A.H. FLANDERS M.D., N.Y. on back; amber; 9"........................... 65.00-70.00

1129 FLETCHERS VEGE-TONIO on front panel; beveled corner; 2½" square; amber; roof shoulder; under bottom *DOC;* 8½".. 10.00-15.00

1130 FLIPPINS; clear; 6½" 2.00-4.00

1131 R.G. FLOWER MEDICAL CO.; amber; 9" 6.00-10.00

1132 THE FLOWERS MANUFACTURING CO.; clear; 6¼"...................... 4.00-6.00

1133 FOLEY & CO.; clear or amethyst; 5½" 2.00-4.00

1134 FOLEY & CO., CHICAGO, FOLEY'S KIDNEY PILLS; 2½"; aqua 2.00-4.00

1135 FOLEY & CO. CHICAGO, U.S.A.; sample bottle; *Foley's Kidney Cure*; round; aqua; 4½" 8.00-10.00

1136 FOLEY'S CREAM on one side; *Foley & Co., Chicago, U.S.A.* on opposite side; square; 4¼"; clear 2.00-4.00

1137 FOLEY'S HONEY AND TAR, FOLEY & CO., CHICAGO, USA vertical on front; rectangular; sample size; 4¼"; aqua............. 2.00-4.00

1138 FOLEY'S HONEY & TAR; *Foley's & Co. Chicago;* 5¼"; aqua............... 4.00-8.00

1139 FOLEY'S KIDNEY PILLS, FOLEY & CO. CHICAGO on front vertically; round; 2½"; clear 3.00-4.00

1140 J. A. FOLGER & CO., ESSENCE OF JAMAICA GINGER, SAN FRA.; tapered top; 6¼"; aqua 8.00-10.00

1141 J. A. FOLGER & CO., ESSENCE OF JAMAICA GINGER, SAN FRANCISCO vertical on front in oval slug plate; graduated collar; oval; 6"; aqua 4.00-6.00

1142 DR. ROBT. B. FOLGER'S, OLOSAONIAN N.Y.; beveled corners; tapered top; 7¼"; aqua 15.00-25.00

1143 THE FORBES DIASTASE CO.; *Cincinnati, O.;* 7⅝"; amber................. 10.00-20.00

1144 same as above except clear......... 8.00-12.00

1145 B. FOSGATES ANODYNE; round; flared top; 4½"; aqua 4.00-8.00

1146 same except ringed top; 5" 4.00-6.00

1147 H. D. FOWLE, BOSTON; 5½"; aqua blue 4.00-8.00

1148 DR. FRAGAS; *Cuban Vermifuge* on two other panels; eight panels; aqua; 3¾" 4.00-6.00

1149 FRANCO AMERICAN HYGENIC CO.; *Perfumer Chicago* other side; clear; 3"... 2.00-4.00

1150 FRASER; cobalt; 4½" 4.00-8.00

1151 FRASER & CO.; amber; 5"......... 2.00-4.00

1152 FRENCH EAU DE QUININE HAIR TONIC, ATLANTA, label; 10½"; clear 8.00-10.00

1153 J. H. FRIEDENWALD & CO.; *Balt. Md., Buchen Gin For All Kidney & Liver Troubles; Friedenwalds Buchen Gin* on other side; 10"; green........................... 8.00-12.00

1154 FROG POND CHILL & FEVER TONIC; cobalt; 7" 8.00-12.00

1155 THE FROSER TABLET CO., label; clear; 5¾" 4.00-6.00

1156 FRUITOLA on side panel; *Pinus Med. Co., Monticello, Ill., U.S.A.* on other side; rectangular; 6½"; aqua 2.00-4.00

1157 F.S. & CO. 229, 2 under bottom; 4"... 2.00-3.00

1159   1160   1162   1164   1165   1168   1183   1186

1187   1199   1201   1203   1204   1205   1209   1216

1158   DR. FURBER'S CORDIAL OF MT. BOLM; flat ring top; 7¾″ 8.00-12.00

1159   GALLED ARMPITS & CO.; one side *For Tender Feet*; other side *Turkish Foot Bath*; 7½″; aqua. 4.00-6.00

1160   GARGLING OIL, LOCKPORT, N.Y.; tapered top; 5½″; green 6.00-8.00

1161   GARRETT DRUG CO.; *R. W. Garrett Mgr., Will Point, Texas*; 4⅛″ and 5¾″; clear 1.00-2.00

1162   D.H. GEER & SON, BOSTON, MASS., STUMP OF THE WORLD TRADEMARK; 9½″; aqua 10.00-20.00

1163   GILBERT BROS. & CO.; *Baltimore Md.*; 7¾″; green 4.00-6.00

1164   J. A. GILKA; *9 Schutzen str. 9* on back; pour spout; plain bottom; amber; 9½″ . . . 60.00-70.00

1165   J.A. GILKA; two men with club and crown on bottom; black; 9″. . . . . 25.00+

1166   GIROLAMO PAGLIANO on front and back in large vertical letters; rectangular; beveled corners; 4⅜″; apple green 15.00-25.00

1167   GLOVER H. CLAY CO., N.Y., on the front panel; rectangular; amber; 5″ 1.00-2.00

1168   GLOVER'S; *412* under bottom; amber; 5″ 2.00-4.00

1169   GLOVER'S IMPERIAL MANGE MEDICINE on the front of panel; *6½ fl. oz., H. Clay Glover Co.* on the left side; *N.Y.* on the right side; rectangular; amber; 6¾″ 1.00-2.00

1170 GLOVER'S IMPERIAL CANKER WASH., H. CLAY GLOVER D.V.S., NEW YORK, vertical on front; rectangular; 5¼"; amber.... 3.00-6.00

1171 GLOVER'S IMPERIAL MANGE MEDICINE 6½ FL. OZ., NEW YORK, H. CLAY GLOVER on front and sides; rectangular; ABM; 7"; amber 3.00-4.00

1172 GLOVER'S IMPERIAL "MANGE REMEDY," H. CLAY GLOVER D.V.S., NEW YORK on front and sides 3.00-4.00

1173 GLYCEROLE on side slot; aqua; applied ring at top; 6¼". 1.00-2.00

1174 GLYCOTHYMOLINE 1 LB. NET; amethyst; 8¼"; oval..................... 3.00-5.00

1175 GLYCOTHYMOLINE 3 FL. OZ. around shoulder; amethyst; oval; 4" and 4¾" . 2.00-3.00

1176 GLYCO THYMOLINE, slanted lower right to top left; square; ABM; 4½"; clear.... 2.00-3.00

1177 S.B. GOFF'S OIL LINIMENT, CAMDEN, N.J. on front and side; rectangular; 5¾"; aqua 3.00-4.00

1178 S.B. GOFF'S COUGH SYRUP, CAMDEN, N.J. on front and opposite side; rectangular; 5¾"; aqua......................... 3.00-6.00

1179 J.P. GOLDBERG, JACKSON'S ORIGINAL AMERICAN MED.; Indian with bow & arrow; pontil; 9"..................... 10.00-15.00

1180 GOLDEN'S LIQUID BEEF TONIC, circular under bottle; in center of the circle, in round sunken panel, *C. N. Crittenton, Prarr, N.Y.*; champagne type bottle; green; 9½"; ring top 4.00-8.00

1181 GOMBAULTS J.E., CAUSTIC BALSAM on front panel; *The Lawrence Williams Co., Sole Props For The U.S. and Canada* on the left and right side of panels; aqua; 6½"; rectangular 4.00-8.00

1182 GOODE'S SARSAPARILLA, W.S.G. GOODE; *Practical Pharmacist, Williamsville, Va.* 10.00-20.00

1183 V.V. GOOGLER; clear; 5"......... 2.00-4.00

1184 GOOSE GREASE LINIMENT, MFG. G.G.L. CO. OF GREENSBORO, N.C.; ring top; picture of a goose on it; 7¼"; aqua.......... 4.00-8.00

1185 W.J.M. GORDON PHARMACEUTIST, CINCINNATI, OHIO on three lines; blob top; 7½"; blue green................... 10.00-20.00

1186 GOURAUD'S ORIENTAL CREAM; *New York* on one side; *London* on the other; 4¼"; clear 1.00-2.00

1187 GRA CAR CERTOSA OF PAVIA; 9½"; aqua 10.00-20.00

1188 GRACE LINEN around shoulder; monogram on bottom; round; 2¼"; aqua 2.00-3.00

1189 GRAHAMS NO. 1 HAIR DYE LIQUID; 3½" 10.00-20.00

1190 GRAND UNION E.T.A. CO., GRAND UNION TEA CO. on each side; 5¼"; clear or amber 2.00-6.00

1191 A.C. GRANT, ALBANY, N.Y., GERMAN MAGNETIC LINAMENT; beveled corners; pontil; 5"; aqua 8.00-12.00

1192 GRANULAR CITRATE OF MAGNESIA; kite with letter inside it; ring top; 8"; cobalt 10.00-30.00

1193 same except 6"................ 10.00-30.00

1194 GRAY'S CELEBRATED SPARKLING SPRAY & EXQUISITE TONIC; blob top; clear 4.00-6.00

1195 GRAY'S ELIXAR, GRAY LAB; 7¼"; amber 4.00-6.00

1196 GRAY'S SYRUP OF RED SPRUCE GUM on opposite sides; sunken panels; rectangular; ABM; 5½"; aqua................. 3.00-4.00

1197 DR. T.W. GRAYDON, CINCINNATI, O., DISEASES OF THE LUNGS vertical on front in slug plate; square collar; 5⅞"; light amber 4.00-8.00

1198 GREAT ENGLISH SWEENY vertical on front in sunken panel; *Specific* on side; *Carey & Co.* on opposite side; rectangular; 6"; aqua .. 3.00-6.00

1199 L. M. GREEN; other side *Woodbury, N.J.*; clear or amethyst; 4¼" 2.00-3.00

1200 DRS. E.E. & J.A. GREENE, N.Y. & BOSTON; 7½"; aqua 4.00-8.00

1201 DRS. E.E. & J.A. GREENE; aqua; 7½" 4.00-8.00

1202 DRS. E E. & J.A. GREENE, on side; *New York & Boston* on opposite side; square collar; rectangular; 7½"; aqua................. 2.00-4.00

1203 GREEVER-LOT SPEICH MFG. CO.; clear; 6¼"............................. 2.00-3.00

1204 GRIMAULT & CO.; clear; 6½"...... 4.00-6.00

1205 GRODERS BOTANIC DYSPEPSIA SYRUP; *Waterville, Me* one side; *U.S.A.* other side; aqua; 8¾"............................. 6.00-8.00

1206 GROVE'S *Tasteless Chill Tonic, Prepared By Paris Med. Co., St. Louis* on the front panel; clear or amethyst; oval; 5¾" and 5⁵⁄₁₆" 2.00-3.00

1207 S. GROVER GRAHAM, DYSPEPSIA REMEDY, NEWBURGH, N.Y. USA vertical on front; rectangular; 6⅛"; clear 2.00-4.00

1208 GUN OIL vertical in sunken panel; rectangular; 4¾"; clear 3.00-4.00

1209 GURRLAIN; other side *Eau Lustrale*; open pontil; 6¼"; raspberry color 4.00-6.00

1210 HAGAN'S MAGNOLIA BALM on front of panel; milk glass or clear; rectangular; 5" 4.00-8.00

1211 HAGAR'S NERVINA TONIC, THE GREAT BLOOD MEDICINE, label; double band collar; 8¾"; light apple green............. 3.00-6.00

1212 HAIR BALSAM; olive green; blob top 4.00-6.00

1213 HAIR HEALTH, DR. HAYS on opposite sides in sunken panels; rectangular; 6¾"; amber 3.00-4.00

1214 same as above except ABM 2.00-3.00

1217

1218

1223

1226

1231

1232

1233

1238

1239

1240

1244

1247

1248

1249

1250

1251

1253

1256

1257

1258

1261

1262

1263

1264

1215 HAIR RESTORATIVE DEPOTS vertical on front in sunken panel; *Professor Woods* on side; *St. Louis & New York* on opposite side; rectangular; sunken panels; 7″; aqua 40.00-50.00

1216 LEON HALE; clear or amethyst; 6″ . 2.00-4.00

1217 LEON HALE; clear or amethyst; 5″ . 2.00-3.00

1218 E. W. HALL; aqua; 3½″ 2.00-4.00

1219 R. HALL & CO., PROP. DR. BARNES, ESSENCE OF JAMAICA GINGER; 5″; aqua 8.00-12.00

1220 HALL'S BALSAM FOR THE LUNGS vertical on front; fancy arch panels; sunken panel; rectangular; 7¼″; aqua................ 4.00-6.00

1221 HALL's BALSAM FOR THE LUNGS on the front panel; *John F. Henry & Co.* on side; *New York* on opposite; rectangular; aqua; 7¾″ and 6⅝″ 4.00-6.00

1222 HALL'S CATARRAH MEDICINE; vertical; round; ABM; 4½″; clear 2.00-3.00

1223 HALL'S HAIR RENEWER, NASHUA, N.H., label; *S&D 112* under bottom; 7¼″; aqua 8.00-12.00

1224 HALL'S on one side; *Hair Renewer* on opposite side of panel; this bottle is prettier than Ayer's Hair Vigor; rectangular; peacock blue; 6½″ 10.00-20.00

1225 HALL'S SARSAPARILLA vertical on sunken arch panel; *J.R. Gates & Co.* on side; *Proprietors, S.F.* on opposite side; rectangular; 9¼″; aqua 25.00-30.00

1226 HALSEY BROS. CO., CHICAGO; 6¾″; amber 4.00-6.00

1227 HAMILTON'S OLD ENGLISH BLACK OIL vertical on three panels; eight vertical panels; 6¾″; aqua 3.00-4.00

1228 HAMLIN'S WIZARD OIL, CHICAGO, USA; aqua; 5¾″; rectangular............ 1.00-3.00

1229 HAMLIN'S WIZARD OIL, CHICAGO, ILL. USA on front and sides; rectangular; sunken panels; 6¼″; aqua................ 2.00-3.00

1230 same as above except 8″ 2.00-3.00

1231 HAMPTON'S; amber; 6½″ 8.00-10.00

1232 HANCE BROTHERS & WHITE; *Phila. U.S.A.* in back; amber; 7″................ 2.00-4.00

1233 HANCOCK LIQUID SULPHUR CO.; *Baltimore Md.* on side; clear............ 3.00-4.00

1234 HAND MED. CO., PHILADELPHIA on front; oval; 5⅛″; aqua 2.00-3.00

1235 HANSEE EUROPEAN COUGH SYRUP, R.H. HANSEE PRO, MONTICELLO, N.Y. vertical on front in sunken panel; rectangular; 5¾″; amethyst........................ 2.00-6.00

1236 HARPER HEADACHE REMEDY, WASH., D.C.; 5″; clear 4.00-8.00

1237 DR. HARRISONS CHALYBESTE TONIC; 7¾″; teal blue 20.00-40.00

1238 DR. HARTER'S IRON TONIC, label; amber; 9″ 10.00-15.00

1239 DR. HARTER'S IRON TONIC; 9¼″; amber 10.00-12.00

1240 DR. HARTER'S LUNG BALM on front; clear 2.00-6.00

1241 E. HARTSHORN & SONS, ESTABLISHED 1850, BOSTON, vertical lettering on slug plate; rare flask shape; aqua.............. 2.00-6.00

1242 HARTSHORN & SONS ESTABLISHED 1850, BOSTON on center front; rectangular; 6¼″; clear 4.00-6.00

1243 same as above except 4⅞″........... 4.00-6.00

1244 DR. HASTINGS NAPHTHA SYRUP on front; *London* other side; aqua; pontil; 6½″ 10.00-15.00

1245 HAVILAND & CO., NEW YORK, CHARLESTON, & AUGUSTA; pontil; tapered top; 5¾″; aqua......................... 10.00-20.00

1246 L. F. H. H. HAY SOLE AGENT on shoulder; *L. F. Atwood* on base; 6½″; aqua 2.00-4.00

1247 R. HAYDEN'S; *H.V.C.* on other side; light blue; 4½″ 4.00-6.00

1248 DR. HAYDEN'S; *Viburnum* on back; aqua; 7″ 2.00-4.00

1249 DR. HAYES; three stars on bottom; clear 2.00-4.00

1250 DR. HAYNE'S ARABIAN BALSAM, E. MORGAN & SONS, PROVIDENCE, R.I. on four consecutive panels; twelve panels; band collar; 4¼″; aqua.................... 2.00-4.00

1251 DR. HAY'S; amber; 6″............. 2.00-6.00

1252 HAY'S on side; *Hair Health* on opposite side; label on back, *adopted April 1, 1912*; ABM; 7½″; amber 6.00-8.00

1253 CASWELL HAZARD & CO.; 7½″; 2¾″ x 2¾″ square; cobalt 6.00-8.00

1254 CASWELL HAZARD & CO, in three lines near top; in center in a circle *Omnia Labor Vincit;* under this in four lines *Chemists, New York & Newport;* 3¾″; square; beveled corner; short neck; 7½″; cobalt................. 6.00-8.00

1255 HEALTH NURSER; 6⅛″; clear or amber 10.00-20.00

1256 HEALTH SPECIALIST SPROULE; clear; 8¼″........................... 4.00-6.00

1257 HEALY & BIGELOW'S INDIAN OIL; 5¼″ tall; 1¼″ round; aqua............... 4.00-6.00

1258 HEALY & BIGELOW; reverse side *Indian Sagwa*; 8¾″; aqua 6.00-8.00

1259 HECEMAN & CO. on front of panel; on one side *Chemists;* other side *New York;* 3″ x 2″ body; 6½″ neck; 3¾″; aqua 4.00-8.00

1260 HECEMAN & CO. vertical in large letters on front; *Chemists* on side; *New York* on opposite side; rectangular; 10½″; aqua 2.00-4.00

1261 G. M. HEIDT & CO.; aqua; 9½″...... 6.00-8.00

1262 H. T. HELMBOLD; *Philadelphia* on side; *Genuine Fluid Extracts* on front; side mold; aqua; 7¼″.......................... 8.00-10.00

1263 H. T. HELMBOLD'S GENUINE PREPARATION; pontil; aqua; 6½″ .... 20.00+

1264 H. T. HELMBOLD; *Philadelphia* other side; *Genuine Fluid Extracts* front side; side mold; aqua; 6½″ 8.00-10.00

1268   1272   1273

1274   1275   1276

1278   1279   1280   1281   1285   1289

1295   1303   1304

1305   1314   1315

1265 HEMOGLOBINE DESCHIENS; 7¾"; cobalt 10.00-15.00

1266 HENRY'S CALCINED MAGNESIA, MANCHESTER; pontil; 4¼" 10.00-15.00

1267 HENRY'S CALCINED MAGNESIA, MANCHESTER vertical on all four sides; rolled lip; 4¼"; clear 6.00-8.00

1268 HENRY'S THREE CHLORIDES; amber; 7¼" 4.00-6.00

1269 THE HERB MED. CO., SPRINGFIELD, O.; reverse side *Lightning Hot Drops No Relief No Pay;* 5"; aqua 4.00-8.00

1270 HERB MED CO., WESTON, W. VA.; 9½"; aqua 8.00-10.00

1271 HERBINE; *St. Louis* on the left side; *Herbine Co.* on the right side; rectangular; 6¾"; clear 1.00-3.00

1272 HERRINGS MEDICINE CO., ATLANTA, GA., label; clear; 7¾" 2.00-4.00

1273 H. 82 under bottom; 7¼"; green...... 2.00-4.00

1274 H on bottom; amber; 4"............. 1.00-2.00

1275 E.H. CO.; aqua; 3½" 4.00-6.00

1276 H.H.H. MEDICINE; *The Celebrated* one side; *D.D.T. 1869* other side; aqua 4.00-10.00

1277 HIAWATHA HAIR RESTORATIVE, HOYT; long neck; 6¾"; light green........ 10.00-20.00

1278 HICKS & JOHNSON; *C.L.C. CO-2* under bottom; clear; 6½".................. 3.00-5.00

1279 HICKS' CAPUDINE; three different sizes; amber 2.00-8.00

1280 HICKS' CAPUDINE; amber; 5¾"... 3.00-5.00

1281 HICKS' CAPUDINE CURES ALL HEADACHES & COLD ETC.; 5¾"; amber 6.00-10.00

1282 DR. H.H. HIGGINS SARSAPARILLA; *Romney Va.;* pontil; 10"; aqua..... 20.00-40.00

1283 DR. H.R. HIGGINS; in back *Romney Va.*; on one side, *Sarsaparilla*; other side *Pure Extract*; pontil; tapered top; 10"; aqua .... 35.00+

1284 HILL'S vertical on front; *Hair Dye No. 1* on back; square; oval sides; 3¼"; aqua 2.00-3.00

1285 HILLSIDE CHEM. CO. on bottom; amber; 7½" 2.00-6.00

1286 HIMALYA; ring top; 7½"; amber ... 3.00-6.00

1287 HIMALYA; 7½"; amber 2.00-4.00

1288 HINDS HONEY AND ALMOND CREAM, A.S. HINDS CO., PORTLAND, MAINE USA, IMPROVES THE COMPLEXION, ALCOHOL 7% on front and sides; rectangular; 2⅞"; clear 3.00-4.00

1289 A. S. HINDS; *Portland, Me* other side; clear; 5½"............................ 2.00-4.00

1290 HOBO MED. CO.; *Beaumont, Texas Registered Trademark; HB* on the front panel in a diamond; 8⅛"; rectangular; clear; screw top ... 2.00-5.00

1291 HOFFMAN'S ANODYNE, label; rectangular; square collar; 5"; clear 2.00-3.00

1292 HOFF'S GERMAN LINIMENT; *Goodrich & Jennings, Anoka, Minn.* vertical on three panels; twelve vertical panels; ring collar; 5¾"; aqua 4.00-6.00

1293 HOFF'S LINIMENT; *Goodrich Drug Co., Anoka, Minn.* vertical on three panels; twelve vertical panels; ring collar; ABM; 7"; aqua blue 3.00-6.00

1294 DR. J.J. HOGAN; *next to post office, Vallejo, Cal.* in circle; *W.T. & CO. U.S.A.* under bottom; ringed top; 7¼"; cobalt blue........... 20.00+

1295 HOLLAND; aqua; 3½"............. 2.00-4.00

1296 HOLLAND DRUG CO. *Prescriptions A Specialty, Holland, Tx.* on the front; on the bottom *USP;* rectangular; 4¾"; amethyst 1.00-2.00

1297 HOLLIS BALM OF AMERICA; cylindrical; square collar; 5"; aqua 6.00-8.00

1298 HOLTONS ELECTRIC OIL on bottle vertically; round; 3¼"; amethyst 2.00-4.00

1299 HOLTON'S ELECTRIC OIL vertical on bottle; cylindrical; square collar; 3¼"; clear 3.00-6.00

1300 THE HONDURAS CO'S. COMPOUND EXTRACT SARSAPARILLA, 1876; 10½"; aqua 30.00-40.00

1301 HONDURAS MOUNTAIN TONIC CO., fancy writing in sunken panel; double band collar; 9"; aqua........................ 20.00-30.00

1302 HONE DEURE on one panel; *Colours* on back panel; six panels; flared top; 2¾"; clear; t.p. pontils; small bottles 6.00-12.00

1303 HOODS SARSAPARILLA; aqua; 8¾" 4.00-6.00

1304 HOOD'S; machine made; 8½"; clear 2.00-4.00

1305 HOOD'S TOOTH POWDER; clear; *C.I. Hood & Co., Lowell, Mass;* 3½" 6.00-8.00

1306 W.H. HOOKER [sic] & CO. PROPRIETORS, NEW YORK, U.S.A. vertical on front in sunken panel; *For the Throat and Lungs* on side; *Acker's English Remedy* on opposite side; 5¾"; cobalt blue 10.00-15.00

1307 same as above except N.&S. AMERICARS; 6½" 8.00-12.00

1308 same except round; and ACKER'S BABY SOOTHER; aqua.................. 6.00-8.00

1309 W. H. HOOPER & CO. *Proprietors New York, U.S.A.* in three lines in sunken panel; on one side in sunken panel *Acker's English Remedy;* on other *For The Throat & Lungs;* 5¾" tall; 1½" neck; ring top; cobalt 6.00-10.00

1310 G. W. HOUSE CLEMENS INDIAN TONIC; ring top; 5"; aqua............... 80.00-100.00

1311 THE HOWARD DRUGS & MEDICINE CO, *Prepared By, Baltimore, Md., Frixie Hair Oil* in sunken panel on front in script, six lines; 2¼" x 1" x 4"; clear or amethyst 2.00-4.00

1312 same size as above except *Rubifoam For the Teeth, Put Up By E.W. HOYTH & CO, Lowell Mass* in six lines, not in sunken panel.. 2.00-4.00

1313 HUGHEL'S DANDER-OFF HAIR TONIC DANDRUFF REMEDY all on front side; square bottle; 6¼"; clear........... 4.00-8.00

1314 HUMPHREY'S; *Humphrey's Homeophathic* on back; clear; 3½"................ 2.00-4.00

1315 HUMPHREY'S MARVEL OF HEALING; clear or amethyst; 5½" 2.00-4.00

1316   1318   1319   1321   1326   1327   1328

1329   1331   1332   1335   1336   1338   1340

1342   1343   1344   1345   1346   1349   1350

1351   1354   1355

1316 HUMPHREY'S MARVEL WITCHHAZEL; machine made; clear; 5½" 2.00-4.00

1317 R. H. HURD PROP., *No. Berwick, Me. U.S.A. Backer's Specific*; 4½"; clear....... 8.00-15.00

1318 HURLEY; clear or amethyst; 5".... 2.00-3.00

1319 HUSBAND'S CALCINED MAGNESIA, PHILA., vertical on all four sides; square; sheared collar; 4¼"; aqua 2.00-6.00

1320 HUSBAND'S CALCINED MAGNESIA, PHILA.; square; sheared lip; 4½"; clear or amber 4.00-6.00

1321 I. G. CO. under bottom; 7"; aqua... 8.00-10.00

1322 IMPERIAL HAIR/TRADE MARK, shield with crown in center; *Regenerator* vertical on front; *Imperial Chemical Manufacturing Co.* on side; *New York* on opposite side; rectangular; beveled corners; square collar; 4½"; light green 4.00-8.00

1323 INDIA CHOLAGOGUE vertical on front; *Norwich, Conn. U.S.A.* on side; *Osgood's* on opposite side; rectangular; beveled corners; machine made; 5½"; aqua 2.00-4.00

1324 same as above except NEW YORK embossed on side; not machine made; 5⅜"; aqua ... 3.00-6.00

1325 DR. H.A. INGHAM'S VEGETABLE PAIN EXTRACT; 4½"; aqua 4.00-6.00

1326 Iodine; machine made; 2¼"; amber ... 2.00-4.00

1327 I.R., label; fancy bottle; graphite pontil; 6½"; aqua .... 25.00+

1328 ISCHIROGENO O BATTISTA FARMACIA INGLESE DEL CERVO—NAPOLI; 7"; amber 10.00-15.00

1329 J & J under bottom; sheared top; cobalt; 2½" 2.00-4.00

1330 JACKSON MFG. CO., COLUMBUS, O.; ring top; 6¼"; clear 4.00-6.00

1331 JACOB'S PHARMACY; other side *Atlanta, Ga., Compound Extract Pine Splinters*; 7½"; clear 2.00-4.00

1332 JACOB'S PHARMACY; *W.T.&CO. C. U.S.A.* under bottom; amber; 6".......... 6.00-10.00

1333 ST. JACOB'S OEL, THE CHARLES A. VOGELER COMPANY, BALTIMORE, MD. U.S.A. vertical around bottle; cylindrical; 6⅝"; aqua......................... 3.00-6.00

1334 same as above except amethyst 3.00-6.00

1335 JAD SALTS, WHITEHALL PHARMACY CO., N.Y., label; screw cap; 5¾"; clear 2.00-4.00

1336 JAMAICA GINGER, label; clear; 5¾" 2.00-4.00

1337 JAMAICA GINGER FRUIT CORDIAL, MANUFACTURED BY C.C. HINES & CO., BOSTON, MASS. on two sides; square; 6½"; clear 4.00-8.00

1338 JAQUES; aqua; 4½".............. 3.00-4.00

1339 DR. D. JAYNES TONIC VERMIFUGE, 242 CHEST ST., PHILA on front; aqua; 5½"; rectangular 2.00-3.00

1340 DR. D. JAYNES EXPECTORANT on front panel; on back *Philada* on each side; three panels; short neck; 6¾"; aqua; pontil 10.00-15.00

1341 DR. D. JAYNES EXPECTORANT vertical on front in sunken panel; *Twenty Five Cents* on side; *Quarter Size* on opposite side; rectangular; square collar; 5¼"; aqua 2.00-4.00

1342 DR. D. JAYNES; *Half Dollar* on one side; *Half Size* on other side 2.00-8.00

1343 DR. D. JAYNES; pontil; aqua; 7"... 7.00-10.00

1344 JAYNES & CO., BOSTON; screw top; 9½"; amber 8.00-10.00

1345 T.E. JENKINS & CO., CHEMISTS, LOUISVILLE, KY.; graphite pontil; 7"; aqua .... 8.00+

1346 JOHNSON'S AMERICAN ANODYNE LINIMENT around bottle; aqua; 4½" or 6½" 4.00-6.00

1347 JOHNSON'S AMERICAN ANODYNE LINIMENT vertical; round; 4¼"; aqua.... 2.00-4.00

1348 same as above except 6½" 2.00-4.00

1349 JOHNSON'S CHILL AND FEVER TONIC; clear; 5¾" 2.00-4.00

1350 JOHNSON & JOHNSON OIL, label; *C1637* under bottom; aqua; 5"............. 2.00-4.00

1351 S. C. JOHNSON & SON, RACINE, WIS. under bottom; clear; 3" 2.00-4.00

1352 DR. E.S. JOHNSON BLOOD SYRUP, FARMINGTON, ME. vertical on front in oval slug plate; large square collar; oval; 9⅝"; aqua 6.00-8.00

1353 DR. JOHNSON'S HORSE REMEDIES PREPARED BY NEW YORK VETERINARY HOSPITAL, vertical on front in slug plate; oval; flared collar; 6¾"; aqua 4.00-8.00

1354 DR. JONES' AUSTRALIAN OIL; *Not To Be Taken* on each side; amber; 5"..... 8.00-10.00

1355 DR. JONES' LINIMENT; aqua; 6¾" 2.00-4.00

1356 J.P.L. under bottom; 7½"; aqua..... 4.00-8.00

1359

1362

1363

1369

1370

1375

1380

1384

1385

1388

1392

1393

1397

1398

1400

1357 L.E. JUNG; machine made; amber; 11″ 4.00-8.00

1358 JUNKET COLORS with monogram on one side; *Little Falls, N.Y., Chas. Hansen's Laboratory;* square; 3½″; aqua 2.00-4.00

1359 KALIUM; 5½″; clear............ 8.00-10.00

1360 KALO COMPOUND FOR DYSPEPSIA, BROWN MFG. CO., GREENVILLE, TENN. (N's in TENN. are backwards) all on front in oval end of sunken panel; rectangular; square collar; 9½″; amethyst.......... 10.00-20.00

1361 KA:TON:KA, THE GREAT INDIAN REMEDY on opposite sides; rectangular; graduated collar; 8¾″; aqua............. 10.00-20.00

1362 KEASBEY & MATTISON CO.; aqua or amber; 3¼″......................... 2.00-6.00

1363 KEASBEY & MATTISON CO.; light blue; 3½″ 2.00-4.00

1364 KEASBEY & MATTISON CO. CHEMISTS, AMBLER, PA. on front; light blue; 5″; rectangular 2.00-3.00

1365 KEASBEY & MATTISON CO, AMBLER, PA. on front; smoky blue; round; 5¾″ ... 2.00-4.00

1366 KEASBEY & MATTISON, PHILADELPHIA around shoulder; cylindrical; ring collar; 6″; cobalt blue 4.00-8.00

1367 THE KEELEY REMEDY NEUROTENE; *Discovered by Dr. L.E. Keeley Dwight;* 5⅝″; clear 8.00-15.00

1368 DR. KELLINGS PURE HERB MED.; pontil; 6½″; green 8.00-15.00

1369 J.W. KELLY & CO.; *C* in a triangle on bottom; clear or amethyst; 6″.............. 4.00-6.00

1370 KEMP'S; *O.F. Woodward* on one side; *Leroy, N.Y.* on other side; light blue; 5½″.... 2.00-4.00

1371 KEMP'S BALSAM, vertical on front; sample size; heavy glass; unusual flask shape; band collar; 2⅞″; aqua 2.00-5.00

1372 KEMP'S BALSAM FOR THROAT AND LUNGS, LEROY, N.Y., O.G. WOODWARD front and sides; rectangular; square band collar; 5¾″; aqua 2.00-4.00

1373 KENDALL'S SPAVIN TREATMENT, on shoulder; *Enosbury Falls, Vt.* on base; amber; 5½″; twelve panels............... 3.00-5.00

1374 DR. KENDALL'S QUICK RELIEF vertical on front in sunken panel; rectangular; double band collar; 5″; aqua................. 2.00-4.00

1375 DR. KENNEDY'S; aqua; 9″; side mold 2.00-6.00

1376 DR. KENNEDY'S FAVORITE REMEDY, KINGSTON, N.Y. U.S.A. vertical on front in sunken panel; 7″; clear 2.00-4.00

1377 DR. D. KENNEDY'S on side; *Favorite Remedy* on front; *Kingston, N.Y. U.S.A.* on opposite side in sunken panels; graduated collar; rectangular; 8¾″; amethyst 2.00-4.00

1378 same as above except aqua 2.00-4.00

1379 DR. KENNEDY'S LINIMENT, RHEUMATIC LINIMENT, ROXBURY, MASS.; 6¼″; aqua 8.00-10.00

1380 DR. KENNEY'S on other side; aqua; 9″ 4.00-8.00

1381 KEYSTONE DRUG CO.; *So. Boston Va.;* tapered; 9″; clear or amber 4.00-10.00

1382 MRS. E. KIDDER CORDIAL; marked vertically *Mrs. E. Kidder Dysentery Cordial, Boston*; round; open pontil; 8″; aqua 10.00-15.00

1383 KIDNEY BOTTLE PILLS, label; kidney shape; ring top; 5½″; clear 15.00-25.00

1384 E.J. KIEFFER & CO.; round back; clear or amethyst; 6½″ 2.00-6.00

1385 E. J. KIEFFER'S; amber; 6½″ 4.00-6.00

1386 KILLINGER on front; aqua; 7⅞″; square 3.00-4.00

1387 DR. KILMER'S; *Swamp Root Kidney Liver and Bladder Remedy, Binghampton, N.Y., U.S.A.* on front; aqua; 7″; rectangular......... 2.00-4.00

1388 DR. KILMER'S; aqua; 7″ 4.00-6.00

1389 DR. KILMER'S; *Swamp-Root, Kidney & Bladder Remedy* on front; *Binghampton, N.Y.* on left; aqua; rectangular; 8″ 3.00-5.00

1390 DR. KILMER'S; *Swamp-Root, Kidney Remedy, Binghampton, N.Y.;* sample bottle; aqua; round; 4¼″......................... 5.00-8.00

1391 DR. KILMER'S U & O ANOINTMENT, BINGHAMPTON, N.Y. on front; round; 1¾″; aqua 2.00-4.00

1392 DR. KILMER'S; clear machine made; 7¼″ 2.00-4.00

1393 KINA; *Laroche* on back; aqua; 7¾″ .. 2.00-4.00

1394 DR. KINGS NEW DISCOVERY on front; *Chicago, Ill.* on side; *H.E. Bucklem & Co.* on right side; rectangular; 4½″; aqua 2.00-4.00

1395 DR. KINGS NEW DISCOVERY FOR COUGHS AND COLDS on front panel; clear; rectangular; 6¾″ 3.00-4.00

1396 DR. KINGS NEW LIFE PILLS on front; clear; square; 2½″........................ 2.00-3.00

1397 KINNEY & CO.; clear or amethyst; 3″ 4.00-6.00

1398 S. B. KITCHEL'S LINIMENT; aqua; 8¼″ 4.00-8.00

1399 KLINKER'S HAIR TONIC, CLEVELAND, vertical on front in fancy panel; ring collar; ring on neck; three ribs on side; base crown shape; fancy shape; 6″; clear 4.00-8.00

1400 KNAPPS; aqua; 4″................. 2.00-4.00

1401 KOBOLE TONIC MED. CO., CHICAGO, ILL.; 8½″; milk glass...................... 25.00+

1402 same as above except amber or aqua 10.00-20.00

1403 DR. KOCH'S REMEDIES, EXTRACTS & SPICES; on one side *Dr. Koch Vegetable Tea Co.;* other *Winona, Minn.;* 9″; clear 3.00-4.00

1404 KODEL NERVE TONIC, FREE SAMPLE; under bottom *E. C. Dewich & Co., Chicago;* wide ring top; 3¼″; aqua 2.00-4.00

1405 KOKEN, ST. LOUIS, U.S.A., 10 FL.OZ. on front; 7″; clear; round.............. 1.00-2.00

1406   1407   1410   1413   1415   1416   1417   1418

1419   1420   1421   1425   1426   1427   1428

1429   1433   1434   1435   1437   1438   1439   1440

1441   1446   1449

1406 KOKO FOR THE HAIR; clear; 4¾".. 2.00-6.00

1407 KOLA-CARDINETTE on each side; *The Palisade Mfg. Co., Yonkers, N.Y.* under bottom; amber; 9" 6.00-10.00

1408 KONING TILLY in vertical line; sheared top; round; ¾"; aqua 4.00-6.00

1409 KONJOLA MOSBY MED. CO., CINCINNATI, U.S.A. on front; *Konjola* on left and right panels; clear; 8¼"; rectangular; screw top 1.00-2.00

1410 THE KREBS-OLIVER CO.; amber; 5¾" 2.00-6.00

1411 KUHLMAN'S KNOXVILLE TENN.; *W.&T. Co. U.S.A.* under bottom; 4½"; clear .. 3.00-4.00

1412 KUTNOW'S POWDER vertical on front in large letters; rectangular; large square collar; corner panels; 4¾"; aqua........... 2.00-4.00

1413 LA AMERICA; clear or amethyst; 5½" 3.00-6.00

1414 L.B. CO.; 11½"; clear 4.00-6.00

1415 LACTO-MARROW CO.; other side *N.Y., U.S.A.*; clear or amethyst; 9¼"; side mold 3.00-6.00

1416 LACTOPEPTINE, NEW YORK; clear or amethyst; 4"..................... 4.00-6.00

1417 LACTOPEPTINE FOR THE DIGESTIVE AILMENTS around cross; dark green; 3"; sheared top...................... 4.00-8.00

1418 LA-CU-PIA under bottom; aqua; four-part mold; 8¼"....................... 2.00-6.00

1419 LAINE CHEM CO.; amber; 5½".... 2.00-4.00

1420 LAINE CHEM CO.; amber; 4".... 2.00-6.00

1421 LAINE CHEM CO.; amber; *341* under bottom; 6½"........................... 2.00-6.00

1422 GEO. L. LAIRD & CO. in horseshoe shape; OLEO-CHYLE in vertical line; cathedral type bottle; ring top; 6¾"; blue....... 25.00-50.00

1423 LAKE SHORE SEED CO., DUNKIRK, N.Y. vertical on front in large sunken panels; rectangular; ring on neck; 5½"; aqua... 2.00-4.00

1424 LANGLEY & MICHAELS, SAN FRANCISCO vertical on front in round sunken panel; round graduated collar; 6¼"; aqua 4.00-8.00

1425 LANMAN & KEMP one side; other side *N.Y.*; aqua; 6" 3.00-4.00

1426 LANMAN & KEMP; aqua; *Cod Liver Oil* one side; other side *N.Y.*; 10½" 6.00-8.00

1427 LANMAN & KEMP; aqua; 8½" 2.00-6.00

1428 LARKIN CO., BUFFALO; 6"; clear 2.00-4.00

1429 LARKIN CO.; clear or amethyst; 4¼" 2.00-4.00

1430 LARKIN SOAP CO., MODJESKA DERMA-BALM, MODJEST DERMA-BALM on three sides; square; flared lip; 4¾"; clear.. 4.00-6.00

1431 LAUGHLIUS & BUSHFIELO WORM POWER, WHEELING, VA. 1850; pontil; 3¼"; aqua.......................... 10.00-20.00

1432 A.J. LAXOL, WHITE, NEW YORK, in two indented panels on front; oval back; triangular; round band collar; 7"; cobalt blue .. 5.00-10.00

1433 LAXOL; 2½" neck; 7"; triangular; cobalt blue 6.00-10.00

1434 L-C 1903 on bottom; blue; sheared top; 4" 3.00-6.00

1435 JOHN P. LEE; clear; 4½" 2.00-4.00

1436 LEGRANDE'S ARABIAN CATARRH REMEDY, N.Y. on front; flask type bottle; 9½"; aqua.......................... 10.00-20.00

1437 LEHN & FINK, NEW YORK on bottom; amber; seven-part mold; 7¼" 4.00-6.00

1438 DR. H.C. LEMKE'S on other side; aqua; 10" 15.00-20.00

1439 LEMON ELIXIR under bottom; paper label reads DR. H. MOYEY'S LEMON ELIXIR HERB COMPOUND, ATLANTA, GA.; 7¼"; aqua.......................... 4.00-8.00

1440 S.B. LEONARDI & CO.; amber; 8¼" 8.00-12.00

1441 JARABE DE LEONARDI; *5* under bottom; aqua; 5½".......................... 2.00-4.00

1442 LEWIS & CO.; 7½"; amber 2.00-4.00

1443 J.A. LIMCRICKS GREAT MASTER OF PAIN, RODNEY, MASS.; pontil; tapered top; 6¼"; aqua...................... 15.00+

1444 DR. LINDSEY'S BLOOD SEARCHER, DR. J.M. LINDSEY, GREENBURG, PA. 1850; *sold (by) agent Robert Emory Sellers & Co., Pittsburg, 1880*; 8½"; clear 12.00-24.00

1445 DR. LINICKS MALZ EXTRACT vertical on front; ring collar; square; shaped like pickle jar; 6"; clear 3.00-8.00

1446 LINIM; 5¾"; clear 8.00-10.00

1447 LINIMENT OR OIL OF LIFE 16 OZ. on front in sunken arch panel; *C.C. TAYLOR* on side; *Fairport, N.Y.* on opposite side; rectangular; graduated collar; 10½"; clear....... 4.00-8.00

1448 same as above except 5⅞"........... 4.00-8.00

1449 LIPPMAN'S LIVER PILLS; aqua; 2¼" 2.00-4.00

1453   1457   1461   1462   1464   1465   1466   1467

1468   1470   1473   1474   1475   1476   1478   1479

1480   1481   1484   1486   1487   1488   1489   1493

1494   1495   1496

1450 LIQUID FRANCONIA, LEROY, N.Y.; *O.F. Woodward* on front and sides; rectangular; 4¼"; amethyst...................... 2.00-4.00

1451 LIQUID PEPTONOIDS, ARLINGTON CHEMICAL CO., YONKERS, N.Y. sunken in arched panel; square; 7⅝"; amber.... 2.00-4.00

1452 LIQUID OPDELDOC; cylindrical; two-piece mold; square band collar; 4½"; aqua 8.00-12.00

1453 LIQUOZONE; 8" tall; 3" diameter; amber 2.00-4.00

1454 LIQUID VENEER under bottom; 6¼"; clear or amber 2.00-6.00

1455 LISTERINE, near shoulder; at bottom *Lambert Pharmacal Co.* in two lines; three sizes; clear or amethyst...................... 2.00-4.00

1456 same except machine made 2.00-3.00

1457 LITTLE GIANT SURE DEATH TO ALL KINDS OF BUGS; *Every bottle warranted, Little Giant Co., Newburgport, Mass*; 8½"; aqua 8.00-10.00

1458 LIVE & LET LIVE CUT RATE DRUG CO.; *Chattanooga, Tenn.*; 3½"; clear 4.00-6.00

1459 L.L.L. in front; ring top; 7¾"; aqua . 4.00-8.00

1460 LOG CABIN EXTRACT, label; *Rochester, N.Y., Pat'd. Sep. 6 1889*; 6¼"; amber... 75.00-100.00

1461 LONDON; pontil; light green; 5½". 8.00-12.00

1462 L.O.R. CO. around an eye; tapered top; 4¾"; cobalt....................... 15.00-30.00

1463 LORD'S OPDELDOC with embossed man breaking and tossing away his crutches, on front in arched panel; oval; square collar; 5"; aqua 8.00-12.00

1464 LORENTZ MED. CO.; amber; 4"   4.00-6.00

1465 DON LORENZO; same on reverse side; 10"; dark olive..................... 10.00-18.00

1466 J.M. LOTRIDGE; *W.T.Co.* under bottom; clear; 6¼"................................. 2.00-4.00

1467 THE LOUIS DAUDELIN CO.; clear; 8¾" 2.00-4.00

1468 LUFKIN ECZEMA REMEDY, label; clear; 7" 4.00-6.00

1469 LUNDBORG, N.Y.; 8⅝"; teal blue ... 3.00-6.00

1470 LUYTIES; 7"; amber.............. 4.00-8.00

1471 LYMAN ASTLEY-CHEYENE, WYO. in a circular panel; 7"; aqua 8.00-15.00

1472 DR. J.B. LYNAR & SON; *Logansport, Ind.*; *J.B.L.* in seal on shoulder; 6"; clear ... 3.00-6.00

1473 DR. J.B. LYNAS & SON; clear or amethyst; 6" 3.00-6.00

1474 LYON'S; pontil; aqua; 6¼" 8.00-12.00

1475 LYON'S; aqua; 6¼" 3.00-6.00

1476 LYON'S LAXATIVE SYRUP, LYON MED. CO.; reverse *Louisville, Ky.*; 6¼"; clear 2.00-4.00

1477 LYON'S FOR THE HAIR, KAT HAIRON, NEW YORK on front, back and sides; sunken panels; rectangular; pontil; 6⅛"; aqua 25.00-35.00

1478 LYON MFG' CO; *Mexican Mustang Liniment* on back; aqua; 7¾"............... 8.00-10.00

1479 LYON MFG' CO; same as above except 7½" 4.00-6.00

1480 LYRIC 3 — Y under bottom; machine made; clear or amethyst; 4½" 1.00-2.00

1481 LYSOL; amber; 3½"............... 2.00-4.00

1482 J. J. MACK & CO., SAN FRANCISCO, DR. A. E. FLINTS HEART REMEDY; 7½"; amber 8.00-12.00

1483 MACK DRUG CO., PROP'S N.Y., DR. FLINTS REMEDY; flat ring top; 7½"; amber 8.00-12.00

1484 MADAME M. YALE FRUITCURA WOMANS TONIC; reverse side *Chicago & N.Y.*; 9"; aqua 6.00-8.00

1485 MAGGI #2; rectangular; tapered neck; 6"; amber 4.00-8.00

1486 MAGNESIE CALCINEE; 8"; clear glass painted brown 10.00-20.00

1487 J. J. MAHER & CO., PROPRIETORS, AUGUSTA, MAINE; 8½"; amber ... 4.00-6.00

1488 P.H. MALLEN CO. CHICAGO; under bottom *W.T. Co. U.S.A.*; 9"; amber 4.00-6.00

1489 THE MALTINE MFG. CO.; *#3* under bottom; 7½"; amber..................... 8.00-10.00

1490 THE MALTINE MFG. CO. CHEMISTS, NEW YORK in five lines on front; various numbers under bottom; amber or brown; 6½"; short neck 4.00-6.00

1491 MALYDOR MFG. CO., LANCASTER, O. U.S.A. on front; large beveled corners; one corner is sunken; 5"; amethyst,....... 3.00-6.00

1492 MANSFIELD MEDICINE, CO. N.Y. and MEMPHIS on front; *Proprietors S. Mansfield* on each side; tapered top; 5½"; aqua .. 8.00-10.00

1493 S. MANSFIELD & CO.; reverse side *Memphis*; 5¾"; aqua 6.00-8.00

1494 CHAS. MARCHAND; amber; 4" ... 2.00-4.00

1495 CHAS. MARCHAND; 8½"; clear or amethyst 3.00-6.00

1496 MARCHAND'S; amber; 5½" 2.00-4.00

1497   1499   1500   1502   1503   1504   1507   1510

1513   1514   1515   1521   1528   1529   1531   1532

1536   1537   1538   1539   1540   1541   1542   1543

1544   1545   1546   1547

1497 J.B. MARCHISI M.D.; aqua; 7½"... 4.00-6.00
1498 MARINE HOSPITAL SERVICE 1798 U.S., 1871 around a crossed anchor and staff; near base *1000 c.c.*; ringed top; 9¼"; clear 15.00-20.00
1499 MARINE HOSPITAL SERVICE; aqua; 5½" and other sizes .... 6.00+
1500 MARSHALL'S; aqua; 4¾"......... 2.00-5.00
1501 DR. MARSHALL'S CATARRH SNUFF on opposite sides in large letters; rectangular; round band collar; 3⅜"; aqua 4.00-6.00
1502 WM. J. MATHESON & CO. LTD; sheared top; 3½"; clear 2.00-6.00
1503 MATHIS QUARTER DOLLAR FAMILY LINIMENT; aqua; 4¼" 2.00-4.00
1504 C. B. MATHIS; aqua; 4" 4.00-6.00
1505 MATHIS QUARTER DOLLAR FAMILY LINIMENT, B. MATHIS, TOMS RIVER, N.J. in seven lines on front; oval; aqua; 4" . 2.00-6.00
1506 MAZON PARFUM vertical on front; square; 4"; aqua......................... 2.00-4.00
1507 J. O. McCANN; clear; 2¾".......... 2.00-4.00
1508 McCANNON & CO., WINONA, MINN. vertical on front in sunken panel; rectangular; double band collar; 7⅛"; aqua 2.00-4.00
1509 McCOMBIE'S COMPOUND RESTORATIVE; pontil...................... 20.00-25.00
1510 McCORMICK & CO.; clear; 3¾"..... 2.00-4.00
1511 DRS. McDONALD & LEVY; *Sacramento City, Calif.*; 4¾"; aqua 10.00-25.00
1512 McELREES WINE OF CARDUI on side; *Chattanooga Medicine Co.* on opposite side; sunken oval panels; graduated collar; 8½"; clear 4.00-6.00
1513 McFADDEN THE DRUGGIST, SENATOBIA, MISS.; 5¾"; clear or amber 2.00-6.00
1514 McKESSON & ROBBINS; amber; 3" 2.00-4.00

1515 McKESSON & ROBBINS in two lines; amber; 2¼" square; 1⅞" wide 2.00-4.00
1516 DOCTOR McLANE'S, AMERICAN WORM SPECIFIC; round; pontil; 4"...... 8.00-15.00
1517 DR. McLEAN'S LIVER & KIDNEY BALMS, ST. LOUIS, MO.; 8¾"; aqua........ 8.00-10.00
1518 McLEAN'S STRENGTHENING CORDIAL; graphite pontil; 9¼"; aqua 15.00-25.00
1519 DR. McLEAN'S LIVER & KIDNEY BALM, ST. LOUIS; 9"; aqua; oval flask 2.00-4.00
1520 DR. J.H. McLEAN'S VOLCANIC OIL LINIMENT on the front; 4"; square; aqua . 3.00-6.00
1521 DR. J.H. McLEAN'S; aqua; sheared top; ten panels; 3½"..................... 2.00-6.00
1522 McMILLAN & KESTER, ESS. OF JAMACIA GINGER, S. F. all on front; flask; graduated collar; 6¾"; aqua 4.00-8.00
1523 McMILLAN & KESTER, ESS. OF JAMAICA GINGER, S. F.; 6"; aqua 8.00-15.00
1524 DR. McMUNN'S ELIXIR OF OPIUM; pontil; round; 4½"; aqua 8.00-15.00
1525 DR. McMUNNS ELIXIR OF OPIUM vertical around bottle; cylindrical; square collar; 4½"; aqua.................................. 3.00-6.00
1526 FURST McNESS CO., FREEPORT, ILL. vertical on front in sunken panel; rectangular; ring and band collar; ABM; 8½"; aqua 2.00-3.00
1527 same as above except 6¼" 2.00-3.00
1528 M.C.W. 10½ OZ under bottom; amber; 7½" 2.00-3.00
1529 M.C.W. 43 under bottom; round; amber; 3" 2.00-4.00
1530 M.D. U.S.A. in center of bottle; ring top; 9½"; amber .... 15.00+
1531 MEADE & BAKER; clear or amethyst; 3½" 3.00-6.00
1532 MEADE & BAKER; clear; 4¼"..... 2.00-4.00
1533 Medicine, plain; square; aqua; applied top; kick-up; pontil; 9¾".................... 8.00-12.00
1534 Medicine, plain; round; cobalt; 3" round; 7½" 4.00-6.00
1535 Medicine, plain; twelve-sided; round; 1¼" x 2½"; pontil.................... 7.00-10.00
1536 Medicine label; 4"; clear 2.00-3.00
1537 Medicine label; pontil; aqua; 6¾" 6.00-8.00
1538 Medicine label; amber; 8" 2.00-3.00
1539 Medicine label; cobalt; 4½" 4.00-6.00
1540 Medicine label; clear or amethyst; *W* on bottom; 6".................................. 2.00-4.00
1541 Medicine label; clear or amethyst; 5" 1.00-2.00
1542 Medicine label; aqua; pontil; 6½"... 6.00-12.00
1543 Medicine label; amber; 7¼"........ 2.00-3.00
1544 Medicine label; free-blown; pontil; 3"; ⁹⁄₁₆" diameter; clear.................. 8.00-12.00
1545 Medicine label; 6"; kick-up; cobalt 2.00-4.00
1546 Medicine label; amber; 7¼" 2.00-4.00
1547 Medicine label; 5¾"; cobalt.......... 4.00-6.00

1548   1549   1550   1551   1552   1554   1555

1556   1557   1558   1559   1560   1561   1562   1563

1564   1565   1566   1567   1568   1569   1570

1571   1572   1573   1574   1575   1576   1577

1578   1579   1580   1581

1548   Medicine label; pontil; aqua; 5¼″; 1½″ diameter
.... 6.00-12.00
1549   Medicine label; aqua; pontil; 2¼″ round
.... 6.00-12.00
1550   Medicine label; clear; pontil; 2¾″ 5.00-8.00
1551   Medicine label; 7½″; light blue; small kick-up
.... 2.00-6.00
1552   Medicine label; W under bottom; clear; 4½″
.... 1.00-2.00
1553   M; plain medicine label; 8½″; amber .. 2.00-4.00
1554   Medicine label; three-cornered bottle; clear; 4″
.... 2.00-3.00
1555   Medicine label; aqua; 4¾″.......... 2.00-3.00
1556   Medicine label; three-part mold; aqua; 6¼″
.... 2.00-6.00
1557   Medicine label; cobalt; 5½″......... 2.00-6.00
1558   Medicine label; B under bottom; aqua. 2.00-4.00
1559   Medicine label; aqua; 6¼″.......... 2.00-3.00

1560   Medicine label; clear; 4½″.......... 2.00-3.00
1561   Medicine label; twelve panels; aqua; 4½″
.... 2.00-3.00
1562   Medicine label; 400 under bottom; 6¼″ amber
.... 2.00-4.00
1563   Medicine label; 5 on bottom; aqua; 8″. 1.00-2.00
1564   Medicine label; 17 on bottom; 7¾″; amber
.... 2.00-4.00
1565   Medicine label; amber; 9″.......... 4.00-6.00
1566   Medicine label; free-blown; pontil; 9¾″; aqua
.... 10.00-15.00
1567   also Pat. March 1893, St. Louis, Mo. under bottom; clear; 7½″.................... 2.00-6.00
1568   Medicine label; aqua; 1¾″.......... 2.00-4.00
1569   Medicine label; clear; 2½″.......... 2.00-4.00
1570   Medicine label; amber; 2423 under bottom; 8″
.... 2.00-4.00
1571   Medicine label; 933 on bottom; amber; 8¾″
.... 2.00-4.00
1572   Medicine label; amber; nine-part mold; machine made; 7½″...................... 2.00-6.00
1573   Medicine label; clear or amethyst; 5″. 2.00-4.00
1574   Medicine label; clear; numbers on bottom; 4″
.... 2.00-3.00
1575   Medicine label; pontil; clear or amethyst; 3½″
.... 4.00-7.00
1576   Medicine label; three-part mold; clear; 5¾″
.... 2.00-3.00
1577   Medicine label; clear; 4″; pontil...... 4.00-6.00
1578   Medicine label; W.T.Co. U.S.A. under bottom; cobalt blue; 5¾″............... 4.00-6.00
1579   Medicine label; three-part mold; cobalt blue; 9½″............................. 4.00-6.00
1580   Medicine label; clear; 4¾″.......... 1.00-2.00
1581   Medicine label; 171 under bottom; aqua; 5″
.... 1.00-2.00

1582   1583   1584   1585   1586   1587   1588   1589

1595   1596   1597   1598   1600   1602   1603

1611   1612   1613   1614   1615   1616   1618   1619

1621   1622   1623

1582   Medicine label; aqua; 6" 1.00-2.00
1583   Medicine label; *E.L. & Co.* under bottom; amber;
        7" 2.00-4.00
1584   Medicine label; round back; clear or amethyst;
        6¾" 2.00-4.00
1585   Medicine label; clear or amethyst; 8½"
        .... 6.00-10.00
1586   Medicine label; front has sunken panel, other
        side flat; *14* under bottom; amber; 7¾" x 2½"x
        2½" 2.00-4.00
1587   Medicine label; amber; 7" 2.00-4.00
1588   Medicine label; cobalt; 3" 2.00-4.00
1589   Medicine label; numbers under bottom; cobalt;
        7½" 4.00-8.00
1590   Medicine label; ringed top; 4½"; milk glass
        .... 6.00-8.00
1591   MEDICAL DEPT. U.S.N.; reverse side *50c.c.*;
        4"; clear or amber. 8.00-15.00
1592   same as above except 8½" 8.00-15.00
1593   C.W. MERCHANT CHEMIST, LOCKPORT,
        N.Y. in vertical lines; tapered top; 5¾"; amber
        .... 8.00-10.00
1594   C.W. MERCHANT, LOCKPORT, N.Y., OAK
        ORCHARD ACID SPRINGS; tapered top; 9¼";
        dark green 40.00-80.00
1595   THE WM. S. MERRELL CO., label; amber;
        machine made; 7¾" 3.00-4.00
1596   THE WM. S. MERRELL CO.; *FGN* on bottom;
        machine made; amber; 7¾" 2.00-4.00
1597   THE MERZ CAPSULE CO.; clear; 3¾"; twelve
        panels 2.00-3.00
1598   T. METCALF & CO.; clear; 8" 4.00-6.00
1599   MRS. S. METTLERS MEDICINE; 6½"; aqua
        .... 4.00-6.00

1600   MEXICAN MUSTANG LINIMENT in three
        vertical lines; round; 4½"; aqua; pontil
        .... 10.00-20.00
1601   same except no pontil 2.00-4.00
1602   MEXICAN MUSTANG LINIMENT on back;
        clear; 7½" 6.00-8.00
1603   A.C. MEYER & CO., BALTO., MD. U.S.A., DR.
        J.W. BULLS COUGH SYRUP; 6½"; aqua
        .... 4.00-6.00
1604   JOHN MEYER CHEMIST, MT. CLEMENS,
        MICH.; 9½"; amber 6.00-10.00
1605   MEYERS MFG. CO. vertical on side; shaped
        like a miniature pop bottle; crown top; 4";
        amethyst 3.00-4.00
1606   DR. MILES NERVINE on the front panel;
        aqua; 8¼"; rectanguar 2.00-3.00
1607   DR. MILES RESTORATIVE NERVINE on the
        front panel; rectangular; aqua; 8¼"; old bubbles
        .... 3.00-5.00
1608   DR. MILES MEDICAL CO. on the front panel;
        8¼"; aqua; rectangular 2.00-3.00
1609   DR. MILES MEDICAL CO. vertical in sunken
        panel on front; label on reverse side; *Dr. Miles
        Alterative Compound*, picture of man with
        diagram of blood veins; double band collar; rec-
        tangular; ABM; 8¼"; aqua 3.00-6.00
1610   DR. J.R. MILLERS on side; *Balm* on opposite
        side; arch panels; rectangular; square collar;
        4¾"; clear 3.00-6.00
1611   MINARDS LINIMENT, BOSTON; seven verti-
        cal panels on front half; back plain; round; round
        band collar; 5⅛"; amethyst 2.00-6.00
1612   MINARDS; clear or amethyst; 5".... 2.00-6.00
1613   MINARDS LINIMENT; six panels; round
        back; clear or amethyst; 6" 3.00-6.00
1614   MINUTE OIL MED CO. LTD, NEW OR-
        LEANS; aqua; 10¼" 40.00-50.00
1615   MITCHELL'S; cobalt; on side *Eye Salve*
        .... 2.00-6.00
1616   M.J. & CO.; amber; 8" 4.00-8.00
1617   MOE HOSPITAL, SIOUX FALLS, SO. DAK.
        vertical on front; side panels show scales; oval
        back; fluting on back; 8¼"; amethyst 4.00-8.00
1618   MONTECATINI SALTS, ITALY; amber; 4"
        .... 2.00-6.00
1619   GEORGE MOORE; clear; 5¾" 2.00-6.00
1620   DR. J. MOORE'S ESSENCE OF LIFE vertical
        around bottle; cylindrical; pontil; 3¾"; aqua
        .... 15.00-25.00
1621   MOORE'S LIVER-AX; aqua; 7" 3.00-5.00
1622   MOORE'S REVEALED REMEDY; 8¾"; amber
        .... 8.00-10.00
1623   DR. MORENO; aqua; 8"; side mold; *W.T. & CO.
        5 U.S.A.* under bottom 6.00-8.00

1624   1625   1629   1634   1635   1636   1637

1638   1642   1643   1644   1648   1649

1650   1656   1657   1659   1661   1670

1624 E. MORGAN & SONS, SOLE PROPRIETORS, PROVIDENCE, R.I. (E left out of Providence); twelve panels; on shoulder *Dr. Haynes Arabian Balsam*; 7½"; aqua............... 10.00+

1625 MORLEY BROS label; aqua; 7".... 2.00-6.00

1626 MORNING CALL-C. LEDIARD, ST. LOUIS; 10½"; olive, amber 4.00-6.00

1627 H.S. MORRELL, N.Y.; pontil; tapered top; 5¾"; aqua.................... 15.00-25.00

1628 MORSES CELEBRATED SYRUP vertically; oval; long tapered neck; graphite pontil; 9½"; aqua.................... 10.00-20.00

1629 MORTON & CO.; clear or amethyst; 5½" 2.00-3.00

1630 MORTON & CO., TAMPA, FLA., W.T. & CO.; 4½"; clear or amber 3.00-4.00

1631 MOXIE NERVE FOOD, TRADE MARK REGISTERED, MOXIE on front and back; round; crown top; 10¼"; aqua 5.00-10.00

1632 MOXIE NERVE FOOD, LOWELL, MASS; thick embossed line; graduated collar; round; 10"; aqua 5.00-10.00

1633 MOYERS OIL OF GLADNESS, BLOOMSBURG, PA. vertical on front in sunken panel; graduated collar; 5⅝"; aqua 4.00-8.00

1634 MUEGGE BAKER, OREGON; *Muegge's* on reverse shoulder; 8"; green 8.00-10.00

1635 H.K. MULFORD CO., PHILA.; 7¼"; amber 4.00-8.00

1636 MUNYON'S in one sunken side panel; other *Paw-Paw*; in front on top a tree; two board lines with *Munyon's Paw-Paw*; plain back; amber; 10"; long tapered top 8.00-12.00

1637 MUNYON'S GERMICIDE SOLUTION; side mold; green; 3¼" 3.00-6.00

1638 MUNYON'S GERMICIDE SOLUTION; green; 3½"..................... 4.00-8.00

1639 MURINE EYE REMEDY CO., CHICAGO U.S.A.; round; 3½"; clear.......... 3.00-4.00

1640 MURPHY BROTHERS, PORTLAND on front in oval end panel; rectangular; square collar; 4⅞"; aqua 2.00-3.00

1641 SIR J. MURRAY'S RE-CARBONATED PATENT MAGNESIA, vertical on front; crude band and small band collar; oval; 7½"; light green 4.00-8.00

1642 NATRIUM; clear; 4¾" 8.00-10.00

1643 NELSON BAKER & CO.; amber; 9". 3.00-4.00

1644 NERVE & BONE LINIMENT; round bottle; old type mold; aqua; 4¼".......... 4.00-6.00

1645 NERVINE; *Prepared by the Catarrhozone Co., Kingston, Ont.* vertical on front in oval sunken panel; rectangular; square collar; 5¼"; amethyst 4.00-6.00

1646 NEWBROS HERBICIDE KILL THE DANDRUFF GERM; ring top; 5½"; clear or amber 4.00-6.00

1647 THE NEW YORK PHARMACAL ASSOCIATION in two lines in a sunken panel on one side; on other side *Lactopeptine*; in front *The Best Remedial Agent In All Digestive Disorders*; 6" body; 1½" neck; 2¾" square; round corners; cobalt......................... 10.00-12.00

1648 N.Y. MEDICAL; reverse side *University City*; 7½"; cobalt..................... 10.00-200

1649 NORTH; pontil; 6¼".............. 8.00-20.00

1650 NORTON; clear or amethyst; 5"..... 1.00-2.00

1651 NOYES, GRANULAR EFFERVESCENT MAGNESIA SULPHATE vertical on front; rectangular; corner panels; square collar; 6"; aqua.................... 4.00-6.00

1652 NUCO-SOLVENT DR. GRIFFIN; 5¼"; aqua 4.00-8.00

1653 NYAL'S EMULSION of COD LIVER OIL; amber; 9" 2.00-4.00

1654 NYAL'S LINIMENT; 7"; amber; ring in neck 2.00-4.00

1655 N.Y. PHARMACAL ASSOCIATION, in two vertical lines; 8½"; cobalt 5.00-8.00

1656 THE OAKLAND CHEMICAL CO.; amber; 4¾" 2.00-4.00

1657 THE OAKLAND CHEMICAL CO.; amber; 5¼" 3.00-6.00

1658 OD CHEM. CO., NEW YORK in two lines; 6¾"; amber 1.00-2.00

1659 ODOJ under bottom; milk glass; *M632* on one panel; 4½"..................... 8.00-12.00

1660 O.K. PLANTATION; triangular; amber; 11" .... 200.00+

1661 OL. AMYGDAL; clear; 5¾"...... 8.00-10.00

1662 OLD DR. TOWNSEND'S SARSAPARILLA; pontil; green 20.00-30.00

1663 OLDRIDGE BALM OF COLUMBIA FOR RESTORING HAIR; 6¼"; aqua .. 40.00-60.00

1664 OMEGA OIL CHEMICAL CO., NEW YORK, in three lines at bottom; above bottom, a leaf with words *Omega Oil It's Green*; ring under this with *Trade Mark*; flared top with ring; under bottom, various numbers in circle; light green; 4½"............................. 3.00-6.00

1665 OMEGA OIL IT'S GREEN, TRADE MARK, all inside of leaf embossed on front; THE OMEGA CHEMICAL CO. NEW YORK at base on front; sheared collar; 6"; clear............ 2.00-4.00

1666 same as above except 4½" 2.00-4.00

1667 same as above except ABM; thread top; 6" 2.00-3.00

1668 OMEGA OIL, vertical on front; cylindrical; 3¼"; aqua 2.00-3.00

1669 Opium bottles, in different sizes; 1 drop to ½ ounce; most are clear, some amethyst 3.00-8.00

1670 Opium; 2½"; aqua................. 4.00-8.00

1671 ORIENTAL CONDENSED COFFEE, TRADE MARK, ORIENTAL TEA COMPANY, BOSTON, MASS. vertical on front in slug plate; square collar; oval; 6½; aqua 4.00-6.00

1673 1674 1675   1676 1683 1685

1686 1689 1690 1692 1693 1694 1695

1696 1701 1703 1704 1705 1706 1707

1711   1714   1715

1672 ORIENTAL CREAM, GOURAND'S, NEW YORK on flat front panel and sides; corner panels; flared lip; rectangular; 5½"; clear 4.00-6.00

1673 OTIS CLAPP & SON; 7½"; amber 6.00-10.00

1674 C. OWENS; clear; 2½" 1.00-2.00

1675 OWL; *J.B. Co., P.C. CO.* in diamond shape on bottom; clear; 3½" 4.00-6.00

1676 OWL DRUG CO.; clear; 5¼" 2.00-6.00

1677 THE OWL DRUG CO. SAN FRANCISCO on bottom; double wing owl on mortar on front; 8⅜"; clear 4.00-10.00

1678 Owl bottle; double wing owl on mortar; thread top; rectangular; 3⅝"; clear......... 2.00-4.00

1679 THE OWL DRUG CO. on back; double wing owl; rectangular; square collar; ABM; 5¾"; clear 2.00-4.00

1680 same as above except 4" 4.00-8.00

1681 THE OWL DRUG CO. on back; single wing owl; hair tonic type bottle; ring collar; tapered neck; round; 7"; amethyst................ 4.00-6.00

1682 OWL DRUG STORE; embossed owl in center; 1½" x 2³⁄₁₆"; diamond and *2* under bottom; clear 4.00-6.00

1683 OX; pontil; cobalt blue; 8½"........... 35.00+

1684 OXIEN PILLS, THE GIANT OXIEN; *Augusta, Me.*; 2"; clear 4.00-6.00

1685 OXIEN PILLS; *The Giant Oxien Co., Augusta Me.*; clear; 2" 2.00-6.00

1686 OZOMULSION; amber; 5½" 4.00-8.00

1687 OZON ANTISEPTIC DRESSING; W.H. DUNCAN, NATURES PINE REMEDY, label; rectangular; square collar; ABM; 6½"; clear 2.00-6.00

1688 THE OZONE CO. OF TORONTO, LIMITED; same in back; double ring top; 7"; clear 8.00-10.00

1689 THE LIQUID OZONE CO.; *8* under bottom; amber; 8"...................... 8.00-10.00

1690 PAINES CELERY COMPOUND; 10"; aqua 8.00-10.00

1691 same as above except amber........ 4.00-8.00

1692 PALACE DRUG STORE; clear; 4½" 2.00-4.00

1693 PALACE DRUG STORE; clear or amethyst; 6" 3.00-4.00

1694 THE PALISADE MFG. CO.; *Yonkers, N.Y.* on bottom; clear or amethyst; 7¾" 6.00-10.00

1695 THE PALISADE MG. CO., YONKERS, N.Y. under bottom; amber; 7¼" 4.00-6.00

1696 JAS. PALMER & CO., PHILADA.; one side *Wholesale*; other side *Druggists*; 5"; aqua 4.00-6.00

1697 PALMOLIVE SHAMPOO, B.J. JOHNSON, TORONTO, ONT. CANADA, on front and back; rectangular; ring collar; ABM; 7¼"; clear 3.00-4.00

1698 10 Panel; 4"; bluish 4.00-6.00

1699 PA-PAY-ANS BELL; ring top; amber 3.00-4.00

1700 PA-PAY-ANS BELL; *(Orangburg, N.Y.)* 6.00-8.00

1701 JOHN D. PARK; *Cincinnati, O., Dr. Cuysotts Yellow Dock & Sarsaparilla* in five vertical lines on front; 8½" body, 2" neck; tapered top; 2¼" x 4¼"; graphite pontil; aqua............. 25.00+

1702 JOHN D. PARK, CINCINNATI, O., DR. WISTARS BALSAM OF WILD CHERRY; 7½"; aqua...................... 8.00-12.00

1703 PARKE DAVIS & CO., label; amber; 5½" 4.00-6.00

1704 PARKE DAVIS & CO., label; *343* under bottom; amber...................... 3.00-6.00

1705 PARKE DAVIS & CO., label; black glass; 3½" 4.00-6.00

1706 PARKE DAVIS & CO., label; *P.D. & CO. 274* under bottom; amber; 5¼" 2.00-4.00

1707 PARKER on one side; *New York* other side; *17* under bottom; amber; 7"........... 2.00-4.00

1708 PARKERS HAIR BALSAM, NEW YORK on front and sides in sunken oval panels; rectangular; ABM; 7½"; amber............. 4.00-8.00

1709 PARKERS HAIR BALSAM, NEW YORK on front and sides; rectangular; 6½"; amber 3.00-4.00

1710 DR. PARK'S INDIAN LINAMENT, WYANOKE; 5⅜"; clear........... 6.00-8.00

1711 PAUL WESTPHAL; clear or amethyst; 8" 4.00-8.00

1712 PAWNEE INDIAN TA-HA; *price 25¢, Jos. Herman Agt.*; 8½"; aqua............. 10.00-15.00

1713 PAWNEE INDIAN, TOO-RE vertical on front in sunken panel; plain sides and back; rectangular; 7¾"; aqua.................. 8.00-10.00

1714 P D & CO. under bottom; amber; 3¼". 2.00-3.00

1715 P D & CO. 119 under bottom; amber; 4" 2.00-4.00

1716   1717   1718   1719   1721   1722   1723

1724   1728   1730   1732   1734   1735   1737   1739

1740   1741   1742   1743   1744   1745   1746

1747   1754   1755   1756

1716 P. D. & CO. under bottom; amber; 3¾" 2.00-3.00

1717 P D & CO.21.S under bottom; machine made; amber; 2½"....................... 2.00-3.00

1718 P D & CO. 334 under bottom; amber; 4¾" 2.00-4.00

1719 PEARL'S WHITE GLYCERINE; cobalt; 6¼" 6.00-10.00

1720 EBENEZER A. PEARL'S TINCTURE OF LIFE, vertical on front in sunken panels; rectangular; 7¾"; aqua.............. 3.00-6.00

1721 PEASE'S EYE WATER; *Newman, Ga.;* 4¼"; aqua................. 2.00-4.00

1722 PROF. W.H. PEEKS'S REMEDY; *N.Y.;* 8"; amber 6.00-8.00

1723 DR. H.F. PEERY'S; on back *Dead Shot Vermifuce;* 4"; amber............... 2.00-4.00

1724 DR. H.F. PEERY'S; clear or amethyst 4.00-6.00

1725 WM. PENDELTON; *Rockland, Me.* vertical on three panels; twelve panels; square collar; 4⅜"; aqua................. 2.00-4.00

1726 PEOPLES CHEMICAL CO., THE SCIENTIFICALLY PREPARED RED CROSS, with cross embossed in circle, BEEF WINE & IRON PROVIDENCE, R.I. all on front; flask shape; flared collar; 7½"; clear 4.00-8.00

1727 PEPERAZINE EFFERVESCENTE MEDY, in three vertical lines; amber; 6¼", 2¾" x 1¼" 2.00-4.00

1728 PEPTENZYME; cobalt; 2½" 4.00-6.00

1729 PEPTENZYNE at slant on front in sunken panel; 3¼"; cobalt blue 3.00-4.00

1730 PEPTO-MANGAN GUDE; six panels; 7"; aqua 6.00-8.00

1731 DR. PETER'S KURIKO on one of the panels; *Prepared By Dr. Peter Fahrney & Sons, Co., Chicago, Ill., U.S.A.* on the other side; amethyst; 9"; square; paneled 2.00-4.00

1732 PETER MOLLER'S PURE COD LIVER OIL, label; clear; 5¾"................. 4.00-6.00

1733 DR. J. PETTITS CANKER BALSAM vertical on front; flask shape; 3¼"; clear 4.00-8.00

1734 PFEIFFER CHEMICAL CO., PHILA & ST. LOUIS on back; aqua; 6" 2.00-6.00

1735 PHALON'S CHEMICAL HAIR INVIGORATOR; pontil; clear; 5½"........... 8.00-12.00

1736 DR. O. PHELPS BROWN vertical on one panel; ring collar; square; wide mouth; 2¾"; aqua 3.00-4.00

1737 JOHN H. PHELPS PHARMACIST, PHELPS RHEUMATIC ELIXIR; *Scranton Pa.;* 5½"; clear 2.00-4.00

1738 PHILLIPS EMULSION COD LIVER OIL, NEW YORK, vertical on front in sunken panel; rectangular; 9¼"; amber........... 3.00-6.00

1739 C.H. PHILLIPS, N.Y.; 9½"; amber... 6.00-8.00

1740 PHILLIPS' EMULSION (N backwards); amber; 9½"..................... 20.00-30.00

1741 PHILLIPS EMULSION; *#1* under bottom; sample; 4¾" 8.00-10.00

1742 PHILLIPS EMULSION; amber; 7½" 2.00-6.00

1743 PHILLIPS MILK OF MAGNESIA; 7"; light blue 3.00-6.00

1744 PHOLON'S VITALIA, same on reverse side; sunken arched panels; rectangular; flared lip; 6⅜"; amethyst 4.00-6.00

1745 PHOSPHOCYCLO-FER on back, label; *Depose* on bottom; 4½"................. 4.00-6.00

1746 DR. GEO. PIERCE'S on front; on back *Indian Restorative Bitters;* on side *Lowell, Mass;* aqua; 7½", 9", and other variants; pontil.. 40.00-60.00

1747 DR. PIERCE'S GOLDEN MED. DISC. on the front panel; *Buffalo, N.Y.* on the left side; *RV Pierce, M.D.* on the right side; rectangular; 8¼"; aqua............................ 2.00-4.00

1748 R.V. PIERCE, M.D. on one side of panel; *Buffalo, N.Y.* on opposite side of panel; aqua; rectangular; 9⅛".................. 1.00-2.00

1749 DR. PIERCE'S ANURIC TABLE FOR KIDNEYS AND BACKACHE on the front; aqua; round; 3½" 1.00-2.00

1750 DR. PIERCE'S FAVORITE PRESCRIPTION on the front panel; *Buffalo, N.Y.* on left side; *R.V. Pierce, M.D.* on right side; aqua; rectangular; 8½"........................ 2.00-4.00

1751 DR. PIERCES, ANURIC embossed inside of kidney, TABLETS FOR KIDNEYS AND BACKACHE all on front; cylindrical; 3"; clear 4.00-6.00

1752 PILL BOTTLES; plain; oval; shear top; screw top; 2½"; clear.................... 4.00-6.00

1753 PILL BOTTLES; plain; oval; shear top; screw top; 1½"; clear.................... 4.00-6.00

1754 PILL BOTTLE; plain; 1¾"; aqua ... 2.00-4.00

1755 PILL BOTTLE; plain; 3½"; clear, amber 2.00-4.00

1756 THE PILLOW-INHALE CO. PHILA.; 7½"; aqua.......................... 4.00-8.00

1762   1764   1765   1767   1768   1769   1770

1771   1772   1774   1775   1776   1778

1779   1781   1782   1787   1788   1791

1794   1795   1797

1757 PINEOLEUM FOR CATARRHAL CONDI-TIONS on both front and back; conical; pewter neck and top; 6⅜"; amber 4.00-6.00

1758 PINE TREE TAR CORDIAL, PHILA. on one panel; on another panel a tree and *patent 1859;* another panel *L.Q.G. Wisharts;* blob top; 8"; green 30.00-50.00

1759 PINE TREE TAR CORDIAL, PHILA. 1859; with tree embossed; 8"; green 18.00-20.00

1760 PINEX on both sides; rectangular; 5¾"; aqua 2.00-3.00

1761 DR. PINKHAM'S EMMENAGOGUE; tapered top; pontil; kick-up in base; 5"; light blue 30.00-50.00

1762 LYDIA E. PINKHAM'S; aqua; *C8* under bottom; 8¼"........................ 2.00-6.00

1763 PINKSTON & SCRUGGS PHARMACISTS, W.T. CO., O, U.S.A. under bottom; 4½" 2.00-4.00

1764 PIPERAZINE; gold; 5" or 6" 3.00-6.00

1765 THE PISO COMPANY, in two lines in front sunken panel; on one side in sunken panel *Trade-Piso's-Mark;* on other side *Hazeltine & Co.;* under bottom, different numbers; green, clear, amber; 5¼"...................... 2.00-6.00

1766 DR. S. PITCHER'S on the side panel; *Castoria* on the other side; rectangular; 5⅞"; aqua 2.00-4.00

1767 PITCHER'S CASTORIA; aqua; 6¼"   2.00-6.00

1768 DR. W.M. PITT'S CARMINATIVE; aqua; 4" 3.00-5.00

1769 DR. W.M. PITT'S CARMINATIVE; clear or amethyst; 4"................... 3.00-6.00

1770 Plain medicine bottle; twelve panels; broken pontil; body 3"; neck 1"; clear 6.00-10.00

1771 Plain label; clear; 4¾".......... 8.00-10.00

1772 Plain label; clear; 4¾".......... 6.00-8.00

1773 DR. PLANETTS BITTERS; iron pontil; amber; 9¾".......................... 40.00-50.00

1774 PLANKS CHILL TONIC CO.; *Chattanooga Tenn.;* 6½"; clear or amber.......... 4.00-6.00

1775 PLANTERS OLD TIME REMEDIES; one side *Chattanooga Tenn.;* other side *Spencer Med. Co.;* aqua.......................... 4.00-8.00

1776 PLATT'S CHLORIDE; quart; clear or amethyst...................... 4.00-6.00

1777 PLUTO WATER; under bottom, a devil and Pluto; round; light green or clear; 3¼" and other sizes.......................... 2.00-4.00

1778 P.M.F.S. & CO. on bottom; amber; 2¼" 2.00-3.00

1779 POMPEIAN MASSAGE CREAM; 2¾"; clear or amber 3.00-4.00

1780 POMPEIAN MASSAGE CREAM on front; barrel shape; ABM; 2¾"; clear 3.00-4.00

1781 POND'S EXTRACT, label; *1846* under bottom; 5½".......................... 2.00-4.00

1782 POND'S EXTRACT CATARRH REMEDY; 5¾"; cobalt .... 10.00+

1783 POND'S MONARCH LINIMENT on front in sunken panel at slant; rectangular; 6½"; aqua 3.00-6.00

1784 PORTER'S PAIN KING on opposite sides; sunken panels; rectangular; 6¾"; clear 3.00-4.00

1785 PORTER'S PAIN KING same as above except ABM 2.00-3.00

1786 DR. PORTER, NEW YORK vertical on front; rectangular; 4¼"; aqua 3.00-6.00

1787 PORTER'S; *Pain King* on other side; *G.H.R.* under bottom; clear or amethyst; 7". 3.00-6.00

1788 POSEN; *Wronkerstr. No. 6;* amber; 10" 20.00+

1789 POTTER & MERWIN on front; plain back; on one side *St. Louis,* on other *Missouri;* beveled corner; roofed shoulder; aqua; tapered top; 5½" 6.00-8.00

1790 same except pontil 8.00-12.00

1791 PP (back to back) label; cobalt; 2½". 4.00-8.00

1792 PRESTON & MERRILL, BOSTON 1871; 4¼"; clear 2.00-4.00

1793 PRESTON OF NEW HAMPSHIRE on front; mold threads; sheared collar; glass stopper with metal cup cover; 3½"; emerald green 2.00-4.00

1794 PROTONUCELN [sic]; amber; 2⅞".. 2.00-4.00

1795 PROTONUCLEIN; amber; 2"; sheared top 3.00-4.00

1796 WM. PRUNDER'S OREGON NO. 7138 (em-bossed child's head with ribbon wreath) on center; REGISTERED MARCH 25th 1879, BLOOD PURIFIER, WM. PRUNDER & CO., PORTLAND, ORE. all on front in slug plate; ring and flared collar; oval; 7½"; amber 10.00-18.00

1797 THE PURDUE FREDERICK CO., NEW YORK; 8"; clear or amber 3.00-4.00

| 1801 | 1802 | 1803 | 1809 | 1812 | 1813 | 1815 |

| 1819 | 1820 | 1821 | | 1823 | 1824 | 1825 |

| 1826 | 1828 | 1829 | 1839 | 1840 | 1841 | 1842 |

1798 PURE COD LIVER OIL, BYNE ATWOOD, PROVINCETOWN, MASS. vertical on front; oval; 7"; aqua 3.00-6.00

1799 PURE & GENUINE FOUR FOLD LINIMENT, R. MATCHETTS on front and sides; rectangular; 5¼"; clear 2.00-4.00

1800 PYNCHON at base on front; *Boston* on opposite side at base; oval; 4¾"; aqua 6.00-10.00

1801 Q BAN; machine made; amber; 6¾"   2.00-4.00

1802 DEL DR. RABELL; reverse side *Emulsion*; 9½"; aqua 4.00-6.00

1803 RACINE de GUIMAUVE; cut glass; 9¼"; blue 15.00-30.00

1804 R.R.R. RADWAY & CO., NEW YORK, ENTD. ACCORD. TO ACT OF CONGRESS on flat front panel and opposite sides in large letters; rectangular; 6⅜"; aqua 3.00-6.00

1805 RADWAY'S on side; SARSAPARILLIAN RESOLVENT on front; *R.R.R.* on opposite side; *Entd. Accord. to Act of Congress*; sunken panels; rectangular; 7¼"; aqua 10.00-15.00

1806 RAMON'S NERVE & BONE OIL, BROWN MFG. CO. PROPRIETORS vertical on front in sunken panel; *Greenville, Tenn.* on side; *New York, NY.* on opposite side; rectangular; 5¾"; aqua 4.00-6.00

1807 RAMON'S NERVE & BONE OIL; *Brown Mfg. Co. Proprietors*; on one side *Greenville Tenn.*; other *St. Louis*; tapered top; 5¾" 2.00-6.00

1808 RAWLEIGH in vertical script; under it in ribbon, *Trade Mark*; 7⅝"; clear or amethyst 3.00-4.00

1809 W.T. RAWLEIGH MED. CO.; *Freeport Ill* other side; clear; 8¼" 4.00-6.00

1810 Rectangular; almost square; no embossing; pontil; 2½"; aqua 4.00-6.00

1811 same as above, concave corner panels; crude flared lip; pontil; 5¼"; aqua 4.00-6.00

1812 RED CROSS FAMILY LINIMENT, label; *Co-operative Drug Mfg., Jackson, Tenn.*; 5½"; clear 2.00-4.00

1813 RED CROSS PHARMACY, W.T. CO. U.S.A.; Savanah [sic] *Ga.*; 5½"; clear 10.00-12.00

1814 REDINGTON & CO., ESSENCE OF JAMAICA GINGER, SAN FRANCISCO vertical on front; 5½"; aqua 4.00-6.00

1815 REED & CARNRICH, JERSEY CITY, N.J. in 3 slanting lines; in back, *Peptenzyme*; 2¾" x 2½"; 8½" tall; cobalt; ring top 10.00-12.00

1816 same, two smaller sides 8.00-10.00

1817 REED & CARNRICH, same except 4½" 10.00-12.00

1818 REED AND CARNRICK PHARMACISTS, NEW YORK in five lines on front panel; 7½"; amber 4.00-6.00

1819 REED & CARNRICK, N.Y. on bottom; amber; 4¾" 2.00-6.00

1820 REED & CARNRICK, N.Y.; dark blue; 6¼" 15.00-25.00

1821 REED & CARNRICK, NEW YORK; *Peptenzyme* on back; cobalt; 4½" 6.00-8.00

1822 REESE CHEMICAL CO., BLOOD & SYSTEM TONIC; ring top; 3¾"; green 8.00-12.00

1823 REID'S; aqua; 5½" 3.00-5.00

1824 RENNE'S; aqua; 5" 2.00-3.00

1825 RESINAL BALTO. MD. CHEMICAL CO. under bottom; milk glass; 3¼" 1.00-2.00

1826 RESTORFF & BETTMAN N.Y.; six panels; 4¼"; aqua 4.00-6.00

1827 REXALL; *3VIII* on shoulder; rectangular; flared lip; 6½"; emerald green 4.00-6.00

1828 C.A. RICHARDS; amber; 9½" 10.00-25.00

1829 RICH-LAX, label; 7½"; aqua 8.00-10.00

1830 F.A. RICHTER & CO. MANUFACTURING, CHEMISTS, NEW YORK, with embossed anchor, vertical on front; anchor on side; *Pain Expeller* on opposite side; rectangular; 5"; aqua 4.00-6.00

1831 RICKER HEGEMAN OR HEGENAK DRUG STORES in center; 5½"; cobalt . . . 10.00-20.00

1832 RIKER'S COMPOUND SARSAPARILLA vertical in sunken panel on front; beveled corners; rectangular; sunken panels on all sides; 10"; aqua blue 30.00-40.00

1833 C.B. RINCKERHOFFS, PRICE ONE DOLLAR; on side, *Health Restorative, New York*; tapered top; 7¼"; olive . . . . 85.00+

1834 THE RIVER SWAMP CHILL and FEVER CURE, with alligator in center; *Augusta Ga.*; 7"; clear or aqua 6.00-15.00

1835 JAMES S. ROBINSON, MEMPHIS, TENN.; 7"; clear 4.00-6.00

1836 ROCHE'S EMBROCATION FOR THE WHOOPING COUGH, W. EDWARDS & SON on consecutive panels; flared lip; 5"; clear 6.00-8.00

1837 RODERIC'S WILD CHERRY COUGH BALSAM; flared collar; ABM; 5½"; clear 2.00-3.00

1838 same as above except amber; 4½" . . . 2.00-3.00

1839 RON-BRE; amber; 6½" 2.00-4.00

1840 ROOT JUICE MED. CO.; aqua; 9" . . 2.00-4.00

1841 ROOT JUICE MED. CO., label; clear or amethyst; 6" 4.00-6.00

1842 DR. ROSE'S; *Philadel* on other side; pontil; aqua 6.00-8.00

1843 ROSHTON & ASPINWALL, NEW YORK; on back *Compound Chlorine Tooth Wash*; flared top; pontil; 6"; golden olive 200.00-300.00

1844 Round; crude ring collar; cylindrical; whittled effect; pontil; 5¾"; aqua blue 4.00-7.00

1845 V. ROUSSIN, DRUGGIST, MUSKEGON, MICH.; 7¼"; clear 4.00-6.00

1846 ROWLANDS MACASSAI (OIL); pontil 4.00-8.00

1847 ROYAL FOOT WASH, EATON DRUG CO.; *Atlanta, Ga* 4.00-8.00

1848   1849   1853   1854   1855   1860

1861   1862   1863   1864   1865   1869

1870   1872   1881   1882   1883   1884

1885   1886   1887

1848 ROYAL GALL REMEDY; machine made; dark amber; 7½"................ 8.00-10.00

1849 ROYAL GERMETUER; same on reverse side; one side *Kings Royal Germetuer Co.*; other side *Atlanta Ga. U.S.A.*; 8½"; amber .. 18.00-25.00

1850 RUBIFOAM FOR THE TEETH, PUT UP E.W. HOYT & CO., LOWELL, MASS., all on front; oval; 4"; clear 3.00-4.00

1851 RUSH'S on one side; REMEDY on reverse; other two sides *A.H.F. Monthly*; double ring top; 6"; aqua 4.00-10.00

1852 RUSH'S vertical on front in small rectangular panel; *Lung* on side; *Balm* on opposite side; *A.H. Flanders, MD.* on back side; sunken panels; rectangular; 7"; aqua 12.00-15.00

1853 RUSHTON'S; *F.V.* on back; *Cod Liver Oil* on side; *N.Y.* other side; ice blue; 10½" 8.00-12.00

1854 RUSS'S AROMATIC; side panel *Schnapps*; other side *N.Y.*; 8"; dark olive 15.00-30.00

1855 JOHN RYAN CITRATE OF MAGNESIA, SAVANNAH, GA. on front in four lines; 7"; aqua; short neck; round .... 12.00+

1856 DR. SAGES on one side; on other side *Buffalo*; *Catarrah Remedy* on front; on back *Dr. Price Propr.*; all on sunken panels; 2¼"; #1 under bottom 4.00-8.00

1857 SALVATION OIL, AC MEYER & CO., BALTIMORE, MD. in four lines in a sunken panel in front; round sides; under bottom, letter D; 2¼" x 1"; rectangular.......... 4.00-6.00

1858 SALAVATION OIL, A.C. MEYER & CO., TRADE MARK, BALTIMORE, MD. USA all on front; arched panel; rectangular; 6¾"; aqua 3.00-6.00

1859 SALVATION TRADE MARK OIL, A.C. MEYER & CO., BALT. MD. U.S.A.; ring top; 6¾"; aqua 3.00-6.00

1860 SAMMY'S MEDICINE; reverse side *Baltimore Md. U.S.A.*; under bottom *S.R. Scoggins*; front side *Reaches Through the Entire System*; 7"; sky blue 4.00-8.00

1861 SAND'S SARSAPARILLA, NEW YORK; pontil; 6¼"; aqua................... 15.00-25.00

1862 DR. SANFORD, NEW YORK on each side; aqua; 7½"...................... 4.00-8.00

1863 SANITAL DE MIDY; clear; twelve panels; 2¾" 2.00-4.00

1864 THE SANITAS CO., label; aqua; 9" 3.00-6.00

1865 SANITOL; *For The Teeth* on other side; clear; 4½"........................... 4.00-6.00

1866 DR. R. SAPPINGTON; reverse side *Flaxseed Syrup*; ring top; 7½"; aqua   4.00-6.00

1867 A. SARTORIUS & CO., NEW YORK on front; round; 2¾"; clear 2.00-3.00

1868 SASSAFRAS, under it an eye cup; *Eye Lotion, Sassafras Eye Lotion Co., Maugh Chunk Pa.*; 6"; cobalt blue 10.00-15.00

1869 SAVE, label; tan; 2¼"............. 1.00-2.00

1870 SAVER; three-sided; amber; 3½"..... 25.00+

1871 same as above except aqua; 4½" ...... 25.00+

1872 E.R. SCHAEFER'S; round back; clear; 4" 2.00-4.00

1873 SCHEFFLER'S HAIR COLORINE, BEST IN THE WORLD on front; rectangular; beveled corners; 4¼"; clear.............. 3.00-4.00

1874 SCHENBS PULMONIC SYRUP; pontil 10.00-15.00

1875 DR. SCHENCK'S PINE TAR FOR THROAT AND LUNGS vertical in oval sunken end panel; rectangular; square collar; 6⅛"; aqua 7.00-10.00

1876 SCHENCK'S PULMONIC SYRUP, PHILADA. on four panels; eight vertical panels; 5¾"; aqua................. 4.00-6.00

1877 SCHENCK'S SYRUP vertical on front; oval end sunken panel; 6¼"; aqua 3.00-6.00

1878 SCHENCK'S SYRUP, PHILADA. on three panels; eight vertical panels; 7¼"; aqua 4.00-8.00

1879 HENDRICK WALTER SCHIEDAM, AROMATIC SCHNAPPS; 7"; olive........ 25.00+

1880 SCHLOTTERBECK & FUSS CO., PORTLAND ME. vertical on front in sunken panel; rectangular; sheared collar; 5"; amber 2.00-3.00

1881 SCHUTZEN STR. NO. 6; *J. E. Gilke* on back panel; 10".......................... 20.00+

1882 SCOTT'S EMULSION; *Cod Liver Oil* on one side; *With Lime Soda* on other side; aqua; various sizes..................... 2.00-4.00

1883 S. & D. 8 under bottom; amber; 6".... 2.00-4.00

1884 S & D 83 2 under bottom; sheared top; amber; 3½"................................ 2.00-4.00

1885 S & D 2S under bottom; amber; 4½" .. 1.00-2.00

1886 S & D 100 under bottom; sheared top; clear; 2½" 2.00-4.00

1887 S & D 73 under bottom; amber; 6¼" .. 2.00-4.00

119

| 1888 | 1889 | 1890 | 1892 | 1895 | 1896 | 1898 | 1899 |

| 1900 | 1902 | 1904 | 1905 | 1908 | 1912 | 1913 | 1916 |

| 1921 | 1922 | 1924 | 1926 | 1928 | 1930 | 1931 | 1935 |

1888 S & D 83 under bottom; amber; 3½" 1.00-2.00

1889 SEABURY; cobalt; sheared top; 3¾" 2.00-6.00

1890 SEABURY; sheared top; amber; 3¾" 4.00-8.00

1891 R. N. SEARLES on side; *Athlophoros* on opposite side; rectangular; 6¾"; aqua .. 3.00-6.00

1892 SHAKE, label; amber; 6" 2.00-4.00

1893 SHAKER FLUID EXTRACT VALERIAN on front and back; square; 3¾"; aqua .. 2.00-4.00

1894 DR. S.&H. AND CO.; *P.R. Registered* on base; amethyst or aqua; round; 9¼" 4.00-10.00

1895 SHARP & DOHME; *Baltimore Md.* under bottom; amber; 5¾" 2.00-4.00

1896 SHARP & DOHME; three corners; round back; 3½"; cobalt 2.00-4.00

1897 SHECUTS SOUTHERN BALM FOR COUGHS, COLD 1840; 6¾"; aqua 20.00-40.00

1898 WM. H. SHEPARD, MARBLEHEAD, MASS, label; aqua; 9" 10.00-12.00

1899 J.T. SHINN; clear; 4¾" 2.00-4.00

1900 S.H.K.C. EXT. P.C.; clear or amethyst; 4"
.... 2.00-4.00

1901 DR. SHOOPS FAMILY MEDICINES; *Racine Wisc.;* aqua; ring top; 5½" 4.00-6.00

1902 SHORES, label; clear; 9½" 4.00-6.00

1903 SHORT STOP FOR COUGHS, H.M. O'NEIL, N.Y. vertical on front in sunken panel; square; 4"; aqua 2.00-3.00

1904 SHULTZ; *Dr. Shultz* on other side; aqua; 6½"
.... 4.00-6.00

1905 SHUPTXINE; in script, *Druggist, Savannah, Ga.,* in two lines on front flat panel; top *31V;* panel each side; round blank back; under bottom *Pat 18/17 C.L.Co., Freen;* 5¼" tall; 2" x 1¼"
.... 8.00-12.00

1906 same as above, 3½" tall; 1½" x ¾" 8.00-12.00

1907 same as above, 2½" tall; 1⅛" x ¾"... 10.00-14.00

1908 SIMMONS; 7"; aqua.............. 3.00-5.00

1909 SIMMONS LIVER REGULATOR in three sunken panels on front; *Philadelphia* on side; *Macon, Ga.* on opposite side; *J.H. Eeilin & Co.* vertical on back; rectangular; 9"; aqua
.... 4.00-6.00

1910 DR. SIMMONS SQUAW VINE WINE COMPOUND, vertical lines; tapered top; 8½"; aqua
.... 4.00-6.00

1911 DR. M.A. SIMMONS LIVER MEDICINE; *St. Louis;* 5¾"; aqua 4.00-6.00

1912 DR. SIMON RANDALL'S; amber; 9"
.... 12.00-20.00

1913 DR. T.J. SIMPSON'S; aqua; 7¼" ... 6.00-10.00

1914 C. SINES one side; *Phila. Pa.* reverse side; front side *Tar Wild Cherry & Hoar Hound;* pontil; 5"; aqua.................... 8.00-10.00

1915 SIPHON KUMY SGEN BOTTLE FOR PREPARING KUMYSS FROM REED & CARRICK, N.Y.; 8¾"; cobalt......... 10.00-30.00

1916 S.J.S. FOR THE BLOOD; on one side *L.G. Gerstle & Co.;* other side *Chattanooga, Tenn.;* 9"; amber 10.00-20.00

1917 SKABCURA DIP CO.; *Chicago U.S.A.;* 5"; aqua............................ 4.00-6.00

1918 SKODA'S SARSAPARILLA; on side *Skoda's;* opposite side *Discovery* with *Belfast, Me,* on indented panel; front indented panel marked *Concentrated Extract Sarsaparilla Compound;* back panel has label; 9"; amber........ 10.00-20.00

1919 same as above except *Wolfville* on one side; *Nova Scotia* on other side.............. 10.00-20.00

1920 SKODA'S WOLEFIRLLE DISCOVERY; 9"; aqua............................ 20.00-30.00

1921 DR. SLEDGE'S HOREHOUND PECTORAL; HOREHOUND PECTORAL in indented front panel; *Memphis, Tenn* one side; *Dr. Sledge's* other side; graphite pontil; 7¼"; aqua
.... 12.00-25.00

1922 SLOAN'S LINIMENT; clear or amethyst; 7"
.... 3.00-6.00

1923 SLOCUM'S COLTSFOOT EXPECTORANT on bottom; flask or oval shape; 2¼"; aqua 2.00-3.00

1924 SLOCUM'S EXPECTORANT COLTSFOOT under bottom; aqua; 2¼".......... 2.00-4.00

1925 T.A. SLOCUM CO. MFG., CHEMISTS, N.Y. & LONDON, with anchor seal; one side reads *For Consumption;* other side *Lung Troubles;* beveled corners; long collar; 9½"; aqua..... 8.00-10.00

1926 T.A. SLOCUM MFG. CO., PSYCHINE CONSUMPTION, 181 PEARL ST. N.Y.; 8½"; aqua
.... 2.00-6.00

1927 MFG. SLOUGH, ELLIMAN'S ROYAL EMBROCATION FOR HORSES; double ring top; 7½"; aqua 8.00-10.00

1928 SMITH'S BILE BEANS; clear; 1¾" 2.00-3.00

1929 SMITH GREEN MT. RENOVATOR; *E. Ga. Vt.;* 6⅛"; olive amber; stoddard glass 200.00 +

1930 DR. SMITH'S WORM OIL; 4"; aqua 2.00-4.00

1931 T.B. SMITH KIDNEY TONIC, CYNTHIANA, KY.; 10½"; aqua................. 8.00-12.00

1932 SOLOMONS CO, in script; *Branch Drug Store, Bull St., Savannah Ga.,* in three lines, in front; under bottom *WTCo, U.S.A.* in two lines; 7"; aqua or amethyst................. 2.00-4.00

1933 same only different sizes........... 2.00-4.00

1934 same only cobalt.................. 4.00-8.00

1935 SOLOMONS & CO., SAVANNAH, GA.; 6"; aqua............................ 4.00-10.00

1936   1937   1938   1942   1943   1948   1949   1952

1955   1956   1957   1959   1961   1962   1963   1964

1966   1969   1970   1971   1972   1975   1976   1983

1936 A.A. SOLOMONS & CO., DRUGGISTS MARKET SQUAE (misspelled *Square*); aqua; 3¾" 8.00-12.00

1937 SOZONDONT on each side; clear; 2½" 2.00-4.00

1938 SPARKLENE; *Registered* on back; amber; 5" 2.00-4.00

1939 SPARKS PERFECT HEALTH; *for Kidney & Liver Diseases*, three lines in sunken panel on front; round; aqua; 4" 3.00-6.00

1940 SPENCER MED. CO. on one side sunken panel; front, *Nubian Tea* and *Trade Mark*, other side panel, *Chattanooga Tenn.*; amber; square; 4" 2.00-6.00

1941 SPENCER MED CO., one side panel; on other *Chatt. Tenn.*; *Nubian Tea* in sunken panel on front; golden; 4" 2.00-6.00

1942 P.H. SPILLANE, PHARMACIST, COHOES, N.Y.; *W.T. CO.* under bottom; clear; 5" 2.00-4.00

1943 SPIRIT OF TURPENTINE, FRANKLIN, OHIO, label; *Pat April 21, 1896* under bottom; clear; 8¾" 4.00-6.00

1944 E.R. SQUIBB 1864; round; 6"; green 4.00-8.00

1945 DR. L.R. STAFFORD OLIVE TAR, label; directions, *J.R. Stafford* on side; *Olive Tar* opposite side; rectangular; double band collar; 6"; clear 3.00-4.00

1946 J.R. STAFFORDS OLIVE TAR on opposite sides; rectangular; 6"; aqua........ 2.00-3.00

1947 STANDARD OIL CO. vertical on front; *Cleveland O.* on one side; *Favorite* on opposite side; rectangular; 6¼"; amethyst........ 2.00-3.00

1948 STAPHYLASE DU DR. DOYEN; clear; 7½" 2.00-6.00

1949 STEIN & CO., APOTHECARIER, JERSEY CITY; *M-W U.S.A.* under bottom; clear or amethyst; 5⅜" 2.00-4.00

1950 STEELMAN & ARCHER, PHILADELPHIA, PA. on front; rectangular; 5½"; clear 3.00-6.00

1951 R.E. STIERAUX PILLS on front in form of circle about the size of a half dollar; 1¾"; clear 2.00-3.00

1952 A. STONE & CO.; inside screw top; *3 Philada* on screw top; aqua; 7½".......... 25.00-35.00

1953 STRAUSS, SPRINGFIELD AVE., N. HIGH ST. NEWARK, N.J.; 5¼"; clear 2.00-4.00

1954 STRONTIUM; 7½"; aqua.......... 4.00-6.00

1955 F.E. SUIRE & CO., CINCINNATI; reverse side *Waynes Duiretic Elixir*; 8"; amber 10.00-15.00

1956 SULPHO LYTHIN; amber; 3"...... 2.00-3.00

1957 SULTAN DRUG CO.; *St. Louis & London* on other side; amber; 7¼"............ 4.00-6.00

1958 SUTHERLAND SISTERS HAIR GROWER, NEW YORK; all seven sisters on front in a sunken panel; *Sutherland Sisters* on the side; *New York* on opposite side; rectangular; ABM; 5¼"; clear.................... 4.00-8.00

1959 THE E.E. SUTHERLAND MEDICINE CO.; aqua; 5½"..................... 2.00-3.00

1960 SUTHERLAND SISTERS HAIR GROWER; 6"; aqua 4.00-8.00

1961 L.B. SUTTON; amber; 5½" 2.00-4.00

1962 SWAIM'S; other panels: *Panacea, Established 1820 Philada*; aqua; 7" 8.00-10.00

1963 SWAIM'S; other panels: *Panacea, Philada*; pontil; olive; 8" .... 75.00+

1964 SWIFT'S; cobalt blue; 9"....... 10.00-20.00

1965 DR. SYKES; *Specific Blood Medicine, Chicago, Ills*; 6½"; clear.................... 1.00-3.00

1966 SYR:RHOEAD; cobalt blue; pontil; 8½" .... 35.00+

1967 SYRUP OF THEDFORD'S BLACK DROUGHT, vertical on front in sunken panel; rectangular; ABM; clear........... 2.00-3.00

1968 DR. TAFT'S ASTHMALENE N.Y. on the front panel; aqua; rectangular; 3½" 2.00-4.00

1969 TANGIN; same on reverse side; 9"; amber 10.00-12.00

1970 TARRANT & CO.; clear; 5¼"..... 3.00-6.00

1971 TAYLOR'S DRUG STORE; clear or amethyst; 4".................................. 2.00-4.00

1972 TAYLOR'S DRUG STORE; clear; 4¾" 4.00-6.00

1973 TAYLOR'S ESSENCE OF JAMAICA GINGER; 5½"; clear 8.00-12.00

1974 TEABERRY FOR THE TEETH & BREATH; 3½"; clear..................... 6.00-8.00

1975 TEINTURE D'FOTIDA; 5½"; amber 20.00-25.00

1976 TEISSIER PREVOS A PARIS; graphite pontil; 7½"; blue 50.00-70.00

1977 A TEXAS WONDER, HALL'S GREAT DISCOVERY; *For Kidney, Bladder Troubles, E.W. Hall, St. Louis, Mo.*; 3½"; clear 2.00-4.00

1978 DR. THACHER'S *Liver and Blood Syrup, Chattanooga, Tenn.* on the front panel; rectangular; 7¼" and 8¼"; amber 2.00-5.00

1979 DR. THACHER'S LIVER AND BLOOD SYRUP on the front; *Chattanooga, Tenn.* on one of the panels; *Sample* on the opposite panel; amber; rectangular; 3½" 2.00-4.00

1980 DR. H.S. THACHER'S DIARRHEA REMEDY, CHATTANOOGA, on one of the panels; amethyst; square; 3⅜" 2.00-5.00

1981 DR. THACHER'S VEGETABLE SYRUP, CHATTANOOGA, TENN. on the front; amethyst; 7"; rectangular 1.00-2.00

1982 DR. H.S. THACHER'S WORM SYRUP on the front panel; *Chattanooga, Tenn.* on other panel; aqua; 4¼"; square 1.00-2.00

1983 DR. THACHER'S; olive; 3¼" 3.00-6.00

| 1984 | 1985 | 1986 | 1989 | 1991 | 1994 | 1996 | 1997 |

| 1998 | 1999 | 2000 | 2004 | 2006 | 2007 | 2010 |

| 2011 | 2012 | 2013 | 2014 | 2021 | 2024 | 2025 | 2026 |

1984 DR. THACHER'S; *Chattanooga Tenn.* on side; aqua; 3¼" 3.00-4.00

1985 DR. H.S. THACHER'S; amber; 2½" 2.00-6.00

1986 HENRY THAYER; 9½"; amber ...... 25.00 +

1987 THOMAS ELECTRIC OIL vertical on front in sunken panel; *Internal & External* on side; *Foster Milburn Co.* on opposite side; rectangular; 4¼"; clear 4.00-6.00

1988 DR. S.N. THOMAS ELECTRIC OIL, vertical on front; *External* on side; *Internal* on opposite side; *Northrup & Lyman, Toronto, Ont.* on back; double band collar; rectangular; 5½"; aqua 4.00-8.00

1989 THOMPSON'S HERBAL COMPOUND, NEW YORK, label; 6¾"; clear or aqua 2.00-4.00

1990 DR. THOMPSON'S SARSAPARILLA, GREAT ENGLISH REMEDY on front indented panel; *Calais, Me. U.S.A.* side; *St. Stephens, N.B.* opposite side; rectangular; 9"; aqua 10.00-20.00

1991 THOMPSON'S; *Philada* other side; *Diarrhea syrup* on back; aqua 4.00-6.00

1992 DR. THOMPSON'S; *Eye Water, New London, Conn.*; aqua; round; 3¾"; pontil... 10.00-20.00

1993 THURSTON & KINGSBURY TAK FLAVORING EXTRACT, BANGOR, MAINE vertical on front in oriental style letters; *Finest Quality Full Strength*; 5"; clear 3.00-4.00

1994 DR. TICHENOR'S; aqua; *Antiseptic* on other side; 3¾" 4.00-8.00

1995 DR. TICHENOR'S on one side of panel; *Antiseptic* on the other side; rectangular; aqua; 5⅞" 1.00-2.00

1996 DR. G.H. TICHENOR'S ANTISEPTIC REFRIGERANT; one side *Sherrouse Medicine Co.*; other side *Ltd.*; *New Orleans La.*; 5¾"; aqua 8.00-10.00

1997 TIKHEEL; light blue; 6½" 4.00-6.00

1998 TILDEN under bottom; amber; 5".. 2.00-4.00

1999 TILDEN; amber; 7½" 2.00-4.00

2000 CLAES TILLY; aqua; 3¾" 2.00-4.00

2001 G.De KONING TILLY; oil; 1"; aqua 2.00-4.00

2002 TIPPECANOE; amber, clear, aqua; 9" 50.00 +

2003 TIPPECANOE; misspelled *Rochester* under bottom; 9"; amber..................... 60.00 +

2004 DR. TOBIAS, NEW YORK; aqua; 8" 4.00-8.00

2005 DR. TOBIAS VENETIAN HORSE LINIMENT, NEW YORK on front and back; rectangular; 8¼"; aqua 4.00-8.00

2006 TOKA; reverse *Blood Tonic*; 8½"; aqua 8.00-12.00

2007 T. TOMLINSON; aqua; 10½"....... 6.00-8.00

2008 TONICIO ORIENTAL PARA EL CABELLO, in three lines on sunken panel on front; on one side *New York*; on other, *Lanman Y Kemp*, both in sunken panels, under bottom *#34*; 6"; aqua; flat collar; ringed neck 4.00-8.00

2009 TO-NI-TA LORENTS MED. CO. TRADE MARK around shoulder; bitters label; amber; 9¾".....................10.00-20.00

2010 R. E. TOOMBS JR.; clear or amethyst; 5¼" 2.00-4.00

2011 TOOTH POWDER, label; 2"; milk glass 6.00-10.00

2012 DR. TOWNSEND; reverse *Sarsaparilla, 1850*; 9½".....................85.00 +

2013 DR. TOWNSEND; *Sarsaparilla* on other sides; pontil; 9½"; amber 60.00-110.00

2014 A. TRASKS; *Magnetic Ointment* on back; aqua; 2½" or 3¼" 4.00-6.00

2015 M. TREGOR SONS, BALTIMORE MD., WASH. D.C.; E.R.B.; 8"; clear 4.00-8.00

2016 J. TRINER, CHICAGO on one panel; six panels; 5¼"; clear..................... 8.00-10.00

2017 TRUAX RHEUMATIC REMEMDY, BEN O. ALDRICH, KEENE, N.H., label; clear 3.00-5.00

2018 DR. TRUES ELIXIR, ESTABLISHED 1851, DR. J.F. TRUE & CO. INC.; *Auburn, Me.*; *Worm Expeller, Family Laxative* on front and opposite side in sunken panel; rectangular; ABM; 5½"; clear.................. 3.00-4.00

2019 same as above except 7¾" 2.00-4.00

2020 H.A. TUCKER M.D., BROOKLYN N.Y., MO.; DIAPHORTIC COMPOUND on front; ring top; 5½"; aqua 4.00-6.00

2021 J. TUCKER, DRUGGIST; reverse *Mobile*; pontil; 7½"; aqua 18.00-20.00

2022 NATHAN TUCKER M.D.; *Star & Shield Specific for Asthma, Hay Fever and All Catarrhal Diseases Of The Res-piratory Organs* all on front; round; 4"; clear 4.00-6.00

2023 TURKISH FOOT BATH, GALLED ARMPITS & CO. 4.00-8.00

2024 TURKISH LINIMENT; 4¾"; aqua.. 2.00-4.00

2025 ROBT. TURLINGTON (TURLINGTON misspelled); on one side *June 14, 1754*; other side *London*; back side *By the Kings Royal Pat. Granted to*; 2¾"; aqua 10.00-20.00

2026 ROBT. TURLINGTON; *By The Kings Royal Patent Granted To* on back; aqua; pontil; 2½" 15.00-30.00

2027 same except no pontil............. 6.00-10.00

2028 TURNER BROTHERS, *New York, Buffalo, N.Y., San Francisco Cal.* on front; graphite pontil; tapered top; 9½"; amber ....75.00 +

2029 2032 2034 2035 2036 2037 2038

2040 2042 2045 2046 2049 2050 2052 2053

2058 2063 2064 2065 2070 2071 2073

126

2029 DR. TUTT'S; *New York* on other side; *Asparagine* on front; aqua; 10¼"... 6.00-10.00

2030 DR. S.A. TUTTLE'S, BOSTON MASS. on vertical panels; twelve vertical panels; 6¼"; aqua 3.00-6.00

2031 TUTTLE'S ELIXIR CO., BOSTON, MASS. on two vertical panels; twelve panels; 6¼"; amethyst.................... 3.00-4.00

2032 UDOLPHO WOLFE'S, on front panel; on back *Aromatic Schnapps* in two lines; right side plain; left *Schiedam*; 2¼" square; beveled corners; 1½" neck; golden amber...... 8.00-12.00

2033 same except 9½"; light amber....... 4.00-6.00

2034 same except olive 6.00-12.00

2035 UDOLPHO WOLFE'S; *Aromatic Schnapps* on back; *Schiedam* on side; other side plain; olive; 8"............................... 10.00+

2036 UDOLPHO WOLFE'S; *Aromatic Schnapps Schiedam* on two sides; green; 7½" 12.00-18.00

2037 UDOLPHO WOLFE'S; *Schiedam Aromatic Schnapps* on three panels; yellow; 8" .. 10.00 +

2038 DR. ULRICH; aqua; 7½" 4.00-8.00

2039 UNCLE SAM'S NERVE & BONE LINAMENT; aqua 4.00-6.00

2040 U.S. MARINE HOSPITAL SERVICE; clear; 5" 6.00-8.00

2041 U.S.A. HOSPITAL DEPT. in a circle; flared top; oval; 2½"; cornflower blue 55.00-80.00

2042 VAN ANTWERP'S; clear; 6½"..... 2.00-4.00

2043 VAN SCOY CHEMICAL CO., SERIAL #879, MT. GILEAD, O. U.S.A.; 6"; clear.. 3.00-4.00

2044 VAN SCOY CHEMICAL CO., SERIAL NO. 8795, MT. GILEAD, O. U.S.A.; 6"; clear 2.00-4.00

2045 VANSTANS; aqua; 2" 2.00-4.00

2046 VAN VLEET & CO.; *W.T. Co.* on bottom; amber; 10" 6.00-8.00

2047 DR. VAN WERTS BALSAM vertical on front in sunken panel; *Van Wert Chemical Co.* on side; *Watertown, N.Y.* opposite side; beveled corners; 5¾"; aqua 4.00-6.00

2048 VASELINE; *Chesebrough New York*, in three lines; 2½"; clear or amethyst 2.00-4.00

2049 VASELINE; dark amber; 3"; machine made 2.00-4.00

2050 VASOGEN; amber; 3¼".......... 2.00-6.00

2051 VICKS, on one side; on other *Drops*; cobalt; screw top; machine made; 1⅞" tall, 1¼" wide, ½" thick; very small 2.00-4.00

2052 VIN-TONE THE FOOD TONIC; amber; 8¾" 8.00-10.00

2053 THE CHARLES A. VOGELER COMPANY; aqua; 6¼" 4.00-8.00

2054 THE CHARLES A. VOGELER CO., ST. JACOBS OIL, BALTIMORE, MD. U.S.A.; round; 6¼" 4.00-6.00

2055 J.C. WADLEIGH, DELIGHTS SPANISH LUSTRAL; tapered top; 6"; aqua... 4.00-6.00

2056 DR. R.B. WAITES, LOCAL ANAESTHETIC, SAFE, RELIABLE, NON-SECRET, vertical around bottle; ring collar; round; 3"; clear 4.00-6.00

2057 DR. R.B. WAITE'S LOCAL ANAESTHETIC; *Safe Reliable Non-Secret, The Antecolor Mfg. Co., Springville, N.Y. U.S.A.*; 2¾"; clear 4.00-6.00

2058 WAIT'S WILD CHERRY TONIC; *The Great Tonic* on back; amber; 8½"........ 10.00-15.00

2059 WAKEFIELDS BLACK BERRY BALSAM vertical on front; rectangular; 5"; blue aqua 3.00-4.00

2060 WAKELEE'S CAMELLINE vertical on front; rectangular; beveled corners; 4¾"; cobalt blue 6.00-8.00

2061 same as above except amber........ 3.00-4.00

2062 WALKER'S TONIC, FREE SAMPLE; 3⅜"; clear 15.00-30.00

2063 HENRY K. WAMPOLE & CO.; clear or amethyst...................... 3.00-4.00

2064 HENRY K. WAMPOLE & CO,; clear or amethyst; 8¾" 3.00-6.00

2065 HENRY K. WAMPOLE & CO. INC.; clear or amethyst; *408* on bottom; 8½" 2.00-4.00

2066 HENRY K. WAMPOLE & CO. INC.; 8½"; clear or amber 2.00-4.00

2067 HENRY K. WAMPOLE & CO. INC., PHILADELPHIA, PA. U.S.A on flat front panel; rectangular; 8¼"; amethyst........... 3.00-4.00

2068 same as above except ABM 2.00-3.00

2069 DR. WARDS TRADE MARK with line through it; *The J.R. Watkins Med. Co.* on side; *Winona, Minn.* on opposite side; 8¾"; amber... 3.00-6.00

2070 W.R. WARNER & CO.; clear; 2¼"... 2.00-4.00

2071 WARNER & CO.; round bottom; sheared top; 2¾"; clear 3.00-6.00

2072 WM. R. WARNER & CO, PHILADELPHIA, in a race track circle in center; *W&Co* on front; 6" body, 1½" neck, 2¼" square; square corners; under bottom *#67*; cobalt 8.00-10.00

2073 WM. R. WARNER & CO., label; amber; 5¼" 2.00-4.00

2074   2075   2077   2082   2085   2086   2087

2088   2089   2090   2091   2092   2093   2095   2096

2097   2098   2099   2105   2106   2107   2108   2110

2113   2114   2115

2074 W.R. WARNER & CO.; clear; 2½"... 3.00-6.00

2075 W.R. WARNER & CO.; *Phila* on back; aqua; 8"; three-part mold 2.00-6.00

2076 WM. WARNERS & CO., PHILADA. vertical on front; round; 4"; clear............. 2.00-3.00

2077 WARNERS SAFE REMEDY; machine made; amber; 9" 8.00-15.00

2078 WARREN'S MOCKING BIRD FOOD; round; sheared top; 7"; aqua 8.00-15.00

2079 WASHINGTONIAN SARSAPARILLA, label; pontil; aqua 10.00-15.00

2080 WATKINS CHILL TONIC, label; picture of J.R. Watkins and *Watkins Trade Mark* embossed on opposite sides; ABM; 8½"; clear 3.00-4.00

2081 WATKINS DANDRUFF REMOVER AND SCALP TONIC on side; *J.R. Watkins Co. Winona, Minn. USA.* on opposite side; rectangular; beveled corners; ABM; 6¾"; clear 3.00-4.00

2082 WATKINS TRIALMARK; 8½"; aqua 2.00-6.00

2083 THE J.R. WATKINS CO, in a sunken panel; 7¹/₁₆"; clear, amber 2.00-4.00

2084 same except machine made 1.00-2.00

2085 J.R. WATKINS MED. CO.; clear or amethyst; 5¼".............................. 2.00-4.00

2086 J.R. WATKINS MEDICAL CO.; 5¼"; clear or amber 2.00-4.00

2087 THE J. R. WATKINS MEDICAL CO.; *Winona Minn. U.S.A.* other side; round bottom; clear; machine made; 3¼" 4.00-6.00

2088 WATSON'S PHARMACY, HOMER, N.Y.; *W.T. CO. U.S.A.* under bottom; 4¾"; clear or amethyst....................... 2.00-4.00

2089 WEB'S A NO. 1 CATHARTIC TONIC; reverse side, *The Best Liver Kidney & Blood Purifier;* amber .... 25.00+

2090 WEBSTER LITTLE; *W.T. CO. M U.S.A.* under bottom; clear; 4¾" 2.00-6.00

2091 WEEDON DRUG CO.; *515 Franklin St. Tampa, Fla.* in two lines; regular medical bottle; clear or amethyst.................... 2.00-4.00

2092 DR. T. WEST; clear; 5" 2.00-4.00

2093 W.D. CO. 6A under bottom; amber; 6" 2.00-4.00

2094 J.B. WHEATLEYS COMPOUND SYRUP, DALLASBURGH, KY.; graphite pontil; 6"; aqua......................... 40.00-70.00

2095 WHEELER'S TISSUE PHOSPHATES, in two lines in a sunken panel; 2½" square; three panels plain; beveled corners; 9"; under bottom monogram *WBYU* or other letters; aqua 4.00-8.00

2096 WHEELOCK FINLAY & CO., PROPRIETORS, DR. WILHOFT'S ANTIPERIODIC OR FEVER & AGUE TONIC, NEW ORLEANS; 5"; clear 2.00-4.00

2097 A.J. WHITE on other panels; *Design Pat 1894* on bottom; green; 7" 8.00-10.00

2098 WHITE & CO.; *Proprietors, New York;* 9½"; amber 10.00-20.00

2099 WHITE'S CREAM; 5¼"; aqua 2.00-3.00

2100 WHITE'S LINIMENT, WHITE & JONES PROPRIETORS, BLAINE, MAINE vertical around bottle; ground top for glass stopper; 5"; clear 3.00-4.00

2101 WHITEHURST vertical on center front; flask shape; 3½"; aqua 2.00-3.00

2102 same as above except ABM 2.00-3.00

2103 WHITE WINE AND TAR SYRUP vertical on front in sunken panel; *Warners* on side; *Coldwater, Mich.;* 7"; aqua.............. 3.00-4.00

2104 WILLIAMS MAGNETIC RELIEF; on one side *A.P. Williams;* other side *Frenchtown N.J.;* 6¼"; aqua........................... 4.00-6.00

2105 WILSON FAIRBANK & CO.; 10".. 8.00-12.00

2106 J.H. WILSON; reverse side *Brooklyn, N.Y.;* front side *Wilsons Carbolated Cod Liver Oil;* 8"; aqua.................. 10.00-12.00

2107 THE WILSON LABORATORIES; machine made; clear.................... 2.00-4.00

2108 WINCHESTER CRYSTAL CLEANER, label; 6¾"; clear 4.00-6.00

2109 J. WINCHESTER, N.Y., DR. J.F. CHURCHILLS, SPECIFIC REMEDY FOR CONSUMPTION, HYPOPHOSPHITES OF LIME & SODA; tapered top; 7¼"; aqua 4.00-6.00

2110 WINGFIELD; clear or amethyst; 5½" 2.00-4.00

2111 MRS. WINSLOW'S SOOTHING SYRUP; *Curtis & Perkins Proprietors,* in four vertical lines; 5¼"; short neck; small round bottle; aqua 2.00-4.00

2112 same as above except pontil 2.00-4.00

2113 MRS. WINSLOW'S TOOTHING SYRUP, CURTIS & PERKINS PROPRIETORS; 5"; aqua.................... 10.00-15.00

2114 WINSTEAD'S; *Lax-Fos* on other side; amber; 7¼"............................. 2.00-4.00

2115 WINTERSMITH; amber; 9¼"...... 6.00-8.00

2116   2123   2126   2127   2131   2132   2133

2134   2135   2136   2137   2139   2140   2144

2145   2146   2150   2154   2155   2156   2157

2158

2159

2116 WINTERSMITH; amber; 8½".... 3.00-5.00

2117 L.Q.C. WISHART'S; pine tree trademark on one side; *Pine Tree Tar Cordial Phila* on other side; different sizes and colors.... 25.00-50.00

2118 DR. WISTAR'S BALSAM OF WILD CHERRY, CINC. O.; 5½"; aqua........ 8.00-10.00

2119 DR. WISTAR'S BALSAM OF WILD CHERRY, 1848-1896; six panels; pontil; clear or aqua 10.00-25.00

2120 DR. WISTAR'S BALSAM OF WILD CHERRY PHILADA. on five consecutive panels; eight panels in all; 5"; aqua 4.00-6.00

2121 DR. WISTAR'S; same as above, 5⅝" 5.00-10.00

2122 DR. WISTAR'S BALSAM OF WILD CHERRY, SETH W. FOWLER & SONS, BOSTON on six consecutive panels; 3⅝"; aqua 4.00-8.00

2123 WOLFE'S; *Schnapps* on one panel; *X* under bottom; amber; 8"................. 15.00-25.00

2124 WOLFSTIRNS RHEUMATIC & GOUT REMEDY, HOBOKEN, N.J. vertical on front; rectangular; 5"; aqua................ 3.00-4.00

2125 THAT WONDROUS LINIMENT on front vertical; *A. Schoenhelt* on side; *San Jose, Cal.* on opposite side; rectangular; beveled corners; 4¼"; aqua.......................... 4.00-6.00

2126 WOOD'S PINE SYRUP COMPOUND; aqua; 5¾"................................ 2.00-4.00

2127 N. WOOD & SON on one side panel; *Portland, Me.* other panel; clear or amethyst; 5¾" 6.00-8.00

2128 WOODARD CLARK & CO. CHEMIST, PORTLAND CO.; 6¼"; clear or amber..... 2.00-4.00

2129 THE WRIGHT RAPID RELIEF CO.; 5¾"; clear 8.00-12.00

2130 WRIGHT'S CONDENSED SMOKE, label with directions; ABM; 9½"; amber 2.00-3.00

2131 W T CO. under bottom; amber; 3¼"   6.00-10.00

2132 W.T.CO. 4 U.S.A. under bottom; aqua; 7¾" 2.00-3.00

2133 W.T. CO. 9 under bottom; aqua; 2½".. 1.00-2.00

2134 W.T. CO. 3 under bottom; amber; 4¾" 1.00-2.00

2135 W & T 50 under bottom; clear; 6½" 1.00-2.00

2136 W.T.U.D. CO. 16 under bottom; amber; 8" 8.00-10.00

2137 WYETH; amber; 6¼"............. 2.00-3.00

2138 WYETH 119 6 under bottom in sunken panel; 1¾" x 1¹³⁄₁₆"; 3⅝" tall; clear, amethyst 3.00-6.00

2139 WYETH under bottom; clear or amethyst; 3½" 2.00-4.00

2140 WYETH under bottom; amber; 3¼".. 1.00-2.00

2141 WYETH & BRO, PHILADA in a circle; saddle type flask; under bottom *226A*; amber; 7½", 1½" neck........................... 2.00-4.00

2142 same except cobalt blue............. 4.00-8.00

2143 WYETH & BRO.; saddle type flask; 7½"; amber 4.00-8.00

2144 JOHN WYETH; clear; 3" 1.00-2.00

2145 JOHN WYETH & BRO., BEEF JUICE on front; round; 3½"; amber 2.00-4.00

2146 JOHN WYETH & BRO.; *Pat May 16th 1899* under bottom; cobalt; 6½" 8.00-15.00

2147 same except 3½" 10.00

2148 JOHN WYETH & BROTHER; *Philadelphia, Liquid Extract Malt;* 9"; squat body; amber 4.00-8.00

2149 JOHN WYETH & BROTHER, PHILA. 1870; round; 9"; blue................. 10.00-20.00

2150 JOHN WYETH & BROTHER; saddle shape; clear; 7¾"...................... 3.00-6.00

2151 JOHN WYETH & BRO., TAKE NEXT DOSE AT around base of neck; *Pat. May 16.;* cap shows hours 1 to 12; square; 5¾"; cobalt blue 5.00-8.00

2152 same as above except ABM 5.00-6.00

2153 DR. WYNKCOPS KATHARISMIC HONDURAS, SARSAPARILLA, N.Y.; 10½" 20.00-40.00

2154 X-LALIA, BOSTON, MASS; clear or amethyst; 7¼" 4.00-6.00

2155 YAGER'S SARSAPARILLA; 8½"; golden amber 10.00-15.00

2156 MADAME M. YALE CO., N.Y. & CHICAGO U.S.A.; on each side *La Freckla;* 6½"; clear 4.00-8.00

2157 BEN LEE YOUNG; clear; 3½"..... 2.00-4.00

2158 BEN LEE YOUNG; clear; 3½"..... 2.00-4.00

2159 YUCATAN CHILL-TONIC, label; embossed *Yucatan Chill-Tonic Improved, Evansville, Ind.;* 6¼"; clear....................... 4.00-6.00

2160 ZIPPS in fancy letters; *Cleveland, O.;* 5½"; clear 3.00-4.00

2161 same except amber................ 4.00-8.00

2162 ZOA-PHORA, c. 1900 .... 4.00-6.00

2163 ZOA-PHORA, WOMAN'S FRIEND in front; on side *Kalamazoo, Mich. USA;* ring top; 7½"; blue green.................... 3.00-6.00

Poison

The colors of poison bottles were likely to be ghastly shades of blues and browns. Bottles were likely to be shaped as coffins or long bones and have ominous embossments of human skulls resting on crossbones. Containers were also likely to have ribbed or quilted surfaces so that they could not be mistaken for medicine bottles even when people would grasp about in the dark.

The skull and crossbones was once a Christian symbol. When eighteenth-century pirates used it on their flags, it came to mean death; and this negative meaning soon became associated with poisons. Legislation to prevent the accidental intake or use of poisons was adopted by the State of New York in 1829. The word "poison" was to be inscribed somewhere on all such containers. As early as 1853 the American Pharmaceutical Association recommended national laws be adapted to identify such substances. The American Medical Association suggested in 1872 that poison containers be uniformly identified by their rough surface on one side and the word "poison" on the other. Yet between the years 1870 and 1930 a variety of poison containers continued to be manufactured. In the 1930's it became known that the many shapes and colors of poison containers intrigued and attracted children; and efforts directed at uniformity in packaging were then made.

John H. B. Howell of Newton, New Jersey, designed the first safety closure in 1886. However, such closures did not become popular until simple bottle designs for poisons were stressed in the 1930's. Most poison bottles range in size from one-half ounce to sixteen ounces, though some are larger than sixteen ounces. Most of the containers were cobalt blue though some manufacturers used amber or green. Use of clear glass for poison bottles is very rare.

TINCT. CAMPHOR.
PREPARED AND SOLD BY
COWLES & LEETE,
Successors to
Dr. NATHANIEL BOOTH,
54 State Street,
NEW HAVEN CONN.

This labeled bottle (similar to #2302) of the early 19th century
was originally in a New England apothecary shop. The bottom
was pushed up into the interior during construction,
resulting in a noticeable kick-up.

2167   2168   2169   2176   2177   2185   2188   2189

2191   2192   2193   2194   2196   2197   2214   2215

2216   2217   2218   2219

2164   ACID; round; clear or green; 6⅜".... 2.00-3.00

2165   Amber; vertical ribs all around; rectangular; ring collar; ABM; 3¼".............. 3.00-6.00

2166   SP. AMMON AR., label; clear; 9½" . 8.00-10.00

2167   BALTIMORE, MD. under bottom; 3"; amber 2.00-3.00

2168   BETUL-OL, W.T. CO. U.S.A. under bottom; clear; 4¼" 2.00-4.00

2169   BOWKERS PLROX; *670-2* under bottom; clear or amethyst; 4½"................. 8.00-12.00

2170   same as above, except 8"......... 10.00-15.00

2171   BOWMANS in script; *Drug Stores* on side panels; ribs; 5¼"; cobalt; hexagonal.... 25.00+

2172   BROWNS RAT KILLER, under it, C. WAKEFIELD CO.; 3"; aqua; applied lip 4.00-8.00

2173   BROWN; three-sided; ABM; 4½".... 2.00-4.00

134

2174 CARBOLIC ACID; *3 oz.* on each side, poison crosses all around it; ring top; 5"; cobalt 15.00+

2175 same as above, except no *Carbolic Acid;* 8½" 25.00-35.00

2176 THE CLARKE FLUID CO., CINCINNATI; *Poison* on side; *8 to 64 oz.* graduated measure on other side; clear or amethyst; quart size 15.00-20.00

2177 C.L.C. CO, PATENT APPLIED FOR under bottom; 2¾"; cobalt 3.00-5.00

2178 C.L.C. & CO., PATENT APPLIED FOR under bottom; emerald green; hexagonal; ½ ounce to 16 ounces 10.00-25.00

2179 same as above, except cobalt ..... 10.00-25.00+

2180 Cobalt blue; seven concave vertical panels on front half; *½ oz.* at top on front; square collar; oval; ABM; 2⅞" 3.00-4.00

2181 COCAINE HYDROCHLOR POISON, label; triangular; 5"; amber; vertical ribs; ring top 8.00-12.00

2182 Crossbones & star; 2¼"; snap-on top; amber 15.00-25.00

2183 CURTICE BROS PRESERVES; *Rochester, N.Y.;* clear or amethyst; 7"; four-part mold 10.00-15.00

2184 DAGGER on front; square; 5"; aqua; pouring lip .... 10.00+

2185 D D D; clear or amethyst; 3¾" and 5½" 2.00-6.00

2186 D.D. CHEMICAL CO., N.Y., SAMPLE on front of panel; amber; 5"; square 1.00-2.00

2187 DEAD STUCK; *Non-poisonous, won't stain* in small letters, *For Bugs* on same line but small letters, in center a bug, on each side *Trade Mark,* under it *Gottlieb Marshall & Co., Cersal, Germany, Philadelphia, Pa.* in three lines; under bottle *X;* aqua; 7" tall, 3½" x 1½"... 12.00-25.00

2188 DEPOSE on bottom; four-cornered; 4⅛" tall, 1¾" x ½" neck; label reads *Riodine Organic Iodine 50 capsules* 4.00-6.00

2189 FINLAY DICKS & CO DISTRIBUTORS, NEW ORLEANS, LA, DICKS ANT DESTROYER; sheared top; clear or amethyst; 6½" 8.00-12.00

2190 DPS below skull and cross on front; *Poison* on each side; cross on four sides; ring top; cobalt .... 25.00+

2191 DURFREE EMBALMING FLUID CO.; *8 to 64 oz.* graduated measure; clear or amethyst; ½ gallon 10.00-18.00

2192 DURFEE EMBALMING FLUID CO.; clear or amethyst; 8¾" 10.00-20.00

2193 ECORC:QUINQUINA PULV:; 5¾"; clear, painted brown; pontil 10.00-20.00

2194 ELI LILLY & CO.; *Poison* on each panel; amber; 2"; four other different sizes .. 6.00-8.00

2195 E.R.S. & S. under bottom; vertical ribbing on all sides; space for label; double ring top; 4½"; square; cobalt................... 10.00-20.00

2196 EVANS MEDICAL LTD, LIVERPOOL, label; *Chloroform B.A., Poison;* number and *U.Y.B.* under bottom; ABM; amber; 6½" 4.00-6.00

2197 EXTRAIT FL: DE QUINQUINA; 6½"; amber 10.00-20.00

2198 FERRIS & CO, LTD., BRISTOL near base; *poison* in center; vertical ribbing; wide ring top; aqua; 7½" 8.00-12.00

2199 FORTUNE WARD DRUG CO., *Larkspur Lotion Poison, 119 Maderson, Memphis, Tenn.* on label; on each side *for External Use Only;* ring top; 5½"; amber 4.00-10.00

2200 FREDERIA, vertical; flask type; hobnail cover; clear; ½ pint .... 40.00+

2201 THE FROSER TABLET CO., *St. Louis—N.Y., Brooklyn, Chicago; Sulphate poison tablets;* label; 5¾"; ABM; clear 4.00-6.00

2202 F.S. & CO. P.M. on base, POISON vertically, surrounded by dots; two sides plain; rectangular; amber; 2¾"; ring top 8.00-12.00

2203 J.G. GODDING & CO., APOTHECARIES, BOSTON, MASS. in three lines in center; ribs on each side; ring top; 4⅛"; hexagon; cobalt 10.00-20.00

2204 GRASSELLI ARSENATE OF LEAD; POISON on shoulder; different sizes 20.00-60.00

2205 HB CO under bottom within an indented circle; glass top ornaments with *Poison* around half of bottle; nobs and lines; very few lines or nobs in back; 6½"; cobalt 4.00-8.00

2206 same as above except smaller; 3¾" ... 4.00-6.00

2207 same as above except plain bottom ... 2.00-4.00

2208 HOBNAIL POISON; collared neck; made using double gather; attributed to N. England; clear; 6" 40.00-60.00

2209 IKEY EINSTEIN, POISON on each side of it; rectangular; 3¾"; ring top; clear... 10.00-20.00

2210 IODINE, POISON TINCT.; machine made; 2¼"; amber...................... 2.00-4.00

2211 IODINE TINCT; no embossing on bottle, but stopper on glass tube is embossed: THE S.H. WETMORE CO./PAT. AUG. 19, 1919; square; ring collar; ABM; light amber; 3½" .. 3.00-4.00

2212 JTM & CO. under bottom; 1¼" slim letters *Poison;* label reads *Milliken's Tri-Sept., Bernays No 2 Unofficial Poison* on two panels; tablet container; amber; 3".................. 4.00-6.00

2213 J.T.M. & CO. under bottom; three-cornered; *Poison* on one side; amber; 10"; two plain sides; ring top........................... 80.00+

2214 LIN, AMMONIAE; label; 6¾"; green 10.00-20.00

2215 LIN BELLAD, label; 7¾"; green .. 15.00-30.00

2216 LIN BELLAD, label; 7"; cobalt ... 40.00-60.00

2217 LIN BELLADON, label; 7"; green; under bottom *Y.G. CO* 10.00-20.00

2218 LIN SAPONIS, label; 6¾"; green.. 10.00-20.00

2219 LIQ. ARSENIC, label; 5¾"; green . 10.00-20.00

2220 2221 2222 2225 2226 2227 2229 2231

2232 2236 2241 2242 2243 2244 2245 2246

2252 2253 2255 2256 2257 2259 2260 2261

2262   2263   2264

2220 LIQ:HYD: PERCHLOR POISON, label; 9″; green 15.00-25.00

2221 LIQ. MORPH. HYDROCHL POISON, label; 4½″; cobalt 20.00-40.00

2222 LIQ. STRYCH. HYD., label; 6″; green 10.00-20.00

2223 LRAY POISON, label; embossed ribs on edges; amber; 3½″ 10.00-15.00

2224 EDWARD R. MARSHALL CO.; *Dead Stuck Insecticide*; 9″; green 25.00-30.00

2225 McCORMICK & CO., REGISTERED TRADE MARK., BALTO, MD., PATENTED; three-sided; cobalt; 4″ 4.00-8.00

2226 same as above except *July 8th 1882* . . . 6.00-8.00

2227 McCORMICK & CO., BALTIMORE; three-sided; clear or amethyst; 3¾″ 4.00-6.00

2228 McCORMICK & CO., BALTO. in a circle; in center a fly or bee, under it, *Patent Applied For*; triangular; 1½″, 2¾″ tall; cobalt; ring top 4.00-6.00

2229 MELVIN & BADGER, APOTHECARIES, BOSTON, MASS; ribbing on side; ring top; 7½″; cobalt . . . . 85.00+

2230 R.C. MILLINGS BED BUG POISON; *Charleston, S.C.*; clear; 6¼″; shoulder strap on side . . . . 10.00+

2231 N 16 OZ; poison label; cobalt; 6½″ . . . . 20.00+

2232 N 8 OZ; poison label; cobalt; 6″ . . . . . . 10.00+

2233 NORWICK on base; coffin shape; *Poison* vertical down center of front, also horizontal in back on shoulder; 7½″; covered with diamond embossing; amber . . . . 10.00+

2234 same as above except cobalt; ABM . . . . 10.00+

2235 same as above except BIMAL 20.00-30.00

2236 THE NORWICK PHARMACY CO, NORWICK, N.Y., label; *M* under bottom; 3½″; ABM; cobalt 8.00-12.00

2237 NOT TO BE TAKEN in center vertically; vertical wide ribbing on sides; rectangular; 6¾″; cobalt; ring top 8.00-12.00

2238 NOT TO BE TAKEN in center of bottle on each side in three vertical lines; *#12* under bottom; 7¾″; cobalt . . . . 35.00+

2239 same as above except in two lines *Poison*, *Not to Be Taken*; cobalt . . . . 35.00+

2240 same as above except emerald green, clear 8.00-20.00

2241 01. CAMPHOR FORTE, label; crystal glass; 5″; amber 15.00-30.00

2242 01. EUCALYPTI, label; crystal glass; 6½″; amber 15.00-30.00

2243 01. SINAP. AETH., label; crystal glass; 5″; amber 15.00-30.00

2244 ORGE MONDE, label; cut glass; blue 15.00-30.00

2245 OWL POISON AMMONIA, label; three-cornered; 5¼″; cobalt . . . . 25.00+

2246 THE OWL DRUG CO.; *Poison* other side; three-cornered; 8″; cobalt . . . . 80.00+

2247 THE OWL DRUG CO. in script on shoulder; on side vertically *Poison*, on other owl sitting on top of a mortar; different sizes; cobalt; ring top 6.00-25.00

2248 POISON BOTTLE on one side; irregular diamond shape; ridges on three corners; amber; four sizes 3.00-6.00

2249 some have *Poison* on two sides 4.00-8.00

2250 some machine made 2.00-4.00

2251 POISON on one panel; nobbed on three sides; *16* on bottom; round back; 3⁹⁄₁₆″; also four other sizes 4.00-12.00

2252 POISON on each side panel; no round back; four-cornered; three sides nobbed, other plain; 2¾″; amber 4.00-6.00

2253 POISON on each side panel; round back; three sides nobbed; four different sizes; machine made; amber 3.00-6.00

2254 POISON, TINCTURE IODINE under a skull and crossbones; ¼ on one side of skull, *Oz.* on other; oval; 5 panels on front; under bottom *At. 1-7-36*; 2¼″ tall; ¾″ x 1″; amber 6.00-10.00

2255 POISON on each side; amber; *P.D. & CO.* on bottom; 2½″ 4.00-6.00

2256 POISON; plain; different sizes; cobalt 6.00-15.00

2257 POISON, label; dark blue; 8″ 6.00-8.00

2258 POISON; ribs in front; black back; 13½″; cobalt; *90* under bottom . . . . 75.00+

2259 POISON; casket type; hobnail finish; amber; 3¼″ 6.00-8.00

2260 POISON; *Use With Caution* on other side; cobalt; 8¾″ 10.00-20.00

2261 POISON DO NOT TAKE (N in Not backward); *DCP* under bottom; 4¼″ . . . . 18.00+

2262 POISON, label; cobalt; 8″ 20.00-25.00

2263 POISON; machine made; ground top; clear; 13½″ 10.00-20.00

2264 POISON; *12* under bottom; *Not To Be Taken* on side; cobalt; 7¾″ 35.00-45.00

2265 2266 2269 2272 2273 2274 2276 2282

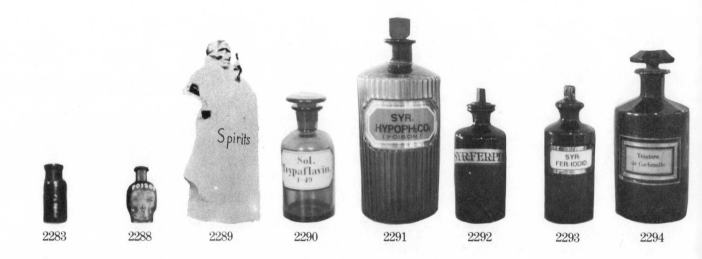

2283 2288 2289 2290 2291 2292 2293 2294

2300 2301 2302 2303 2304 2305 2306

2307   2308   2309

2265 POISON, label; three-cornered; *74* under bottom; cobalt; 2½".................. 2.00-4.00

2266 POISON, label; cobalt; 5" 10.00-20.00

2267 POISON; flask; made rough to avoid a mistake in the dark; sheared top; ½ pint; aqua 85.00-150.00

2268 same as above except, pontil; green 35.00-50.00

2269 POISON on each side panel; *WRW & CO.* under bottom; amber; 2¾" 4.00-6.00

2270 X around POISON in one panel; *X* around plain side, *1 oz. use with caution;* diamond shape with letter *D* under bottom; ring top; 3¼"; cobalt .... 18.00+

2271 POISON, label; dark blue; 8" .... 10.00+

2272 POISON, label; 3½"; cobalt or amber 4.00-8.00

2273 POISON, label; 3¼"; cobalt 6.00-10.00

2274 POISON, skull; *Pat. Applied For* on bottom rim; *S* under bottom; ceramic reproduction; 3½"; cobalt .... 25.00+

2275 POISON; clear; 6½"; embossed picture of rat on front; machine made.............. 4.00-8.00

2276 PYROX BOWKER INSECTICIDE CO., BOSTON & BALTIMORE; cream crock; glass top; 7½" 8.00-10.00

2277 RAT POISON horizontal on round bottle; 2½"; clear or amethyst 10.00-20.00

2278 RDDES, 7073 under bottom; 6½"; three-cornered with ribs or ridges; ring top; aqua 10.00-20.00

2279 REESE CHEMICAL CO., CLEVELAND, OHIO; *For External Use Only,* etc.; rectangular; 5½"; sides ribbed; flat and ring top; cobalt, green, clear 8.00-20.00

2280 RIGO embossed on base; vertical on left panel; *Use with Caution;* in center *Not to be Taken;* right usage extreme with stars all around bottle; ring top; cobalt.................... 25.00+

2281 ROMAN INC. vertical in script in center; ribbed on each side; hexagonal; ring top; 5¼"; emerald green......................... 15.00+

2282 S & D 173 under bottom; ABM; poison label; 2½"; cobalt 10.00-20.00

2283 SHARP & DOHME on one panel; *Phila* on other panel; label; *X126-1* under bottom; three-cornered; cobalt; 2" 6.00-10.00

2284 SHARP & DOHME/BALTIMORE on two panels; six vertical panels; bulbous shoulder; ring collar; amber; ABM; 2½" 3.00-4.00

2285 SHARP & DOHME on one panel; *Baltimore, Md.;* three-cornered; 3½"; cobalt.... 4.00-6.00

2286 SHARP & DOHME on one panel; other *Phila;* label reads *Ergotole D & D;* three-cornered; 2"; cobalt; under bottom *X-126-1.*...... 6.00-10.00

2287 Skull & crossbones on each of six vertical panels, also GIFT embossed on each panel, (*gift* means poison in German); aqua or clear; flared collar; 8⅛" 8.00-15.00

2288 Skull, POISON on forehead; crossbones under bottom; 2" round, 3" tall, 1" neck; ring top; cobalt; *Pat. Appl'd For* on base in back . 50.00+

2289 SPIRITS; silver and milk glass; 9"..... 20.00+

2290 SOL. TRYPAFLAVIN; *1 + 49;* crystal glass; 5"; amber 15.00-30.00

2291 SYR: HYPOPH: CO.; 9"; green ... 15.00-25.00

2292 SYR: FER: PA: CO:; 7"; cobalt ... 35.00-55.00

2293 SYR: FER: IODID; 7"; cobalt 60.00-75.00

2294 TEINTURE de COCHENILLE, label; 7½"; amber 10.00-15.00

2295 F.A. THOMPSON & CO., DETROIT on front; *Poison* on sides; ribbed corner; coffin type; ring top; 3½" .... 15.00+

2296 TINCT CELLADON, POISON; round bottle; vertical ribbing; aqua and green ... 25.00-35.00

2297 TINCTURE IODINE in three lines under skull and crossbones; square; flat ring and ring top; amber; ABM 4.00-6.00

2298 same as above except BIMAL 6.00-10.00

2299 same as above except 2¾"........... 4.00-6.00

2300 TINCT. ACONITI., label; 6"; green 10.00-20.00

2301 TINCT: ACONITI:, label; 7¾"; green; *Y.G. CO* under bottom.................. 15.00-30.00

2302 TINCT: CAMPH: CO: POISON, label; 9"; green...................... 15.00-25.00

2303 TINCT. CHLOROF. et MORPH. CO., label; 7¾"; green 15.00-30.00

2304 TINCT. CONII, POISON, label; 6"; cobalt 20.00-40.00

2305 TINCT: ERGOTAE. AMM; *Y.G. Co* under bottom; 7¾"; green.................. 15.00-30.00

2306 TINCT. IODI MIT., label; 7¾"; green 15.00-30.00

2307 TINCT. LOBELIAE AETH, label; 6"; green 10.00-20.00

2308 TINCT. NUX VOM, label; 6"; green 10.00-20.00

2309 TINCT. OPII, label; 6"; green.... 10.00-20.00

2310   2311

2310   TINCT. OPII.; *POISON* on base; 7"; cobalt
       .... 20.00-40.00
2311   TINCTURE: SENEGAE, label; under bottom
       numbers *6 U.G.B.*; ABM; amber; 6" 8.00-10.00
2312   TRILETS vertical; other side *poison;* triangu-
       lar; 3½"; cobalt; ribbed corner; ABM 4.00-8.00
2313   same as above except BIMAL 8.00-15.00
2314   TRILOIDS on one panel of triangular bottle;
       Poison on another; the other plain; corners
       nobbed; number under bottom; 3¼"; cobalt
       .... 4.00-6.00

2315   TRI-SEPS; *Milliken Poison;* one ribbed side;
       two for label; under bottom in sunken panel *JTM
       & Co.;* ring top; 1½" x 2" tall, ¾" neck; 1¼" let-
       ters *Poison* on side 3.00-6.00
2316   U.D.O. on base; *Poison* vertically on two panels;
       triangular; 5¼"; ring top; cross stitch around
       Poison; cobalt 10.00-20.00
2317   same as above, except 8½"....... 15.00-25.00
2318   VAPO-CRESOLENE CO. vertical on one panel
       with four rows of nail heads; *Patd. U.S. July
       1794 Eng. July 23, 94* on next panel with nail
       heads; square; double band collar; aqua; ABM;
       5½"............................. 3.00-6.00
2319   same as above except clear; 4"...... 3.00-6.00
2320   same as above except *S* is reversed; dated *July
       23, 94.*......................... 4.00-10.00
2321   VICTORY CHEMICAL CO.; *Quick Death In-
       secticide, 148 Fairmount Ave., Phila, Pa., 8 oz.;*
       7"; clear 8.00-12.00
2322   W.R.W. & CO. under bottom; *Poison* on each
       side; ribbed corner; rectangular; 2½"; ring top
       .... 10.00+
2323   JOHN WYETH & CO., PHILA on front; oval;
       cobalt; 4"; cross around base and side; flat ring
       collar............................ 4.00-6.00
2324   JOHN WYETH & BROS., PHILA. in two lines
       on side; square; 2¼"; 10.00-20.00
2325   WYETH POISON vertical in back; round ring
       base and top; 2¼"; cobalt 8.00-10.00
2326   same as above, except amber 4.00-6.00

*After 18th-century pirates began using the
skull and crossbones, up until then a Christian
symbol, on their Jolly Roger flags, it took on a
negative connotation and soon became associated
with poisons. This gruesome poison
bottle was patented in 1894.*

141

Soda

On a May afternoon in 1886, "Doc" Pemberton of Atlanta, Georgia, patiently stirred a mixture in a three-legged pot in his back yard. When at last it was ready, he sampled it and thought that he had been successful. Just to be sure he took a portion to Willis Venable, the proprietor of Jacob's Drug Store. Venable added ice and tap water to the syrup, tasted it and liked it, and agreed to sell it as a headache cure. Only one drink of Coca-Cola was consumed that day, but now over ninety-five million drinks of it are downed daily. "Doc" Pemberton was never able to cash in on the worldwide success of the new drink and made only fifty dollars in the first year of its existence.

Business did improve, however, after that hard first year when it was discovered that the addition of carbonated water made the drink taste better. Pemberton, unaware of the reverberations his discovery would cause, died in 1888, four years before a corporation was formed to manufacture the drink on a larger scale. The recipe for Coca-Cola was and still is a guarded secret and has never been exactly copied.

It occurred to Joseph A. Biedenharn in 1894 that if he could put Coca-Cola in bottles he could sell a great deal more of the beverage. He loaded the containers on his truck and peddled the drink, already a favorite of the rural people when they came to town, throughout the countryside around Vicksburg, Mississippi.

Alex Samuelson is credited with designing the familiar "Coke" bottle in 1915. A supervisor of the Root Glass Company in Terre Haute, Indiana, he studied drawings of cola nuts, the brown, bitter-tasting oval seeds from which Coca-Cola syrup was made. The result was the "hobble skirt" or "Mae West" bottle adopted by the Coca-Cola company in 1916. Though it resembled the cola nut in shape, it was dubbed "hobble skirt" after its similarity to a ladies' fashion fad of the day. Except for a minor trimming in the middle, the bottle has remained the same. Prior to 1916, a variety of shapes can be found.

Many people attempted to cash in on the rising popularity of Coca-Cola by mixing their own cola drinks. The most successful of these was Caleb D. Bradham of New Bern, North Carolina, who began producing Brad's Drink in 1890. In 1896 he changed its name to Pep-Kola and two years later to Pipi-Cola. It was not until 1906 that it finally became known as Pepsi-Cola.

Ever since it was discovered that some mineral springs contained natural carbonation, people had been trying to duplicate nature. It was a task assigned to sixteenth-century scientists, but Joseph Priestley, the English scientist who discovered oxygen, is credited with carbonating water in 1772. He hastily proclaimed the medicinal values of carbonated water, which were proved false. Small quantities of soda water were sold by Professor Benjamin Silliman of Yale in 1806. By 1810 a New York fountain sold homemade seltzers as sure cures for over-

These soda bottles (#2607) were made sometime between 1845 and 1870 as evidenced by their improved or graphite pontils, easily noted upon examining the indented bottle bottom for a smooth circular mark, red to reddish-black in color.

weight. Flavored soda appeared in 1881, five years before Pemberton made his Coca-Cola, when a drink called Imperial Inca Cola was marketed. In the years that followed, many other flavored sodas— strawberry, orange, lemon, grape—were manufactured and sold.

Most of the early soda bottlers made their own products and sold them in the immediate area. It was not until the turn of the nineteenth century that the local plants began to expand. Many early soda bottles can be found with pontil scars—a pontil is a rod that holds the bottle at the bottom while it is eased away from the blowpipe at the neck. Most soda bottles, however, are unscarred.

In the days of sailing vessels they often served as ballast; more than just dead weight, they could be sold for a profit at the destination. The flat bottoms made upright stacking impossible, which was the precise intention since they were stopped with cork. Cork expands when moist, thereby securely locking the contents within. If the cork was allowed to dry, it was quite likely that it would be expelled with a loud "pop," hence the nickname for soda.

One of the most popular bottles among collectors today is the John Ryan bottle. In addition to soda, John Ryan bottled ale, beer, bitters and cordials in containers that ranged in color from amber and aqua to cobalt blue and lime green. Ryan's first plant was built in Savannah, Georgia, in 1852 and others quickly followed in Atlanta, Augusta and Columbus. Prior to 1883, most of the bottles were embossed without a date with the exception of those that bore the dates 1852, 1859 and 1866.

| 2327 | 2328 | 2329 | 2330 | 2331 | 2332 | 2334 |

| 2339 | 2340 | 2341 | | 2342 | 2344 | 2348 |

| 2349 | 2350 | 2356 | 2361 | 2362 | 2370 | 2378 |

2327 A.B. CO., ALLIANCE, O.; Hutchinson type; 6½"; aqua 4.00-6.00

2328 ABILENA #1 under bottom; amber; label; 6" 4.00-6.00

2329 THE ACME SODA WATER CO. PITTSBURG, REGISTERED; reverse side *W.A.S. Co.* in hollow letters; 6½"; aqua or clear . . . 4.00-6.00

2330 ALABAMA BOTTLING CO.; aqua; *a* under bottom; 7½"; in back—a bird in a circle *This Bottle Prop. of A.B.Co. Not To Be Sold* . . 3.00-6.00

2331 ALABAMA GROCERY CO.; *Registered* on shoulder; clear; 8" 2.00-4.00

2332 ALA COLA; aqua; 7¾" 2.00-6.00

2333 ALEXANDRIA BOTTLING, INDIANA; 7½"; aqua 8.00-12.00

2334 ALPHA; *B.H.A.* in back; light green or aqua; 6" 2.00-4.00

2335 ALVAN VALLEY BOTTLE WORKS, EVERETT, WASH.; 8½"; aqua 4.00-6.00

2336 H. AMAN, CHEYENNE, WYO. in a circle; Hutchinson type; 6½"; aqua 4.00-16.00

2337 THE A.M. & B. CO., REG. WACO TEXAS & ST. LOUIS, MO.; reverse side, *We Pay For Evidence Conv. Thieves For Refilling Our Bottles*; 8½"; aqua 8.00-10.00

2338 AMERICA SODA WORKS, TRADE MARK, PORTLAND, OR.; 7¾"; green 4.00-6.00

2339 AMOS POST; *Not To Be Sold* on back base; clear or amethyst; 7¾" 4.00-6.00

2340 AQUA DIST & BOT CO.; aqua; 8½" 4.00-6.00

2341 ARIZONA BOTTLING WORKS; *A* under bottom; *This Bottle Must Be Returned* on base; aqua; 7" 4.00-6.00

2342 ARTESIAN BOTTLING WORKS, DUBLIN, GA., in sunken circle; with ribs; bottom; or ten panels; *C.C. Co.* on one panel; 7"; aqua 4.00-6.00

2343 AUGUSTIN VITALE, PROVIDENCE, R.I., A.V. monogram all in slug plate on front; blob top; 9¼"; clear 4.00-6.00

2344 AUSTIN ICE & BOTTLING; *Reg. Must Not Be Sold* on back; *71* under bottom; 7¼"; aqua 4.00-8.00

2345 WM. AYLMER FARGO, O.T.; 7"; blue 6.00-12.00

2346 B on front; gravitating stopper made by John Matthews; *N.Y. Pat. Oct. 11, 1864* on bottom; 7¼"; blue aqua 4.00-8.00

2347 BABB & CO., SAN FRANCISCO, CAL. in three lines; graphite pontil; 7½"; green 25.00+

2348 DANIEL BAHR; light blue; *D.B.* in back; 7½" 4.00-6.00

2349 JOHN C. BAKER & CO.; aqua; 7½" 4.00-8.00

2350 J. ED BAKER; clear; 9½" 3.00-8.00

2351 J. ED BAKER, 417 WASHINGTON ST. NEWBURGH, N.Y. on front slug plate; 7⅛"; aqua 4.00-6.00

2352 THE PROPERTY OF MRS. J. ED BAKER, NEWBURGH, N.Y. on front in oval slug plate; blob top; 9"; clear 4.00-8.00

2353 JOHN S. BAKER SODA WATER T.B.I.N.S.; eight-sided; 7½"; green 4.00-8.00

2354 BARCLAY STREET; in center 41, N.Y.; applied lip; 7"; green 10.00-20.00

2355 BARTLETT BOTTLING WORK; 6½"; clear or amethyst 8.00-10.00

2356 BARTOW BOTTLING WORKS; aqua; *root* under bottom; 7½" 2.00-6.00

2357 F. BAUMAN, SANTA MARIA, CAL. in a circle; SODA WORKS in center; 7¼"; aqua 4.00-8.00

2358 BAY CITY POP WORKS M.T. REGISTERED BAY CITY, MICH. on front in slug plate; *This Bottle Not To Be Sold*, on opposite side; blob top; quart; 8¾"; apple green 5.00-10.00

2359 BAY CITY SODA WATER CO., S.F.; star symbol; 7"; blue 10.00-15.00

2360 B. & C., S.F.; applied lip; 7¼"; cobalt 25.00-35.00

2361 R.M. BECKER'S; aqua; *B* under bottom; 6½" 2.00-6.00

2362 R.M. BECKER; aqua; *B* on bottom; 7¼" 4.00-6.00

2363 R.M. BECKER'S HYGEIA BOTTLE WORKS TRADE MARK in a shield; *B* on the bottom; crown top; 7½"; aqua 4.00-8.00

2364 M.O. BENNETT, CHEYENNE, WYO.; 7½"; aqua 6.00-12.00

2365 same as above except in arched panel; Hutchinson; 6½"; aqua 4.00-6.00

2366 THE BENNINGTON BOTTLE CO., NO. BENNINGTON, VT. in a sunken panel; under bottom *E.S. & H.*; ten-sided base; 7¾"; clear or amber 10.00-15.00

2367 BELFAST COCHRAN & CO. on front and back of tear drop bottle; ⁷⁄₁₆" size letters; aqua; 9¼" 8.00-12.00

2368 BELFAST & DUBLIN, *Cantrell, Cochrane*; see that cork is branded around bottles on bottom; pop type; 9½"; aqua; round bottom . . . 4.00-6.00

2369 BELFAST; round bottom; 9¼"; aqua. 3.00-6.00

2370 BELFAST; plain flat bottom; 9"; aqua 2.00-4.00

2371 BELFAST ROSS; round bottom; 9¼"; aqua 3.00-5.00

2372 BELFAST ROSS; plain; 9½"; aqua and clear 3.00-5.00

2373 C. BERRY & CO., 84 LEVETT ST., BOSTON, REGISTERED on shoulder in oval slug plate; crown top; 9⅜"; emerald green 4.00-6.00

2374 C. BERRY & CO., 84 LEVERETT ST., BOSTON in oval slug plate; crown top; 9½"; clear 2.00-4.00

2375 same as above except 9¼"; amber 2.00-4.00

2376 same as above except blob top; 9"; clear 4.00-6.00

2377 SAMUEL BESKIN, FISHKILL LANDING, N.Y. on front in oval slug plate; blob top; 9⅜"; aqua 4.00-6.00

2378 BESSEMER COCA-COLA; aqua; 6½". 65.00+

145

2382   2383   2385   2387   2388   2390

2391   2393   2394   2396   2398   2400

2417   2420   2421   2422   2425   2427

2379 BEVERAGE; plain; 6¼"; aqua; opalescent; pop type 3.00-5.00

2380 BEVERAGE; plain; 9"; Belfast type; aqua 3.00-4.00

2381 BEVERAGE; plain; clear; aqua 3.00-4.00

2382 BIEDENHARN CANDY CO.; *B* under bottom; aqua; 7¼" 4.00-8.00

2383 BIEDENHARN CANDY CO.; *BCC* under bottom; aqua; 7¼" 10.00-20.00

2384 WEISS BIER; under bottom *Carl Hutten, N.Y.*; blob top; 7¼"; aqua 8.00-12.00

2385 BIG 4 MF'G. CO.; *1120* and three dots under bottom; aqua; 7¾" 4.00-6.00

2386 E.L. BILLINGS, SAC. CITY, CAL.; reverse *Geyser Soda*; blob top; 7"; blue 8.00-10.00

2387 CHAS. BINDER; *C.B. Mongroft C.B.* on back; *C.B.* bottom; aqua; 7" 4.00-8.00

2388 BIRMINGHAM BOTTLING CO.; aqua; 7" . . . . 40.00+

2389 R.W. BLACK BOTTLER, OKLAHOMA, TEXAS, in slug plate; panel base; Hutchinson; 6¾"; aqua . . . . 40.00+

2390 BLACKHAWK GINGER ALE; dark green; 6½" 2.00-6.00

2391 J.A. BLAFFER & CO., NEW ORLEANS; squat type; blob top; 6½"; amber . . . 10.00-20.00

2392 T. BLAUTH, 407 K. ST., SACRAMENTO, CALIF., BOTTLING WORKS; 6¾"; aqua 4.00-6.00

2393 BLUDWINE BOTTLING CO.; aqua; 7½"; machine made 4.00-6.00

2394 BLUDWINE; clear or amethyst; 8" 2.00-4.00

2395 BLUFF CITY BOTTLING in horseshoe shape; in center of horseshoe *Co. Memphis, Tenn.*; on bottom, on one panel, *B.G. Co.* in very small letters and next to it *199*; aqua 3.00-6.00

2396 BOARDMAN; blue; ground pontil; 7½" 25.00-30.00

2397 GEO BOHLEN, *Brooklyn*; in a round slug plate in center *358 Hart St.*; blob top; 7¼"; aqua 4.00-6.00

2398 BOLEN & BYRNE; in a dome shape under it EAST 54th ST. N.Y.; reverse *T.B.N.T.B.S.*; 7¾"; aqua 10.00-20.00

2399 BOLEN & BYRNE; opposite side *N.Y.*; aqua; 8¼" . . . . 12.00+

2400 BOLEN & BYRNE, NEW YORK; round bottom; aqua; 9" 4.00-8.00

2401 BOLEY & CO., SAC. CITY, CAL., UNION GLASS WORKS, PHILA.; 7½"; cobalt 10.00-20.00

2402 BOLEY & CO., SAC. CITY, CAL. in slug plate; reverse *Union Glass Works, Phila.*; graphite pontil; blob top; 7¼"; cobalt 20.00-40.00

2403 THE BONHEUR CO. INC., SYRACUSE, N.Y. in script; clear; 7½"; *14 fl. ounce* on bottom; under bottom diamond shape figure; machine made 2.00-4.00

2404 BONODE 5; 6¾"; clear or amber . . . 4.00-6.00

2405 BORELLO BROS. CO., FRESNO (B.B. CO.) on bottom; crown top; 7¾"; lt. aqua blue 2.00-6.00

2406 R. BOVEE, TROY, N.Y.; 7½"; clear 8.00-12.00

2407 W.H. BRACE, AVON, N.Y. on front in slug plate; blob top; 9¼"; aqua 4.00-6.00

2408 C.W. BRACKETT & CO., 61 & 63 ANDREW ST., LYNN, MASS on front in oval slug plate; 9⅛"; clear 4.00-6.00

2409 H. BRADER & CO.; *Penalty For Selling This Bottle, XLLR Soda Work, 738 Broadway, S.F.* on eight-panel bottle; blob top; 7¼"; aqua 10.00-20.00

2410 BREIG & SCHAFFER, S.F.; picture of a fish under it; 6½"; aqua 4.00-12.00

2411 BREMEKAMPF & REGAL, EUREKA, NEV.; 7¼"; clear or aqua 6.00-10.00

2412 BRENHAM BOTTLING WORK; 8¼"; aqua 4.00-8.00

2413 W.E. BROCKWAY in hollow letters; NEW YORK; graphite pontil; squat type; blob top; 6¾"; blue green 25.00-40.00

2414 BROWN BROS CHEMISTS, GLASGOW; round bottom; blob top; 9½"; aqua 4.00-8.00

2415 H.L. & J.W. BROWN in hollow letters; HARTFORD, CT.; squat type; tapered top; 7"; olive 10.00-30.00

2416 I. BROWNLEE in dome shaped lines; under it, NEW BEDFORD; in back *T.B.N.S.*; blob top; blue 10.00-30.00

2417 J. BRUNETT; big hollow letter *A*, big *B*; aqua; 7" 8.00-12.00

2418 THE BRUNNER BOTTLING CO., 669 to 673 GRAND ST., BROOKLYN, N.Y., 1889, AUG.; blob top; 7½" 8.00-10.00

2419 FILLIPPO BRUNO & CO., 298-300 NORTH ST. & 50 FLEET ST., BOSTON, MASS. on front in oval slug plate on shoulder; 8⅞"; clear 4.00-6.00

2420 R. W. BUDD; aqua; 7¼" 4.00-6.00

2421 BURKE; *E & J* under bottom; amber; 7½" 4.00-6.00

2422 HENRY BURKHARDT; *H.B.* under bottom; aqua; 6¾" 4.00-6.00

2423 W.H. BURT, SAN FRANCISCO; blob top; graphite pontil; 6½"; aqua 30.00-40.00

2424 W.H. BURT, SAN FRANCISCO; 7½"; aqua 4.00-8.00

2425 BUTEL & ERTEL, TIPTON, IND.; *B & E* under bottom; aqua; 6¾" 4.00-6.00

2426 J.G. BYARS in center; *1882 No. Hoosick, N.Y.*; reverse *T.B.N.T..S.*; 7"; aqua 8.00-12.00

2427 C.A.; aqua; 10" 6.00-8.00

2428 CALHOUN FALLS in center; BOTTLING WORKS, CALHOUN FALLS, S.C.; 7½"; clear or amber 6.00-8.00

2429 CALIFORNIA BOTTLING WORK, T. BLAUTH, 407 K ST., SACRAMENTO; 7"; clear 4.00-6.00

2433   2434   2436   2437   2442   2443   2444

2447   2448   2450   2451   2455   2457

2458   2459   2460   2461   2462   2463   2465

2468   2469   2471

2430   CALIFORNIA SODA WORKS; eagle in center; 7"; aqua 4.00-10.00

2431   CALIFORNIA SODA WORKS with an arrow under it; H. FICKEN, S.F.; in back an embossed eagle; blob top; 7"; green 10.00-20.00

2432   CALVERT BOTTLE WORKS, *Calvert, Texas*; aqua; soda water; 7¼" 2.00-4.00

2433   CAMDEN BOTTLING COMPANY; clear; 8" 6.00-8.00

2434   CAMEL BOTTLING WORKS; clear; 7" 4.00-6.00

2435   D. CAMELIO CO., 10 LEWIS ST., BOSTON, MASS. on shoulder in oval slug plate; 8⅞"; clear 4.00-8.00

2436   CAMPBELL & LYON; aqua; 9" 4.00-6.00

2437   CANADA DRY; *14 I Ginger Ale Incorporated* under bottom; carnival glass; crown top; machine made; 10½" .... 10.00+

2438   P. CANTERBURY, GALVESTON TEXAS; blob top; 6¼"; aqua 4.00-8.00

2439   M. J. CANTRELL, YONKERS N.Y., M. J. C. monogram; 6½" or 11½"; amethyst or clear 4.00-8.00

2440   CANTRELL & COCHRANE'S; *Aerated Water, Dublin & Belfast*; 8¾"; aqua; round bottom 3.00-6.00

2441   CANTRELL & COCHRANE'S; *Aerated Waters, Dublin & Belfast* runs up and down; round bottom; 8¾"; aqua 4.00-6.00

2442   CANTRELL & COCHRANE; *Belfast & Dublin Medicated Aerated Water* around bottle; round bottom; aqua; 9¼" 6.00-10.00

2443   CANTRELL & COCHRANE; *Belfast & Dublin* around bottle; round bottom; aqua; 9" 6.00-10.00

2444   CAPITAL S.W. CO.; aqua; 6½" 4.00-6.00

2445   N. CAPPELLI, 327 ATWELLS AVE., PROVIDENCE, R.I., REGISTERED on front; blob top; 8¼"; clear 4.00-8.00

2446   CAPRONI BROS. CO., PROV., R.I., REGISTERED written inside of shield; blob top; 9¼"; clear 4.00-8.00

2447   CARBONATING APPARATUS COMPANY, BUFFALO, N.Y. REG.; marble inside bottle; clear 8.00-12.00

2448   CARDOVA BOTTLING WORKS; aqua; 6¾" 6.00-8.00

2449   M. CARNEY & CO., LAWRENCE, MASS., with MC & Co. mono. all inside of slug plate circle; blob top; 9¼"; clear............ 4.00-8.00

2450   E. CARRE, MOBILE, ALA; 7¼"; aqua 6.00-8.00

2451   OWEN CASEY EAGLE SODA WORKS on front; *Sac. City* on back; blob top; 7¼"; aqua blue 4.00-8.00

2452   HUGH CASEY EAGLE SODA WORKS, 51 K ST., SAC., CAL.; 7¼"; aqua........ 4.00-6.00

2453   OWEN CASEY EAGLE SODA WORKS; 7¼"; dark blue 8.00-12.00

2454   CASWELL & HAZARD & CO., NEW YORK, GINGER ALE in vertical line; round bottom; blob top; 9"; aqua................ 8.00-12.00

2455   C. B. SODA; *Quality Coca Cola Bottling Co.* on back; aqua; machine made; *St. Louis* on bottom; 8" 2.00-4.00

2456   C.C., PORTLAND, ORG., T.M., REG., T.B.N.T.B.S.; 7½"; amber 6.00-10.00

2457   C. C. S. & M. CO., 1118 TOLL 26 ROYAL ST., NEW ORLEANS; crown top; 8"; aqua 4.00-6.00

2458   C.C.S. & M.F.; aqua; 8" 6.00-8.00

2459   CELERY COLA; *C* under bottom; amber; 7½" 4.00-6.00

2460   CELERY COLA; clear or amethyst; 7½" 2.00-4.00

2461   CENTRAL CITY BOTTLING CO.; clear or amethyst; 7¾" 2.00-4.00

2462   CENTRAL CITY BOTTLING CO.; on back *Bottle Not To Be Sold*; clear or amethyst; 7¾"; (note misspelling)................... 8.00+

2463   CENTRAL CITY BOTTLING CO.; (note misspelled *Selma*); *Bottle Not To Be Sold* on back; 7¾"; clear 10.00-20.00

2464   CHADSEY & BRO.; 2" hollow letters, N.Y.; blob top; graphite pontil; 7½"; cobalt 25.00-40.00

2465   CHCRO-COLA; *Savannah, Ga.* on back; aqua; 7½" 3.00-6.00

2466   CHECOTAH BOTTLING WORKS, CHECOTAH I.T.; 7¼"; light blue.. 8.00-12.00

2467   CHERO COLA BOTT. CO.; raised square X pattern; *Tyler, Texas*; aqua; 7⅝".... 1.00-2.00

2468   CHICAGO BOTTLING CO.; *Root* on bottom; aqua; 7"................................ 4.00-8.00

2469   CHRISTIAN SCHLEPEGRELL & CO.; eight panels; ground pontil; blue; 8¼" ... 35.00-50.00

2470   THE CINCINNATI on shoulder; under it in horseshoe letters SODA WATER & GINGER ALE CO. in center; aqua 8.00-10.00

2471   THE CITY BOTTLING CO. on label; marble in center of neck; aqua; 7¼" 6.00-8.00

2472 2474 2476 2477 2479 2480 2485

2486 2488 2489 2491 2492 2493 2495 2498

2504 2512 2513 2514 2515 2516 2518

2472 CITY BOTTLING WORKS, CLEVELAND, OHIO; aqua; 7" 8.00-10.00

2473 CITY BOTTLING WORK, DETROIT, MICH.; in back *G. Norris & Co.; A.&D.H.G.* on base; blob top; 7¾"; blue............. 10.00-20.00

2474 CITY ICE & BOTTLING WORKS; aqua; 7½" 4.00-6.00

2475 C & K in hollow letters; EAGLE SODA WORK, SAC. CITY; blob top; 7"; cobalt ... 20.00-40.00

2476 C. CLARK; ground pontil; green; 7½" 20.00-25.00

2477 CHARLES CLARK; ground pontil; green; 7¾" 20.00-25.00

2478 CLEBURNE BOTTLING WORK; *Cleburne, Tex.*; paneled trunk; 7¼"; wire "pop" stopper 4.00-8.00

2479 CLINTON BOTTLING WORKS; aqua; 8" 6.00-8.00

2480 CLYSNIC under bottom; green; 7½". 2.00-4.00

2481 G. B. COATES, G.B.C. monogram, LYNN, MASS. in a slug plate; 8½"; clear 2.00-4.00

2482 M.H. COBE & CO. BOTTLERS, BOSTON in large letters on front; clear; 8⅛".... 4.00-6.00

2483 COCA COLA bottle, (Christmas Coke); *Patd. Dec. 25. 1923, Zanesville, Ohio* on bottom; ABM; crown top; 7⅝"; aqua 4.00-8.00

2484 COCA COLA CO., SEATTLE, WASH.; 8½"; clear or aqua.................... 4.00-6.00

2485 COCA COLA IDEAL BRAIN TONIC SUMMER & WINTERS BEVERAGE FOR HEADACHE AND EXHAUSTION all on label; 9½"; clear......................... 25.00+

2486 COCA COLA, TOLEDO, OHIO; 7"; amber 8.00-15.00

2487 COCA COLA BOTTLING WORKS, TOPEKA, KAN.; 6"; aqua 4.00-8.00

2488 COCA COLA, BUFFALO, N.Y.; clear or amethyst; 7¾" 6.00-8.00

2489 DAYTONA COCA COLA BOTTLING CO.; clear or amethyst; 8½" 6.00-10.00

2490 COCA COLA; *Wilmington N.C.* around bottom of bottle; under it small letters *D.O.C. 173*; aqua; 7¼"; clear 2.00-4.00

2491 COCA COLA MACON GA.; *Property of the Coca Cola Bottling Co* on back; aqua; 7¾" 4.00-6.00

2492 COCA COLA BOTTLING CO., ROME, GA; *Trade Mark Reg.* on back; *This Bottle Not To Be Sold* on base; clear; 7½" 4.00-6.00

2493 COCA COLA MACON (reverse N), GA; aqua; 7"....................................... 8.00-15.00

2494 same as above with different towns in U.S.A. 2.00-4.00

2495 COCA COLA in center of bottle; under it *Trade Mark Registered*; around bottom of bottle *Waycross, Ga.*; on back, in small letters, *O.B.Co.*; aqua; clear; 7¼" 2.00-4.00

2496 same as above with different town in U.S.A. 2.00-4.00

2497 COCA COLA BOTTLING WORK; *6¼ Flu ozs* on lower trunk; also in center of shoulder; clear or aqua; 7¼" or various sizes 2.00-4.00

2498 also in amber; vertical arrow, under it the name of different towns; some have only *Coca Cola* 4.00-15.00

2499 also machine made 4.00-8.00

2500 COCA COLA on crown top; 7¼"; amber; under the bottom *S B & G CO. #2*; diamond shape label 4.00-6.00

2501 COCA COLA, name on shoulder in center, also on trunk; 7¾"; aqua, clear.......... 2.00-4.00

2502 COCA COLA BOTTLING CO, *Charleston, S.C.* on front of shoulder; other side *Trade Mark Registered*; under the bottle *Root*; aqua or clear; 7¼"....................................... 2.00-4.00

2503 COCA COLA (not in script) in center; clear or aqua; 8½" 4.00-6.00

2504 COCA COLA; around bottom base *Trade Mark Registered*; around shoulder *Portland, Oregon, this bottle never sold*; amber; 7½" ... 3.00-6.00

2505 COCA COLA in ½ circle; under it *Berlin, N.H.*; slim bottle; green; around bottom *Contents 7 fl. oz.*; 8¾"; machine made 2.00-4.00

2506 PROPERTY OF COCA COLA BOTTLING CO. on small embossed bottle; 7¾"; aqua; four square panels; six panels above shoulder.... 2.00-4.00

2507 PROPERTY OF COCA COLA; six stars on shoulder; *Tyler, Texas* on bottom; square; aqua; 7¾"....................................... 3.00-4.00

2508 COCA COLA on two sides of sample bottle; *Clear Soda Water*; 2½" 1.00-2.00

2509 COCA COLA BOTTLING CO.; *Property of Waco, Drink Delicious Bludwine For Your Health Sake*; sunken middle; aqua; *7 flu. ozs.*; 7½"....................................... 2.00-4.00

2510 COCA COLA, some bottled in pottery and pop bottles or Hutchinson with diamond shape labels in 1900's 7.00-15.00

2511 COCA COLA BOTTLING CO, *Lakeland, Fla.* in a circle; above it in script, *Indian Rock Ginger Ale*; on bottom panel, *7 fluid oz*; ten pin type; about 1908; aqua; 8½" 3.00-6.00

2512 COCA COLA; 6"; amber......... 8.00-15.00

2513 COCA COLA; on back shoulder *Trade Mark Registered*; aqua; 3¾" round; *root* on bottom; semi-round bottom 5.00-8.00

2514 COCA COLA; clear or amethyst; 7¾"; semi-round bottom 4.00-6.00

2515 COCA COLA; amber; 6"; *S.B.&G. CO.* on bottom 6.00-15.00

2516 COCA COLA; aqua; 7"............ 4.00-8.00

2517 COCA MARIANI, PARIS FRANCE; 8½"; green..................... 4.00-8.00

2518 COCHRAN & CO.; tear drop shape; *Belfast* on back; 9" 6.00-10.00

2519 COD SODA, embossing: STAR BRAND SUPER STRONG with star at base on front; marble closure; 9¼"; aqua......... 4.00-8.00

2520	2522	2524	2528	2529	2530	2531

2534	2536	2538	2543	2544	2547

2550	2552	2553	2554	2563	2565	2569

2520 L. COHEN NEW YORK; *This Bottle is Reg. Not To Be Sold* on back; *2* under bottom; aqua; 7½" 4.00-6.00

2521 COLE'S SODA by N. J. COLE, SO. ACTON, MASS.; 7"; clear or amber 8.00-10.00

2522 COMANCHE BOTTLING WORKS; aqua; 6¾" .... 10.00+

2523 COMSTOCK COVE & CO., 139 FRIEND ST., BOSTON on front; *C.C. & CO.* in large letters on back; blob top; 7"; aqua 6.00-10.00

2524 F.A. CONANT., 252 GIROD ST. N.O.; graphite pontil; blob top; 7¼"; olive 30.00-45.00

2525 CONCORD BOTTLING CO., CONCORD, N.H.; 6½"; aqua 8.00-10.00

2526 JAS. CONDON., WALDEN, N.Y., C. J. monogram; *Cont. 7 oz.*; 6¾"; amethyst or clear 4.00-8.00

2527 CONKLIN BOTTLING WORK, PEEKSKILL, N.Y. on front in arched shape slug plate; blob top; 7⅛"; aqua 6.00-8.00

2528 CONNOR & McQUAIDE; aqua; 8"; on back *C & S* 4.00-8.00

2529 CONNOR & MCQUAIDE; aqua; 6½" 4.00-6.00

2530 CONSUMERS; *C* under bottom; aqua; 7¾" 2.00-6.00

2531 CONSUMERS B.B. CO.; amber; 9" .. 3.00-6.00

2532 H. CORTES, GALVESTON, TEXAS; 7"; clear 4.00-8.00

2533 H. CORTES & BRO., TEXAS BOTTLING WORK, GALVESTON, TEXAS; in back *Belfast Ginger Ale & Soda Water*; blob top; aqua 10.00-12.00

2534 H. CORTES & CO. PROP; *Texas Bottling Works, Galveston, Texas; A & D.H.C.* around base; Hutchinson; 8"; aqua......... 4.00-8.00

2535 COSCROUL JAMES; *Charleston, S.C.* in a circle; in center of circle *& Son*; in back *this bottle not to be sold*; aqua; 8¼" 2.00-4.00

2536 J. COSGROVE; aqua; 7" 4.00-6.00

2537 COTTAN & MAGG (C & M mono.), BOSTON, MASS on front; 7½"; aqua 4.00-6.00

2538 JOHN COTTER; aqua; 7¾"........ 4.00-6.00

2539 COTTLE POST & CO., PORTLAND; blob top; 7½"; blue.................... 15.00-25.00

2540 COTTLE POST & CO.; in center an eagle; under it, PORTLAND, ORG.; blob top; 7¼"; green......................... 10.00-20.00

2541 JOHN COYLE, NEWBURGH, N.Y. inside of circular slug plate on front; THIS BOTTLE NOT TO BE SOLD also on front; blob top; 9¼"; clear 4.00-8.00

2542 C.R. CRAMER & JACKY; in a dome line under it, PHILLIPSBURG, MON.; 6¾"; aqua 4.00-8.00

2543 W.A. CRAWLEY, CLARKSDALE, MISS.; 7½"; clear 8.00-10.00

2544 C.W. CRELL & CO.; ground pontil; blue green; 7".................... 25.00-35.00

2545 M. CRONAN, 230 K ST., SACRAMENTO on front; *Sac. Soda Works* on bottom; 6¾"; green aqua.......................... 6.00-10.00

2546 M. CRONAN, 230 K ST., SACRAMENTO, SODA WORKS; blob top; 6½"; aqua . 4.00-6.00

2547 CROWN BOTTLING & MFG. CO.; aqua; 6½" 6.00-8.00

2548 CROWN BOTTLING & MFG. CO., ARDMORE I.T., with crown in center; aqua..... 6.00-12.00

2549 CROWN BOTTLING WORKS, DELAWARE O. in a circle; 6¾"; light green 8.00-10.00

2550 THE CROWN CORK & SEAL CO. BALTIMORE; crown top; sample; clear; 3¾" .... 10.00+

2551 CRYSTAL BOTTLING CO., CHARLESTON, W. VA.; panel base; 7¼"; aqua 4.00-10.00

2552 CRYSTAL BOTTLING WORKS; *C.B.W.* under bottom; aqua; 7½" 3.00-6.00

2553 CRYSTAL BOTTLING WORKS; *C.B.W* under bottom; aqua; 7¾" 2.00-6.00

2554 CRYSTAL SODA WORKS, HONOLULU, H.I.; Hutchinson; 7"; aqua 4.00-8.00

2555 CRYSTAL SODA WORKS, HONOLULU, H.I.; 6¾"; aqua 15.00-30.00

2556 CRYSTAL SODA WORKS CO., S. F.; 7¼"; aqua or light green................ 4.00-8.00

2557 CRYSTAL SPRING BOTTLING CO., BARNET, VT.; clear or amber; 7¼" 4.00-6.00

2558 CRYSTAL (*Soda* in center) WATER CO.; in back, *Pat. Nov. 12-1872, Taylors U.S.P.T.*; blob top; 7½"; blue 4.00-8.00

2559 A.W. CUDWORTH & CO., S.F.; 7¼"; aqua 4.00-6.00

2560 CULVER HOUSE PURE NATURAL LEMONADE SPECIALITY; in back *Registered Trade Mark* with house in center; 9"; golden amber .... 25.00+

2561 CUNNINGHAM & CO., PHILA.; blob top; 7"; aqua.......................... 4.00-8.00

2562 T. & J. CUNNINGHAM., PHILA.; blob top; 7"; green......................... 15.00-30.00

2563 JOHN CUNEO; *269* under bottom; aqua; 9" 4.00-6.00

2564 DR. DADIRRIANS ZOOLAK vertical around neck on two lines; 7¼"; aqua 4.00-6.00

2565 M.D'AGASTINO; aqua; *1223* under bottom; 7¼".......................... 4.00-6.00

2566 DANNENBURG BROS., C.C. T.M.R., in center GOLDSBORO, N.C.; 7¾"; clear or aqua 8.00-10.00

2567 E. DANNENBURG, AUTHORIZED BOTTLER of C.C. WILSON-GOLDSBORO, N.C., U.S.A.; in a circle on the base T.B.N.T.B.S.; 8"; clear or amber.................. 8.00-15.00

2568 C. DAVIS., PHOENIXVILLE in slug plate; squat type; graphite pontil; 7"; green 20.00-45.00

2569 DAVIS & WORCESTER; *E.HE CO. No. 3* on base; green aqua; 6½" 4.00-6.00

2571   2573   2574   2575   2577   2580   2586   2588

2594   2595   2596   2597   2599   2601   2603   2608

2609   2610   2611   2612   2614   2615   2618   2619

2570 J. DAY & CO. in two lines; blob top; 7¾"; aqua
.... 8.00-12.00

2571 DEACON BROWN MFG. CO., MONTGOMERY, ALA.; on base T.BN.T.B.S.; 8¾"; aqua
.... 2.00-4.00

2572 DEAMER in hollow letters; *Glass Valley* in back; *W.E.D.* in hollow letters; blob top; 7¼"; aqua 3.00-6.00

2573 H. E. DEAN., GREAT BEND, KANS.; Hutchinson; 7"; clear or amber 4.00-8.00

2574 W. DEAN; small kick-up pontil; blue green; 6½"
.... 15.00-25.00

2575 WM. DEAN; 7¾"; pale blue 8.00-12.00

2576 DEARBORN, 83 3rd AVE., N.Y.; blob top; 7"; green 25.00-40.00

2577 DEIS & TIBBALS, LIMA, OHIO; Hutchinson; 7"; aqua 4.00-6.00

2578 E. T. DELANEY & CO. in center; BOTTLERS PLATTSBURG, N.Y.; 7"; aqua.... 8.00-15.00

2579 H. DELMEYER; in center, 1861 BROOKLYN; in back *XX*; in hollow letters, *Porter*; squat bottle; blob top; 6½"; aqua 10.00-15.00

2580 DELTA MF'G. CO.; *Delta* in a triangle under bottom; aqua; 7¼"....................... 6.00-8.00

2581 DeMOTT'S CELEBRATED SODA or MINERAL WATER; in back, *Hudson County, N.J.*; 7¼"; cobalt.................... 25.00+

2582 G.V. DeMOTT'S; graphite pontil; 7½"; green .... 25.00+

2583 DeMOTT'S PORTER & ALE; squat type; blob top; 6½"; green 20.00-35.00

2584 H. DENHALTER, SALT LAKE CITY, UT. in four lines; Hutchinson; 6½"; aqua ..... 25.00+

2585 H. DENHALTER & SONS in a dome-shaped line; in center SALT; under it, SALT LAKE CITY, UT.; 7"; aqua 4.00-10.00

2586 D.G.W. script type letters; blob top; 7¼"; aqua 8.00-10.00

2587 DIAMOND SODA WORK CO., S.F., TRADE MARK; *D* in diamond; Hutchinson; 6"; aqua 8.00-10.00

2588 DIEHL & DANBURY, MEMPHIS, TENN.; *D* under bottom; *D* in back on shoulder; aqua; 6½"
.... 6.00-8.00

2589 JOHN DIETZE, WINONA, MINN. on front inside of slug plate; crown top; 8⅛"; aqua
.... 2.00-4.00

2590 J. DINETS, SUPERIOR SODA WATER, CHICAGO in panel; six panels; graphite pontil; 8"; blue 25.00-40.00

2591 DISTILLED & AERATED WATER CO., MITCHELL, S.D.; 3½"; aqua 10.00-20.00

2592 DISTILLED SODA WATER CO. OF ALASKA; 7½"; aqua 6.00-12.00

2593 DISTILLED SODA WATER OF ALASKA in a sunken panel; ten-sided; Hutchinson; 7¼"; aqua
.... 10.00-20.00

2594 DIXIE CARBONATING CO.; thick bottom; clear or amethyst; 9".............. 4.00-6.00

2595 DIXIE CARBONATING CO.; back shoulder *Trade Mark, Augusta, Ga.*; 8"; clear or amethyst.................... 4.00-6.00

2596 DIXIE CARBONATING CO.; aqua; 8"
.... 4.00-6.00

2597 HENRY DOWNES; aqua; 7½"; on back *The City Bottling Works of New York*..... 4.00-6.00

2598 DOOLY, CORDELE, GA.; panel base; 7"; clear or amber...................... 7.00-10.00

2599 DR. PEPPER, label; aqua; 7" 2.00-4.00

2600 DR. PEPPER KING OF BEVERAGE; *Reg. Dallas Bottling Co., Dallas, Tx.*; amethyst; 8¼"
.... 3.00-5.00

2601 DR. PEPPER in script; under it *King of Beverages*; on shoulder *Registered*; on base *Artesian Mfg. & Bot. Co., Waco, Tex.*; clear, amethyst
.... 4.00-6.00

2602 D.S. & CO., SAN FRANCISCO; blob top; 7"; cobalt blue 10.00-15.00

2603 E. DUFFY & SON; 7"; green 30.00-40.00

2604 FRANCIS DUSCH, T.B.N.T.B.S., 1866; blob top; 7¼"; blue.................. 10.00-15.00

2605 DUTCHESS BRAND BEVERAGES MADE IN VERBANK VILLAGE, 7 OZ. on front; 8½"; amethyst.................... 2.00-4.00

2606 JAMES N. DYER, CATSKILL, N.Y.; *This Bottle Not To Be Sold*; 6½"; aqua 4.00-10.00

2607 DYOTTVILLE GLASS WORKS, PHILA.; squat type; graphite pontil; 6¼"; green
.... 30.00-60.00

2608 Eagle symbol in a circle; marble closure; 8"; aqua.................... 8.00-10.00

2609 WM EAGLE, N.Y. PREMIUM SODA WATER; paneled; blob top; graphite pontil; 7¼"; cobalt.................... 70.00-90.00

2610 W. EAGLE, CANAL ST., N.Y.; reverse side, *Phila. Porter*; blob top; squat type; 6¾"; dark green.................... 35.00-55.00

2611 EAGLE BOTTLING WORKS; *D* under bottom; clear; 7¾".................... 4.00-6.00

2612 EAGLE BOTTLING WORKS, BIRMINGHAM, ALA.; eagle symbol; crown top; 8"; aqua 6.00-8.00

2613 ALEX EASTON, FAIRFIELD, IOWA in a circle; Hutchinson; 6½"; aqua 4.00-6.00

2614 E.B. CO., EVANSVILLE, IND.; *B* under bottom; panels around bottle; aqua; 7" 4.00-6.00

2615 G. EBBERWEIN, *Savannah, Geo.* on front; Ginger Ale vertical on back; short neck; 7¾"; amber 18.00-20.00

2616 EEL RIVER VALEY SODA WORKS in center; SPRINGVILLE, CAL.; 7"; aqua
.... 6.00-8.00

2617 EL DORADO; tapered top; 7¼"; aqua
.... 4.00-10.00

2618 ELECTRIC BOTTLING WORKS, WEST POINT, MISS.; Hutchinson; 6¾"; aqua
.... 4.00-8.00

2619 ELECTRO BRAND; *Jackson Tenn* on back; *R.O. Co.* under bottom........... 3.00-6.00

| 2620 | 2621 | 2622 | 2627 | 2629 | 2630 | 2631 | 2633 |

| 2635 | 2638 | 2640 | 2641 | 2642 | 2645 | 2650 |

| 2653 | 2654 | 2656 | 2660 | 2663 | 2664 | 2665 | 2668 |

2620 ELEPHANT BOTTLING COMPANY; *D.O.C. Co.* on base; *D* under bottom; aqua; 8″ 4.00-6.00

2621 ELEPHANT BOTTLING CO.; *D* under bottom; aqua; 7¾″ 4.00-6.00

2622 ELEPHANT STEAM BOTTLING WORKS; *D* under bottom; 6¼″ 4.00-8.00

2623 ELLIOTT, TRENTON, N.J.; blob top; 7¼″; aqua..................... 10.00-15.00

2624 EL RENO, B. W.; 7¼″; aqua 6.00-12.00

2625 ELSBERRY BOTTLING WORKS, ELSBERRY, MO. on front in oval slug plate; ABM; crown top; 8″.................... 2.00-4.00

2626 G. L. ELWICK, LINCOLN, NEB.; light blue; 6¾″.................... 3.00-4.00

2627 EMMERLING; amber; 9½″ 2.00-4.00

2628 EMPIRE SODA WORKS, VALLEJO, CAL.; crown top; 6½″; aqua 4.00-6.00

2629 EMPSORRS in fancy script; tall blob top; panel base; 9¼″; amber 4.00-10.00

2630 F. ENGLE; big *E* in back; aqua; 7½″ 8.00-12.00

2631 ENSLEY BOTTLING WORKS, ENSLEY, ALA.; crown top; 7½″; clear or aqua 2.00-4.00

2632 ENTERPRISE BOTTLING WORKS, DAVIS & CO. PROP., LINCOLN, ILL. on panels; ten panels; 6¼″; aqua 10.00-12.00

2633 EPPS-COLA; *John C Epping, Louisville, Ky, Reg. 7 Fluid Oz.* around bottle; *E* under bottom; snap-on top; 8″; aqua............. 8.00-10.00

2634 C. ERNE'S CITY BOTTLING WORKS, 348 & 350 PIENVILLE ST. N.O., T.B.N.T.B.S.; blob top; 8¼″ 8.00-10.00

2635 JOHN M. ERTEL; *B & E* under bottom; clear; 6¾″.................... 4.00-6.00

2636 J. ESPOSITO, 812 & 814 WASHINGTON AVE., KACA KOLA; Hutchinson; 7¾″ 4.00-8.00

2637 CHARLES EUKER; reverse *T.B.N.T.B.S., 1866, Richmond, Va.;* blob top; 7″; light blue 10.00-15.00

2638 EUREKA BOTTLING WORKS, FT. SMITH, ARK.; the words STOLEN FROM are at the top.; Hutchinson; 7″; aqua 10.00-12.00

2639 STOLEN FROM EUREKA BOTTLING WORKS; 6¾″; aqua 30.00-40.00

2640 HENRY EVERS; aqua; 7½″ 8.00-12.00

2641 JAMES EVERADO, NEW YORK; clear or amethyst...................... 4.00-6.00

2642 F.A.B., in a large horseshoe symbol, with GALVESTON inside; 7½″; aqua.... 6.00-8.00

2643 M. FAIRBANKS & CO., HOWARD ST., BOSTON, MASS. on front; large *F & Co.* on back; aqua 4.00-8.00

2644 F.B.W., FAIRFIELD, IOWA; tenpin type; blob top; 6½″; aqua.................... 8.00-12.00

2645 J. A. FALSONE; clear or amethyst; 6¾″ 2.00-4.00

2646 S. H. FARNHAM in center; AMERICAN FLA., WESTERLY, R.I., vertical; 7½″; aqua 8.00-15.00

2647 J. E. FARRELL, MAIN ST., COLD SPRING on front in oval slug plate; 9⅛″; clear 3.00-6.00

2648 FEIGENSON BROS., REG. DETROIT, MICH. on front in oval slug plate; 6⅛″; aqua 4.00-8.00

2649 FEIHENSPAN P.O.N. TRADE MARK AGENCY, NEWBURGH, N.Y. in oval slug plate; crown top; 9¼″; aqua.............. 2.00-4.00

2650 H. FELLRATH, PEORIA, ILL.; reverse side, at base, *SB & Co.;* Hutchinson; 7″; aqua 4.00-6.00

2651 FERBER BROS., PHOEBUS, VA.; 7¼″; aqua 4.00-12.00

2652 E.M. FERRY, ESSEX, CONN.; blob top; 9¼″; clear 4.00-6.00

2653 C. P. FEY & CO.; 7½″; light blue ...... 40.00+

2654 S.C. FIELDS SUPERIOR SODA WATER; eight panels; ground pontil; 7¼″; cobalt 60.00-80.00

2655 B.H. FINK; *J* instead of *F;* in back *To Be Returned;* ground pontil; 7¼″; blue green .... 50.00+

2656 HENRY FINKS SONS; *Harrisburg, Pa.;* clear or amethyst; 9½″ 4.00-8.00

2657 FLEMING BROS., MEADVILLE., PA. in four lines; 6½″; aqua 4.00-10.00

2658 J.C. FOX & CO., FOX T.M., SEATTLE, WASH.; 7½″; aqua 4.00-8.00

2659 WM. FREIDMAN, CHAMPION SODA FACTORY, KEY WEST, FLA., T.B.N.T.B.S.; 6½″; clear or amber 4.00-6.00

2660 J. FURLA BOTTLING CO.; aqua; 6½″ 8.00-12.00

2661 GADSDEN; in center, BOTTLING WORKS, GADSEN, ALA.; 6¾″; clear 4.00-8.00

2662 GAFFNEY & MORGAN, AMSTERDAM, N.Y. in a circle; panel base; 7½″; aqua.... 8.00-10.00

2663 C.H. GAHRE BOTTLER, BRIDGETOWN, N.J.; aqua; 7″ 8.00-12.00

2664 GALLITZIN BOTTLING CO.; *326* under bottom; aqua 4.00-6.00

2665 GALLITZIN BOTTLING CO.; amber; 9½″ 4.00-6.00

2666 GALVESTON BREWING CO.; *Guaranteed Pure, Galveston Tex.;* aqua; 7¾″; round 2.00-4.00

2667 HENRY GARDENER TRADE MARK, WEST BROMWISH; 7½″; emerald green ... 4.00-8.00

2668 GEO. GEMENDEN, *Savannah Ga.* on front; Eagle, Shield and Flag on back; improved pontil; 7¼″; green; blob top 35.00-85.00

2669 WILLIAM GENAUST, WILMINGTON, N.C. in a circle; blob top; reverse side T.B.N.T.B.S.; 9¼″; aqua 4.00-10.00

2670 GEYSER SODA; in back *Natural Mineral Water, From Litton Springs, Sonoma Co. Calif.;* blob top; 7″; aqua 10.00-20.00

2671 GHIRARD ELLIS BRANCH, OAKLAND, three lines on front; blob top; 7¾″; blue 10.00-15.00

2673   2678   2679   2681   2683   2685   2686   2690

2693   2696   2697   2698   2700   2706   2712   2714

2717   2719   2720   2726

2672   CHAS. GIBBONS, PHILAD., in a horseshoe shape; reverse a star; long neck; blob top; 8″; amber 20.00-40.00

2673   T.W. GILLETT, NEW HAVEN; eight panels; graphite pontil; 7½″; blue............ 75.00+

2674   GLOBE BOTTLING WORKS; *Savannah, Ga.,* in a circle in center on bottom; in back *This Bottle Is Never Sold;* clear; 8½″........ 3.00-6.00

2675   G.M.S. CO.; crown in center, REGISTERED; ALLIANCE, OHIO; panel base; 7⅜″; aqua 6.00-8.00

2676   GOLDEN GATE BOTTLING WORK in a horseshoe; under it SAN FRANCISCO; 7¾″ 8.00-10.00

2677   GOLDEN WEST S. & E. SODA WORKS, SAN JOSE, CAL.; four-piece mold; 8⅜″; aqua green 4.00-6.00

2678   JOHN GRAF, MILWAUKEE; panel base; reverse *T.B.N.T.B.S.;* 8½″; blue..... 7.00-10.00

2679 JOHN GRAF; on other panels *This bottle never sold, Please Return, When Empty, To The Owner, Cor. 17th & Greenfield Ave, Trade Mark The Best What Gives* 10.00-30.00

2680 JOHN GRAF, MILWAUKEE, WIS. on front; reverse *T.B.N.T.B.S., The Best What Gives* trade mark; eight panels on base; 6⅜"; aqua green 4.00-8.00

2681 GRAMERCY BOTTLING WORKS, GRAMERCY, LA.; Hutchinson; 7½"; clear or aqua 4.00-8.00

2682 GRANT & UPTON in a horseshoe shape; under it, COLUMBUS, OHIO; 6½"; aqua .. 8.00-12.00

2683 J & J GRANTHAM; star under bottom; *Kiner Bros Ltd* on back; green; 8" 15.00-20.00

2684 JOHN GRANZ, CROTON FALLS, N.Y. on front; *T.B.N.T.B.S.* on reverse side; blob top; 7½"; aqua 4.00-8.00

2685 GRAPE PRODUCTS CO. WALKERS on bottom; clear or amethyst; 11" 2.00-4.00

2686 GRATTAN & CO. LTD.; 9"; aqua ... 6.00-8.00

2687 GREAT BEAR SPRINGS, FULTON, N.Y.; round bottom; 12"; aqua 10.00-20.00

2688 GREENWOOD BOTTLING & SUPPLY CO., GREENWOOD, S.C. in a circle; crown top; 7½"; aqua...................................... 6.00-8.00

2689 GEO. GRUBEL, KANSAS CITY, KANSAS in three lines; Hutchinson type; 6¾"; aqua 10.00-20.00

2690 G.T.B. under bottom; marble in center; aqua; 7¾"...................................... 3.00-6.00

2691 GUYETTE & COMPANY, DETROIT, MICH.; REGISTERED in center; *G* under bottom; 6¾"; cobalt...................................... 30.00-50.00

2692 H in hollow letter, also SAC. with hollow P; 7"; clear or aqua...................... 4.00-8.00

2693 THE PROPERTY OF THE HAAS CO in half circle in center; monogram *THCo,* on each side *Trade Mark;* under circle *Registered Chicago;* under bottom monogram *THCo;* aqua; on back *This Bottle is Never Sold;* 7"........ 4.00-8.00

2694 HABENICHT BOTTLING WORKS; *Columbia, S.C.* in sunken panel; aqua; 9" 4.00-6.00

2695 HABENICHT; next line *Bottling Work; Columbia, S.C.* in round sunken circle; 9½"; blob top; amber 4.00-6.00

2696 HAIGHT & O BRIEN; graphite pontil; aqua; 7½"...................................... 20.00-30.00

2697 H. HALL, HILLTOWN; *Ireland & New York* at base in three lines; in center a hand in shield; under it *Trade Mark;* tapered top; semi-round; 9"; aqua...................................... 8.00-10.00

2698 HANIGAN BROS; *Denver, Colo.* on back; aqua; *H.B.* on bottom; 7" 4.00-6.00

2699 HANIGAN BROS.; *Denver, Colo.* vertical letters; Hutchinson; 6½"; clear or amethyst 4.00-8.00

2700 HANNE BROTHERS; *This Bottle Not To Be Sold* in back; clear; 7½".............. 6.00-8.00

2701 HANSSEN BROS., GRASS VALLEY, CAL.; in center G.W.B.; 7¼"; aqua......... 6.00-8.00

2702 C. J. HARGAN & CO., MEMPHIS, TENN.; blob top; 6¾"; aqua............. 10.00-15.00

2703 P. HARRINGTON, MANCHESTER, N.H., P.H. monogram all inside slug plate; blob top; 9¼"; clear....................... 3.00-6.00

2704 J. HARRISON; in center 197 FULTON, N.Y.; reverse, *Phila. XXX Porter & Ale;* squat type; 6½"; green 20.00-30.00

2705 C. HARTMAN, CLEVELAND, O; light blue and blue green................... 8.00-12.00

2706 F. HARVEY & CO.; *This Bottle Not To Be Sold* on back; amber; 8½".............. 4.00-6.00

2707 J. HARVEY & CO. in hollow letters; *65½ Canal St., Providence, R. I.;* graphite pontil; tapered top; 7¾"; green..................... 35.00+

2708 J. HARVEY & CO. in hollow letters; *65½ Central St., Providence, R.I.;* blob top; graphite pontil; 7½"; green..................... 20.00-40.00

2709 J. & J.W. HARVEY, NORWICH, CONN.; reverse hollow letter *H;* graphite pontil; blob top; 7¾"; green..................... 20.00-40.00

2710 HARVEY & BRO. in a dome shape; under it HACKETTSTOWN, N.J.; in back, hollow letter *H;* 7"; green................... 20.00-35.00

2711 HAWAIIAN SODA WORKS, HONOLULU, T.H.; 7½"; aqua................. 4.00-10.00

2712 HAYES BROS.; *This Bottle Never Sold* in back; 7"........................... 4.00-6.00

2713 J.S. HAZARD, WESTERLY, R.I.; reverse side *XX* in hollow letters; blob top; 7¼"; aqua 8.00-15.00

2714 H & D in raised letters 1½" tall; under this in two lines *Savannah, Geo;* squat bottle; aqua; 7"; blob top 8.00-12.00

2715 HEADMAN, PHILA., reverse F.W.H. in hollow letters; graphite pontil; 7¼"; green 30.00-60.00

2716 M.C. HEALD & CO. (M.C.H. CO) LYNN, MASS. inside of slug plate on front; crown top; 7½"; amethyst 2.00-4.00

2717 HEATLY BROS., MANGUM, O.T.; Hutchinson; 6⅜"; clear.................... 25.00+

2718 HEATLY BROS., MANGUM; *This Bottle Not To Be Sold* reverse side; 6¾"; aqua ..... 50.00+

2719 JOHN HECHT, BROOKLYN, N.Y. 1862; aqua; 7½".......................... 10.00-15.00

2720 J. J. HEINRICH & CO.; *J.J.H.* under bottom; aqua; 7¼" 4.00-8.00

2721 JOHN HEINZERLING, BALTIMORE, MD.; 7½"; aqua 6.00-8.00

2722 GEO. N. HEMBDT, MONTICELLO, N.Y., REG. on front in slug plate; 6¾"; aqua 4.00-6.00

2723 HEMPSTEAD BOTTLING WORK; *Hempstead Tx.* in a circle; amethyst; 8"; fluted bottom 2.00-4.00

2724 HENNESSY & NOLAN GINGER ALE, ALBANY, N.Y.; in panels; reverse H. & N. monogram; *1876;* blob top; 7¼"; aqua 10.00-12.00

2727

2728

2729

2733

2734

2738

2743

2750

2751

2756

2759

2762

2763

2770

2771

2772

2775

2776

2777

2778

2725 ED HENRY, NAPA, CAL.; monogram in center; 6¾''; aqua 4.00-6.00

2726 GEO HENRY; aqua; 7½''.......... 8.00-12.00

2727 F. T. HELLER; aqua; 7½''.......... 4.00-8.00

2728 HERANCOURT BRG. CO.; amber; 8¼'' 4.00-6.00

2729 J.C. HERRMANN, SHARON, PA.; Hutchinson; 9''; aqua..................... 8.00-10.00

2730 HEWLETT BROS., SALT LAKE CITY, UTAH; reverse *T.B.N.:T.B.S.*; 6½''; aqua 4.00-8.00

2731 T.E. HICKEY, PROVIDENCE, R.I.; 6¼''; aqua 4.00-8.00

2732 E. HIGGINS, OROVILLE in two lines; blob top; 7"; aqua 10.00-15.00

2733 O.G. HILLE & CO.; *w.b.* under bottom; aqua; 7" 8.00-10.00

2734 E. HINECKE; *Louisville, K.Y.,* H under bottom; 7"; aqua 8.00-10.00

2735 HIPPO SIZE SODA WATER, *Prop. Of Alamo Bottling Wks., San Antonio, Tx., Nov. 2-1926;* clear; 9½"; picture of hippopotamus . 2.00-4.00

2736 HIRE'S on bottom; old crown top; 9¾"; aqua 2.00-4.00

2737 H.L. & J. W. HARTFORD, CONN.; 6½"; amber 4.00-8.00

2738 HOBART BOTTLING WORKS; aqua; 5½" 25.00-35.00

2739 HOFFMAN BROS., CHEYENNE, W.; aqua .... 35.00+

2740 LAWRENCE L. HOLDEN, FALL RIVER, MASS. written at an angle; fancy; blob top; 9¼"; clear 4.00-8.00

2741 same as above except amber; 8½" ... 4.00-8.00

2742 HOLDENVILLE BOTTLING WORKS; 7½"; aqua 8.00-15.00

2743 HOLIHAN BROS; clear or amethyst; 9¼" 4.00-6.00

2744 HOLLAND RINK BOTTLING WORKS, BUTTE, MONT. in a sunken panel; Hutchinson; 6½"; aqua 10.00-20.00

2745 HOLLAND RINK, BUTTE, MONT.; in center, BOTTLING WORKS; 6¼"; aqua... 8.00-10.00

2746 HOME BREWING CO., RICHMOND, VA. (1895); 6¾"; aqua 8.00-12.00

2747 R. A. HORLOCK CO., NAVASOTA, TEXAS; 8¼"; clear or amber 4.00-8.00

2748 HOUCK & DIETER CO., DOUGLAS, ARIZ.; Hutchinson; 6"; aqua 10.00-15.00

2749 HOUCK & DIETER in one of the six cathedral panels; *Company* in one; *El Paso* in another; *Texas* in another; two blank panels; under bottle *H&D Co.*; applied crown top; 8"; aqua 5.00-7.00

2750 HOUCK & DIETER; *H & D Co.* on bottom; aqua; 8" 4.00-10.00

2751 HOUPPERT & WORCESTER; aqua; 6½"; *H. & W.* under bottom 4.00-6.00

2752 L. HOUSE & SONS, SYRACUSE, N.Y.; 7"; aqua 4.00-8.00

2753 J.F. HOWARD; *Haverhill, Mass.* around the lower part of the trunk; round; fluted around; clear; 7¼" 1.00-2.00

2754 JOHN HOWELL; hollow letters under it, BUFFALO, N.J.; blob top; 7"; aqua 8.00-15.00

2755 HOXSIE, ALBANY; *XOSI* in back; blob top; 6½"; aqua 6.00-10.00

2756 HULSHIZER & CO., PREMIUM all on panels; graphite pontil; 8½"; green 60.00-80.00

2757 HUNT & CO, *Trade Mark,* in two lines; *Hunt & Co* in script inside a square below; word *Hinckley* below; in back near base, *Dan Hylands Ld Sole Marke, Barnsley;* 2½" at base to pinch shoulder; neck tapers to applied top; also in neck a pinch; inside of neck a marble; 8¾"; aqua 6.00-8.00

2758 same as above except no pinch in neck; 6½"; 1¾" at base; (Japan); light green 6.00-8.00

2759 HUNTINGTON; machine made; 7½"; amber 6.00-10.00

2760 HUTCHINSON SODA BOTTLING WORKS, HUTCHINSON, MINN.; 7"; aqua .. 4.00-8.00

2761 E.L. HUSTING, MILWAUKEE, WIS. vertical on side; 6½"; aqua 4.00-6.00

2762 HYDE PARK, ST. LOUIS; crown top; 9¾"; amber 2.00-4.00

2763 HYGEIA BOTTLING WORKS; aqua; 6¾" 4.00-6.00

2764 HYGEIA SODA WORKS, KAHULUI, H. in three lines; star under bottom; 7¼" ... 25.00+

2765 HYGENIC DISTILLED WATER CO.; in horseshoe shape lines under it, BROOKLYN, & FAR ROCKAWAY L.I.; in back *H.D.W. Co.,* interlocking hollow letters; 7"; aqua.. 8.00-12.00

2766 IMPERIAL BOTTLING WORKS, PORTLAND, OREGON; 7¾"; aqua 6.00-12.00

2767 INGALL'S BROS., PORTLAND, ME.; squat type; 7"; green 10.00-20.00

2768 INGALL'S BROS., PORTLAND, ME., BELFAST ALE, vertical lines; round bottom; 8¼"; aqua 6.00-8.00

2769 ITALIAN SODA WATER MANUFACTOR, SAN FRANCISCO, in a horizontal line; reverse *Union Glass Works, Phila;* graphite pontil; 7½"; emerald green 40.00-80.00

2770 IRON CITY; *11* on bottom; *96* on base; aqua; 6½" 4.00-6.00

2771 IUKA; *C* in center of diamond shape under bottom; clear or amethyst; 6½" 8.00-15.00

2772 JACKSON BOTTLING WORKS, JACKSON, TENN.; 8"; aqua 4.00-6.00

2773 J. L. JACOBS, CAIRO, N.Y. in a round sunken panel; 7"; green 8.00-10.00

2774 J.L. JACOBS, CAIRO, N.Y.; reverse side, *This Bottle Not To Be Sold;* blob top; 7¾" 8.00-10.00

2775 THE JAMES BOTTLING CO.; aqua; 6¾" 6.00-8.00

2776 JEFFERSON BOTTLING WORKS, JEFFERSON, TEXAS; 7½"; aqua 6.00-8.00

2777 F.W. JESSEN BOTTLING WORKS; amber; 9½" 3.00-6.00

2778 J.L. & C. LDC 1449 under bottom; aqua; 9½" 2.00-4.00

2779 JOHNSON & BRO., DELTA, PA.; 6¾"; olive 20.00-30.00

161

| 2780 | 2783 | 2784 | 2786 | 2787 | 2790 | 2791 | 2794 |

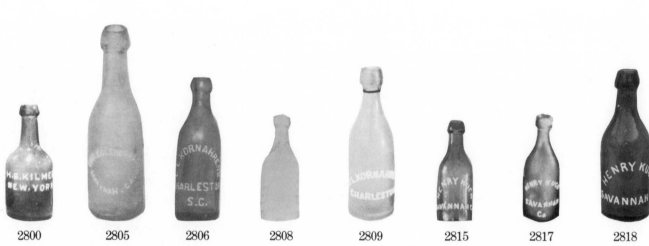

| 2800 | 2805 | 2806 | 2808 | 2809 | 2815 | 2817 | 2818 |

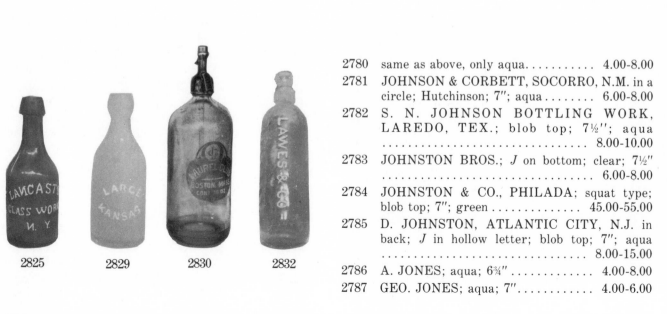

| 2825 | 2829 | 2830 | 2832 |

2780   same as above, only aqua.......... 4.00-8.00

2781   JOHNSON & CORBETT, SOCORRO, N.M. in a circle; Hutchinson; 7″; aqua........ 6.00-8.00

2782   S. N. JOHNSON BOTTLING WORK, LAREDO, TEX.; blob top; 7½″; aqua 8.00-10.00

2783   JOHNSTON BROS.; *J* on bottom; clear; 7½″ 6.00-8.00

2784   JOHNSTON & CO., PHILADA; squat type; blob top; 7″; green 45.00-55.00

2785   D. JOHNSTON, ATLANTIC CITY, N.J. in back; *J* in hollow letter; blob top; 7″; aqua 8.00-15.00

2786   A. JONES; aqua; 6¾″ 4.00-8.00

2787   GEO. JONES; aqua; 7″............ 4.00-6.00

2788 GEO. JONES, FONDA, N.Y. on front; G-J Co. monogram on back; 7¼"; clear 4.00-8.00

2789 DANIEL KAISER, KEOKUK, IOWA, P.A. & CO. in four lines; 7½"; aqua 10.00-20.00

2790 G. KAMMERER; *A.G.W.L.* on base; aqua; 7" 4.00-8.00

2791 KANTER BROS; aqua; 6½"....... 6.00-8.00

2792 NICK KARL, GLOVERSVILLE, N.Y. on front in oval slug plate; *This Bottle Not To Be Sold* on back; 9¼"; aqua 4.00-8.00

2793 JOHN KARSCH & SONS, EVANSVILLE, IND.; Hutchinson; 6½"; aqua 4.00-8.00

2794 K.B. LD 7-122-1 under bottom; aqua; 7½" 2.00-4.00

2795 KEENAN MFG. CO., BUTTE, MT. in a circle; ten panels at base; Hutchinson; 7¼"; aqua 5.00-10.00

2796 P. KELLETT, NEWARK, N.J.; squat type; graphite pontil; 6¾"; green 25.00-35.00

2797 P. KELLETT, NEWARK, N.J.; reverse *K, 1857*; 7½"; green 20.00-30.00

2798 KERYER & CO., EST. 1851, BELFAST in center; in center of *Trade Mark* a five-leaved flower; round bottom; aqua; tapered top; 9½" 8.00-12.00

2799 KIA-ORA. T.M. REG. BEVERAGES LEMON ORANGE & LIME MADE FROM REAL FRUIT JUICE, O-T LTD. INC., S.F., CAL.; 11"; clear or amber 8.00-10.00

2800 H.B. KILMER N.Y.; *Philada Porter & Ale* in back; graphite pontil; green; 6½" . 35.00-45.00

2801 GEORGE KIMMERER, CANAJOHARIE, N.Y. on front in oval slug plate; 9½"; aqua 3.00-6.00

2802 KINSELLA & HENNESSY, ALBANY, N.Y.; blob top; 6¾"; aqua 10.00-12.00

2803 KINSELLA & HENNESSY; in a dome shape under it, ALBANY; blob top; 7½"; aqua 8.00-10.00

2804 G.A. KOHL, LAMBERT, N.J.; in back, *K* in hollow letter; graphite pontil; 7½"; green 25.00-50.00

2805 CHAS. KOLSHORN & BRO., SAVANNAH, GA; blob top; aqua; 8" 4.00-6.00

2806 C. L. KORNAHRENS; aqua; 7½"; *C.L.K.* in back 6.00-8.00

2807 C.L., KORNAHRENS, *Charleston S.C.* in circle; *Trade Mark* in center; in back *This Bottle Not To Be Sold*; 7¾"; aqua 4.00-6.00

2808 C.L. KORNAHRENS in horseshoe shape; under it *Charleston, S.C.*; blob top; 7"; aqua 4.00-6.00

2809 C.L. KORNAHRENS; blue; 7⅜" .. 20.00-30.00

2810 KROGER BROS., BUTTE, MT. in a slug plate; 6¾"; aqua 14.00-16.00

2811 KROGER BROS., BUTTE, MT., in a circle; Hutchinson; 8"; aqua .... 35.00+

2812 H.O. KRUEGER, GRAND FORKS, N.D.; 7½"; aqua 6.00-10.00

2813 A. KRUMENAKER, *New York* in a slug plate circle; in center, two lines, *512 & 514 West 166th St.*; under it *Registered*; in back *This Bottle Not To Be Sold*; blob top; 7¼"; aqua 4.00-6.00

2814 HENRY KUCK, 1878, *Savannah Ga.* in four lines on front; 7½"; green; blob top 10.00-20.00

2815 same as above, no date............ 6.00-10.00

2816 HENRY KUCK, *Savannah Ga* in a slug plate on front; blob top; short neck; 7½"; aqua 8.00-10.00

2817 HENRY KUCK, *Savannah, Ga.* in three lines; green; 7"; blob top 6.00-10.00

2818 same except no *Ga.*............... 8.00-15.00

2819 THE JOHN KUHLMANN BREWING CO., ELLENVILLE, N.Y. on front in oval slug plate; 6¾"; aqua 4.00-6.00

2820 J. H. KUMP in hollow letters, MEMPHIS, TENN.; blob top; 7½"; aqua....... 4.00-10.00

2821 Le LAGHTLEBEN-HACKENSACK, N.J. REGISTERED slanted on front; blob top; 9¼"; aqua.......................... 4.00-8.00

2822 J. LAKE in hollow letters, SCHENECTADY, N.Y.; semi-round bottom; graphite pontil; 8"; cobalt.......................... 20.00-40.00

2823 LANCASTER GLASS WORKS, N.Y.; graphite pontil; 7¼"; blue 20.00-40.00

2824 LANCASTER GLASS WORKS, N.Y.; reverse in center *XX*; blob top; graphite pontil; 6¼"; aqua.......................... 40.00-80.00

2825 LANCASTER GLASS WORKS, N.Y.; (reverse N in LANCASTER); graphite pontil; 7½"; cobalt blue.......................... 35.00+

2826 F. LANCKAHR, HIGGINSVILLE, MO.; 6¼"; aqua.......................... 4.00-10.00

2827 A. LANDT, LIVINGSTON, MT.: 7"; aqua .... 35.00+

2828 LARAMIE BOTTLE WORKS, LARAMIE, WYO.; crown top; 6½"; aqua 4.00-8.00

2829 LARGE, KANSAS; reverse side on base, *A. & D. H.C.*; 7"; blue 10.00-20.00

2830 LAUREL CLUB, BOSTON; clear; 10" 4.00-6.00

2831 LAWERENCE & SHAVER, GEORGETOWN, WASH.; 8¼"; aqua.............. 4.00-6.00

2832 LAWES & CO.; *Belfast Ginger Ale* around bottle; aqua 6.00-8.00

2833 L. & B. in hollow letters; blob top; graphite pontil; 7¼"; green 25.00-45.00

2834 L & B in 2" hollow letters; blob top; 7"; aqua 3.00-6.00

2835   2836   2837   2839   2841   2845   2846   2847

2852   2853   2856   2858   2861   2863   2864   2866

2867   2868   2871   2872   2877   2880   2885   2888

2835 LEBANON BOTTLING WORKS; aqua; 7½"
.... 4.00-6.00

2836 JULIUS LIEBERT; *C 4* under bottom; aqua; *This Bottle Not To Be Sold* in back; 9½"
.... 4.00-8.00

2837 LIME COLA on both sides; aqua; under bottom *Duro-glas 9-47-G999*; machine made 2.00-4.00

2838 J.A. LINDSEY; a harp on back; *33* under bottom; aqua; 7".................. 7.00-10.00

2839 J.A. LINDSEY; clear or amethyst; 6¾"
.... 4.00-6.00

2840 L. LINDY, SAVANNAH in sunken panel; under it, *Union Glass Works Phila* in two lines; cobalt blue; slug plate; improved pontil; 6½"
.... 8.00-20.00

2841 LIFE PRESERVER; clear; 7" 6.00-10.00

2842 C.C. LITTLE, GREENFIELD, MASS.; 7¼"; aqua.......................... 6.00-12.00

2843 LOCKE & BELTZ BOTTLERS, BROWNSVILLE, PA. in a slug plate; 7"; aqua
.... 4.00-6.00

2844 LODI SODA WORKS; 6¼"; aqua... 4.00-6.00

2845 ANDREW LOHR; 6½"; aqua; ridge on back mold; *C & CO LIM* on base........ 6.00-8.00

2846 J A LOMAX; *J.L.* under bottom; cobalt; 7¼"
.... 20.00+

2847 J.A. LOMAX, CHICAGO; reverse *T. B. M. B. R.*; 7"; cobalt.................... 35.00+

2848 LONGMONT BOTTLING WORKS, LONGMONT, COLO.; 6¾"; clear 4.00-10.00

2849 LOS ANGELES; in center, a star and SODA WORKS; crown top; 6½"; clear..... 4.00-6.00

2850 LOS ANGELES SODA CO.; in a dome shape line under it, MINERAL WATER FACTORY; reverse side *H.W. Stoll*; blob top; 6¾"; aqua
.... 8.00-15.00

2851 LOS BANOS; in center, L & B SODA WORKS; crown top; 6½"; clear............ 4.00-6.00

2852 JOHN S. LOW; aqua; 7" 6.00-10.00

2853 HENRY LUBS & CO.; *1885, Savannah Ga*; green; 7½"; blob top............. 8.00-15.00

2854 HENRY LUBS & CO.; *1885, Savannah Ga.* in a sunken circle; short neck; aqua; blob top
.... 8.00-12.00

2855 LYMAN ASTLEY, CHEYENNE, WYO.; 7"; aqua............................ 4.00-10.00

2856 MACON MEDICINE CO.; *Guinns Pioneer Blood Renerver* on other side; amber; 11"
.... 8.00-10.00

2857 MACKS BEVERAGE, SAN ANGELO, TEXAS; 7½"; light green 4.00-6.00

2858 GEORGE E. MADDEN; aqua; 7"... 4.00-6.00

2859 M. MADISON, LARAMIE, W.T.; blob top; 7"; aqua............................ 35.00-50.00

2860 MAGNOLIA BOTTLING CO., PASO, TEXAS; *Contents 7 fl. oz.* around bottom and shoulder; crown top; 7⅝"; aqua 2.00-4.00

2861 THOS MAHER, in small letters on slug plate; ground pontil; 7½"; dark green 15.00-30.00

2862 same, except larger ½" size letters . 15.00-30.00

2863 THOS MAHER; 6¾"; green; slug plate
.... 30.00-40.00

2864 THOS MAHER; slug plate; dark green; 7"
.... 15.00-20.00

2865 MANUEL BROS., NEW BEDFORD, MASS. on front in slug plate; blob top; 9¼"; amethyst
.... 4.00-8.00

2866 Marble bottle, Japan; two round holes on shoulder; green; 7½"............. 6.00-8.00

2867 Marble teardrop type bottle; aqua; 9¾"
.... 8.00-15.00

2868 THE MAR-COLA CO.; aqua; 7¾" ... 4.00-6.00

2869 MARION BOTTLE WORKS; in center M. & B. monogram, MARION, N.C.; 6½"; aqua
.... 8.00-15.00

2870 A. MAROTTA, 249-251 NORTH ST., BOSTON, MASS.; 9¼"; clear............. 4.00-6.00

2871 MARQUEZ & MOLL; ground pontil; aqua; 7¼"
.... 15.00+

2872 MARTHIS & CO.; aqua; 8"........ 2.00-4.00

2873 C.H. MARTIN & CO., SODA WORKS, AVON, WASH.; 7¼"; aqua 4.00-6.00

2874 B. MARSH & SON, DETROIT, MICH.; ten panels; blob top; 7½"; aqua......... 0000-0000

2875 MASON & BURNS, RICHMOND, VA. 1859; blob top; 7"; dark green 10.00-25.00

2876 S.M. MATTEAWAN, N.Y.; S.M.M. monogram on back; ten panels at base; 6¼"; clear 4.00-8.00

2877 MAYFIELDS, CELERY-COLA, J. C. MAYFIELD MFG. CO., BIRMINGHAM, ALA.; 6¾"; aqua 4.00-6.00

2878 M. B. & CO., 145 W. 35th ST., N.Y., 1862; blob top; 7¼"; aqua 8.00-12.00

2879 J.W. McADAMS TRADE MARK in center of a bunch of grapes, RICHMOND, VA.; panel base; 7"; aqua........................ 8.00-10.00

2880 M. McCORMACK; *W.McC & CO.* on back; amber; 7"......................... 15.00+

2881 S.E. McCREEDY, PROVIDENCE, R.I., in a circle; panel base; Hutchinson; 6¼"; aqua
.... 4.00-10.00

2882 THOS. McGOVERN, ALBANY, N.Y.; blob top; 7½"; aqua 4.00-10.00

2883 J. McLAUGLIN; 7½"; green..... 20.00-30.00

2884 McMAHONS WELL'S, FT. EDWARD, N.Y.; T.B.N.T.B.S.; blob top; 7½"; clear or amber
.... 6.00-8.00

2885 McMINNVILLE BOTTLING WORKS; *This Bottle Not To Be Sold* in back; amber; 7½"
.... 4.00-6.00

2886 DAN McPALIN, PARK CITY, UTAH in a circle; Hutchinson; 6½"; clear or amber 5.00-10.00

2887 MEEHAN BROS., BARBERTON, OHIO in script; 6½"; aqua.................. 8.00-12.00

2888 MEINCKE & EBBERWEIN; in horseshoe shape in center *1882*; under it in two lines *Savannah, Geo; Ginger Ale* vertical on back; amber; short neck; 8¼"; blob top ..... 15.00+

2889 MEMPHIS BOTTLING WORKS, R.M. BECKER; 7½"; aqua............. 6.00-8.00

2891   2892   2894   2895   2898   2899   2900   2901

2902   2907   2909   2916   2917   2919   2923   2930

2931   2933   2937   2939   2940   2941   2942

2890 JOSEPH MENTZE, MILTON, PA.; blob top; 7¼"; aqua 8.00-15.00

2891 MERCER BOTTLING CO.; *This Bottle Is Registered Not To Be Sold* on back; aqua; 9½" 6.00-8.00

2892 MERRIT MOORE JR. BOTTLER; *This Bottle Not To Be Sold* on back; clear or amethyst; 7" 4.00-8.00

2893 MERRITT & CO., HELENA, MONT.; blob top; 7¼"; aqua 8.00-10.00

2894 MEXOTA; *Root* under bottom; 11½" 4.00-8.00

2895 A.W. MEYER 1885, SAVANNAH, GA. in four lines on front; short neck; 8"; green; blob top 8.00-15.00

2896 same except aqua 8.00-15.00

2897 JOHN P. MEYER, FREEHOLD, N.J. on front in oval slug plate; 9"; clear 4.00-8.00

2898 MIAMI BOTTLING WORKS; clear or amethyst; 7½" 4.00-6.00

2899 MIGUEL PONS & CO., MOBILE; blob top; graphite pontil; 7½"; teal blue . . . . 20.00+

2900 A.H. MILLER; aqua; 6½" 4.00-6.00

2901 C. MILLER; aqua; 9¼" 4.00-6.00

2902 MILLERS BOTTLING WORKS; aqua; *M* under bottom; 8" 2.00-4.00

2903 MILLER, BECKER & CO., M.B. & CO., CLEVELAND, OHIO; apple green; blob top; 6¾" 4.00-6.00

2904 MILWAUKEE BOTTLING CO., N. PLATTE, NEB. in a sunken panel; Hutchinson; 7¼"; aqua 10.00-20.00

2905 M. MINTZ, M.M.; in center GLOVERSVILLE, N.Y., REGISTERED; blob top; 8"; clear 4.00-6.00

2906 MIRRIANS on shoulder; graphite pontil; 7¼"; cobalt 20.00-40.00

2907 MISSION ORANGE DRY REG. under bottom; black glass; 9½" 2.00-6.00

2908 J.M. MOE, TOMAHAWK, WIS. in three lines; Hutchinson; 5¾"; clear 12.00-15.00

2909 C.A. MOELLER; *Karl Hutter 33 n New York* under bottom; aqua; 9¼" 6.00-10.00

2910 CHAS MOHR & SON; *5¢ for return of bottle, Mobile Ala.*; 7"; clear 4.00-8.00

2911 MONTANA BOTTLING CO., BUTTE CITY, MON.; blob top; 6¾"; clear or aqua 8.00-12.00

2912 MONROE CIDER & VINEGAR CO., EUREKA, CAL.; 7¼"; clear or aqua 4.00-8.00

2913 MORGAN & BRO., 232 W. 47th ST., N.Y.; reverse, *M.B. Trade Mark*; blob top; 7"; aqua 10.00-15.00

2914 T. & R. MORTON, NEWARK, N.J. in three lines; squat type; graphite pontil 6¾"; green 40.00-60.00

2915 L.C. MOSES BOTTLER, PARSONS, KANSAS AND BARTLESVILLE; crown top; aqua . . . . 25.00+

2916 MOUNT BOTTLING CO.; *This Bottle Not To Be Sold* on back; *3* under bottom; aqua; 9½" 6.00-8.00

2917 C. MOTEL; aqua; 7"; big *M* on bottom 6.00-8.00

2918 MOXIE; 6¾"; aqua or clear 4.00-8.00

2919 E. MOYLE; aqua; 7¼" 4.00-8.00

2920 EDWARD MOYLE, SAVANNAH, GA. on front; *Ginger Ale* vertical on back; amber; 7½" 18.00-20.00

2921 E. MOYLE, SAVANNAH, GA. in sunken circle; blob top; 7¼"; *1880*; aqua 4.00-6.00

2922 JOHN E. MUEHLECK, NELLISTON, N.Y. on front in arch slug plate; *T.B.N.T.B.S.* on reverse side; 6¾"; aqua 4.00-6.00

2923 MUFF CO., label; marble in center of neck; aqua; 7¼" 6.00-8.00

2924 JAS. MULHOLLAND, SOUTH AMBOY, N.J. on front in oval slug plate; reverse side, *T.B.N.T.B.S.*; 9½"; blue aqua 4.00-8.00

2925 B.J.E. MULLENS; eagle in center; STANDARD GRADE BOTTLING WORK, ALBANY, N.Y. in script; crown top; 9¼"; aqua 4.00-8.00

2926 T.F. MURPHY, BROOKFIELD, MASS. on front in slug plate; blob top; 9¼"; aqua 3.00-6.00

2927 P.C. MURRAY, MONTICELLO, N.Y. on front in slug plate; 7"; aqua 6.00-8.00

2928 MUSKOGEE BOTTLING WORKS, MUSKOGEE, I.T.; 6¾"; aqua . . . . 25.00+

2929 N.A. PA. (star under it), WOODS (star under it), SODA; in back, *Natural Mineral Water*; blob top; 7¼"; blue . . . . 25.00+

2930 NATIONAL DOPE CO.; aqua; 8" tall; 2¼" diameter 6.00-8.00

2931 NATIONAL DOPE CO.; aqua; 8" . . 4.00-6.00

2932 OTIS S. NEALE CO., HOWARD ST., BOSTON, REGISTERED 1893, with OSN monogram, all on front; blob top; 9¼"; amethyst 4.00-8.00

2933 NERVE PEPSIN CO.; *Trade Mark Registered* on shoulder; clear; 8" 4.00-6.00

2934 NEUMANN & FUNKE, DETROIT, MICH.; Hutchinson; 7"; aqua 4.00-10.00

2935 NEW ALAMADEN/MINERAL WATER, W & W, 1870; same on reverse in large letters; blob top; 7½"; aqua 4.00-8.00

2936 NEW CASTLE BOTTLING CO., MT. KISCO, N.Y. on front in oval slug plate; 9"; amethyst 4.00-6.00

2937 NEWTON BOTTLING WORKS; aqua; 8" 2.00-4.00

2938 NO. MAIN ST. WINE CO., 208-212 NO. MAIN, ST., PROVIDENCE, R.I.; with *H* in center inside of slug plate; blob top; 9¼"; clear 4.00-6.00

2939 G. NORRIS & CO., CITY BOTTLING WORKS, DETROIT, MICH.; 6¼"; cobalt . . . 10.00-15.00

2940 same as above except aqua 6.00-8.00

2941 NORTHERN COCA-COLA BOTTLING WORKS INC., MASSENA, N.Y.; seltzer bottle type with pewter nozzle; 9¼"; cobalt . . 35.00+

2942 NOVA KOLA; *This Bottle Not To Be Sold* on base; clear or amethyst; 7¾" 3.00-6.00

2946

2953

2956

2962

2963

2964

2965

2966

2967

2968

2972

2974

2975

2976

2977

2978

2979

2980

2982

2986

2987

2992   2993   2994

2943 OAKLAND PIONEER SODA WORK CO.; TRADE MARK (embossed bottle inside of O); 8¼"; blue aqua................... 4.00-6.00

2944 OAKLAND STEAM SODA WORKS INC., in center in a wheel; on base, *Bottle Not To Be Sold*................... 4.00-12.00

2945 OCCIDENTAL BOTTLE WORKS, OCCIDENTAL, CAL.; O.B.W. monogram; 6¾"; aqua or clear................... 4.00-8.00

2946 ODIORNE'S; clear; 8½"........... 2.00-4.00

2947 O'KEEFE BROS. BOTTLERS, MATTEAWAN, N.Y. REGISTERED on front; O.K.B. monogram on back; ten panels at base; 6½"; aqua or clear................. 4.00-8.00

2948 same as above except 9¼"......... 6.00-8.00

2949 O.K. SODA WORKS in three lines; 7"; aqua 4.00-8.00

2950 OLSEN & CO., MEMPHIS, TENN.; blob top; 7½"; cobalt......................... 75.00+

2951 D.L. ORMSBY in 2" hollow letters; graphite pontil; blob top; 7½"; cobalt 35.00-50.00

2952 E. OTTENVILLE, NASHVILLE, TENN.; Hutchinson; 6¾"; blue 25.00-50.00

2953 E. OTTENVILLE; *McC* on base; *25* under bottom; cobalt; 6"................ 20.00-30.00

2954 OZARK FRUIT CO., MEMPHIS, TENN in a circle; panels around base; 7½"; aqua 8.00-10.00

2955 same except crown top........... 4.00-8.00

2956 OZO-OLA THE HAPPY DRINK; clear; 7½" 2.00-4.00

2957 J. PABST & SON, HUMILTON, OHIO in a circle; 6½"; aqua 8.00-15.00

2958 PACIFIC & PUGET SOUND SODA WORKS, SEATTLE, WASH.; 7"; aqua 10.00-15.00

2959 PACIFIC BOTTLING WORKS, PACIFIC, MO.; ABM; 8"; aqua 2.00-4.00

2960 PACIFIC SODA WORKS, SANTA CRUZ.; R in a hollow letter in center 3.00-6.00

2961 D. PALLISER, MOBILE, ALA.; 6¾"; aqua 4.00-8.00

2962 D. PALLISER; *Arthur Christian 1875 Pat. April 13* under bottom; glass plunger for stopper; aqua 8.00-10.00

2963 D. PALLISIER (Palliser, misspelled); aqua; 7½" .... 12.00+

2964 D. PALLISER; aqua; 7½" 6.00-8.00

2965 D. PALLISERS SONS; aqua; 7" ... 4.00-6.00

2966 D. PALISER; (Palliser, misspelled); aqua; 6¼" 12.00-16.00

2967 PALMETTO BOTTLING WORKS; clear or amethyst; 9¼" 6.00-10.00

2968 PARKER; graphite pontil; blue; 5" 25.00-40.00

2969 E. PARMENTER, GLENHAM, N.Y. on front in crude slug plate; 9¼"; aqua........ 4.00-8.00

2970 E. PARMENTER, MATTEAWAN, N.Y. on front in slug plate; *T.B.N.T.B.S.* reverse side; blob top; aqua 4.00-6.00

2971 PEARSON BROS.; Hutchinson; 6"; aqua 4.00-8.00

2972 PEARSON'S SODAWORKS; aqua; 7" 4.00-6.00

2973 PEPSI-COLA in center in script, also on bottom; *7* on top of shoulder; clear or aqua; crown top; not machine made............ 4.00-6.00

2974 PEPSI COLA, in script; *Trade Mark* on top; *Memphis, Tenn.* under it on slug plate; on back, *Registered*; *2322* under bottom; amber; crown top; not machine made............... 25.00+

2975 PEPSI COLA; *Newberry, S.C., This Bottle Not To Be Sold* on back; 8" tall; 2¼" diameter; aqua 4.00-6.00

2976 PEPSI COLA; aqua; 8¾" 3.00-6.00

2977 PEPSI COLA; aqua; 7¾" 2.00-6.00

2978 PEPSI COLA; aqua; 8" 2.00-6.00

2979 PEPSI COLA, ALBANY BOTTLING CO., INC.; amber; 8" 6.00-15.00

2980 PEPSI-COLA, NORFOLK, VA; *This Bottle Not To Be Sold Under Penalty Of Law* on back; cross under bottom; amber; 8¾" .... 25.00+

2981 P.W. PERKINS, TANNERSVILLE, N.Y.; 6½"; aqua 4.00-10.00

2982 PERRY MFG. CO., INC., SONORA, KY.; reverse side on base, *REG. T.B.N.T.B.S.*; 8¼"; aqua................... 3.00-6.00

2983 N.C. PETERS, LARAMIE, WYO.; Hutchinson; 6"; clear 4.00-8.00

2984 M. PETERSON SODA WORKS, SAN RAFAEL, (VA. CITY, NEV.); blob top; 7¾"; aqua................... 4.00-8.00

2985 JOHN V. PETRITZ in a dome; ANACONDA, MONT.; 6¾"; aqua 8.00-10.00

2986 HENRY PFAFF, EL PASO; clear or amethyst; 8¼"................... 8.00-12.00

2987 HENRY PFAFF; clear or amethyst; 9¼" 10.00-15.00

2988 GEO. PFEIFFER JR. in a dome; CAMDEN N.J.; blob top; 7½"; aqua 10.00-20.00

2989 PHILLIPSBURG (BOTTLE WORK in center) PHILLIPSBURG, MONT.; reverse side *T.B.N.T.B.S.*; 6¾"; aqua........... 8.00-10.00

2995

3000

3002

3003

3004

3008

3010

3011

3012

3014

3015

3016

3017

3018

3024

3025

3026

3027

3030

3032

3034

3039

3040

3041

2990 PHOENIX BOTTLING WORKS on three panels; other seven panels are blank; 6½"; light blue 2.00-8.00

2991 PHOENIX GLASS WORK in a circle, under it BROOKLYN; blob top; graphite pontil; 7¼"; aqua. 20.00-40.00

2992 R.V. PIERCE M.D., BUFFALO, N.Y.; *C2 1182* under bottom; aqua; 7" 4.00-6.00

2993 DR. PIERCES ANURID TABLETS, label; aqua; 3¼" 4.00-8.00

2994 B. PIETZ, PIQUA, O.; *This Bottle Never Sold* on back; aqua; 7¾" 10.00-15.00

2995 PIONEER BOTTLING WORKS; *P.B.W.* under bottom; aqua; 7¾" 4.00-6.00

2996 PIONEER SODA WORKS; a shield with word TRADE on one side, MARK on the other; blob top; 7½"; aqua 40.00-80.00

2997 PIONEER SODA WORKS, GILROY in large letters; 7⅞" 4.00-6.00

2998 PIONEER SODA WATER CO., S.F. in center of a bear; 6½"; aqua 4.00-8.00

2999 PIONEER SODA WORKS, SMITH & BRIAN, RENO, NEV.; 6"; aqua 6.00-8.00

3000 W. PIPE; sky blue; 7" 8.00-15.00

3001 JOSEPH C. PLANTE & CO., 631-635 ELM ST., MANCHESTER, N.H. on front inside of slug plate; blob top; 9¼"; amethyst 4.00-6.00

3002 PAUL POMEROY, LUDINGTON, MICH; aqua; 7" 4.00-6.00

3003 P. PONS & CO.; large P on back; ground pontil; aqua 30.00-50.00

3004 Pop bottle, label; aqua; 7" 4.00-6.00

3005 C.M. POPE BOTTLING, HOLLIDAYSBURG, PA.; blob top; 6¾"; aqua 6.00-8.00

3006 PORTLAND; picture of an eagle; above that, TRADE MARK, THE EAGLE SODA WORKS, P.O.; blob top; 7¼"; aqua 8.00-15.00

3007 POST EXCHANGE BOTTLING WORK, FORT RILEY, KAN. in a circle; crown top; 7"; aqua 4.00-6.00

3008 PRATT BOTTLING WORKS; amber; 8" 4.00-8.00

3009 PRESCOTT BOTTLING WORKS, PRESCOTT, A.T. in four lines; 6½"; aqua 8.00-12.00

3010 S. PRIESTER & BRO., HOUSTON, TEXAS; 7¼"; aqua 8.00-10.00

3011 PURITY BOTTLING & MFG. CO.; clear or amethyst; *purity* on bottom; 8" 4.00-6.00

3012 M.T. QUINAN, in horseshoe shape; in center, *1884*; under it in two lines, *Savannah, Geo*; in back, 2" monogram *MTQ*; on top, *Mineral* and under, *Water*; under bottom, monogram *MTQ*; cobalt; 7¾"; blob top . . . . 25.00+

3013 QUINAN & STUDER 1888, SAVANNAH, GA.; 7½"; aqua; blob top 8.00-12.00

3014 RADIUM SPRINGS BOTTLING CO.; machine made; *R* on bottom; clear; 7¾" 2.00-4.00

3015 RANDALL; clear or amethyst; 5¼" . . 2.00-4.00

3016 JAMES RAY'S SONS, SAVANNAH, GA. in center; *Hayo-Kola* in sunken circle; blob top; clear; 8" 4.00-6.00

3017 JAMES RAY, SAVANNAH, GEO. in sunken circle; on back in one vertical line, *GingerAle*; cobalt; 8"; blob top 15.00-25.00

3018 JAMES RAY, SAVANNAH, Ga.; in watermelon circle on back, monogram *JR*; 7½"; dark amber 15.00-25.00

3019 JAMES RAY, SAVANNAH, GA.; in watermelon circle on back, monogram, *JR*; 7½"; aqua 15.00-25.00

3020 JAMES RAY & SONS 1876, SAVANNAH, Ga.; in a sunken circle on back, *This bottle Registered, Not To Be Sold*; under bottom, *B*; 7½"; clear or amethyst 8.00-12.00

3021 JAMES RAY, SAVANNAH, Ga. in a sunken circle; aqua; blob top; under bottom *C24*; 7½" 6.00-10.00

3022 JAMES RAY, SAVANNAH, Ga. in a sunken circle on front; 7½"; blob top; aqua . . . 4.00-8.00

3023 JAMES RAY & SONS 1876; same except on back *RJ*, hollow letters 4.00-10.00

3024 JAMES RAY; 8"; aqua 8.00-10.00

3025 JAMES RAY; aqua; 7¼" 6.00-10.00

3026 RAYNERS SPECIALTIES; aqua; 7½" 6.00-10.00

3027 R.C. & T., NEW YORK; graphite pontil; aqua; 7½" 35.00-45.00

3028 R CROWN SODA WORKS in large slug plate; ABM; 7⅞"; aqua 2.00-4.00

3029 READ'S DOG'S HEAD, LONDON on front around base; crown top; ABM; 9¼"; emerald green 2.00-4.00

3030 P.H. REASBECK, BRADDOCK, PA.; 7"; aqua 4.00-6.00

3031 REGISTERED in oval slug plate; T.B.N.T.B.S.; crown top; 9¼"; amethyst 2.00-4.00

3032 RICHARD & THALHEIMER; clear or amethyst; *Dixie* on bottom; 7½" 6.00-8.00

3033 C.H. RICHARDSON; in a dome shape under it, TRENTON, N.J.; 7"; green 10.00-25.00

3034 N. RICHARDSON, TRENTON, N.J.; graphited pontil; dark green; 7" 30.00-35.00

3035 THE RICHARDSON BOTTLING CO., MANSFIELD, OHIO in a circle; 6¾"; aqua 4.00-6.00

3036 RICHMOND PEPSI COLA BOTTLING CO., RICHMOND, VA. in a circle; slim shape; 9"; aqua 8.00-10.00

3037 W.R. RIDDLE, PHILAD.; reverse, large monogram; graphite pontil; blob top; 7½"; blue . . . . 35.00+

3038 C.W. RIDER, WATERTOWN, N.Y.; 6¾"; frost green . . . . 50.00+

3039 C.W. RIDER, WATERTOWN, N.Y.; Hutchinson; 7"; amber 8.00-15.00

3040 RIGGS & DOLAN; clear; 7" 2.00-4.00

3041 T. & H. ROBER, SAVANNAH, GEO.; graphite pontil; 7"; green 20.00-30.00

3044   3045   3047   3050   3051   3052

3053   3054   3056   3057   3058   3059   3062

3064   3066   3084   3085   3086   3088

3042 JAMES M. ROBERTSON, PHILADA; reverse side *T.B.N.T.B.S.*; blob top; 7¼"; aqua 4.00-8.00

3043 A.B. ROBINSON; in a dome under it BANGOR, ME.; blob top; 7¾"; aqua 8.00-12.00

3044 A.B. ROBINSON, BANGOR, ME.; aqua; 7½" 6.00-8.00

3045 A.R. ROBINSON; aqua; 7" tall; 2¼" diam. 4.00-6.00

3046 J.P. ROBINSON, SALEM, N.J.; reverse side, hollow letter *R;* blob top; 6½"; green 10.00-25.00

3047 R ROBINSON'S; *402 Atlantic Av. Brooklyn N.Y.* on back; aqua; 7¼" .... 10.00+

3048 ROBINSON, WILSON & LEGALLSE, 102 SUDSBURYS, BOSTON; blob top; 6⅜"; ice blue 8.00-12.00

3049 ROCKY MOUNTAIN BOTTLING CO., BUTTE, MONT. in large letters; 6⅜"; aqua 4.00-8.00

3050 THE ROCKY MOUNTAIN BOTTLE WORKS; aqua; 6¾" 4.00-6.00

3051 A.I. ROE; *Arcadia Fla.* on panel; *Coca Cola Bottling Co.* on bottom; clear; 7¾"; machine made 2.00-3.00

3052 C. ROOS; aqua; 7⅝" 4.00-6.00

3053 ROSS'S BELFAST; 9"; aqua 4.00-8.00

3054 HENRY ROWOHLT; *HR Trade Mark Registered* on back; aqua; 7½" 4.00-8.00

3055 R. & W., LAS VEGAS, N.M. in a sunken panel; ten-sided base; Hutchinson; 7½"; aqua 10.00-20.00

3056 JOHN RYAN in 2" letters around bottle; hollow letters under it *Savannah, Geo;* ground pontil; 7"; cobalt .... 20.00+

3057 JOHN RYAN in 2" hollow letters around bottle; under it *Savannah, Geo;* under it *1859;* cobalt; 7".............................. 20.00+

3058 JOHN RYAN SAVANNAH, GA. in vertical line; in back, also vertical line *Gingerale;* on shoulder, *1852 Excelsior;* amber or golden; 7½" .... 15.00-20.00+

3059 JOHN RYAN *1866* in front; in back *Excelsior Soda-works, Savannah, Geo.;* cobalt, olive, blue, green and red; 7¼".............. 10.00-25.00

3060 JOHN RYAN; in small no. *1866;* blue; 7¼" .... 15.00+

3061 JOHN RYAN; cobalt; 7¾"; round; on front *J.R. S. 1852. T, Columbus, Ga.;* on back *This bottle Is Never Sold 1883;* on bottom *R* 10.00-25.00

3062 JOHN RYAN 1866 SAVANNAH, GA. on front; in back, 1" letters *Cider;* 7½"; amber.. 15.00+

3063 JOHN RYAN SAVANNAH, GA.; in center of it, *1852;* blue; 7½"............... 10.00-20.00

3064 JOHN RYAN SAVANNAH, GA. in three vertical lines; round bottom; 8" .... 20.00+

3065 JOHN RYAN JAMAICA GINGER in vertical line; 6"; aqua 6.00-8.00

3066 RYAN BROS; *Gravitating Stopper Made By John Mathews N.Y. Pat 11, 1864* in a circle under bottom; aqua; 7" 15.00-20.00

3067 JOHN RYAN, SAVANNAH, GEO.; reverse *XX, Philadelphia Porter;* squat shape; blob top; 6½"; green 35.00-50.00

3068 same as above except long tapered, blob top; graphite pontil; 6¾"; cobalt 50.00-75.00

3069 JOHN RYAN EXCELSIOR MINERAL WATER SAVANNAH, GA.; reverse side *This Bottle Never Sold, Union Glass Works, Phila.;* graphite pontil; 7½"; cobalt 50.00-75.00

3070 JOHN RYAN EXCELSIOR MINERAL WATER, SAVANNAH, GA.; reverse side *U.G.W.P., T.B.N.T.B.S.;* blob top; graphite pontil; 7¼"; blue 50.00-75.00

3071 same as above except no pontil; blob top; peacock blue 35.00-50.00

3072 same as above except on base *1859;* and graphite pontil; cobalt 50.00-75.00

3073 same as above except no pontil.... 35.00-50.00

3074 JOHN RYAN in 2" hollow letters; SAVANNAH, GA. 1859; 7½"; cobalt 50.00-75.00

3075 same as above except no date; graphite pontil 50.00-75.00

3076 JOHN RYAN in 1" hollow letters; PHILA. XX PORTER & ALE; squat type; 6¼"; blue 35.00-60.00

3077 JOHN RYAN, SAVANNAH, GEO.; reverse side *XX Philadelphia Porter;* squat type; 5¾"; cobalt............................ 60.00-80.00

3078 JOHN RYAN 1866 SAVANNAH, GA.; reverse side in 1" hollow letters, *Cider;* blob top; 7½"; blue or amber 40.00-80.00

3079 JOHN RYAN in 1" hollow letters; PHILADELPHIA, 1866; reverse side *XX Porter & Ale;* squat type; green 40.00-80.00

3080 JOHN RYAN 1852, AUGUSTA & SAVANNAH, GA.; reverse *Philadelphia XX Porter & Ale;* blob top; 6¾"; cobalt 40.00-80.00

3081 JOHN RYAN, SAVANNAH, GA.; in a circle in center *1852;* blob top; aqua....... 35.00-50.00

3082 same except amber 40.00-80.00

3083 JOHN RYDER, MT. HOLLOW, N.J.; blob top; 7"; aqua 10.00-25.00

3084 RYE- OLA BOTTLING WORKS; *DOC 1166* on base; clear or aqua; 8"............. 4.00-6.00

3085 ST. JAMES GATE, DUBLIN; machine made; amber 2.00-4.00

3086 ST. PETERSBURG BOTTLING WORK; clear or amethyst; 8" 2.00-6.00

3087 SALINAS SODA WORKS, STEIGLEMAN, SALINAS, CAL.; BOTTLE NEVER SOLD; 7⅞"; aqua 4.00-6.00

3088 SALSA DIABLO on panels around bottle; clear; 6¾"........................... 4.00-6.00

3089 SAMMIS & HENTZ, HEMSTEAD, L.I.; 7¼"; aqua.......................... 8.00-10.00

3090 SAN ANSELMO BOTTLING CO., SAN RAFAEL, CAL.; 6¾"; aqua 4.00-6.00

3091 H. SANDERS, SAVANNAH, GA.; 8½"; amber 20.00-30.00

| 3092 | 3098 | 3100 | 3101 | 3104 | 3110 | 3112 | 3114 |

| 3115 | 3116 | 3117 | 3119 | 3120 | 3121 | 3122 | 3123 |

| 3127 | 3129 | 3130 | 3135 | 3136 | 3138 | 3140 | 3141 |

3092 JOHN L. SANDERS; *This bottle Not To Be Sold* on back; aqua; 7″ 4.00-8.00

3093 SAN FRANCISCO GLASS WORKS; blob top; 7⅛″; aqua 8.00-12.00

3094 SAN JOSE SODA WORKS, A.J. HENRY, SAN JOSE, CAL. all on front; 8¼″; light blue 4.00-6.00

3095 SAN JOSE SODA WORKS (K missing in WORKS); blob top; 7½″; aqua 8.00-12.00

3096 SANTA BARBARA BOTTLING CO.; in center, SANTA BARBARA, CAL.; 7″; aqua 4.00-8.00

3097 SAPULA BOTTLING WORKS; 7¼″; clear 8.00-12.00

3098 SASS & HAINER, CHICAGO, ILL; *C & I* on back; aqua; 7¼″ 6.00-10.00

3099 C.L SCHAUMLOLEFFEL, TRENTON, N.J. REG., T.B.N.T.B.S.; crown top; 7½″; aqua 6.00-8.00

3100 SCHENK'S; *Syrup Philada* on other panels; clear 8.00-15.00

3101 P. SCHILLE; fancy script SP; COLUMBUS OHIO; Hutchinson; 7″; aqua 4.00-6.00

3102 P. SCHILLE in center; monogram S. P. under it; COLUMBUS, O.; 6¾″; aqua . . . 4.00-8.00

3103 C. SCHINERS & CO., SACRAMENTO, CAL., CAPITAL SODA WORKS; Hutchinson; 6½″; aqua 6.00-12.00

3104 A. SCHMIDT BOTTLER; aqua; 6¾″ 4.00-6.00

3105 F. SCHMIDT, LEADVILLE, COLO.; Hutchinson; 6¼″; aqua 4.00-8.00

3106 SCHOONMAKER & WILKLOW in center; ELLENVILLE, N.Y. in a sunken circle; blob top; 7½″; aqua 8.00-10.00

3107 ALEX SCHOONMAKER, ELLENVILLE, N.Y. in an oval slug plate; 6¾″; clear . 4.00-8.00

3108 CARL H. SCHULT top vertical line; in center *C-P*; monogram *M-S*; three lines *Pat. May 4 1868 New York*; tenpin type; 8½″; aqua 8.00-10.00

3109 FRANK SCUTT BOTTLER, VERBAND VILLAGE, N.Y. 702 inside of slug plate; crown top; 7½″; amethyst 2.00-4.00

3110 JOHN SEEDORFF; ground pontil; blue; 7½″ 20.00-50.00

3111 SEITZ BROS., EASTON, PA.; large *S* on reverse side; blob top; graphite pontil; 7½″; cobalt 50.00

3112 SEITZ BR. CO.; large *S* in back; amber; 7¼″ 6.00-8.00

3113 SEITZ BROS., EASTON, PA.; large *S* on reverse side; blob top; 7¼″; green . . . . . 25.00+

3114 SEITZ BROS; large *S* on back; blue green; 7″ 10.00-15.00

3115 F. SETZ, EASTON, PA. on back; ground pontil; green; 7¼″ 25.00-35.00

3116 7 UP; crown top; brown; squat type bottle; 6″ 4.00-8.00

3117 E.P. SHAW'S, label; marble in center of neck; aqua; 7¼″ 6.00-8.00

3118 E. SHEEHAN 1880, AUGUSTA, GA.; blob top; *Return This Bottle* reverse side; 9″; aqua 8.00-10.00

3119 E. SHEEHAN 1880, AUGUSTA, GA.; blob top; 7¼″; amber . . . . 35.00+

3120 E. SHEEHAN 1880, AUGUSTA, GA. in an oval slug plate; reverse side *R.T.B.*; 7½″; cobalt . . . . 100.00+

3121 E. SHEEHAN, AUGUSTA, GA.; blob top; 7½″; amber 18.00-20.00

3122 E. SHEEHAN, 1880, AUGUSTA, GA.; blob top; 7¼″; green 18.00-25.00

3123 E. SHEEHAN, 1880 AUGUSTA, GA.; reverse side *R.T.B.*; 8¼″; amber 18.00-25.00

3124 SHERIDAN BOTTLE WORK, SHERIDAN, ARK; Hutchinson; 6″; aqua 4.00-8.00

3125 SHEYENNE BOTTLING, VALLEY CITY, N.D., STEVENS & CO. PROP; 6¼″; aqua 10.00-12.00

3126 SHINER BOTTLING WORKS, SHINER, TEX. in a circle slug plate; 6½″; aqua 4.00-8.00

3127 SINALCO; *C* in a triangle and *8* under bottom; snap-on; machine made; amber; 7½″ . 2.00-6.00

3128 SIOUX BOTTLING WORKS, WATERTOWN, S.D.; 7″; clear 4.00-8.00

3129 SIP DRINKS TASTES LIKE MORE; around base SIP BOTTLING CORP; reverse side, a hand with crossed fingers and embossing reading *Make This Sign*; crown top; 7½″; clear 8.00-10.00

3130 A.P. SMITH; ground pontil; 7¼″ . . 25.00-35.00

3131 B. SMITH REG. POUGHKEEPSIE, N.Y. in a slug plate; blob top; 9¼″; clear 4.00-6.00

3132 D. SMITH, YONKERS, N.Y. on front in shield slug plate; T.B.N.T.B.S.; 9″; aqua . . . 4.00-8.00

3133 D.H. SMITH, YONKERS, N.Y. in shield slug plate; blob top; 11½″; clear 4.00-8.00

3134 JOHN J. SMITH, LOUISVILLE, KY.; 6¼″; aqua 10.00-20.00

3135 SMITH & CO.; panels around base; blue 25.00-35.00

3136 SMITH & CO.; seven panels; ground pontil; green 30.00-40.00

3137 SMITH & SWEENEY, MIDDLETOWN, N.Y. on front in oval slug plate; blob top; 7″; aqua 4.00-8.00

3138 Soda, label; graphite pontil; 7½″; green 15.00-20.00

3139 Soda, plain; blob top with sunken circle; under it, *Registered*; aqua; 7½″ 4.00-6.00

3140 Soda, label; *1589 C* on bottom; aqua; 7½″ 2.00-4.00

3141 Soda, label; clear or amethyst; 7½″ . . 2.00-4.00

3142   3143   3144   3145   3146   3147   3150   3151

3153   3154   3157   3158   3159   3160   3161   3162

3165   3166   3167   3168   3171   3172   3173   3174

3176　　　　3178　　　　3181

3142 Soda, label; aqua; 9"; marble in neck 4.00-8.00

3143 Soda, label; tear drop; flat top; aqua; 8½"
.... 8.00-10.00

3144 Soda, label; dark amber; 7½"...... 8.00-12.00

3145 Soda, label; small kick-up; dark green; 7½"
.... 2.00-4.00

3146 Soda, label; *This Bottle Not To Be Sold* on back;
aqua; 9¼"........................ 2.00-4.00

3147 Soda, label; *Reg. This Bottle Not To Be Sold* on
back; anchor under bottom; clear or amethyst;
7½"............................... 4.00-6.00

3148 SODA WATER BOTTLING CO., PROPERTY
OF COCA COLA, PAT'D JUNE 1, 1926,
MEMPHIS on four panels on center; six panels
on neck with stars; ABM; 9¼"; green 2.00-6.00

3149 SOLANO SODA WORKS, VACAVILLE,
CALIF. in four lines; 6¼"; aqua ... 4.00-10.00

3150 A. SOLARY; aqua; 7"............. 4.00-8.00

3151 SOUTH McALISTER BOTTLE WORKS;
South McAlister, Ind. Ter; aqua; 7"... 65.00+

3152 SOUTHERN BOTTLING CO., ATLANTA,
GA.; 6¼"; aqua 3.00-6.00

3153 SOUTHERN PHOSPHATE CO., COLUMBUS,
MISS; clear; 8".................... 4.00-6.00

3154 SOUTHERN PHOSPHATE CO.; aqua; 8"
.... 3.00-6.00

3155 THE SOUTHWESTERN BOTTLING CO.,
TULSA; crown top; 7¾"; aqua .... 25.00+

3156 SOUTHWICK & TUPPES, NEW YORK on
eight panels; graphite pontil; 7½"; green
.... 35.00+

3157 SQUEEZE; clear or amethyst; *Ybor City Fla* on
bottom; 8"; machine made......... 2.00-6.00

3158 STANDARD BOTTLING & EXTRACT CO.;
aqua; 9¼"...................... 2.00-4.00

3159 THE STANDARD BOTTLING & MFG. CO.;
clear; *#20* on bottom; 6½".......... 4.00-6.00

3160 THE STANDARD BOTTLING & MFG. CO.;
clear or amethyst; 8".............. 2.00-4.00

3161 STANDARD BOTTLING CO.; machine made;
a star on bottom; aqua............. 2.00-4.00

3162 STANDARD BOTTLING CO., ATLANTA;
reverse side *This Bottle To Be Returned;*
Hutchinson; 8"; aqua 4.00-8.00

3163 STANDARD BOTTLING CO., PETER
ORELLO PROP., SILVERTON, COLO.; 6¾";
aqua.......................... 6.00-10.00

3164 STANDARD BOTTLING WORKS, MIN-
NEAPOLIS, MINN.; 6¼"; amber .. 8.00-12.00

3165 Star under bottom; aqua; 9½" 2.00-6.00

3166 STAR BOTTLING WORKS, ANADARKO
O.T., T & M; Hutchinson; 7"; aqua.... 25.00+

3167 STAR BOTTLING WORKS, HOUSTON,
TEXAS, written in a circle around a large star;
tear drop shape; blob top; 8"; aqua ... 50.00+

3168 STAR MAIL ORDER HOUSE; *243* under bottom; clear or amethyst; 12¼"...... 8.00-12.00

3169 M & M STAR BOTTLING CO., OSKALOOSA,
LA.; 6¾"; clear or aqua........... 6.00-8.00

3170 STAR SODA WORKS, GRIBLE & CO. in a circle in center; *Nevada City*; 7"; clear 4.00-8.00

3171 E.B. STARSNEY; clear or amethyst; 8¼"
.... 2.00-4.00

3172 STEAM BOTTLING WORKS, SHAWNEE,
OKLA., I.T.; 7"; clear.............. 65.00+

3173 STEINKE & KORNAHRENS on one panel;
Charleston S.C. other panel; eight panels; dark
olive; ground pontil; 8½"......... 35.00-50.00

3174 H. STEWART, 253 ROOM ST., N.O.; blob top;
graphite pontil; 7½"; aqua .... 25.00+

3175 STILLMAN BOTTLING CO., 42 STILLMAN
ST., BOSTON in a slug plate; blob top; 9¼"
.... 4.00-6.00

3176 PETER STONITSCH; aqua; 9" 4.00-6.00

3177 STRAWHORN & SLAGO, REGISTERED,
GREENWOOD, S.C., T.B.N.T.B.S. & MUST BE
RETURNED; crown top; 7¾"; aqua 6.00-10.00

3178 P. STUMPF & CO; *This Bottle Not To Be Sold* on
back; amber; 8½"................ 20.00-30.00

3179 J.P. SULLIVAN, SANTA ROSA; blob top;
6½"; aqua 4.00-6.00

3180 SUMMERS & ALLEN, ALEXANDRIA,
VIRGINIA in three vertical lines; 7½"; aqua
.... 4.00-8.00

3181 SUNSET BOTTLING WORKS; aqua; 7"
.... 8.00-10.00

3182 SUPERIOR BOTTLING WORK, SUPERIOR,
WASH.; 6½"; aqua............... 4.00-8.00

3183 SUPERIOR SODA WATER, J.F. MILLER,
DAVENPORT, IOWA; blob top; fancy shoulder; five panels; blue........... 40.00-50.00

3184   3186   3188   3189   3190   3191

3195   3196   3197   3199   3200   3204   3205

3206   3207   3211   3213   3215   3216

| 3218 | 3219 | 3224 |

3184 SUPERIOR SODA WATER other side; ground pontil; blue; 7½" 30.00-60.00

3185 SUPREME BOTTLING CO., WAUKESHA, WIS. on front in a slug plate; 6¼"; aqua 4.00-8.00

3186 SWIDLER & BERNSTEIN, CHICAGO; *S.B.* under bottom; aqua; 6½" 6.00-8.00

3187 ALBERT H. SYDNEY, PROVIDENCE, R. I., AHS monogram all inside of slug plate; blob top; 9¼"; clear 4.00-8.00

3188 SYPHON CORP. OF FLORIDA; *Bottle Made in Czechoslovakia* under bottom; emerald green; 9" 10.00-20.00

3189 TAMPA BOTTLING WORKS; pale green; 8" 4.00-8.00

3190 TAMPA CIDER & VINEGAR CO.; aqua 4.00-6.00

3191 THE TAMPA PEPSI COLA BOTTLING CO.; semi-round bottom; 6"; aqua 6.00-8.00

3192 TANGO-COLA, RICHMOND, VA. REG.; star around neck; 7½"; clear........... 4.00-8.00

3193 B. F. TATMAN, OWENSBORO, KY. in center on 3-4" panel; other panels are plain; semi-round bottom; aqua 4.00-8.00

3194 TAYLOR SODA WATER MFG. CO., BOISE, IDA.; panel base; 6¾"; clear........ 4.00-8.00

3195 TAYLOR, ERIE, PA, REG. around bottle; large *I* under bottom; aqua; 6¼" 4.00-6.00

3196 C. TAYLOR, ERIE, PA. around bottle; large *T* under bottom; aqua; 6¼".......... 4.00-6.00

3197 TAYLOR & WILSON; aqua; 8½"; round bottom 8.00-12.00

3198 Tear drop (or sunbeam); 8½"; aqua; there are three or four different sizes 4.00-8.00

3199 Tear drop shape; crude blob top; 8"; dark olive .... 50.00+

3200 W. Z. THOMAS, NILES, OHIO in a circle; T.B.N.T.B.S. on the base; Hutchinson; 8¼"; clear 4.00-6.00

3201 TOLLE BOTTLING WORKS, in center big T; LITCHFIELD, ILL.; 6½"; clear or amethyst 6.00-8.00

3202 C.A. TOLLE in a circle in the center; a big *C* in center; REGISTERED LITCHFIELD, ILL.; 6½"; aqua 4.00-8.00

3203 TONOPAH SODA WORKS, TONOPAH, NEV. in three lines; Hutchinson; 6"; clear 8.00-12.00

3204 TOWNE'S; aqua; 7" 4.00-6.00

3205 TRINIDAD BOTTLING WORKS; clear or amethyst; 6¾" 2.00-6.00

3206 TRI STATE BOTTLING CO.; *D.O.C. 1209* around base in back; 7½" 8.00-12.00

3207 TRY-ME BEVERAGE CO.; machine made; clear; 9" 1.00-2.00

3208 T. & S. PORT TOWNSEND SODA WORKS, P.T. W.T.; 6¼"; aqua 25.00-50.00

3209 T S, SAVANNAH, GEO. in three lines; on back, *This Bottle Is Never Sold*; emerald green; improved pontil; 6½"; blob top 8.00-15.00

3210 TUCSON BOTTLING WORKS, TUCSON, ARIZ., I.P.G. CO.; crown top; 7¼" .. 3.00-6.00

3211 TUSKALOOSA BOTTLING WORKS, C.C. SIMPSON MGA., TUSKALOOSA, ALA.; reverse *T.B.N.T.B.S.*; Hutchinson; 6¾"; aqua 4.00-8.00

3212 T. & W.; in hollow letter under it *1875*; reverse side 141 Franklin St. N.Y.; blob top; 6½"; aqua 10.00-15.00

3213 TWITCHELL; aqua; 7½"........ 8.00-15.00

3214 G.S. TWITCHELL; in center, hollow letter T; under it PHILA.; reverse hollow letter *T*; blob top; 7"; green 10.00-30.00

3215 TWITCHELL, PHILADA; in center, hollow letter T; same on back; green; 7½" 20.00-35.00

3216 TYLER BOTTLING WORKS; aqua; 7¼" 2.00-4.00

3217 TYLER UNION BOTTLING WORKS, T.B.N.T.B.S., TYLER, TEX.; panel base; 7"; clear or amethyst 6.00-8.00

3218 U.C.B. CO.; *Contents 8 Fl. Oz.* under bottom; clear; machine made; 8" 2.00-4.00

3219 WM. UNDERWOOD & CO. BOSTON around base; amber or aqua; 7½" 10.00-15.00

3220 UNION BEVERAGE CO., JITNEY-COLA, KNOXVILLE, TENN., 6½ FLO. OZ. on shoulder; 7¾"; amber.............. 4.00-8.00

3221 UNION BOTTLING CO., WILMINGTON, DEL., REGISTERED; 7½"; aqua .. 8.00-12.00

3222 UNION BOTTLING WORK in dome shape; under it VICTOR, COLO.; 6¾"; aqua 6.00-10.00

3223 UNION GLASS WORK, PHILA.; blob top; graphite pontil; 7"; green 10.00-30.00

3224 UNION SODA WATER CO.; *W & C* under bottom; *This Bottle Never Sold Please Return* on back; aqua; 7½"................. 3.00-6.00

3225 3226 3229 3230 3231 3232 3235 3236

3238 3239 3241 3246 3248 3249 3250

3252 3253 3259 3260 3262 3263 3264

3225 UNITED GLASS LTD. ENGLAND; map of world and *1759-1959;* these bottles were dropped in the ocean in 1959 with maps, etc., sealed inside to commemorate the Guinness Brewing Co. bicentennial; machine made; amber; 9″ 6.00-8.00

3226 A. URMANN; *649* under bottom; aqua; 7¼″ 6.00-8.00

3227 PROPERTY OF VALLEY PARK BOTTLING WORKS, VALLEY PARK, MO. on front; ABM; 7½″; aqua 2.00-4.00

3228 VANCOUVER SODA WORKS, VANCOUVER, WAS.; star and trade mark in a sunken panel; Hutchinson; 7¼″; aqua 10.00-15.00

3229 VERNON & O'BRYAN; *X* under bottom; aqua; 7″ 4.00-6.00

3230 JOHN VICKERY, ENNIS, TEXAS; *Registered* on shoulder; *62* under bottom; aqua; 8¼″ 2.00-6.00

3231 VICKSBURG STEAM BOTTLING WORKS; *P* under bottom; aqua; 6¾″ 4.00-6.00

3232 VIG-O; *T. E. McLaughlin, Lynchburg, Va;* aqua; 9½″ 2.00-4.00

3233 VINCENT & HATHAWAY, BOSTON; reverse side, hollow letters *V. & H.*; 7″; aqua 10.00-15.00

3234 VINCENT HATHAWAY & CO., BOSTON; blob top; round bottom; 7¼″; aqua 4.00-10.00

3235 VIRGINIA FRUIT JUICE CO.; machine made; clear or amethyst; thick bottom; 7½″ 2.00-6.00

3236 VIVA BOTTLING WORKS; *This Bottle Not To Be Sold* on base; *CS6G CO* under bottom; clear; 9″ 2.00-4.00

3237 VOGELS BEVERAGES, SYLACAUGA, ALA.; 6¾″; aqua.................. 2.00-6.00

3238 VOGEL SODA WATER CO., ST. LOUIS, MO.; squat; crown top; 7¼″; aqua....... 8.00-10.00

3239 ALBERT VON HARTEN, SAVANNAH, GA. in two vertical lines; in back, same except one line *Ginger ale;* 7″; dark green; blob top 12.00-15.00

3240 ALBERT VON HARTEN, SAVANNAH, GA., in two lines; on back *Ginger Ale;* 7″; 2″ neck; blob top; green 10.00-20.00

3241 VON HARTEN & GROGAN, SAVANNAH, GA., on front; dark green; 7¼″; blob top 12.00-18.00

3242 WABASH BOTTLING WORKS, B.F. HEILMAN, 702 WABASH, IND.; ABM; crown top; 7⅝″; light blue 2.00-4.00

3243 WAGONER BOTTLING WORKS; panel base; 7″; aqua .... 10.00+

3244 WAINSCOTT'S DISTILLED WATERS, WINCHESTER, KY. in a circle; 7¼″; aqua 8.00-12.00

3245 H.S. WARTZ & CO., 78, 80 & 82 LEVERETT ST., BOSTON, MASS. in oval slug plate; blob top; clear........................ 4.00-8.00

3246 WEACLE VESTRY, VARICK & CANAL ST.; *Prem Soda Water* on back; graphite pontil; cobalt; 7½″ .... 40.00+

3247 WEBB & RILEY, JOLIET, ILL., TRADE MARK; Hutchinson; 7″; aqua 4.00-8.00

3248 WEBBS; *London* on back; amber; 9½″ 10.00-15.00

3249 JOSEPH WEBER; aqua; 7¼″; *J.W.* inside clover leaf..................... 8.00-12.00

3250 R.B. WEBSTER; *New York Ginger Ale* around bottle; 7½″; aqua .... 10.00+

3251 A. WEGENER & SONS, DETROIT, MICH. in oval slug plate; 6⅜″; aqua........... 4.00-6.00

3252 H. WEIGEL; big *W* under bottom; aqua; 6¾″ 4.00-6.00

3253 J.W. WELCH; *This Bottle Not To Be Sold* on back; *4-X* under bottom; aqua; 9¾″.. 8.00-10.00

3254 GEO. WELLER, SCHENECTADY; blob top; 7½″; aqua 8.00-10.00

3255 R. WELLER; in center 176 SPRING ST., SARATOGA N.Y.; reverse *T.B.N.T.B.S.*; blob top; 7½″; aqua 8.00-15.00

3256 CHAS. WESTERHOLM & CO., CHICAGO, ILL., TRADE MARK, W. CO. in a monogram on front; blob top; 6½″; aqua........... 2.00-6.00

3257 WESTERN; in center a deer head and trade mark; under it SODA WORK, P.O.; 6¾″; aqua 8.00-10.00

3258 W.F. & S.; star in the center and MIL.; Hutchinson; 6¾″; aqua 4.00-12.00

3259 HIRAM WHEATON & SONS; *Registered* on bottom rim; *19* under bottom; 7½″.... 4.00-6.00

3260 H. WHEATON & SONS TRADE MARK, NEW BEDFORD, MASS. REG.; 7½″; aqua 6.00-10.00

3261 WHEELER BROS., WAUKESHA SODA WATER CO., WAUKESHA, WIS. in a slug plate; blob top; 6½″; light green 4.00-6.00

3262 WHEELER & CO. UD CROMAC SPRING in line around base of round bottom bottle; under it *Belfast;* under bottom big *W;* in center a wagon wheel; between top spoke *E.R.;* on bottom of wheel between spokes *& Co;* under wheel *Registered;* aqua; 9½″; blob top 6.00-10.00

3263 WHITE SPRING CO.; light aqua; 8″ 3.00-5.00

3264 W.P. WHITE; clear or amethyst; 7″.. 6.00-8.00

3265 WILLIAMS BROS., SAN JOSE in oval slug plate; crown top; 7⅝″; light aqua 2.00-6.00

3266 S.M. WILLIAMS, MATTEAWAN, N.Y.; SMW monogram on reverse side; ten vertical panels; blob top; 6½″; clear 4.00-8.00

3267 WILLITS SODA WORKS, WILLITS, CAL.; crown top; 7¾″; aqua............... 4.00-6.00

3268 C.C. WILSON, MARKED TREE, ARK.; 7″; clear 4.00-8.00

3269 HENRY WINKLE in a dome shape; SAC. CITY; blob top; graphite pontil; 7¼″; aqua 10.00-20.00

3270 HERMAN WINTER in ½ circle; *Savannah, Ga.* under it; in back *This Bottle Not To Be Sold* in three lines; aqua; 8¼″; round; blob top 4.00-6.00

3274   3275   3276   3277   3280   3281   3284

3285   3286   3288

3271   HERMAN WINTER in a horseshoe shape; under it *Savannah, Ga;* 8"; blob top; aqua; 3" diameter 6.00-8.00

3272   A.J. WINTLE & SONS, BILL MILLS, NR ROSS, T. TURNER & CO., MAKERS, DEWSBURY; 6¼"; golden 8.00-15.00

3273   JACOB WIRTH & CO. INC.; JW monogram; PROV., R.I. in a diamond slug plate; 9¼"; clear 4.00-10.00

3274   WISEOLA; star under bottom; clear or amethyst; 8¼" 3.00-6.00

3275   WISEOLA BOTTLING CO.; star under bottom; clear; 7" 6.00-8.00

3276   THE P.H. WOLTERS BREWING CO.; *This Bottle Never Sold* in back; aqua; 9½" . . 2.00-4.00

3277   BY WOOTAN WELLS CO. (written vertically on bottle), WOOTAN WELLS, TEXAS; Hutchinson; 6½"; aqua 4.00-8.00

3278   W. & P. CO. in ½" letters; blob top; 7"; aqua 8.00-12.00

3279   W.S. WRIGHT under bottom; PACIFIC GLASS WORKS; blob top; 7½"; green 10.00-30.00

3280   WRIGHT'S; *Coca Cola* on back; amber; 7" 8.00-15.00

3281   W.T. & CO.; star under bottom; aqua; 7¼" . . . . 25.00+

3282   W. & W. in large letters; BURLINGTON, IOWA; blob top; 6¾"; aqua 8.00-10.00

3283   YALE BOTTLING CO., in center 268½ WOOSTER ST., NEW HAVEN, CONN.; 7¾"; aqua 4.00-12.00

3284   YETTER & MOORE; clear or amethyst; 8" 4.00-6.00

3285   J.H. YETTER; aqua; 7½" 15.00-20.00

3286   PHILIP YOUNG & CO., SAVANNAH, GA. on front; on back, eagle, shield and flag; improved pontil; 7½"; green; blob top . . . . 25.00+

3287   MRS. B.Z. ZIMMERMAN, NEW BRUNSWICK, N.J. in a circle; under it, T.B.N.T.B.S.; 6⅛"; clear or amethyst 4.00-8.00

3288   OTTO J. ZIPPERER; *This Bottle Is Never Sold* on back; amber; 8½" 4.00-8.00

This nostalgic advertisement promoting Coca-Cola in the straight-walled bottle (#2510) appeared between 1900 and 1916, before the introduction of the now famous contour-shaped or hobble-skirt bottle in 1916.

Mineral Water

Before it became stylish for wealthy folk to flock to the seashore or retreat to the mountains, America's nobility gathered at resorts established around the healthful, sparkling waters of mineral springs. They bathed in it, drank it, and because that somehow wasn't enough, they took it home with them in bottles.

Mineral water had been sought for its medicinal properties since ancient times. The Greek physician Hippocrates described the value of mineral waters in 400 B.C. The traditional appeal of the healing waters was maintained through the generations, and by the eighteenth century, the European leisure class was congregating in large numbers at health spas. In America, practical Yankees designed less elaborate spas than their European counterparts. Still, they were resorts complete with hotels, gambling, horse racing and other diversions reserved solely for those who could afford them. The rich could frolic in the cure-all waters, while the less fortunate could only dream of its wonderful taste. However, that was remedied in 1767 when a Boston spa began to bottle its waters. It was followed in 1800 by a spa in Albany and in 1819 by one in Philadelphia.

Competition soon developed among the spas. Claims of the healing virtues of the various bottled mineral spring waters often were as extravagant as those of their medicine cousins. The sparkling waters purportedly cured rheumatism, diabetes, kidney and urinary diseases, gout and nervous disorders. Doctors recommended it to their patients.

European immigrants to America were so convinced of the powers of these salted waters that they imported their favorite brands from the "old country." These arrived in crudely fashioned pottery bottles. The first American bottles were unadorned, but made of glass. Glassmaking had, after all, been the first industry in the New World. The first commodity produced by the earliest glasshouse in Jamestown in 1608 was probably a bottle.

Development of a spa was likely to be a successful commercial venture. George Washington had a speculative eye on Saratoga Springs in Saratoga County, New York, and in August of 1783 attempted to invest in it. His attempt to purchase failed and several years later the springs were opened to the public. But the cooling, curing mineral waters

In the late 1800's, Waukesha, Wisconsin, was nicknamed the "Saratoga of the Midwest" as a result of the discovery of the curing effects of its spring water. Tourists flocked to the area seeking good health and returned to their homes with enough bottled mineral water to see them through the cold winter.

found there were not bottled until 1820 when the Reverend Mr. D. O. Griswold, who slyly chose to stamp his bottles with the pseudonym "Dr. Clarke," began to market the water. Just thirty years later over seven million bottles were needed annually to keep up with the demand for Saratoga Springs water.

Promoters of mineral water were quick to capitalize on stories about its properties. Since a mineral spring was located near the Gettysburg, Pennsylvania, Civil War battlefield, it was only natural that Gettysburg Katalysine Spring Water be bottled. Its bottling was prompted by the story that many soldiers wounded in that battle had been cured by the spring waters.

Following the Civil War, at a time when sales of mineral water began to drop, excessive boasts began to appear that lithium, an alkali metal supposedly with healing properties, was in the water. An investigation after the passage of the Pure Food and Drug Act in 1907 found only infinitesimal traces of lithium in the bottled water. "Lithia Water" abruptly disappeared from bottle labels.

Bottled spring water began to replace mineral water in the late nineteenth century. Most of the collectable bottles were closed with cork and are from the 1850-1900 period.

3293   3303   3304   3305   3309   3311   3312

3313   3319   3320   3321   3322   3333   3336

3337   3343   3344

3289   ABILENA NATURAL CATHARTIC WATER
on the bottom; 11½"; amber or brown   4.00-8.00

3290   ABILENA NATURAL CATHARTIC WATER
on bottom; blob top; 10⅛"; amber ...   8.00-10.00

3291   AETNA MINERAL WATER; 11½"; aqua
.... 4.00-6.00

3292   AETNA SPOUTING SPRING in horseshoe letters in center; *A & E* in block letters; *Saratoga,
N.Y.*; pint; aqua 40.00-60.00

3293   AKESION SPRINGS; *Owned By Sweet Springs
Co., Saline Co., Mo.*; 8"; amber 10.00-15.00

3294   ALBERT CROOK; *Saratoga Co. N.Y.* in a circle; through center of it *Paradise Spring*;
tapered top; six rings; pint; green or aqua
.... 60.00-80.00

3295   ALEX EAGLE in center, 1861 MINERAL
WATER; tapered top; 7¼"; aqua ...   8.00-15.00

3296 ALHAMBRA NAT. MINERAL WATER CO., MARTINEZ, CAL.; applied top; 11¼"; aqua 8.00-12.00

3297 ALLEGHANY SPRING, VA.; amber 10.00-20.00

3298 ALLEN MINERAL WATER, horizontal letters placed vertically on bottle; blob top; 11½"; golden amber 8.00-12.00

3299 ALLEN MINERAL WATER; big ring top; 7½" 8.00-15.00

3300 AMERICAN KISSINGER WATER in vertical lines; tapered top and ring; pint; aqua 50.00+

3301 AMERICAN MINERAL WATER CO., NEW YORK, M.S. monogram all inside slug plate; THIS BOTTLE NOT TO BE SOLD at base; blob top; 9¼"; aqua 8.00-10.00

3302 ARTESIAN BALLSTON SPA; green 20.00-30.00

3303 ARTESIAN SPRING, BALLSTON, N.Y.; same on back; green; 8" 15.00-30.00

3304 ARTESIAN SPRING CO., BALLSTON, N.Y.; Ballston Spa. Lithia Mineral Water on back; dark aqua; 7¾" 25.00-30.00

3305 ARTESIAN WATER; pontil or plain; Dupont on back; dark olive; 7¾" .... 40.00+

3306 ASTORG SPRINGS MINERAL WATER, S.F., CAL.; blob top; 7"; green 4.00-10.00

3307 JOHN S. BAKER; Mineral Water, this bottle never sold on panels; blob top; eight panels; pontil; aqua .... 35.00+

3308 BARTLETT SPRING MINERAL WATER, CALIFORNIA in a slug plate; blob top; 11⅝"; aqua 8.00-15.00

3309 BEAR LITHIA WATER; aqua; 10" 4.00-8.00

3310 J. & A. BEARBOR, NEW YORK MINERAL WATER; eight panels; star on reverse side; graphite pontil; 7¼"; blue 20.00-45.00

3311 BEDFORD WATER; label in back; aqua; 14" 4.00-8.00

3312 BITTERQUELLE SAXLEHNERS JANOS on bottom; 10½"; whittle mark or plain; avocado green; ring top 4.00-6.00

3313 BLOUNT SPRINGS NATURAL SULPHUR; cobalt; 8" .... 15.00+

3314 J. BOARDMAN & CO. MINERAL WATER; eight panels; graphite pontil; 7¾"; cobalt, ... 30.00-80.00

3315 BOLEY & CO., SAC. CITY, CAL; reverse side Union Glass Work, Phila. slug plate; blob top; graphite pontil; 7½"; blue 50.00-75.00

3316 J. BORN MINERAL WATER, CINCINNATI; reverse hollow B, T.B.N.T.B.S.; blob top; 7¾"; green 8.00-20.00

3317 J. BORN MINERAL WATER, CINCINNATI in three lines; reverse side large B and T.B.N.T.B.S.; blob top; 7½"; blue .. 30.00-40.00

3318 BOWDEN LITHIA WATER, under it a house and trees; under that Lithia Spring Ca.; blob top; aqua 8.00-12.00

3319 BUCKHORN MINERAL WATER, label; aqua; 10¼" 8.00-10.00

3320 BUFFALO LICK SPRINGS; clear or amethyst; 10" 3.00-6.00

3321 BUFFALO LITHIA SPRING WATER; aqua; 10½" 8.00-12.00

3322 BUFFALO LITHIA GIN; clear or amethyst; 10¼" 8.00-12.00

3323 BUFFALO LUTHIS' WATER; Natures Materia Medica; lady sitting with pitcher in hand; under it, Trade Mark; round; 11½"; aqua; ½ gallon 6.00-12.00

3324 same with whittle effect 7.00-14.00

3325 BYTHINIA WATER; 10¼"; tapered top; amber 4.00-8.00

3326 CAL. NAT. MINERAL WATER, CASTALIAN around shoulder; 7¼"; amber... 6.00-8.00

3327 CALIFORNIA NATURAL SELTZER WATER; reverse side picture of a bear, H.&G.; blob top; 7¼"; aqua 10.00-20.00

3328 W. CANFIELD; Agt. for S.H.G.; graphite pontil; squat; blob top; 6¼"; green .... 35.00+

3329 CARLSBAD L.S.; sheared collar; cylindrical; ground top; 4"; clear 3.00-6.00

3330 CARLSBAD L.S. on bottom; short tapered top; quart; 10¼"; green 6.00-10.00

3331 CARTERS SPANISH MIXTURE; pontil; 8½" .... 50.00+

3332 C.C. & B., SAN FRANCISCO in two lines; reverse side Superior Mineral Water; ten-sided base; blob top; graphite pontil; 7"; blue 35.00-80.00

3333 CHAMPION SPOUTING SPRING; amber; 7¾" .... 35.00+

3334 CHASE & CO. MINERAL WATER, SAN FRANCISCO, STOCKTON, MARYSVILLE, CAL. in six lines; graphite pontil; blob top; 7¼"; green 35.00-65.00

3335 CITY BOTTLING WORK, under it a girl seated; Mt. Vernon, O.; tapered top; 11"; clear 15.00-30.00

3336 C. CLARK on front; Mineral Water on back; dark olive; 7"; ground pontil 15.00-30.00

3337 JOHN CLARKE, NEW YORK around shoulder; three-piece mold; pontil; 9¼"; olive 45.00-60.00

3338 JOHN CLARK, N.Y. SPRING WATER; 7"; green .... 35.00+

3339 LYNCH CLARK, N.Y.; aqua 30.00-40.00

3340 CLARK & WHITE in U; under it New York; in center C Mineral Water; 9¼"; olive green .... 10.00+

3341 CLARK & WHITE in horseshoe; in center big C; in back, Mineral Water; 9½"; olive green .... 10.00+

3342 CLARKE & CO., N.Y. in two lines; tapered top and ring; 7¾"; pontil; blue green.. 35.00-55.00

3343 CLARKE & WHITE; wide mouth; dark olive; 7" x 3¾" diameter 35.00-45.00

3344 CLARKE & WHITE; green; 7½" .... 20.00+

3345

3349

3350

3351

3352

3353

3354

3356

3357

3358

3362

3363

3364

3365

3368

3369

3370

3376

3377

3383

3384

3385

3389

3391

3345 CLARKE & WHITE; olive; 8"...... 20.00+

3346 C. CLEMINSON SODA & MINERAL WATER, TROY, N.Y.; blob top; 7¼"; blue 12.00-20.00

3347 COLUMBIA MINERAL WATER CO., ST. LOUIS, MO.; 7¼"; aqua 4.00-6.00

3348 COLWOOD, B.C., HYGENIC MINERAL WATER WORKS; blob top; crock; white and brown; 8"..................... 8.00-12.00

3349 CONGRESS & EMPIRE SPRING CO.; *Hotchkiss Sons & Co. New York, Saratoga, N.Y.,* large hollow letters; *CW* in center; 7"; olive 65.00+

3350 CONGRESS & EMPIRE SPRING CO., SAROTOGA, N.Y.; reverse side *Congress Water;* 7¾"; dark olive.......... 20.00-30.00

3351 CONGRESS & EMPIRE SPRING CO. in horseshoe shape; big *C* in center; above it *Hotchkiss Sons;* under the big *C, New York, Saratoga, N.Y.;* pint; 7¾"; under bottom two dots; green; wood mold .... 15.00+

3352 CONGRESS & EMPIRE SPRING CO in a horseshoe shape; in center of it a big *C* in a frame; under it, *Saratoga, N.Y.;* tapered and ring top; 7¾"; emerald green 35.00-55.00

3353 CONGRESS & EMPIRE SPRING CO.; on back *Empire Water;* dark green; under bottom a star; 7½" tall; 3" diameter .... 20.00+

3354 CONGRESS & EMPIRE SPRING CO., NEW YORK, SARATOGA; olive green; 7½" 15.00+

3355 CONGRESS & EMPIRE SPRING CO. in U; under it *Saratoga, N.Y.;* in center of big *C, Mineral Water;* 9¼"; blue green ... 8.00-10.00

3356 CONGRESS SPRING CO., SARATOGA, N.Y.; dark green; quart; tapered top and ring 25.00-35.00

3357 CONGRESS SPRING CO. in horseshoe shape; in center large *C;* under it *Saratoga, N.Y.;* in back *Congress Water;* quart; 7¾"; dark green .... 15.00+

3358 CONGRESS SPRINGS CO. S S, N.Y. in a circle; under the bottle in center *#4;* old beer type; wood mold; blue green; 9½" 8.00-10.00

3359 CONGRESS SPRINGS CO. in horseshoe shape; in center a *G, Saratoga, N.Y.;* emerald green; 8"; tapered top and ring............ 25.00-50.00

3360 CONGRESS WATER in two lines; tapered and ring top; green; 8" 25.00-50.00

3361 P. CONWAY BOTTLER, PHILA.; reverse side *No. 8 Hunty, 108 Filbert, Mineral Water;* blob top; cobalt; 7¼".................. 10.00-30.00

3362 COOPERS WELL WATER; *BCOO* on back base; aqua; 9¾"..................... 20.00-30.00

3363 COULEY'S FOUNTAIN OF HEALTH, No. 38 BALTIMORE'S BALTIMORE; symbol of a fountain in the center; tall whiskey bottle shape; pontil; 10"; aqua.............. 15.00-25.00

3364 COURTLAND STREET 38 N.Y.; *T. Weddle's Celebrated Soda Mineral Water* on back; graphite pontil; cobalt; 7½" .... 65.00+

3365 COWLEYS FOUNTAIN OF HEALTH; pontil; aqua; 9½".................. 10.00-40.00

3366 CROWN on shoulder; 8½"; olive green; beer type bottle 6.00-8.00

3367 CRYSTAL SPRING WATER in horseshoe shape; under it, *C.R. Brown Saratoga Spring, N.Y.;* quart; 9½"; green .... 10.00+

3368 CRYSTAL SPRING WATER CO., N.Y. around base; aqua; 9½".................... 4.00-8.00

3369 DEEP SPRING; three-part mold; *C* in a diamond under bottom; amber; 12¾" 12.00-18.00

3370 DOBBS FERRY MINERAL WATER CO., DOBBS FERRY, N.Y.; 6½"; aqua... 4.00-6.00

3371 DOBBS FERRY MINERAL WATER CO. WHITE PLAINS, N.Y. all inside slug plate; *CONTENTS 7 OZ. REGISTERED* on front at base; 8"; amethyst and clear 4.00-6.00

3372 D.P.S. CO.; *Rochester, N.Y. U.S.A.;* 3½"; amber 2.00-3.00

3373 EAGLE SPRING DISTILLERY CO. on front; rectangular; 7"; amethyst......... 3.00-4.00

3374 G. EBBERWEIN, *Savannah, Geo* in three lines on front; on back between words *Mineral Water,* monogram *EGB;* under bottom monogram *E;* light blue; 7½"; blob top 12.00-20.00

3375 same except aqua .... 10.00+

3376 same except amber or dark blue .. 10.00-30.00

3377 same except short neck; 8"; vertical in back *Ginger Ale*..................... 12.00-30.00

3378 same except amber............. 15.00-30.00

3379 ELK SPRING WATER CO., BUFFALO, N.Y. on front in oval slug plate; blob top; ½ gallon; clear 4.00-10.00

3380 C. ELLIS & CO., PHILA.; short neck; graphite pontil; 7"; green .... 35.00+

3381 EMPIRE SPRING CO.; *E* in center, *Sarotoga, N.Y., Empire Water;* 7½"; green; tapered top and ring 20.00-30,00

3382 EMPIRE WATER; pint; star under bottom; green........................... 10.00+

3383 A.C. EVANS SUPᴿ MINERAL WATER, WILMINGTON, N.C. written vertically; graphite pontil; 7½"; green .... 35.00+

3384 EXCELSIOR SPRINGS, MO.; *Roselle* under bottom; clear or amethyst; 8" 2.00-4.00

3385 THE EXCELSIOR WATER; blue; 7"; ground pontil........................ 35.00+

3386 THE EXCELSIOR WATER on eight panels; blob top; graphite pontil; 7¼"; green 30.00-50.00

3387 FARREL'S MINERAL WATER, EVANSVILLE, IND.; graphite pontil; 7½"; aqua .... 25.00+

3388 FRIEDRICHSHALL, C. OPPEL & CO. on the bottom; label; blob top; 9"; green ... 6.00-10.00

3389 J.N. GERDES; *S.F. Mineral Water;* blob top; green; 7½" 4.00-8.00

3390 J.N. GERDES S.F. MINERAL WATER vertical on four panels; eight panels in all; blob top; 7⅛"; aqua blue 18.00-30.00

3391 GETTYSBURG KATALYSINE WATER; *X* under bottom; green; 10" 20.00-25.00

189

3392   3394   3398

3400   3404   3405

3406   3409   3410   3411   3412

3417   3418   3419   3430   3432   3434

3392 GEYSER SPRING, SARATOGA SPRING, STATE OF N.Y.; light blue; 7¾" ...... 20.00+

3393 GEYSER SPRING, SARATOGA SPRINGS in horseshoe; in center *State of New York*; in back vertically *The Saratoga Spouting Spring*; 7¾"; about a quart; light blue 25.00-30.00

3394 GILBEYS SPEY ROYAL, label; three dots and number under bottom; golden amber; 8" 10.00-15.00

3395 GLACIER SPOUTING SPRING in horseshoe shape; letters under it *Saratoga Spring, N.Y.*; in back a fountain; pint; green; *Glacier* misspelled 100.00-150.00

3396 GLENDALE SPRING CO., THIS BOTTLE NOT TO BE SOLD; blob top; 7"; aqua 8.00-12.00

3397 GRANITE STATE SPRING WATER CO., AKINSON DEPOT, N.H., TRADE MARK embossed; two Indians taking water from stream and large granite rock; crown top; 10"; aqua 4.00-8.00

3398 GREAT BEAR SPRING; *Fulton N.Y., This Bottle Is Loaned And Never Sold* on bottom; aqua; 11½" 8.00-10.00

3399 CHARLES S. GROVE & CO. SPARKLING MINERAL WATER, NO. 30 CANAL ST., BOSTON in a diamond shape; reverse side *T.B.N.S. Deposit On Same, Refund When Returned*; 7½"; aqua 14.00-18.00

3400 GUILFORD MINERAL SPRING WATER; blue green; 9¼" 20.00-35.00

3401 GUILFORD MINERAL SPRING WATER; green 10.00-20.00

3402 GUILFORD & STAR SPRING; green or amber 10.00-15.00

3403 GUILFORD MINERAL SPRING WATER inside of a diamond in center, also *G.M.S.*; under it *Guilford, Vt.*; short neck; 10"; dark green 20.00-40.00

3404 HANBURY SMITH; light olive; 8" 6.00-8.00

3405 HANBURY SMITH'S MINERAL WATERS; 7¾"; dark green 15.00-30.00

3406 HARRIS; amber; 9¼" 4.00-8.00

3407 HARRIS ALBANY MINERAL WATERS; graphite pontil; tapered top; 7¼"; aqua 8.00-12.00

3408 DR. HARTLEY'S MINERAL WATER, PHILA. in front; in back *Improved Patent*; pontil; flared top; 6¾"; light emerald green 65.00+

3409 HATHORN; amber; 9¼" 15.00-25.00

3410 HATHORN SPRING in horseshoe shape; under this, *Saratoga, N.Y.*; dark amber; under bottle a "drop" and a letter *H*; 7½"; round.. 8.00-20.00

3411 same except bottom plain; very dark green 8.00-15.00

3412 HATHORN WATER, SARATOGA, N.Y., paper label; 9½"; amber 4.00-6.00

3413 HEADMAN, in a dome shape under it *Excelsior Mineral Water*; reverse *F.W.H.* in hollow letters; graphite pontil; 7¼"; green .. 25.00-40.00

3414 HECKINGS MINERAL WATER; green 20.00-30.00

3415 HIGHROCK CONGRESS SPRING; aqua 10.00-20.00

3416 same except amber............. 15.00-30.00

3417 HOLMES & CO. MINERAL WATER; ground pontil; 7½"; blue................... 20.00+

3418 HOLMES & CO.; graphite pontil; *Mineral Water* in back; light blue; 7¼".... 20.00-25.00

3419 HONESDALE GLASS WORKS, AP ("PA" backwards); *Mineral Water* in back; aqua; 7½" 18.00-22.00

3420 HONESDALE GLASS WORKS, PA. in a dome shape; reverse side *Mineral Water*; graphite pontil; blob top; green 40.00-60.00

3421 J. HOPKINS, PHILA; pontil; short neck; dark aqua................ 20.00-35.00

3422 HYGEIA WATER; *Cons. Ice Co., Memphis, Tenn.* around base; 9¼"; aqua 4.00-10.00

3423 HYPERION SPOUTING SPRING in a horseshoe shape; tapered top and ring; pint; aqua 40.00-60.00

3424 IMPROVED MINERAL WATER; short tapered top; graphite pontil; 7½"; cobalt 25.00-50.00

3425 IMPROVED MINERAL WATER; blob top; graphite pontil; 6¼"; blue 20.00-40.00

3426 INDIAN SPRING in center; Indian head under bottom; 10½"; aqua............. 10.00-15.00

3427 JACKSON NAPA SODA on front; in back *Natural Mineral Water, Jacksons T.B.I.N.S.*; 7½"; aqua................ 10.00-20.00

3428 JACKSON'S NAPA SODA SPRING on front; reverse side *Natural Mineral Water*; blob top; 7½"; aqua................ 8.00-12.00

3429 JOHNSTON & CO. PHILA. in large block letters; on back large fancy 2" *J*.; tapered top; 6¼"; sea green 16.00-35.00

3430 JUBILEE SPRING WATER CO.; *101* under bottom; *5 pt* on back; aqua; 11½" . 10.00-20.00

3431 J. KENNEDY, MINERAL WATER, PITTSBURG in three lines on back; script letters *J.K.*; graphite pontil; blob top; 7½"; green 35.00-40.00

3432 KISSINGER WATER; dark olive; 6¼" 25.00-35.00

3433 KISSINGER WATER PATTERSON & BROZEAU; tapered top; 7"; olive 15.00-20.00

3434 D.A. KNOWLTON in a dome shape; under it *Saratoga, N.Y.*; tapered top; 9½"; olive 30.00-50.00

3435 R.T. LACY, NEW KENT CO., VA., PROP. BELMONT LITHIAWATER; in circle in center two men turning a hand drill; under that *DEUS AQUAM CREAVIT BIBAMUS* and *AD 1877*; 10"; blue green............... 20.00+

3436 J. LAMPPIN & CO. MINERAL WATER, MADISON, LA.; in back *Madison Bottling Establishment*; graphite pontil; blob top; 6½"; blue green................ 40.00-80.00

3438   3440   3441

3443   3446   3453

3454   3455   3456   3457   3462   3467   3472

3474   3475   3480

3481   3487   3488

192

3437 LIVITI DISTILLED WATER CO., PASADENA, CAL. around base in small letters; crown top; *I.P.G. CO. 841 LIVITI* on bottom; round; ABM; tapered neck; 7¾"; aqua 4.00-6.00

3438 J.A. LOMAX, 14 & 16 CHARLES PLACE, CHICAGO; four-piece mold; 9¾"; amber 10.00-20.00

3439 LYTTON SPRING; in center a pelican; *SWEET DRINKS* under it; in three lines *P.M.H. Co., San Franciso, C.H.B.*; 6½"; aqua 12.00-15.00

3440 MADDEN MINERAL WATER CO., label; aqua; 7" 8.00-10.00

3441 MAGEE'S; aqua; 10½" 8.00-15.00

3442 MAGNETIC SPRING; amber 20.00-35.00

3443 J. MANKE & CO, SAVANNAH in two lines; in back *Mineral Water*; blob top; 7"; aqua 10.00-15.00

3444 FREDERICK MEINCKE, in horseshoe shape; in center of horseshoe *1882*; under it, in two lines, *Savannah, Geo.*; on back 2" monogram F.M.; on top of it *Mineral Water*; under it *Water*; cobalt; 7¾"; under bottom is monogram M.......................... 18.00+

3445 MEINCKE & EBBERWEIN, *Savannah, Geo.* in horseshoe shape; in center *1882*; on back monogram between words *Mineral Water*, M&E; under bottom, monogram ME; cobalt; blob top...................... 30.00-50.00

3446 MICUELPIRIS MINERAL WATER, NO. 334 ROYAL ST., N.O.; ground pontil; 7½"; aqua 20.00-35.00

3447 MIDDLETOWN HEALING SPRING; amber 15.00-30.00

3448 MIDDLETOWN SPRING, VT.; amber 15.00-20.00

3449 J. & D. MILLER, MARIETTA, OHIO; reverse side *Mineral Water*; blob top; 7½"; aqua 8.00-20.00

3450 MILLS SELTZER SPRING; under bottom *M*; blob top; 7½"; aqua............ 12.00-20.00

3451 MINERAL WATER; tapered top; graphite pontil; 7¼"; green.............. 20.00-40.00

3452 same as above except cobalt 30.00-65.00

3453 MINERAL WATER; tapered top; six panels; improved pontil; dark green; 7"... 12.00-18.00

3454 MINERAL WATER, label; light green; 10¾" 4.00-8.00

3455 MINERAL WATER; ground pontil; 7¼"; green 30.00-40.00

3456 MINERAL WATER, label; green; 6½" 10.00-12.00

3457 MINERAL WATER, label; dark olive; pontil; 6" .... 15.00+

3458 MINERAL WATER in two lines on front; 7½"; blob top; aqua 5.00-10.00

3459 same except pontil .... 35.00+

3460 MINNEGUE WATER; *Bradford Co., Pa.*; 8"; aqua; tapered top and ring.......... 35.00+

3461 MISSISQUOI, *A* in center; *Spring* on reverse side, also an Indian woman carrying a baby; olive .... 50.00+

3462 MISSISQUOI; olive; 9¾" 20.00-35.00

3463 NAPA SODA, PHIL CADUC; reverse *Natural Mineral Water*; tapered neck; blob top; 7½" 20.00-35.00

3464 NATURAL in center; a man with sleeping cap and handkerchief around neck; under it MINERAL WATER; blob top; 7½" 10.00-20.00

3465 NEW ALMADEN in a horseshoe shape; under it MINERAL WATER; blob top; 6¾"; aqua 8.00-12.00

3466 NEW ALMADEN MINERAL WATER, W&W on panels; ten panels; tapered top; blob top; graphite pontil; 7½"; green....... 20.00-50.00

3467 N.Y. BOTTLING CO., N.Y.; star on shoulder; *10cts. Deposit* on back; *This Bottle is Loaned, 10¢ Will Be Paid For Its Return* under bottom; aqua; 12" 6.00-8.00

3468 OAK ORCHARD ACID SPRING, on shoulder *H.W. BOSTWICK AGT., NO. 574 BROADWAY, N.Y.*; on bottom *From F. Hutchins Factory Glass, Lockport, N.Y.*; 9"; light amber ... 20.00-35.00

3469 O.K. BOTTLING CO., O.K.; in center *526, 528, 530, W. 38th St., N.Y.*; reverse side Indian holding a flag; 10¾"; aqua 10.00-25.00

3470 O'KEEFE BROS. HIGH GRADE MINERAL WATER, MATTEWAN, N.Y., with monogram; crown top; 7¾"; amethyst.......... 4.00-8.00

3471 OLYMPIA WATER CO. in a dome shape; under it MINERAL WELLS, TEX.; blob top; several different sizes; aqua............. 10.00-20.00

3472 OLYMPIA WATER CO., MINERAL WELLS, TEX; aqua; 9½" 8.00-15.00

3473 ORIGINAL CALIF. MINERAL WATER CO.; *Sweetwater Springs, San Diego, Calif.*; 11"; aqua......................... 10.00-12.00

3474 E.O. OTTENVILLE, large *E.O.* on front; reverse *Ottenville, Nashville, Tenn.*; 9¼"; amber 25.00-30.00

3475 PABLO & CO.; *Mineral Water Factory* on back; aqua; 7½"..................... 12.00-15.00

3476 PACIFIC CONGRESS WATER on bottom; crown top; four-piece mold; 8¼"; aqua 6.00-8.00

3477 PACIFIC CONGRESS in horseshoe shape; under it WATER; applied top; 7"; light blue 10.00-20.00

3478 B. PAGE JR. & CO.; *Pittsburgh, Pa.* other side; side mold; aqua; 7½" 15.00-25.00

3479 PARAISO MINERAL WATER BOTTLED BY P. STEGELMAN, SALINAS, CAL. on front; four-piece mold; crown top; 8¼"; aqua 4.00-8.00

3480 PATTERSON & BRAZEAU, VICHY WATER, N.Y.; dark green; 6¾" 6.00-10.00

3481 PAVILION & UNITED STATE SPRING CO.; dark olive; 7¾" tall; 3" diameter...... 25.00+

3482 P.H. CRYSTAL SPRING WATER COMPANY N.Y. around base; crown top; tenpin shape; 9¼"; aqua................... 4.00-10.00

| 3489 | 3490 | 3492 | 3496 | 3499 | 3502 | 3504 | 3516 |

| 3519 | 3527 | 3528 | 3536 |

3483 POLAND WATER; aqua 20.00-35.00

3484 PRIEST NATURAL WATER; aqua
. . . . 6.00-10.00

3485 PRIST NAPA; *A Natural Mineral Water Recarbonated At St. Helena From The Priest, Mineral Spring, Napa Co., Calif.*; applied crown; 7¼"; aqua 4.00-8.00

3486 PURE NATURAL WATERS CO., PITTS-BURG, PA. inside fancy shield, with house embossed in center; crown top; ABM; 12¼"; aqua
. . . . 4.00-6.00

3487 THE PURITAN WATER CO., N.Y.; aqua; 12¼" 4.00-8.00

3488 ROCKBRIDGE ALUM WATER; aqua; 9½"
. . . . 10.00-20.00

3489 ROUND LAKE MINERAL WATER; amber 7¾" 75.00-90.00

3490 RUTHERFORDS PREMIUM MINERAL WATER; ground pontil; dark olive; 7½"
. . . . 45.00-55.00

3491 RUTHERFORD & KA on shoulder; three-piece mold; graduated collar; 10½"; olive amber
. . . . 30.00+

3492 JOHN RYAN; *Excelsior Mineralwater, Savannah* in front; back *Unionglass Work, Phila, This Bottle Is Never Sold*; cobalt; 7"; improved pontil
. . . . 25.00+

3493 ST. REGIS MASSENA WATER; green
. . . . 10.00-15.00

3494 SAN FRANCISCO GLASS WORKS; tapered neck; blob top; 6⅞"; sea green 20.00-30.00

3495 SAN SOUCI SPOUTING SPRING in a horse-shoe shape; in center a fountain and *Ballston Spa, N.Y.*; tapered top and ring; pint; aqua
. . . . 50.00+

| 3537 | 3538 | 3539 | 3541 |

3496 SARATOGA, under it a big *A*, under it *Spring Co, N.Y.;* tapered top and ring; olive green; 3¾" x 9"; round .... 20.00+

3497 SARATOGA SELTZER SPRING; olive green; 8"; quart; tapered top and ring 25.00-35.00

3498 same except pint; 6¼" 25.00-75.00

3499 SARATOGA VICHY SPOUTING SPRING in a horseshoe shape; in center a hollow letter *V;* under it *Saratoga, N.Y.;* tapered top; 7½"; aqua 25.00-40.00

3500 SEVEN SPRINGS MINERAL WATER CO. GOLDSBORO, N.C.; 8"; aqua 4.00-8.00

3501 SHASTA WATER CO; *Mineral Water Co.;* 10½"; amber...................... 4.00-8.00

3502 E.P. SHAW & CO. LTD, WAKEFIELD, paper label; 5"; green 4.00-8.00

3503 SHOCO LITHIA SPRING CO., LINCOLN, NEB.; crown top; 7¾"; aqua 2.00-6.00

3504 S. SMITHS, KNICKERBOCKER MINERAL & SODA WATER, N.Y.; pontil; 7"; green 35.00+

3505 SPARKLING LONDONBERRY SPRING LETHA WATER, NASHUA, N.H., label; 11⅝"; green 2.00-6.00

3506 STAR SPRING; aqua............. 8.00-10.00

3507 STEINIKE & WEINLIG SCHUTZ MARKE, embossed hand holding some tools; *Seltzers* in large letters on back; three-piece mold; blob top; 9¾"; emerald green 8.00-12.00

3508 STODDARD MAGNETIC SPRING, HENNIKER, N.H.; amber 60.00-80.00

3509 SUMMIT MINERAL WATER, J.H. in three lines; blob top; 7½"; green 8.00-15.00

3510 SUNSET SPRING WATER, CATSKILL MT., HAMES FALLS, N.Y.; on base *This Bottle Loaned Please Return;* 13"; aqua ... 8.00-10.00

3511 THOMPSONS, in center PREMIUM MINERAL WATERS; tenpin shape; reverse side *Union Soda Works, San Francisco*; blob top; 7½"; aqua 10.00-15.00

3512 TOLENAS SODA SPRINGS; reverse side *Natural Mineral Water*; tapered neck; blob top; 7"; aqua blue..................... 7.00-12.00

3513 TRITON SPOUTING SPRING in horseshoe shape; in center block letter *T,* under it, *Saratoga, N.Y.;* pint; green .... 40.00+

3514 TWEDDLES CELEBRATED SODA OR MINERAL WATER; reverse side *Courtland Street,* in center *#38,* under it *New York;* tapered top; graphite pontil; 7½"; cobalt 30.00-60.00

3515 UNDERWOOD SPRING, FALMOUTH FORESIDE, ME. on front in oval slug plate; crown top; 8⅞".................... 4.00-8.00

3516 UNGARS OFNER BITTERWASSER; green; 9½"............................. 4.00-8.00

3517 same as above with no embossing..... 2.00-4.00

3518 UNION GLASS WORKS, PHILA., under it SUPERIOR MINERAL WATER; panel base; blob top; graphite pontil; 7½"; blue 30.00-50.00

3519 UNION SPRING; green; 8" 50.00-100.00

3520 UTE CHIEF OF MINERAL WATER; *Maniton, Colo., U.T.* on base; crown top; clear or purple; 8" 4.00-6.00

3521 VARUNA MINERAL WATER WELLS in a horseshoe shape; *Richwood, Ohio,* under it *I. Miller, Prop., T.B.N.S. and must be returned;* 6½"; clear.......................... 15.00+

3522 VERMONT SPRING SAXE & CO.; green 10.00-20.00

3523 VERONICA MEDICINAL SPRING WATER; 10½"; amber.................... 4.00-10.00

3524 VERONICA MINERAL WATER around shoulder; 10¼"; square; amber, clear 6.00-10.00

3525 same as above except ABM 4.00-8.00

3526 VERONICA MINERAL WATER on square shoulder; square; 10½"; amber..... 6.00-10.00

3527 VICHY ETAT, label; reverse side embossed *Establishment Thermal De Vichy*; 6¾"; cobalt 15.00-20.00

3528 VICHY WATER CULLUMS SPRING, CHOCTAW CO., ALA.; 7¼"; dark olive 30.00-40.00

3529 VICHY WATER, PATTERSON & BRAZEAU, N.Y. vertically on front; pint size; 6¾"; dark green......................... 8.00-15.00

3530 WASHINGTON SPRING, picture of Washington's head; pint; 6¼"; emerald green 25.00-75.00

3531 same except quart; 8¼" 20.00-35.00

3532 WELLER BOTTLING WORKS, SARATOGA, N.Y.; blob top; aqua.............. 6.00-10.00

3533 G.W. WESTON & CO 10.00-20.00

3534 G.W. WESTON & CO., MINERAL WATER, SARATOGA, N.Y.; amber 15.00-20.00

3535 WHELAN TROY; embossed tulips; Hutchinson; 7½" 10.00-12.00

3536 D.J. WHELAN; *Mineral Water* on back; aqua; 7½"........................... 8.00-12.00

3537 WHITE SULPHUR WATER; blue green; 8¾" 4.00-8.00

3538 WITTER; *Witter Medical Spring* under bottom; amber; 9½"...................... 4.00-8.00

3539 WITTER SPRING WATER; *Witter Medical Springs Co.* under bottom; amber; 9½" 4.00-8.00

3540 WITTER SPRINGS WATER, W.M.S. CO., SAN FRANCISCO around shoulder and bottom; 9¼"; amber 8.00-12.00

3541 W.S.S. WATER; machine made; *9-2-8 O.I.* with diamond shape under bottom; green; 5½" 1.00-2.00

3542 XXX ($\overset{X}{XX}$) in two lines; blob top; graphite pontil; 7"; green .... 25.00+

3543 ADAM W. YOUNG, CANTON, OHIO in slug plate; squat shape; graduated collar; 9¼"; aqua 4.00-8.00

3544 ZAREMBO MINERAL SPRING CO., SEATTLE, WASH.; blue; 7½"; tapered top 10.00-20.00

Ale and Gin

Ale and gin were both alcoholic beverages that the average person could afford. Ale could conveniently be made at home, while gin could be produced cheaply and was therefore affordable. Early ale bottles were usually of pottery and nearly always from England. The first ones had a matte surface, while later examples are shiny. The home brewer of ale in the early seventeenth century was aware of the hazards of cork closures: If the corks became dry, the carbonation would expel them from the bottles and the contents would be ruined.

Francisco de la Boe, a Dutch doctor seeking a medicinal compound to treat kidney disease, discovered gin in the mid-seventeenth century. The product was sold as medicine and soon the druggists, who knew a good thing when they tasted it, devoted full-time work to the distillation of gin. By the end of the eighteenth century it was a favorite drink throughout most of Europe.

The shape of gin bottles has not varied a great deal since the seventeenth century. Their square bodies allowed twelve to be packed in a special wooden case, and they came to be called case bottles. The first case bottles were octagonal in shape, however. Early case bottles had particularly short necks, while the later ones had long, stretched necks. Many case bottles in this country were imported from Holland. Because English and American glasshouses made use of Dutch craftsmen, it is difficult to differentiate between Dutch, English and American bottles.

Most of the case bottles with tapered collars can be dated to the nineteenth century. Plate molds began to be used in bottle making in the late 1800's; such molds were designed to hold plates with lettering or designs on them to be easily transferred to the bottle. Some case bottles are embossed with animals, people and stars.

Case bottles range in size from a half-pint to the multiple-gallon container. Though they vary in size, most have the traditional shape. The early bottles are crudely made and have pontil scars.

Left: Though this bottle is
an 18th-century American wine bottle,
so identified by its seal, this method of identification
is not foolproof, as bottles containing rum and even
mineral water often had attached seals.
Below: Originally, this pine box held
twelve 18th-century Dutch gin bottles (#3621-3631),
possibly the most distinguished of all bottles
containing distilled liquors.

3546   3548   3549   3550   3551   3552   3553   3554

3555   3556   3557   3558   3559   3560   3561   3562

3563   3564   3565   3566   3567   3568   3569   3570

3571   3572   3573   3577   3578   3579   3580   3581

3545   ABMYERSAM; *Rock Rose, New Haven, Md.;* 9⅛"; dark green.................... 4.00-6.00

3546   A & D.H.C.; yellow amber; 9½"..... 8.00-18.00

3547   A.H. in seal; roll top; 11⅜"; green amber .... 35.00+

3548   A.I., with an anchor in seal on shoulder; honey amber; 8¾"........................... 50.00+

3549   Ale, label; dark green; 9½"; turn mold 2.00-6.00

3550   Ale, label; olive; 8½"; turn mold; kick-up 2.00-4.00

3551   Ale, label; green; 6"; kick-up........ 2.00-6.00

3552   Ale, label; *1716 A* under bottom; olive; 9½" 2.00-4.00

3553   Ale, label; 9½"; aqua 2.00-6.00

3554   Ale, label; aqua; kick-up; 8"........ 2.00-3.00

3555   Ale, label; aqua; *Root* under bottom; 11¾" 2.00-4.00

3556   Ale, label; dark olive; 9½"; turn mold 6.00-12.00

3557   Ale, label; amber; ground pontil; 11¼".. 20.00+

3558   Ale, label; amber; 8¾"............. 8.00-12.00

3559   Ale, label; light green; small kick-up pontil; 9" 8.00-10.00

3560   Ale, label; olive; kick-up; 7½"...... 6.00-12.00

3561   Ale, label; olive; kick-up with broken pontil; 12" .... 15.00+

3562   Ale, label; olive; kick-up pontil; three-part mold; 8¾" 15.00-20.00

3563   Ale, label; amber; pontil; 9"....... 20.00-24.00

3564   Ale, label; milk glass; 11"........ 10.00-20.00

3565   Ale, label; five dots under bottom; small kick-up; black; 10".................... 4.00-8.00

3566   Ale, label; light aqua; 9½" 2.00-6.00

3567   Ale or wine, label; three-part mold; *B* under bottom; dark olive; 10"................ 4.00-6.00

3568   Ale or wine, label; kick-up; dark olive; 9½" 2.00-4.00

3569   Ale or wine, label; kick-up; dark olive; 10" 2.00-4.00

3570   Ale, plain 7¼"; free-blown; 2" diameter; pontil crude top...................... 10.00-15.00

3571   Ale, plain; aqua; free-blown; kick-up; pontil; light-weight bottle; 9½"; very crude top; 2¾" diameter...................... 12.00-20.00

3572   Ale, plain; free-blown; aqua; kick-up; pontil; 8½"; 2¼" diameter; crude top...... 10.00-15.00

3573   Ale, plain; quart; 6"; 3" neck; very crude applied top; pontil in kick-up; very light blue 10.00-20.00

3574   Ale, plain; eight panels; graphite pontil; 7"; green...................... 18.00-25.00

3575   Ale, plain pottery; 8½"; brown and white 3.00-4.00

3576   Ale, plain pottery; 8½"; white 2.00-4.00

3577   Ale, plain; 11½"; white; pottery 3.00-4.00

3578   S. ALVARES on seal; clear; 11½"; kick-up 3.00-5.00

3579   AMELIORATED SCHIEDAM HOLLAND GIN; 9½"; amber............... 15.00-25.00

3580   ANTEDILUVIAN LUYTIES BROTHERS NEW YORK; small kick-up; olive; 12" 6.00-8.00

3581   ASCR in a seal; olive; kick-up; 10½"; pontil or plain .... 35.00+

3588   3589   3590   3591   3596   3597

3603   3604   3605   3614   3615   3628   3629

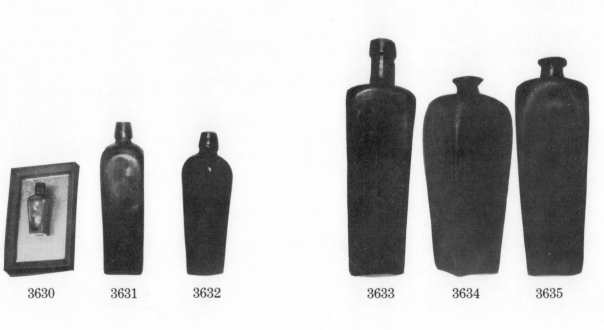

3630   3631   3632   3633   3634   3635

3582 ASPARAGUS GIN, THE ROTHENBERG CO. on front in circle; slug plate, S.F. CALIF.; same shape as a Duffy malt; graduated collar; 10⅛"; aqua........................ 10.00-20.00

3583 AVAN HOBOKEN & CO. on front; seal on shoulder AVH; case bottle; 11¼"; olive 28.00-35.00

3584 BAIRD DANIELS CO. DRY GIN; tapered and ring top; 9"; aqua................ 8.00-10.00

3585 same as above except MISTLETOE DRY GIN; 8½"; clear or amethyst............ 8.00-10.00

3586 same as above except CORONET under bottom; aqua......................... 8.00-10.00

3587 BART E.L. in Old English type on one line; on the other *Dry Gin;* 8½"; light green . 2.00-4.00

3588 BASS' PALE ALE, label; three-part mold; amber; 9½"...................... 2.00-6.00

3589 B.B. EXTRA SUPERIOR; whiskey; amber; 10½"......................... 12.00-18.00

3590 B. C. W.; dark olive; pontil; 9" ... 40.00-60.00

3591 Benedictine; dark green; 8¾"; kick-up; *F22* on bottom......................... 6.00-8.00

3592 BERGOMASTER; *Geneva Gin, Cobb Hersey Co., Boston* on round label; also ship on bottom of label; case type; 10½"; olive 8.00-12.00

3593 BERGOMASTER; *Geneva Gin, Cobb Hersey Co.,* (no label); case type; 10½"; olive 6.00-10.00

3594 BERRY BROS.; *323 E. 38th St. N.Y.* in circle on front; aqua; 11¼" 2.00-4.00

3595 BIG 6 GIN, ORIGINAL; tapered top; 6½"; clear or amethyst 4.00-8.00

3596 BILL & DUNLOP; dark olive; 11½" 15.00-25.00

3597 Black bottle, beer or ale; three-part mold; kick-up with one dot; 4½" body; 2" neck; 7¾"; crude top; bottom 3"; dark olive......... 8.00-12.00

3598 Black bottle; 4¾" body; 2" neck; 3" bottom; three-part mold; kick-up; dark olive 8.00-12.00

3599 Black bottle; 5½" body; 2½" lady's leg neck; improved pontil; 2¾" bottom; crude top 8.00-12.00

3600 Black bottle, beer or ale; three-part mold; 6½" body; 3" neck; 2½" bottom; dark olive 8.00-12.00

3601 Black glass; plain; three-part mold; 7¾"; kick-up........................... 4.00-10.00

3602 Black glass; *C.W. & Co.* under bottom; three-part mold; kick-up 4.00-10.00

3603 BLAKE BROS PALE ALE, LANGPORT, label; *P & R B* under bottom; three-part mold; olive; 9½" 8.00-10.00

3604 BLANKENHEYM & NOLET on front, ½" letters; case bottle; 9½"; olive .... 15.00+

3605 BLANKENHEYM & NOLET; dark olive; 7½" 15.00-25.00

3606 BLANKENHEYM & NOLET, 1912; 9½"; green or amber...................... 10.00-20.00

3607 same as above except 8½"; brown or amber 10.00-20.00

3608 same as above except 7⅞"; brown ...... 15.00+

3609 same as above except 9⅜"; clear 8.00-15.00

3610 same as above except 9½"; green....... 15.00+

3611 BOUVIER'S BUCHU GIN on front; on back, *Louisville, Ky.;* square fancy shoulder and neck; purple 10.00-14.00

3612 DR. C. BOUVIER'S BUCHU GIN vertical in two lines; 11¾"; fancy quart bottle ... 4.00-6.00

3613 BOUVIER'S BUCHU GIN; 11¾"; clear or amethyst......................... 2.00-4.00

3614 BOUVIER'S BUCHU GIN; clear; 6"; machine made 1.00-2.00

3615 BOWER & TUFT'S; *New Albany, Ind.* around bottom in ten panels; *L & W* under bottom; dark amber; 9½"...................... 25.00-35.00

3616 E. J. F. BRANDS (ale) in seal; case type; ribbed sides; tapered top; 9½" .... 45.00+

3617 B. R. P. CO.; mold-blown; tapered top; 8⅞"; green or amber................. 20.00-30.00

3618 BUNGALOW; gin label; tapered top; 10½"; amber 20.00-35.00

3619 C.A. & C. DOS VINHOS DO PORTO, vertical; 11¾"; whittle mold; olive, amber 4.00-8.00

3620 CARL MAMPE, BERLIN; ale; small kick-up; tapered top.................... 10.00-20.00

3621 Case bottle with two dots under bottom; crude applied top; 9½" .... 15.00+

3622 Case bottle, plain; broken pontil; curved bottom; dark olive; 10"; short neck 35.00-45.00

3623 Case bottle, plain; curved bottom; dark olive; crude applied top; full of bubbles; short neck; 9¼" .... 25.00+

3624 Case bottle, plain; clear; 9"; long neck; on front, sunken circle 10.00-15.00

3625 Case bottle, plain; 10½"; five dots under bottom; short neck; crude top; olive .... 15.00+

3626 Case bottle, plain; 10½"; short neck; crude top; olive .... 15.00+

3627 Case bottle, plain; 9½"; small kick-up; dark olive .... 15.00+

3628 Case bottle, plain; 9½"; milk glass; roof type shoulder; 2" neck and top; 1¼" deep circle under bottom....................... 40.00-50.00

3629 Case bottle, plain; curved or plain bottom; dark olive; tapered top; short neck; 10" .... 15.00+

3630 Case bottle, plain; curved or plain bottom; dark olive; tapered top; short neck; 3⅞"..... 15.00+

3631 Case bottle, plain; curved or plain bottom; brown-olive, light olive; tapered top; short neck; 10"............................ 15.00+

3632 Case bottle, label; black; 8" 10.00-15.00

3633 Case gin, label; green; 10"; cross on bottom 15.00-25.00

3634 Case gin, label; pontil; 10"; black .. 10.00-20.00

3635 Case gin, label; dark olive, green; 9" 10.00-15.00

3636   3638   3639   3640   3643   3644   3645   3647

3650   3651   3652   3653   3654   3657   3659

3660   3664   3665   3666   3667   3669   3670   3671

3672   3674   3675   3681

3636   Case gin, label; green; 8½"......... 4.00-8.00

3637   Case gin; much larger............... 10.00+

3638   E.P. CAWET in seal; deep kick-up; light green; 12"...................... 4.00-6.00

3639   RICHARD CHAMBERY; turn mold; kick-up; aqua; 12½"..................... 4.00-8.00

3640   P. CHAPMAN; inside screw top; *N & Co. 2401* and a spike under bottom; green; 9"   8.00-12.00

3641   Chinese letters under bottom; label; crown top; ale; 8¾"; green................ 8.00-10.00

3642   S. COBBS in seal; ale; squat bottle; slim ring near top; 6½"; olive................. 75.00+

3643   ROGER COMERBACK 1725 in a seal; pontil; blue green; 7"..................... 100.00+

3644   Crown seal, label; kick-up; aqua; 11". 2.00-4.00

3645   C.S. & CO. under bottom; three-part mold; olive; 10".......................... 6.00-8.00

3646   C.W.&CO. under bottom; kick-up; dot in center; three-part mold; 5" body; 2" bob neck type; 3" bottom; dark olive................ 8.00-12.00

3647   JOHN DE KUYPER & SON; olive; 10¼" 10.00-15.00

3648   DE KUYPER GIN, label; 10½"; dark amber 20.00-30.00

3649   DE KUYPER, L.G. CO.; square face gin; 7⅜"; dark green.................... 8.00-12.00

3650   Demijohn, sample label; 4"; clear or amethyst 3.00-8.00

3651   Demijohn; olive; 12".......... 4.00-12.00

3652   Demijohn, label; cobalt; 12"...... 25.00-30.00

3653   Demijohn; pontil; dark green; 16½" x 6½" x 8" 25.00-35.00

3654   DE MONDARIZ V.H.P. ACUAR around shoulder; snap-on top; olive; machine made; 8½" 4.00-6.00

3655   Double Eagle Seal; kick-up on bottom; turn mold; ring top; 9¾"; light green.... 10.00-15.00

3656   DREWS DOPPEL KRONENBIER; squat bottle; ale; 8"; dark amber.......... 25.00-30.00

3657   D^R K in center of a circle with INTRODUCED ON MERIT around edge of circle; on bottom, *Established D^R K 1851* inside a circle; applied top; quart size; amber .... 15.00+

3658   D-SEARS in a seal; ale; tapered collar; 10½"; olive........................ 20.00-30.00

3659   DUB & G in seal; olive; 8¼" and 6½".. 35.00+

3660   Dunmore or squat, label; different sizes and heights; dark olive, green; pontil; free-blown 35.00-125.00

3661   J. & R. DUNSTER on front panel; tapered top; 9½"; olive green 20.00-60.00

3662   F. DUSCH, RICHMOND, VA., T.B.I.N.S., reverse side *XXX Porter*; squat type; 6¾"; aqua .... 25.00+

3663   DUTCH ONIONS; ale; free-blown; open pontil; olive .... 45.00+

3664   DYOTTVILLE GLASS WORKS, PHILA. under bottom; three-part mold; olive 10.00-15.00

3665   DYOTTVILLE GLASS WORKS, PHILA. 5 under bottom; three-part mold; amber; 11" 8.00-12.00

3666   W. EAGLE, CANAL ST, NY. (missing period after N); *Philadelphia Porter 1860* on back; ice blue; 7"..................... 20.00-25.00

3667   EMON COLL in seal; kick-up; olive; 11½" 10.00-15.00

3668   D.H. EVANS, ST. LOUIS; ale; three-piece mold; tapered top and ring; quart; black glass .... 35.00+

3669   F under bottom, label; amber; 6" ... 4.00-8.00

3670   FABRICADE GIJON under bottom; dark olive; 11"............................. 4.00-8.00

3671   F.C.G. CO., LOU., KY. under bottom; 12"; amber 8.00-12.00

3672   F E S & CO. GIN; aqua; 9¾"........ 10.00+

3673   FINEST OLD WINDMILL GIN; tapered top; 10½"; clear................. 15.00-30.00

3674   FLORA TEMPLE HARNESS TROT 219; horse on front; amber; 8½"...... 90.00-100.00

3675   GARNET DRY GIN; clear; 8¾"... 6.00-10.00

3676   GINEBRA DE LA CAMPANA; in center a bell in seal; dog bottle; a Star of David on base; TRADE MARCA REGISTRADA; tapered case gin; 9⅛"; green .... 50.00+

3677   Gin, label; free-blown; open pontil; wide collar; 11"; green........................... 25.00+

3678   Gin, label; free-blown; flared lip; open pontil; 13"; amber green.................... 25.00+

3679   Gin, label; free-blown; roll lip; pontil; 15½"; green or amber.................. 40.00-60.00

3680   Gin, label; free-blown; improved pontil; 8½"; dark green 20.00-60.00

3681   Gin, label; 9½"; clear or amethyst 2.00-3.00

3682   3683   3684   3689   3690   3695   3699

3701   3702   3706   3707   3708   3709   3710

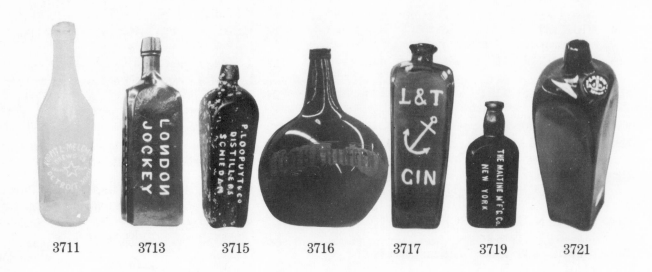

3711   3713   3715   3716   3717   3719   3721

3725   3726   3727   3728

3682   Gin, label; green; 10½" 6.00-8.00

3683   Gin, plain; clear; 3¼" 2.00-3.00

3684   GOLDEN SPRAY; clear or amethyst; 9½" 4.00-6.00

3685   GORDON'S DRY GIN on front; on one side *England*; the other *London*; under bottom in sunken circle a wild boar; 8½" or 8⅝"; green or clear; seam to top 4.00-6.00

3686   same, except seam to top ring; the boar is a little different; amber 6.00-8.00

3687   GRAVES GIN, label; 6"; clear 4.00-6.00

3688   H D B & C; roll lip; 6¼"; green or amber 25.00+

3689   P. F. HEERING; amber; 11" 12.00-20.00

3690   P. F. HEERING on a seal; amber; 10¼" 35.00+

3691   P.F. HEERING on ribbon shield; kick-up; double ring top; dark green; 8¾" .... 60.00+

3692   J.H. HENKES, DELFSHAVEN; tapered top; 8½"; green 20.00-30.00

3693   J.H. HENKES; tapered top; 10⅜"; green 25.00-35.00

3694   HIGHEST MEDAL, VIENNA 1873 in circle; head in circle; 8¼"; green 30.00-60.00

3695   I.C. HOFFMANN in seal; kick-up; dark olive; 9" .... 30.00+

3696   P. HOPPE, SCHIEDAM in seal; flared top; improved pontil; 9⅜"; dark green .... 35.00+

3697   same as above; 9½"; green .... 25.00+

3698   A. HOUTMAN & CO., SCHIEDAM; same on reverse side; roll lip; 11"; amber green 25.00+

3699   H.T. & CO. LONDON & N.Y. under bottom; *Capacity 24½ oz* on shoulder; sheared top; aqua 4.00-8.00

3700   HERMAN JANSEN, SCHIEDAM HOLLAND in seal; 9⅜"; dark green .... 25.00+

3701   JAVOI; *908* under bottom; dark olive; 8" 8.00-12.00

3702   C.A. JOURDE BORDEAUX; dots under bottom; olive; 10½" 6.00-8.00

3703   JUNIPER BERRY GIN, BOTTLED BY QUININE WHISKEY CO., LOUISVILLE KY.; wide ring top; 10"; aqua 10.00-20.00

3704   JUNIPER LEAF GIN; case type; 10½"; amber 18.00-30.00

3705   KAISERBRAUEREI, BREMEN vertically in ¾" letters; 9¼"; olive; inside screw top 10.00-15.00

3706   Key seal; dark olive; 9½" .... 35.00+

3707   E. KIDERLEN; dark olive; 5¾" ... 15.00-30.00

3708   H.B. KIRK & CO. N.Y.; *Bottle Remains The Property Of* in back; right face; amber; 11" 4.00-6.00

3709   same as above, except left face 4.00-6.00

3710   A.B. KNOLL REGISTERED ERIE, PA.; amber; 9½" 4.00-6.00

3711   KOPPITZ MELCHERS; DETROIT, MICH.; *A B & Co.* under bottom; aqua; 9½" 4.00-6.00

3712   L.M.G. CO. in seal; flared top; improved pontil; 9½"; brown, green .... 40.00+

3713   LONDON JOCKEY; N's in London backward; *Club House Gin* on one side; man riding a horse on back; dark olive; 9¾" .... 150.00+
      same except N is correct .... 100.00+

3714   LONG NECK PORTER; free-blown; open pontil; olive 30.00-60.00

3715   P. LOOPUYT & CO. DISTILLERS, SCHIEDAM; dark olive; 9½" 15.00-30.00

3716   LOTHARINGEN; pontil; dark olive; 10" x 18" .... 150.00+

3717   L & T GIN; anchor on front; olive; 9" 60.00-80.00

3718   MADISON ORIGINAL ALE, *John Femnell Louisville, Ky.* on front; tapered ring top; star under bottom; 7⅛"; amber 8.00-15.00

3719   THE MALTINE M'F'G CO., NEW YORK; amber; 6" 10.00-15.00

3720   V. MARKER & CO. semi-script; tapered top; 9⅜"; green or amber 20.00-30.00

3721   J. MEBUS in seal; olive; 9¾" .... 45.00+

3722   MEDER & ZOON; swan with *W.P.* in center, all in a seal; 9¼"; amber or green .... 25.00+

3723   J. MEEUS; anchor with *J.M.* over it; improved pontil; 9¾"; clear or amber .... 40.00+

3724   L. MEEUS, ANTWERP; key in center; 10¼"; green, brown .... 50.00+

3725   V. MEIER, INDIANAPOLIS, IND.; dark amber; 8¾" 25.00-30.00

3726   MELCHER GIN, label; dark olive; 10¾" 10.00-20.00

3727   J.J. MELCHERSWZ COSMOPOLIET on top; *J.J. Melcherswz* under; in center, a man holding a bottle; on base *Schiedam*; case type; short neck; tapered top; dot under bottom; dark olive; 10" 40.00-50.00

3728   Monk label; amber; 10" .... 60.00+

3729   3735   3740   3742   3745   3746   3747   3748

3749   3750   3751   3752   3754   3755   3756   3759

3761   3763   3764   3766   3767   3768   3773   3775

3729 NATHAN BROS, 1863, PHILA.; amber; 9½" 50.00-60.00

3730 A.C.A. NOLET, SCHIEDAM; 8⅞"; greenish brown 20.00-35.00

3731 I.A.I. NOLET, SCHIEDAM; 8¼"; dark green, amber 20.00-40.00

3732 NOLETS MISTLETOE BRAND; dark green, amber 40.00-60.00

3733 PALMBOOM, with palm tree; in a seal, *Ilyes & Co., Schiedam*; improved pontil; 11"; green .... 35.00+

3734 P & C; tapered top; 11¾"; green ... 20.00-40.00

3735 J.J. PETERS on one side; *Hamburg* other side; sunken panel under bottom; green; 8½" x 3¼" x 3¾" 15.00-30.00

3736 J.J.W. PETERS; tapered top; figure of dog on one side; 7¾" x 2½" x 2½"; green .... 25.00+

3737 J.J.W. PETERS, HAMBURG on bottom; dog figure; tapered lip; two-piece mold; oval; 7¾"; amber .... 35.00+

3738 same as above except 8¼"; dark amber.. 35.00+

3739 J.J.W. PETERS in vertical line; tapered lip; case type; dog figure; 10½ x 3¼" x 3"; green .... 50.00+

3740 P.G. & OLD BRISTOL seal; pontil; dark olive; 9" .... 85.00+

3741 PHILANTROP; *only imported by Lrucipsoila Demerara Mein;* crown over head; 10¾"; amber, green 40.00-60.00

3742 G.W., PORTER, XX PORTER & ALE; hollow *P* on reverse side; tapered top with ring; 7¼"; light green .... 40.00+

3743 POSEN, WRONKERSTR. NO 6, HARTWIG KANTOROWIC; eagle under bottom; 10"; amber .... 20.00+

3744 P.S. in seal; ale; double ring top; pontil; 10"; olive .... 40.00+

3745 JAMES RAY, SAVANNAH, GA., in front; in back, XX Ale; 4" body, 2¾" neck; blob top; aqua 18.00-25.00

3746 T.M. REEVE 1732 in a seal on shoulder; square; refined pontil; olive; 10½" .... 75.00+

3747 RELYEA, CARTER & CO's; on one side *Royal;* other side *Schiedam Schnapps;* olive; 9½" .... 25.00+

3748 Roman bottle; teardrop catcher; free-blown; aqua; 4" .... 25.00+

3749 Roman bottle; teardrop catcher; pontil; aqua; 4½" .... 25.00+

3750 ROSS'S IRISH GIN, label; three-part mold; quart; aqua 4.00-6.00

3751 ROYAL CHAMPI; dark olive; 8¾" 25.00-35.00

3752 RUCKER DRY GIN; *1* under bottom; aqua; 9" 6.00-8.00

3753 R.W. in a seal on shoulder; squat body; ale; long neck; 6¼"; olive .... 45.00+

3754 JOHN RYAN, SAVANNAH, GA.; two dots under *a*, in front; *XX Philadelphia Porter* on back; cobalt; 6½"; improved pontil ..... 20.00+

3755 JOHN RYAN in 1" letters around bottle; ½" letters under John Ryan, *XX Porter & Ale, Philada;* blue; 7¾"; ground pontil ...... 20.00+

3756 JOHN RYAN 1866 in 1" hollow letters around bottle; ½" under J.R., *XX Porter & Ale, Philada;* blue; 4¾" .... 20.00+

3757 JOHN RYAN 1866 SAVANNAH, GA. in front; *Philadelphia XXX Star* on each side of *Ale* on back; squat body; blue; 7¼" 10.00-20.00

3758 JOHN RYAN 1866 SAVANNAH, GA. in front; *Philadelphia XXX Star* on each side of *Porter* on back; squat body; blue; 7¼" .... 10.00+

3759 JOHN RYAN PORTER & ALE, PHILADA, XX 1859; graphite pontil; cobalt; 7" ... 25.00+

3760 Sample, label; square; 6"; free-blown; black glass 40.00-50.00

3761 SARGENT 1830; (reverse 3 on front); dark amber; 8½" .... 50.00+

3762 SEAHORSE HOLLANDS GIN; tapered top; three dots under bottom; 9⅝"; green 40.00-60.00

3763 ST. ANGELINE; *#1136* under bottom; dark amber; 11" .... 85.00+

3764 ST. DOMINIC; indentation in back for label; dark olive; 9¼" 15.00-25.00

3765 T.C.C.R. in a seal at the base; three-piece mold; 11"; dark green 20.00-30.00

3766 A. THELLER, label; *Theller Arnold* under bottom; dark olive; 8¾" 6.00-10.00

3767 VANDENBURGH & CO; bell in a seal on shoulder of bottle; case gin; avocado or olive, crude top; 11" .... 45.00+

3768 same except 9" .... 45.00+

3769 VANDENBURGH & CO.; bell with ribbon in center; flared top; 8⅞"; dark amber.... 30.00+

3770 VANDENBURGH & CO.; bell with ribbon in center; improved pontil; 9"; green or amber .... 85.00+

3771 J. VANDERVALK & CO., ROTTERDAM; 9½"; green 30.00-60.00

3772 VANDERVEER'S MEDICATED GIN, OR REAL SCHIEDAM SCHNAPPS; flared top; 8½"; amber 10.00-20.00

3773 VAN DUNCK'S GENEVER, TRADE MARK; *Ware & Schmitz* in back; amber; 9" ... 100.00+

3774 S. VAN DYKE, AMSTERDAM; cross in center; 10¼"; dark green 20.00-25.00

3775 H. VAN EMDEN POSTHOORN GIN; *M* in a ring under bottom; clear or amethyst; 10⅝" 8.00-12.00

3776 J.H. VANGENT, SCHIEDAM; tapered top; three dots under bottom; 9⅜"; brown 20.00-25.00

3777 A. VANPRAAG & CO'S. SURINAM GIN; 9¾"; dark green 40.00-50.00

3778 same except dark amber 40.00-60.00

3779 V.G.&C.; flared top; pontil; 10"; green or amber .... 40.00+

3780

3781

3782

3783

3785

3786

3788

3789

3780 VH & C under bottom; dark olive; 9½″
.... 15.00-20.00

3781 VHOYTEMAEC, vertical; case bottle; 9″, 2¼″ x
2¼″; short neck; tapered top; dark olive
.... 18.00-25.00

3782 V.H.P.; *Aquas De Mondariz* around shoulder;
three-part mold; olive; 6½″ 4.00-8.00

3783 VIII; pontil; dark olive; 9″....... 25.00-35.00

3784 DANIEL VISSER & ZONEN, SCHIEDAM;
tapered top; 9″; amber 30.00-40.00

3785 WARNERS IMPORTED; *B Gin* in back; sky
blue; 9″ 20.00-30.00

3786 WATSON BILTONPARK; olive; 9″   50.00+

3787 WEISS BIER on front; *KARL HUTTER, N.Y.*
on botton; blob top; 7¼″ 4.00-10.00

3788 R. WHITE & SONS LD, LONDON around a *W*
on bottle top; on bottom *J* in a shield; whittle
mark; dark olive; 10¼″ 12.00-16.00

3789 WOODMAN'S; pontil; three-part mold; black
glass; 8″ .... 150.00+

Assorted clear bottles including an embossed whiskey (#4858), a miniature case or gin, a perfume figural resembling a woman's boot (#6791), and a whiskey figural (#4905) are appealing when artistically displayed.

Handcrafted, Blown and Molded

***From the kiln to the assembly line,
from the craftsman to the factory worker,
bottles have been a product of man's pride and his resourcefulness***

Overleaf: Until the introduction of automation, no two bottles were exactly alike. This collection includes (from left to right), a beer bottle (#3885), a bitters bottle (#345), a medicine bottle (#1485), a case gin bottle (#3548), another bitters (#264) and a whiskey bottle (#4505).

Above: This artistic yet utilitarian earthenware jug
was made in 1798. Opposite: Of contrasting color, design
and quality are these two bottles, one a crude free-blown
flask and the other an embossed perfume bottle (#6930)
with matching glass stopper.

Left: These pottery containers include (from left to right), a cylin-drical wine jug, a coffin-shaped spirits jug (#4489), a miniature whiskey jug (#4796), a beer bottle, an ink crock (#6254), and another whiskey jug (#6131). Above: A delight to all bottle fanciers are these miniature whiskey jugs: #6309, #6135, #6349, #6210, #6300 and #6232.

Overleaf: This array of amber bottles includes (left to right), a lady's leg whiskey bottle (similar to #5044), a drop or medicine bottle (#1050), an obsolete fire extinguisher (#7154), a famous Plantation Bitters bottle (#157), a simple, but classic wine bottle, and an ornate whiskey bottle flask.

Opposite: *An emerald green perfume bottle (#6928), a pottery whiskey jug,
and a unique spirits bottle (#5060) constitute this display.* Above *and* below: *Bottles
originally containing mineral water, produced as early as 1767, and soda, originally artificially
carbonated water, unflavored until around 1838, make up this colorful collection. (#3239, #2668,
#3492, #3286 and below #3018, #3386, #3057, and #3313.)*

Above: *An ink bottle (similar to #6541) and a poison bottle (#2288) in the shape of a human skull. Opposite: Two types of poison bottles, a common container (#2255) and a unique figural made so that it was easily identifiable in the dark or by a blind person.*

Overleaf: *A variety of containers including (from left to right), a medicine bottle (#7279), a beverage bottle, a whiskey bottle (#4806) with a rare off-center neck, a soda bottle (#2522) sold in the Comanche Indian Territory in the 1800's, and a bitters bottle (#55).*

Above: *These aqua containers include a conical ink (#6540), a miniature spirits bottle and an igloo ink (#6529). Opposite: Produced by nature, the colors and patterns on this aged whiskey bottle are easily erased by soaking in kerosene or scrubbing. The pottery Harper Whiskey bottle is still in mint condition.*

Embossed "Price's Patent Candle Company Limited," this bottle
(#7267) was imported from England in the 19th century and contained
an ingredient used in making candles.

In contrast with the ornate, cathedral-type craftsmanship of this bottle (#6812) is the crude top. The bottle was made from a detailed mold and the top was added later.

Overleaf: *Medicines were bottled in a variety of containers in the 18th century with closures ranging from applied ring tops using cork closures to glass stoppers to blob tops.*

Left: *The design of ink containers was determined by the writing device. Because quills and early steel pens had to be dipped frequently, ink bottles were designed to minimize tipping.* **Below:** *Bottles such as this cologne figural provided a unique means of attracting the customer's attention.*

Overleaf, left to right: *A whiskey flask with a metal screw-on top, a medicine bottle (#856), a plain whiskey bottle, a soda bottle (#2674), a miniature spirits bottle and a square ink container complete this arrangement.*

Left: *With the exception of the Coco-Cola bottle (#2498), all these beverage bottles (#2674, #2522, #2680, #856) employ an internal Hutchinson-stopper, invented in 1879.* Below: *A common pickle jar and a pottery beverage bottle.*

Milk glass barber bottles (similar to #6789) were found in barber shops as well as homes from the mid-1800's until the turn of the century and were often retained by the owner for many years because they were easy to refill.

The trademark on this bottle (#619), containing a supposed liver and kidney cure, circa 1900, assured the user that the contents were safe for consumption.

Left: These bitters bottles are colorful conversation pieces, especially the white German case bottle. Above: Perhaps the best-known mineral bottles are the crude and unusually heavy Saratoga bottles (#3352), first produced in 1844 in shades of dark olive-green and olive-amber.

Beer

Beer was consumed in Mesopotamia several thousand years ago, and each medieval monastery had its own brewery. The beverage sailed on the *Mayflower* with the Pilgrims in 1620, and George Washington and Thomas Jefferson brewed their own beers at home. It was as common a drink one hundred years ago as it is today.

Most of the first beer in America was tapped from barrels in taverns. The first bottles were made of pottery; those imported from England between the years 1860 and 1890 were recycled by American breweries. Bottled beer often served as ballast on sea vessels.

By the end of the Civil War, most American cities boasted at least one brewery. By 1870 most beer bottles followed a standard pattern—they were usually glass, contained a quart of beer and were closed with cork. The embossing of brewery names and emblems was not popular until after 1870.

C. Conrad and Company, a wholesaler for Adolphus Busch in St. Louis, sold the original Budweiser bottle from 1877 to 1890. The Budweiser name was a trademark of C. Conrad but in 1891 the company sold it to the Anheuser-Busch Brewing Association. By that time, Adolphus Busch, founder of the brewery, had already established two companies to make beer bottles. In addition to providing bottles for Budweiser, they supplied other breweries from about 1880 to 1910.

Herman F. Graw, a German immigrant to the United States, had hopes of establishing the country's largest brewery. To aid him in the quest of his dream, he shrewdly married a brewer's daughter in New York in 1871. By 1899 his Buffalo Brewery was established in Sacramento, California. Unfortunately, his venture never attained the desired proportions and folded in 1929. His bottles were brown and were embossed with the trademark of a horseshoe and buffalo.

David Nicholson of St. Louis manufactured ordinary beer under the pretentious but intriguing title, "Liquid Bread—A Pure Extract of Malt." To further enhance salability, he bottled it in cobalt blue glass.

Nineteenth-century Americans found it difficult to avoid connecting available products with one's general well-being. Hoff's Malt Extract was advertised as a beer to be drunk in order to maintain good health. The bottle's label insists that the brew is a "remedy recommended by European physicians for complaints of the chest, dyspepsia, obstinate cough, hoarseness, and especially consumption."

Closures on beer bottles were greatly improved by the invention in 1891 of the crown cork closure by William Painter of Baltimore. The same type of closure is used on beer bottles today.

When production of beer was resumed after Prohibition ended in 1933, use of green glass in the bottles was discontinued since it was believed that the color let in too many of the sun's harmful rays. Bottle shapes took their traditional form, minus embossing, which was replaced by paper labels. Today, many of the bottles have been replaced by aluminum cans.

*Anheuser-Busch bottled their brew
in this standard container (#3802) using a wire-porcelain
closure during the 1880's and 1890's.*

3790   3792   3793   3795   3797   3798   3799

3802   3804   3806   3810   3814   3815   3816   3817

3818   3819   3820   3821   3833   3838   3844

3790 ABC Co.; aqua; 9½"............ 2.00-4.00

3791 A.B.C.M. CO.; *E27* on bottom in circle; aqua; 11½"........................ 1.00-3.00

3792 A.B.G.M.CO.; *C13* under bottom; aqua; 9½" 2.00-4.00

3793 A.B.G.M. CO.; *S4* under bottom; aqua; 10" 3.00-4.00

3794 A.B.G.M. CO. in a circle·under bottom; in center *E27*; aqua; 11¼" 4.00-6.00

3795 A.B.G.M. CO. under bottom; aqua; 9¾" 2.00-6.00

3796 ABERDEEN BREWING CO., ABERDEEN, WASH.; 9¼"; blob top; amber, clear 3.00-6.00

3797 AB6G; *4* under bottom; aqua; 9½" .. 2.00-4.00

3798 A,661,2 under bottom; aqua; 9½".... 2.00-4.00

3799 ACME BREWING COMPANY; aqua; 9½" 6.00-8.00

3800 ALABAMA BREWING CO., BIRMINGHAM, ALA.; 9½"; aqua. 4.00-8.00

3801 AMERICAN BREWING & C. I. CO., BAKER CITY, ORE.; crown top; 11¼"; amber 3.00-6.00

3802 ANHEUSER BUSCH INC; amber; machine made; 9½"...................... 1.00-2.00

3803 ARNAS under bottom; amber; round; 8" 2.00-3.00

3804 AROMA; *F* under bottom; amber ... 2.00-6.00

3805 AUGUSTA BREWING CO., AUGUSTA, GA. around outside of circle; in center of circle, a large *A* with bottle shape embossed over *A*; crown top; 9¼"; aqua 4.00-10.00

3806 same except 7"................. 4.00-6.00

3807 THE BAKER CO., DAYTON, OHIO on front in oval slug plate; blob top; quart; 11½"; amber 4.00-6.00

3808 BEADLESTON & WOERZ; *Excelsior Empire Brewery* in a circle; in center of it two ladies, eagle, monogram, *New York, This Bottle Not To Be Sold*; 9"; round; aqua 2.00-4.00

3809 BECHER & CO. BOTTLE BEER, LANCASTER, O.; blob top; 10½"; aqua.. 4.00-8.00

3810 THE GEORGE BECHTEL BREWING CO.; *This Bottle Not To Be Sold* on back; aqua; 9" 8.00-10.00

3811 Beer; amber; *A.B.G.M. Co.* in center, *K 17* all under bottom of bottle; 9½"; opalescent 2.00-6.00

3812 Beer; brown; 11½" 2.00-3.00

3813 Beer; green; 11¼"............. 2.00-3.00

3814 Beer, label, plain; amber; 8½" 2.00-4.00

3815 Beer, label, plain; light amber; 8¾".. 2.00-4.00

3816 Beer, label; *M.G.Co.* under bottom; amber; 9¼" 2.00-4.00

3817 Beer, label; star under bottom; amber; 7¾" 4.00-8.00

3818 Beer, label; dark green; 9"...... 4.00-8.00

3819 Beer, label; cobalt; 9¼"........ 15.00-25.00

3820 Beer, label; on bottom, *I* inside ring; clear or amethyst; 9½"............... 2.00-4.00

3821 Beer, label; *Root 8* on bottom; amber; 9½" 2.00-4.00

3822 Beer, label; crown top; 11½"; amber 2.00-4.00

3823 Beer, label; lady's leg neck; 12"; amber 4.00-6.00

3824 Beer, label; blob top; 9½" 4.00-8.00

3825 Beer, label; pontil; 10½"; aqua.... 14.00-18.00

3826 Beer; milk glass; wine type; crown top; 10¼" 8.00-12.00

3827 Beer, plain; 8¾"; amber.......... 2.00-4.00

3828 Beer, plain; 11½"; amber.......... 2.00-4.00

3829 Beer, plain; 11¼"; blue, light green.. 2.00-4.00

3830 Beer, plain; 11¾"; blue............ 2.00-4.00

3831 BERGHOFF on shoulder; FT. WAYNE, IND at base; crown top; ABM; aqua..... 2.00-3.00

3832 BERGHOFF, FORT WAYNE, IND.; blob top; amber .... 4.00+

3833 B. 42 on bottom; dark green; turn mold; 9½" 3.00-6.00

3834 BIERBAUER BREWING CO., CANAJOHARIE, NY on front in slug plate; blob top; aqua; 9⅜"...................... 3.00-6.00

3835 BLATZ, MILWAUKEE on shoulder; olive; 9¼" 2.00-4.00

3836 BLATZ, OLD HEIDELBERG; stubby bottle; amber .... 5.00+

3837 BLATZ, PILSNER; amber; 10½" ... 3.00-4.00

3838 BLATZ, VAL BREWING CO., MILWAUKEE; on shoulder in a star VB; under bottom *V.B. & Co., Milw.*; blob top; amber; 12" 4.00-8.00

3839 BOHEMIAN LAGER BEER, BODIE BOTTLING WORK, BODIE, CAL.; crown top; aqua 4.00-10.00

3840 BORN & CO., COLUMBUS, OHIO, in a diamond shape; blob top; quart; amber .. 4.00-6.00

3841 BOSCH LAKE, LINDEN, MICH. on front; *T.B.N.T.B.S.* on bottom; blob top; 12"; amber 4.00-6.00

3842 BOSCH LAKE, LINDEN, MICH., T.B.N.T.B.S. on bottom; blob top; 12"; amber...... 4.00-8.00

3843 BOSCH LAKE LINDEN, MICH; blob top; quart; amber 3.00-4.00

3844 R. BOVEE, large block outline of a *B*; *Troy, N.Y.*; reverse *T.B.N.T.B.S., N.B.B. & Co.*; 12"; aqua................................ 4.00-8.00

3845 BUFFALO BREWING CO., SACRAMENTO, CAL. in form of circle, horseshoe with buffalo jumping through; blob top; quart; 12"; amber 8.00-10.00

3846 BUFFALO BREWING CO., S.F. AGENCY, BB Co. monogram; crown top; 9⅛"; amber 8.00-10.00

3847 E & J BURKE; *E & B* on bottom (cat); ABM; 8"; amber 2.00-4.00

3848 C.W. BURR, RICHMOND, VA. in a circle; reverse *T.B.N.T.B.S.*; blob top; 9¼"; aqua 4.00-8.00

3851   3852   3856   3857   3858   3859   3860   3861

3868   3871   3872   3873   3875   3876   3877   3878

3879   3880   3882   3884   3885   3888   3893   3898

3849 CAIRO BREWING CO. on shoulder; amber; 9″; round; wire-porcelain stopper 3.00-5.00

3850 same as above except aqua 3.00-6.00

3851 CAMDEN CITY BREWERY; amber; 9″; various numbers on bottom. 2.00-6.00

3852 CANTON, OHIO; star under bottom; 9¾″; aqua 8.00-10.00

3853 CAS-CAR-RIA BOTTLE with 45 in a circle; 9½″; amber 8.00-10.00

3854 CB CO., monogram in circle; under it, *Chattanooga, Tenn.*; 11½″; light amber . . . 2.00-4.00

3855 CB CO., monogram near shoulder; under it *Chattanooga, Tenn.*; 11¼″; amber. . . . 2.00-4.00

3856 THE CENTRAL BRAND EXTRA LAGER BEER, label; aqua; 9¼″ 2.00-4.00

3857 CHAS JOLY; *Phila* on back; amber; 9¼″ 8.00-10.00

3858 CHATTAHOOCHEE BREWING CO.; *This Bottle Not To Be Sold, Phoenix City, Ala.* on back; aqua; 9½″ 6.00-8.00

3859 CHATTAHOOCHEE BREWING CO., COLUMBUS, GA; aqua; 9½″ 6.00-8.00

3860 CHATTAHOOCHEE BREWING CO., BROWNSVILLE, ALA.; aqua; 9½″ 6.00-8.00

3861 CHATTANOOGA BREWING CO.; aqua; 9½″; *C* on bottom 4.00-6.00

3862 CLAUSSEN BREWING ASS'N., SEATTLE, WASH.; crown top; 9½″ 2.00-4.00

3863 CLAUSSEN SWEENEY BREWING CO.; blob top; 10½″; aqua 4.00-6.00

3864 THE CLEVELAND & SANDUSKY BREWING CO.; under bottom *M*; in center of bottle C.S.B.C. monogram; blob top; 9″; aqua 3.00-4.00

3865 Cobalt blue beer, label; graduated and flared band collar; 9¾″ 8.00-12.00

3866 THE CONNECTICUT BREWERIES CO.; *The Connecticut, Bridgeport, Conn.* in a circle; in center *Breweries Co.*; 9½″; blue green. 2.00-3.00

3867 same except *Registered* on shoulder. . . 2.00-4.00

3868 C. CONRAD & CO, *Original Budweise, U.S. Patent no. 6376;* under bottom *CCCO;* short tapered top with ring; 9¼″; aqua. . . 8.00-12.00

3869 CONSUMERS ICE CO.; *Hygeia Water, Memphis, Tenn.,* around lower bottom; round; tapers to small neck; 10″ tall; base 4¼″; porcelain-spring stopper 2.00-5.00

3870 THE COOK & BERNHEIMER CO. on one side; other side *Refilling Of This Bottle Prohibited*; on the bottom, *C&B.Co. Bottling;* 2¼″ x 4″; amber; 6¾″. 4.00-10.00

3871 THE COOK & BERNHEIMER COMPANY; *Refilling Of This Bottle Prohibited* other side; amber 10.00-12.00

3872 COOK BOCK BEER, label; amber; 9¼″ 2.00-4.00

3873 COOKS 500 ALE, label; aqua; 9½″. . 2.00-6.00

3874 Crown on shoulder, label; applied lip; twisted neck; deep grooves; three-piece mold; iron pontil; 8½″; dark olive 10.00-20.00

3875 CRYSTAL BREWAGE, BALTIMORE, MD. U.S.A.; 10½″; amber 4.00-8.00

3876 C 6 CO.; *I* on bottom; aqua; 9¼″ 2.00-4.00

3877 DALLAS BREWERY; machine made; amber; 7½″. 2.00-4.00

3878 DALLAS BREWERY; clear or amethyst; 9″ 4.00-6.00

3879 DAYTON BREWERIES; amber; 9½″ 6.00-8.00

3880 DIAMOND JIMS BEER, label; aqua; 9¼″ 2.00-6.00

3881 DIEHL, DEFIANCE, OHIO; wine type; blob top; 9½″; amber 6.00-10.00

3882 DIXIE BREWERY, PHENIX [sic] CITY, ALA; aqua; 9½″ 6.00-8.00

3883 DU BOIS; blob top; 8″; amber. 4.00-6.00

3884 DUBUQUE BRG. & MALTING CO.; *Dubuque, IA* under bottom; amber; 8¾″. 6.00-8.00

3885 DUKEHART & CO., *Maryland Brewery, Baltimore* on front, three lines; squat body; long neck; 8″; amber; round 8.00-12.00

3886 EAGLE SPRING DISTILLERY CO. on front; rectangular; 7″; amethyst 3.00-4.00

3887 E.B. CO., ESCANABA, MICH.; 8½″; amber 4.00-6.00

3888 E.B. & CO. LD 11614 on bottom; aqua; 12″ 2.00-6.00

3889 THE EBLING BREWING CO., NEW YORK, USA on front; crown top; 9¼″; aqua 3.00-6.00

3890 same as above except blob top 4.00-6.00

3891 THE JOHN EICHLER BREWING CO., NEW YORK, REGISTERED (written fancy) on front; blob top; 9″; aqua 4.00-6.00

3892 EL DORADO BREWING CO., E.D.B. Co. monogram, STOCKTON, CAL.; crown top; four-piece mold; quart; 12″; amber 10.00-12.00

3893 EL PASO BREWERY; amber; 8″ . . 4.00-6.00

3894 same as above except aqua 5.00-8.00

3895 ENGEL & WOLF'S NO. 26 & 28, DILLWYN ST., PHILA.; applied lip; graphite pontil; 7¾″; blue green. 10.00-20.00

3896 ENTERPRISE BREWING CO., S.F., CAL. vertical on front; four-piece mold; quart; blob top; 11¾″; light amber. 10.00-12.00

3897 C.H. EVANS & SONS ALE on shoulder; crown top; 9″; amber. 2.00-4.00

3898 EXCELSIOR; *M* under bottom; 9¾″; aqua . . . . 10.00+

3899 EXCELSIOR LAGER BIER FROM VALENTINE BLATZ BOTTLING DEPT., CHICAGO in a circle; blob top; *T.B.I.N.S.* on reverse side; 9″; aqua 8.00-10.00

3900 FALSTAFF LEMP, ST. LOUIS inside of shield; crown top; 9″; aqua. 3.00-6.00

3901 FEE BROS., ROCHESTER, N.Y., BEL ISLE; *8 fl. oz.;* 6″ 4.00-6.00

3903	3916	3919	3920	3924	3927	3929	3932

3934	3937	3944	3945	3956	3957	3961	3965

3902   JOHN E. FELDMAN, RICHFIELD SPRINGS, N.Y. in oval slug plate; blob top; 9¼"; clear 4.00-6.00

3903   F.H.G.W.; *4* under bottom; amber; 10" 2.00-3.00

3904   F.H.G.W.S.; tapered top with ring; blob neck; 12" 4.00-8.00

3905   FINLEY BREWING CO., TOLEDO, O. under bottom; trade mark, an *F* in a diamond on shoulder; blob top; quart; aqua 4.00-6.00

3906   FINLEY BREWING CO., TOLEDO, O.; *Trade Mark* on top of a diamond shape in center of which is an *F*, all on bottom; 10¾"; aqua 4.00-6.00

3907   THE FLORIDA BREWING CO., TAMPA, FLA. in sunken panel; aqua; under bottom *F.B.Co.*; 6¾" 2.00-4.00

3908   THE FOSS-SCHNEIDER BREWING CO.; 7½"; aqua 4.00-6.00

3909   THE FOSS-SCHNEIDER CO. in a horseshoe shape; under it BREWING CO., CINCINNATI, O.; crown top; 11"; aqua 4.00-6.00

3910   J. GAHM & SON TRADE MARK (mug with J.G. monogram) BOSTON, MASS. on front; blob top; 9"; amethyst 4.00-6.00

3911   same as above except old crown top . 4.00-6.00

3912   same as above except amber; ABM.. 4.00-6.00

3913   GALLITZIN BOTTLING CO.; *326* under bottom; clear; 10" 4.00-6.00

3914   GALLITZIN BOTTLING CO.; aqua; 9½" 2.00-4.00

3915   GALVESTON BREWING CO.; *Guaranteed Pure, Galveston Tex.*; aqua; 7¾"; round 2.00-4.00

3916 GALVESTON BREWING, GALVESTON, TEX.; reverse *T.B.N.T.B.S.*; 9½"; aqua 4.00-6.00

3917 G-B-S (with arrow); *Baltimore, Md., Trade Mark* on the shoulder; clear; 9¼"; round; porcelain wire top................. 2.00-3.00

3918 GEO. CH. GEMUNDEN, SAVANNAH, GEO. in a circle in center; *Lager Beer* on back, *This Bottle Is Loaned Only* in three lines; blob top; 8" 8.00-12.00

3919 GEORGIA BREWING ASSOCIATION; aqua; 9¾"............................... 4.00-8.00

3920 THE GERMANIA BREWING CO.; aqua; 7½" 6.00-8.00

3921 A. GETTLEMAN BREWING CO.; *Pure Malt & Hops, Milwaukee;* round; hand holding hops; amber; 9¼"..................... 4.00-8.00

3922 GREAT SEAL STYRON, BEGGS & CO., NEWARK, OHIO; round; 9"; clear   4.00-6.00

3923 CHARLES S. GROVE CO.; *78 & 80 Merrimac Street Boston, Sparkling Lager Beer*, with CSG Co. monogram all inside of diamond-shaped panel on front; blob top; 9"; clear ... 4.00-6.00

3924 GUTSCH BREW. CO.; *13* under bottom; red or amber; 8½" .... 10.00+

3925 A. HAAS BREWING CO, HOUGHTON, MICH. in circle on front; blob top; large size; REGISTERED at base; 12"; amber   3.00-4.00

3926 A. HAAS BREWING CO. written fancy at slant; blob top; 9½"; amber......... 3.00-6.00

3927 HACK & SIMON; aqua; 9½"...... 2.00-6.00

3928 THE JOHN HAUCK BREWING CO.; *Cincinnati O.;* on the bottom *A.B. Co.;* round; 11⅜"; clear or amber 4.00-6.00

3929 HENNINGER; machine made; amber; 11½" 4.00-6.00

3930 HEUSTIS' E.M.; *Main St., Charleston, Mass., This Bottle Not To Be Sold, Registered;* 9"; aqua; round............................. 2.00-4.00

3931 H.G. CO. on base; tapered top; blob top; 9½"; amber 4.00-8.00

3932 HOME BREWING CO., RICHMOND, VA. on shoulder; number under bottom; aqua; 9½" 4.00-6.00

3933 HOME BREWING CO., INDIANAPOLIS; blob top; clear....................... 4.00-10.00

3934 HOSTER CO, O.; *665* and mark under bottom; amber; 11¾"..................... 8.00-10.00

3935 HOSTER'S in script, COLUMBUS, O., WEINER BEER; blob top; quart; amber 2.00-4.00

3936 same as above except 7½"; dark amber 8.00-10.00

3937 HOUSTON ICE & BREWING CO.; crown top; ABM; 7¾"; aqua................. 8.00-10.00

3938 HUDSON, N.Y., EVANS ALE on shoulder; crown top; ABM; 10"; amber...... 2.00-3.00

3939 A. HUPFEL'S SON'S; *161-St. & 3rd Ave. New York;* blob top; 9⅜"; amber 3.00-6.00

3940 same as above except crown top; 9"... 3.00-4.00

3941 INDEPENDENT BR'G ASS'N on bottom in circle form with big *E* and building on top and small *B* at bottom of *E*; 11¼"; amber...... 4.00-6.00

3942 INDEPENDENT BREWING CO. OF PITTSBURGH on front; crown top; 9"; light amber 3.00-4.00

3943 same as above except PITTSBURGH misspelled PITTSBRUGH 10.00-15.00

3944 IND. BR'G. ASSN., MARION in a circle; 9½"; amber 2.00-8.00

3945 INDIANAPOLIS BREWING CO.; *R.C. Co.* under bottom; 7¼"; amber 4.00-6.00

3946 INDIANAPOLIS BREWING CO., INDIANAPOLIS, IND.; angel holding a glass of beer, sitting on a wheel on world, USA, all on front; 9½"; aqua................. 6.00-12.00

3947 IROQUOIS BRG. CO., BUFFALO inside of circle, INDIAN HEAD in center; crown top; ABM; amber 3.00-6.00

3948 JACKSON & CO.; hop leaves with *B* in center, YONKERS, N.Y. on front; *1904* on bottom; blob top; 9½"; clear 3.00-6.00

3949 JACOB JACKSON, 803 & 805 DICKINSON ST., PHILADA.; blob top; reverse *T.B.N.T.B.S.*; 9½"; aqua 4.00-8.00

3950 THE KANSAS CITY BREWERIES CO. on front; crown top; 9"; amber........ 3.00-4.00

3951 KAUFMAN BEV. CO., CINCINNATI, O. USA.; 7"; clear 4.00-8.00

3952 A.W. KEMISON CO. in horseshoe shape; blob top; blob neck; 7¾"; amber...... 4.00-8.00

3953 KESSLER MALT EXTRACT; squat body; crown top; amber.................. 4.00-6.00

3954 KOPPITZ-MELCHERS BREWING CO.; trademark star in center; *Reg. Detroit Mich.* in a circle slug plate; blob top; 11¼"; aqua. 4.00-8.00

3955 M. KRESS, REDWOOD CITY, T.B.N.T.B.S. .... 25.00+

3956 THE KRESS WEISS BEER CO.; amber; 7¼" 4.00-6.00

3957 C.A. KRUEGER; *D.O.C. 36* under bottom; amber; 9¾"...................... 6.00-8.00

3958 K.S. monogram, KUEBELER STRONG, SANDUSKY, OHIO; blob top; 7½"; aqua.. 4.00-6.00

3959 same as above except 11" 4.00-10.00

3960 K.S. monogram on front; crown top; ABM; 9"; aqua............................. 2.00-3.00

3961 THE JOHN KUHLMAN BREWING CO., ELLENVILLE, N.Y.; aqua; 7" 4.00-6.00

3962 JOHN KUHLMAN BREWING CO., ELLENVILLE, N.Y. on front in oval slug plate; crown top; 9¼"; aqua 3.00-6.00

3963 LAKE ERIE BOTTLING WORKS, TOLEDO, OHIO in a circle; 10½"; aqua 4.00-10.00

3964 Large aqua bottle; round blob-top; THIS BOTTLE LOANED NOT SOLD, SIX PINTS; near base, place for large label; 13¼"; 4.00-6.00

3965 LEECHEN BEER, GERMANY, label; amber; 9¼".......................... 2.00-6.00

| 3966 | 3967 | 3971 | 3972 | 3974 | 3979 | 3980 | 3982 |

| 3983 | 3988 | 3993 | 3996 | 4000 | 4004 | 4006 | 4011 |

| 4014 | 4015 | 4024 |

3966 LEISY; *Peoria, Ill* on back; amber; 9½"
.... 4.00-6.00

3967 LEMP; *AB Co.* under bottom; aqua; 9½"
.... 2.00-3.00

3968 LEXINGTON BREWING CO., LEXINGTON, KY.; blob top; *S.B. & CO.* under bottom; 12"; amber 4.00-8.00

3969 LIMP, ST. LOUIS in a shield; blob top; 8¾"; amber 4.00-8.00

3970 D. LUTZ & SON BREWING CO., ALLEGHENY, PA. on front in oval slug plate; blob top; 9¾"; aqua................ 4.00-6.00

3971 MALZBIER BEER GERMAN; 8½"; amber
.... 2.00-6.00

3972 THE MARYLAND BREWING COMPANY; amber; 9"................ 8.00-10.00

3973 MASSACHUSETTS BREWERIES CO., BOSTON; crown top; 9½"; amber... 2.00-3.00

3974 M. MAYER; *This Bottle Not To Be Sold* in back; 5 under bottom; aqua; 9"........ 4.00-6.00

3975 McAVOY BREWING CO., LAGER BEER, CHICAGO; blob top; 9½"; aqua..... 4.00-8.00

3976 D.W. McCARTHY, D.W. McC. monogram; STOCKTON, CAL. on front; blob top; four-piece mold; quart; 12"; amber 10.00-15.00

3977 same as above except 9½" 8.00-10.00

3978 McLYMAN & BRADY, TOLEDO, OHIO; blob top; 11½"; aqua 4.00-8.00

3979 GEORGE MEYER BEER; aqua; 9" 4.00-8.00

3980 GEORGE MEYER, SAVANNAH, GA.; 7½"; aqua .... 15.00+

3981 C. & J. MICHEL BREWING CO., LACROSSE, WIS.; reverse side *B.N.T.B.S.*; blob top; 7½"; amber 8.00-10.00

3982 MILLER BECKER CO.; on back *Send Me Home When I Am Empty*; on base *This Bottle Not To Be Sold*; machine made; aqua; 11½" 2.00-6.00

3983 MINERAL SPRING BEER, label; aqua; 9" 2.00-4.00

3984 MOBILE BREWERY, MOBILE, ALA; 10"; aqua.................. 8.00-10.00

3985 THE CHRISTIAN MOERLEIN BREWING CO., CINCINNATI, O. in a circle; in center of circle monogram *M.*; aqua; 9½" 2.00-4.00

3986 THE CHRISTIAN MOERLEIN BREWING CO., CINTI., O. in four lines; amber; fifth; blob top; blob neck 7.00-10.00

3987 MOFFATS-ALE BREWERY-INC. on both sides; large *M* on bottom; ABM; crown top; 9⅜"; grass green................ 3.00-4.00

3988 MUNCHNER BAVARIAN TYPE BEER; aqua; 9¼" 2.00-6.00

3989 NATIONAL LAGER BEER, H. ROLTRBACHER AGT., STOCKTON, CAL., H.R. monogram all on front; four-piece mold; blob top; amber; 11½"............. 6.00-10.00

3990 same as above except pint size 4.00-12.00

3991 same as above except 8" 4.00-12.00

3992 NEBRASKA BREWING CO, OMAHA, NEB. in a circle; amber; 9"................ 6.00-8.00

same except clear................... 3.00-6.00

same except red or amber 10.00-15.00

3993 T.L. NEFF'S SONS; case bottle trade mark on back; aqua; 11" 8.00-10.00

3994 DYSON NELSON; *Trade Mark*; round; aqua; 6¾"; inside screw................. 2.00-6.00

3995 OAKLAND BOTTLING CO., OAKLAND, CAL. around shoulder; blob top; 9"; amber 4.00-8.00

3996 O.B. CO. under bottom; label; amber; 9¾" 3.00-6.00

3997 OCONTO BREWING CO.; blob top; amber 4.00-10.00

3998 THE PROPERTY OF OHLSSON'S CAPE BREWERY; inside screw cap 10.00-15.00

3999 W. OLMSTED & CO. on one side; reverse NEW YORK; roof type shoulders; on roof in front CONSTITUTION; pontil; 10½" .... 50.00+

4000 PABST BREWING CO. OF MILWAUKEE; amber; 12" 4.00-8.00

4001 PABST; *Milwaukee, Trade Mark*, crown top; 9¼"; amber..................... 4.00-8.00

4002 PABST, MILWAUKEE in circle in center, leaves and in circle big *P*, *Trade Mark* under it; on bottom *Registered, This Bottle Not To Be Sold*; amber; 9¼".................. 3.00-4.00

4003 THE PALMEDO BREWING CO, CHARLESTON, S.C.; in a circle in center, large monogram *P*; 7¾"; aqua........... 2.00-4.00

same except no *P*; 9½"; crown top; aqua 2.00-4.00

4004 C. PFEIFFER BREWING CO., C.P.B. CO., DETROIT, MICH. in circle on shoulder; blob top; 9¼"; amber 4.00-6.00

4005 PHOENIX BREWING CO., an eagle with trade mark under it, VICTORIA, B.C.; tapered top; 8¼"; amber................. 10.00-15.00

4006 PIEL BROS; *This Bottle Not To Be Sold* on back; 9"; clear............. 4.00-6.00

4007 PIEL BROS, P.B. and arrow in shield, EAST NEW YORK BREWERY, all on front; crown top; 9¼"; amber 4.00-6.00

4008 same as above except dark aqua 4.00-6.00

4009 PIEL BROS; above *P.B.* inside of circle; under that *East New York Brewery*; aqua; 9" 2.00-4.00

4010 PITTSBURGH BREWING CO.; crown top; 12¼"; amber.................. 4.00-8.00

4011 ROBERT PORTNER BREWING CO.; amber; 7¼".................... 10.00-20.00

4012 PROSPECT BREWERY, CHAS WOLTER'S PHILA.; reverse *T.B.N.T.B.S.*; blob top; 8"; amber 10.00-15.00

4013 same as above except 7¼" 8.00-10.00

4014 W.O. PUTNAM; clear; 9½" 4.00-6.00

4015 RAHR'S BEER, label; amber; 9¼".. 2.00-6.00

4016 JOHN RAPP & SON, S.F., CAL. on front; blob top; quart; 11½"; light amber...... 6.00-10.00

4017 same as above except 9½" 8.00-10.00

4018 same as above except 8¼" 4.00-8.00

4019 R.C. & A.; reverse NEW YORK; tapered top; 9"; cobalt blue 20.00-30.00

4020 RENO BREWING CO., RENO, NEV.; tapered top; 10¾"; amber 4.00-8.00

4021 ROSE NECK BREWING CO., RICHMOND, VA., embossed star; round; crown top; 9¾"; aqua.................... 4.00-8.00

4022 ROSESSLE BREWERY, BOSTON, T.B.T.B.R. on front; *Premium Lager* on back; crown top; 9"; aqua 3.00-6.00

4023 ROTH & CO. in center monogram, letters RCO, SAN FRANCISCO in a circle; tapered top; 10¼"; amber...................... 8.00-12.00

4024 ROYAL RED; *Not To Be Refilled, No Deposit No Return*, on base; ABM; 9½"; red... 8.00-12.00

4028   4032   4036   4037   4040   4042   4048   4050

4052   4056   4059   4064   4070   4071   4072   4074

4075   4076   4079   4081

4025 **RUBSAM & HORRMANN BREWG. CO.** in horseshoe shape in center; *Staten Island, N.Y., Registered;* in four lines on back near bottom *This Bottle Not To Be Sold;* blob top; under bottom *KH, 1906;* aqua; 9″ 4.00-6.00

4026 **JACOB RUPPERT BREWER, NEW YORK** on shoulder in circle; crown top; 9¼″; yellowish green or amber 3.00-4.00

4027 **JOHN RYAN;** *All XXX Star 1866;* blob top; 8¼″; cobalt 20.00-30.00

4028 **SAKURA BEER** on base; foreign writing on back; 11¼″; dark amber 4.00-6.00

4029 **SANTA CLARA COUNTY BOTTLING CO., SAN JOSE;** four-piece mold; ½ pint; 7¾″; light amber 4.00-8.00

4030 **F. & M. SCHAEFER MFR'G. CO., NEW YORK** around base on front; crown top; 9″; aqua 2.00-4.00

4031 **THE SCHAEFER-MEYER BRO. CO., TRADE MARK LOUISVILLE, KY.** in a shield; 11″; amber 8.00-10.00

4032 SCHELLS BEER, label, SCHELLS BREWING CO., NEW ULM, MINN.; 9½"; amber 2.00-4.00

4033 PHIL SCHEWERMANN BREWERY, HANCOCK, MICH.; *T.B.N.T.B.S.* on bottom; 12"; amber 4.00-6.00

4034 same as above except quart size 4.00-6.00

4035 SCHLITZ, MILWAUKEE under bottom; tapered top; 5½"; amber .... 35.00+

4036 JOS SCHLITZ BREWING CO.; 7½" 2.00-4.00

4037 SCHLITZ BREWING CO.; *124* on bottom; amber; 9½" 6.00-10.00

4038 C. SCNEER & CO. in horseshoe letters, under it SACRAMENTO, CAL.; blob top; blob neck; 7½"; amber 4.00-6.00

4039 CHAS SEILER, MILWAUKEE, BEER, in two lines on front; on back *Empty Bottle to Be Returned*; blob top; aqua; 8" 4.00-6.00

4040 G.B. SELMER, CALIFORNIA POP BEER; reverse *Pat. Oct. 29 1872*; tapered top; 10½"; amber 30.00-50.00

4041 SMITH BROS. BREWERS, NEW BEDFORD, MASS. inside of slug plate; TO BE WASHED AND RETURNED on front also; blob top; clear 4.00-6.00

4042 SOUTHERN BREWING CO.; 9½"; machine made; green 2.00-3.00

4043 L. SPEIDEL & CO., BOSTON, MASS., *Hop Leaf* and *B* on center front; *Registered* LS Co. monogram on back; blob top; 9"; clear 4.00-6.00

4044 SPRINGFIELD BREWERIES CO., BOSTON BRANCH, BOSTON, MASS., TRADE MARK, S.B. Co. monogram; blob top; 9"; clear 4.00-6.00

4045 STETTNER & THOMAS, WEISS BEER BREWERS, ST. LOUIS, MO.; blob top; 9½"; amber 10.00-15.00

4046 ST. MARY'S BOTTLING WORKS, ST. MARY'S, OHIO in a circle; quart; blob top; aqua 4.00-8.00

4047 JOHN STROHM, JACKSON, CAL., J.S. monogram on front; four-piece mold; 7¾"; light amber 8.00-10.00

4048 PETER STUMPF; *This Bottle Not For Sale* on back; amber; 8½" 8.00-10.00

4049 TEIKOKU BEER; Japanese writing on back; graduated collar and ring; 11¾"; amber 4.00-6.00

4050 TERRE HAUTE BREWING CO.; 9½" tall; 2½" diameter; *R.G.CO.* on bottom; aqua 4.00-6.00

4051 GEO. A. TICOULET SAC. on front; four-piece mold; 7¾"; amber 8.00-12.00

4052 TOLEDO BREWING & MALTING CO.; amber; 9½" 2.00-6.00

4053 JOHN TONS, JT monogram; STOCKTON, CAL, on front; four-piece mold; blob top; quart; 11½"; amber 6.00-10.00

4054 S.A. TORINO; gray snake around bottle; RED EYE, RED TONG; 12¼"; clear ... 10.00-15.00

4055 same as above except aqua 8.00-12.00

4056 TROMMER'S EVERGREEN BR'Y; aqua; 9¼" 2.00-6.00

4057 UNION BREWING CO., LTD., BEER, TARRS, PA.; on bottom *Union Made C & CO.*; 8"; brown 8.00-10.00

4058 UNITED STATES BREWING CO., CHICAGO, ILL.; 9"; aqua 4.00-8.00

4059 VA. BREWING CO.; 9¾"; aqua 4.00-6.00

4060 A.G. VAN NOSTRAND, CHARLESTOWN, MASS.; inside of ribbon, BUNKER HILL LAGER, BUNKER HILL BREWERIES, EST. 1821 REG.; 9¾"; amber 20.00-30.00

4061 C.J. VATH & CO., SAN JOSE on front in slug plate; blob top; 12"; amber 8.00-12.00

4062 VICTORIA BREWING CO.; on base *Not To Be Sold, Victoria, B.C.*; 9½"; amber 4.00-8.00

4063 same except red amber 6.00-10.00

4064 THE WACKER & BIRK BREWING CO., CHICAGO; reverse *T.B.N.T.B.S.*; 9½"; aqua 4.00-6.00

4065 SIDNEY O. WAGNER, on shoulder; crown top; 11¼"; amber 4.00-6.00

4066 THE J. WALKER BREWING CO., CINCINNATI, OHIO, in a circle; 11¼"; amber 3.00-8.00

4067 HENRY K. WAMPOLE & CO., PHILADA. around shoulder; graduated collar and ring; 8½"; light amber 4.00-6.00

4068 WASHINGTON BREWING CO., trade mark with picture of eagle; REG. WASH. D.C.; 9¼"; aqua 8.00-16.00

4069 WEST END written fancy; BRG. CO. UTICA, N.Y.; crown top; ABM; 9½"; amber 2.00-4.00

4070 W.F. & G.P MIL under bottom; clear; 9¼" 3.00-6.00

4071 W.F. & S. on bottom; crown top; 9½"; aqua 2.00-3.00

4072 W.F. & S MIL under bottom; aqua; 9" 2.00-4.00

4073 same except *#39* and amber 2.00-4.00

4074 WIEDEMANN; *0179* under bottom; amber; 9½" 6.00-8.00

4075 WISCONSIN SELECT BEER; aqua; 9¼" 2.00-6.00

4076 THE P.H. WOLTERS BREWING CO.; *This Bottle Never Sold* in back; aqua; 9½" 2.00-6.00

4077 WUNDER BOTTLING CO., W.B. Co. monogram, SAN FRANCISCO, CAL., on front; 7⅝"; amber 4.00-8.00

4078 same as above except OAKLAND.... 4.00-8.00

4079 Y under bottom, label; 9¾"; amber ... 4.00-6.00

4080 YOERG BREWING CO., ST. PAUL, MINN.; 9½"; aqua 2.00-6.00

4081 GEO. YOUNG CALIFORNIA POP BEER; reverse *Pat. 29th 1872*; 10½"; amber 30.00-50.00

4082 THEO. YOUNG with large stars, hop leaves, buds, in a monogram, *T.Y. Union Ave., 165th & 166th St. N.Y.*, all on front; crown top; 9"; amber 4.00-6.00

Flasks

During the 1800's the equivalent of the sayings and sentiments expressed on today's automobile bumpers were the embossed whiskey flasks. These containers picked sides in Presidential campaigns, ironically warned of the evils of their contents and kept the new spirit of nationalism that followed the War of 1812 within reach of the common man by putting American eagles on his favorite whiskey flasks.

The earliest American flasks were probably from the Pitkin glasshouse built in 1783 near Hartford, Connecticut. The first were freeblown, or made without the aid of a mold. By 1850 there were four hundred design varieties. These containers have black graphite pontil marks caused by the coating of the pontil with powdered iron to enable the bottle's bottom to be broken away without damaging the glass. The several hundred additional types of flasks made between the years 1850 and 1870 have no such markings due to the invention of the snap-case, a spring device which cradled the bottle in the finishing process.

Flasks were immediately popular. In addition to carrying a "message" they also contained whiskey, a combination that was simply unbeatable. Glassmakers realized that such containers brought profits and nearly every glasshouse in the country was producing them. Plagiarism of mold designs by rival companies was common.

Thomas W. Dyott, a poor English immigrant who worked his way up from a boot polisher to the owner of the Philadelphia and Kensington Glass Works, manufactured several popular flasks. In recognition of his own triumphant career he produced a flask with his portrait embossed on one side and Benjamin Franklin's on the other. Another of Dyott's flasks honors the French general, Lafayette. The general was beloved by the American people as a champion in the struggle for human liberty. He received tumultuous welcomes wherever he appeared when he visited the United States in 1824. Dyott, always with an eye on publicity, personally presented Lafayette with a flask that same year.

The Masons were literally builders of the nation, and were strong politically as well, despite growing anti-Mason sentiment. Many Masonic flasks appeared with emblems of the order on one side and the symbolic American eagle on the reverse. Public opinion was enraged against the Masons when William Morgan of Batavia, New York, who

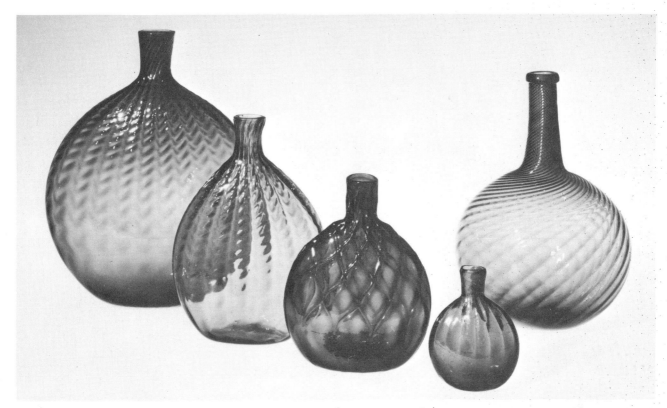

These pattern-molded flasks, circa 1815–1835, include (from left to right), two chestnut-shaped midwestern flasks, an expanded diamond-designed flask, a vertically ribbed chestnut flask and a swirled flask.

threatened to make public secrets of the order, was mysteriously abducted. The incident caused the formation of an anti-Mason party, but public anger eventually subsided.

George Washington was a popular subject for flasks, despite the belief that he had had ambitions to be king of America. Upon his death in 1799, the press chose to eulogize him as the "Father of his Country." At first he appeared on the flasks as a soldier in uniform, but as his accomplishments as first President became more apparent in retrospect, he was shown on whiskey flasks in a classic portrait pose. Not a few citizens pointed out the inconsistency of having a likeness of the father of one's country appear on a whiskey bottle.

Even the Temperance people had a flask of sorts—it bore the inscription, "Use me, don't abuse me."

Singer Jenny Lind, "the Swedish Nightingale," was also honored on a flask. She was brought to the U.S. by P.T. Barnum for a two-year tour in 1850 and was enthralled with America. The people were enthralled with her, too, paying as much as $650 a ticket to hear her sing.

Flasks extolled the qualifications of Presidential candidates John Quincy Adams and Andrew Jackson in the elections of 1824 and 1828. Adams was elected in 1824 and by 1828 was publicized as an aristocratic man of privilege. Jackson, who was popularized as a friend of the common man, was elected in 1828.

An echoing cry of gold and easy fortune in the Colorado mountains prompted many men, unemployed by the depression of 1857, to pack a pick ax and head toward Pike's Peak. Of the approximate 100,000 who set out for the region in the spring of 1858, half soon turned back, according to *Harper's Weekly*, "deluded and suffering, ... retracing their steps back to quiet farms in the West." The magazine reported them to be in a "starving condition, barefooted, ragged and penniless." Nevertheless, flasks bearing the slogans "For Pike's Peak" and "Pike's Peak or Bust" appeared in 1859.

4084   4088   4096   4113   4128   4129   4130   4131

4132   4133   4134   4135   4140   4149   4151

4083   JOHN Q. ADAMS in a circle; eagle facing to right; on base J.T. & CO.; beaded edge; sheared top; pontil; pint; green .... 800.00+

4084   A.G.W.L. under bottom; saddle flask; amber; ½ pint 4.00-8.00

4085   All Seeing Eye; star and large eye in center; under it A.D.; in back, six-pointed star with arms; Masonic emblem; under it G.R.J.A.; pontil; sheared top; pint; amber..... 90.00-185.00

4086   Anchor flask; double ring; ½ pint, quart; amber or clear....................... 10.00-30.00

4087   Aquamarine; pint 20.00-40.00

4088   BALTIMORE GLASS WORKS; aqua; very thin glass; pontil; on back a stack of wheat .... 65.00+

4089   B.P. & B.; ½ pint; yellow green... 30.00-40.00

4090   BRIDGETON, NEW JERSEY around a man facing to left; in back a man facing to the left with *Washington* around it; ribbed sides; sheared top; pontil; pint; aqua.. 100.00-150.00

4091 CALABASH; hunter and fisherman; quart; aqua.................... 30.00-40.00

4092 Cannon and Capt. Bragg; pint; aqua .. 55.00+

4093 Cannon and clasped hands; pint; aqua 60.00-100.00

4094 CHAPMAN P., BALT., MD; soldier with a gun, on front; a girl dancing on a bar in back; sheared top; pint; aqua.............. 100.00-150.00

4095 Clasped hands and cannon; pint; aqua 30.00-60.00

4096 CORN FOR THE WORLD; amber; 8¼" .... 100.00+

4097 Corn and Balt. monument; quart; citron .... 100.00+

4098 Cornucopia; pint; emerald green .. 30.00-50.00

4099 Cornucopia and eagle; ½ pint; aqua .. 100.00+

4100 same as above except inverted cornucopia .... 100.00+

4101 Cornucopia and urn; olive; pint ... 40.00-50.00

4102 Cornucopia and urn; ½ pint; amber 40.00-50.00

4103 Cornucopia and urn with twig; open pontil; ½ pint; olive or amber 60.00-80.00

4104 CUNNINGHAM, PITTSBURGH, PA.; Indian, hunter and eagle................... 50.00+

4105 Delicate powder blue; ½ pint 20.00-40.00

4106 18 diamond quilted flask; 6¼"; green 80.00-90.00

4107 Dog in center; in back man in uniform on a horse; pontil; sheared top; quart; aqua . 90.00-110.00

4108 Double eagle (eagles lengthwise); open pontil; olive green 80.00-100.00

4109 Double eagle; pint; aqua 100.00-125.00

4110 Double eagle; pint; light green... 80.00-100.00

4111 Double eagle, STODDARD, N.H.; pint; olive or amber 80.00-100.00

4112 Duck flask; picture of a duck in water; under duck SWIM; above duck WILL YOU HAVE A DRINK; pint; aqua 90.00-125.00

4113 Eagle flask; circle below eagle; 6"; aqua 50.00+

4114 Eagle facing to right resting on a shield and rock pile; pint; aqua 40.00-60.00

4115 Eagle and Masonic flask; large eagle with rays over head and OHIO in a circle under eagle; under that J. SHEPARD & CO.; on shoulder ZANESVILLE; reverse Masonic arch; ornaments under arch; pontil; pint; green, amber or olive...................... 125.00-225.00

4116 Eagle resting on arrows and olive branch with ribbon in beak; an oval panel under eagle; CUNNINGHAM & CO., PITTSBURGH, PA.; ring neck; quart; olive green 100.00-130.00

4117 Eagle and clasped hands; pint; aqua 30.00-50.00

4118 Eagle and cornucopia; ½ pint; clear 100.00-150.00

4119 Eagle and DYOTTVILLE G.W.; pint; aqua 80.00-100.00

4120 Eagle and flag; pint; aqua 90.00-125.00

4121 Eagle and girl on bicycle; A & DHA; pint; aqua 40.00-80.00

4122 Eagle, Masonic; pint; blue green..... 100.00+

4123 Eagle and stag; ½ pint; aqua....... 100.00+

4124 Eagle and tree; pint; aqua 40.00-90.00

4125 Flask, plain; amber; ½ pint........ 4.00-8.00

4126 Flask, plain; ½ pint; bulbous neck; 6¾" 3.00-5.00

4127 Flask, plain; ½ pint; bulbous neck; 7" 4.00-6.00

4128 same as above except clear........ 3.00-5.00

4129 same as above except 7" 4.00-6.00

4130 Flask, label; 6"; pontil; very pale olive 35.00+

4131 Flask, label; dark olive; 5½"......... 10.00+

4132 Flask, label; ribbed base; clear; 6¾" 8.00-12.00

4133 Flask, label; amber; 7½" 8.00-10.00

4134 Flask, round label; amber; 6½" 8.00-12.00

4135 Flask, label; pontil; clear; 6¾".... 10.00-20.00

4136 Flask, plain; sheared top; pontil; pint; green 100.00-150.00

4137 same as above except clear..... 100.00-150.00

4138 FLORA TEMPLE; pint; aqua.. 150.00-200.00

4139 FLORA TEMPLE; handle pint; puce or amber 150.00-200.00

4140 FLORIDA UNIVERSAL STORE BOTTLE; clear; pint....................... 2.00-6.00

4141 FRANK TEA & SPICE CO; *Turpentine, Cinti*; aqua; 5⅜"....................... 4.00-8.00

4142 H. FRANK, PAT'D. AUG. 6th 1879 under bottom; two circles in center; reverse plain; ring top; ribs on sides 20.00-40.00

4143 H. FRANK, PAT. AUG. 6, 1872 all on bottom; circular shaped flask; two circles in center on front; reverse side plain; wide rib on sides; ring neck; pint; aqua................ 25.00-50.00

4144 FRANKLIN & FRANKLIN; quart; aqua 100.00-125.00

4145 Gen. MacArthur and GOD BLESS AMERICA; ½ pint; purple or green 8.00-10.00

4146 G.H.A.; *Concord, N.H. 1865*; ½ pint; aqua 10.00-20.00

4147 GIRL FOR JOE; girl on bicycle; pint; aqua 40.00-80.00

4148 GRANITE GLASS CO. in three lines; reverse *Stoddard, N.H.*; sheared top; pint; olive 100.00-150.00

4149 GUARANTEED FLASK; clear or amethyst; 6¼"......................... 2.00-6.00

4150 GUARANTEED FULL; 6½"; clear.. 4.00-8.00

4151 History flask, label; aqua; side panels; 7¼" .... 10.00+

4152 Hunter and dog; pint; puce .... 300.00+

4153 Iron pontil; double collared; pint... 20.00-40.00

4154 ISABELLA G.W.; sheaf of wheat; pint 40.00-80.00

4155   4168   4183   4188   4202

4203   4207   4216   4217   4226

4155   JENNY LIND with wreath; reverse picture of glass works; above it FISLERVILLE GLASS WORKS; wavy line on neck; pontil; tapered top; quart; aqua.................. 85.00-100.00

4156   same except S. HUFFSEY .... 35.00+

4157   JENNY LIND LYRE; pint; aqua. 90.00-100.00

4158   KEENE Masonic; tooled lip; pontil; pint .... 200.00+

4159   KEENE sunburst; green...... 200.00-300.00

4160   Lafayette and eagle; amber....... 60.00-70.00

4161   Lafayette and eagle, KENSINGTON; open pontil; pint; aqua.................. 90.00-125.00

4162   Lafayette and Dewitt Clinton; ½ pint; olive, amber......................... 200.00+

4163   Lafayette and liberty cap; pint; aqua 90.00-110.00

4164   Lafayette and Masonic; ½ pint....... 200.00+

4165   L.C. & R. CO. on bottom, eagle in a circle; reverse plain; ½ pint clear....... 20.00-40.00

4166   LEGENDARY GRANDFATHER; broken swirl pattern; reddish amber.......... 90.00-100.00

4167   LOUISVILLE G.W. and eagle; ½ pint; aqua 50.00-100.00

4168   LOUISVILLE GLASS WORKS; aqua; 7½" .... 60.00+

4169   LOWELL R.R.; ½ pint; olive, amber 100.00-125.00

4170   LYNDEBORO, L.G. CO.; PATENT on shoulder; pint; aqua............. 10.00-20.00

4171   LYNDEBORO, L.G. CO.; quart; golden amber 25.00-35.00

4172   Man with a gun and bag; reverse side running dogs; double ring top; pint; aqua.... 100.00+

4173   Man with a gun and bag and a feather in hat; reverse side grape vine, with bunches of grapes and leaves; ribbed sides; sheared top; pontil .... 100.00+

4174   Marked double eagle; pint; olive or amber 40.00-80.00

4175   Masonic and eagle, J.F.B.; pint...... 300.00+

4176   Masonic and eagle; pint; olive or amber 90.00-125.00

4177   Masonic and eagle; pint; blue-green 100.00-150.00

4178   Monument and corn in a circle under this, BALTIMORE; reverse side a large ear of corn; quart; aqua.................. 90.00-125.00

4179 same as above except amber.... 100.00-160.00

4180 Mounted soldier and dog; quart; citron 200.00+

4181 PIKES PEAK man with pack and cane walking to left; reverse eagle with ribbon in beak in oval panel; pint; aqua............... 60.00-90.00

4182 same except several colors .... 60.00+

4183 FOR PIKE'S PEAK; reverse side, man shooting a gun at a deer; 9½"; aqua........... 25.00+

4184 FOR PIKE'S PEAK; old rye; pint; aqua 30.00-40.00

4185 PIKES PEAK; traveler and hunter; pint; olive, amber 150.00-200.00

4186 PITTSBURGH, double eagle; pint; citron 150.00-200.00

4187 PITTSBURGH, double eagle; pint; aqua 20.00-30.00

4188 PITTSBURGH, PA. in raised oval circle at base, with an eagle on front; back same except plain for label; pint; aqua; applied ring at top; 7½" .... 35.00+

4189 Pitkin type; pint; light green.... 30.00-60.00

4190 Pottery flask; figure of a man and horse; same on reverse side; pint.......... 210.00-225.00

4191 Quilted pattern flask; sheared top; pontil; ½ pint; reddish brown, amber, green, olive amber .... 400.00+

4192 same except amethyst .... 500.00+

4193 same except white bluish cast... 110.00-175.00

4194 Quilted poison flask; ½ pint; olive green 80.00-120.00

4195 RAVENNA GLASS WORKS in three lines; ring top; pint; yellow green 60.00-125.00

4196 RAVENNA in center; anchor with rope; under it GLASS COMPANY; ring top; pint; aqua 90.00-125.00

4197 RAVENNA TRAVELERS COMPANION; pontil; quart; amber.......... 150.00-300.00

4198 REHM BROS, *Bush & Buchanan Sts & O'Farrel & Mason Sts*, in a sunken circle; ribbed bottom; two rings near shoulder; coffin type; metal and cork cap; ½ pint; clear or amethyst 6.00-10.00

4199 Ribbed flask; fluted base to shoulder; sheared top; pontil; ½ pint; aqua 100.00-160.00

4200 same except yellow or amber ... 125.00-200.00

4201 Sailing vessel and COLUMBIAN JUBILEE; pint; amber 60.00-90.00

4202 Sailor bottle; dancing sailor on back; amber; 7½" .... 50.00+

4203 Scroll; aqua; one star; 7"; smooth base 6.00-8.00

4204 same as above except two stars....... 25.00+

4205 Scroll; ½ pint to quart; one star; clear, aqua or amber; pontil................. 35.00+

4206 same as above except two stars....... 35.00+

4207 Scroll; 9"; aqua.............. 200.00-300.00

4208 Scroll; open pontil; pint; aqua 20.00-30.00

4209 Scroll; M.C. on side in script; pint; blue or aqua 30.00-50.00

4210 Scroll; D.C. MOTT; ½ pint....... 20.00-30.00

4211 Scroll; pint; green 40.00-60.00

4212 Scroll; banded neck; aqua 30.00-40.00

4213 Scroll; quart; aqua............. 60.00-90.00

4214 Scroll; pint; iridescent blue..... 80.00-125.00

4215 Scroll; 2½ quart; aqua 100.00-125.00

4216 S.G. CO. and anchor on bottom; aqua; 6¼" 8.00-15.00

4217 same as above except amber...... 6.00-12.00

4218 Sheaf of wheat and grapes; open pontil; ½ quart; aqua......................... 85.00-110.00

4219 SOUTH CAROLINA DISPENSARY with palm tree; pint; aqua................. 30.00-65.00

4220 same except ½ pint; amber 40.00-85.00

4221 Spiral flask; spiral to the left; pontil; sheared top; ½ pint; amber 185.00-285.00

4222 same except spiral to the right; pint; green 110.00-175.00

4223 SPRINGFIELD G.W. and CABIN; ½ pint; aqua 40.00-60.00

4224 SPRING GARDEN in center; anchor; under it GLASS WORKS; reverse side, log cabin with a tree to the right; ring top; ½ pint; aqua 90.00-125.00

4225 Stag and tree; pint; aqua 40.00-60.00

4226 Star with a circle around it on shoulder; ½ pint; light amber; saddle flask.......... 6.00-12.00

4227 Stoddard double eagle; GRANITE GLASS CO., STODDARD, N.H.; pontil; pint; golden amber 80.00-90.00

4228 STODDARD, N.H. in panel under eagle facing left; reverse same except blank panel; sheared top; pontil; pint; amber........ 60.00-125.00

4229 same except tapered top; olive green 60.00-125.00

4230 Strongman and two gentlemen; ½ pint; clear 60.00-120.00

4231 S.T.R.A. in a five point star; reverse plain; ring; collared top; ½ pint; amber...... 50.00-110.00

4232 SUCCESS TO THE RAILROAD with a horse and a cart on rail around it; same on reverse side; sheared top; pontil; pint; olive or aqua 115.00-225.00

4233 SUCCESS TO THE RAILROAD around a horse and cart on a rail; in back an eagle with wings spread; also an arrow and a branch; 17 stars around this; sheared lip and pontil; ½ pint; amber 150.00-200.00

4234 SUCCESS TO R.R.; eagle; pint; olive 80.00-125.00

4235 same except pint; aqua 100.00-125.00

4236 same except pint; olive green or amber 80.00-100.00

4237 Summer and winter flask; ½ pint; aqua 60.00-80.00

4238 same except quart.............. 60.00-80.00

4239 Sunburst flask; pint; olive, amber or light green .... 100.00+

4240 same except ½ pint; aqua or green ... 100.00+

4241 Sunburst flask; pint; aqua 60.00-80.00

4242 Sunburst; KEENE; pint; olive or amber 100.00-150.00

4243 Sunburst; KEENE P & W; pint; olive or amber 100.00-150.00

4244 Sunburst; KEENE; ½ pint; amber 100.00-150.00

4245 Swirled Pitkin; amber 100.00-125.00

4246 Swirled Pitkin; pint; blue green .. 40.00-80.00

4247 Taylor & Ringgold; pint; aqua.... 40.00-80.00

4248 TRAVELERS; in center a sunflower; under it COMPANION; in back *Ravenna*; in center sunflower; under it *Glass Co.*; sheared top; pint; amber 90.00-110.00

4249 TRAVELERS COMPANION and sheaf; quart; amber 80.00-100.00

4250 TRAVELERS COMPANION and star; ½ pint; aqua........................ 40.00-60.00

4251 UNION; side mold; ball and cannon on back; 7½"; aqua........................ 70.00+

4252 UNION; clasped hands in shield; eagle with banner on reverse side; pint 30.00-60.00

4253 U 2266 on bottom; clear or amethyst; 5" 2.00-3.00

4254 Violin flask; curled ornaments in a heart shape, with a panel with two stars and a C; reverse same except no C; collared neck; pint; green 90.00-175.00

4255 WARRANTED FLASK; clear or amethyst; 7½".......................... 6.00-10.00

4256 G. Washington; prune color; pontil; 10½" .... 85.00+

4257 Washington and Albany; ½ pint; aqua 90.00-125.00

4258 G. Washington and A. Jackson; pint; olive green 100.00-125.00

4259 G. Washington and T. Jefferson; pint; dark amber 100.00-150.00

4260 G. Washington and sheaf of wheat; pint; aqua 100.00-125.00

4261 G. Washington, and Z. Taylor; open pontil; aqua; pint 30.00-40.00

4262 G. Washington and Z. Taylor; quart; green 40.00-80.00

4263 same except aqua 30.00-50.00

4264 same except pint; green......... 30.00-50.00

4265 G. Washington and Z. Taylor; Washington in a circle; over it THE FATHER OF HIS COUNTRY; reverse Taylor in a circle; over it GEN. TAYLOR NEVER SURRENDERS; sheared top; pontil; quart; aqua 60.00-120.00

4266 WHEELING, VA.; a bust facing to the right; in a horseshoe shape WHEAT PRICE & CO., WHEELING, VA.; reverse a building; around it FAIRVIEW WORKS; sheared top; pontil; green 350.00-450.00

4267 WESTFORD GLASS CO. in ½ circle; under it WESTFORD, CONN.; reverse side a stack of wheat; pint; green 50.00-100.00

4268 Whiskbroom; 7½"; clear .... 10.00+

4269 Whiskey flask; quilt design; 8"; clear or amethyst...................... 8.00-10.00

4270 WILLINGTON GLASS CO., WEST WILLINGTON, CONN. on four lines; reverse eagle & shield; under it a wreath; on shoulder LIBERTY; pint; amber........ 60.00-100.00

4271 WILL YOU TAKE A DRINK? WILL A DUCK SWIM?; pint; aqua 100.00-125.00

4272 Winter and summer flask, tree with leaves and a bird on right side; above it SUMMER; reverse side tree without leaves and bird; above it WINTER; tapered top; quart and pint; aqua 60.00-110.00

4273 same as above with Summer on front and Winter on back 40.00-90.00

4274 ZANESVILLE CITY GLASS WORKS in oval panel; reverse plain; ring top; amber 60.00-110.00

4275 same except aqua 40.00-60.00

4276 ZANESVILLE OHIO, J. SHEPARD CO.; S is backwards; reverse side Masonic; with pontil; aqua............................... 100.00+

4251   4253   4255   4256   4268   4269   4276

Produced by the Baltimore Glass Works in the 1840's, this mold-blown flask (#4096) commemorates the great quantities of corn shipped from Baltimore's port, bringing economic prosperity to many of her citizens.

Spirits

Dr. Billy J. Clark, a physician, managed to attract a group of concerned citizens to a meeting in 1808 at Moreau, New York. Before the gathering adjourned, forty-four had placed their signatures on a document vowing to "use no rum, gin, whisky, [sic] wine or any distilled spirits . . . except by advice of a physician, or in the case of actual disease." The American Temperance Movement had begun.

The great majority of Americans did not pledge to avoid the evils of spirits, however, and their favorite beverages were bottled in increasing numbers. They believed that the Irish had the right idea when they gave us the word "whiskey" from a Gaelic phrase meaning "water of life." Irish tradition claims that it was St. Patrick himself who taught them the art of distilling.

In 1860, E. G. Booz of Philadelphia manufactured a whiskey bottle in the shape of a cabin. His name, the year 1840, the phrase "Old Cabin Whiskey," and the company address were proudly embossed on the bottle. Many claim that this bottle accounts for the origin of the phrase "bottle of booze;" others insist that the colloquial "booze" actually comes from the word "bouse," a word for liquor in the seventeenth century.

The Booz bottle is credited with starting the practice of embossing brand names onto spirits bottles. Dedicated drinkers could order their favorite by name, an innovation that added a certain amount of distinction to alcohol consumption. Jack Daniel was a popular brand. As a child, young Jack exhibited an independent nature. He ran away from home and managed to obtain a full partnership in a distillery. By 1866, just three years later, he owned his own whiskey company in Tennessee. His enterprise was a success and Jack Daniel whiskey is still produced today.

Other spirits bottles are found in the figural shapes of cannons, clocks and barrels. These and other figurals are the most sought-after bottles today. At the turn of the century until Prohibition began in 1920, small bottles—called nips—were given away by tavern owners to their steady customers, especially during the holiday season. All liquor bottles after the repeal of Prohibition in 1933 bore the inscription, "Federal Law Forbids Sale or Re-Use of This Bottle." That practice was discontinued in 1964.

The making of wine is an art that has been passed down through generations from antiquity. Wine bottles usually hold a pint of liquid. The one- to ten-gallon capacity containers used to transport or store wines were called carboys or demijohns. Carboys were so durable that they were also used to store corrosives; demijohns had characteristic long necks. Both types of containers were reusable and weighed thirty to forty pounds.

The shapes of wine bottles came to be associated with certain wine types by the mid-nineteenth century. Seal bottles were also popular, especially among the wealthy. Family crests and coats-of-arms were stamped on these bottles in the finishing process. The practice dwindled in the late 1800's after invention of the plate molds which eliminated the hand stamping. Though some wines today still use seals to identify the contents, paper labels have largely replaced them.

Above: *An elaborate bottle is this blown three-mold decanter (similar to #5059), circa 1815-1841, manufactured by the Keene Glass Works.* Right: *This square-shaped whiskey bottle was made in the early 1800's.*

4277   4279   4280   4281   4287   4288   4289

4291   4294   4295   4297   4298   4299   4300

4305   4306   4307   4308   4310   4312   4315

| 4316 | 4318 | 4319 | 4322 |

4277 ACKER MERRALL, label; *A9* under bottom; amber; 11″ 6.00-8.00

4278 F.P. ADAMS AND CO.; *Boston, Mass., USA* under bottom; decanter with handle; ring top; clear .... 25.00+

4279 ADAMS, TAYLOR & CO.; *Full Qt. Registered* on back; clear; 12½″ 12.00-15.00

4280 ADAMS, TAYLOR & CO.; *Boston, Mass., Royal Hand Made Sour Mash Whiskey*; clear; quart 10.00-15.00

4281 AGCS CO.; birds or eagle all around bottle on base; clear; 12″ 8.00-15.00

4282 AGW on base; cefrin type; aqua; quart 4.00-8.00

4283 ALAMEDA COMPANY; *Tremont and Bromfield Streets, Boston* on front written in slug plate; flask; ring collar; side bands; amethyst; 8″ 4.00-8.00

4284 ALAMEDA same as above except ½ pint; monogram on center; 6⅛″ 4.00-8.00

4285 ALCOHOL on label, also *Brandy*; square bottle; clear; 8¼″ 2.00-4.00

4286 ALDERNEY OLD RYE WHISKEY around a cow; *Chris Gallagher, 806 Lombard Street, Philadelphia*; 7½″ 8.00-12.00

4287 ALMADEN VINEYARDS; green; 10″ 1.00-2.00

4288 AMBROSIAL B.M. & EAW & CO. in a seal on shoulder; pontil; amber; 9″ .... 100.00+

4289 AMERICUS CLUB; amber; 7½″ 4.00-8.00

4290 AMERICUS CLUB PURE WHISKEY; clear or amethyst; 9½″ 6.00-10.00

4291 AMETGAN THERAPEUTIC CO.; green; 8″ 10.00-25.00

4292 AMIDON'S UNION; *Ginge Brandy Registered*; in center lady with long hair; clear or amethyst; 11¾″.................... 6.00-8.00

4293 E.L. ANDERSON DISTILLING CO.; *Newport, Ky.* on front in circle; round; tapered; graduated top and ring; clear 8.00-10.00

4294 ANDRESEN & SON; *Western Importers, Minneapolis, Minn. & Winnipeg* on back; amber; 5″ x 4¾″ x 3″ 200.00-300.00

4295 ANGELO MYERS; clear or amethyst; 6½″ 2.00-4.00

4296 ARCADE GROCERY CO.; whiskey; clear; quart............................. 10.00+

4297 ASPASIA; tan and white crock; 10″ x 9″ 200.00-225.00

4298 BAILEYS WHISKEY; clear or amethyst; 9¾″ 8.00-10.00

4299 Banjo; label; lavender camphor glass; 10″ .... 25.00+

4300 THE BANTAM COCK, NORTHAMPTON; under bottom *64 H.32*; aqua 25.00-30.00

4301 same as above except clear............ 25.00+

4302 Bar bottle; label; clear; 10¾ .... 25.00+

4303 Bar bottle; fancy; plain rib on bottom; clear; 10¼″ 8.00-12.00

4304 Bar bottle; clear cut glass type; plain; quart; 10¾″ 18.00-25.00

4305 Bar bottle; label; red; 10¾″ .... 75.00+

4306 Bar bottle; label; pontil; dark amber; 10¼″ 10.00-20.00

4307 BARCLAY; amber; 12″ 34.00-60.00

4308 BARCLAY 76; machine made; amber; 12″ 8.00-12.00

4309 BARKHOUSE BROS & CO.; *Golddust, Ky., Bourbon, John Van Bergen, Sole Agents*; amber; quart............................. 100.00+

4310 A. BAUER & CO.; *Pineapple Rock & Rye, Chicago, USA*; under bottom *Design Patented*; clear; 9¾″ 10.00-15.00

4311 same as above except amber; 8½″ ... 8.00-10.00

4312 B & B; clear or amber 2.00-4.00

4313 B.B. EXTRA SUPERIOR WHISKEY; in center a hand holding playing cards; blob neck; amber; 4½″........................ 10.00-20.00

4314 SOL. BEAR & CO.; *Wilmington, North Carolina*; ring top; clear or aqua; 6″ x 2½″ x 1½″ 8.00-10.00

4315 BEECH HILL DISTILLING CO.; *B* under bottom; amber; 12″ 8.00-10.00

4316 same as above except letters closer together and longer neck...................... 10.00-20.00

4317 BELFAST MALT WHISKEY FOR MEDICINE USE in a circle; aqua; 11″ ..25.00-90.00

4318 BELLE OF NELSON, label; whiskey; top *one full quart*; *M.M.* under bottom; clear; 12″ 4.00-6.00

4319 BELSINGER & CO. DISTILLERS; *Guar. Full Qt.* on back; clear; 10″ 6.00-10.00

4320 BENEDICTINE; liquor crescent above shoulder; olive green................. 12.00-18.00

4321 same as above except machine made 2.00-4.00

4322 BERNARD CONATY CO., INC. PROVIDENCE, R.I.; *TBNTBS* on base; letters and number under bottom; smoke; 9″... 6.00-10.00

4323   4324   4326   4329   4330   4333

4334   4335   4337   4338   4339

4346   4350   4377

4323   BERNHEIM BROS AND URI, LOUISVILLE, KY, on seal; amber; 9½" . . . . 12.00+

4324   E.R. BETTERTON & CO.; amber; 11" 8.00-15.00

4325   E.R. BETTERTON & CO.; *Distilleries Chattanooga, Tenn.* in 3 lines in sunken panel in back; raised panel plain; flask; three ribs on each side; twenty ribs around neck; under bottom a diamond with letter *Y*; brown; ½ pint . . 4.00-8.00

4326   E.R. BETTERTON & CO.; *White Oak* on back; *C* in diamond under bottom; amber; 12" 15.00-20.00

4327   GEORGE BIELER & SONS, CINCINNATI on base; *Brookfield Rye; B* in center; clear; 9¼" 10.00-15.00

4328   GEORGE BIELER & SONS, CINCINNATI RYE; fancy fluted neck; ring top; clear; 9½" 8.00-15.00

4329   A. M. BININGER & CO.; *Distilled in 1848* around base; pontil; 8" . . . . 100.00+

4330 A.M. BININGER & CO.; *Kentuckey* [sic] on front; *No. 19 Broad St. N.Y., Biningers Old Kentuckey Bourbon 1849 Reserve Dist in 1848* on side; amber; 9¼".................... 85.00+

4331 BINSWANGER & BRO.; *Simon W.L. Co., St. Joseph, Mo.* on front; whiskey; clear or amethyst; 6¾"..................... 2.00-4.00

4332 BINSWANGER & BRO.; *Simon* in horseshoe, *W.L. Co. St. Joseph, Mo.* under it; flask; clear 2.00-4.00

4333 BLACK AND WHITE WHISK Y, E left out of whiskey; three-part mold; olive; one 10½"; other 11½"............................ 10.00-20.00

4334 G. O. BLAKE; clear or amethyst; 12⅝" 8.00-12.00

4335 G. O. BLAKE'S KY. WHISKEY; aqua; 12½" 8.00-10.00

4336 BLUTHENTHAL & BECKART / ATLANTA "B & B" CINCINNATI / HIGH GRADE LIQUORS vertical in slug plate; flask; clear; ½ pint; 6½"....................... 4.00-6.00

4337 BLUTHENTHAL & BICKART; clear or amethyst; 6¼" 2.00-4.00

4338 BOB TAYLOR WHISKEY; *Jos A. Magnus & Co.; Cincinnati O. U.S.A.;* lion and arrow monogram on back; amber; 9½".... 75.00-95.00

4339 C.T. BOND, MERCHANT & TRADER, NEW ALBANY, MISS.; on back eagle in circle, *C.T. Bond;* golden amber; 6¼" 300.00-400.00

4340 W.E. BONNEY in center of barrel-shaped bottle; two rings encircling bottle; three rings on top and bottom; stands up on one side; aqua; 2½" tall; 3" long x 1½" wide 4.00-8.00

4341 BONNIE BROS. on top of circle; *Louisville, Ky.* on bottom; in center circle *Bonnie & Twiges;* whiskey; clear; quart; 6½"........ 4.00-5.00

4342 BONNIE BROS. in circle; foliage and BONNIE in center; LOUISVILLE, KY. on front; rectangular; amethyst; ½ pint; 7"...... 4.00-6.00

4343 E.C. BOOZ'S; broad sloping collar; smooth with circular depression; *Old Cabin Whiskey* on one roof; on back roof *1840;* short neck on front door; three windows on back; plain on one side; *120 Walnut St.,* two dots under *St.; Philadelphia* on other side; *E.C. Booz's Old Cabin Whiskey* on another side...................... 75.00+

4344 same as above except no dot under *St.;* very short neck with large round collar; smooth with circular depression; pale green .... 75.00+

4345 same as above except reproduction or machine made 2.00-6.00

4346 BOURBON in center; over it inside a diamond *131 F;* amber; 3" round bottle; 7½" body; 2¾" neck with a handle from neck to shoulder .... 25.00+

4347 BOURBON WHISKEY; bitters; 1875; amber; 9¼"............................. 90.00-100.00

4348 same as above except puce 100.00-150.00

4349 JOHN BOWMAN AND CO.; *Old Jewell Bourbon, San Francisco;* amber.......... 75.00+

4350 S.W. BRANCH; amber; ½ gallon; 9½" 15.00+

4351 THE HENRY BRAND WINE CO.; *Toledo, Ohio;* crown top; hock wine shape; amber; 14" 4.00-8.00

4352 BRANDY, CHICAGO FANCY; clear or amethyst; 11¾"................... 4.00-6.00

4353 BRANDY, CHICAGO FANCY; ruby red; 11¾" 8.00-12.00

4354 Brandy; crescent on shoulder; amber; 10" 3.00-6.00

4355 Brandy; no crescent; clear or amethyst; 9¼" 4.00-6.00

4356 Brandy, plain; amber; 9¼" 2.00-4.00

4357 Brandy, plain; amber; 8½" 2.00-4.00

4358 Brandy, plain; olive; 12" 2.00-4.00

4359 Brandy, plain; olive; 11½" 2.00-4.00

4360 Brandy, plain with crescent; green; 11½" 2.00-3.00

4361 Brandy, plain; blob neck; red amber; 10½" 3.00-5.00

4362 Brandy; square type with crescent on shoulder; amber; 10" 3.00-6.00

4363 Brandy, plain; square type; clear or amethyst; 9¼"........................... 4.00-6.00

4364 Brandy, plain; square type; amber .. 2.00-4.00

4365 Brandy, plain; beer type; amber; 8½" 2.00-4.00

4366 Brandy, plain; round; lady's leg neck; olive green; 12"........................... 2.00-4.00

4367 Brandy, plain; round; lady's leg neck; olive green; 11½" 2.00-4.00

4368 Brandy, plain; crescent; round; amethyst or clear; 11⅝" 1.00-3.00

4369 Brandy, plain; crescent; round; clear or amethyst; 12" 1.00-3.00

4370 Brandy, plain; beer type; blob neck; olive green; 9¾"........................... 2.00-4.00

4371 Brandy, plain; round; short neck; amber; 11½" 2.00-4.00

4372 BROOK SUNNY; *the Pure Food Whiskey;* left medallion *Grand Prize St. Louis 1904;* right medallion *Gold Med. St. Louis 1904;* clear or amethyst; 10¾" 10.00-12.00

4373 BROOK SUNNY; *the Pure Food Whiskey;* with two shields on front, *Grand Prize, St. Louis 1904* on one side, *Gold Medal St. Louis 1904* other side; clear; 10¾".................. 10.00-14.00

4374 BROOKVILLE DISTILLING CO. CINCINNATI, O. USA in circle; DISTILLERIES in center; *Guaranteed full quart* on back; fluting on neck and shoulders; graduated top and ring; amethyst; 9⅞" 8.00-12.00

4375 BROWN'S CATALINA; tapered; barber type neck; amber; 11" 25.00-60.00

4376 BROWN-FORMAN CO. DISTILLERS LOUISVILLE, KY on front; flask; double band collar; clear; pint; 7½" 4.00-6.00

4377 BROWN-FORMAN CO. LOUISVILLE, KY; machine made; clear or amethyst; quart 4.00-8.00

4381   4382   4386   4388   4390   4391   4393

4397   4400   4401   4402   4403   4404   4407

4408   4409   4410   4412   4413   4414   4417

4378 BROWN-FORMAN CO. on one line; *Louisville, Ky.* on shoulder; whiskey; clear or amethyst 2.00-4.00

4379 BROWN-FORMAN CO, DISTILLER, LOUISVILLE, KY; flask; clear; ½ pint; 6¼" 4.00-8.00

4380 BROWN THOMPSON & CO. on one line; *Louisville, Ky.* on shoulder; beer type; lady's leg neck; opalescent; amber; 11" 4.00-8.00

4381 SURSH BROWN, label; *R.B.J. & Co.* under bottom; clear; 8" 10.00-20.00

4382 BROWNSVILLE FRUIT DISTILLING CO.; *Native Wine Maker, Brooklyn, N.Y.*; clear; 13¼" 10.00-12.00

4383 BUFFALO OLD BOURBON; *George Dierssen & Co. of Sacramento, Calif.*; clear; quart 20.00-40.00

4384 BUFFALO SPRING, with buffalo in center; *Stomping Ground, Ky. Co.*; 7" 4.00-12.00

4385 SIR R. BURNETT & CO., TRADE MARK; between *Co.* and *Trade* is a circle with a crown in it on top of shoulder; under it *This Bottle Not To Be Sold But Remains Property of Sir R. Burnett & Co. London, England*; under the bottom *B & Co.*; in center of bottom *K B 57*; whiskey; clear or aqua; 12" 4.00-6.00

4386 SIR R. BURNETT & CO.; aqua; 8½" 6.00-10.00

4387 SIR R. BURNETT/& CO./ LONDON / ENGLAND TRADE MARK (crown); *This Bottle Is Not To Be Sold But Remains Property of*; bulbous neck; gloppy square and ring top; round; aqua; 11¾" 4.00-8.00

4388 BURNS & O'DONOHUE; amber; 10¼" 8.00-15.00

4389 BURROW MARTIN & CO.; *Norfolk, Virginia*; round ring top; clear or aqua; 6"... 8.00-15.00

4390 CAHN, BELT & CO.; clear; 8½" ... 4.00-6.00

4391 CAHN, BELT & CO.; clear; ½ pint; 7" 2.00-4.00

4392 CALEDONIA WHISKEY; B.C. DISTILLERY CO. L.T.D. NEW WESTMINSTER B.C.; oval shape; graduated top; emerald green; quart 4.00-6.00

4393 CALLAHAN WHISKEY; clear or amethyst; 12⅛" 5.00-6.00

4394 CALLAHAN / WHISKEY / J. CALLAHAN & COMPANY (written fancy) BOSTON, MASS / REGISTERED; round; amethyst; 12⅛" 4.00-8.00

4395 J.F. CALLAHAN & COMPANY / BOSTON, MASS at slant; clear; ½ pint; 6⅝".... 4.00-6.00

4396 JOHN F. CALLAHAN, BOTTLED ONLY BY BOSTON, MASS; round; slug plate; graduated top and ring; amethyst; 11" 8.00-12.00

4397 D. CANALE & CO.; *Memphis, Tenn. Old Dominick Bourbon* other side; clear or amethyst; 11" 10.00-15.00

4398 T.F. CANNON & COMPANY / BOSTON, MASS / GUARANTEED FULL PINT all in slug plate; *12 Devonshire St.* on side; *28-30 Exchange St.* on opposite side; rectangular; clear; pint; 8" 4.00-6.00

4399 CARTAN, McCARTHY & COMPANY, SAN FRANCISCO, CALIF. FULL QUART with monogram at top, all vertically; rectangular; graduated top and ring; amber; 10¾" 8.00-15.00

4400 CASCADE; clear; 9½" 8.00-15.00

4401 J.W. CASHIN FAMILY LIQUOR STORE; clear or amethyst; 6¼" 4.00-8.00

4402 CASPERS WHISKEY; cobalt; 10½"... 75.00+

4403 CEDARHURST; *Cont. 8 Oz.* on back shoulder; amber; ½ pint; 7" 6.00-8.00

4404 CENTURY LIQUOR & CIGAR CO.; *B-8* under bottom; amber; pint 6.00-10.00

4405 Champagne; cylindrical; 2" indented bottom; pale green; 11⅞" 5.00-8.00

4406 Champagne, plain; kick-up; opalescent; green; 12" x 10" x 9" 1.00-3.00

4407 Champagne, plain; green; 4¼" 4.00-6.00

4408 Champagne, plain; kick-up; dark green; 8" 4.00-8.00

4409 CHAPIN & GORE, CHICAGO; *Hawley Glass Co.* under bottom; amber; 8¼" .... 65.00+

4410 CHAPIN & GORE; diamond shape on back for label; amber; 8¾" 25.00-30.00

4411 HENRY CHAPMAN & COMPANY; *sole agents, Montreal* in circle; pumpkin seed type; inside screw; *Patent 78* on screw cap; amber; 5¼" 50.00-80.00

4412 CHEATHAM & KINNEY; *W. Mc & Co.* under bottom; aqua; 8¾" 10.00-20.00

4413 Chestnut bottle; kick-up; handle; ring around top neck; squat; amber; 2" neck; 4" body; 3" x 4" 18.00-25.00

4414 same as above except larger; amber 10.00-16.00

4415 same as above except machine made .. 4.00-8.00

4416 same as above except clear or blue... 8.00-10.00

4417 Chestnut bottle; kick-up; ring around top; pontil; blue; 4" body; 2" neck 8.00-12.00

4418 Chestnut bottle; 25 ribs; Midwestern; l.h. swirl; sheared top; green; 7½" 60.00-80.00

4419 Chestnut bottle; 24 vertical ribs; sheared neck; attributed to Zanesville; golden amber; 5¼" 90.00-150.00

4420 Chestnut bottle; light vertical rib plus 18 r.h. swirl ribs; sheared neck; attributed to Kent; green.......................... 60.00-70.00

4421 Chestnut bottle; 16 vertical ribs; sheared neck; 6½".................................... 80.00-90.00

4422 Chestnut bottle; swirl tooled top; pontil; green; 5¾" .... 100.00+

4423 same as above except deep amber; 5¼" 100.00+

4436   4439   4441   4442   4446   4447

4448   4450   4451   4452   4454   4455   4456

4457   4458   4459   4460   4462   4463   4468

4424 Chestnut bottle; long outward flared neck; bluish aqua; ½ pint............. 30.00-60.00

4425 Chestnut bottle; diamond; ¼" ground off top; attributed to Zanesville; yellow green; 10"
.... 20.00+

4426 Chestnut bottle; aqua; 5½".......... 20.00-30.00

4427 Chestnut bottle; twelve diamonds quilted over 24 vertical ribs; tooled mouth; clear; 5¾"
.... 200.00+

4428 Chestnut bottle; diamond; yellow green or clear; 5¼"......................... 20.00-30.00

4429 Chestnut bottle; sixteen ribs; sheared neck; mantua; 6¼".................... 60.00-80.00

4430 Chestnut bottle; sixteen ribs; l.h. swirl; mantua; aqua; 6½"................. 60.00-80.00

4431 Chestnut bottle; kick-up; ring around top; pontil; amber; 6"............... 15.00-20.00

4432 same as above except clear......... 8.00-12.00

4433 Chestnut bottle; kick-up; squat body; handle ring around neck; light amber; 6"... 8.00-10.00

4434 same as above except machine made; clear 4.00-8.00

4435 CHEVALIERS OLD CASTLE WHISKEY; *San Francisco;* spiral neck; aqua or amber; quart................... 200.00-300.00

4436 CHICAGO FANCY BRANDY, label; amber; 12"............................ 8.00-15.00

4437 CHICAGO FANCY BOTTLER BRANDY; ribs on shoulder and bottom; clear or amethyst; 11¾"
.... 4.00-8.00

4438 CHICAGO FANCY BOTTLER BRANDY; ribs on shoulder and bottom; ruby red; 11¾"
.... 8.00-10.00

4439 Cigar bottle, cigar-shaped; amber; 7½"
.... 6.00-18.00

4440 Cigar bottle; cigar-shaped; amber; 5½"
.... 6.00-18.00

4441 CLARKE BROS & CO.; amber; 11½" 4.00-8.00

4442 Clown bottle (front and back of bottle pictured); frosted clear or amethyst; 17"..... 85.00-95.00

4443 COCA MARIANI on one line; *Paris* on line near shoulder; liquor; whittle mold; green; 8¾"
.... 2.00-6.00

4444 COCA MARIANI PARIS in two lines; whittle effect; short body; long neck; green; 8½"
.... 3.00-5.00

4445 Coffin type; all basket weave except neck; clear or amethyst; ½ pint 6.00-10.00

4446 Coffin type; two rings on shoulder; checker type body except neck; in center on front, a circle for label; clear; amethyst; 5"; 1¾" at bottom
.... 6.00-10.00

4447 COGNAC CASTILLON; *Depose* under bottom; curved back; clear; 6½".......... 5.00-10.00

4448 GEO. COHN & CO.; amber; 4½"..... 4.00-6.00

4449 GEORGE COHN & COMPANY; *Louisville, Ky.;* blob neck; amber; 4¾" ... 10.00-12.00

4450 CONGRESS HALL WHISKEY BLEND; *The Fleischmann Company, Cincinnati, USA;* amber; 11"................... 8.00-12.00

4451 same as above except dark amber 10.00-15.00

4452 COOK & BERNHEIMER CO.; *Mount Vernon Pure Rye* on one side; amber; 6".. 10.00-15.00

4453 VERY OLD CORN; *From Casper Winston, North Carolina, Louist Price Whiskey House; write for private terms;* fancy with handle and glass top..................... 40.00-60.00

4454 COWIE & CO. LTD.; clear; 8¾".. 10.00-20.00

4455 S. CRABFELDER & CO.; amber; 7"; 4" x 2"
.... 6.00-8.00

4456 CREAMDALE; *Hulling, Mobile, Alabama, Cincinnati, Ohio; Refilling of This Bottle Will Be Prosecuted By Law* under bottom; amber; 11¼"
.... 4.00-10.00

4457 CREAM OF KENTUCKY "THEE" WHISKEY; clear; 11¼"........ 20.00-25.00

4458 CREME DE MENTHE; gold claws; green; 11"
.... 10.00-20.00

4459 THE CRIGLER & CRIGLER CO.; clear or amethyst; 4½".................. 4.00-6.00

4460 CRIGLER & CRIGLER DISTILLERS; *Full Qt. Union Made* other side; clear or amethyst; quart
.... 6.00-8.00

4461 CRIGLER & CRIGLER DISTILLERS, COVINGTON, KY. vertical on one panel; *Full Quart Union Made* on next side; square body; lady's leg neck; graduated top and ring; amethyst; 10⅛".................. 8.00-12.00

4462 GET THE BEST, ORDER YOUR WHISKEY FROM J. CROSSMAN SONS; *New Orleans, La.;* amber; quart 8.00-10.00

4463 CROWN, label; whiskey pinch bottle; machine made; amber; 8½".................. 6.00-8.00

4464 CROWN DISTILLERIES CO.; around monogram *Crown & Co.* in center; inside screw thread; amber; 10" 4.00-6.00

4465 CROWN DISTILLERIES COMPANY; under bottom, *Sample Whiskey;* round; clear or amethyst........................ 3.00-4.00

4466 CROWN DISTILLERIES COMPANY in circle; CROWN & SHIELD, CD CO. monogram, on center; *S.F. Whiskey;* inside threads; embossed cork; round; amber; 11¼"........ 15.00-20.00

4467 same as above except reddish amber; quart
.... 4.00-8.00

4468 CUCKOO; clear or amethyst; 11¾" 15.00-25.00

4469 CUCKOO/(bird, branches, leaves on center) WHISKEY/M. BURKE/BOSTON/TRADE MARK; flask; clear; ½ pint; 6½"... 10.00-20.00

4470 CUCKOO/WHISKEY/M. BURKE/BOSTON/ TRADE MARK all with embossed cuckoo bird in branches and leaves; *Full M.B. Quart* on back; graduated top; round; amethyst; 12"
.... 20.00-30.00

4471 CURNER & COMPANY; *80 Cedar Street, New York;* three-part mold; olive, amber; 11½"
.... 35.00-50.00

4472 J.H. CUTTER OLD BOURBON; *A.P. Hotaling & Company, Portland, Oregon;* pewter screw cap; round top; amber............. 400.00+

4478 4483 4485 4489 4490 4491 4492

4501 4502 4503 4504 4507 4517 4518

4519 4524 4525 4526

4473 J.H. CUTTER OLD BOURBON; *A.P. Hotaling & Co., Portland, Oregon;* quart....... 50.00+

4474 J.H. CUTTER OLD BOURBON; *Moorman Mfg. Louisville, Ky., A.P. Hotaling & Company;* amber; quart 60.00-80.00

4475 J.H. CUTTER OLD BOURBON; *E. Martin & Company;* amber; quart 90.00-125.00

4476 J.H. CUTTER/TRADE MARK (star and shield) /E. MARTIN & COMPANY/SAN FRANCISCO, CAL. in circle; slug plate; graduated top; round; amber; 11" 10.00-15.00

4477 J.H. CUTTER OLD BOURBON; *by Milton J. Hardy & Company, Louisville, Ky.;* barrel in center; amber; 12" .... 50.00+

4478 J.H. CUTTER OLD BOURBON; *Louisville, Ky.;* amber; quart............... 10.00-20.00

4479 J.H. CUTTER OLD BOURBON; barrel and crown in center; *C.P. Moorman Mfg., Louisville, Ky., A.P. Hotaling & Co;* amber; quart 60.00-80.00

4480 CUTTER HOTALING; coffin type; 1886; amber 75.00-100.00

4481 DALLEMAND & CO. INC.; *Chicago* around bottom; brandy; fancy; blob neck; amber; 11¼" 3.00-6.00

4482 DALLEMAND & CO.; *Cream Rye* around bottom; fancy shoulders; amber; 2¾"... 3.00-4.00

4483 DALLEMAND & CO. CHICAGO; *Design Pat 21509 Apr. 26, 1892* under bottom; amber; 11" 10.00-12.00

4484 B.B. DAVIS & COMPANY, NEW YORK, CONTENTS 8 FL. OZS.; flask; graduated collar and ring; amethyst; ½ pint; 6¾" 4.00-8.00

4485 DAVIS' MARYLAND, label; *Guaranteed Full Pint* in back; *Davis & Drake;* clear; 8½" 4.00-6.00

4486 PETER DAWSON LTD, DISTILLERS on bottom; graduated and flared collar; concave and convex circles (thumb prints) around shoulder and base; green; 11¾" 4.00-6.00

4487 DEEP SPRING; *Tennessee Whiskey;* amber; quart; 7" 10.00-15.00

4488 DeKUYPER'S SQUAREFACE; WHO DeKUYPER'S NIGHTLY TAKES, SOUNDLY SLEEPS AND FIT AWAKES on two panels; vertical at slant; vase gin shape; ABM; thread top; grass green; 7⅞" 3.00-4.00

4489 R. DENNER WINE & SPIRIT MERCHANT; *Bridgewater* in three lines on one side shoulder; crock with handle; coffin flask type; ring top; short neck; tan and cream; 8½" tall, 2¼" x 3" .... 10.00+

4490 DEVIL'S ISLAND ENDURANCE GIN; clear or amethyst; pint.................. 4.00-6.00

4491 DE IL'S ISLAND; V missing from Devil's; clear; 9" 10.00-12.00

4492 DIAMOND PACKING CO., BRIDGETON, N.J.; *Pat. Feb 11th 1870* on shoulder; aqua; 8" 8.00-12.00

4493 Diamond quilted flask; double collar; very light aqua, almost clear; quart; 9" 10.00-20.00

4494 DIEHL & FORD; *Nashville, Tennessee* around bottle each letter in a panel; light amber; 9" .... 25.00+

4495 Dip mold wine; kick-up; pontil; dark amber 5.00-10.00

4496 J.E. DOHERTY COMPANY, BOSTON, MASS written vertically; flask; clear; ½ pint; 6¾" 4.00-6.00

4497 J.E. DOHERTY CO./BOSTON, MASS on shoulder; *Regist. Full Qt.* on back; three-piece mold; graduated top; lady's leg neck; amethyst; 11" 6.00-10.00

4498 N.F. DOHERTY, 181-185 CAMBRIDGE ST., BOSTON, GUARANTEED FULL PINT vertically in slug plate; rectangular; graduated collar and ring; amethyst; pint; 8¾" ... 4.00-8.00

4499 NEIL DOHERTY; *176 North St. Boston* in circle; in center of circle *Wine & Liquors;* strap flask; light amber; 9⅝".......... 5.00-8.00

4500 DONALDSON & COMPANY FINE OLD MADERA, MADCIRA HOUSE, FOUNDED 1783, label; aqua; quart; 12¼" 4.00-8.00

4501 DREYFUSS-WEIL & COMPANY, DISTILLERS, PADUCAH, KY, USA; clear; ½ pint 4.00-6.00

4502 DREYFUSS-WEIL & CO; clear or amethyst; 6½"............................ 2.00-6.00

4503 D.S.G. COMPANY under bottom; light amber; 7¾" .... 20.00+

4504 DUFF GORDON SHERRY; three-part mold; aqua; 12"...................... 7.00-10.00

4505 THE DUFFY MALT WHISKEY CO.; *Rochester N.Y.U.S.A.* on front in watermelon circle; in center monogram *D.M.W.Co.;* under bottom *pat'd Aug.24-1886;* different number or letter on bottom; round; amber; 10¼" 3.00-6.00

4506 same as above except ½ pint or pint..... 20.00+

4507 same as above except miniature..... 5.00-10.00

4508 same as above except machine made .. 2.00-3.00

4509 THE DUFFY MALT WHISKEY COMPANY; *Baltimore, Md. U.S.A.* in a circle monogram; in center of circle *D.C.O.;* under bottom *Pat. Aug. 24-86, Baltimore Md.;* some have letters or numbers; amber; approximate quart 4.00-8.00

4510 same as above except machine made .. 2.00-4.00

4511 same as above except approx. pint.. 10.00-20.00

4512 same as above except machine made; approx. pint 8.00-10.00

4513 same as above except approx. ½ pint 10.00-20.00

4514 same as above except machine made; approx. ½ pint 8.00-10.00

4515 same as above except sample 8.00-10.00

4516 THE DUFFY MALT WHISKEY CO.; *Baltimore Md., U.S.A.* in watermelon circle; in center of circle monogram *D.M.W. Co.;* under bottom *Pat. Aug. 24 '86, Baltimore Md.;* ½" ring around neck; amber; 8.00-15.00

4517 THE DUFFY MALT WHISKEY COMPANY; *Patd Aug. 1886* in back; plain bottom; amber; 10½".......................... 12.00-15.00

4518 DUKEHART & CO.; amber; 4" ... 15.00-25.00

4519 DURHAM; amber; 11½" .... 75.00+

4520 DURKIN WHOLESALE AND RETAIL WINE AND LIQUOR; *Hill and Sprague Street, Spokane, Washington* in front; tapered; ring top; 13½" .... 15.00+

4521 JAMES DURKIN WINE & LIQUORS; *Wholesale & retail, Durkin Block, Mill & Sprague, Spokane, Washington, Telephone Main 731; 32 ounce* on front; blob neck; tapered top and ring; amber; 11⅜" 8.00-12.00

4522 DYOTTVILLE GLASS WORKS, PHILA on bottom; gloppy graduated and flared lip; round; green; quart; 11½" 6.00-10.00

4523 DYOTTVILLE GLASS WORKS, PHILA.; green; 6½" .... 35.00+

4524 EAGLE LIQUEUR DISTILLERIES; olive; 7¾"............................ 40.00-50.00

4525 NATIONAL'S EAGLE BLENDED WHISKEY, label; light amber; 4½". 4.00-6.00

4526 F.H. EARL, SPRING ST., NEWTON N.J.; *Full Qt.* on shoulder; light green; 7½".... 4.00-8.00

4527   4528   4529   4530   4531   4532   4533

4535   4536   4540   4541   4542   4544

4545   4548   4549   4553   4554   4558   4559

4561   4562   4564

4527 EDGEMONT WHISKEY BLEND, label; *The I. Trager Co., Cincinnati, Ohio*; clear; 8" 8.00-12.00

4528 EDGEWOOD in gold lettering; clear; quart; 11" 15.00-20.00

4529 EDGEWOOD; panels on shoulders and base; clear or amethyst; 11" 15.00-20.00

4530 WEISS EICHOLD LIQUOR CO.; sheared top; 3 dots on bottom; clear or amethyst; 7" 6.00-8.00

4531 ELK RUN BR'G CO. PUNX'Y, PA.; golden amber; 9½" 6.00-8.00

4532 ERIE CLUB; clear or amethyst; quart or fifth; 11" 8.00-12.00

4533 ESSENCE OF JAMAICA, label; clear or amethyst; 5" 8.00-10.00

4534 same as above except 7½" 10.00-12.00

4535 N.J. ETHRIDGE; *Macon, Ga., pure old Winchester rye whiskey*, label; clear; 6½" 8.00-12.00

4536 EUREKA; clear or amethyst; 7¼" .. 4.00-8.00

4537 EVANS & O'BRIEN; *1870 Stockton*; amber or green.................. 80.00-150.00

4538 FARMVILLE DISPENSARY, FARMVILLE, VA. in a circle; REGISTERED FULL PINT; ring collar; and below it tapered ring top; clear or amethyst 8.00-15.00

4539 FARMVILLE DISPENSARY, FARMVILLE, VA. REGISTERED FULL PINT; clear; pint flask; 8" 8.00-12.00

4540 FARRELL; *A Merry Christmas and a Happy New Year*, label; sheared top; clear or amethyst; 4½" .... 10.00+

4541 FRED FERRIS, ELMIRA, N.Y.; amber; 6¾" 8.00-10.00

4542 JOHN F. FITZGERALD WHISKEY; clear or amethyst; quart 6.00-12.00

4543 same as above except ½ pint....... 8.00-10.00

4544 FLEMING'S; *Bottled Expressly For Family & Medicinal Purposes* in back; *1 Qt.* on side; clear or amethyst; 8½"................ 20.00-25.00

4545 JAMES FOX; *Full* under bottom; clear or amethyst; 9½" .... 25.00+

4546 FRAIELLT BRANCA, MILANO in crude blob seal on shoulder; two ring collar; turn mold; green; 14"...................... 4.00-8.00

4547 THE PURDUE FREDERICK CO, NEW YORK inside of oval circle; PF CO. monogram in center; oval flask; amethyst; pint; 8" 4.00-6.00

4548 FRIEDMAN KEILER & CO; *Distillers and Wholesale Liquor Dealers, Paducah, Ky., 1* under bottom; amber; 12"........ 8.00-10.00

4549 FRIEDMAN KEILER & SON; amber; 12" 8.00-12.00

4550 JOS FUHRER & SONS; *3701 Butler Street, Pittsburgh, Pa.*; tapered top; clear or amethyst; 9½".................. 8.00-15.00

4551 GAELIC OLD SMUGGLER on bottom; round; square and ring collar; fat neck; olive green; quart; 10"...................... 8.00-10.00

4552 GAGLE GLEN WHISKEY; *29 Market Street, San Francisco, Werle & Willow*....... 50.00+

4553 GAHN, BELT & CO.; clear or amethyst; 8" 4.00-6.00

4554 GANNYMEDE; amber; 7½" 4.00-8.00

4555 GARRETT & CO.; *Established In 1835* on top; in center eagle and shield with *American Wines*; on each side of it *St. Louis, Mo., Norfolk, Va.*; at bottom *Registered Trade Mark, Refilling Prohibited*; fancy; clear or amethyst; quart; 12" 4.00-8.00

4556 same as above except amber...... 12.00-18.00

4557 same as above except sample with *Norfolk, Va.*; 4¾".................. 4.00-8.00

4558 GARRETT & CO.; two types: crown top—14"; applied top—12"; clear or amethyst; 14" 4.00-6.00
12" 6.00-8.00

4559 GARRETT WILLIAMS CO.; clear; 6½" 4.00-6.00

4560 C.R. GIBSON, SALAMANCA, NEW YORK in shield; amber; pint.............. 8.00-12.00

4561 OLD JOE GIDEON WHISKEY; amber; 11½" 12.00-20.00

4562 OLD JOE GIDEON; amber; ½ pint   4.00-6.00

4563 GILBERT BROS. & CO. BALTIMORE, MD on front; oval; graduated collar and ring; thick glass; aqua; pint; 8¼" 6.00-8.00

4564 H & A GILBEY LTD.; aqua; 12"... 3.00-6.00

4565 J.A. GILKA vertically; *J.A. GILKA/BERLIN* vertically on side; *THIS BOTTLE D* vertically on corner panel; *NOT TO BE SOLD* on corner panel; *SCHUTZEN STR. NO. 9* on side; graduated collar and ring; light amber; quart; 9¾" 10.00-20.00

4566 J.A. GILKA BERLIN on side; *J.A. GILKA* on back; *SCHUTZEN STR. NO. 9* on opposite side; same as above except embossing; gloppy collar; red amber; quart; 9¾" 20.00-30.00

4567   4571   4572   4573   4577   4578   4579   4582

4584   4586   4587   4591   4592   4593   4594   4595

4596   4597   4601   4602   4604   4605   4606   4608

4567 W. GILMORE & SON, PAVILION, N.Y.; kick-up; teal blue; 10¼".............. 10.00-15.00

4568 GLENBROOK DISTILLING CO/BOSTON, MASS vertically; oval flask; aqua; ½ pint; 6¾" 4.00-6.00

4569 GLENBROOK on bottom; flask; amber; ½ pint; 6¾"............................ 4.00-6.00

4570 same as above except aqua 4.00-6.00

4571 THE GLENDALE CO.; three-part mold; clear or amethyst; 12"................ 8.00-12.00

4572 I. GOLDBERG DISTILLER; five panels; clear; 13¼"............................ 10.00-12.00

4573 I. GOLDBERG on one panel; next panel *171E Broadway*; next *Houston or Clinton St., 5th Ave. cor, 115th St*; next *New York City, Brooklyn*; next *Graham Ave. cor. Debevoise St. Pitkin cor. Rockaway Ave.*; three panels blank for label; under bottom different number; on shoulder *I. Goldberg* and *Est. 1873*; 12¼" 20.00-30.00

4574 I. GOLDBERG on one panel; next *Distiller*; next *171-E Broadway*; next *Houston cor Clinton St.*; next *5th Ave cor 115th St New York City*; three panels blank for label; plain shoulder; amber; 12¼".......................... 15.00-20.00

4575 I. GOLDBERG vertically on one panel; *171 E. BROADWAY* on next; *Houston Cor Clinton St. 5th Ave. cor 115th St.* on next panel; *New York City, Brooklyn* on next panel; *Gram Cor Debevoise Pitkin cor Rockaway Ave;* on next panel; eight large vertical panels; graduated collar; amber; quart; 12½"......... 30.00-40.00

4576 GOLDEN & CO, SAN FRANCISCO, CAL. inside of circle; *Net Contents One Quart Full Measure* on front; round; graduated collar and ring; amber; 11¾"............... 15.00-25.00

4577 GOLDEN CREAM 1878 WHISKEY; *Weiss Echold Liquor Co., Mobile, Ala., Proprietors;* clear or amethyst; 8½".......... 8.00-10.00

4578 GOLDEN CREAM; seven panels; clear; fifth 8.00-12.00

4579 GOLDEN GATE CO. BALTIMORE CELERY RYE; *Pat Apl. For* under bottom; clear; quart 4.00-8.00

4580 same as above except amethyst 4.00-8.00

4581 GOLDEN HILL on base; *#2* under bottom; two ring top; amber; 4½" 8.00-10.00

4582 GOLDEN WEDDING; *Jos. S. Fench & Co. Schenley Pa*, label; whiskey sample; 4" 8.00-10.00

4583 GOLDIE—KLENERT CO, STOCKTON, CAL in slug plate; graduated collar; round; clear; quart; 11¼" 4.00-8.00

4584 GOLD THIMBLE SCOTCH WHISKEY; *Blck Bros Glasgow;* pinch bottle; amber; 8½" 15.00-25.00

4585 GOLDTREE BROS in slug plate; *1880; San Luis;* amber; quart .... 100.00+

4586 MORRIS T. GOMBERT, HOUSTON; clear or amethyst; 6" 8.00-10.00

4587 GEO. H. GOODMAN.; *B* on bottom; clear or amethyst; fifth 6.00-10.00

4588 GORDONS DRY GIN, LONDON, ENGLAND; square with wide beveled corners; boar on bottom; graduated and flared collar; aqua; quart; 8⅝".................... 4.00-8.00

4589 same as above except oval back; old .. 2.00-6.00

4590 same as above except ABM 2.00-6.00

4591 G.P.R.; whiskey label; clear or amethyst; 7½" 2.00-6.00

4592 G.P.R.; *Baltimores G. Gump & Sons* on shoulder; clear; 10¾".............. 8.00-10.00

4593 S. GRABFELDER & CO.; *I* on bottom; amber; 5¾".......................... 4.00-6.00

4594 S. GRABFELDER & CO.; *99A* on bottom; amber; 7" 6.00-8.00

4595 S. GRABFELDER & CO.; *J* on bottom; amber; 7¼"............................ 6.00-10.00

4596 S. GRABFELDER & CO.; clear or amethyst; 6" 3.00-6.00

4597 GRAFFING & CO. N.Y. under bottom; boy and girl climbing trees; clear; 12¼" 20.00-30.00

4598 C.E. GRANGER, WINE & LIQUORS, SUNBURY, OHIO; double collar; bottom—*AMF & CO.;* clear; ½ pint; 6½" 8.00-15.00

4599 C.E. GRANGER, WINES & LIQUORS; double collar; flask; under bottom—*AMF & CO. warranted full measure;* clear; ½ pint; 6½" 8.00-12.00

4600 E.E. GRAY & CO/IMPORTERS/BOSTON, MASS vertically; *Full Quart Registered* on back; round; graduated collar, seven rings; amethyst; quart; 12½" 8.00-12.00

4601 GREAT SEAL STYRON BEGGS & CO. NEWARK O.; clear or amethyst; 6".. 4.00-6.00

4602 GREAT SEAL; clear or amethyst; 6" 2.00-6.00

4603 GREEN & CLARK MISSOURI CIDER; *Registered, Aug. 27, 1878* in vertical lines under bottom; *A B & M Co.;* blob top; amber; 9½" 10.00-15.00

4604 GREENBRIER WHISKEY, label; *The Old Spring Distilling Company, Cincinnati; H2* under bottom; clear; 11"............ 4.00-6.00

4605 B.S. GREIL & CO, CINCINNATI, OHIO; clear or amethyst; pint................. 10.00-15.00

4606 THE GRIM REAPER; *Sandemong Cherry Black* on back; *Royal Doulton China* under bottom; black; 10½"............ old 25.00-30.00
.... new 10.00-15.00

4607 GUARANTEED on ribbon; FULL PINT under ribbon at top; long graduated collar with ring; rectangular; 8¾" 4.00-6.00

4608 GUARANTEED FULL; amber; 6½". 4.00-8.00

4609 4610 4611 4612 4615 4617 4619

4621 4622 4623 4626 4629 4630 4631 4632

4636 4639 4640 4641 4643 4652 4653

4609 GUITAR WHISKEY, label; amber; 15"
.... 8.00-12.00

4610 H on bottom; whiskey label; clear or amethyst;
6½".................... 2.00-4.00

4611 L. HAAS & CO. TOLEDO, O., label; horseshoe
seal; clear; 12½"................ 4.00-6.00

4612 HAIG & HAIG; clear; 8"......... 4.00-8.00

4613 same as above except amber...... 10.00-15.00

4614 HALL, LUHRS & CO. SACRAMENTO;
monogram on the front pumpkin seed; amethyst;
6¾"........................ 8.00-20.00

4615 Ham on shoulder; shape of a whole ham; screw
top; sheared top; amber; 6¼" tall, 3½" wide
.... 15.00+

4616 Handled whiskey jug; Chestnut type; amber;
7⅝"...................... 10.00-25.00

4617 HANDMADE SOUR MASH; clear; 4½"
.... 4.00-8.00

4618 same as above except amber....... 8.00-12.00

4619 HANNIS DISTLG CO.; *Pat April 1890* under
bottom; amber; 8¾"............. 20.00-30.00

4620 I.W. HARPER; with like-new wicker; name
shows through window in wicker; graduated collar; light amber; quart; 9¾"...... 15.00-30.00

4621 I.W. HARPER; *Medal Whiskey* in center; gold
on front; anchor in gold; rope around neck; 3"
pottery; very light tan; 4" square tapering to
3½" on shoulder 10.00-20.00

4622 I.W. HARPER; whiskey; amber; 9½"
.... 8.00-15.00

4623 I.W. HARPER; clear or amethyst; 4¼"
.... 8.00-10.00

4624 ADOLPH HARRIS AND CO.; *San Francisco*;
amber; quart 30.00-40.00

4625 ADOLPH HARRIS & CO. (deer head) SAN
FRANCISCO; cylindrical; amber; fifth
.... 70.00-85.00

4626 ALBERT H. HARRIS N.Y., label; turn mold;
amber; quart 4.00-8.00

4627 HARVARD RYE, with interlocking HR, inside
of rectangle; slug plate; vertical panels on neck
and shoulder; fancy; graduated collar; round;
amethyst; quart; 12"............. 4.00-8.00

4628 HARVARD RYE with interlocking HR
monogram in center; rectangular; double band
collar; heavy glass; clear; pint; 7½" .. 4.00-8.00

4629 HARVARD RYE; clear or amethyst; 7½"
.... 8.00-10.00

4630 THE HAYNER DISTILLING CO.; *Dayton,
Ohio & St. Louis Mo. Distillers; W* on bottom,
also *Nov. 30th 1897*; whiskey; amethyst; 11½"
.... 6.00-14.00

4631 THE HAYNER DISTILLING CO., DAYTON,
ST. LOUIS, ATLANTA, ST. PAUL, DIS-
TILLERS; *Design Patented Nov. 30th, 1897*
under bottom; amber; 11½"....... 8.00-10.00

4632 HAYNER RICH PRIVATE STOCK PURE
WHISKEY; in back *H.W. Distillers, Troy, Ohio;*
under bottom, *Distillers, Pat. Nov 30th, 1897-F;*
clear; 11½"................... 6.00-8.00

4633 THE HAYNER WHISKEY DISTILLERS,
TROY, OHIO; *Design Patented Nov. 30th, 1897*
on bottom; fluting around base 1" high, also on
shoulder and neck; graduated collar and ring;
round; ABM; clear; quart; 11½".... 4.00-8.00

4634 HAYNER WHISKEY DISTILLERY, TROY O.
lower trunk and paneled shoulder; *Nov. 30th
1897, F* on bottom; round; amethyst 6.00-14.00

4635 HAYNERS DISTILLING CO., DAYTON,
OHIO, USA, DISTILLERS & IMPORTERS in
circle; *Design Patented Nov. 30th, 1897* on bottom; 14 fancy vertical panels on shoulder and
neck; 14 vertical 1" panels around base; graduated collar and ring; amethyst; liter; 12"
.... 4.00-8.00

4636 W.H. HECKENDORN & CO., label; *2* under
bottom; three-part mold; golden amber; 12"
.... 7.00-10.00

4637 EDWARD HEFFERMAN in center, REG.
FULL PINT at top, 88 PORTLAND ST.
BOSTON, MASS all on front in slug plate;
rectangular; light green; pint; 8½"... 3.00-6.00

4638 W.H. HENNESSEY, 38 TO 44 ANDREW ST.,
LYNN, MASS. vertically; slug plate; rectangular; graduated collar and ring; amethyst; ½ pint;
6¾"........................ 4.00-8.00

4639 HERE'S A SMILE TO THOSE I LOVE; clear;
5½"...................... 10.00-15.00

4640 HERE'S A SMILE TO THOSE I LOVE; clear
or amethyst; 5½"................ 14.00-18.00

4641 HERE'S HOPING—; clear; 8"....... 10.00+

4642 HEWONTS SQUEAL; hog bottle 15.00-35.00

4643 HIGHCLIFF WHISKEY CINI O, label; amber;
½ pint 4.00-6.00

4644 HOCK WINE, label; sheared top and ring; red
ground pontil; mold; 14"........ 10.00-20.00

4645 same as above except old; teal blue; 11½"
.... 4.00-8.00

4646 same as above except old; teal blue; 14"
.... 4.00-10.00

4647 same as above except old; red amber; 11½"
.... 3.00-6.00

4648 same as above except old; light amber; 7"
.... 4.00-8.00

4649 same as above except old ABM; light amber; 14"
.... 3.00-6.00

4650 same as above except old ABM; green; 13½"
.... 2.00-4.00

4651 HOFHEIMER'S EAGLE RYE BLEND (large
eagle embossed on shield) M. HOFHEIMER &
CO. NORFOLK, VA; rectangular; clear; ½ pint;
6"......................... 4.00-8.00

4652 HOFHEIMER'S EAGLE RYE BLEND; clear
or amethyst; 6".................. 4.00-6.00

4653 HOLBERG MERCANTILE CO.; amber; 11"
.... 10.00-12.00

4654 HOLLANDS in gold letters; around it gold circle; glass top with *H*; fancy; 9½" ..... 50.00+

4655 HOLLYWOOD WHISKEY; round; graduated
collar and ring; amber; quart; 11" 10.00-20.00

4657   4658   4659   4660   4661   4665   4666

4667   4669   4673   4674   4676   4677   4678   4679

4680   4682   4683   4684   4686   4688   4690

4695   4696   4697   4699

4656 same as above except golden amber 15.00-30.00

4657 HOLLYWOOD WHISKEY; amber; 12" 8.00-12.00

4658 HOLLYWOOD WHISKEY; kick-up; amber; 11¼" 8.00-12.00

4659 HOME SUPPLY CO.; wine label; three-part mold; amber; 11¼" 4.00-8.00

4660 HOME SUPPLY CO.; whiskey label; three-part mold; amber; 11¼" 4.00-8.00

4661 HONEST MEASURE; clear; 4¾"... 6.00-8.00

4662 HONEST MEASURE; half pint on shoulder; saddle flask; amber; ½ pint........ 4.00-8.00

4663 same as above except clear 2.00-4.00

4664 same as above except clear; pint 4.00-6.00

4665 W. HONEY GLASS WORKS under bottom; amber; 7½".................... 15.00-30.00

4666 HOTEL WORTH BAR, FORT WORTH, TEXAS; inside screw; amber; 6" 80.00-100.00

4667 HUBER KUEMMEL LIQUEUR, B.S. FLERSHEIM MERC. CO., label; amber; 10" 8.00-15.00

4668 H.W. HUGULEY CO., 134 CANAL ST. BOSTON; Full Quart on back; round; graduated collar and ring; amethyst; 12".. 4.00-8.00

4669 H.W. HUGULEY CO.; clear or amethyst; 11¾" 8.00-10.00

4670 HURDLE RYE; clear panels; neck; letters etched; 3"....................... 8.00-15.00

4671 THE IMPERIAL DISTILLING CO; Kansas City, Mo. in center; IDCO; fancy shoulder; clear; 4" 8.00-12.00

4672 IMPERIAL in ribbon; Pint on back in ribbon; oval; aqua; 9" 4.00-6.00

4673 IMPERIAL in back; aqua; ½ pint; 7¾" 10.00+

4674 IMPERIAL WEDDING WHISKEY BLEND, label; clear or amethyst; 8" and other sizes 6.00-10.00

4675 IMPORTERS vertically; flask; clear; ½ pint; 6½"....................... 3.00-6.00

4676 G. INNSEN & SONS, PITTSBURGH under bottom; green; quart 18.00-20.00

4677 JACK CRANSTON'S DIODORA CORN WHISKEY; Jack Cranston Co., Baltimore, Md. in back; U blank seal; clear; 12" ... 8.00-15.00

4678 JACK DANIEL'S GOLD MEDAL OLD NO. 7; clear; 7¾"..................... 18.00-25.00

4679 JAMES BUCHANAN & CO. LTD.; ½ ring on each side; 106 under bottom; dark green; 7¼" 10.00-20.00

4680 JESSE MOORE-HUNT CO.; amber; 11¼" 10.00-15.00

4681 J.M. & CO. BOSTON, MASS in slug plate; oval flask; aqua; 10".................. 4.00-6.00

4682 JOHANN MARIA FARINA NO. 4, JULICRSPLATZ NO. 4; clear or amethyst; 4" 3.00-6.00

4683 JOHN HART & CO. on each side; amber; 7¼" 25.00-35.00

4684 W.L. JOHNSON KENTUCKY; pontil; amber; 8¼"...................... 65.00-75.00

4685 W.H. JONES & CO. ESTABLISHED 1851 (shield with bear) IMPORTERS/HANOVER AND/BLACKSTONE STS/BOSTON, MASS all on front; flask; light green slug plate; pint; 8¾"...................... 6.00-10.00

4686 W.H. JONES AND CO.; clear; 9½" 8.00-15.00

4687 Jug; round base; bulbous neck; light green; gallon; 13½" tall, 5¼" across...... 10.00-20.00

4688 L.E. JUNG & CO, PURE MALT WHISKEY, NEW ORLEANS, LA.; amber; 10¾" 8.00-12.00

4689 J & W HARDIE EDINBURGH on bottom; three-piece mold; large square collar; emerald green; 10¼" 4.00-6.00

4690 J&W.N. & CO. under bottom; aqua; 11" 2.00-4.00

4691 same as above except clear; 10"..... 3.00-5.00

4692 KELLY & KERR; 222 Colleges St., Springfield, Mo.; C.W. Stuart's; machine made; clear, amber or aqua; quart.................... 4.00-6.00

4693 KELLY & KERR; 222 College St., Springfield, Mo.; machine made; clear or aqua... 2.00-4.00

4694 KENTUCKY GEM, S.M. COPPER DISTILLERS, WHISKEY; T.G. Cockrill, San Francisco; quart................... 50.00+

4695 KEYSTONE BURGUNDY; tapered top; amber; 8¾"...................... 35.00-40.00

4696 KEYSTONE; whiskey label; clear or amethyst; 7½"...................... 10.00-15.00

4697 KING BEE; ten panels; clear; 11¼" 10.00-20.00

4698 KIRBY'S; 222 Colleges St., Springfield, Mo., 1870; quart; clear or aqua........ 4.00-12.00

4699 H.B. KIRK & CO.; amber; 11⅛" 8.00-15.00

4700 REMAINS THE PROPERTY OF H.B. KIRK & CO. N.Y. on back; three Indian heads embossed in circle on shoulder; trademark in ribbon; Registered U.S. on front; graduated collar and ring; round; amber; quart; 11¼".... 6.00-10.00

4705   4707   4713   4718   4720   4722   4723

4725   4726   4727   4728   4729   4733   4734   4735

4737   4739   4742   4743   4745   4747   4748

4701 HENRY KLINKER, JR.; *The Owl, 748-10th ave., SE corner 51st Street, N.Y.* in circle under it; *Full Measure;* double collar; under bottom—*LCMG, 182 Fulton Street, N.Y.;* amber; 1½ pint 8.00-10.00

4702 C.F. KNAPP, PHILADELPHIA; pig slope; clear or amethyst; 3¼" x 2"....... 20.00-40.00

4703 CHATEAU LAFIETE 1896 in circle; blob seal on shoulder; crude band collar; kick-up; green; 12".................... 4.00-8.00

4704 LAKE DRUMMOND PURE RYE, J & E MAHONEY; rectangular; clear; ½ pint; 6½" 4.00-8.00

4705 LAKE KEUKA VINTAGE CO., BATH, NEW YORK WINERY NO. 25; same shape and design as a Hayner Whiskey; graduated collar and ring; amethyst; 12" 4.00-6.00

4706 LAMBE & DENMARKE FINE WHISKEY; *Arkansas City, Ark.;* under bottom, *L.C. & R CO.;* tapered top and ring; fancy bottom; clear or aqua; 8"................ 15.00-30.00

4707 JOHN LATREYTE; under bottom *C. Pat'd, April 1, '84;* clear or aqua; 7¼"... 10.00-12.00

4708 LEIPPS in script; *Chicago;* tapered top; amber; 4½".......................... 8.00-12.00

4709 LILIENTHAL, CINCINNATI, SAN FRANCISCO & NEW YORK, 1885; yellow amber 100.00-200.00

4710 LILIENTHAL DISTILLERS; coffin type with crown; amber .... 75.00+

4711 LILIENTHAL CO.; slask; amber.... 200.00+

4712 LOS ANGELES CO., 51 & 53 SUMMER ST., BOSTON, MASS., LA CO. monogram; flask; ring collar; amethyst; ½ pint 4.00-8.00

4713 LOUISVILLE, KY. GLASS WORKS; aqua; 8¾".......................... 65.00+

4714 LYNDEBORS; *L.G. CO.* on base; cylindrical; honey amber 20.00-30.00

4715 LYONS, E.Y. AND RAAS; *San Francisco, California;* cylindrical; clear or amethyst 10.00-15.00

4716 MACKENZIE & CO. FINE TAWNY PORT, MEDAL OF HONOR S.F. 1915, label on front and back; round and flared band collar; slight bulbous neck; emerald green; 11½".. 4.00-6.00

4717 JOS MAGNUS & CO.; embossed dragon and CINCINNATI, OHIO; rectangular; square collar; clear; ½ pint; 6" 4.00-6.00

4718 JOS. A. MAGNUS & CO.; clear or amethyst; 6½".......................... 4.00-8.00

4719 J & E MAHONEY DISTILLERS, PORTSMOUTH AND ALEXANDRIA, VA.; rectangular; flask; clear; 6¼"....... 4.00-8.00

4720 MAILHOUSE RYE; clear or amethyst; 8¼" .... 100.00+

4721 MALLARD DISTILLING CO., BALTIMORE AND NEW YORK, PATENT APPLIED FOR; sunken sides; ½ pint; 6¼" 3.00-6.00

4722 MALLARD DISTILLING CO.; clear or amethyst; pint.................. 2.00-4.00

4723 Man's face figural whiskey bottle, label; clear or amethyst; 7½".................... 35.00+

4724 ISAAC MANSBACH & CO., in a dome shaped line; under it, *Fine Whiskeys, Philadelphia;* square; flat collar; ring; amber; quart 10.00-20.00

4725 ISAAC MANSBACH & CO.; *Philadelphia* other side; *Millionaires Club Whiskey* around shoulder; amber; 4¾" 10.00-15.00

4726 ISAAC MANSBACH & CO. in back; *Millionaire Club* on shoulder; amber; 4½" 6.00-8.00

4727 THE J.G. MARK'S LIQUOR CO. WHOLESALE on back; clear or amethyst; 9" 15.00-25.00

4728 THE J.G. MARKS LIQUOR CO.; three barrels trademark in back; clear or amethyst; 9¼" 15.00-25.00

4729 Marriage bottle; crock; black, white, blue, tan; 8¾" .... 40.00+

4730 MARTINI COCKTAILS, FOR MARTINI COCKTAILS USE ONLY MARTINI VERMOUTHS; champagne shaped; sand blasted or etched lettering; ABM; green; 12½" 4.00-6.00

4731 MAY & FAIRALL GROCERS, BALTIMORE; three-piece mold; slug plate; amber; quart; 11¼" 10.00-15.00

4732 MAYSE BROS. DISTILLERS RYE with seal; clear or amethyst; 10"............... 50.00+

4733 McAVDY BREW CO.; amber; 8½".. 4.00-6.00

4734 McDONALD & COHN; *San Francisco, Cal.;* amber; quart 8.00-12.00

4735 McKNIGHTS; amber; 10½" 6.00-8.00

4736 same as above except clear; 9¼" 4.00-6.00

4737 JOHN A. McLAREN; in center, PERTH MALT WHISKEY, PERTH, ONT; saddle flask; *193* under bottom; two-ring top; 8" 10.00-15.00

4738 MERIDITH'S CLUB PURE RYE WHISKEY; *East Liverpool, Ohio;* white; 7¼".. 10.00-15.00

4739 MERRY CHRISTMAS HAPPY NEW YEAR; quilted back; sheared top; clear; 6" ... 25.00+

4740 MERRY CHRISTMAS & HAPPY NEW YEAR in center; clear or amethyst; 5"... 10.00-20.00

4741 MERRY CHRISTMAS & HAPPY NEW CENTURY; in back a watch with Roman letters and *B I Co.* in center; pocket watch type; milk glass 15.00-25.00

4742 Mexican drinking bottle; clear; 10" tall, 7" round 6.00-12.00

4743 MEYER PITTS & CO.; clear or amethyst; 6" 2.00-4.00

4744 H. MICHELSEN in center; on top *Bay Rum;* under it *St. Thomas;* clear or amethyst; fifth 5.00-6.00

4745 I. MICHELSON & BROS; clear or amethyst; 11".......................... 8.00-12.00

4746 MIDLAND HOTEL; *Kansas City, Mo.;* panels on neck; clear; 3"................ 4.00-8.00

4747 Milk glass; 7¼" .... 20.00+

4748 J.A. MILLER, HOUSTON, TEXAS; clear or amethyst; ½ pint.............. 8.00-10.00

4749   4750   4751   4755   4756   4757   4758

4761   4762   4764   4768   4769   4771   4773   4774

4775   4776   4779   4781   4782   4783   4785

| 4786 | 4787 | 4788 |

4749 M & M T CO.; clear or amethyst; 3¼" 4.00-6.00

4750 J. MOORE OLD BOURBON; amber; 12"
.... 10.00-12.00

4751 J. MOORE; amber; 11"............. 25.00+

4752 JESSE MOORE & CO. LOUISVILLE, KY.;
*Ringdeer Trade Mark; Bourbon & Rye; Moore
Hunt & Co.; sole agents;* flask; amber
.... 100.00-200.00

4753 JESSE MOORE & CO. LOUISVILLE, KY.
outer circle; C.H. MOORE BOURBON & RYE
center; JESSE MOORE HUNT CO./SAN
FRANCISCO at base; graduated collar and
ring; quart; 11½" 15.00-30.00

4754 same as above except golden amber; 11¾"
.... 15.00-30.00

4755 G.T. MORRIS; a bunch of flowers on back;
amber; 12"...................... 200.00+

4756 Moses in bulrush; clear or amethyst; 5"
.... 10.00-20.00

4757 MOUNT VERNON; machine made; amber; 8¼"
.... 8.00-10.00

4758 MOUNT VERNON PURE RYE WHISKEY in
three lines; back *Hannis Dist'l'G Co., Full Five*
in two lines; two more lines *Re-Use of Bottle
Prohibited;* under bottom *Patented March 25
1890;* amber; 3¼" square, 4¼" tall, neck 4"
.... 10.00-20.00

4759 same as above except sample; 3¼".. 8.00-10.00

4760 same as above except machine made 2.00-4.00

4761 MULFORD'S DISTILLED MALT EXTRACT;
embossed, *J.F. Mulford & Co., chemists, Philadelphia;* amber; 8¾" 4.00-6.00

4762 MURRAY HILL MARYLAND RYE;
Sherbrook Distilling Co., Cincinnati, label; clear
or amethyst; 6".................. 6.00-8.00

4763 JOHN MURRAY (JM) RYE WHISKEY, label
only; flask; amber; ½ pint; 7" 4.00-6.00

4764 ANGELO MYERS; clear or amethyst; 6¼"
.... 4.00-8.00

4765 H.C. MYERS COMPANY/NEW YORK, N.Y./
AND/COVINGTON, KY., GUARANTEED
FULL ½ PINT all on front; flask; amethyst;
6⅜" ....

4766 NEALS AMB PHTH in seal on shoulder; cobalt
blue; 9⅛"................... 40.00-80.00

4767 NEWMAN'S COLLEGE; *San Francisco and
Oakland;* round like football; amber; 4¼"
.... 8.00-15.00

4768 O'HARE MALT, H. ROSENTHAL & SONS;
#1 under bottom; amber; 10¾" 8.00-12.00

4769 O'HEARN'S WHISKEY; *#1919* under bottom;
side mold; inside screw; amber; 10¼"
.... 15.00-30.00

4770 OHIO; expanded swirl bottle; 24 rib pattern:
vertical over swirl to left; club shaped; deep blue
aqua; 7¾"..................... 50.00-75.00

4771 OLD ASHTON; clear; 8½"....... 5.00-10.00

4772 THE OLD BUSHMILLS DISTILLING CO.,
LIMITED TRADEMARK; *pure malt, established 1734;* 10"; to 1903 .... 6.00-10.00;
1915 up 4.00-6.00

4773 OLD CHARTER WHISKEY, LOUISVILLE,
KY., label; amber; 11¾" 4.00-6.00

4774 OLD DUFFY'S 1842 APPLE JUICE,
VINEGAR STERILIZED 5 YEARS around
shoulder; amber; 10" 6.00-8.00

4775 OLD EDGEMONT WHISKEY, label; clear; ½
pint; 6½" .... 8.00+

4776 OLD EDGEMONT WHISKEY, THE I.
TRAGER CO. CINCINNATI, OHIO, label;
clear; ¼ pint; 5" 8.00-10.00

4777 OLD FAMILY WINE STORE (diamond
design)/ESTABLISHED 1857/JOS. CLEVE &
CO/19821 CAMBRIDGE ST. BOSTON in slug
plate; narrow flask; ring collar; clear; ½ pint;
6½"......................... 6.00-8.00

4778 OLD HENRY RYE in script; ring top; clear or
aqua; 9½" 8.00-10.00

4779 OLD HUDSON; pinch bottle; clear; 6½"
.... 20.00-30.00

4780 OLD IRISH WHISKEY (trademark—shield
and crown); *This Is the property of Mitchell &
Co. of Belfast, Ltd, Imperial Pint,* all on front;
flask shape; graduated collar and flared band;
ABM; aqua; 9½" 3.00-4.00

4781 OLD IRISH WHISKEY; *Imperial Pint* on back;
aqua; 10" 10.00-20.00

4782 OLD J.H. CUTTER V.F.O. RYE,
LOUISVILLE KY., label; clear or amethyst;
11"......................... 4.00-6.00

4783 OLD JOE GIDEON WHISKEY BROS.; *F*
under bottom; 11½" 10.00-20.00

4784 OLD KAINTUCK BOURBON; clear; 3¾"
.... 6.00-10.00

4785 THE OLD KENTUCKY CO.; clear or
amethyst; 11" 8.00-12.00

4786 OLD PORT HALEY WHISKEY; *Swope &
Mangold, Dallas, Texas;* clear or aqua; quart
.... 15.00+

4787 OLD PRENTICE WHISKEY, label; in back
embossed *J.T.S. Brown & Sons, Distillers,
Louisville, Ky.;* clear; 11"......... 4.00-6.00

4788 OLD QUAKER; *1234* under bottom; clear; 6½"
.... 3.00-6.00

4789   4790   4791   4792   4793   4794

4796   4799   4805   4806   4808   4809   4811

4812   4813   4814   4815   4816   4828

4829   4830   4831

4789 OLD SERVITOR DISTRIBUTING CO. N.Y.; amber; 11″ 4.00-6.00

4790 THE OLD SPRING DISTILLING CO.; clear or amethyst; 8½″ 2.00-4.00

4791 OLD SPRING WHISKEY; clear or amethyst; 9¼″ 10.00-12.00

4792 OLD TIME; *First Prize Worlds Fair 1893;* clear; 9½″ .... 10.00+

4793 OPPENHEIM; *Fine Whiskey, Atlanta, Ga.;* amber; 8″ 10.00-20.00

4794 THE ORENE PARKER CO.; clear or amethyst; 11¼″ 8.00-10.00

4795 E. OTLENVILLE, A.G. D.H. CO.; in back *E.O., Nashville, Tenn.;* tapered top; amber; 9″ .... 25.00+

4796 J.W. PALMER, NELSON COUNTY KY. WHISKEY in four lines; in back *Compliments of J.W. Seay, Savannah, Ga.;* pottery jug, with handle; brown and tan; 3″ 4.00-6.00

4797 PARKER RYE in front of squat bottle; ribs under bottom; six panels on neck; flat top; clear; 1½″ neck; 3¼″ 4.00-6.00

4798 PARKER RYE; six panels; fancy; clear; 1¾″ neck; 1½″ body 6.00-10.00

4799 PAROLE; amber; 10½″ 35.00-60.00

4800 PATENT on shoulder; three-part mold; round; amber; 10½″ 2.00-4.00

4801 PATENTED APRIL 3d, 1900 at base on concave panel; oval back; two rings on neck; unusual shape; amber; ½ pint; 6½″ .. 3.00-6.00

4802 PATTERSON'S LIQUOR STORE; *Wapakoneta, Ohio;* flask; clear; 6½″ 8.00-12.00

4803 PATTERSON'S LIQUOR STORE; *Wapakoneta, Ohio* in a circle; lined at bottom; clear; 6¼″ 8.00-15.00

4804 PAUL JONES 1908 N8 under bottom; amber; pint 4.00-6.00

4805 PAUL JONES BOURBON, LOUISVILLE, KY. in seal; amber; quart 10.00-15.00

4806 PAUL JONES PURE RYE, LOUISVILLE, KY. on blob seal; round; amber; 9¼″ 8.00-14.00

4807 same as above except WHISKEY .. 8.00-14.00

4808 same as above except OLD MONONGAHELA RYE 10.00-18.00

4809 PAUL JONES & CO. in script on curved 1½″ x 3″ panel on one side; front and back of bottle curved; off center neck; light green; 6½″ to top, 4½″ to curved shoulder.......... 12.00-20.00

4810 PAUL JONES; (enameled) ground pontil; clear 20.00-30.00

4811 PAUL JONES WHISKEY, label; amber; quart 10.00-15.00

4812 PAUL JONES WHISKEY; amber; 4″ 6.00-8.00

4813 PAUL JONES & CO.; *718* in diamond shape under bottom; machine made; amber; 12″ 6.00-8.00

4814 PAUL JONES 1905 22 under bottom; amber; 9″ 4.00-8.00

4815 PAUL JONES PURE GIN, LOUISVILLE, KY. in seal; green; 9½″ 15.00-20.00

4816 PAUL JONES PURE RYE, LOUISVILLE KY. in circle; small kick-up; amber; 5¾″ 6.00+

4817 PEARSONS/PURE OLD/MALT WHISKEY at top; REDINGTON & CO./PACIFIC COAST AGENTS at base; round; graduated collar; clear; quart 4.00-6.00

4818 PEDRO; *1880;* glop top; amber; quart 60.00-80.00

4819 S.F. PETTS & CO./IMPORTERS/BOSTON/ U.S.A./REGISTERED horizontally; round; graduated collar and ring; amethyst; 12½″ 6.00-8.00

4820 Picnic flask or pumpkin seed; there are many different sizes and colors, some embossed, some not 3.00-10.00

4821 S.N. PIKES MAGNOLIA, CINCINNATI, OHIO; *The Fleischman;* clear or amethyst; 12¼″ 10.00-15.00

4822 PIKES PEAK OLD RYE; aqua; pint 40.00-50.00

4823 PIKESVILLE RYE; clear; 4″ 4.00-6.00

4824 same as above except *Patented* under bottom 5.00-8.00

4825 PLANTER RYE, REGISTERED ULLMAN & CO., OHIO; amethyst; ½ pint 10.00

4826 PLANTER MARY LOU RYE; *Ullman & Co., Cincinnati;* ground top; clear; 5½″ 6.00-10.00

4827 PLANTER MARY LOU RYE; *Ullman & Co., Cincinnati;* clear; 5½″ 8.00-10.00

4828 POND'S ROCK & RYE WITH HOREHOUND; R missing in Rock, E missing in Rye; aqua; 10″ 10.00-20.00

4829 PREACHER WHISKEY; curved bottle; 3″ round sides; off-center neck; clear or amethyst; ½ pint; 6½″ 10.00-20.00

4830 P & SP under bottom; three-part mold; dark olive; 9½″ 8.00-12.00

4831 same as above except 11½″ 12.00-18.00

4832   4833   4841   4842   4843   4845   4846   4847

4849   4850   4853   4855   4856   4857   4858

4859   4860   4864   4865   4866   4867   4870   4871

4872   4873   4874   4875

4832 Pumpkin seed; small; on back and front, sunburst pattern; clear or amethyst; 5" 14.00-18.00

4833 Pumpkin seed; plain; clear or amethyst; all sizes 5.00-10.00

4834 Pumpkin seed picnic flask; double band collar; amethyst; 5½" 3.00-6.00

4835 Pumpkin seed; amethyst; 6" 4.00-6.00

4836 Pumpkin seed, label; amber; 4" . . . 10.00-20.00

4837 same as above except dark aqua; 4½" 10.00-20.00

4838 PURE MALT WHISKEY, PRIDE OF CANADA; tapered top; amber; 10½" 10.00-20.00

4839 QUAKER MAID WHISKEY; girl in center of label; *S. Hirsch & Co. Kansas City, Mo.*; fancy shoulder; clear; 3½" 8.00-20.00

4840 QUAKER MAID WHISKEY in center; *S.C.H. & Co.* in circle, embossed; fancy shoulder; clear; 3½" 8.00-20.00

4841 QUAKER MAID WHISKEY; *Patented* under bottom; clear or aqua; quart 10.00-15.00

4842 QUARTERBACK RYE WHISKEY; *S. Silberstein, Philadelphia, Pa.*; clear; quart 10.00-20.00

4843 QUEEN MARY SCOTCH WHISKEY; amber; quart 12.00-15.00

4844 QUEENSDALE WHISKEY, label; amber; quart 2.00-3.00

4845 QUININE WHISKEY CO. LOUISVILLE, KY. on bottom; amber; 5¼" 6.00-12.00

4846 F. R. QUINN; *This Bottle Not To Be Sold* on back base; aqua; 11½" 6.00-10.00

4847 W.J. RAHILY CO.; *W.J.R.* on back shoulder; three-part mold; clear or amethyst; 11" 4.00-6.00

4848 FRED RASCHEN CO. SACRAMENTO, CAL. in form of circle; *F.R. CO.* monogram; round; graduated collar and ring; amber; quart; 12" 10.00-20.00

4849 FRED RASCHEN, SACRAMENTO, CAL.; amber; quart 8.00-20.00

4850 REBECCA AT THE WELL; pontil; clear or amethyst; 8" . . . . 65.00+

4851 RECORDS AND GOLDBOROUGH, BALTIMORE, MD. vertically on slug plate; rectangular; ring collar; clear; pint; 6" 4.00-6.00

4852 RED CHIEF; *Fort Hood, Indiana, Ballina Rye*; clear; 12" 10.00-15.00

4853 RED TOP with *Top* on shoulder; *R.D. Westheimer & Sons* on bottom; under bottom, different numbers; flask; extra ring on bottom of neck; amber; ½ pint 4.00-6.00

4854 REGISTERED HONEST ONE PINT at top half; rectangular; graduated collar and ring; amethyst; pint and ½ pint 3.00-4.00

4855 REGISTERED; clear or amethyst; 8" 6.00-8.00

4856 E. REMY; champagne; cognac; machine made; *A.R.* on bottom; green; 4" 1.00-2.00

4857 RHEINSTROM BROS, PROPRIETORS; on other side, *Mother Putnam's Blackberry Cordial*; amber; 11" 10.00-25.00

4858 J. RIEGER & CO. KANSAS CITY, MO.; clear or aqua; 11½" 6.00-10.00

4859 W.R. RILEY DISTILLING CO. KANSAS CITY, MO.; clear; quart 8.00-10.00

4860 H.H. ROBINSON, BOSTON, label; *Guaranteed Full Pt* on back; clear or amethyst; 8¾" 2.00-4.00

4861 ROMA CALIFORNIA WINE, PRIDE OF THE VINEYARD, R.C.W. CO. monogram all on front; ABM; thread top; amber; 12⅛" 2.00-3.00

4862 L. ROSE & CO.; rose & vine bottle; applied crown; tapered; aqua; 7½" 4.00-10.00

4863 ROSEDALE OK WHISKEY; *Siebe Bros. & Plagermann, San Francisco*; clear or amber; quart . . . . 50.00+

4864 ROSSKAM GERSTLEY & CO.; *Old Saratoga Extra Fine Whiskey* on back; *Philadelphia* in seal; small kick-up; clear or amethyst; 9¼" 8.00-12.00

4865 ROSSKAM GERSTLEY & CO.; *Monogram No. 6*; clear; 8¼" 75.00-85.00

4866 ROSSKAM GERSTLEY & CO.; clear; 9½" . . . . 25.00+

4867 ROSS'S BRAND; aqua; 14¼" 10.00-12.00

4868 ROTH & CO., SAN FRANCISCO, CALIFORNIA; pocket flask 10.00-12.00

4869 ROTH & CO., SAN FRANCISCO; amber; quart 75.00-85.00

4870 ROXBORO LIQ. CO.; clear or amethyst; 8" 6.00-8.00

4871 AQUA DE RUBINAT; aqua; 11" 2.00-4.00

4872 CHAS. RUGERS, WINE & LIQUORS, HOUSTON, TEXAS; *#181* under bottom; amber; 6" 8.00-10.00

4873 RUM; five rings; clear; 3¾" 4.00-6.00

4874 RYE; three-part mold; clear; 11" . . 8.00-10.00

4875 RYE; ground pontil; silk glass; hand painted; 11" 18.00-30.00

4876 4877 4878 4879 4880 4884 4885 4886

4888 4889 4890 4891 4892 4893 4897 4898

4899 4900 4902 4904 4905 4908 4910 4913

4914   4915   4917   4918

4876 RYE; decanter; gold trim; clear; 9¼" 25.00+

4877 SAFE WHISKEY; aqua; 9¼" 40.00-50.00

4878 Sailor's flask; crock; tan and brown; 8¼"
.... 75.00+

4879 ST. JACOBS; 10½" 6.00-8.00

4880 ST. JACOBS MALT WHISKEY, CINCIN-
NATI O. U.S.A.; amber; 9¾"..... 8.00-10.00

4881 ST. THOMAS DOUBLE DISTILLED BAY
RUM, ST. THOMAS, V.I., label; ABM; 10⅛"
.... 4.00-6.00

4882 ST. THOMAS BAY RUM on bottom; *St.
Thomas, V.I. USA*; graduated ring collar;
emerald green; quart; 11" 4.00-6.00

4883 L.A. CHRTEN, ST. THOMAS, D.W.I. BAY
RUM all on label; graduated collar and ring;
slight bulbous neck; emerald green; 11½"
.... 3.00-4.00

4884 SALLADE & CO.; aqua; 8"........ 4.00-8.00

4885 M. SALZMAN CO., NEW YORK, label; same in
back with *Purity* above all; *Old Doctrine Club
Whiskey*; quart; 11¼" 4.00-8.00

4886 THE SAM'L LEHMAN CO., CINCINNATI,
OHIO; amber; 11½" 12.00-18.00

4887 THOS. D. SAMUEL, WHOLESALE LIQUOR
DEALER; *11 East 5th Street, Kansas City, Mo.*;
8¾".............................. 4.00-12.00

4888 T.W. SAMUELS BOURBON WHISKEY, label;
clear; 11" 4.00-8.00

4889 SAW PALMETTO; *Genuine Vernal Buffalo
N.Y.* on other sides; clear or amethyst; 10"
.... 6.00-12.00

4890 S.B. CO. CHICAGO in back; clear; 3"
.... 8.00-10.00

4891 S.B. & CO. under bottom; amber; 12". 2.00-4.00

4892 S.B.& G. CO. under bottom; aqua; 8"   2.00-6.00

4893 S.C. DISPENSARY; under monogram *SCD*;
under bottom *C.L.F.G.C.O.*; with palm tree also;
clear; ½ pint, pint, quart   4.00-20.00

4894 DANIEL SCHAEFFER'S LOG CABIN
WHISKEY..................... 40.00-60.00

4895 SCHLESINGER & BENDER, PURE WINE &
BRANDIES, SAN FRANCISCO, CAL.;
amber; quart 50.00-100.00

4896 BARNEY SCHOW; *Wholesale & Retail Wine &
Liquors, Willits, California; net contents, 8 oz.*;
screw cap; amber; 6" .... 25.00+

4897 SCHUTZ-MARKE; *Eigenthym von A. Schenk
Altona* in back; amber; 11½" 10.00-15.00

4898 SCHWARZ ROSENBAUM & CO.; *B* under bottom; amber; 11½" 8.00-12.00

4899 SCOTCH, label; clear; 10"............ 8.00+

4900 G.B. SEELY'S SON; clear; 11".... 8.00-12.00

4901 SHEA-BACQUERAZ CO., SAN FRANCISCO,
CAL. vertically; round; graduated collar and
ring; dark amber; quart; 11½".... 10.00-20.00

4902 A.A. SHEAFFERS, label; three-part mold;
amber; quart 4.00-6.00

4903 SHEEHAN'S MALT WHISKEY with
monogram in center; *Utica, N.Y.*; same shape as
The Duffy Malt; round; graduated collar;
amethyst; 10½" 4.00-8.00

4904 SHEFFIELD CO, NEW YORK; amber; 9¾"
.... 10.00-15.00

4905 Shell figural; whiskey; sheared top; clear or
amethyst; 5" 20.00-40.00

4906 S.H.M. SUPERIOR; *Old Bourbon*; quart
.... 100.00+

4907 Shoe fly or coffin flask; graduated collar and
ring; clear; pint and ½ pint........ 3.00-6.00

4908 Shoe figural, label; dark purple; 6" x 3½" x 1¼"
.... 65.00+

4909 SHOOMAKERS; *1331 Famous Resort, Pa.
Avenue, Washington, D.C.; Registered Full
Pint*; side strap; ring top; clear; quart
.... 10.00-20.00

4910 S.I.G.W. 1 under bottom; aqua; 12"   2.00-4.00

4911 SILVER LEAF PURE RYE WHISKEY;
*Virginia, Carolina Co., owners, Richmond,
Virginia, U.S.A.*; clear; ½ pint..... 8.00-10.00

4912 SILVER LEAF RYE; *Virginia, Carolina Grocery Co., Richmond, Virginia*; under bottom,
B.R. G. CO.; clear or amethyst; 6¼" 8.00-10.00

4913 SIMON BROS; horseshoe seal on back shoulder;
clear; 10" 4.00-8.00

4914 SIMON BROS; plain seal on back; clear or
amethyst; 13" 8.00-12.00

4915 SM & CO.; ground pontil; amber; 11" 85.00+

4916 THOS. L. SMITH & SONS/BOSTON, MASS on
shoulder; three-piece mold; bulbous neck;
round; graduated collar and ring; amethyst;
quart; 12¼" 4.00-8.00

4917 SOL. BEAR & CO.; clear or amethyst; 13¾"
.... 10.00-12.00

4918 SOUTH CAROLINA DISPENSARY; clear;
9¼"............................. 15.00-25.00

4919   4920   4925   4926   4927   4929   4930

4932   4936   4937   4942   4943   4948   4951

4952   4953   4954   4955   4956   4957   4958

4959   4960   4962

4919 SOUTH CAROLINA DISPENSARY; aqua; 9½" .... 85.00+

4920 SOUTHERN COMFORT; clear; 11½" 1.00-2.00

4921 SOUTHERN LIQUOR CO., DALLAS, TEXAS in a circle; tapered top; clear or amethyst; 10½" 7.00-15.00

4922 WILLIAM H. SPEARS OLD PIONEER WHISKEY; bear in center; *A. Fenkhauser & Co., sole agents, San Francisco*; amber; quart .... 100.00+

4923 JARED SPENCER; flask; flared top; green; pint 1,000.00-2,000.00

4924 R.A. SPLAINE & CO., HAVERHILL, MASS. on shoulder; *It Pays To Buy the Best* written on shoulder on opposite sides; three-piece mold; round; graduated collar and ring; amethyst; quart; 11½" 6.00-8.00

4925 S.S.T. PATENT; amber; quart 6.00-10.00

4926 Star in center with stars circling; clear; 4¼" 6.00-8.00

4927 Star whiskey label; saddle strap; amber; pint 4.00-6.00

4928 STEIN BROS. CHICAGO on bottom; round; graduated rows of beads swirled around on shoulder; graduated band and ring collar; amethyst; quart; 11¾" 6.00-10.00

4929 C.B. STEWART, ATLANTA, GEORGIA; double top; clear; pint 8.00-12.00

4930 C.B. STEWART, ATLANTA, GEORGIA; clear or aqua; pint 4.00-8.00

4931 STODDARD, label; wine; iron pontil; olive or amber; 8½" 10.00-20.00

4932 STONE BROOK; turn mold; amber; 9½" tall, 4" diameter 4.00-8.00

4933 OLD HENRY WHISKEY, STRAUS GUNST & CO., RICHMOND, VA.; panels on shoulder; clear or amethyst; 11" 10.00-20.00

4934 STRAUS GUNST & CO., PROPRIETORS, RICHMOND, VIRGINIA; amber; ½ pint 10.00-20.00

4935 STRAUSS BROS. CO., CHICAGO, U.S.A.; deep green; 12¼" 8.00-10.00

4936 STRAUSS PRITZ & CO.; sheared top; clear or amethyst; 5½" 4.00-8.00

4937 THE STRAUSS PRITZ CO.; clear or amethyst; 6¼" 4.00-6.00

4938 C.W. STUARTS; amber; quart...... 10.00+

4939 LOUIS TAUSSIG & CO./SAN FRANCISCO/NEW YORK vertically on one side; *Union Made*; *C.B.B.A. Branch No. 22* on opposite side; square; graduated collar; clear; scant quart; 10¼" 4.00-8.00

4940 LT & CO inside of circle; *Patented Feb. 4th, 1902* on bottom; oval front paneling; ribbed; panels at base on back; rectangular; graduated collar and ring; amber; quart; 10½" 4.00-8.00

4941 LOUIS TAUSSIG, MAIN STREET, SAN FRANCISCO; flask; amber.......... 100.00+

4942 TAYLOR & WILLIAMS; clear or amethyst; 3¼" 4.00-6.00

4943 TAYLOR & WILLIAMS; side strap; clear; 6½" 2.00-3.00

4944 TAYLOR & WILLIAMS in a horseshoe shape; under it *Louisville, Ky*; in center *Whiskey*; ring top; clear or amethyst; 4¾" round... 4.00-6.00

4945 same as above except 11⅜" 4.00-10.00

4946 Tea cup; *Old Bourbon; Shea Bacqueraz & Co., San Francisco*; amber; quart .... 100.00+

4947 TEAKETTLE OLD BOURBON; *San Francisco*; amber; quart................. 100.00+

4948 TEXAS; flask; tapered top; whiskey; clear; quart; 11" tall, 1¾" neck, 8" wide at center, 4" x 3" at bottom 8.00-10.00

4949 JAS. THARP'S SONS in center; *Wine & Liquor, Washington, D.C.*; saddle flask; ring top; amber; 7¾" 15.00

4950 A. THELLER on shoulder; under bottom of bottle, in a circle, *Theller Arnold*; applied top; kick-up; dark olive; 9½" 4.00-6.00

4951 THEODORE NETTER; *1232 Market St. Phila., Pa*; cobalt; 6".......................... 100.00+

4952 TOKJ in seal; small kick-up; clear; 11" 4.00-8.00

4953 TONSMEIRE & CRAFT, MOBILE, ALABAMA; amber; 11" 10.00-20.00

4954 THE I. TRAGER CO.; amber; 12" .. 8.00-10.00

4955 THE I. TRAGER CO., CINCINNATI, OHIO; inverted V instead of A in Cincinnati; amber; 12" .... 20.00+

4956 THE I. TRAGER CO.; ring top; amber; ½ pint 4.00-6.00

4957 THE I. TRAGER CO.; amber; 8½"... 2.00-6.00

4958 THE I. TRAGER CO.; amber; ½ pint 3.00-6.00

4959 TROST BROS; clear; 6½" 4.00-6.00

4960 TUCKER ALA on one panel; four running legs in circle on back panel; amber; 9¼"..... 60.00+

4961 F.G. TULLEDGE & CO. PURE POP CORN WHISKEY, CINCINNATI, OHIO; clear; quart 4.00-8.00

4962 Two Fish Whiskey; clear or amethyst; 7½" .... 25.00+

4963   4967   4968   4969   4970   4972   4974

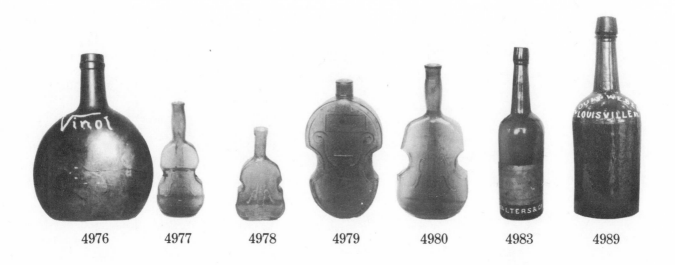

4976 4977 4978 4979 4980 4983 4989

4991 4992 4994 4995 4996 4997 4998

4999   **5002**   **5005**

4963 ULLMAN & CO.; *Planter Rye Registered* on
back; clear or amethyst; 6¼" 6.00-8.00

4964 UNION MADE C.B.B.A. OF US & C TRADE-
MARK in circle; flask; clear; pint; 8¾"
.... 3.00-6.00

4965 same as above except ½ pint 4.00-8.00

4966 UNION SQUARE COMPANY, 239 UNION
ST., LYNN, MASS. GUARANTEED FULL ½
PINT all in slug plate; rectangular; clear; 7"
.... 2.00-3.00

4967 N.M. URI & CO.; *B* on bottom; amber; 4¾" tall;
1½" diameter 6.00-8.00

4968 N.M. URI & CO. LOUISVILLE, KY.; amber;
5¾".............................. 6.00-8.00

4969 U.S. MAIL; clear; 5½" 12.00-18.00

4970 W.B. VAIL; golden amber; 11½" ..... 12.00+

4971 VARWIG & SON, PORTLAND, ORE.;
monogram in center; *Full Measure;* round; graduated collar and ring; amber; 12¼" 20.00-30.00

4972 L. VERETERRA OVIEDO on bottom; ring top;
12"............................... 2.00-4.00

4973 THE NORTH VERNON DISTILLING CO.,
DISTILLERY OFFICE CINCINNATI, O.;
round; ten fancy vertical panels on neck and
shoulder; graduated collar and ring; amethyst
.... 6.00-8.00

4974 VI on base; whiskey label; pontil; clear; 5¼"
.... 10.00-15.00

4975 VIEUX COGNAC; three-part mold; small kick-
up; old top; aqua; 8¾" 4.00-8.00

4976 VINOL; *Private Mold Pat April 18, 1898* under
bottom; amber; 6½" 6.00-8.00

4977 Violin, plain back; different colors & sizes
.... 8.00-10.00

4978 Violin, label; plain back; different colors & sizes
.... 15.00-20.00

4979 Violin, label; amber; 8½"........ 15.00-25.00

4980 Violin, label; music score on back; pontil;
different colors; 9¾"............. 10.00-15.00

4981 Violin; in back, musical score; plain bottom;
many colors; various sizes........ 6.00-10.00

4982 WALKERS KILMARNOOK WHISKEY 1807
on bottom; square; square band and ring; ABM;
emerald green; 10¼"............... 4.00-8.00

4983 WALTERS & CO. BALTIMORE on back base;
amber; 11¾" .... 25.00+

4984 WALTERS BROTHERS & CO.; *115-6-7 Front
Street, San Francisco;* red; quart . 20.00-40.00

4985 WARRANTED; flask; dark amber and golden
amber; pint or ½ pint............. 4.00-8.00

4986 WARRANTED; flask; light aqua; pint and ½
pint 3.00-6.00

4987 WARRANTED; flask; side bands; double band
collar; amber; pint and ½ pint 4.00-8.00

4988 WARRANTED; flask; side bands; double band
collar; amethyst; pint and ½ pint.... 4.00-8.00

4989 LOUIS WEBER, LOUISVILLE, KY.; *H.W.M.
Colly & Co., Pittsburg* under bottom; three-part
mold; olive; 10".................. 25.00+

4990 EDWARD WEISS; *leading West End Liquor
House; corner of West and Calvert, Annapolis,
Md.;* ring top; clear or aqua; 6"..... 4.00-6.00

4991 WEST BEND OLD TIMERS LAGER BEER,
label; aqua; 9¼" 2.00-4.00

4992 WEST END WINE & SPIRITS CO.; *Full Qt.
Registered* on back; amber; 12¼".. 12.00-18.00

4993 FERDINAND WESTHEIMER & SONS, CIN-
CINNATI, USA in circle; rectangular; graduated collar and ring; amber; ½ pint.. 3.00-4.00

4994 FERDINAND WESTHEIMER & SONS;
amber; 6"....................... 6.00-8.00

4995 FERDINAND WESTHEIMER & SONS;
amber; 9½"..................... 10.00-15.00

4996 W.F. & S. under bottom; aqua; 9½" 2.00-4.00

4997 WHARTON'S WHISKEY; *Witter Glass Work
Glasboro N.J.* under bottom; amber; 10"
.... 200.00-300.00

4998 Whiskey decanter; inlaid with silver; crystal
glass; clear or aqua; 11¼"........ 8.00-15.00

4999 Whiskey; ½ barrel shape; in front a rooster in
center; in 1¾" x 2¾" panel *A Merry Christmas
and a Happy New Year;* in center of panel *M.C.
& H.N.Y.* and a woman in an old dress holding a
glass while sitting on barrel; ½ pint; 1¾" neck; 4"
body........................... 20.00-30.00

5000 Whiskey; ribs on shoulder and bottom; clear or
amethyst; fifth 4.00-6.00

5001 Whiskey; ribs on shoulder and bottom; clear or
amethyst; fifth; 4½"............... 6.00-8.00

5002 Whiskey, plain; 3¼" round; 4½" body tapering to
a blob neck 4¼"; ring around top and bottom of
body with plain seal on shoulder; amber; quart
.... 12.00-20.00

5003 Whiskey, plain; side strap or shoe fly, Union
oval; light green, clear or amber; ½ pint
.... 6.00-12.00

5004 same as above except pint........ 6.00-12.00

5005 same as above except quart 6.00-12.00

5006   5009   5011   5014   5015   5016   5017   5018

5019   5020   5021   5022   5023   5024   5025   5026

5027   5028   5029   5030   5031   5032   5033   5034

5035   5036   5037   5038   5039   5040   5041   5042

5006	Whiskey, plain; turn mold; emerald green; quart; 11¼" 8.00-12.00	
5007	Whiskey, plain, with ribbed shoulder; various numbers under bottom; clear or amethyst; quart 2.00-4.00	
5008	same as above except pint.......... 2.00-4.00	
5009	Whiskey, plain, with ribbed shoulder; with various numbers under bottom; amber; pint 4.00-8.00	
5010	same as above except quart 4.00-8.00	
5011	Whiskey, plain; turn mold; kick-up; pontil; light olive; 11½" tall, 2½" diameter..... 10.00-16.00	
5012	Whiskey, plain; three-piece mold; round; amethyst; 11" 4.00-6.00	
5013	Whiskey, plain; round; tapered shoulder; amethyst; 9⅞" 2.00-4.00	
5014	Whiskey, plain; green; fifth........ 8.00-12.00	
5015	Whiskey, label; sheared top; also pewter top; clear; 6" .... 6.00+	
5016	Whiskey, label; aqua; 6½" 6.00-10.00	
5017	Whiskey, label; milk glass; sheared top; 8" 10.00-15.00	
5018	Whiskey, label; seal on shoulder; *H999* on bottom; 11½" tall, 2½" diameter 6.00-8.00	
5019	Whiskey, label; three-part mold; whittle mark; a dot on bottom; aqua; 11½" tall, 3" diameter 6.00-10.00	
5020	Whiskey, label; clear or amethyst; 8" 2.00-6.00	
5021	Whiskey, label; small kick-up; turn mold; red amber; 10½"..................... 3.00-6.00	
5022	Whiskey, label; clear or amethyst; ½ pint 2.00-6.00	
5023	Whiskey, label; shallow kick-up; turn mold; amber; 8¼".................... 6.00-10.00	

5024	Whiskey, label; amber; 6¼" 2.00-6.00
5025	Whiskey, label; clear; 10" tall, 4" diameter 3.00-6.00
5026	Whiskey, label; three-part mold; clear or amethyst; 11"..................... 4.00-6.00
5027	Whiskey, label; sample; *B* on bottom; amber; 4" 2.00-4.00
5028	Whiskey, label; sample; round; amber; 4½" 2.00-4.00
5029	Whiskey, label; sample; amber; 4½".. 2.00-4.00
5030	Whiskey, label; sample; round; amber; 5" 4.00-6.00
5031	Whiskey, label; sample; round; amber; 4⅞" 2.00-4.00
5032	Whiskey, label; sample; round; #4 on bottom; amber; 5½".................... 2.00-4.00
5033	Whiskey, label; press glass; clear or amethyst; 6½".............................. 4.00-6.00
5034	Whiskey, label; amber; 10" 10.00-20.00
5035	Whiskey, label; two stars under bottom; clear; 6½".............................. 2.00-4.00
5036	Whiskey, label; sample; kick-up; amber; 4½" 4.00-6.00
5037	Whiskey, label; sample; amber; 3¾".. 2.00-4.00
5038	Whiskey, label; sample; three-part mold; dark amber; 5¾".................... 4.00-6.00
5039	Whiskey, label; sample; dark amber; 5¼" 2.00-4.00
5040	Whiskey, label; sample; *B* under bottom; dark amber; 5¾"..................... 2.00-4.00
5041	Whiskey, label; sample; kick-up; light amber; 5⅛" 4.00-6.00
5042	Whiskey, label; turn mold; small kick-up; dark amber; 10" tall, 3½" diameter........ 6.00-8.00

5043   5044   5045   5046   5047   5048   5049   5050

5051   5052   5053   5054   5055   5056   5057   5058

5059   5060   5061   5062   5063   5064   5065   5066

296

5067   5068   5069   5070   5071   5072   5073   5074

5043   Whiskey, label; machine made; amber; 6¾" 2.00-4.00

5044   Whiskey or bitters, label; amber; 9" 8.00-15.00

5045   Whiskey, label; brown crock; 6½"... 6.00-8.00

5046   Whiskey, label; sample; amber; 5½" 4.00-6.00

5047   Whiskey, label; amber; 9" 3.00-5.00

5048   Whiskey, label; amber; quart....... 4.00-6.00

5049   Whiskey, label; diamond shape with # under bottom; amber; 5"................. 2.00-4.00

5050   Whiskey, sample or medicine; clear; 3" 2.00-4.00

5051   Whiskey, label; two dots under bottom; amber; 4"................................. 2.00-3.00

5052   Whiskey, label; sample; sheared top; 4" 3.00-6.00

5053   Whiskey, label; light gold; 6½" 2.00-6.00

5054   Whiskey, label; amber; 12"........ 3.00-8.00

5055   Whiskey or bitters, label; nine rings top and bottom; graphite pontil; amber.......... 50.00+

5056   Whiskey, decanter; *E.B. & CO. LP REG. No709209 1886* under bottom; 7"... 8.00-10.00

5057   Whiskey, decanter, label; clear; 10" 10.00-20.00

5058   Whiskey, decanter, label; *1 Qt.* on shoulder; clear or amethyst.................. 20.00+

5059   Whiskey, decanter; painted with gold and other colors; 10½"....................... 40.00+

5060   Whiskey, label; olive; 3½"........ 15.00-25.00

5061   Whiskey, label; dark green; 8¼" ... 8.00-10.00

5062   Whiskey, label; clear; 3½".......... 4.00-6.00

5063   Whiskey, label; pontil; amber; 7¾" 45.00-90.00

5064   Whiskey, label; pontil; amber; 5½".... 25.00+

5065   Whiskey, label; turn mold; small kick-up; clear; 11½"............................. 2.00-4.00

5066   Whiskey, label; three-part mold; olive; 8¼" 8.00-10.00

5067   Whiskey, label; pontil; aqua; 9"... 70.00-90.00

5068   Whiskey, label; sheared top; clear or amethyst; 9½"............................. 8.00-10.00

5069   Whiskey, sample; plain; amber; 4½" 2.00-4.00

5070   Whiskey, sample; plain; clear or amethyst; 3½" 2.00-4.00

5071   Whiskey, sample; plain; clear; 4¼".. 2.00-4.00

5072   Whiskey, sample; plain; clear; 4½".. 2.00-4.00

5073   Whiskey, sample; plain; clear; 4" ... 2.00-4.00

5074   Whiskey, sample; plain; *506* under bottom; olive; 3¾"........................ 2.00-4.00

5075   5076   5077   5078   5079   5080   5081   5084

5085   5086   5087   5088   5089   5090   5091   5092

5093   5094   5095   5096   5097   5098   5099   5100

5101	5102	5103	5104	5105	5106	5107	5108

5075 Whiskey, sample; plain; *506* under bottom; amber; 3½".................... 2.00-4.00

5076 Whiskey, sample; plain; clear; 3¾".. 2.00-4.00

5077 Whiskey, sample; plain; seal; clear; 3¾" 4.00-6.00

5078 Whiskey, sample; plain; *2* under bottom; clear; 3¾"............................ 4.00-6.00

5079 Whiskey, sample; plain; *5* under bottom; clear; 4½"............................ 4.00-6.00

5080 Whiskey, sample; plain; clear; 3¾".. 2.00-4.00

5081 WHITE RYE, label; clear or amethyst; 11¾" 2.00-6.00

5082 WILLIAM WHITELEY LEITH; *Reuse of Bottle Prohibited* in back; *Whiteleys Leith Scotch Whiskey;* applied top; aqua; 8½".. 15.00-35.00

5083 same as above except double ring top 8.00-20.00

5084 Wine, decanter; clear; 8¼" 4.00-8.00

5085 Wine, decanter; leather cover; Italy machine made; lion head with ring in mouth; two small lion heads 8.00-12.00

5086 Wine, label; cobalt; 12".............. 35.00+

5087 Wine, label; amber; 4"........... 8.00-10.00

5088 Wine, label; clear or amethyst; 11".. 4.00-8.00

5089 Wine, label; aqua; 12" 10.00-15.00

5090 Wine, label (fish); French wine; aqua; 11" 20.00-30.00

5091 Wine, label; also with wicker; green; 9" 1.00-2.00

5092 Wine tester; turn mold; green; 8½" 4.00-8.00

5093 Wine, label; clear; 11"............. 2.00-4.00

5094 Wine, label; kick-up; aqua; 7¼"..... 2.00-4.00

5095 Wine, label; kick-up; clear; 4"...... 4.00-6.00

5096 Wine, label; *WT* under bottom; carnival glass; 10½"............................ 4.00-6.00

5097 Wine, label; machine made; clear; 8" 2.00-4.00

5098 Wine, label; 200 to 300 yrs. old; pontil; blue green; 5½" tall, 3½" diameter........ 25.00+

5099 Wine, label; three-part mold; kick-up; pontil; whittle mark; light green; 14½" tall; 5" x 4" 10.00-18.00

5100 Wine, label; kick-up; olive; 13"..... 2.00-6.00

5101 Wine, label; very crude; free blown; kick-up; olive; 11½"...................... 8.00-15.00

5102 Wine, label; pontil; small kick-up; light aqua; 9¾"............................ 8.00-15.00

5103 Wine, label; small kick-up; amber; 11¼" 4.00-6.00

5104 Wine, label; aqua; 7¼" 3.00-6.00

5105 Wine, label; small kick-up; turn mold; dark green; 12"........................ 2.00-6.00

5106 Wine, label; pontil; double collar; olive green; 9" 10.00-20.00

5107 Wine, plain; lady's leg; kick-up; light green; body 7"; neck 6½" .... 25.00+

5108 Wine, plain; turn mold; olive green; 8", 9½" or 11½".............................. 2.00-4.00

5111 5112 5113 5114 5122 5123 5124

5125 5127 5128

5109 Wine, plain; turn mold; green; 9¾" or 11¼"
.... 2.00-4.00

5110 Wine, plain; turn mold; jade green; 9¾" or 11¼"
.... 2.00-4.00

5111 Wine, plain; *P* on bottom; three-part mold;
aqua; 12"........................ 2.00-6.00

5112 Wine, plain; turn mold; aqua; 12½"... 2.00-4.00

5113 A.J. WINTLE & SON; *Pint Imperial* on
shoulder; dark olive; 8"........... 4.00-10.00

5114 W.M. in circle on shoulder; *Whyle & MacKay* on
back; three-part mold; aqua; 8¾".... 4.00-8.00

5115 WOOD POLLARD & CO / BOSTON, MASS
slanted on front lower left to upper right; FULL
QUART on front; blob seal on back; round;
bulbous neck; graduated collar and ring;
amethyst; 12½" 6.00-10.00

5116 WORMER BROS., SAN FRANCISCO embossed vertically; flask; clear 15.00-20.00

5117 WORMER BROS. in semicircle; SAN FRAN-
CISCO in horizontal lines; flask; clear
.... 15.00-20.00

5118 same as above except S.F. instead of SAN
FRANCISCO 15.00-20.00

5119 WORMER BROS., SAN FRANCISCO; *Fine
Old Cognac;* double rolled collar; flask; amber
.... 80.00-90.00

5120 WORMER BROS., S.F.; *Fine Old Cognac 1872;*
double rolled collar; flask; amber .. 80.00-90.00

5121 WRIGHT & TAYLOR DISTILLERS
LOUISVILLE, KY. in large letters on one side
on shoulder; *Full Quart Registered* on opposite
side; large base; round; graduated collar and
ring; amber; 9" 5.00-10.00

5122 WRIGHT & TAYLOR; *Full Quart Registered*
on back; *A B Co.* under bottom; amber; 10½"
.... 8.00-12.00

5123 WYETH & BRO.; saddle flask; amber; 7½"
.... 4.00-8.00

5124 JOHN WYETH & BRO.; amber; 9"   6.00-8.00

5125 JNO. WYETH & BRO.; amber; 9" ... 6.00-8.00

5126 YE OLD MOSSROFF BOURBON, label on
panel; *R.S. Roehling, 1 Schutz. Inc., Chicago;*
cabin shape; amber; 9½".......... 8.00-12.00

5127 ZELLER SCHWARZE KATZ on base in
center; *Golden Cat* on round base; under bottom
AC and misc. numbers; machine made; green;
13¼"............................ 8.00-10.00

5128 same as above except a monkey wrapped around
bottle......................... 8.00-10.00

5129 ZWACK, label seal; ZWACK around shoulder;
each letter in a flower; amber; 4¼"   8.00-10.00

This highly decorative, early 18th-century, clear-glass
decanter was made from an ornately sculptured mold. The
ground-away pontil and matching ground stopper are evidence
that the bottle was made to be retained for many years.

Food

Milk in the nineteenth century was not hidden from the public in plastic gallon jugs or shrouded behind cardboard container walls. Catsup did not come in tiny individual squeeze packages. Milk, pickles and condiments were all bottled in glass. While a large portion of bottles manufactured today are for containing food, the burgeoning plastic industry is replacing many of them.

Peppersauce bottles were fashioned in the shape of a Gothic cathedral with arches and windows on each side. The connection between the peppersauce and the cathedral design is not apparent; most were manufactured between 1860 and 1890, and the earlier bottles are pontil scarred. These bottles came in shades of green, while tomato sauce bottles appeared in clear glass.

Mustard jars came in a variety of shapes. Differences include varying numbers of rings around the jar and differing sizes of jar mouths. Colors used were the practical, easy-to-produce bottle green or clear. Older mustard jars have pontil scars, and some are embossed, as are some chili sauce bottles. One chili sauce bottle bears a Maltese cross.

Cooking oil bottles were tall and slim in shape; most were produced after 1890. A few are embossed, though most embossing was dropped at the turn of the century because paper labels were much cheaper.

Though round bottles traveled better in shipments because they could withstand more pressure, pickle or chutney bottles resisted the laws of physics and were large and square in shape. Spice bottles, too, could not travel exceptionally well due to their concave front and back panels. Both the early pickle and spice bottles have pontil scars.

Worcestershire sauce, originally made in Worcester, England, was a common flavoring in demand by household gourmets in the last century. The sauce bottles are quite common and easy to find, particularly the Lea and Perrins brand. Most are in shades of green.

Henry J. Heinz began to manufacture "good things for the table" in 1869. The company began production on a small scale; the goal was to give consumers confidence in the purity of foods not preserved in the home. One innovation was to use clear glass to show that there were

Durkee Famous Sauce (#5249-#5258), developed in 1857, was unique at that time because it was ready for immediate table use. The embossed gauntlet (far right) was a warranty that the ingredients were pure.

no impurities in the product. The company's first bottled product was horseradish. It was a success and the company began to bottle catsup in 1889. Both products are seen in familiar bottles in supermarkets today.

Before effective glass packaging techniques, milk came directly from the family cow or from a churn or milkcan. A Brooklyn milkman was reported to have been delivering milk in bottles to the steady customers on his route as early as 1878. The ancestor of the present-day milk bottle was not invented, however, until 1884 by Dr. Harvey D. Thatcher, a druggist in Potsdam, New York. Thatcher's first milk bottle was embossed with a Quaker farmer milking his cow while seated on a three-legged stool. The words "Absolutely Pure Milk" were stamped into the glass on the bottle's shoulder. Today, waxed cardboard and plastic containers have largely replaced glass milk bottles.

5130   5133   5134   5135   5136   5137   5139   5140

5142   5144   5145   5146   5148   5149   5154

5155   5156   5157   5158   5159   5160   5162   5165

5167   5168   5169   5171

5130   THE ABNER ROYCE CO.; *The Abner Royce Co. Pure Fruit Flavor, Cleveland, Ohio* in back; clear; 5¼".......................... 2.00-6.00

5131   THE ABNER ROYCE CO.; aqua; 5½"
.... 3.00-6.00

5132   A.E.B.B., PURE OLIVE, DEPOSE FRANCE; aqua; 10"......................... 2.00-3.00

5133   A.G. 5 & CO.; *4-Patented April 5, 1898*; clear; quart...................... 8.00-12.00

5134   ALART & McGUIRE TRADEMARK "OK" PICKLES; amber; 7"............. 6.00-8.00

5135   ALART & McGUIRE N.Y. under bottom; aqua; 5".................................... 4.00-6.00

5136   ALEXIS GODILLOT JEUNE; *Bordeaux* on back panel; eight panels; green; 6¼" 8.00-14.00

5137   AMERICAN GROCERY CO. PAT APP. FOR N.Y. under bottom; clear; 10"...... 2.00-8.00

5138   ANCHOR; screw top; clear or amethyst; quart; 9".................................... 30.00-45.00

5139   THE A-1 SAUCE; aqua; 7¾"...... 4.00-6.00

5140   THE A-1 SAUCE; aqua; 11"...... 4.00-6.00

5141   ARMOUR AND COMPANY, CHICAGO in four lines on cathedral type panels; round corner; lady's leg neck; milk glass; 5¼".... 6.00-12.00

5142   ARMOUR & CO. PACKERS, CHICAGO under bottom; milk glass; 2¼".......... 2.00-3.00

5143   ARMOUR & CO.; aqua; 4"........ 2.00-4.00

5144   ARMOUR & CO.; milk glass; 5¼".. 1.00-15.00

5145   ARMOUR'S TOP NOTCH BRAND, CHICAGO under bottom; clear or amethyst; 5¾" 2.00-3.00

5146   A-10 under bottom; clear or amethyst; 8"
.... 2.00-4.00

5147   BABBLIN BROOK; milk bottle; clear; pint
.... 2.00-4.00

5148   BABY TOP; two-face milk bottle; *Brookfield* on other side; *1 qt. liquid 2 Reg. Sealed 157* on base; clear........... 8.00-15.00

5149   BAKER'S; aqua; 4¼"............ 2.00-4.00

5150   BAKER'S FLAVORING EXTRACTS, BAKER EXTRACTS CO.; on one side *Strength & Purity*; on the other side *Full Measure*; machine made; clear.............. 1.00-2.00

5151   BANQUET BRAND CHARLES GULDEN, N.Y. on slug plate; flared lip; amethyst; 5⅛"
.... 3.00-4.00

5152   Barrel mustard, plain; two rings on top, three on bottom; amethyst or clear; 4½"...... 2.00-3.00

5153   Barrel mustard, plain; three rings on top and bottom; clear or amethyst; 4½"...... 2.00-3.00

5154   B.B.G. CO. 326 under bottom; clear or amethyst; 8"........................ 1.00-2.00

5155   B.B.G. CO. 78 on bottom; clear or amethyst; 7½"
.... 2.00-3.00

5156   B & CO. LD. B, 13 under bottom; aqua; 8½"
.... 2.00-3.00

5157   B C CO.; clear or amethyst; 4½"..... 3.00-6.00

5158   BECKER'S PURE HORSE-RADISH, BUFFALO; aqua; 4¼"............ 4.00-8.00

5159   B.F.B. CO. 109 2845 on bottom; aqua; 8"
.... 2.00-3.00

5160   B & FB CO. 2445 under bottom; aqua; 8"
.... 2.00-3.00

5161   BIRELEY'S TRADEMARK REG. HOLLYWOOD, CAL.; milk bottle; clear; 5¼" 4.00-6.00

5162   BISHOP & COMPANY under bottom; clear or amethyst; 5½".................... 4.00-6.00

5163   BISHOP & COMPANY on bottom; fourteen vertical panels; ring at base; catsup; amethyst; 9¾"........................ 2.00-4.00

5164   same as above except 7⅝".......... 2.00-4.00

5165   A. BOOTH & CO. BALT., label; *Oyster Cocktail Catsup Salad Dressing* under bottom; clear or amethyst; 7½".................... 2.00-4.00

5166   same as above except 6"........... 1.00-2.00

5167   BORDENS CONDENSED MILK CO.; milk glass; clear or amethyst; 4½"........ 4.00-8.00

5168   Breast pump; sheared top; clear; 4".. 2.00-6.00

5169   H. B. BROOKS; amber; 10¼"........ 18.00+

5170   same as above except clear........ 4.00-10.00

5171   B-33 on bottom; aqua; 5".......... 1.00-2.00

| 5175 | 5176 | 5177 | 5178 | 5181 | 5182 | 5185 | 5186 |

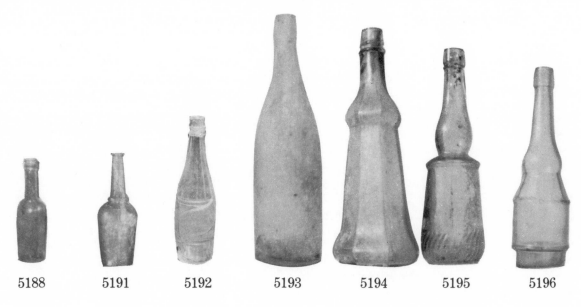

| 5188 | 5191 | 5192 | 5193 | 5194 | 5195 | 5196 |

| 5197 | 5198 | 5199 | 5200 | 5201 | 5202 | 5203 | 5205 |

5206	5207	5208	5209	5212	5213	5214	5215

5172   BURNETT'S STANDARD FLAVORING EXTRACTS in sunken panel; aqua; 5¼" . 2.00-3.00

5173   BURNETT'S STANDARD FLAVORING EXTRACTS; long neck; medicine bottle type; clear or amethyst; 4½"; 1.00-2.00

5174   same as above except 5⅝"........... 1.00-2.00

5175   BWCA in monogram; eight panels; clear or amethyst; 10".................. 4.00-8.00

5176   JOSEPH CAMPBELL PRESERVE CO.; clear or amethyst; 8" 2.00-4.00

5177   CANDY BROS MFG. CO. CONFECTIONERS, label; aqua; 12" 8.00-15.00

5178   Cannon bottle; amber or olive; 9½"   20.00-30.00

5179   Caper, plain; green; 6½"........... 6.00-8.00

5180   same as above except machine made   2.00-3.00

5181   Caper bottles; several different sizes and colors; some embossed, some not 6.00-12.00

5182   Capers; eight indented panels in neck; two-ring top; three sizes................ 8.00-18.00

5183   DON CARLOS CYLINDER; *Pat. June 19, 1894 N.Y.* under bottom; clear; 5¼"....... 4.00-8.00

5184   CARNATION'S FRESH MILK; *Chicago Sealed 1 qt.*; milk bottle; amber 1.00-2.00

5185   Cathedral pickle, label; light blue; 9½" 15.00-20.00

5186   Cathedral; ground pontil; blue green; 8½" .... 50.00+

5187   Catsup, plain; clear or amethyst; 7½"   1.00-2.00

5188   Catsup; ten panels; amethyst or clear; 8" or 9¾" 2.00-4.00

5189   Catsup; ten panels; top and bottom panels alternate; clear or amethyst; 10"........ 2.00-4.00

5190   Catsup; two mid-sections; ten panels; clear or amethyst; 8"................... 3.00-5.00

5191   Catsup, plain; tapered body; ring at shoulder; tapered neck; ring top; clear, amethyst; 7½" 3.00-6.00

5192   Catsup, plain; clear or amethyst; 10" tall; 2½" diameter 4.00-6.00

5193   Catsup, label; *1600* on bottom; clear or amethyst; 10".................... 1.00-2.00

5194   Catsup, label; clear or amethyst; 9¾"   3.00-6.00

5195   Catsup, plain; clear or amethyst; 9" .. 3.00-5.00

5196   Catsup, plain; clear or amethyst; 8½"   4.00-6.00

5197   Catsup, label; *403* on bottom; clear or amethyst; 7½"........................ 2.00-3.00

5198   Catsup, label; aqua; 8" 3.00-6.00

5199   Catsup, plain; clear or amethyst; 8½"   3.00-6.00

5200   Catsup, label; clear or amethyst; 10½"   4.00-6.00

5201   Catsup, label; swirl design; clear or amethyst; 8" 4.00-6.00

5202   Catsup, label; *10F* under bottom; clear or amethyst........................ 4.00-6.00

5203   Catsup, label; clear; 9½" 2.00-4.00

5204   Catsup and preserve bottles; embossed 2.00-4.00

5205   C B B under bottom; aqua; 8" 6.00-8.00

5206   C.B.K. and 1233 on bottom; aqua; 7¼"   2.00-3.00

5207   C B W under bottom; clear or amethyst; 10¼" 4.00-6.00

5208   C & D under bottom; aqua; 7¾" .... 8.00+

5209   CENTRAL MFG. COMPANY; clear or amethyst; 5" 2.00-4.00

5210   Champagne Catsup; round; screw top; amethyst or clear; 7½" 3.00-5.00

5211   Champagne Catsup; applied top; one ring; amethyst; 9¾" 3.00-5.00

5212   CHAMPION VERMONT MAPLE SYRUP, label; clear or amethyst; 8½"....... 3.00-6.00

5213   CHAMPION'S VINEGAR; aqua; 14½" 10.00-30.00

5214   CHAMPION'S VINEGAR; aqua; 15½" 15.00-25.00

5215   R.C. CHANCES SONS, TABLE TALK KETCHUP, PHILA, label; clear or amethyst; 9¼"................................ 4.00-6.00

5216   5217   5218   5225   5226   5227   5228

5229   5230   5231   5232   5238   5240   5241

5243   5244   5245   5254   5255   5256   5257

5258   5259   5260

5216   Cherry, label; *B* under bottom; clear; 4½"
.... 1.00-2.00

5217   Cherry, plain; *33* and a star on bottom; clear or amethyst; 6¼"...................... 2.00-4.00

5218   Cherry pickle, plain; clear or amethyst; 6"
.... 2.00-3.00

5219   THE C.I. CO. LTD; *This Trademark Registered, Maple Sap & Boiled Cider Vinegar*; on front, *East Ridge, NH*; three rings near base; flint shoulder; tapered neck and ring top; cobalt; 11½"............................. 25.00+

5220   THE J.M. CLARK PICKLE CO. LOUISVILLE, KY.; round; clear; 5"
.... 4.00-10.00

5221   N.L. CLARK & CO., PERUVIAN SYRUP; aqua; 8½".................. 4.00-8.00

5222   CONDIMENT; plain milk bottle type; clear or amethyst; 6½".................. 2.00-3.00

5223   same as above except vase type bottle; 4"
.... 2.00-3.00

5224   COTTAGE CHEESE; ten panels; clear or amethyst; 4½".................. 4.00-6.00

5225   COURTENAY & CO.; *A & P* under bottom; clear or amethyst; 7"............. 4.00-6.00

5226   COURTENAY & CO.; clear or amber; 7"
.... 2.00-4.00

5227   C.R.B. under bottom; label; aqua; 8"   2.00-4.00

5228   CROWN under bottom; pickle label; 14"
.... 20.00+

5229   CRUIKSHANK BROS & CO.; *Allegheny Pa.* under bottom; clear or amethyst; 8". 2.00-3.00

5230   C.S. & CO. LD5302 on bottom; eight panels; aqua; 6½".................. 2.00-6.00

5231   CURTICE BROTHERS CO.; *1613* under bottom; clear or amethyst; 8" tall, 2¼" round
.... 2.00-4.00

5232   CURTICE BROS.; machine made; clear or amethyst; 10".................. 2.00-4.00

5233   CURTICE BROS. CO.; *Preserves* on the shoulders; ridges all around; round; amethyst or clear; 7¼"...................... 2.00-4.00

5234   CURTICE BROTHERS CO. PRESERVES ROCHESTER, NY in circle on tapered neck; 8", 10½" or 12¼".............. 2.00-6.00

5235   CURTIS BROS. PRESERVES; clear; 10½" or 12½"............................ 8.00-10.00

5236   GEORGE M. CURTIS, PURE OLIVE OIL; clear; 17"...................... 2.00-4.00

5237   GEO M. CURTIS, PURE OLIVE OIL; slim; round............................ 1.00-2.00

5238   CURTIS & MOORE; clear or amethyst; 10" tall, 2¼" x 2¼".................. 6.00-10.00

5239   DAVIS OK BAKING POWDER; round; aqua; 4½"............................ 2.00-4.00

5240   DAWSON'S PICKLES; ten panels; clear or amethyst; 7½".................. 2.00-4.00

5241   D. & C.; pontil; clear or amethyst; 11½"
.... 8.00-10.00

5242   D. & CO; mustard; clear or amethyst; 4½"
.... 2.00-3.00

5243   DIXIE under bottom; clear; 7¾".... 2.00-6.00

5244   DODSON & HILS MFG CO.; aqua; 8"
.... 2.00-4.00

5245   DUNDEE; gray................. 6.00-8.00

5246   J. DUPIT BORDEAUX ELIXIR DE SOULAC LES BAINS; amber; 3"........ 10.00-20.00

5247   A. DURANT & FILS BORDEAUX; round; aqua and blue; 7⅛"................. 2.00-4.00

5248   same as above except no embossing; fancy
.... 2.00-4.00

5249   E. R. DURKEE & CO., N.Y.; pontil; aqua; 4½"
.... 10.00-20.00

5250   E. R. DURKEE & CO. CHALLENGE SAUCE; sample; amethyst; 4".............. 4.00-6.00

5251   E.R. DURKEE & CO. SALAD DRESSING, N.Y. vertically; *Bottle Patented April 17,1877* on bottom; round; amethyst; 6½"....... 1.00-3.00

5252   E.R. DURKEE & CO., N.Y.; round; screw top; amethyst; 3½"................... 1.00-2.00

5253   E.R. DURKEE & CO., SALAD DRESSING, N.Y.; round shoulder; *Patented April 17, 1877* on the bottom; round; clear; 4½" or 7¾"
.... 1.00-2.00

5254   E.R. DURKEE & CO., NEW YORK in vertical lines; clear or amethyst; 5", 6¾" or 8¼"
.... 2.00-3.00

5255   E. R. DURKEE AND CO.; sheared top; eight panels; clear or amethyst; 4"........ 4.00-8.00

5256   E. R. DURKEE & CO.; clear or amethyst; 6"
.... 3.00-6.00

5257   E.R. DURKEE & CO.; clear or amethyst; 7"
.... 3.00-4.00

5258   E. R. DURKEE & CO.; clear or amethyst; 4" tall; 1½" diameter................. 2.00-6.00

5259   E.E. DYER & CO. EXTRACT OF COFFEE, BOSTON MASS; graphite pontil; green; 6"
.... 25.00+

5260   E.H.V.B.; graphite pontil; six panels; light blue; 9½".................... 25.00-50.00

5262   5263   5264   5265   5267   5268   5270

5274   5275   5279   5283   5286   5287

5288   5289   5290   5292   5294   5295   5296

5298   5299   5300

5261 EIFFEL TOWER LEMONADE; *G. Foster Clark & Co. Manufacturer* on opposite side; clear; 2¾" 3.00-4.00

5262 CHARLES ELLIS SON & CO. PHILA.; aqua; 6" 2.00-4.00

5263 ENO'S FRUIT SALT; *W* on botton; 7" tall, 1½" x 2½" 4.00-8.00

5264 ESKAY'S; *pat. J11-93 Albumenized 163 Food* on bottom; sheared top; amber; 7½" 4.00-8.00

5265 ESKAY'S; *pat July 93 Albumenized 179 Food* on bottom; machine made; amber; 7½" 2.00-4.00

5266 EVANGELINE PEPPERSAUCE; *Made in St. Martinville, La., U.S.A.* on one side panel; twelve panels; tiny screw top; 5¼" ... 2.00-3.00

5267 EXTRACT TABASCO under bottom; clear; 4¾" 2.00-3.00

5268 F in center of bottle; refined pontil; clear; 5" 4.00-8.00

5269 FANCY OLIVE OIL; small base with five rings; six rings at shoulder; long bulbous neck; aqua; 7" 8.00-10.00

5270 F.G.W. under bottom; clear; 7¾".... 4.00-6.00

5271 J.A. FOLGER & CO; *Golden Gate High Grade Flavoring Extracts, 2 oz Full Measure* on front panel; rectangular; amethyst; 5½" .. 2.00-3.00

5272 FOLGERS GOLDEN GATE FLAVORING on panel; rectangular; amethyst; 5¼" .. 1.00-2.00

5273 FORBES DELICIOUS FLAVORING EXTRACTS, *Made By Forbes Bros. & Co, St. Louis* on front panel; rectangular; clear; 4¾" 1.00-2.00

5274 4N under bottom; clear or amethyst; 9¼" 2.00-4.00

5275 THE FRANK TEA & SPICE CO.; machine made; clear; 5½" 2.00-4.00

5276 FRANK TEA & SPICE CO, CINCINNATI O. *Jumbo Peanut Butter, Made from No 1 Spanish and No 1 Va. Peanuts, Salt Added, 5 oz;* embossed head of elephant; round ridges on bottle; clear 1.00-2.00

5277 LOUIT FRERES & CO. BORDEAUX; mustard barrel; three rings at base and shoulder; crude ring collar; open pontil; amethyst; 4¾" 4.00-8.00

5278 same as above except graphite pontil 4.00-10.00

5279 G.A.J. under bottom; sheared top; 7" 2.00-4.00

5280 GARRETTS FOOD PRODUCTS; *Garrett & Co. Inc. Monticello, N.Y., St. Louis Est. U.S. Pat. Off.;* round; green; 10½" and 12⅛".... 4.00-8.00

5281 GEBHARDT EAGLE on the side panel; *Chile powder* on the opposite panel; *Eagle* embossed on the front with *Trademark;* screw top; rectangular; clear or amethyst; 3½" or 5½".... 2.00-4.00

5282 THE M.A. GEDREY PICKLING CO.; aqua; 9¼" 4.00-6.00

5283 GIBBS; *B* on bottom; clear or amethyst; 8¼" 2.00-3.00

5284 GOLDBERG-BOWEN & CO.; *Sierra Madre Olive Oil San Francisco, Cal;* shaped like a gin bottle; flared collar; bulbous type neck; amethyst; quart; 11¼" 3.00-4.00

5285 GOLDEN TREE PURE SYRUP; crown top; aqua; 11¼" 2.00-4.00

5286 THE GRADUATED NURSING BOTTLE; clear; 6¾" 4.00-6.00

5287 Grape juice, plain; aqua; 6" 2.00-4.00

5288 GRAPETTE PRODUCTS CO. CAMDEN ARK. under bottom; ABM; clear; 7¼" 2.00-4.00

5289 GRARY & CO; stag head on shoulder; *Worcestershire Sauce* on side; a stag on neck; clear or amethyst...................... 4.00-6.00

5290 CHARLES GULDEN; clear or amethyst; 4¾" 2.00-4.00

5291 CHAS. GULDEN, NEW YORK on bottom; pickle jar; four large bulbous rings; flared collar; clear; 5½" 3.00-6.00

5292 CHAS. GULDEN; *16* under bottom; aqua or clear; 8½" 6.00-8.00

5293 CHAS. GULDEN, NEW YORK; four rings on base; three on shoulder; mustard barrel; amethyst; 4⅝" 3.00-4.00

5294 CHAS. GULDEN, N.Y. under bottom; clear; 4¼" 2.00-6.00

5295 CHAS. GULDEN, N.Y. under bottom; clear or amethyst; 4¼" 2.00-4.00

5296 H under bottom; clear; 4½" 2.00-6.00

5297 HALFORD LEIGESTERSHINE; aqua; 7⅛" 2.00-3.00

5298 HANANC; aqua; 6" 2.00-4.00

5299 THOMAS L. HARDIN CO.; clear or amethyst; 7" 3.00-6.00

5300 GEO HARM; *This Bottle To Be Washed And Returned, Not To Be Bought Or Sold* on back; clear; quart 8.00-12.00

5301 H.J. HEINZ CO. NO. 37 GOTHIC HORSERADISH; aqua; 6" 2.00-4.00

5302 H.J. HEINZ CO. on bottom; also large notch on bottom; 18 panels; round; clear; 8¾".. 2.00-5.00

5303 H.J. HEINZ CO.; patent on the bottom; eight panels; amethyst; 9¼".............. 2.00-4.00

5304 5305 5306 5307 5308 5309 5311 5312

5313 5314 5315 5316 5320 5321 5323 5324

5325 5328 5329 5331 5332 5333 5334 5336

5337   5338   5339   5340

5304   H.J. HEINZ CO. 69 PATD. under bottom; clear; 6".................... 4.00-6.00

5305   H.J. HEINZ CO.; *122 Patd* under bottom; ten panels; clear or amethyst; 4¾"...... 2.00-4.00

5306   H.J. HEINZ CO.; *7 Patented* and an *X* on bottom; clear or amethyst; 8¼"........ 4.00-8.00

5307   HEINZ; clear or amethyst; 6"....... 3.00-6.00

5308   HEINZ; *No. 28* under bottom; aqua; 7¼".................... 2.00-3.00

5309   HEISEY RELISH, label; eight panels; lead glass; clear or amethyst; 4"........ 4.00-8.00

5310   HERB JUICE on panel; rectangular; clear; 8⅜".................... 2.00-4.00

5311   HILL'S, label; machine made; *L.B.CO* monogram on back; aqua; 11"...... 8.00-12.00

5312   HIRES IMPROVED ROOT BEER; panel, *Mfg. by The Charles Hires Co.*; panel, *Philadelphia Pa. U.S.A.*; panel, *Make Five Gallons of a Delicious Drink*; aqua; 4¾"......... 3.00-6.00

5313   HOLBROOK & CO.; *P.B.* on bottom; aqua; 7½".................... 3.00-4.00

5314   HOLBROOK & CO.; aqua; 4½"..... 8.00-12.00

5315   HOLBROOK & CO.; *R.B.B.* under bottom; aqua; 8¾".................... 8.00-10.00

5316   HONEY; clear or amethyst; 8"...... 5.00-8.00

5317   HONEYWELL; sauce type bottle; rolled lip; concave panels, front and back; three concave on sides; open pontil; aqua; 6¾"....... 6.00-8.00

5318   HORLICK'S TRADEMARK, RACINE, WIS., MALTED MILK M.M. U.S.A. 1 GAL.; round; clear; 10¾"..................... 1.00-3.00

5319   HORLICK'S twice on shoulders; round; screw top; clear; 2¾".................. 1.00-2.00

5320   HORLICK'S; clear or amethyst; 5".. 2.00-4.00

5321   HORLICK'S; aqua; different sizes... 2.00-4.00

5322   HORTON-CATO MFG CO, DETROIT, MICH. in three lines; three round panels; on bottom *T.P.*; clear; 5½".................... 2.00-6.00

5323   HORTON-CATO CO.; clear; 7"..... 3.00-6.00

5324   HORTON-CATO & CO., DETROIT; reverse side *Crown Celery Salt*; gold; 8"... 15.00-25.00

5325   HORTON-CATO MFG. CO., DETROIT, MICH under bottom; clear; 6"............. 3.00-6.00

5326   J.W. HUNNEWELL & CO. on side; *Boston* on opposite side; three concave panels; aqua; 1½" 4.00-6.00

5327   same as above except aqua green..... 4.00-6.00

5328   H.W.P. 394 under bottom; sheared top; clear; 6" 6.00-8.00

5329   HYMAN PICKLE CO., LOUISVILLE, KY. under bottom; yellow; 8".......... 6.00-10.00

5330   INDIA PACKING CO., PORTLAND, ORG.; moon in center; aqua; 6"........ 10.00-20.00

5331   Jelly, label; *Patented June 9-03 June 23 03* under bottom; clear; 3½"............... 2.00-3.00

5332   Jelly, label; *2* under bottom; clear or amethyst; 4¾"............................... 2.00-4.00

5333   Jelly, label; sheared top; 2¼"....... 2.00-4.00

5334   Jelly, label; *Patented June 9-03 June 23 03* under bottom; clear or amethyst; 2½"..... 2.00-4.00

5335   JOSLYN'S MAPLE SYRUP; eight sides; ground lip; aqua; 8".............. 5.00-10.00

5336   J.P.S. under bottom; clear or amethyst; 7¼" 2.00-3.00

5337   J.P.S. under bottom; pickles; green; 6" 4.00-6.00

5338   J.P.S. under bottom; green; 6"...... 4.00-6.00

5339   J.P.S. under bottom; clear or amethyst; 5" 4.00-6.00

5340   J. Wm JUNKINS CATSUP, BALTIMORE MD.; clear or amethyst; 8"........ 8.00-10.00

5341   KELLOGGS on base; oval; clear; 4¼", 6" or 7" 1.00-2.00

5342   KEPLER on four sides on shoulder; tapered bottle; ring top; under bottom *Snowhill RW&CO, London*; green; 1¾" x 2¼"; 5¼" tall; 1¼" neck 6.00-10.00

5343   same except no *Kepler* on shoulder; 7½" tall; 2¼" x 3¼" 10.00-15.00

5344   KARL KIEFER PAT in glass lid to fit pickle bottle; round; amethyst or clear; 6". 3.00-4.00

5345   KITCHEN BOUQUET on bottom; round; ABM; aqua; 5¾".................... 2.00-3.00

5342   5346   5347   5348   5351   5352   5353   5354

5356   5357   5358   5359   5360   5361   5362   5363

5364   5367   5368   5369   5370   5371   5372   5373

| 5374 | 5375 | 5376 | 5380 | 5381 | 5382 | 5383 | 5386 |

5346 LAM A & F under bottom; green; 9¼" 16.00-18.00

5347 Lamp candy bottle; aqua; 3" 4.00-8.00

5348 LEA & PERRINS; *J10D,S* on bottom; aqua; 11½"......................... 4.00-6.00

5349 same as above except 8½"......... 2.00-4.00

5350 same as above except 7¼"......... 2.00-3.00

5351 LEVER BROS. CO. NEW YORK, label; amber; 10"..................................... 2.00-4.00

5352 LINCOLN BANK BOTTLE on base; *Pat 1959 Lincoln Foods Inc. Lawrance Mass 3-17-3* under bottom; clear; 8½" 2.00-4.00

5353 LIPTON; number on bottom; aqua; 8½" 2.00-6.00

5354 JOSHUA LONGFIELD; *North of England Sauce* around shoulder; aqua; 7".... 4.00-8.00

5355 LONG SYRUP REFINING CO., S.F. CAL.; wine color; 4¾" 4.00-8.00

5356 LUNDBORG; clear or amethyst; 2½" 2.00-4.00

5357 E.G. LYONS & RAAS CO.; clear or amethyst; 4".............................. 4.00-6.00

5358 M under bottom; amber; 6½"....... 4.00-8.00

5359 MANDER WEAVER & CO.; cream crock; 4" 8.00-10.00

5360 MANSFIELD DAIRY; clear; quart 4.00-10.00

5361 SGDG GRAND MARNIER on back; snap on; machine made; light amber; 6" 6.00-15.00

5362 D. MAURER & SON under bottom; 3" 1.00-3.00

5363 F.E. McALLISTER'S; aqua; 7" 3.00-6.00

5364 McCORMICK & CO. SPICE GRINDERS, BALTIMORE; eight panels; sheared top; clear or amethyst; 3¾"...................... 2.00-4.00

5365 McCORMICK & CO., EXTRACTS, SPICES & ETC., BALTIMORE MD.; clear; 4½" 4.00-8.00

5366 McCORMICK & CO., BALTIMORE; triangular; clear; 3½"......................... 3.00-6.00

5367 McCORMICK & CO.; clear or amethyst; 4¾" 3.00-6.00

5368 McCORMICK & CO.; clear; 5¼".... 2.00-4.00

5369 McCORMICK & CO.; round; aqua; 5¼" 2.00-6.00

5370 McILHENNY CO., AVERY ISLAND LA.; clear or amethyst; 8".............. 4.00-6.00

5371 McILHENNY CO., AVERY ISLAND LA.; swirl pattern; clear; 8" 8.00-12.00

5372 MELLINS FOOD, FREE SAMPLE; *P* on bottom; aqua; 3¾" 2.00-3.00

5373 MENLEY-JAMES LIMITED; *N.Y., London* on bottom; milk glass; 1¾"............ 1.00-2.00

5374 Milk bottle; *HA* under bottom; clear 2.00-4.00

5375 MILKS' EMULSION; *F.C.W.* under bottom; machine made; amber; 6¼"........ 2.00-3.00

5376 MILKS' EMULSION; *#1054* under bottom; machine made; amber; 6¼"........ 2.00-4.00

5377 M&M on one line; T in center; CO. on bottom line; pumpkin seed type bottle; clear; 3¾" 6.00-10.00

5378 MOUTARDE DIAPHANE/LOUIT FRERES & CO.; mustard barrel; three rings at base and shoulders; crude ring collar; graphite pontil; amethyst; 5" 6.00-10.00

5379 same as above except clear........ 4.00-8.00

5380 MUSKOGEE WHO. GRO. CO.; clear; 8¼" 4.00-6.00

5581 Mustard, label; clear or amethyst; 4½" 2.00-3.00

5582 Mustard, label; small kick-up; six-part mold; clear or amethyst; 5½"............ 2.00-4.00

5383 Mustard, label; *Patented* under bottom; twelve panels; clear or amethyst; 4¾"...... 2.00-4.00

5384 Mustard barrel; plain; three rings at top and bottom; sheared top; clear or amethyst; 1¾" round, 4½" tall 4.00-8.00

5385 same as above except no sheared top 2.00-4.00

5386 MY WIFE'S SALAD DRESSING; machine made; blue green; 8" 8.00-10.00

5389   5392   5395   5396   5397   5398

5399

5400   5401   5402   5403   5404   5405   5410

5411   5412   5414   5415   5416   5417   5418   5419

| 5420 | 5421 | 5422 | 5423 | 5424 | 5426 | 5427 |

5387 BIBO NEWMAN & KENBERG; BNI monogram; *San Francisco, Cal.*; round; ring collar; clear; 5¼" 4.00-8.00

5388 NUT HOUSE; figure of house and other writing; store jar; ball shape; clear 8.00-15.00

5389 OLD DUFFY'S 1842 5 YEAR OLD APPLE JUICE VINEGAR on top shoulder; *Duffy's* in diamond shape and *1842* in circle on neck; eight panels; amber; 6¾".................. 15.00+

5390 Olive oil; long neck; ring collar; graphite pontil; light aqua; 12½" 6.00-8.00

5391 Olive oil, plain; old flared lip; round with tapered neck; aqua; 11¼".................. 4.00-8.00

5392 Olive oil, plain; three-part mold; flat ring top; under bottom, sunken circle; cobalt; 4¼" tapered body, 2½" neck.................. 8.00-12.00

5393 Olive oil; amber; 1½" round, 6¼" tall, 2½" neck 3.00-4.00

5394 Olive oil; slim, bulbous neck; clear or aqua; three sizes: 7¼" to 12½"............... 6.00-10.00

5395 Olive oil, label; aqua; 7½" 2.00-6.00

5396 Olive oil; aqua; 10¼" 2.00-4.00

5397 Olive oil; free-blown; pontil; small kick-up; aqua; 10" 8.00-12.00

5398 Olive oil, label; clear; 6½" 2.00-3.00

5399 Olive oil, label; kick-up; aqua; 12¼" 6.00-12.00

5400 Olive oil, label; clear or amethyst; 8" 3.00-4.00

5401 Olive oil; aqua; 10"............... 3.00-6.00

5402 Olive oil, label; clear or amethyst; 5½" 2.00-3.00

5403 Olive oil, label; free-blown; pontil; aqua; 13½" 15.00-20.00

5404 Olive oil, label; free-blown; pontil; aqua; 10" 6.00-10.00

5405 Olive oil, label; applied ring top; deep kick-up; aqua; 9½" 4.00-8.00

5406 J. M. OLIVER & SONS on blob seal; olive oil; aqua; 7" 4.00-8.00

5407 F.A. OSTEN'S PURE SALAD OIL; eight-ring top; long neck; flared bottom; aqua 5.00-10.00

5408 PARKER BROS. vertically; on shoulder, *London Club Sauce*; crude top; round; aqua; 7¼" 4.00-6.00

5409 PASKOLA'S, THE PRE-DIGESTED FOOD CO., TRADEMARK; embossed *Pineapple*; amber; 6"...................... 4.00-8.00

5410 PEPPERMINT; marble in center of neck; aqua; 7¼"............................... 8.00-12.00

5411 Peppersauce; 20 rings around bottle; round; space for label; clear or aqua; 6¼" 6.00-12.00

5412 Peppersauce; 22 rings around bottle; space for label; oval; clear or aqua; 7" 6.00-12.00

5413 Peppersauce; cathedral; gothic arch in lower half of six panels; two windows in upper half of each panel; aqua; 8½" 12.00-18.00

5414 Peppersauce; clear; 8"............ 6.00-12.00

5415 Peppersauce, label; 4¾"............ 2.00-3.00

5416 Peppersauce, label; *X* on bottom; aqua; 9" 8.00-12.00

5417 Peppersauce; clear or amethyst; 6½" tall, 1½" square.......................... 10.00+

5418 Peppersauce, label; clear or amethyst; 6½" 1.00-2.00

5419 Peppersauce, label; aqua; 7"........ 2.00-6.00

5420 Peppersauce, label; aqua; 10½" 8.00-12.00

5421 Peppersauce, label; 24 rings; clear; 8¼" 6.00-12.00

5422 Peppersauce, label; *NYMM* and monogram under bottom; aqua 8.00-15.00

5423 Peppersauce, label; leaded glass; clear or amethyst; 7¼" 4.00-6.00

5424 Peppersauce, label; swirl pattern; clear or amethyst; 8½" 4.00-6.00

5425 Peppersauce; fifteen rings; cathedral type; *G.C.O. Pat. Sept 26, 1875* on base; double ring top; aqua; 8½".................. 10.00-20.00

5426 Peppersauce, label; *C & B* on base; clear or amethyst; 7½" 8.00-15.00

5427 Peppersauce, label; clear; 12½" 4.00-6.00

5428   5429   5430   5431   5432   5433   5435

5437   5438   5439   5440   5441   5442   5443

5444   5445   5446   5447   5448   5449   5450

5451	5452	5453	5454	5455	5456	5457

5458	5459	5460	5461

5428 Peppersauce, label; amber; 7¾" ... 10.00-15.00

5429 Peppersauce, label; *D.E.* under bottom; aqua; 8"
.... 4.00-8.00

5430 PEPSINE CHAPOTEAUT; ten panels; clear or amethyst; 3½" 2.00-4.00

5431 PEPTOGENIC MILK POWDER around shoulder; machine made; tin measure top; amber; 5¾" 4.00-6.00

5432 PHOENIX BRAND; machine made; clear; 6"
.... 3.00-5.00

5433 Pickle bottle; cathedral; square; four gothic panels; applied ring and lip; aqua; 11½"
.... 15.00-30.00

5434 Pickle; cathedral; cobalt; 5½"; ½" square
.... 20.00-25.00

5435 Pickle, plain; paneled corner; tapered neck; yellow; 7¼"; 2½" square 10.00-15.00

5436 same except no panel; under bottom *Pat. Apr 4 1882, Heinz 16* in circle; aqua...... 2.00-6.00

5437 Pickle, label; clear or amethyst; 13½" tall, 3¾" square 6.00-10.00

5438 Pickle, label; machine made; *165* under bottom; clear or amethyst; 7".............. 2.00-3.00

5439 Pickle, label; pontil; aqua; 10"..... 8.00-12.00

5440 Pickle, label; broken pontil; aqua; 7¼" 50.00+

5441 Pickle, label; kick-up; pontil; aqua; 8½"
.... 10.00-20.00

5442 Pickle, label; *W.T. & CO.* under bottom; aqua; 6¼".............................. 1.00-2.00

5443 Pickle, label; aqua; 8¼"............ 2.00-6.00

5444 Pickle, label; aqua; 6½"............ 2.00-4.00

5445 Pickle, label; green; 11" 6.00-8.00

5446 Pickle, label; clear or amethyst; 6¾" 6.00-10.00

5447 Pickle, label; small kick-up; aqua; 9" 4.00-8.00

5448 Pickle, label; clear or amethyst; 7½" 2.00-4.00

5449 Pickle, label; *Patented Aug. 20, 1901* under bottom; clear or amethyst; 7" 1.00-2.00

5450 Pickle, label; *Pat Applied For #16* under bottom; clear; 11¼" 4.00-6.00

5451 Pickle, label; *Pat July 11th 1893* under bottom; sheared top; clear; 7".............. 4.00-6.00

5452 Pickle, label; *3* under bottom; aqua; 3½"
.... 4.00-8.00

5453 Pickle, label; sheared top; clear or amethyst; 5"
.... 3.00-5.00

5454 Pickle, label; sheared top; aqua; 12¾"
.... 25.00-35.00

5455 Pickle, label; aqua; 10½"........... 4.00-6.00

5456 Pickle, label; clear or amethyst; 5".. 4.00-6.00

5457 Pickle, label; small kick-up; green; 7½"
.... 10.00-12.00

5458 Pickle, label; eight panels; clear or amethyst; 6½".............................. 2.00-4.00

5459 Pickle, label; amber; 6¾" .... 10.00+

5460 Pickle, label; clear; 7"............ 4.00-6.00

5461 Pickle, label; clear or amethyst; 11" tall, 2½" x 3¼"................... 4.00-8.00

5462   5463   5464   5465   5466   5467   5468

5469   5470   5471   5472   5473   5474   5475

5476   5477   5478   5479   5480   5481   5482

5483 5484 5485 5486 5487 5488 5489 5490

5491 5492 5493 5494

5462 Pickle, label; green; 5½" 2.00-8.00
5463 Pickle, label; ten panels; clear or amethyst; 10¼"
.... 2.00-4.00
5464 Pickle; *AM* on bottom; clear....... 2.00-3.00
5465 Pickle, label; *Pat Apr. 20, 1901* on bottom; clear
or amethyst; 8¼"................. 2.00-4.00
5466 Pickle, label; *Pat O.P. 1900* on bottom; clear or
amethyst; 6" 3.00-6.00
5467 Pickle, label; sunken bottom; aqua; 9" tall, 2½"
diameter....................... 2.00-6.00
5468 Pickle, label; aqua; 8½".......... 6.00-10.00
5469 Pickle, label; pontil; aqua; 9"....... 6.00-8.00
5470 Pickle, label; clear; 4½"........... 3.00-4.00
5471 Pickle, label; broken pontil; aqua; 6½"
.... 8.00-10.00
5472 Pickle, label; improved pontil; amber; 10"
.... 30.00-40.00
5473 Pickle, label; cathedral design; blue green; 13½"
.... 50.00+

5474 Pickle, label; sheared top; green; 3¼" 2.00-5.00
5475 Pickle, label; small kick-up; amber; 7½"
.... 8.00-10.00
5476 Pickle, label; four side panels; pontil; aqua; 6¼"
.... 20.00-30.00
5477 Pickle, label; green; 8½" 8.00-10.00
5478 Pickle, label; *Pat. App. For* under bottom; aqua;
9¼"............................. 6.00-8.00
5479 Pickle, label; pontil; aqua; 7½"..... 8.00-20.00
5480 Pickle, label; three-piece mold; light blue; 12"
.... 4.00-8.00
5481 Pickle, label; aqua; 9" 2.00-4.00
5482 Pickle, label; ten panels halfway down; small
kick-up; aqua; 12" 4.00-8.00
5483 Pickle or cherry, label; *Pat. App. For* under bottom; clear or amethyst; 5" 4.00-6.00
5484 PICKMAN'S CHOCOLATE; machine made;
aqua............................. 2.00-4.00
5485 E. D. PINAUD; aqua; 2¼"........ 4.00-8.00
5486 PIN MONEY; clear; 5¼" 4.00-8.00
5487 PLANTERS; same in back; peanut figures on
each corner; glass top with a peanut nob; clear
.... 45.00-60.00
5488 PLANTERS; same in back; square; glass top
with peanut nobs; clear 15.00-20.00
5489 PLANTERS SALTED PEANUTS; same in
back; glass top with peanut nob; clear
.... 15.00-30.00
5490 PLANTERS; same in back on base; glass top
with peanut nob; clear........... 15.00-30.00
5491 PLANTERS on shoulder; PENNANT 5c
SALTED PEANUTS on front; on each side a
Planters Peanut Man figure; glass top with
peanut nob; clear 30.00-40.00
5492 P/P CO. under bottom; clear; 5" tall; 1¼"
diameter........................ 2.00-4.00
5493 DR. PRICE'S; clear or amethyst; 5¾" 2.00-3.00
5494 PRICE-BOOKER MFG. CO.; clear or
amethyst; 8" 2.00-6.00

5495   5496   5498   5502   5503   5504   5505

5506   5507   5508   5509   5510   5511   5512   5513

5514   5515   5516   5518   5519   5520   5521   5522

| 5523 | 5524 | 5525 | 5526 | 5533 | 5535 | 5536 |

5495 PRIDE OF LONG ISLAND; clear or amethyst; 9¾"............................ 2.00-4.00

5496 POMPEIAN BRAND VIRGIN LUCCA OLIVE OIL in four lines; aqua; 7½" 2.00-4.00

5497 same as above except other sizes.... 2.00-6.00

5498 THE POTTER PARLIN CO. under bottom; sheared top; clear or amethyst; 4" .. 4.00-6.00

5499 PRIMROSE SALAD OIL WESTERN MEAT CO. vertically on one panel; aqua; 9½" 3.00-4.00

5500 same as above except quart 4.00-6.00

5501 PURE OLIVE OIL S.S.P.; bulb shaped base; long neck; amethyst; 7¼" 3.00-5.00

5502 QUERUS; pontil; aqua; 5¼" .... 25.00+

5503 Radish, label; eight panels; clear or amethyst 2.00-6.00

5504 Radish, label; ten panels; clear; 4½" 2.00-3.00

5505 Radish, label; square on bottom; clear or amethyst; 7" 2.00-4.00

5506 Radish, label; 2 on bottom; sheared top; clear or amethyst; 10¾".............. 3.00-6.00

5507 Radish, label; green; 5½".......... 4.00-6.00

5508 Radish, label; clear or amethyst; 9½" 2.00-3.00

5509 Radish, label; clear or amethyst; 5¼" 2.00-4.00

5510 Radish, label; *Pat April 2nd 1901* under bottom; clear or amethyst; 5½".............. 2.00-4.00

5511 Radish, label; ribbed base; clear or amethyst; 7½"................................ 2.00-4.00

5512 Radish, label; eight panels; clear or amethyst; 6½"................................ 2.00-4.00

5513 Radish, label; *169* under bottom; clear or amethyst; 8¾" 2.00-3.00

5514 Radish, label; clear or amethyst; 6" 2.00-4.00

5515 Radish, label; clear or amethyst; 5¼" 2.00-4.00

5516 Radish, label; *56S* in triangle under bottom; clear; 4½".............................. 2.00-3.00

5517 RED SNAPPER SAUCE CO., MEMPHIS, TENN.; six sides; clear; 9½" 4.00-10.00

5518 RED SNAPPER; clear or amethyst; 7½" 3.00-4.00

5519 RESTORFF & BETTMANN, N.Y. under bottom; light green; 4½".............. 2.00-6.00

5520 RESTORFF & BETTMANN F.F., N.Y. under bottom; mustard; aqua; 4½"....... 8.00-12.00

5521 R.J. RITTER CONSERVE CO. under bottom; clear; 8¼" or 10½" 4.00-6.00

5522 ROWAT & CO.; same in back; light green; 10" 8.00-10.00

5523 ROYAL LUNCHEON CHEESE; milk glass; 2½"................................ 2.00-3.00

5524 ROYAL LUNCHEON CHEESE under bottom; milk glass; 3"..................... 2.00-3.00

5525 Salad dressing, label; clear or amethyst; 6¼" 2.00-6.00

5526 M. SALZMAN CO., PURITY ABOVE ALL; *855* under bottom; amber; 10½".... 8.00-15.00

5527 Sauce; round; tapered neck; sixteen concave vertical panels all around; aqua; 8".. 4.00-6.00

5528 Sauce; coffin shape; ring on base and top of neck; clear; 8¼" 3.00-4.00

5529 Sauce; olive oil shape; round; tapered neck; graduated collar; pontil; aqua; 5¾".. 4.00-8.00

5530 Sauce; square; tapered neck; sixteen rings; sunken panel on front; aqua; 8⅜"..... 2.00-4.00

5531 Sauce; tapered neck; 23 rings; oval; sunken panel on front; ABM; aqua; 8"....... 2.00-4.00

5532 Sauce; triangular; tapered neck; diamond shape down center on all three sides; crude collar; amethyst; 8¾" 4.00-6.00

5533 SKILTON FOOTE & COS., BUNKER HILL PICKLES; light olive; 11½" 15.00-30.00

5534 SKILTON FOOTE & COS., BUNKER HILL PICKLES in outer ring; picture of pickle barrels, trees, fence, tower, all in center; round; aqua; 6⅜" 4.00-8.00

5535 same as above except gold; 7½" 12.00-15.00

5536 SNOWHILL B.W. & CO. LONDON on bottom; amber; 6½"............................ 2.00-4.00

5538   5540   5541

5543   5544   5545

5546   5547   5550   5551   5553   5554

5555   5556   5557   5558   5559

5537 SOCIETE HYGIENIQUE, NO. 5 RUE J.J. ROUSSEAU, PARIS vertically around bottle; cylindrical; graphite pontil; clear; 6³⁄₈″ 6.00-8.00

5538 STRONG COBB & CO., CLEVELAND O., *Pure Concentrated Flavoring Extracts* embossed; clear; 6½″ 4.00-6.00

5539 TILLMANN'S in small panel at top; star with T in center in circular panel; OIL in square panel at base; square; aqua; 8″ 4.00-6.00

5540 Tabasco or dry food; wide mouth—2½″ opening; pontil; dark green; 7½″.............. 25.00+

5541 TOURNADES KITCHEN BOUQUET; clear or amethyst; 5¼″ 3.00-6.00

5542 TRAPPEYS TABASCO PEPPERS on center panel; vertical panels on upper and lower half; four large rings divide the panels; crown top; oval; ABM; clear; 6¾″ 2.00-4.00

5543 WILLIAM UNDERWOOD & COMPANY around bottom; aqua; 10″ 8.00-12.00

5544 U. S. NAVY; pepper; eight panels; aqua 4.00-10.00

5545 VALENTINES; amber; 3¼″........ 3.00-6.00

5546 V.D.CO.; *Pat April 27, 1875* under bottom; aqua; 7″........................ 8.00-12.00

5547 Vinegar, label; milk glass; 5½″ 4.00-8.00

5548 VIRGINIA FRUIT JUICE CO., NORFOLK, VA. in script on front; machine made; tenpin shape; clear or amethyst; 7½″ 2.00-4.00

5549 M.T. WALLACE & CO. PROP. BROOKLYN N.Y.; *Brasst's Purifying Extract 1850*; pontil; aqua; 9½″ 25.00-50.00

5550 WM. R. WARNER & CO.; clear; 8¼″ 4.00-8.00

5551 WARSAW PICKLE CO.; aqua; 8¾″ 10.00-15.00

5552 WATERS BROS. OLIVE OIL AND EXTRACTS, OAKLAND, CAL.; round; light aqua; 11½″ 4.00-6.00

5553 WDS N.Y.; graphite pontil; dark green; 8″ .... 50.00+

5554 C. WEISBECKER, MANHATTAN MARKET, NEW YORK; pickle jar; corner panels; square; ring on neck; square collar; aqua; 6¼″ 3.00-6.00

5555 WELLCOME CHEMICAL WORKS under bottom; *Kepler* around top; machine made; amber; 6½″.................................. 2.00-4.00

5556 THE J. WELLER CO.; clear or amethyst; 7½″ 4.00-6.00

5557 WELLS & RICHARDSON CO.; *Cereal Milk* on each side; amber; 7¾″ 8.00-12.00

5558 H. WICKERT; aqua; 7¼″.......... 6.00-8.00

5559 THE WILLIAMS BROS CO., pickle label; clear; 7½″ 2.00-4.00

5560 WOOD COOPER PURE OLIVE OIL, SANTA BARBARA, CA. inside of crude blob seal on shoulder; band collar; round; aqua; 11″ 4.00-6.00

Embossed *"Skilton Foote & Co., Bunker Hill Pickles,"* this container (#5533) was not the usual cathedral-styled pickle bottle of 1880-1900. Cathedral bottles had four or more side panels that formed a gothic arch design.

Fruit Jars

In 1795 the French army under Napoleon was deeply involved in military conflicts. A good food supply was often a determining factor in victory—and in how long victory and conquest would persevere. Napoleon, determined that an empire would be his, offered a government prize of twelve thousand francs (about four thousand dollars) to anyone who could invent an effective food preservation process. Nicolas Appert claimed the prize fourteen years later. His idea was incredibly uncomplicated: Enclose the food in glass, seal it, then boil it to destroy bacteria. He put his theory in a book, which was translated and published in New York in 1812. The book was well-received in America, where people were always looking for better ways of living.

The public soon clamored for glass jars in which to preserve fruit. Thomas W. Dyott, a prominent American bottle maker, was promoting sales of his fruit jars by 1829 in Philadelphia. It was his advertising campaign that gave preserving bottles the name fruit jars.

The most common closure used during the first fifty years in the development of food preservation was cork sealed with wax. The process was improved in 1855 by Robert Arthur who invented an inverted saucerlike lid to be inserted into the jar to insure its airtight integrity. The Hero Glass Works of Philadelphia developed a glass lid in 1856.

The first significant improvement in the glass food jar and the sealing of its contents came with the patent on November 30, 1858, of a screw-type glass jar by John Landis Mason. The jars could be easily and tightly sealed, but they were not without disadvantage. The lids were made of zinc and it was not healthy to have food exposed for long periods of time to that metal. But this problem was circumvented by the Hero company's development of a glass lid for Mason's jar in 1868. Mason transferred his patent rights on the jar to the Consolidated Fruit Jar Company, which subsequently let the rights expire. The competition was then opened and Ball Brothers of Muncie, Indiana, began distributing Mason jars on a national basis in 1880.

Meanwhile, Mason had gone on to pursue other ideas—he invented a folding life raft, a soap dish, a brush holder and a sheet metal cap dye.

Use of a semiautomatic bottle-making machine in 1898 in Buffalo, New York, increased production of the Mason jars. The biggest impetus to the industry probably was the automatic bottle-making machine in 1903. John Landis Mason did not live to see his fruit jars attain national popularity—he died in poverty in 1902.

Embossed "John M. Moore & Co.," the fruit jar on the far left, circa 1863, employs the use of a glass lid held on by a yoke and thumbscrew as does the second jar from the left of the same period. "The Salem Jar" at one time probably had some type of wire closure. A closure known as a Lightning stopper, modified in 1875 from a beverage bottle stopper, is atop the jar on the far right.

5580

5592

5616

5635

5561 A.B.G.A. MASON IMPROVED; green; quart
.... 2.00-4.00

5562 A.B.G.A. MASON PERFECT, MASON MADE
IN U.S.A.; green; quart 2.00-6.00

5563 A & C, 1885; glass lid and wire clip; aqua green;
quart........................ 40.00-60.00

5564 ACME in shield, stars; 1920; square wire lid;
pint, ½ gallon.................... 4.00-8.00

5565 ADLER on lid; clear or green; ½ pint, pint,
quart, gallon.................... 4.00-14.00

5566 ADVANCE; 1885; glass lid with metal clamp;
aqua; quart 25.00-60.00

5567 same as above except TRADEMARK, PAT.
APL'D FOR, J.W. monogram; green; quart
.... 15.00-30.00

5568 AGEE QUEEN; 1925; clear; quart 14.00-18.00

5569 AGEE in script; *Utility Jar*; round, screw top,
clear; pint...................... 6.00-12.00

5570 AGEE in script; *Victory*; clear; quart
.... 4.00-10.00

5571 AGEE LIGHTNING FRUIT JAR; square; wire
clamp; clear.................... 8.00-12.00

5572 AGNEW; 1876-1892; wax sealer; aqua; quart
.... 20.00-30.00

5573 A.G.W.L.; 1865; *Pitts, Pa.*; wax seal; aqua
.... 20.00-30.00

5574 AIRTIGHT; 1877; wax sealer; barrel shape;
green; quart.................... 60.00-90.00

5575 ALL RIGHT; 1868; glass lid with wire clamp;
green; quart.................... 30.00-45.00

5576 ALMY; glass cap; aqua; quart ... 25.00-40.00

5577 THE ALSTON; metal lid and wire clip; clear;
pint, quart 20.00-30.00

5578 AMAZON SWIFT SEAL; glass lid with full
wire bail; 1920; blue; pint, quart, ½ gallon
.... 6.00-10.00

5579 AMERICAN FRUIT JAR; 1885-95; aqua,
green; several sizes 20.00-40.00

5580 ANCHOR with figure of anchor; quart; 9"
.... 30.00-45.00

5581 ANCHOR HOCKING in center; an anchor with
an *H* under it; *Mason* under bottom; clear; 7"
.... 2.00-3.00

5582 same as above except with glass top; 1915; metal
band; clear or amethyst; quart ... 10.00-20.00

5583 ANCHOR HOCKING LIGHTNING; 1937;
glass top; clear; different sizes 4.00-6.00

5584 ANCHOR HOCKING MASON; 1937; screw
top; clear; quart.................. 2.00-4.00

5585 ANCHOR MASON'S PAT.; screw top; clear;
quart........................... 4.00-6.00

5586 ANDERSON PRESERVING CO., 1920; screw
top; clear; quart.................. 6.00-8.00

5587 ATHORHOLT, FISHER & CO.; 1875; wire
clamp; clear; quart.............. 20.00-35.00

5588 ATLAS CLOVER; in center, GOOD LUCK;
clear; 4¾"...................... 2.00-4.00

5589 ATLAS E-Z SEAL; 1896; wire bail and glass
lid; amber, green or clear; quart.. 10.00-20.00

5590 ATLAS E-Z SEAL; green or clear; 4½" or 5¼"
.... 2.00-4.00

5591 same as above except green; 6¾" or 7" 2.00-3.00

5592 ATLAS; *Atlas E-Z Seal, Trade Mark Reg.* on
bottom; aqua; quart; 7¼" 2.00-6.00

5593 ATLAS GOOD LUCK; 1930; glass lid; full wire
bail; clear; ⅓ pint, ½ pint, pint, quart, ½ gallon
.... 6.00-8.00

5594 ATLAS GOOD LUCK with cloverleaf; wire top;
aqua or amber; different sizes 10.00-15.00

5595 ATLAS with HA in center; MASON; clear; 9"
.... 1.00-2.00

5596 ATLAS H-A MASON; 1920; glass insert; metal
screw band; clear; pint, quart 2.00-4.00

5597 ATLAS H-A MASON; metal screw band; clear;
½ pint........................... 2.00-4.00

5598 ATLAS IMPROVED MASON; 1890's; glass lid; metal screw band; aqua or green . 4.00-8.00

5599 ATLAS MASON'S PATENT; 1900; zinc lid; blue green; quart 10.00-20.00

5600 ATLAS MASON'S PATENT NOV. 30, 1858; zinc lid; green; ½ gallon 4.00-8.00

5601 ATLAS MASON'S PATENT NOV. 30th, 1858; screw top; green; quart. 3.00-4.00

5602 ATLAS MASON'S PATENT; screw top; green; quart. 2.00-3.00

5603 ATLAS SPECIAL; screw top; 1910; clear or blue 4.00-8.00

5604 ATLAS SPECIAL MASON; 1910; zinc lid; wide mouth; aqua; quart 2.00-8.00

5605 ATLAS STRONG SHOULDER MASON; green or clear; 5⅛" or 6⅞" 2.00-3.00

5606 ATLAS STRONG SHOULDER MASON; 1915; zinc lid; aqua, green, clear or blue; pint, quart 6.00-10.00

5607 ATLAS WHOLEFRUIT JAR; glass lid and wire bail; wide mouth; clear; pint, quart, ½ gallon. 4.00-8.00

5608 ATMORE & SON; glass lid and metal screw band; wide mouth; aqua, green; quart 15.00-19.00

5609 THE AUTOMATIC SEALER; 1895; glass lid with spring wire bail; aqua, green; quart 14.00-25.00

5610 BAKER BROS; 1865; wax sealer; groove ring; green or aqua; pint 30.00-40.00

5611 BALL; vaseline glass; screw top; pint, quart 4.00-6.00

5612 BALL; 1890; screw top; green; three sizes 5.00-10.00

5613 THE BALL; 1890; screw top; green; quart 10.00-15.00

5614 BALL in script, IDEAL; wire top clamp; clear; 3" or 4¾" 4.00-6.00

5615 BALL in script, IDEAL; in back, *Pat. July 14, 1908*; wire top clamp; green or clear; three sizes 3.00-4.00

5616 BALL IDEAL PATD JULY 14 1988 (error in date); blue green; pint 15.00-20.00

5617 BALL IDEAL PAT'D JULY 14, 1908; wire and glass lid; aqua or blue; quart; 7¼" 4.00-6.00

5618 BALL IDEAL PATD JULY 14, 1908; lid and wire; aqua or blue; quart 2.00-4.00

5619 BALL IMPROVED; aqua; pint 2.00-3.00

5620 THE BALL JAR, MASON'S PATENT NOV. 30, 1858; screw-on lid; aqua; quart . . . 4.00-8.00

5621 BALL in script, MASONS PATENT 1858; green; three sizes. 2.00-3.00

5622 BALL in script, MASON; clear or green; six sizes. 2.00-6.00

5623 BALL MASON; aqua; quart. 2.00-3.00

5624 BALL in script, PERFECT MASON; screw top; six sizes. 2.00-4.00

5625 BALL PERFECT MASON; clear; quart 2.00-3.00

5626 BALL (printed) PERFECT MASON; deep aqua; pint 3.00-4.00

5627 BALL PERFECT MASON; aqua; quart 2.00-3.00

5628 BALL PERFECT MASON, no line under BALL; zinc lid; aqua; pint, quart 3.00-4.00

5629 BALL PERFECT MASON; 1900; zinc lid; vertical lines around sides are cup and pint measurements; amber, olive, blue or clear . . 25.00-35.00

5630 BALTIMORE GLASS WORKS; 1865; aqua; quart 30.00-40.00

5631 BANNER TRADE MARK WARRANTED; glass top; aqua; quart 8.00-10.00

5632 BANNER WIDEMOUTH WARRANTED; 1910; glass lid; full wire bail; wide mouth; blue; quart 6.00-12.00

5633 B. B. G. M. CO.; 1887; glass lid and metal screw band; blue, green or aqua; quart . . . 30.00-50.00

5634 BEAVER; 1897; glass lid and screw band; amber, green, clear or amethyst; pint, quart 12.00-25.00

5635 BEAVER; 4 under bottom; amber; 7¼" 20.00+

5636 BEECH NUT TRADE MARK with leaf; green; quart 4.00-6.00

5637 BEE HIVE; zinc band and glass insert; blue 20.00-30.00

5638 BENNETT'S; 1875; green; quart . 35.00-40.00

5639 BERNARDIN MASON; zinc lid; clear; quart 25.00-30.00

5640 BEST; zinc screw band and glass insert; wide mouth; green; quart. 18.00-25.00

5641 THE BEST; 1875; glass stopper that screws into the neck; quart 18.00-30.00

5642 THE BEST FRUIT KEEPER; glass lid and wire clamp; green; quart. 25.00-35.00

5643 BEST WIDE MOUTH; zinc band and glass insert; aqua or clear 2.00-4.00

5644 BOLDT MASON JAR; zinc lid; blue green 10.00-20.00

5645 BORDEN'S MILK CO.; 1885; hexagonal; metal band and glass insert; clear; pint . 10.00-20.00

5646 BOSCO DOUBLE SEAL; glass lid and full bail; clear; quart 4.00-8.00

5647 BOYD MASON; 1910; zinc lid; olive green; pint, quart 4.00-8.00

5648 BOYD PERFECT MASON; zinc lid; green; ½ pint, pint, quart. 4.00-6.00

5649 BRAUN SAFETEE MASON; zinc lid; aqua 3.00-5.00

5650 BRELLE JAR; glass lid and wire clamp; wide mouth; clear; quart 15.00-30.00

5651 BRIGHTON; 1890; glass lid; metal wire clamp; clear, amber or amethyst; quart . . 35.00-60.00

5652 GEO. D. BROWN & CO.; 1875; glass lid and heavy metal clamp; green; quart.. 20.00-40.00

5653 THE BURLINGTON; 1880; zinc band; clear or aqua; quart 20.00-40.00

5654 BURNHAM & CO.; 1865; iron lid; green; quart . . . . 60.00+

| 5657 | 5664 | 5670 | 5678 | 5679 | 5741 |

5655 CANADIAN KING; glass lid and full wire bail; clear; quart 4.00-8.00

5656 CANADIAN SURE SEAL; metal lid and wire metal screw band; wide mouth; clear; quart 2.00-4.00

5657 CANTON DOMESTIC FRUIT JAR; 1895; glass lid and wire bail; clear; quart 20.00-30.00

5658 CASSIDY; 1885; glass lid and wire bail; clear 35.00-50.00

5659 C. F. J. CO.; 1871; glass lid and metal band; green; quart 12.00-20.00

5660 C. G. CO.; 1890; screw lid; clear; quart 10.00-20.00

5661 A. & D. H. CHAMBERS UNION FRUIT JAR, PITTS; clear; quart 8.00-10.00

5662 THE CHAMPION, PAT. AUG. 31, 1869; glass lid and top metal screw band; aqua; quart 25.00-35.00

5663 CLARKE FRUIT JAR CO.; 1886; glass lid and wire bail with lever lock clamp; aqua; quart 40.00-50.00

5664 CLARKE FRUIT JAR CO., CLEVELAND O.; 54 under bottom; aqua; 7¼" 20.00-30.00

5665 CLARK'S PEERLESS; 1882; wire bail and glass lid; blue; quart 10.00-20.00

5666 CLIMAX; full wire bail and glass lid; green; pint 8.00-16.00

5667 CLYDE LIGHTNING; screw top; clear or green; quart 8.00-10.00

5668 CLYDE MASON; 1880; screw top; green; quart 10.00-20.00

5669 COHANSEY; 1870; glass lid and clamp; barrel shaped; aqua; quart 18.00-20.00

5670 COHANSEY GLASS MFG. CO.; Pat MCH 20 77 under bottom; barrel shaped; aqua 20.00+

5671 COLUMBIA; glass lid with clamp; amber; quart 20.00-35.00

5672 COMMONWEALTH FRUIT JAR; glass lid and wire bail; green; quart 20.00-40.00

5673 CORONA JAR IMPROVED; beaded neck design; clear; all sizes 4.00-10.00

5674 CROWN; 1890; glass lid and zinc screw band; aqua; quart 18.00-25.00

5675 CROWN; 1870; glass lid and zinc screw band; aqua; all sizes 6.00-12.00

5676 CROWN; glass lid and zinc screw band; all sizes 2.00-4.00

5677 CROWN MASON; zinc screw band; white opal insert; round with vertical ribs on the sides; all sizes 2.00-4.00

5678 CRYSTAL JAR; clear or amethyst; 6½" 10.00-20.00

5679 CRYSTAL JAR C.G.; sheared top; clear; quart 6.00-10.00

5680 CUNNINGHAM & IHMSEN; 1868; wax seal; cobalt blue; quart . . . . 40.00+

5681 CUNNINGHAM'S & CO.; 1879; wax seal; aqua; quart; . . . . 25.00+

5682 THE DAISY in a circle; glass lid and wire bail; aqua; quart 8.00-20.00

5683 THE DAISY JAR; 1885; heavy iron clamp; round; aqua; quart 25.00-45.00

5684 DALBEY'S FRUIT JAR; 1866; glass lid; round extending wax seal neck; deep aqua; quart 45.00-70.00

5685 THE DANDY; 1885; glass lid and wire clamp; round and slender; light green; quart 20.00-30.00

5686 THE DANDY; Gilberds 9 under bottom; amber; 7½" . . . . 20.00+

5687 THE DARLING; 1885; zinc screw band and glass insert; round tapering sides; aqua; quart 20.00-30.00

5688 DECKER DEPENDABLE FOOD, JACOB E. DECKER & SON, MASON CITY, IOWA; clear; quart 2.00-4.00

5689 DECKER'S IOWANA; glass lid and wire bail; clear; quart 8.00-12.00

5690 DEXTER; 1865; zinc band with glass insert; aqua; quart 20.00-40.00

5691 DIAMOND FRUIT JAR; glass lid and full wire bail; clear; quart 4.00-10.00

5692 DICTATOR D.D.I. HOLCOMB PATENTED DEC. 14TH, 1869; wax seal; blue; quart 15.00-30.00

5693 DILLON; 1890; wax seal; round; aqua; quart 20.00-30.00

5694 DOMINION; 1886; zinc band and glass insert; round; clear; quart 25.00-40.00

5695 DOMINION WIDEMOUTH SPECIAL; zinc lid; round; clear; quart 4.00-8.00

5696 DOOLITTLE, THE SELF SEALER; glass lid; wide mouth; clear; quart 20.00-30.00

5697 DOUBLE SAFETY; glass lid and full wire bail; clear; quart 2.00-4.00

5698 DOUBLE SAFETY in script; *Smalley Kiviare Onthank, Boston Mass.*; in center #4; clear; 7⅜" 2.00-4.00

5699 DOUBLE SEAL in script; clear; 7¼" 2.00-4.00

5700 DREY EVER SEAL; glass lid and full wire bail; clear or amethyst; quart 2.00-4.00

5701 DREY IMPROVED EVER SEAL; glass lid and full wire bail; round; clear; quart 2.00-4.00

5702 DREY MASON; screw top; round; aqua; all sizes 2.00-4.00

5703 DREY in script, PERFECT MASON; screw top; clear or green; several sizes 2.00-4.00

5704 DREY PERFECT MASON; zinc lid; green; pint, quart 2.00-4.00

5705 DREY SQUARE MASON; zinc lid; square; clear or amethyst; quart 1.00-2.00

5706 THE DUNKLEY CELERY CO., KALAMAZOO; four-piece mold; ground top; amethyst; quart 25.00-35.00

5707 THE DUNKLEY PRESERVING CO.; 1898; glass lid, metal clamp; clear; quart . 12.00-15.00

5708 DU PONT; screw top; round; aqua; quart 14.00-20.00

5709 DURHAM; glass lid and wire bail; round; aqua; quart 10.00-20.00

5710 DYSON'S PURE FOOD PRODUCTS; metal band; round; clear; quart 4.00-8.00

5711 EAGLE; 1876; glass lid and iron thumbscrew to tighten; green; quart .... 85.00+

5712 EASI-PAK MASON-METRO; screw top; clear 4.00-6.00

5713 EASY VACUUM JAR; 1895; glass lid; tall and round; clear; quart 15.00-25.00

5714 THE ECLIPSE; 1868; wax seal; aqua; quart 25.00-50.00

5715 ECLIPSE WAX SEALER; 1868; wax seal; green; quart .... 40.00+

5716 ECONOMY; metal lid and spring wire clamp; amethyst; pint, quart, ½ gallon 2.00-6.00

5717 ECONOMY, TRADE MARK; clear or amethyst; quart 2.00-4.00

5718 ECONOMY, TRADE MARK, PAT. JUNE 9, 1903; clear or amethyst; quart 2.00-4.00

5719 E.G.CO. (monogram) IMPERIAL; clear; quart 8.00-10.00

5720 ELECTRIC; glass lid and wire bail; round; aqua; quart 15.00-25.00

5721 ELECTRIC FRUIT JAR; 1900-1915; glass lid and metal clamp; round; aqua; quart 25.00-35.00

5722 ELECTROGLAS N.W.; clear; quart 2.00-4.00

5723 EMPIRE in maltese cross; clear; quart 2.00-4.00

5724 EMPIRE; 1860; glass stopper; deep blue; quart 50.00-60.00

5725 THE EMPIRE; 1866; glass lid with iron lugs to fasten it; aqua; quart 35.00-50.00

5726 ERIE FRUIT JAR; 1890; screw top; clear; quart 10.00-25.00

5727 ERIE LIGHTNING; clear; quart.... 4.00-6.00

5728 EUREKA; 1864; wax dipped cork or other; extending neck; aqua; pint 20.00-30.00

5729 EUREKA, PAT. FEB 9TH, 1864, EUREKA JAR CO., DUNBAR, W. VA.; 1870; aqua; quart 12.00-25.00

5730 EVERLASTING IMPROVED JAR in oval; 1904; quart 4.00-6.00

5731 EVERLASTING JAR; 1904; glass lid and double wire hook fastener; round; green; pint, quart, ½ gallon 10.00-17.00

5732 EXCELSIOR; 1880-1890; zinc screw band and glass insert; aqua; quart 20.00-27.00

5733 EXCELSIOR IMPROVED; 1890; green; quart 4.00-6.00

5734 EXWACO; clear or green; quart .. 10.00-20.00

5735 F.A. & CO.; 1860; glass stopper; green; quart 30.00-40.00

5736 FAHNSTOCK FORTUNE & CO.; green; quart .... 20.00+

5737 FAMILY FRUIT JAR; wire top; clear; quart 10.00-15.00

5738 FARLEY; glass lid and full wire bail; square; slender; clear; quart 4.00-6.00

5739 F.C.G. CO.; 1875; metal cap; amber or green; quart 35.00-50.00

5740 FEDERAL FRUIT JAR; 1895; glass lid and wire bail; olive green; quart 20.00-30.00

5741 FHANESTOCK ALBREE & CO.; pontil; sheared top; aqua; 7¼" 50.00-100.00

5742 FINK & NASSE, ST. LOUIS; green; quart 10.00-20.00

5743 FLACCUS CO., E.C. TRADE MARK; elk and floral design; milk glass .... 90.00+

5744 W.L.J. FLEET LIVERPOOL; glass stopper; aqua; quart 30.00-50.00

5745 FOSTER SEALFAST; glass lid and full wire bail; clear or amethyst; quart 4.00-10.00

5746 FRANKLIN DEXTER FRUIT JAR; 1865; zinc lid; aqua; quart 12.00-20.00

5747 FRANKLIN FRUIT JAR; 1866; screw-on lid; green; quart 20.00-40.00

| 5749 | 5750 | 5751 | 5752 | 5753 | 5754 | 5770 |

| 5792 | 5801 | 5821 |

5748 FRUIT GROWER'S TRADE CO.; wax dipped cork; oval; extending wax seal neck; green; quart 10.00-30.00

5749 Fruit jar, label; graphite pontil; seal top; aqua; 9½" 90.00-100.00

5750 Fruit jar, label; sheared top; 4¼" . . . 4.00-6.00

5751 Fruit jar, label; pontil; clear; quart 100.00-150.00

5752 Fruit jar; ground pontil; blue green; 8¼" . . . . 60.00+

5753 Fruit jar, label; 4 under bottom; sheared top; black; 7" 50.00-100.00

5754 Fruit jar, label; graphite pontil; aqua; 10" 100.00-125.00

5755 FRUIT KEEPER; glass lid and metal clamp; deep green; quart 20.00-30.00

5756 THE GAYNER; glass lid and wire bail; clear; quart 10.00-15.00

5757 THE GEM; 1856; zinc band and glass insert; amber, aqua or green; quart 6.00-12.00

5758 GEM; 1868; zinc screw band and glass insert; green; quart 10.00-12.00

5759 GEM; 1869; zinc screw band and glass insert; aqua; quart 10.00-15.00

5760 THE GEM, C.F.J. monogram; 1882; wide zinc screw band and glass insert; aqua green; quart 10.00-20.00

5761 GEM; 1884; zinc screw band and glass insert; green; quart 10.00-20.00

5762 GEM with maltese cross; aqua; quart 2.00-4.00

5763 GEM HGW; aqua; quart 2.00-6.00

5764 GEM IMPROVED MADE IN CANADA; clear; quart 2.00-4.00

5765 GEM IMPROVED; 1860; zinc band and glass insert; round; green; pint 10.00-20.00

5766 THE GEM, PAT. NOV. 26, 1867; clear; quart 4.00-8.00

5767 GENUINE BOYDS MASON; 1900; zinc lid; green; quart 6.00-8.00

5768 GENUINE MASON; 1900; zinc; olive green; pint, quart 20.00-25.00

5769 G.G. CO.; screw top; clear 6.00-10.00

5770 GILBERDS; *Gilberds Improved Jar Cap Jamestown N.Y. Oct. 13, 1885 Pat July 31, 82* on top; small kick-up; sheared top; aqua; quart 60.00-80.00

5771 GILBERDS IMPROVED JAR; 1885; glass lid and wire bail; aqua; quart 35.00-44.00

5772 GILBERDS JAR; 1884; glass lid and screw band; aqua; quart 50.00-60.00

5773 GILCHRIST; 1895; zinc lid and dome shaped opal liner; wide mouth; aqua green; quart 4.00-8.00

5774 GILLAND & CO., 1890; glass stopper; aqua; quart 10.00-20.00

5775 G.J. monogram; clear; quart 4.00-8.00

5776 Glass screw- cap jar; *Pat. Oct. 24, 1905;* six panels; *Warm Cap Slightly To Seal Or Unseal* on top of cap; amethyst; 5" 4.00-8.00

5777 GLASSBORO, trademark; 1880-1900; zinc band and glass insert; light to dark green; three sizes 15.00-24.00

5778 GLASSBORO IMPROVED; 1880; wide zinc screw band and glass insert; aqua or pale green; quart 20.00-25.00

5779 GLENSHAE G. MASON (G in square); clear; quart 2.00-4.00

5780 GLOBE; glass lid; metal neck band; top wire bail and bail clamp; amber, green or clear; quart 10.00-20.00

5781 GLOCKER, PAT. 1911 OTHERS PENDING SANITARY; aqua; quart 2.00-4.00

5782 GOLDEN STATE, S in a triangle; *Pat. Dec. 20, 1910, Pat. Pending* under it; amethyst 4.00-8.00

5783 GOLDEN STATE; metal screw-on lid; wide mouth; clear; four sizes 8.00-10.00

5784 GOLDEN STATE IMPROVED; thin metal screw-on lid; clear; two sizes 6.00-10.00

5785 GOOD HOUSE KEEPER'S MASON JAR; 1935-1946; screw-on metal lid; clear; quart 2.00-4.00

5786 GOOD HOUSE KEEPER'S, R in circle, WIDE MOUTH MASON; screw top; clear; quart 2.00-4.00

5787 GREEN MOUNTAIN G.A. CO.; wire clamp; aqua 2.00-4.00

5788 G SQUARE MASON; metal screw-on lid; clear; quart 4.00-8.00

5789 HAINES; 1882; glass lid and iron clamp; green; quart 35.00-50.00

5790 HAINES IMPROVED; 1870; glass lid and top wire bail; aqua green; quart..... 30.00-40.00

5791 HAMILTON GLASS WORKS; green; quart 10.00-20.00

5792 HANSEE'S PLACE HOME JAR; *Pat. Dec. 19 1899* under bottom; aqua; 7"...... 20.00-30.00

5793 HARRIS; 1860; metal lid; deep green; quart 50.00-60.00

5794 HARRIS IMPROVED; 1875-1880; glass lid and iron clamp; green; quart........ 40.00-50.00

5795 HASEROT COMPANY; 1915-1925; zinc lid; green; quart................... 10.00-20.00

5796 THE HASEROT COMPANY, CLEVELAND MASON PATENT; screw top; green; quart 2.00-4.00

5797 E.C. HAZARD & CO., SHREWSBURY N.J.; wire clamp; aqua; quart 4.00-8.00

5798 HAZEL; glass lid and wire bail; aqua; quart 10.00-15.00

5799 HAZEL-ATLAS LIGHTNING SEAL; full wire bail and glass lid; green; quart 10.00-12.00

5800 H. & D.; 1915; glass top; metal band 4.00-6.00

5801 HELME'S RAILROAD MILLS; amber; 7¼" 8.00-15.00

5802 HELMES RAILROAD MILLS; amber; quart 8.00-16.00

5803 THE IMPROVED HERO; glass top; metal band; green 8.00-10.00

5804 HERO with cross and lightning at top; green; quart................... 8.00-16.00

5805 THE HEROINE; wide zinc screw band and glass insert; light green; quart ... 18.00-20.00

5806 THE HIGH GRADE; zinc screw-on top; clear 12.00-20.00

5807 HOLZ, CLARK, & TAYLOR; 1878; screw-on glass lid; aqua; quart.......... 25.00-40.00

5808 HOM-PAK; metal lid; clear....... 2.00-4.00

5809 HOM-PAK MASON; two-piece lid; clear; pint, quart................... 4.00-8.00

5810 THE HOUSEHOLD; in center W.T. CO.; under it FRUIT JAR; aqua; quart...... 8.00-10.00

5811 H & R; 1886; round wax sealer; blue; quart 8.00-16.00

5812 HUDSON BAY; picture of a beaver on side coat of arms; rawhide clamp top; square; clear; quart 8.00-12.00

5813 THE IDEAL; 1890; zinc lid; clear; pint, quart 10.00-20.00

5814 IDEAL WIDE MOUTH JAR; flat metal lid; clear; quart 2.00-4.00

5815 THE IMPERIAL; 1886; glass lid and wire clamp; green; quart 15.00-25.00

5816 IMPERIAL IMPROVED QUART; glass lid and wide zinc screw band; aqua or green; quart 8.00-10.00

5817 IMPROVED EVERLASTING JAR in a water-melon panel; under bottom *Illinois Pacific Glass Co. S.F. Cal., Pat.* in center; amethyst; 6½" 4.00-8.00

5818 INDEPENDENT; 1888; screw-on glass lid; clear or amethyst; quart........ 25.00-30.00

5819 INDEPENDENT JAR; 1882; screw-on glass lid; clear or amethyst; quart 20.00-30.00

5820 IVANHOE; glass lid and wire bail; clear; quart 8.00-10.00

5821 IVANHOE; 4 under bottom; clear; 4¼" 4.00-8.00

5822 J. & B. FRUIT JAR; 1898; zinc lid; light green; pint, quart 12.00-16.00

5823 JEANNETTE, a J in a block under it, MASON HOME PACKER; clear; quart 2.00-3.00

5824 JEWEL JAR; wide zinc screw band and glass lid; clear or amethyst; quart 2.00-4.00

5825 same as above except also made in Canada 2.00-4.00

5826 J.G. CO. monogram; zinc lid and domed opal liner; wide mouth; green; quart... 14.00-25.00

5827 JOHNSON & JOHNSON, NEW BRUNSWICK, N.J. U.S.A.; 1890; ground top; square; amber; 4¼" or 6½" 4.00-8.00

5828 JOHNSON & JOHNSON, NEW BRUNSWICK, N.J. U.S.A.; cobalt blue .... 100.00+

5844   5869   5874   5886   5902   5903   5904

5905   5909

5829 same as above except amber...... 12.00-20.00

5830 JUG; glass ears with wire handle; round; amethyst; gallon 6.00-10.00

5831 KALAMAZOO, THE JAY B. RHODES; 1875; wax seal; *Kalamazoo, Mich.*; quart 6.00-10.00

5832 K.C. FINEST QUALITY in banner, MASON; square, spacesaver style; zinc lid; clear or amethyst; quart 6.00-10.00

5833 KEFFERS GLASS; screw-on top; aqua; quart 25.00-35.00

5834 KERR ECONOMY TRADE MARK; *Chicago* on base; metal lid and narrow clip band; clear or amethyst; pint, quart 2.00-4.00

5835 KERR ECONOMY in script, under it TRADE MARK; under bottom *Kerr Glass Mfg. Co., Sand Spring, Okla.*; clear; 3¾"........... 2.00-3.00

5836 same as above except *Chicago Pat.* under bottom 1.00-2.00

5837 KERR GLASS TOP MASON; flat metal lid; clear; pint, quart................. 2.00-3.00

5838 KERR SELF SEALING, TRADE MARK REG. in banner, PAT. MASON; clear; quart 2.00-3.00

5839 same except indigo blue........... 4.00-8.00

5840 KERR SELF SEALING WIDE MOUTH MASON; base reads: *Kerr Glass Mfg. Co., Sand Springs, Okla., Pat. Aug. 31, 1915*; clear 2.00-3.00

5841 KERR in script, SELF SEALING TRADE MARK in a ribbon; under it MASON; clear; 6¾" 1.00-2.00

5842 same as above except square; clear; 9" 1.00-2.00

5843 KERR SELF SEALING TRADE MARK 65TH ANNIVERSARY; 1903-1968....... 4.00-8.00

5844 KERR WIDE MOUTH MASON; clear; ½ pint 8.00-15.00

5845 KG in oval; wire clamp; clear; quart 2.00-6.00

5846 THE KILNER JAR; zinc screw band and glass insert; clear; quart................ 6.00-8.00

5847 KING; full wire bail and glass lid; clear or amethyst; quart 8.00-10.00

5848 KINSELLS TRUE MASON; 1874; zinc lid; clear; quart 6.00-8.00

5849 KLINE PAT. OCT. 27, 1863 A on glass stopper; aqua; quart 8.00-10.00

5850 KLINE A.R.; 1863; glass fitting lid and clamp; aqua; quart 18.00-25.00

5851 KNIGHT PACKING CO.; screw top; clear; quart.......................... 2.00-4.00

5852 KNOWLTON VACUUM FRUIT JAR with star in center; clear or amethyst; quart.. 4.00-8.00

5853 KNOWLTON VACUUM FRUIT JAR; zinc lid and glass insert; blue; quart...... 16.00-25.00

5854 KNOX MASON; zinc lid; clear; quart 2.00-4.00

5855 KOHRS; glass lid and half wire bail; clear; quart.......................... 2.00-4.00

5856 KYGW CO. on base; clear; quart   15.00-30.00

5857 LAFAYETTE; 1864; wax dipped cork, with profile; aqua or blue; quart .... 40.00+

5858 LAMB MASON; zinc lid; clear; pint, quart 4.00-8.00

5859 THE LEADER; glass lid and wire clamp; amber; quart..................... 50.00+

5860 LEE & CO., J. ELWOOD; zinc screw; amber 8.00-10.00

5861 LEGRAND IDEAL CO., L.I.J. monogram; screw top; blue; quart.......... 8.00-20.00

5862 LEOTRIC in oval; glass lid; medium green; quart..................... 8.00-10.00

5863 LIGHTNING TRADE MARK REGISTERED U.S. PATENT OFFICE; *Putnam 4* on bottom; lid with dates; aqua; pint 4.00-6.00

5864 LIGHTNING TRADE MARK; *Putnam 199* on bottom; aqua; ½ gallon............. 4.00-6.00

5865 same as above except wire and lid; pint 4.00-6.00

5866 LIGHTNING TRADEMARK; glass top; round; aqua; 6″ 4.00-10.00

5867 same as above except *Putnam* on base; aqua; quart, ½ gallon................... 6.00-10.00

5868 same as above except amber; pint, quart, ½ gallon........................ 12.00-20.00

5869 LIGHTNING; *Putnam 824* under bottom; sheared top; aqua................... 10.00+

5870 LINDELL GLASS CO.; 1870; wax sealer; amber; quart................... 30.00-50.00

5871 LOCKPORT MASON; zinc top; aqua; ½ gallon 4.00-10.00

5872 LOCKPORT MASON, IMPROVED; zinc screw band; glass insert; aqua; quart 6.00-12.00

5873 LORILLARD & CO. on base; glass top; metal clamp; amber; pint.............. 9.00-17.00

5874 P. LORILLARD & CO.; sheared top; amber; 6¼″ .... 10.00+

5875 LUSTRE R.E. TONGUE & BROS. CO. INC. PHILA. in circle or shield; wire clamp; quart 2.00-4.00

5876 LUSTRE; glass top and wire bail; aqua 4.00-8.00

5877 L. & W.; 1860; wax sealer; green; quart 20.00-35.00

5878 W.W. LYMAN; 1862; glass top and wire clamp; aqua; quart 25.00-30.00

5879 LYON & BOSSARD'S JAR; glass lid and iron clamp; aqua; quart............. 40.00-50.00

5880 LYON & BOSSARD'S JAR, EAST STROUDS-BURG PA.; 1890; iron clamp; aqua; quart .... 90.00+

5881 MACOMB POTTER CO. PAT. APPLIED FOR on base; screw top; white crock... 10.00-12.00

5882 THE MAGIC FRUIT JAR; 1890; glass top and iron clamp; amber; quart 50.00-70.00

5883 THE MAGIC FRUIT JAR; star in center; clear; quart 4.00-8.00

5884 MALLINGER; zinc top; clear; quart 6.00-10.00

5885 MANSFIELD IMPROVED MASON; clear; quart........................... 2.00-4.00

5886 THE MARION JAR; #5 under bottom; sheared top; aqua; quart 10.00-20.00

5887 THE MARION JAR; 1858; zinc top; green; quart 8.00-12.00

5888 THE MASON; zinc top; light green; quart 4.00-6.00

5889 MASON FRUIT JAR; zinc lid; clear; quart 4.00-8.00

5890 MASON FRUIT JAR; zinc top; clear; quart 4.00-12.00

5891 same as above except amber..... 35.00-50.00

5892 MASON FRUIT JAR; zinc top; aqua; quart 8.00-12.00

5893 MASON FRUIT JAR PATENT NOV. 30TH, 1858; zinc top; aqua; quart....... 10.00-20.00

5894 THE MASON JAR OF 1858; zinc top; aqua; quart..................................... 8.00-20.00

5895 MASON KEYSTONE; clear; quart   2.00-4.00

5896 MASON PATENT NOV. 30TH, 1880; zinc top; clear; pint, quart.................... 10.00-20.00

5897 MASON PATENT NOV. 30TH, 1858 with dots on letters; hand painted with hot glass; screw top; green; quart 8.00-10.00

5898 MASON PAT. NOV. 30TH, 1858; 1910; clear; quart 2.00-4.00

5899 MASON PORCELAIN; tan; quart 10.00-12.00

5900 same as above except black .... 200.00+

5901 MASON star design jar; zinc top; clear; pint 10.00-20.00

5902 MASON'S; sheared top; pale green; 7¼″ 2.00-6.00

5903 MASON'S; *Pat Nov. 26-67* under bottom; aqua; 5½″..................................... 8.00-12.00

5904 MASON'S; sheared top; black; 7¼″ 100.00-200.00

5905 MASON'S; swirled milk glass; 7¼″ 60.00-75.00

5906 MASON'S CG, PATENT NOV 30, 1858; zinc lid; green; quart................... 8.00-14.00

5907 MASON'S-C-PATENT NOV. 30TH 1858; green; 7″..................................... 4.00-8.00

5908 MASON'S IMPROVED; zinc screw band and glass insert; aqua or green; pint .. 10.00-25.00

5909 MASON'S IMPROVED BUTTER JAR; sheared top; aqua; ½ gallon 8.00-10.00

5910 MASON'S IMPROVED; *Hero F J Co.* in cross above; zinc band and glass lid covered with many patent dates, earliest *Feb 12, '56*; aqua; quart 8.00-12.00

5911 MASON'S KEYSTONE; 1869; zinc screw band and glass insert; aqua; quart 10.00-20.00

5912 MASON'S "M" PATENT NOV. 30TH 1858; green; 7″..................................... 4.00-8.00

5913 MASON'S, under it "M" PATENT NOV. 30TH 1898; screw top; aqua; quart 6.00-8.00

5914 MASON'S PATENT 1858; zinc lid; amber or green; pint..................................... 20.00-30.00

| 5925 | 5934 | 5965 | 5970 | 5986 | 5990 | 5998 |

5915 MASON'S PATENT 1858; zinc top; aqua; quart 6.00-8.00

5916 MASON'S PATENT NOV. 30 1858; zinc top; amber or yellow; quart 6.00-12.00

5917 MASON'S PATENT NOV. 30, 1858; zinc top; aqua or green; pint .... 45.00+

5918 MASON'S PATENT NOV. 30, 1858; zinc top; clear; quart 8.00-13.00

5919 MASON'S (cross) PATENT NOV. 30TH, 1858; *Pat. Nov. 26, 67, 45* in center on bottom; blue or aqua; pint...................... 6.00-8.00

5920 MASON'S PATENT NOV. 30TH 1858, C.F.J. Co. monogram; aqua; pint 4.00-6.00

5921 MASON'S, under it an arrow, under that PATENT NOV. 30TH 1858; sheared top; quart 10.00-15.00

5922 MASON'S with flat type cross; *H.F.J. Co.* in each corner; *Patent Nov. 30th 1858;* ½" letters; sheared top; aqua; gallon 8.00-15.00

5923 MASON'S PATENT; zinc lid; aqua, green or clear; quart 4.00-8.00

5924 MASON'S PATENT, NOV. 30TH 1858; three errors on M, P, N; reads ASONS ATENT, OV.; aqua; quart 15.00-20.00

5925 MASON'S PAT. NOV. 30TH 1858 (backward *S*); *New Reproduction;* sheared top; amber; pint 10.00-20.00

5926 MATHIA'S & HENDERSON; glass lid and heavy wire clamp; clear; quart ... 15.00-25.00

5927 M. C. CO. on base; screw top; amber; quart 10.00-20.00

5928 McDONALD NEW PERFECT SEAL; wire bail and glass lid; blue; quart..... 8.00-12.00

5929 McDONALD NEW PERFECT SEAL, PATENT JULY, 14 1908; clear; quart 2.00-4.00

5930 METRO EASI-PAK MASON; threaded neck; clear; quart 2.00-4.00

5931 M.F.A.; metal screw-on top; clear; quart 8.00-16.00

5932 MICHIGAN MASON; zinc top; clear; quart 10.00-20.00

5933 MID WEST; wide zinc band and glass top; clear or amethyst; quart............... 2.00-6.00

5934 MILLER'S FINE FLAVOR; three bees in circle in center; aqua; quart........... 15.00+

5935 MILLVILLE ATMOSPHERIC FRUIT JAR; in back *Whitall's Patent June 18, 1861;* clamp top........................ 10.00-15.00

5936 MILLVILLE IMPROVED; 1885; zinc lid and glass insert; aqua; quart......... 20.00-30.00

5937 MISSION, a bell and trademark on each side, under it MASON JAR, MADE IN CALIF.; on bottom *Los Angeles Calif. Mfg. by W. J. Latchford Co.;* screw top; clear or green; three sizes........................ 3.00-10.00

5938 MODEL MASON; 1910; zinc top; green; quart 8.00-14.00

5939 JOHN M. MOORE; 1865-1875; glass top and heavy iron clamp; aqua; quart.... 50.00-85.00

5940 MOORE'S PATENT, DEC. 3, 1861; glass top with cast iron clamp and screw; aqua or green; quart........................ 35.00-65.00

5941 NATIONAL; 1885; metal top; quart 25.00-40.00

5942 NATIONAL SUPER MASON; 1870; glass top and iron clamp; clear; quart...... 18.00-35.00

5943 NEWARK; zinc top; clear; quart.. 8.00-15.00

5944 NEWARK SPECIAL EXTRA MASON JAR 4.00-6.00

5945 NEWARK; zinc top; clear; quart.. 4.00-10.00

5946 NEW GEM; wide zinc top; clear; quart 2.00-4.00

5947 N STAR; metal top and wax seal; blue; quart 10.00-20.00

5948 N.W. ELECTROGLASS WIDE MOUTH MASON; screw top; clear or amethyst; quart 2.00-4.00

5949 N.W. ELECTROGLASS WIDE MOUTH MASON; zinc top; clear or amethyst; quart 4.00-8.00

5950 OC on base; glass top; wire clamp; quart 8.00-10.00

5951 OHIO QUALITY MASON; clear; quart 4.00-6.00

5952 OPLER BROTHERS INC., OB monogram, COCOA AND CHOCOLATE, NEW YORK U.S.A.; glass top; wire clamp; clear 4.00-6.00

5953 OSOTITE in diamond; clear; quart.. 2.00-4.00

5954 PACIFIC GLASS WORKS; zinc band and glass insert; green; quart 40.00-50.00

5955 PACIFIC MASON; zinc top; clear; quart 10.00-20.00

5956 PACIFIC S.F. GLASS WORKS; 1880; green; quart....................... 20.00-30.00

5957 PARAGON, NEW; glass top and iron clamp; green; quart.................... 35.00-40.00

5958 PATENT APPLIED FOR; metal top and wax seal, extending wax seal neck; green; quart 10.00-20.00

5959 P.C.G. CO.; wax seal; aqua; quart 10.00-25.00

5960 THE PEARL; zinc screw band and glass insert; green; quart.................... 20.00-30.00

5961 PEERLESS; wax dipped cork; green; quart 50.00-60.00

5962 THE PENN; metal cap and wax seal; green; quart....................... 25.00-30.00

5963 PEORIA POTTERY; metal top and wax seal; glazed brown stoneware; quart 6.00-12.00

5964 PERFECTION; double wire bail and glass top; clear; quart 20.00-30.00

5965 THE NEW PERFECTION; clear or amethyst; ½ gallon........................ 15.00-25.00

5966 PERFECT SEAL; full wire bail and glass top; clear; quart 2.00-6.00

5967 PERFECT SEAL in shield, MADE IN CANADA; clear; quart........... 2.00-4.00

5968 PET.; glass stopper; green; quart 40.00-50.00

5969 PET.; glass stopper and wire bail; aqua; quart 25.00-30.00

5970 H.W. PETTIT, WESVILLE N.J. under bottom; aqua; quart 4.00-10.00

5971 THE GORAGAS PIERIE CO., PHILA., ROYAL PEANUTENE; sheared top; clear 8.00-10.00

5972 PINE DELUXE JAR; full wire bail and glass top; clear; quart 2.00-6.00

5973 PINE (P in square) MASON; zinc top; clear; quart....................... 2.00-6.00

5974 PORCELAIN LINED; zinc top; aqua; quart 12.00-20.00

5975 same as above except green; 2 gallon 10.00-15.00

5976 POTTER & BODINE PHILADELPHIA; glass top and clamp; aqua; quart....... 35.00-50.00

5977 PREMIUM COFFEYVILLE KAS.; wire ring and glass top; clear or amethyst; quart 15.00-30.00

5978 PREMIUM IMPROVED; glass top and side wire clips; clear; quart 10.00-15.00

5979 PRESTO; screw-on top; clear 2.00-4.00

5980 PRESTO FRUIT JAR; screw-on top; clear 2.00-4.00

5981 PRESTO GLASS TOP; half wire bail and glass top; clear or amethyst; quart....... 2.00-6.00

5982 PRESTO SUPREME MASON; threaded neck; clear; pint...................... 2.00-4.00

5983 PRESTO WIDEMOUTH GLASS TOP; threaded neck; clear; quart 2.00-4.00

5984 PRINCESS; fancy shield; glass top and wire bail; clear; quart................ 12.00-20.00

5985 PROTECTOR; flat zinc cap and welded wire clamp; aqua; quart 15.00-20.00

5986 PROTECTOR; 6 under bottom; sheared top; six panels; aqua.................. 10.00-20.00

5987 THE PURITAN; glass top and wire clamp; aqua; pint...................... 25.00-30.00

5988 PUTNAM GLASS WORKS on base; wax seal; green; quart.................... 25.00-30.00

5989 THE QUEEN; circled by *Pat. Dec 28th Patd. June 16th 1868*; wax seal; green; quart 20.00+

5990 THE QUEEN; *Patd. Nov. 2 1869, #39* under bottom; clear; quart............. 20.00-30.00

5991 THE QUEEN; 1875; zinc band; aqua or green; quart......................... 16.00-22.00

5992 QUEEN IMPROVED; shield design; glass lid and wire clamps; clear; quart....... 4.00-8.00

5993 QUICK SEAL in circle; glass lid and wire bail; green, blue or clear; quart 2.00-4.00

5994 QUONG HOP & CO., 12 OZ. NET; glass lid and wire bail; Chinese writing; clear; pint 2.00-4.00

5995 QUONG YEUN SING & CO.; half wire bail and glass lid; clear; pint.............. 4.00-6.00

5996 RAMSEY JAR; glass lid; twelve-sided jar; aqua; quart 40.00-50.00

5997 RAU'S IMPROVED GROOVE RING JAR; 1910; wax sealer; pink; pint, quart 25.00-35.00

5998 RED KEY MASON; 2 under bottom; clear or amethyst; 6½" 20.00-30.00

5999 RED MASON'S, embossed key, PATENT NOV. 30TH 1858; zinc lid; aqua or green; pint 10.00-14.00

6000 REID MURDOCK & CO. CHICAGO; zinc lid; clear; quart 4.00-10.00

6001 RELIABLE HOME CANNING MASON; 1940's; zinc screw band and glass insert; clear; quart........................ 2.00-3.00

6002 RELIANCE BRAND WIDE MOUTH MASON; screw-on lid; clear; three sizes 2.00-4.00

6003 ROOT; 1925; clear; quart......... 2.00-6.00

6004 ROOT MASON; 1910; zinc screw-on lid; aqua, green or blue; quart............. 4.00-7.00

6005 ROOT MASON; 1925; clear; quart.. 2.00-6.00

6007

6026

6044

6055

6074

6006	THE ROSE; 1920; screw-on lid; clear; three sizes. 10.00-20.00
6007	ROYAL; sheared top; clear 3.00-6.00
6008	ROYAL OF 1876; screw top; clear; quart . . . . 25.00+
6009	ROYAL TRADE MARK with crown; glass lid and full wire bail; light green or clear; pint, quart, ½ gallon. 4.00-8.00
6010	ROYAL TRADE MARK FULL MEASURE; 1900, REGISTERED with crown; green; quart 2.00-4.00
6011	SAFE SEAL, PATD. JULY 14, 1908; clear; quart 2.00-4.00
6012	SAFE SEAL; 1935; glass lid and wire bail; aqua or clear; pint, quart 3.00-4.00
6013	SAFETY; 1900; full wire bail and glass lid; amber; pint, quart, ½ gallon 40.00-50.00
6014	SAFETY SEAL MADE IN CANADA; half wire bail and glass lid; clear; pint, quart 2.00-4.00
6015	SAFETY VALVE PATD. MAY 21, 1895, with emblem in center on bottom; amethyst; pint 6.00-10.00
6016	SAFETY VALVE PATD. MAY 21, 1895; midget jar; ground top; clear; 3¾" 25.00-30.00
6017	SAFETY WIDE MOUTH MASON, SALEM GLASS WORKS, SALEM N.J.; zinc lid; aqua or green; quart, ½ gallon. 8.00-14.00
6018	SAMCO in center, GENUINE MASON; zinc screw band and opal insert; clear; all sizes 1.00-2.00
6019	SAMCO SUPER MASON; 1920; zinc screw band and opal insert; clear; all sizes. 1.00-2.00
6020	SAMPSON IMPROVED BATTERY; 1895; screw-on lid; aqua; quart 10.00-16.00
6021	SANETY WIDE MOUTH MASON; 1920; zinc lid; wide mouth; aqua; quart 12.00-19.00
6022	SANFORD; 1900; metal screw band and glass insert; clear; quart. 15.00-21.00
6023	SANITARY; 1900; glass lid and wire bail; aqua; quart 10.00-17.00
6024	SAN YUEN CO.; 1925; glass lid and half wire bail; clear; quart. 6.00-10.00
6025	THE SCHAFFER JAR, ROCHESTER N.Y., monogram S.J.C.; aqua; quart 15.00-20.00
6026	SCHRAM; *Schram St. Louis* on bottom; clear or amethyst; 4" 6.00-8.00
6027	SCHRAM AUTOMATIC SEALER in ribbon; flat metal lid and wire clamp; clear; all sizes 7.00-13.00
6028	THE SCRANTON JAR; 1870-1880; glass stopper and wire bail; aqua; quart. . . . 40.00-50.00
6029	SEALFAST; *sold by W.H. Vanlew, Dayton, Wash. Bakery & Grocery* in an oval; wire clamp top; green; 6¼" 4.00-8.00
6030	SEALFAST; 1915; full wire bail and glass lid; clear or amethyst; all sizes. 2.00-4.00
6031	SEALTITE TRADE MARK; green; quart 2.00-4.00
6032	SEALTITE WIDE MOUTH MASON; flat metal top and screw band; green; quart 6.00-10.00
6033	SEASON'S MASON; metal band and glass insert; clear; three sizes. 8.00-20.00
6034	SECURITY; glass top and wire bail; clear; quart. 8.00-12.00
6035	SECURITY SEAL; half wire bail and glass top; green or blue; pint, quart 6.00-10.00
6036	SELCO SURETY SEAL; half wire bail and glass top; green or blue; pint, quart 6.00-10.00
6037	SELCO SURETY SEAL in circle, PATD. JULY 14, 1908; green; quart. 2.00-4.00
6038	SILICON GLASS COMPANY, PITTSBURG, PENN.; wire bail and glass top; clear or aqua; quart. 10.00-18.00
6039	SIMPLEX; glass screw top; clear; pint, quart 10.00-25.00

6040 SIRRA MASON JAR; zinc top; clear; pint, quart 10.00-15.00

6041 SMALLEY; zinc screw band and milk glass insert; amber; quart 15.00-20.00

6042 SMALLEY; zinc top; clear; quart . . 4.00-8.00

6043 THE SMALLEY FRUIT JAR, SEPT. 23, 84; aqua; quart . . . . 20.00+

6044 SMALLEY FULL MEASURE QUART; *Patented Dec. 1889, Apr. 1896, Dec. 1896* under bottom; sheared top; clear or amethyst 4.00-6.00

6045 SMALLEY SELF-SEALER WIDE MOUTH; full wire bail and glass top; clear; pint, quart 6.00-8.00

6046 SMALLEY'S ROYAL; ROYAL TRADE MARK NU-SEAL; crown; clear; pint 2.00-4.00

6047 J.P. SMITH, SON & CO., PITTSBURGH; clear; quart 10.00-20.00

6048 SPENCER; 1865; glass top and iron clamp; aqua; quart 30.00-40.00

6049 SPENCER'S PATENT; 1868; wax dipped cork; aqua; quart 25.00-35.00

6050 STANDARD MASON LYNCHBURG; aqua; quart 2.00-6.00

6051 STANDARD with ribbon and MASON inside; aqua; quart 4.00-8.00

6052 STANDARD, W.C. & CO.; aqua 4.00-8.00

6053 STANDARD; wax sealer; aqua; quart 10.00-16.00

6054 STANDARD MASON; zinc top; light aqua or light green; pint, quart 4.00-8.00

6055 STAR; *6* under bottom; aqua; 6½" 30.00-40.00

6056 STAR; 1895; zinc band and glass insert; clear; quart 15.00-20.00

6057 STAR GLASS CO., NEW ALBANY IND.; aqua 10.00-20.00

6058 STERLING MASON; zinc top; clear; pint, quart 2.00-4.00

6059 STEVEN'S; 1875; wax sealer; green; quart 40.00-50.00

6060 A. STONE & CO. PHILA; aqua . . 10.00-20.00

6061 STONE MASON FRUIT JAR, UNION STONEWARE CO., RED WING MINN.; sand crock; ½ gallon 10.00-15.00

6062 STONE MASON FRUIT JAR; zinc top; white crock; quart 6.00-12.00

6063 SUEY FUNG YUEN CO.; Chinese writing; clear; quart 4.00-8.00

6064 SUN; glass top and metal clamp; light green; quart 25.00-30.00

6065 SUPREME MASON; screw top; clear; quart 4.00-8.00

6066 SURE SEAL; full wire bail and glass top; deep blue; quart 4.00-6.00

6067 SWAYZEE'S FRUIT JAR; zinc top; aqua; pint, quart 8.00-15.00

6068 SWAYZEE'S IMPROVED MASON; blue or aqua; pint 4.00-6.00

6069 SWAYZEE'S IMPROVED MASON; zinc lid; green or aqua; pint 4.00-8.00

6070 TAYLOR & CO.; wire bail and glass top; aqua; quart 6.00-11.00

6071 TELEPHONE JAR; full wire bail and glass top; green; quart 15.00-20.00

6072 THE TELEPHONE JAR, TRADE MARK, REG. WHITNEY GLASS WORKS; clear; quart 2.00-6.00

6073 THE WIDE MOUTH TELEPHONE JAR, TRADE MARK REG; clear; quart . . 2.00-6.00

6074 TEXAS MASON; *made in Tx by Tx* under bottom; clear; 6¾" 4.00-8.00

6075 TF monogram on base; clear; quart 2.00-4.00

6076 TIGHT SEAL PAT'D. JULY 14, 1908; half wire bail and glass lid; green or blue; all sizes 2.00-4.00

6077 TROPICAL CANNERS; metal top; clear; quart 2.00-4.00

6078 TRUE FRUIT; 1900; glass top and metal clamp; clear; quart 12.00-16.00

6079 TRUE SEAL; glass top and wire bail; clear 8.00-10.00

6080 UNION; 1865; wax seal and metal lid; extending neck; deep aqua; quart 18.00-20.00

6081 UNION FRUIT JAR; 1866; wax seal and metal top; aqua; quart 10.00-20.00

6082 UNITED DRUG CO., BOSTON MASS.; clear; quart 2.00-4.00

6083 UNIVERSAL; screw top; clear; quart 4.00-8.00

6084 UNIVERSAL L.F. & CO.; clear; quart 2.00-6.00

6085 VACU-TOP on base; flat metal lid and clamp; light green; quart 15.00-30.00

6086 THE VACUUM SEAL; glass top; slender extending neck; clear; quart 8.00-12.00

6087 THE VALVE JAR CO., PHILADELPHIA; 1864; *Patent March 10th 1868*; screw top; aqua . . . . 35.00+

6088 THE VALVE JAR; 1868; zinc screw-on top; aqua; quart 20.00-30.00

6089 THE VAN VLIET; glass top and iron band with screw; aqua or green; quart . . . . 60.00+

6090 VETERAN; bust of soldier; clear; quart 8.00-12.00

6091 THE VICTOR; 1899; flat metal top and clamp; light green; quart 8.00-12.00

6092 THE VICTOR, PAT. FEB 20, 1900, M monogram in circle and diamond; clear; quart 10.00-15.00

6093 VICTORY; 1875; flat glass top and side wire clips; clear; quart 6.00-10.00

6094 VICTORY HOM-PAK MASON; clear; quart 2.00-4.00

6095 "W"; 1885; wax seal; green; quart 4.00-10.00

6096 W & CO. on base; green; quart . . . 10.00-20.00

6120

6097 GEO. E. WALES on base; glass lid and metal clamp; clear; quart.............. 6.00-15.00

6098 WALLACEBURG GEM; glass insert and zinc screw band; clear or amethyst; quart 4.00-8.00

6099 WAN-ETA COCOA, BOSTON; zinc top; amber, blue; quart 10.00-15.00

6100 WAN-ETA COCOA, BOSTON; ½ pint; 4¾" 8.00-12.00

6101 THE WARSAW SALT CO. in center, monogram W.S. CO., under it *Choice Table Salt Warsaw, N.Y.*; screw top; quart ... 8.00-12.00

6102 WEARS JAR; glass top and wire clamp; clear; quart....................... 8.00-16.00

6103 WEIDEMAN BOY BRAND, CLEV.; clear; quart....................... 8.00-10.00

6104 THE WEIR, PAT. MAR. 1ST 1892; wire bail; crock; quart.................... 6.00-12.00

6105 WEIR SEAL; white stoneware lid and wire bail; white; quart.................... 6.00-8.00

6106 WESTERN PRIDE; 1880; wax seal; clear; quart....................... 40.00-50.00

6107 WHEATON on base; clear; quart... 2.00-4.00

6108 WHEELER; 1889; glass top and wire bail; aqua or green .... 40.00+

6109 WHITALL'S; glass top and clip with screw tightener; green; quart 20.00-25.00

6110 WHITALL'S PATENT, JUNE 18, 1861 in form of circle; on back, *Millville Atmospheric Fruit Jar;* aqua; quart 15.00-29.00

6111 WHITE CROWN MASON framed in circle and oblong; aqua; quart 2.00-4.00

6112 WHITNEY MASON PATD. 1858 in a circle; clear; 9" 4.00-8.00

6113 WHITNEY MASON; 1858; zinc lid; aqua or light green; quart.............. 24.00-32.00

6114 WILCOX; 1867; flat metal lid and clamp; green; quart......................... 20.00-26.00

6115 WILLS & CO., 1880-1885; glass stopper and metal clamp; blue green 35.00-44.00

6116 WINSLOW JAR; 1870-1873; glass lid and wire clamp; green; quart 30.00-36.00

6117 WOODBURY; 1884-1885; glass lid and metal band clamp; aqua; quart 18.00-26.00

6118 WOODBURY IMPROVED, WGW monogram; *Woodbury Glass Works, Woodbury, N.J.* on bottom; aqua; quart................ 8.00-10.00

6119 WOODBURY IMPROVED; 1885; zinc cap; aqua; three sizes................ 20.00-30.00

6120 WOODBURY; *Woodbury Glass Works Woodbury, N.J. 2* under bottom; aqua; 7" 20.00-25.00

6121 WORCESTER; clear or amber; quart 25.00-45.00

6122 JOSHUA WRIGHT, PHILA.; pontil; barrel type........................... 150.00+

6123 XNOX in center, a block with K in middle, MASON under it; XNOX is an error, should read KNOX; clear; quart 10.00-20.00

6124 YELONE JAR; 1895-1900; glass lid and wire bail; clear..................... 10.00-14.00

6125 YEOMAN'S FRUIT BOTTLE; 1855-1870; wax sealer; small mouth; aqua 30.00-40.00

This arrangement of fruit jars (from left to right) includes
a conveniently shaped Mason jar (#5898), a light blue jar
(#6076) with a half-wire bail and glass lid closure, an early
20th-century Kerr jar (similar to #5840) and a Root Mason
jar (#similar to #6004) with a zinc screw-on cap.

Pottery Bottles, Crocks and Jugs

When the best method known for making glass was blowing it by hand, it was recognized that the ancient process of taking wet clay from the earth and shaping and baking it was a more economical means of making containers. Pottery had several advantages: It kept beverages cooler and it shielded the contents from harmful sunrays.

Pottery containers were being made in this country as early as 1641 by John Pride of Salem. The majority of early pottery bottles were imported, however, mostly from England. The bottles were primitive and, since each was handmade, each was unique. The first settlers in Pennsylvania and Ohio were famous for their pottery—bottles, jugs and mugs of the fired clay held beverages, medicines, condiments and inks. Many early jugs were decorated with flowers, birds, people and, of course, the American eagle.

Chinese immigrants to the United States brought a variety of pottery containers with them. The Chinese worked hard and demanded little, and many were brought to help build the railroads. Others had been beckoned to California by the discovery of gold in 1848. Wherever they settled they formed their own community to maintain their traditions—often arousing the suspicions of American observers.

The Chinese contained their food and household items in earthenware jugs. Western Americans held the belief that these containers were burial urns in which the newcomers shipped the cremated ashes of their dead to China. In reality, the jugs contained pickles or vinegar. Another popular theory, possibly correct, was that the two-inch high medicine bottles held opium. Beverages were also stored in pottery— one Chinese whiskey was ninety-six proof.

Chinese bottles are often highly glazed and colorful, with the several colors running together. Some are embossed with Oriental characters, though most designs were impressed into the clay, rather than embossed.

After the discovery of the role of the microbe in disease-causing bacteria in the late 1800's, it seemed only logical that enterprising medicine sellers would attempt to blame every disease known to

One interesting feature of early 18th-century American pottery containers, such as this (similar to #6148), is that most were marked with a large number indicating the capacity, whether it be pint, quart or gallon. In order for this unusual numbering system to be effective, however, the user had to have a good idea of the container's capacity.

humanity on the organism and then invent cures to do away with it. One of the more infamous of these "cures" was marketed in pottery containers by William Radam, a Prussian immigrant living in Texas. He was granted a patent for his "Microbe Killer" in 1886. The Pure Food and Drug Act of 1907 put an end to his lucrative business. It was discovered that his "cure" was a simple combination of wine and water. Since the wine was only a fraction of one percent of the total contents, he was making a profit of twenty thousand percent.

Most household pottery jars were made in the nineteenth century. Jugs glazed on the inside are later than 1900. The advent of the automatic glassblowing machine in 1903 made glass bottles cheaper and easier to produce, and pottery began to decline in popularity. But pottery containers had inherent disadvantages anyway—it was difficult to determine how much of a substance remained in the jugs or if the insides were clean. Today a collector must exercise extreme caution when purchasing pottery or crocks as it is quite difficult to ascertain what is old and what is in fact new.

6128 6129 6131 6133 6134 6135 6136 6137

6139

6138 6140 6142 6144 6145 6146 6147

6149

6148 6150 6151 6152 6153 6154 6155

6156   6158   6160   6162

6157   6159   6161   6163

6126	ALASKAN YUKON 1909 PACIFIC EXPO. OF SEATTLE; flower on shoulder; jug; 2¾″ 8.00-20.00
6127	P. H. ALDERS, COMPLIMENTS OF THE EAGLE SALOON, ST. JOSEPH, MO.; cream and brown; 3″ 8.00-10.00
6128	Ale, label; tan; 8½″ 8.00-10.00
6129	Ale, label; brown; 6″ 2.00-4.00
6130	THE ALTMAYOR & FLATAU LIQUOR CO., FINE LIQUORS, MACON GA.; round; tan; 6½″ 20.00-30.00
6131	F. A. AMES & CO.; *Owensboro Ky* in back; flat; tan and brown; 3½″ 8.00-12.00
6132	ANDERSON'S WEISS BEERS; 7¼″ 3.00-6.00
6133	ARMOUR & COMPANY, CHICAGO; jug; pouring spout; white; 7¼″ 10.00-20.00
6134	B. & J. ARNOLD, LONDON ENGLAND; *Master Ink*; dark brown; 9″ 8.00-10.00
6135	B & H; cream; 3″ 8.00-12.00
6136	BASS & CO. N.Y.; cream; 9½″ 8.00-10.00
6137	Bean pot, label; light blue; 4¼″ 2.00-4.00
6138	COMPLIMENTS OF BENISS & THOMPSON, SHELBYVILLE, KY; tan and brown; 3¾″ 10.00-15.00
6139	JAS. BENJAMIN, STONEWARE DEPOT, CINCINNATI, O.; blue stencil lettering; mottled tan; 9″ 18.00-20.00
6140	same as above except tan; 13½″ ... 15.00-20.00
6141	Bitter, label; olive, brown trim; 10¼″ 25.00-30.00
6142	B. B. BITTER MINERAL WATER, BOWLING GREEN, MO.; white; five gallon; 15″ 20.00-25.00
6143	BLACK FAMILY LIQUOR STORE stamped in blue glaze; brown and tan; gallon 10.00-12.00

6144	BOSTON BAKED BEANS; *HHH* on back; brick color; 1½″ 2.00-6.00
6145	BOSTON BAKED BEANS; *OK* on back; brick color; 1½″ 2.00-6.00
6146	BOWERS THREE THISTLES SNUFF; cream color with blue lettering; two to three gallon 10.00-30.00
6147	BRYANT & WOODRUFF, PITTSFIELD, ME.; handled jug; blue gray; 7″ 18.00-20.00
6148	Butter crock; no label; handle; blue-gray decoration; 4″ 15.00-25.00
6149	Butter crock; no label; blue-gray decoration; 5¼″ 12.00-15.00
6150	CALIFORNIA POP; *Pat. Dec. 29, 1872*; blob top; tan; 10½″ 60.00-70.00
6151	Canning crock; inscribed *Hold Fast That Which is Good*; dark brown; 6½″ 18.00-20.00
6152	Canning crock; wax sealer; 6″ 18.00-20.00
6153	Canning crock; wax sealer; reddish brown; 8″ 10.00-12.00
6154	Canning crock; blue with a gray decorative design; 8½″ 18.00-20.00
6155	Canning crock; mustard color; 7″ 10.00-12.00
6156	Canning crock; maple leaf design in lid; caramel color; 6″ 6.00-8.00
6157	Canning crock; brown; 5″ 8.00-10.00
6158	Canning crock; wax channel; brown; 8½″ 10.00-12.00
6159	Canning crock; reddish brown, green on the inside; 6¾″ 12.00-14.00
6160	Canning crock; crude; brown; 4″ 6.00-8.00
6161	Canning crock; wax sealer; dark brown; 5½″ 8.00-10.00
6162	Canning crock; wax sealer; tan; 5½″ 8.00-10.00
6163	Canning crock; wax sealer; dark brown; 5½″ 5.00-8.00

6164   6165   6166   6167   6168   6169   6170   617

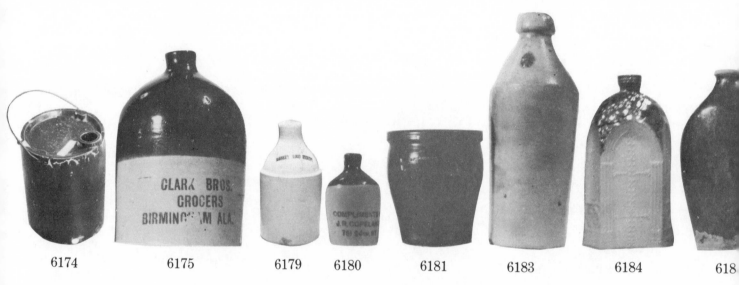

6174   6175   6179   6180   6181   6183   6184   618

6186   6187   6188   6189   6190   6191   6192   6193

| 6194 | 6195 | 6198 | 6199 | 6200 | 6201 |

6164 Canning crock; wax sealer; dark brown; 6½"
.... 5.00-8.00

6165 Canning crock; wax sealer; mottled gray; 5"
.... 4.00-6.00

6166 Canning crock; wax sealer; brown; 5½"
.... 8.00-10.00

6167 Canning crock; barrel; dark brown; 5½"
.... 8.00-10.00

6168 Canning crock; lid; star design; dark brown; 8¾"
.... 12.00-15.00

6169 Canning crock; dark brown; 7½"... 8.00-10.00

6170 Canning crock; tan; 9".......... 10.00-12.00

6171 Canning crock; wax channel; brown; 7½"
.... 10.00-12.00

6172 CHINESE CROCK JUG; vase; wide, flared mouth; black or dark brown; 6"..... 6.00-8.00

6173 same as above, except with *Federal Law Forbids*
.... 2.00-4.00

6174 CLARK BROS.; *Pat. May 17, 1899, Zanesville, Ohio*; brown; 7½"............. 10.00-20.00

6175 CLARK BROS. GROCERS, BIRMINGHAM, ALA.; handle; jug; white and brown; 10½"
.... 12.00-15.00

6176 COMPLIMENTS OF M. A. CLAUTON, 26 FARM ST.; brown and tan; 3".... 8.00-10.00

6177 COMPLIMENTS OF MARTIN COLLINS, CARTERSVILE, GA.; brown and tan; 3"
.... 8.00-12.00

6178 COMPLIMENTS OF COLUMBIA LIQUOR COMPANY, AUGUSTA, GA.; handle; tan and brown; 3"...................... 8.00-15.00

6179 CONNER'S BLOOD REMEDY; cream; 6⅜"
.... 8.00-10.00

6180 COMPLIMENTS OF J.R. COPELAND, 781 24TH ST.; miniature jug; brown and white, blue lettering; 5¼".............. 18.00-20.00

6181 COWDEN & CO., HARRISBURG, PA.; dark brown; 6½"...................... 18.00-20.00

6182 CRAMER'S KIDNEY CURE, ALBANY N.Y.; N's are backward; aqua; 4½"...... 10.00-20.00

6183 Crock bottle; gray; 10"............. 5.00-8.00

6184 Crock, label; cathedral type; brown and tan; 8½"
.... 25.00-30.00

6185 Crock flask; red and brown glaze; 7½"
.... 50.00-100.00

6186 Crock, label; brown, green and tan; 7"
.... 8.00-10.00

6187 Crock, label; light gray; 6½"...... 8.00-12.00

6188 Crock, label; brown; 7"........... 8.00-10.00

6189 Crock with seal; *Amsterdam*; tan; 12"
.... 8.00-10.00

6190 Crock, label; tan and cream; 6¾"..... 6.00-8.00

6191 Crock, label; tan and cream; 5½"..... 6.00-8.00

6192 Crock, plain; ring top; two tone, tan and cream; 8½"............................... 2.00-4.00

6193 Crock, plain; *Kinney* on base; ring top; two tone, tan and cream; 8½"................. 4.00-8.00

6194 Crock, plain; bottle type; tapered crown; cream and tan; 7½"..................... 2.00-6.00

6195 Crock, plain; roof type shoulder; cream and tan; 8".............................. 2.00-4.00

6196 DR. CRONK'S SARSAPARILLA BAR; blob top; sand color; 9½".............. 10.00-20.00

6197 CROWN GINGER BEER CO., CLEVELAND, OHIO in a circle in center; brown; 6¾"
.... 6.00-12.00

6198 CRUISKEEN LAWN; cream and brown; 8"
.... 4.00-10.00

6199 PRESENTED BY, P. J. CURRIN; A MERRY CHRISTMAS AND HAPPY NEW YEAR; pint jug; brown and tan with blue stencil lettering; 6½"..................................... 15.00-20.00

6200 DAWSON SALTS & WATER CO. DISTRIBUTORS HAMBY SALTS, IRON AND LITHIA WATER, DAWSON SPRINGS, KY.; large 5 above; jug; brown and white, blue lettering; 18"
.... 20.00-25.00

6201 D. C.; gray; 11".................. 5.00-8.00

6204   6206   6207   6208   6209   6210   6211   6213

6214   6218   6220   6221   6222   6223   6224   6225

6226   6227   6228   6229   6231   6232   6233   6234

6235   6237   6238

6202 same as above except tan; 10½".... 4.00-6.00

6203 THE D.C.L. SCOTCH WHISKEY DISTILL-ERS LIMITED, LONDON, EDINBURGH, GLASGOW, GOLD MEDALS, EDINBURGH 1886; under bottom *Bengimark, Doulton, Shicon, England* .... 35.00+

6204 GEO. A. DICKEL & CO., CASCADE DIS-TILLERY, HAND MADE SOUR MASH TEN-NESSEE WHISKEY; white with black letter-ing, blue bands; 9½".............. 15.00-18.00

6205 D. J. AND CO., NO. 2A LUMBER STREET, N. YORK, 1795; preserves crock; seal top; salt glaze; 5"........................ 100.00+

6206 A. P. DONAGHHO, PARKERSBURG, W. V.; canning crock; tan, blue stencil; 8" 18.00-20.00

6207 A. P. DONAGHHO, PARKERSBURG, W. V. written at a slant; blue-gray stencil; 8" 18.00-20.00

6208 DOSTER-NORTHINGTON DRUG CO., BIR-MINGHAM, ALA; jug with handle; white and brown; 11"..................... 12.00-15.00

6209 DOSTER-NORTHINGTON DRUG CO., BIR-MINGHAM, ALA; brown and cream; ½ gallon 15.00-25.00

6210 COMPLIMENTS OF A. J. DRESEL, SECOND & MAGNOLIA AVE., LOUISVILLE KY., brown and tan; 2¼" 8.00-12.00

6211 DRINKOMETER in back; tan; 5" .. 4.00-8.00

6212 EAGLE LIQUEUR DIS., CINCINNATI O.; ring top; eagle and shield in center; green; 2¼" 10.00-20.00

6213 EELAARKI, ADRSV., SCHIEDARN; crock with handle; ring around bottom; tan; 4" 4.00-6.00

6214 same as above except 12" 4.00-8.00

6215 ENGLAND NATOINE in two lines on base; four rings near shoulder; spout; brick brown; 10" 4.00-8.00

6216 same as above except in all colors and sizes; some with panels; some with plain tops .. 4.00-10.00

6217 ETRUIA STONE CHIN; *2518* under bottom; syrup label; tan; 6" 10.00-20.00

6218 J. W. M. FIELD & SONS WHOLESALE LI-QUORS, OWENSBORO, KY.; cream; 3¼" 10.00-12.00

6219 FOCKIN, WYNAND, AMSTERDAM; beer jug with handle; tan; 12"............ 8.00-15.00

6220 Football figural; whiskey label; brown; 3¾" x 2½".................................. 10.00-15.00

6221 FOWLKES & MYATT CO. CIDER VINE-GAR; miniature jug; brown and white, blue let-tering; 3" 18.00-20.00

6222 J FRIEDER; hand-painted picture; ring around bottom; tan; 12" 18.00-20.00

6223 same as above except B. FRANKFER 18.00-20.00

6224 G. W. FULPER & BROS., FLEMINGTON, N.J.; tan and blue decorations; 11¼" 20.00-25.00

6225 GALLAGHER & O'GARA, DEALERS IN FINE WHISKEY, BESSEMER, ALA.; tan 8.00-10.00

6226 GALLOWAY'S EVERLASTING JAR; *Pat'd Feb. 8th Pat. Applied for 1870*; canning crock with wax sealer; gray; 7¾"....... 15.00-18.00

6227 Ginger pot; fancy decoration; no lettering; tur-quoise; 3½"..................... 6.00-8.00

6228 Gold Tester; crock; 4" 2.00-4.00

6229 CHARLES S. GOVE COMPANY, WHOLE-SALE LIQUOR DEALERS, BOSTON, MASS.; jug with handle; brown top and cream base; 9" 12.00-15.00

6230 COMPLIMENTS OF H. GRAFF & CO., FRESNO, CAL. in three lines; jug with handle; letters stamped in blue glaze; ivory and dark brown; 3½".................... 15.00-25.00

6231 GRASSELLI ARSENATE OF LEAD; poison crock; cream; 6½".............. 10.00-15.00

6232 THE O. L. GREGORY VINEGAR CO.; tan and brown; 3½".................... 4.00-8.00

6233 HAPPY PATTY; with handle; brown and tan; 8½".................................. 4.00-8.00

6234 I. W. HARPER, NELSON CO., KY.; cream; 3¼".................................. 8.00-12.00

6235 I. W. HARPER, GOLD MEDAL WHISKEY; square base; long twisted neck; cobalt; 8¾" .... 25.00+

6236 W. P. HARTLEY, LIVERPOOL & LONDON; London Tower in center; under it *Trademark Reg.*; eleven panels; tan; 4"........ 4.00-8.00

6237 VINCENT HATHAWAY & CO.; blob top; tan; 9½".................................. 5.00-8.00

6238 HAYNER LOCK, BOX 290, DAYTON, OHIO; white; 8"...................... 15.00-20.00

6239 HELMENT RYE; blue lettering; cream; 3" 8.00-16.00

6240   6241   6242   6243   6244   6245   6246

6247   6249   6250   6251   6253   6254   6255

6256   6257   6258   6259   6261   6262   6263

| 6264 | 6265 | 6266 | 6268 | 6269 | 6270 | 6271 | 6274 |

6240 DISTILLED BY JAMES R. HOGO, JIM WHISKEY, POPLAR BLUFF, MO.; white and brown, blue lettering; 9¾"....... 15.00-18.00

6241 COMPLIMENTS OF HOLBERG, MOBILE AND CINCINNATI; brown and white; 3¼" 6.00-12.00

6242 E. J. HOLLIDGE, label; cream; 6" 7.00-10.00

6243 J. W. HOOPER & BRO., GROCERIES AND LIQUORS NASHVILLE, TENN.; jug; tan with brown top and blue lettering; 8¼" 15.00-20.00

6244 HORTON CATO MFG. CO., DETROIT, MICHIGAN, ROYAL SALAD DRESSING; wide mouth jug; white and brown with black lettering; 10¼" 15.00-18.00

6245 R. M. HUGHES & CO.'S, monogram, VINEGAR; blue label; white; 9¼" 20.00-25.00

6246 HUMPHREY & MARTIN; tan and brown crock; 8¾" 25.00-40.00

6247 Ink crock; conical; light gray; 2¾" .. 4.00-8.00

6248 Ink crockery; round pouring lip; cream; 10¼" 4.00-8.00

6249 Ink crockery; round pouring lip; brown; 7¾" 4.00-8.00

6250 Ink crock, plain; roof type shoulder; pouring lip; 6"................................ 8.00-12.00

6251 Ink crock, plain; tan; 2¾" 4.00-8.00

6252 Ink crock, plain; no neck; round collar; brown; 1¾" round, 1¾" tall 6.00-8.00

6253 Ink crock, label; light gray; 5¾" .. 10.00-20.00

6254 Ink crock, label; tan; 2½" 4.00-8.00

6255 Ink crock, label; tan; 2½" .... 10.00+

6256 Ink crock, label; tan; 2¾" 6.00-10.00

6257 Ink crock, label; tan; 7"........... 6.00-8.00

6258 Ink crock, label; cream; 5" 4.00-8.00

6259 Ink pottery; light blue; short neck .. 6.00-8.00

6260 Ink pottery; some have embossing; brick brown; 10".................................... 6.00-8.00

6261 Ink pottery; plain; conical; light gray; 2¾" around bottom, 2⅛" tall;........... 4.00-8.00

6262 same as above except brown........ 4.00-8.00

6263 Ink pottery; plain; ring top; light brown; 1¾" round, ¼" neck 6.00-8.00

6264 JONES BROS. & CO.; brown and tan; 3½" 2.00-6.00

6265 JONES BROS., COMPLIMENTS OF J. CARR MFG.'S OF HIGH GRADE CIDER & VING., LOUISVILLE, KY.; tan and cream; 3½" 6.00-12.00

6266 Jug; very crude bell shape; red and tan; 7" 6.00-8.00

6267 KAEHLER BROS., FRESNO CAL. in a circle with a medicine trademark; ivory and brown; gallon.......................... 10.00-20.00

6268 JAMES KEILLER & SONS, DUNDEE MARMALADE, LONDON, 1862, GREAT BRITAIN; gray; 4" 6.00-8.00

6269 KENNEDY; tan and beige; 8½" 8.00-10.00

6270 THE KINTORE; cream and brown; 8¼" 4.00-10.00

6271 C.B. KIRBY, LATE R. CROOK & CO., HERVEY STREET, IPSWICH; tan and cream; two gallon..................... 15.00-25.00

6272 J.W. KOLB & SON, 4471 ST. LOUIS AVE., ST. LOUIS, MO.; jug; stamped letters; dark brown and cream; 3¼" 5.00-8.00

6273 RETURN TO KUTNER & GOLDSTEIN & CO., WHOLESALE GROCERS, FRESNO, CALIF.; wire handle; cream; gallon 10.00-15.00

6274 LAMBRECHT in script, BUTTER; white and blue lettering; 2⅞"............... 5.00-8.00

6275 LITTLE BROWN JUG; engraved; brown pottery; 2¾"...................... 4.00-8.00

6276 LITTLE BROWN JUG 1876; dark brown; 3" 8.00-15.00

6277 6279 6280 6281 6282 6283 6284 6285

6286 6287 6288 6291 6292 6294 6295

6297 6298 6300 6301 6302 6305 6307 6308

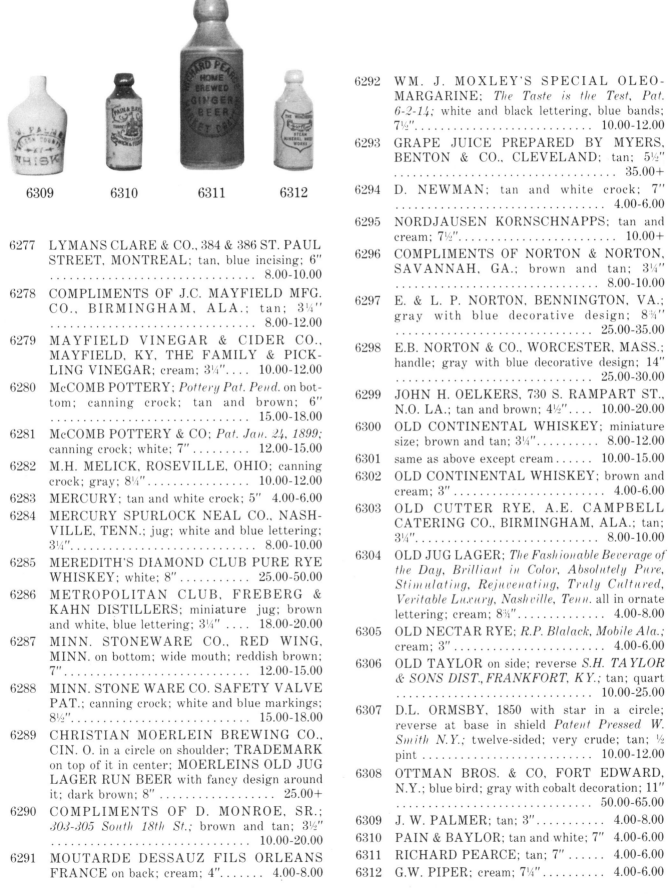

6309   6310   6311   6312

6277 LYMANS CLARE & CO., 384 & 386 ST. PAUL STREET, MONTREAL; tan, blue incising; 6" 8.00-10.00

6278 COMPLIMENTS OF J.C. MAYFIELD MFG. CO., BIRMINGHAM, ALA.; tan; 3¼" 8.00-12.00

6279 MAYFIELD VINEGAR & CIDER CO., MAYFIELD, KY, THE FAMILY & PICKLING VINEGAR; cream; 3¼".... 10.00-12.00

6280 McCOMB POTTERY; *Pottery Pat. Pend.* on bottom; canning crock; tan and brown; 6" 15.00-18.00

6281 McCOMB POTTERY & CO; *Pat. Jan. 24, 1899*; canning crock; white; 7" 12.00-15.00

6282 M.H. MELICK, ROSEVILLE, OHIO; canning crock; gray; 8¼" 10.00-12.00

6283 MERCURY; tan and white crock; 5" 4.00-6.00

6284 MERCURY SPURLOCK NEAL CO., NASHVILLE, TENN.; jug; white and blue lettering; 3¼" 8.00-10.00

6285 MEREDITH'S DIAMOND CLUB PURE RYE WHISKEY; white; 8" 25.00-50.00

6286 METROPOLITAN CLUB, FREBERG & KAHN DISTILLERS; miniature jug; brown and white, blue lettering; 3¼" 18.00-20.00

6287 MINN. STONEWARE CO., RED WING, MINN. on bottom; wide mouth; reddish brown; 7" 12.00-15.00

6288 MINN. STONE WARE CO. SAFETY VALVE PAT.; canning crock; white and blue markings; 8½" 15.00-18.00

6289 CHRISTIAN MOERLEIN BREWING CO., CIN. O. in a circle on shoulder; TRADEMARK on top of it in center; MOERLEINS OLD JUG LAGER RUN BEER with fancy design around it; dark brown; 8" .... 25.00+

6290 COMPLIMENTS OF D. MONROE, SR.; *303-305 South 18th St.*; brown and tan; 3½" 10.00-20.00

6291 MOUTARDE DESSAUZ FILS ORLEANS FRANCE on back; cream; 4"....... 4.00-8.00

6292 WM. J. MOXLEY'S SPECIAL OLEO-MARGARINE; *The Taste is the Test, Pat. 6-2-14*; white and black lettering, blue bands; 7½" 10.00-12.00

6293 GRAPE JUICE PREPARED BY MYERS, BENTON & CO., CLEVELAND; tan; 5½" .... 35.00+

6294 D. NEWMAN; tan and white crock; 7" 4.00-6.00

6295 NORDJAUSEN KORNSCHNAPPS; tan and cream; 7½" .... 10.00+

6296 COMPLIMENTS OF NORTON & NORTON, SAVANNAH, GA.; brown and tan; 3¼" 8.00-10.00

6297 E. & L. P. NORTON, BENNINGTON, VA.; gray with blue decorative design; 8¾" 25.00-35.00

6298 E.B. NORTON & CO., WORCESTER, MASS.; handle; gray with blue decorative design; 14" 25.00-30.00

6299 JOHN H. OELKERS, 730 S. RAMPART ST., N.O. LA.; tan and brown; 4½".... 10.00-20.00

6300 OLD CONTINENTAL WHISKEY; miniature size; brown and tan; 3¼" 8.00-12.00

6301 same as above except cream 10.00-15.00

6302 OLD CONTINENTAL WHISKEY; brown and cream; 3" 4.00-6.00

6303 OLD CUTTER RYE, A.E. CAMPBELL CATERING CO., BIRMINGHAM, ALA.; tan; 3¼" 8.00-10.00

6304 OLD JUG LAGER; *The Fashionable Beverage of the Day, Brilliant in Color, Absolutely Pure, Stimulating, Rejuvenating, Truly Cultured, Veritable Luxury, Nashville, Tenn.* all in ornate lettering; cream; 8¾" 4.00-8.00

6305 OLD NECTAR RYE; *R.P. Blalack, Mobile Ala.*; cream; 3" 4.00-6.00

6306 OLD TAYLOR on side; reverse *S.H. TAYLOR & SONS DIST., FRANKFORT, KY.*; tan; quart 10.00-25.00

6307 D.L. ORMSBY, 1850 with star in a circle; reverse at base in shield *Patent Pressed W. Smith N.Y.*; twelve-sided; very crude; tan; ½ pint 10.00-12.00

6308 OTTMAN BROS. & CO, FORT EDWARD, N.Y.; blue bird; gray with cobalt decoration; 11" 50.00-65.00

6309 J. W. PALMER; tan; 3" 4.00-8.00

6310 PAIN & BAYLOR; tan and white; 7" 4.00-6.00

6311 RICHARD PEARCE; tan; 7" 4.00-6.00

6312 G.W. PIPER; cream; 7¼" 4.00-6.00

6313   6314   6315   6316   6317   6320   6321   632

6323   6325   6329   6330   6331   6333   6334   6336

6337   6338   6339   6340   6341   6342   6344   6345

| 6346 | 6347 | 6348 | 6349 |

6313 M. QUINN, WHOLESALE GROCER, KANSAS CITY, MO.; wire handle with wooden grip; white with blue lettering; 10".... 12.00-15.00

6314 WM. RADAM'S MICROBE KILLER NO. 1; handle on jug; white with blue lettering; 10¾"
.... 20.00-25.00

6315 RANDOLPH & CO.; brown and tan; 3"
.... 2.00-6.00

6316 THEO RECTANUS CO.; *Pure Old Hand Made Sour Mash Louisville*; brown and cream; 3¼"
.... 4.00-6.00

6317 RELIABLE MIDDLE QUALITY FRUIT PRESERVES; gray with black lettering; 6"
.... 12.00-15.00

6318 JACOB RICHTER CO., FRESNO, CAL.; *Best Wines & Liquors $5 per gal.* in four lines; brown and ivory; gallon............... 25.00-35.00

6319 H.E.N. ROSS in a circle; in a circle under it a cross and *Cross Flag;* under it in one line *Phein Preussen; Pottery* or *Crock* on shoulder; handle; tan; 12" tall, 3¼" round.......... 4.00-10.00

6320 SANFORD'S INKS, THE QUALITY LINE PASTES; jug with pouring spout; white with blue lettering; 10½"............. 18.00-20.00

6321 SATTERLEE & MORY, FT. EDWARDS, N.Y.; gray with blue decorative design; 7½"
.... 20.00-25.00

6322 JAMES SCHAM; *Pat. July 13, 1909;* embossed *Sherwood;* canning crock; glass lid; white; 7½"
.... 8.00-10.00

6323 CHRISTIAN SCHMIDT, SHENANDOAH, PA.; cream; 7" 8.00-10.00

6324 COMP. OF H. SCHRODER, 401 & 403 BROUGHTON; brown and tan; 3½" 8.00-10.00

6325 FRED L. SCHWANTZ, UP-TO-DATE GROCER, FINE LIQUOR, 63 BEALE ST. MEMPHIS, TENN.; jug; tan with brown top; 8½"............................ 20.00-25.00

6326 SCOTLAND EXPORT CO. LTD. CHIVAS REGAL; tan; 12".................. 30.00+

6327 B. J. SIMOND'S; blob top; 10" ... 30.00-50.00

6328 D. F. SMITH & SNOWS; *Whitefoot, Pat. July 17, 66;* blob top; tan; 10"........ 30.00-50.00

6329 J. L. SMITH inside under lip; crude Southern pottery; brown; 11" 12.00-15.00

6330 SMOKY MT. 1880; vinegar jar; brown; 5"
.... 8.00-10.00

6331 COMP. OF SOUTHERN GRO. CO., 114 BERNARD ST.; brown and tan; 3½" ... 8.00-12.00

6332 SOY SAUCE; pottery jug; short neck; ring top; side spout; brown; 5".............. 6.00-8.00

6333 W. M. SPENCER; *Clarks improved, Pat. May 19th 92, Zanesville, Ohio* on bottom; white with blue lettering; 9"................. 18.00-20.00

6334 STONE MASON PAT'D. APPLIED FOR on shoulder; canning crock; tan and brown
.... 12.00-15.00

6335 THE WEIR STONEWALL FRUIT JAR, PAT. 1892; tan and brown; 6½"........ 10.00-15.00

6336 E. SWASEY & CO., PORTLAND, ME.; butter crock; white and brown; 3½" 10.00-12.00

6337 DR. SWETT'S ORIGINAL ROOT BEER, REGISTERED, BOSTON, MASS.; brown and tan; 7¾" 6.00-8.00

6338 E. B. TAYLOR, RICHMOND VA. at an angle; gray with blue stencil lettering; 8" 18.00-20.00

6339 TODE BROS; *T.B.* and arrow through a ring on bottom; dark tan................. 4.00-6.00

6340 N.M.URI & CO. R.H. PARKER; tan; 2¾"
.... 2.00-6.00

6341 Vase, label; 3½".................. 3.00-4.00

6342 Voodoo face jug; *2* under bottom; gray; 6" x 6"
.... 40.00+

6343 WALKDENS COPYING INK; salt glaze; 7½"
.... 100.00+

6344 WATERLOW & SONS, LIMITED; brown; 7½"
.... 10.00-12.00

6345 WESSON OIL; blue lettering; 5" 10.00-12.00

6346 WESTERN STONEWARE CO.; *Pat. Jan 24, 1899* on bottom; brown and tan; 7" 12.00-15.00

6347 WEYMANS SNUFF on base; tan; 6¾"
.... 10.00-20.00

6348 same as above except cream...... 10.00-20.00

6349 Whiskey, label; tan and cream; 4".. 8.00-15.00

6350   6351   6352   6355   6356

6350 N. A. WHITE & SONS, UTICA, N.Y.; blue iris
     flower on front; tan; 6¾"......... 20.00-25.00
6351 WHITE-HALL, W. H. monogram; *S. P. & S. Co.
     Whitehall, Ill.*; canning crock; 7".. 18.00-20.00
6352 WING LEE WAI, HONG KONG under bottom;
     CHINESE RICE WINE; *Federal Law Forbids
     Sale or Re Use of This Bottle* on back; brown; 6"
     .... 8.00-10.00
6353 WOAPOLLINARIS-BRANNEN; M with an
     anchor in center of the seal; under it CEBRY
     KREUYBER AHR WEILER, RHEIN
     PRAUSSE; under it #65; handle; tan; 12"
     .... 14.00-18.00
6354 COMP. OF WORRELL & FOSTER, WEST
     END, ALA.; tan and brown; 3¼".. 8.00-12.00
6355 X on shoulder; brown pottery; 6½" tall, 3¾"
     diameter 4.00-6.00
6356 COMPLIMENTS OF MRS. J. M. YOCKERS,
     500 WILKINSON ST.; tan and cream; 3¼"
     .... 6.00-12.00

*This early 19th-century stoneware jug (similar to
#6147) is typical of most in that it was delightfully
painted with heat-resistant cobalt blue coloring, one
of the few coloring additives that could withstand
the high temperatures of firing stoneware.*

*This earthenware crock (#6151-#6171) of the early 1800's has a
granular or pitted surface, the result of salt glazing. During firing, common
salt was thrown into the kiln. The intense heat turned the salt to vapor, releasing
chlorine and leaving the soda to combine with the acid in the clay.
This results in a crock that is extremely hard and acid resistant.*

Ink

Ink has been a part of man's civilization, aiding it in organization and communication. The Egyptians and Chinese used it as early as 2500 B.C., and in the first century B.C., ink was made from mixing glue with coal. People of that era were fascinated by the cuttlefish, or ink fish, a clever creature that ejects a black fluid to conceal itself when endangered. The Romans managed to extract the liquid from the fish's pouch and use it as ink.

The first patent for the manufacture of ink was granted in England in 1792. The first American patent was granted to the firm of Maynard and Noyes in Boston in 1816. Since England and France were famous for their high quality inks, the first ink in the United States was imported. Most of the bottles were crudely fashioned of pottery, usually brown or white in color. The first American-made master bottles—bottles that contained a pint or quart of ink and were used primarily to store ink—were of poor quality glass containing many bubbles and tears.

The ink industry in America had difficulty catching on partly because of a lack of effective writing instruments. Quills—feathers fashioned into pens by pointing and slitting the lower end—were used well into the 1850's, though other innovations preceded them. Peregine Williamson of Baltimore invented a metal pen in 1809 but it did not find widespread acceptance until 1858. In that year Richard Esterbrook opened a factory to produce the pens in Camden, New Jersey. They were not an immediate success—they had to be dipped in the ink often which frequently resulted in messy ink spills at the writing tables. American engineering and ingenuity were set to work to come up with an ink bottle that would not topple. This resulted in over one thousand types of ink bottles, many designed not to tip. Umbrella-shaped ink bottles were a popular shape as were the teakettle shapes, complete with pouring spouts. Other shapes included turtles, barrels, shoes, buildings, boats, schoolhouses and cathedrals.

Three prime examples of ink bottles designed not to tip and spill are (left to right), an umbrella-shaped ink bottle (#6742), circa 1800-1850; an "Underwood Inks" (#6755), circa 1880-1900; and a sheared-lip bottle (#6529), often referred to as an igloo ink, circa 1800-1850.

The first ink bottles were fancy since they adorned the writing table. D. Hyde of Reading, Pennsylvania, invented the fountain pen in 1830. Upon its commercial manufacture in 1884, the extravagance of fancy ink bottles became unnecessary since small and round or square ink containers could be conveniently placed in a drawer. Many ink bottles were embossed, and the paper labels, when used, were ornate.

The familiar Carter ink bottle was first manufactured by William Carter in Massachusetts in 1858. A few Carter bottles were of pottery, but they were expensive—particularly when so many broke in transit—and their manufacture was discontinued.

6360   6364   6367   6373   6374   6375   6376   6392

6393   6397   6398   6399   6400   6405   6406   6409

6410   6411   6417

6357   ALLING'S; sheared top and teapot spout; green; 2¼" 8.00-12.00

6358   ALLING'S INK; triangular; green; 1⅞" x 2¼" 20.00-30.00

6359   ALONZO FRENCH; barrel; *Pat. March 1st. 1870;* aqua; 2" tall, 2" long 30.00-40.00

6360   ANGUS & CO.; cone; aqua; 3½" 4.00-6.00

6361   ANTOINE ET FILS; straight top with pouring lip; brown pottery; 8⅜" 6.00-8.00

6362   P & J ARNOLD; collar with pouring lip; brown; 9¼" 10.00-12.00

6363 ARNOLD'S; round; clear or amethyst; 2½" 4.00-6.00

6364 A3; *Pat July 9, 1895* under bottom; aqua; 2¼" 6.00-8.00

6365 B & B; pottery bottle; tan; 7½" 4.00-8.00

6366 Bell; sheared top; clear or amethyst; 3" 4.00-6.00

6367 Bell, label; crock; double ring top; tan 10.00-20.00

6368 BERTINGUIOT; sheared top; amber; 2" 18.00-30.00

6369 BILLING & CO.; *Banker's Writing Ink*; *B* in center; aqua; 2" x 1½" 4.00-10.00

6370 BILLING & CO.; *Banker's Writing Ink*; *B* embossed in center on bottom; aqua; 2".. 4.00-6.00

6371 BILLINGS, J. T. & SON; sheared top; aqua; 1⅞" 4.00-8.00

6372 BILLINGS/MAUVE INK near base; dome shaped; sheared top; aqua; 1¾" tall, 2¹¹⁄₁₆" deep base 10.00-20.00

6373 S. M. BIXBY & CO.; aqua; 2½" 10.00-20.00

6374 BIXBY on bottom; aqua; 2½" 2.00-4.00

6375 BIXBY on bottom; clear or amethyst; 2½" 2.00-3.00

6376 BIXBY under bottom; ink or polish; *Patented Mch, 83* under shoulder; square base; round corners slanting upward so the bottle gradually becomes round; bulbous shoulder; amber; 4" tall; 1⅛" base 4.00-8.00

6377 same as above except plain, no BIXBY 2.00-6.00

6378 BIXLEY MUSHROOM INK; aqua; 2" 15.00-20.00

6379 C. BLACKMAN; green; 2½" 10.00-20.00

6380 Boat shaped; plain; blue; 1¾" 4.00-6.00

6381 same as above except clear 4.00-6.00

6382 BONNEY BARREL INK; aqua; 2½" 10.00-20.00

6383 BONNEY CONE INK; *Bonney Premium French Ink, South Hanover, Mass*; aqua; 2½" 30.00-50.00

6384 W. E. BONNEY INK, SOUTH HANOVER, MASS; aqua; 2¼" 8.00-10.00

6385 W. E. BONNEY; aqua; 2½" x 3" x 1½" 13.00-16.00

6386 J. BOURNE & SONS NEAR DERBY on base; *Carter's Ink*; tan; 7" 8.00-15.00

6387 J. BOURNE & SON, PATENTEES, DERBY POTTERY NEAR DERBY, P. J. ARNOLD, LONDON, ENGLAND embossed near the base; pottery; round; pouring spout lip; light brown; 9½" tall, 3¾" diameter 6.00-8.00

6388 BOURNE DERBY; crock; brown; 8½" 4.00-6.00

6389 BRICKETT J. TAYLOR INK; cylindrical; flared lip; 4½" 100.00-150.00

6390 D. B. BROOKS & CO. INK; blue green; 2⅛" 8.00-12.00

6391 D. B. BROOKS & CO.; amber; 2" x 2½" 15.00-25.00

6392 Bulldog head; milk glass; 4" .... 50.00+

6393 J. J. BUTLER; aqua; 2" 6.00-8.00

6394 CALUMBINE INK between four pointed stars; ring top; aqua; 1¾" x 1½" x 1½" .... 15.00+

6395 CARDINAL BIRD INK; turtle; aqua; 60.00-70.00

6396 CARDINELL INK OU TRADE MARK, MONTCLAIR, N.J.; *Cardinell Erado Trade Mark Montclair, N.J.* on back; square; collar; ABM; amber; 1" x 2⅛" 2.00-4.00

6397 CARTER; *#11* under bottom; aqua; 2½" 2.00-6.00

6398 CARTER under bottom; milk glass; 3" 6.00-10.00

6399 CARTER INK; *Made in U.S.A.* under bottom; tea kettle; clear; 2½" x 4" .... 10.00+

6400 CARTER INK; clear or amethyst; 2¼" 2.00-4.00

6401 CARTER'S on bottom; double V band collar; ring on shoulder and base; round; aqua or amethyst; 2⅝" 3.00-4.00

6402 same as above except CARTER'S 7½ MADE IN USA on bottom; aqua 4.00-6.00

6403 CARTER'S on bottom; cone; large and small raised ring at base of neck; two round bands on collar; aqua; 2½" x 2⅞" 4.00-6.00

6404 CARTER'S on lid; screw-on top; *13* embossed on bottom; clear; 1⅛" 4.00-6.00

6405 CARTER'S; cobalt; 6½" 6.00-8.00

6406 CARTER'S; eight panels; aqua; 1¾" 4.00-8.00

6407 CARTER'S on shoulder; three-part mold; ring collar and pouring lip; light green; pint 8.00-16.00

6408 CARTER'S; one ring tapers at neck; round base; amethyst; 2¼" 2.00-4.00

6409 CARTER'S; three dots close together under bottom; aqua; 2½" 2.00-6.00

6410 CARTER'S FULL ½ PINT on shoulder; applied ring; round; aqua; 6¼" 5.00-12.00

6411 CARTER'S on back; *Full ½ Pint* on bottom; *Pat Feb. 14-99*; 6" tall, 2½" round 4.00-10.00

6412 CARTER'S FULL QUART on top shoulder; under that *Made in U.S.A.*; aqua; 9½" 6.00-10.00

6413 CARTER'S FULL QUART, MADE IN U.S.A. around shoulder; *Pat. Feb. 14, 99* on base; round; applied lip; aqua; 9⅝" 8.00-15.00

6414 CARTER'S; *House Ink*; turtle; double door with two windows on dome near spout, *Ink*, and below that, *Carter's* .... 100.00+

6415 CARTER'S INK; plain; three-part mold; round; pouring lip; light green; ½ pint, quart; 10¼" tall, 3" bottom, 2¼" neck 8.00-16.00

6416 same as above except ring collar; two-part mold 8.00-16.00

6417 CARTER'S INK MADE IN U.S.A. under bottom, label; aqua; 2¾" 4.00-6.00

6419   6422   6425   6432   6433   6435   6437

6439   6441   6443   6444   6447   6448

6449   6458   6460   6461   6464   6465   6466

6418 CARTER'S INK CO.; two bottles, one in the shape of a man and one in the shape of a woman; woman has red blouse, red and white skirt, black shoes, yellow hair, and rolling pin in her left hand; man has tan trousers, blue jacket and red tie; 3⅝"........................ 25.00-40.00

6419 CARTER'S KOAL BLK INK, label; machine made; clear; 2".................. 2.00-4.00

6420 CARTER'S MADE IN U.S.A. on shoulder; also *Full Qt. Bulk Ink*; aqua; 9¾"........ 3.00-6.00

6421 CARTER'S; on base *Made in U.S.A. 1897*; round base; tapers at neck; one ring; green or aqua; 2½" tall, base 2⅜"........... 3.00-7.00

6422 same as above except brown........ 8.00-12.00

6423 CARTER'S / NON-COPYING / CARMINE / WRITING / FLUID imprinted on jug; *The Carter's Ink Co.*; seal, powderhorn, etc.; brown and tan glaze; gallon........... 15.00-30.00

6424 CARTER'S NO. 1 on base; round; cobalt blue; 32 fluid ounces; 9½"............. 5.00-10.00

6425 CARTER'S NO. 5 MADE IN U.S.A. on bottom; machine made; clear or amethyst... 2.00-4.00

6426 CARTER'S NO. 5 MADE IN USA on bottom; ring collar; large ring forms shoulder; cone; ABM; amethyst; 2½"............. 2.00-4.00

6427 CARTER'S #6 MADE IN USA on bottom; round; ring collar; ring on shoulder and base; aqua; 2½" diameter, 3" tall........ 3.00-5.00

6428 CARTER'S #6½ MADE IN USA on bottom; 16 FLUID OZ. on shoulder; sheared type collar and ring on neck; bulbous shoulder; ring at base; round; ABM; amethyst; 3" diameter, 7½" tall 6.00-10.00

6429 CARTER'S #9 MADE IN USA on bottom; double ring collar; step on shoulder; amethyst; 2"x 2" x 2"............................. 2.00-4.00

6430 CARTER'S #9 on bottom; ring collar; ABM; square; clear; 2"................. 2.00-3.00

6431 CARTER'S 1897 on bottom; cone; wide and narrow raised rings; rings at base of neck; narrow, round band collar; aqua; 2½"....... 4.00-6.00

6432 CARTER'S 1897 MADE IN U.S.A. under bottom; cone; aqua.................. 6.00-7.00

6433 CARTER'S 1897 MADE IN U.S.A. under bottom; cone; emerald.............. 7.00-10.00

6434 CARTER'S PENCRAFT COMBINED OFFICE & FOUNTAIN PEN FLUID; clear; 7½" 4.00-8.00

6435 CARTER'S PRO WRITING FLUID, label; machine made; *G 11 Sk No. 1* under bottom; on shoulder, *32 Fl. Oz.*; cobalt; 9½".... 8.00-15.00

6436 CARTER'S RYTO PERMANENT; *Blue-black ink for fountain pen and general use, The Carter's Ink Co.*; *Carter* embossed near base; *The Cathedral*, label; 9¾"....... 30.00-40.00

6437 CARTER'S 2 C-101 under bottom; cathedral type; in bottom of each window *Ca*; machine made; cobalt blue; 10".............. 18.00+

6438 same as above except 8".......... 25.00+

6439 CAW'S BLACK FLUID INK; light blue; 7¾" 20.00-25.00

6440 CAW'S INK; *New York* on one side; circle on top of shoulder with raised square on top of circle; clear, aqua or light blue; 2¼" x 1¾" . 2.00-4.00

6441 CAW'S INK; aqua; 3½" x 2" x 2"... 4.00-8.00

6442 CHALLENGE; green; 2¾"........ 4.00-10.00

6443 CHASE BROS. *Excelsior Office Ink, Haverhill, Mass.*, label; under bottom *Feb. 15, 1886*; cobalt; 9"........................ 8.00-15.00

6444 CLAR-O-TYPE CLEANER, label; *Clar-O-Type* embossed on each side; *3* under bottom; cobalt; 2½"..................... 3.00-6.00

6445 CLIMAX on shoulder; machine made; square; curved bottom; clear; 3¾"......... 4.00-6.00

6446 THE CLUB INK CARTER HEXAGONAL; four-leaf clover; cobalt; 4 ounces.. 15.00-30.00

6447 Confederate hat ink well; copper and tin; 3¾" x 1½"................................ 30.00-50.00

6448 CONQUEROR, label; blue or aqua; 2¼" 12.00-15.00

6449 CONTINENTAL JET BLACK INK MFG. CO., PHILADELPHIA, label; two dots under bottom; clear....................... 3.00-6.00

6450 CONTINENTAL INK; long tapered collar and pouring lip; aqua; 7¾"............. 8.00-10.00

6451 COVENTRY GEOMETRIC INK; open pontil; amber; 1⅝"..................... 60.00-70.00

6452 CROSS PEN CO.; aqua; 2¾"...... 10.00-12.00

6453 CROSS PEN CO. INK; CPC trademark; aqua; 2¾"............................. 8.00-10.00

6454 APPLE GREEN CROSS PEN CO., embossed monogram; 2½".................... 8.00-10.00

6455 CURRIER & HALL, CONCORD, N.H. POT INK; brown; quart.............. 20.00-40.00

6456 CURRIER & HALL POTTERY MASTER INK; two-tone label............. 8.00-10.00

6457 CURRIER & HALL'S INK, CONCORD, N.H.; *1840*, label; twelve-sided; open pontil; aqua; 2½" 20.00-40.00

6458 DAVID'S ELECTRO CHEMICAL WRITING FLUID, label; *M 3* under bottom; machine made; cobalt blue; 9"............ 10.00-15.00

6459 DAVID'S TURTLE INK; green.. 20.00-40.00

6460 T. DAVID'S & CO.; aqua; 1¾"..... 4.00-6.00

6461 THAD DAVID'S CO. N.Y. on bottom; amber; 2¾"............................. 4.00-6.00

6462 THAD DAVID'S INK; beveled edges; slope shoulder; green; 1¾" square........ 4.00-8.00

6463 THADDEUS DAVID'S CO.; pinched pouring lip; clear; 6⅜".................... 10.00-15.00

6464 THADDEUS DAVID'S & CO., label; *Writing Fluid, New York*; cream crock; 5¾" 25.00-35.00

6465 DAVIES; sheared top; *Patd Sept 4-80* under bottom; clear or amethyst; 2½".... 25.00-40.00

6466 W.A. DAVIS CO. in back; U.S. TREASURY on front shoulder; clear or amethyst ... 8.00-12.00

6467 W.A. DAVIS; clear; 2¼".......... 3.00-5.00

6469   6470   6472   6490   6494   6495   6497

6501   6502   6505   6507   6508   6509   6511

6516   6530   6533

6468   W.A. DAVIS CO/BOSTON, MASS/U.S.A. embossed on shoulder; decorated cylinder with sixteen curved panels at top of body, and sixteen near base of body; base pedestal flared; double rings at base of neck; mold lines end at base of neck; flared ring on lip; greenish aqua; 8" 8.00-15.00

6469   DIAMOND & ONYX; aqua; 9" 6.00-12.00

6470   DIAMOND & ONYX; aqua; 9¼" 2.00-6.00

6471   DIAMOND & ONYX; aqua; 3" 3.00-5.00

6472   DIAMOND INK CO., MILWAUKEE in a circle under bottom; pinch type bottle; in each pinch a diamond; round ring on shoulder; ring at base; clear; ½" neck.................... 8.00-12.00

6473   DIAMOND INK CO., MILWAUKEE on base; *Patented Dec 1st, 03; No. 622;* square; amethyst; 1⅝" 3.00-5.00

6474   DIAMOND INK CO.; clear; 1½" 3.00-5.00

6475 DIAMOND INK CO.; wash pen point; one large and small connected jar........... 8.00-15.00

6476 DOULTON, LAMBETH; pouring lip; brown pottery; 4½"................. 5.00-10.00

6477 DOVELL'S PATENT; cone; blue; 2½"................. 3.00-6.00

6478 S.O. DUNBAR; stopper or cork; aqua; 2½"................. 5.00-10.00

6479 S.O. DUNBAR, TARINTON; cone; eight-sided; open pontil; aqua 15.00-30.00

6480 S.O. DUNBAR, TAUNTON; cone; eight-sided; open pontil; aqua 15.00-30.00

6481 S.O. DUNBAR, TAUNTON, MASS; round; graduated collar; aqua; 5¾" tall, 2¾" diameter 8.00-10.00

6482 EARLES INK CO.; pouring lip; crock; beige; 6⅛"................. 4.00-10.00

6483 E.B.; inside threads; cone; clear or amethyst; 2⅛"................. 4.00-6.00

6484 E D I S O N   F O U N T A I N   P E N   I N K, PETERSBURG VA.; under bottom *A.C.W. 232*; ring tip and neck; square; clear..... 6.00-10.00

6485 ESBINS INDELIBLE INK; aqua; small bottle 4.00-6.00

6486 ESTES, N.Y. INK; pontil; aqua; 6¾"... 10.00+

6487 FARLEY'S INK; open pontil; olive or amber; 2" x 2" 85.00-100.00

6488 FARLEY'S INK; eight-sided; open pontil; aqua; 2" x 2"................. 60.00-70.00

6489 L.P. FARLEY CO.; sheared top; dark green; 2" .... 15.00+

6490 FINE BLACK WRITING INK, label; pontil; aqua; 5"................. 10.00+

6491 H.B. FORSTER; aqua; 7¾"....... 6.00-10.00

6492 PATENT FORTSCHMITT, CANADA; long metal cap with *P*; clear; 6".......... 35.00+

6493 FOUNTAIN INK CO., N.Y., USA; clear; 3½" 8.00-15.00

6494 FOXBORO; clear; 2½".......... 2.00-8.00

6495 FRANKLIN INK; aqua; 4" long, 2" at tallest part................. 15.00+

6496 FRENCH INK CO., HANOVER, MASS 30.00-50.00

6497 FULLER'S BANNER INK, DECATUR, ILL.; aqua; 8" 10.00-20.00

6498 GATES; round; clear; 6" 1.00-2.00

6499 Geometric ink well; *Coventry Black Glass;* round open pontil; dark olive amber or olive green; 1½" x 2½"................. 75.00-125.00

6500 GLENN & CO.; round; clear; 1⅝" .. 8.00-10.00

6501 Glue or ink, label; clear; 2¾" 2.00-4.00

6502 Glue or ink, label; eight panels; aqua 6.00-10.00

6503 G.M.W.C.A.A.S.; turtle; ink pen rest slot; oval; aqua................. 8.00-12.00

6504 GREENWOOD'S; sheared top; under bottom *Patd March 22, 92*; tapered; clear or aqua green; 1½"................. 6.00-10.00

6505 HALEY INK CO.; aqua; 2¾" 6.00-8.00

6506 same as above except clear.......... 4.00-6.00

6507 HALEY INK CO., MADE IN USA; two rings on shoulder; four rings on base; clear or amethyst; 6¾" 8.00-10.00

6508 same as above except brass spout; aqua 10.00-15.00

6509 HARRIS INK, label; pontil; black glass; 10½" 10.00-15.00

6510 HARRISON'S COLA INK 2; open pontil; aqua 40.00-60.00

6511 HARRISON'S COLUMBIAN INK; eight panels; pontil; aqua; 2"......... 10.00-20.00

6512 HARRISON'S/COLUMBIAN/INK; eight-sided squat; open pontil; aqua; 1¾" tall, 1¾" base 40.00-50.00

6513 HARRISON'S COLUMBIAN INK; open pontil; cobalt; 1½" x 1½" 100.00-125.00

6514 HARRISON'S/COLUMBIAN/INK embossed vertically on three of twelve panels; *Patent* embossed on shoulder; iron pontil; aqua; 7½" x 4" .... 25.00+

6515 HARRISON'S/COLUMBIAN/INK; open pontil; aqua; 3⅛" x 1½".................. 40.00+

6516 CHAS. M. HIGGINS & CO.; aqua; 7½" 4.00-8.00

6517 HIGGINS DRAWING INK under bottom; machine made; clear; 3".......... 2.00-4.00

6518 HIGGINS INKS, BROOKLYN, N.Y. on bottom; round; squat; clear; 3¾" 4.00-6.00

6519 same as above except ABM 2.00-3.00

6520 HIGGINS INKS, BROOKLYN, N.Y.; round; amethyst or clear; 2"............... 2.00-6.00

6521 H.J.H. WRITING INK; *B.B.* on panels; sheared top; clear or aqua; 2½" 15.00-25.00

6522 HOGAN & THOMPSON; *Phila.;* cone; open pontil; aqua; 2" x ⅜" 50.00-75.00

6523 JOHN HOLLAND, CINCINNATI; square bottle with rounded corners; ring top and neck; aqua; 2¼" 4.00-6.00

6524 HOOKER'S; sheared top; round; aqua; 2" 8.00-10.00

6525 HOUSE INK; light blue; 2⅞" 4.00-6.00

6526 HOVER, PHILA. on two panels; eight panels; umbrella shape; aqua; 2" 25.00-50.00

6527 HUNT MFG. CO., SPEEDBALL, U.S.A., STATESVILLE, N.C. embossed on bottom; cone; clear; 2¾" 2.00-3.00

6528 HUNT PEN CO. SPEEDBALL, U.S.A., CAMDEN, N.J. embossed on bottom; round; clear; 2¾" 2.00-3.00

6529 IGLOO INK; dome shaped; plain with neck on side; sheared top; panels on bases; aqua; 1¾" or 1¼" tall, 2" round 4.00-10.00

6530 same as above except cobalt........ 150.00+

6531 IMPROVED PROCESS BLUE CO.; aqua; 2⅜" 2.00-4.00

6532 Ink; ring around base, base of shoulder and neck; amber; 2⅝" x 1⅞" 2.00-6.00

6533 same as above except aqua or clear ... 2.00-4.00

6541   6548   6551   6552   6554   6555   6556

6557   6558   6559   6560   6561   6562   6563

6564   6565   6566   6567   6568   6569   6570

6571   6572   6573   6574   6575   6576 6577

6534   Ink; cone; ring collar; bulbous ring forms shoulder; ring on base of neck; amber; 2½″ x 2½″ 4.00-6.00

6535   Ink; square; ABM; cobalt blue; 2″ x 2¼″ 3.00-4.00

6536   Ink; round; cobalt blue; 2½″ x 3″ 4.00-6.00

6537   Ink; round; ABM; cobalt blue; 1⅞″ x 2¾″ 4.00-6.00

6538   Ink; cone type, yet not a true cone; base is cone shape with two large graduated flared bands on shoulder and neck; sheared collar; aqua; 3⅜″ 4.00-6.00

6539   Ink; cone; honey amber; 2½″ 4.00-15.00

6540   Ink; cone; aqua; 2½″ 4.00-5.00

6541   Ink; cone; cobalt blue; 2½″ 8.00-15.00

6542   Ink; cone; amber; 2⅝″ 8.00-15.00

6543   Ink; cone; light blue; 2¾″ 6.00-8.00

6544   Ink; cone; plain; clear or amethyst; 2½″ 2.00-3.00

6545   same as above except blue or amber   8.00-12.00

6546   Ink; cone; amethyst; 3″ 4.00-8.00

6547   Ink; *design Patd. Feb 16th, 1886* under bottom in sunken circle; five different size rings on top of shoulder; one 1¼″ ring on base; clear; 12¼″ 6.00-10.00

6548   same as above except one ring near shoulder; green 6.00-10.00

6549   Ink; three-piece mold; crude graduated collar; ice blue; pint; 7⅜″ 6.00-10.00

6550   Ink; ice cube shaped; solid glass; heavy; small well; metal collar; desk type; clear; 2″ x 2″ x 2″ 3.00-4.00

6551   Ink, label; three-part mold; aqua; 2¾″ 8.00-15.00

6552   Ink, label; black; 7½″ .... 20.00+

6553   Ink, label; cone; ring shoulder; 2½″... 4.00-8.00

6554   Ink, label; crock; tapered neck; brick red; 4″ 4.00-6.00

6555   Ink, label; aqua; 2¾″ 3.00-6.00

6556   Ink, label; crock; green and white; 2½″ x 2½″ 4.00-8.00

6557   Ink, label; clear; 2½″ 2.00-4.00

6558   Ink, label; light blue; 2¾″ 2.00-6.00

6559   Ink, label; tin box; 1½″ 8.00-15.00

6560   Ink, label; dark aqua; 2¾″ 3.00-6.00

6561   Ink, label; clear; 6½″ 2.00-8.00

6562   Ink, label; clear; 2½″ at base tapering to 2″ at top 8.00-10.00

6563   Ink, label; wood; brick red; 3″ 6.00-8.00

6564   Ink, plain; checked bottom; clear; 3″ tall, 1¾″ x 1¾″ base 8.00-12.00

6565   Ink, label; aqua; 5¾″ 4.00-6.00

6566   Ink, label; three-part mold; green; 9¼″ 10.00-20.00

6567   Ink, label; sheared top; pontil; clear; 2″ 2.00-6.00

6568   Ink, label; desk bottle; sheared top; clear or amethyst; 1¾″ 4.00-6.00

6569   Ink, label; *Pat Oct. 17, 1865* around bottom; clear or amethyst; 2¾″. 10.00-20.00

6570   Ink, label; desk bottle; sheared top; clear or amethyst; 1½″ 4.00-6.00

6571   Ink, label; clear; 1½″ 4.00-8.00

6572   Ink, label; sheared top; panels on shoulder; clear or amethyst; 1¼″ x 1½″ x 1½″ 8.00-10.00

6573   Ink, label; green; 2½″ 15.00-20.00

6574   Ink, label; broken pontil; green; 7½″ 10.00-20.00

6575   Ink, label; sheared top; aqua; ½″ tall, 5½″ long .... 25.00+

6576   Ink, label; long square body; neck on end; clear; 3¾″ x ¾″ 10.00-15.00

6577   Ink, label; round; dark green; 2¼″   8.00-12.00

6578   Ink; pen rest on both sides at shoulder; sheared collar; amethyst; 2⅝″ x 2⅜″ x 2⅜″... 6.00-10.00

6579   same as above except aqua; 2″ x 2¼″ x 2¾″ 4.00-8.00

6580   6581   6584   6587   6591   6592   6595

6609   6616   6617   6623   6625   6626   6628

6629   6633   6636

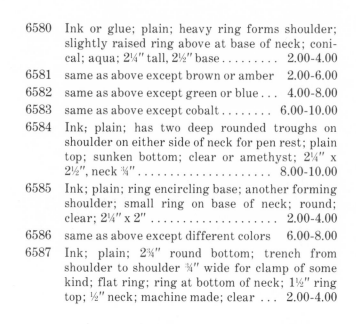

6580   Ink or glue; plain; heavy ring forms shoulder; slightly raised ring above at base of neck; conical; aqua; 2¼″ tall, 2½″ base 2.00-4.00

6581   same as above except brown or amber   2.00-6.00

6582   same as above except green or blue ...   4.00-8.00

6583   same as above except cobalt 6.00-10.00

6584   Ink; plain; has two deep rounded troughs on shoulder on either side of neck for pen rest; plain top; sunken bottom; clear or amethyst; 2¼″ x 2½″, neck ¾″ 8.00-10.00

6585   Ink; plain; ring encircling base; another forming shoulder; small ring on base of neck; round; clear; 2¼″ x 2″ 2.00-4.00

6586   same as above except different colors   6.00-8.00

6587   Ink; plain; 2¾″ round bottom; trench from shoulder to shoulder ¾″ wide for clamp of some kind; flat ring; ring at bottom of neck; 1½″ ring top; ½″ neck; machine made; clear ...   2.00-4.00

6588 Ink; plain; round; inside of flower stand; two prongs on left top to hold pen; all metal is gold color; clear; 2½" tall, 3½" round.... 15.00-30.00

6589 Ink; plain; round; green, clear or amethyst; 2⅝" 2.00-4.00

6590 Ink; plain; round bottom; green; 9"   4.00-10.00

6591 Ink; plain; square top; on top and bottom fancy gold colored metal stand; round base; clear; 2" 10.00-20.00

6592 Ink; plain; square; green or clear; 2"   2.00-4.00

6593 Ink; square; squat; cobalt blue; 2⅜".. 4.00-8.00

6594 Ink; square; amethyst or aqua; 2½" .. 2.00-4.00

6595 Ink; *2 oz.* on short neck; square; rounded corners; machine made; cobalt, clear or blue; 2" x 2" 2.00-4.00

6596 Ink well; sunken desk type; flat; round; ABM; clear; 3" x 1½" 2.00-4.00

6597 IRVING; square; aqua; 2½" 20.00-25.00

6598 J & IEM imprinted in each panel; turtle with six panels; on base *Patd Oct 31, 1865*; under bottom *J*; aqua .... 35.00+

6599 same as above except no patent date; amber .... 35.00+

6600 same as above except cobalt 35.00-75.00

6601 same as above except J & IEM around bottle in ⅘" ring 4.00-10.00

6602 JASMINE INK CORP., NORFOLK VIRGINIA; square; labeled *Perfumed Jasmine Ink*; ABM; clear 2.00-4.00

6603 J. M & S IGLOO INK; early 10.00-15.00

6604 JOHNSON INK CO., WILLINGTON, CONN., fancy label; *Stoddard*; tapered and sheared top; dark green; 5⅞"................ 20.00-30.00

6605 KEENE GEOMETRIC INK; open pontil; amber 75.00-85.00

6606 KEENE UMBRELLA INK; eight-sided; open pontil; green 35.00-45.00

6607 KELLER; double ring top; clear or amethyst; 2½".......................... 4.00-8.00

6608 KELLER INK, DETROIT; square; screw top; machine made; clear or amethyst ... 2.00-4.00

6609 THE ROBERT KELLER INK CO.; clear; 9¼" 6.00-8.00

6610 KELLERS INK under bottom; clear; 1¼" x 1½"; ½" neck..................... 10.00-15.00

6611 F. KIDDER IMPROVED, INDELIBLE INK around bottle; square; aqua; 2½" x 1½" x 1½" 25.00-30.00

6612 same as above except 5"; clear.... 20.00-25.00

6613 KIRKLAND WRITING FLUID; ring on shoulder and base; aqua; 2¼" x 1½"   4.00-8.00

6614 L & B monogram in center; cone; aqua; 2½" 8.00-12.00

6615 LAKE'S; cone; aqua; 2½"........ 15.00-20.00

6616 LEVISON'S; machine made; clear; 7¼" 6.00-8.00

6617 LEVISON'S INKS; amber; 2½"   85.00-115.00

6618 LOCHMAN'S LOCOMOTIVE INK; train shaped; trademark, *Patd, Oct, 1874*; plain collar; aqua; 2³⁄₁₆" x 2" .... 25.00+

6619 LOMBARD'S LILAC INK, diamond shape label; house type; clear; 2⅜" 4.00-6.00

6620 LYNDEBORO; rectangular; slots for two pens; aqua; 2¼" 8.00-15.00

6621 LYNDEBORO; rectangular; slots for two pens; green; 2¼" x 2⅜" 8.00-10.00

6622 MAGNUS; tan pottery; 4⅝" 5.00-10.00

6623 CARL MAMPE BERLIN; amber; 2" .. 15.00+

6624 MANCHESTER NOVELTY CO.; aqua; 2⅝" 10.00-14.00

6625 MANN'S, label; *Design Patd Feb 16, 1886* under bottom; amber; 9¼"............ 10.00-20.00

6626 MASSACHUSETTS STANDARD RECORD INK on shoulder; clear; 7¾"....... 10.00-15.00

6627 MAYNARD'S WRITING INK; sheared top; amber case; eight panels; umbrella type; dark green; 2".......................... 35.00+

6628 JULES MIETTE, PARIS; sheared top; blue green; 2¾" .... 10.00+

6629 MON-GRAM INK; round; clear or amethyst; 2½".......................... 4.00-6.00

6630 MOORE; square or cylindrical; aqua; 2" 4.00-8.00

6631 MOORE & SON; sheared top; aqua or clear; 1⅝" 6.00-10.00

6632 MOORE J & IEM; igloo; round; 2½" to 6½"; several other types and sizes 6.00-35.00

6633 M.S. CO.; *Sanford's #216* on bottom; clear 2.00-6.00

6634 MT. WASHINGTON GLASS CO; *New Bedford, Mass; Bubble Ball Inkwell*; clear; 2" 20.00-40.00

6635 MY LADY INK on base; *Carbonine Ink Co., N.Y.*; aqua; 1⅜" 6.00-10.00

6636 NATIONAL INK N.W.W. & CO., label; clear; 2" 2.00-4.00

6637 NATIONAL SURETY INK; round; two rings on shoulder and base; *32 oz.* on shoulder; ABM; clear; 9" 4.00-10.00

6638 NAYMARD & MOYES, [sic] BOSTON, label; pontil; clear..................... 35.00+

6639 P. NEWMAN & CO., GILSUM, N.H., label; umbrella type; eight panels; olive green; 1½" 30.00-50.00

6640 NICHOLS & HALL, label; house type; clear; 2⅞" 4.00-10.00

6641 OCTAGON INK; mushroom shaped; pontil; aqua.......................... 20.00-30.00

6642 THE OLIVER TYPEWRITER; round; clear; 2" 4.00-8.00

6643 1 X L; fancy ink; ring top; clear; 2½" 8.00-10.00

6644 OPDYKE; barrel shaped bottle with four rings around it; opening in center; clear; 2" 10.00-12.00

6645 same as above except panels around bottom; ring top; *Opdyke* under bottom; clear; 2¼" 18.00-30.00

| 6651 | 6658 | 6663 | 6672 | 6675 | 6677 | 6678 | 6679 |

| 6681 | 6684 | 6694 |
| 6680 | 6682 | 6691 | 6692 | 6697 |

6646   OPDYKE BROS. INK; barrel with opening in center; ring top; aqua; 2½" x 2⅜" .. 15.00-30.00

6647   OPDYKE BROS. INK; barrel; *Patd March 11, 1870;* opening in center; aqua; 2½" x 2⅜" 18.00-30.00

6648   PALMER; round; sheared top; golden amber; 4¼" .... 45.00+

6649   PARKER; panels on shoulder; ring top; ABM; clear; 2½" 10.00-20.00

6650   same as above except *Parker's "Quink"* under bottom; *Made in U.S.A. #1;* ABM; 1½" 5.00-10.00

6651   PAUL'S INKS; *N.Y., Chicago* on back; cobalt; 9½".............................. 12.00-20.00

6652   PAUL'S SAFETY BOTTLE & INK CO. N.Y. on shoulder; squat; ring top; clear; 1⅜" 10.00-20.00

6653   PAUL'S WRITING FLUID; *N.Y., Chicago;* flared neck; ring top; three-part mold; 5½" 10.00-20.00

6654   P.B.CO. INK; round; aqua; 2½" 8.00-10.00

6655   PEERLESS on two panels; eight panels; umbrella type; bulbous shoulder; sheared top; clear or amethyst................ 10.00-20.00

6656 J.W. PENNELL embossed on eight panels on base; round top; ring top; aqua; 2″ 10.00-20.00

6657 PENN. MFG. WORK, PHILA.; eight flat sides; white; 2½″ .... 50.00+

6658 PERRY & CO., LONDON, PATENT in two lines; on top ½″ hole for ink and funnel hole for pen; flared ring bottom 3″ to 2¼″ top; sunken bottom; cream pottery; 3″ round, 1¾″ tall .... 15.00+

6659 PITKIN INK KEENE; open pontil; dark aqua; 1¾″........................ 100.00-150.00

6660 PITKIN INKWELL; 36-rib mold, swirls to left; flared lip; lime green; 1¾″ x 2½″ x 2¼″ 200.00+

6661 POMEROY INK, NEWARK, N.J., label; two rings on base and shoulder; ring top; aqua; 2¾″ 6.00-8.00

6662 G.A. POTTER; pottery; tan; 9⅞″... 6.00-10.00

6663 RAVEN'S, label; *Design Patd Feb 16th 1886* under bottom; 7¾″............... 10.00-20.00

6664 READING INK CO., READING, MICH., SUPERIOR BLUE INK, label; round; wide collar; flared top; aqua; 6$^{3}/_{16}$″ x 1$^{9}/_{16}$″ ... 8.00-12.00

6665 READING INK CO., READING, MICH., diamond shaped label; on base *Pat. April 18, 1875;* round; crude pouring lip; aqua; 6⅛″ 8.00-15.00

6666 READING INK CO.; *Violet Ink*, label; crude cone with pronounced mold lines; 2¾″ x 2⅝″ 8.00-15.00

6667 READS INKSTAND & INK; *Pat. Nov. 25, 1872;* ring top; aqua blue; 2″ 18.00-25.00

6668 SAFETY BOTTLE & INK CO., N.Y.; *Paul's pat.* on shoulder; diagonal swirls; sunburst pattern on base; clear; 2⅛″ x 2⅜″ 12.00

6669 SANFORD HORSE-SHOE INK; *Sanford 21/7 Pat. apl. for;* aqua 8.00-10.00

6670 SANFORD/INKS/ONE QUART/AND LIBRARY PASTE vertically; raised ¾″ ring around base and shoulder; round; square collar and ring; ABM; amber; 3¾″ diameter, 9⅜″ tall 4.00-8.00

6671 same as above except embossing on pouring cap, *Pat. Feb. 27, '06;* 10½″............. 8.00-16.00

6672 SANFORD MFG. CO.; *Pat. May 23, 1899* on bottom; clear or amethyst; 3″ 3.00-4.00

6673 SANFORD'S BELLWOOD, ILL.; *Made in U.S.A. 44CC.* embossed on bottom; metal screw-on top; red plastic; 1½″............. 4.00-6.00

6674 SANFORDS MFG. CO. vertically in sunken panel; *1 oz* on next panel; *S.I. Co.* monogram on next panel; square collar; ABM; amethyst; 1½″ x 2½″ 3.00-4.00

6675 SANFORD'S FREE SAMPLE NEVER SOLD; sheared top; 3½″ 4.00-8.00

6676 SANFORDS #6 on bottom; *1½ oz.* on one panel; large step on shoulder; double band collar; clear; 1¾″ x 2¼″ 2.00-3.00

6677 SANFORD'S #8 under bottom; light green; 2½″ 2.00-6.00

6678 SANFORD'S 9 under bottom; machine made; clear or amethyst; 2½″ 3.00-4.00

6679 SANFORD'S 25-8 on bottom; aqua; 2½″ 2.00-6.00

6680 SANFORD'S #27 on bottom; machine made; clear; 2½″ 2.00-3.00

6681 SANFORD'S #29 PAT APP'D FOR on bottom; boat shaped; clear; 2″ x 2¾″ x 2¼″... 8.00-12.00

6682 SANFORD'S 30 PATENT APPLIED FOR on bottom; boat shaped; aqua; 2″ tall, 2¼″ x 1¾″ base.............................. 8.00+

6683 SANFORD'S #39 on bottom; large ring with deep groove at base and shoulder; step on shoulder; small and large ring collar; round; aqua or amethyst; 2″ x 2⅜″ 3.00-4.00

6684 SANFORD'S #39 3N on bottom; aqua; 2½″ 2.00-5.00

6685 SANFORD'S #88; bell shaped; sheared collar; amethyst; 2½″ diameter, 3⅜″ tall 4.00-8.00

6686 SANFORD'S #89; somewhat conical; sheared collar; amethyst; 2¼″ diameter, 2½″ tall 2.00-4.00

6687 SANFORD'S #98 CHICAGO, NEW YORK 1½ OZ. on bottom; large ring on base and shoulder; two rings on collar; round; ABM; clear; 1¾″ x 2½″.......................... 2.00-3.00

6688 SANFORD'S, CHICAGO, #187 under bottom; round; flared top; clear; 1½″ x 1½″ 10.00-15.00

6689 SANFORD'S #219 on bottom; large ring on base and shoulder; large ring and small ring collar; round; ABM; clear; 1⅞″ x 2¼″ ... 2.00-3.00

6690 SANFORD'S #276 on bottom; *S.I. Co.* monogram in sunken bull's-eye panel; rings at base of neck; ABM; three other plain bull's-eyes; clear; 1⅞″ x 2⅝″.............. 2.00-3.00

6691 SANFORD'S PREMIUM WRITING FLUID, label; ABM; amber; 9″............. 4.00-8.00

6692 SCHLESINGER'S HYDRAULIC INK; white and black crock, copper top; 6″......... 25.00

6693 SHEAFFER'S/SKRIP/THE SUCCESSOR TO INK embossed on metal plate in top of wooden cylinder; container for an ink bottle; wooden threaded screw-on top; 3⅝″ tall, 2$^{7}/_{16}$″ diameter 4.00-6.00

6694 Shoe, label; clear; 6″ long 8.00-12.00

6695 Shoe with buckle; clear; 3⅞″ long ... 6.00-10.00

6696 SIGNET INK; threaded for screw top; cobalt blue; 7¾″.................... 16.00-20.00

6697 S. SILL- (cannot decipher balance); *Chester, Conn.*; blue label under bottom; 3¼″ round ring at bottom and top; vase shaped; four different side holes to hold quill pens; in center top a bottle for ink; all wood; brown; 1¾″.......... 15.00+

6698 SISSON & CO.; sheared top; round; pale aqua green; 1⅝″ 4.00-10.00

6699 SKRIP; *tighten cap, tip bottle to fill the well* on metal top; *Pat'd 1759866* on bottom; ink well; screw-on top; clear; 2¾″.......... 10.00-15.00

6700   6703   6705   6706   6707   6708   6709   6710

6715   6716   6722   6724   6725   6726   6728   6729

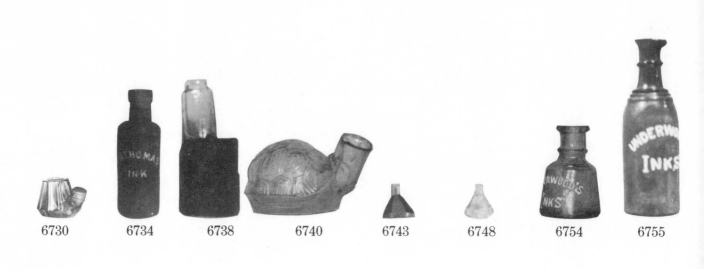

6730   6734   6738   6740   6743   6748   6754   6755

6700 S.M. CO 6 under bottom; aqua; 2¼" .. 6.00-8.00

6701 SONNEBORN & ROBBINS; flared lip; cork stopper topped with brass; tan pottery; 5½" 6.00-8.00

6702 SO. STAMP & STATIONERY CO., MFG. STATIONERS, RICHMOND, VIRGINIA; amber; 9½".......... 20.00-30.00

6703 STAFFORD'S COMMERCIAL INK; round; *Pat. Jan 13-85, S.M. CO*; clear; 2".. 8.00-10.00

6704 STAFFORD'S INK in two lines, running vertically; two rings on shoulder and bottom; amber; 4¼" body, 2" neck 6.00-12.00

6705 STAFFORD'S INK; green; 8" 10.00-15.00

6706 STAFFORD'S INK; round; aqua; 3" 4.00-6.00

6707 S.S. STAFFORD INK, MADE IN U.S.A. in two lines in a sunken panel; under it *This Bottle Contains One Full Quart*; two rings on bottom, two on shoulder; short neck; aqua; 2".... 8.00-16.00

6708 same as above except 7" 8.00-16.00

6709 same as above except 6" 10.00-18.00

6710 same as above except 4¾" 10.00-18.00

6711 STAFFORD'S INKS, MADE IN U.S.A.; pouring spout; cobalt blue; 6" 10.00-20.00

6712 STAFFORD'S INK SS, MADE IN U.S.A. in sunken panel; under it, *This Bottle Contains One Full Qt.*; aqua or light blue; 9½"...... 5.00-8.00

6713 STAFFORD'S NO. 5, PAT NOV. 17, 1896, NOV. 22, 1892 on base; shoe shaped; aqua; 2½" neck, 3¼"........................ 12.00-16.00

6714 STAFFORD'S VERMILION INK; two pen slots; aqua with blue label.......... 8.00-10.00

6715 STANFORD; square roof and 1½" chimney; ½" base; *Stanford's Fountain Pen Inks*; machine made; 2" x 2" 4.00-6.00

6716 STANFORD'S BLUE INK label around body; ring on base, neck and shoulder; 2⅜" neck, 2" tall, 2" round........................ 4.00-6.00

6717 HENRY C. STEPHENS, LTD.; pouring spout; dark brown; 9".................. 6.00-10.00

6718 STODDARD MASTER INK; olive amber around pontil; 9⅜".......... 25.00-35.00

6719 STODDARD UMBRELLA INK; eight-sided; open pontil; amber.............. 40.00-60.00

6720 SUPERIOR INK; tan and brown; 2" 6.00-10.00

6721 SWIFT & PEARSON; top and neck drawn out and shaped by hand; bulbous neck; dark green; 7⅝" 30.00-40.00

6722 SYR-RHEL INK; pontil; cobalt; 8"...... 30.00+

6723 BRICKETT J. TAYLOR INK; cylindrical; flared lip; Keene; open pontil; 4½" 100.00-150.00

6724 Tea kettle; stars on eight panels; metal top; cobalt; 2½"...................... 100.00+

6725 same as above except no stars and long neck; clear; 6" .... 50.00+

6726 same as above except no stars and short neck with eight panels; metal top; blue...... 50.00+

6727 Tea kettle; place for two pens on top; *Pat. App for* and cloverleaf under bottom; aqua; 2" .... 20.00+

6728 TEA KETTLE INK, label; eight panels; 2½" sheared top; cobalt; 2" x 4" .... 85.00+

6729 same as above except clear........ 40.00-50.00

6730 same as above except neck is close to the eight panels; metal top; aqua.......... 40.00-50.00

6731 THOMAS on bottom; cone; bulbous shoulder; double collar; amethyst 4.00-8.00

6732 L.H. THOMAS & CO.; clear or aqua; 2¼" x 3⅛" 2.00-4.00

6733 L.H. THOMAS CHICAGO CO. #57 on bottom; double band collar; large and small ring on shoulder; large ring on base; round; aqua; 2½" 6.00-8.00

6734 L.H. THOMAS INK; aqua; 5¼" ... 10.00-15.00

6735 L.H. THOMAS INK; bell shaped; aqua; 2¾" 15.00-25.00

6736 L.H. THOMAS INK; *Pat. April 13, 1875* under bottom; aqua; 8" 10.00-15.00

6737 W.B. TODD; ring top; round; green; 2⅞" 5.00-10.00

6738 TRAVEL INK, label; with fitted hard leather case; six panels; aqua; 2" 8.00-10.00

6739 Turtle; plain rim around bottle at bottom; spout extends 1¹/₁₆" on side; sheared top; aqua; 1½" wide, 2⅛" tall 4.00-8.00

6740 Turtle; aqua; 2" x 4" .... 25.00+

6741 Turtle; twelve lines lower half; granite; aqua 20.00-40.00

6742 Umbrella ink; eight-sided; tapers into small round neck; open pontil; clear; 2½" tall, 2½" base 5.00-10.00

6743 same as above except brown........ 6.00-12.00

6744 same as above except blue.......... 7.00-14.00

6745 same as above except no pontil...... 5.00-10.00

6746 same as above except no pontil; brown or blue 6.00-10.00

6747 Umbrella ink; six panels; aqua or blue; 2½" 4.00-10.00

6748 same as above except with pontil... 10.00-15.00

6749 same as above except smaller type 10.00-12.00

6750 Umbrella ink; rolled lip; eight vertical panels; aqua; 2⅝" 4.00-8.00

6751 Umbrella ink; rolled lip; open pontil; light emerald green; 2½" diameter, 2⅜" tall 35.00-45.00

6752 Umbrella ink; eight vertical panels; rolled lip; whittled effect; open pontil; emerald green; 2⅜" 40.00-50.00

6753 Umbrella ink, label; twelve panels; open pontil; aqua.......... 15.00-25.00

6754 UNDERWOOD; aqua; 3".......... 4.00-8.00

6755 UNDERWOOD INKS; cobalt blue; 6½" 15.00-25.00

6756 UNDERWOOD INKS; embossed; cylindrical; two pen rests on shoulder; flared lip, cloudy; mold line ends at base of neck; aqua; 1⅞" tall, 2⅛" base 10.00-20.00

6757 UNDERWOOD INKS under bottom; circle or ring; tapered bottle; space for label; aqua; 3¼" x 2¼".......... 40.00+

6758 JOHN UNDERWOOD & CO.; cobalt blue; 9½"
.... 20.00-35.00
6759 UNION INK CO.; ring top; aqua; 2¼"
.... 10.00-20.00
6760 UNION INK CO./SPRINGFIELD/MASS. on sloping front; dome shaped; sheared top; aqua; 1½"...................... 15.00-30.00
6761 UNION INK CO./SPRINGFIELD MASS; aqua; 2"...................... 8.00-15.00
6762 VOLGERS INK, label; house type; *T.C.V.* under bottom; ring top; clear; 2" 8.00-15.00
6763 SAMUEL WARD & CO.; sheared top; clear; 3"
.... 10.00-20.00
6764 WARD'S INK; pouring spout; round; olive green; 4¾" 10.00-20.00
6765 WATERLOW & SONS, LIMITED, COPYING INK, label; crock; brown; 7½"...... 8.00-10.00
6766 L.E. WATERMAN CO.; squat band; ABM; aqua...................... 2.00-4.00
6767 E. WATERS; aqua; 6½".......... 5.00-10.00

6768 WATERS INK, TROY, N.Y. on panels; six panels; pontil; ring on shoulder and ring top; tapered; aqua; 2½" x 2" .... 100.00+
6769 J.M. WHITALL; round; green; 1¾" 4.00-10.00
6770 WHITTEMORE BROS & CO.; dark green; 9½"
.... 10.00-20.00
6771 WILLIAMS & CARLETON, HARTFORD, CONN.; round; aqua............ 15.00-20.00
6772 GEORGE W. WILLIAMS & CO.; *Hartford, Conn.*; cone; aqua; 2½" 15.00-25.00
6773 WOODS, PORTLAND, MAINE BLACK INK; tapered; ring top; aqua; 2½" 15.00-25.00
6774 WRIGHT-CLARKSON, MERC. CO. DULUTH, MINN. on base; clear; 6½" 4.00-6.00
6775 WRITEWELL & CO/INK/CHEMICALLY PURE, label; cobalt blue; 7¼" x 2¹⁵/₁₆"
.... 10.00-15.00
6776 YALE; *Dickinson & Co., Rutherford, N.J.*; amber; 1¾"...................... 4.00-8.00

6761

6765

6766

6774

6776

The two basic types of ink containers are shown here.
The larger bottle (#6496) is the master ink or bulk container and was used
primarily for storage. The other two vessels, known as ink bottles
(#6512 and #6448), were placed on the desk top within easy access.

Perfume and Cosmetic

The world's oldest known glass bottles are from Egypt and Mesopotamia and once contained cosmetics and medicines. Egypt's Eighteenth Dynasty in 3000 B.C. made perfumes in religious ceremonies and used them in embalming and religious celebration. Guests at banquets would be splashed with perfume.

Greeks esteemed perfume so highly that they arranged to meet their friends in perfume shops, rather than cafes or street corners, despite protests of the practice from Socrates. During the European Age of Extravagance of the eighteenth century, social custom required men to bring a trinket or small present to their lady when they came to call. The favorite of the women was a scent bottle.

One of the prime reasons for using perfume was to cover up personal body odors, since sanitary facilities were not what they are today. Martha Washington reportedly carried a small perfume bottle with her that she could discreetly slip into her glove. Her bottle was said to have been made by Caspar Wistar who owned the first successful American glasshouse. The plant was founded in New Jersey in 1739 and Wistar's work became known for its functional qualities.

Henry William Stiegel entered glassmaking in 1763. His bottles, in contrast to Wistar's simplicity, are decorative. They are of the pattern-molded and expanded variety—blown into a mold, then removed and finished to the desired shape by blowing. Stiegel's diamond-patterned perfume bottles are particularly ornate.

In the 1840's Solon Palmer of Cincinnati, Ohio, began to manufacture and sell perfumes. A few had rather unusual names, Jockey Club and Baby Ruth among others. A greater availability of resources prompted his move to New York in 1871. By 1879 his products were familiar to all drugstores, and are interesting to collectors because of the brilliant emerald green color of the glass.

Perfume bottles embossed with a child's face appeared around 1880. Known as Charley Ross bottles, they commemorate the abduction in 1874 of the youngest of seven children of a grocer in Germantown, Pennsylvania. Young Charley was only four years old and easily fooled by the two men who offered him candy. The father did not pay the ransom and the child was never seen again. The case remained unsolved but the father never gave up the search for his son. He advertised in major newspapers for people willing to help him locate information. Extra impetus was given in the five-thousand-dollar reward he offered. He encouraged the Charley Ross bottles to be produced to keep public conscience concerning the kidnapping alive.

Perfume was not only for ladies. Trade cards—advertisements usually with a full-color picture on one side and a product description on the other, often inserted in packages at the factory or mailed—were

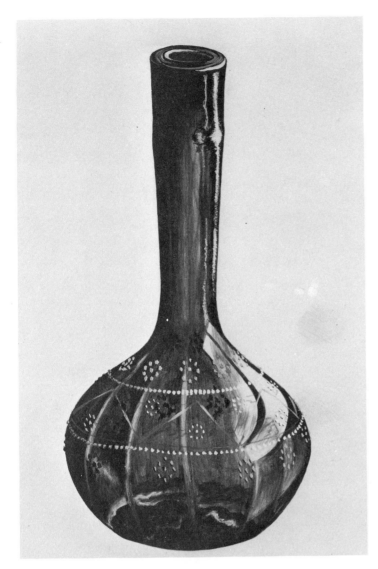

Above left: *Around 1850 barbers began providing special customers with personalized hair tonic bottles. They also had sets of decorative tonic bottles (barber bottles) for other customers.* Above right: *This mold-blown American scent bottle, circa 1780-1820, contained perfume and ammonia.*

a popular form of proclaiming the virtues of the various products available. A trade card for Florida Water, a gentleman's after-shave fragrance, boasted it to be "the richest, most lasting yet most delicate of all perfumes for use on the handkerchief, at the toilet and in the bath, delightful and healthful in the sick room, relieves weakness, fatigue, prostration, nervousness, and headache." The product was undoubtedly noticed when applied; it was about seventy-five percent alcohol.

In the mid-1880's, David H. McConnell, a door-to-door book salesman, began to entice his prospective customers by giving away free samples of perfume. His book sales increased, but he found that his customers were more interested in the perfume than in the books. Thus, in 1886 he established the California Perfume Company in New York City which later, in 1939, became known as Avon.

Demand for perfume and cologne increased at the turn of the century. The perfection of the automatic bottle-making machine in 1903 by Michael Owens helped supply keep pace with demand. Prior to that time, all bottles were expensive to make. A variety of products including hair balsam, dyes, lotions, washes, unguents and oils were contained in bottles usually under six inches in height. Fortunes were amassed, and still are today, through sales of these products.

6777   6778   6782   6783   6784   6785   6786   6787

6788   6789   6790   6791   6792   6795   6796   6797

6798   6802   6803   6805   6808   6812   6815   6816

378

6817   6821   6822   6823

6777 AUBRY SISTERS; *Pat Aug 22, 1911* under bottom; milk glass; 1″ 1.00-2.00

6778 C. R. BAILEY; aqua; 3½″ 2.00-6.00

6779 BAKER'S PERFUME; ring top; clear; 3″ 3.00-4.00

6780 BALDWINS QUEEN BESS PERFUME; reverse side *Sample Baldwins Perfume*, label; ring top; 5½″ 8.00-10.00

6781 Barber bottle; milk glass; ring top; 4¾″ x 2½″ sunken panel on front of bottle for label; round; 9″ 10.00-20.00

6782 Barber bottle, label; clear or amethyst; 7¼″ 6.00-8.00

6783 Barber bottle, label; milk glass; 12″ 12.00-20.00

6784 Barber bottle, label; clear or amethyst; 10½″ 8.00-12.00

6785 Barber bottle, label; aqua; 8″ 4.00-8.00

6786 Barber bottle, label; blue green; 8½″ .. 12.00+

6787 Barber bottle, label; aqua; 8½″ 6.00-8.00

6788 Barber bottle; plain; red; 3½″ 10.00-20.00

6789 BAY RUM on one panel; barber bottle; six 1¾″ panels; roof type shoulder; lady's leg neck; neck 3¼″; ring top; milk glass; body, neck and shoulder 4½″ tall 15.00-25.00

6790 Bell; plain; perfume; clear; 3″ tall, 2″ round 4.00-6.00

6791 Boot; perfume label; clear or amethyst; 3½″ 8.00-15.00

6792 BRUNO COURT PARFUMEUR; green with gold neck; 5½″ 6.00-10.00

6793 CALIF. PERFUME CO.; fruit flavors on the front of panel; rectangular; amethyst; 5½″ 4.00-10.00

6794 CARD COLOGNE or OPIUM SQUARE; decorated; frosted; tapered 3.00-4.00

6795 C CO.; perfume; fancy shape; screw top; clear; 3¼″ 3.00-6.00

6796 CHAPOTEAUT; reverse side *Paris*; *BL4063* on bottom; clear or amethyst; 2¾″ 2.00-4.00

6797 CHAPOTEAUT; on back *Paris*; clear 2.00-5.00

6798 CHRISTIAN DIOR; clear; 4″ 6.00-8.00

6799 CHRISTIANI DE PARIS; perfume; fancy shape; thin flared lip; open pontil; aqua; 3⅜″ 25.00-35.00

6800 CLARKE & CO.; *Woodard* under bottom; cosmetic; square; cobalt; 4¼″ 1.00-2.00

6801 C. L. G. CO. under bottom; inside screw; clear or amethyst; 4¼″ 8.00-10.00

6802 C.M., label; clear; 1¾″ 2.00-4.00

6803 COLGATE & CO.; clear or amethyst; 6¼″ 3.00-6.00

6804 COLGATE & CO. NEW YORK in a circle; through center of circle PERFUMERS; clear or amethyst; 3⅝″ 2.00-3.00

6805 COLGATE & CO.; *New York* on back; clear; 4¾″ 2.00-4.00

6806 COLGATE & CO. NEW YORK on bottom; fancy shape; five concave panels on side; step on shoulder; ring collar; amethyst; 5¼″ .. 2.00-4.00

6807 COLGATE & CO. N.Y. COLEO SHAMPOO; *X* on sides; flask; AMB; amethyst 3.00-4.00

6808 COLGATE & CO. PERFUMER 4 N.Y. on bottom; machine made; clear; 4¼″ 2.00-3.00

6809 COLGATE & CO. PERFUMERS, NEW YORK; rectangular; long neck; amethyst; 3⅝″ 3.00-4.00

6810 COLGATE AND CO. PERFUMER'S N.Y. on one panel; rectangular; amethyst or clear; 3¾″ 3.00-4.00

6811 Cologne; decorated trunk and shoulder; applied lip; six panels; amethyst or clear; 5¼″ 3.00-5.00

6812 Cologne; cathedral type; ring top; 1¼″ square at bottom; improved pontil; cobalt; 5¾″ ... 25.00+

6813 Cologne, label; fancy shape; panels; milk glass; 7¼″ 18.00-25.00

6814 Cologne, label; fancy shape; open pontil; flared lip; aqua; 4¾″ 35.00-45.00

6815 Cologne, label; *603* on bottom; clear or amethyst; 3″ 2.00-3.00

6816 Cologne or peppersauce, label; five stars on three panels; light green; 7½″ 10.00-15.00

6817 Cologne, label; pontil; cobalt; 8¾″ .. 8.00-10.00

6818 Cologne; plain; round; clear or opalescent; 2¾″ 1.00-2.00

6819 Cosmetic jar; round; cream; 2¼″ tall, 1¾″ base 3.00-4.00

6820 Cosmetic; plain; square; metal screw top; cobalt; 6″ 1.00-2.00

6821 Cream, label; milk glass; 2¼″ 1.00-2.00

6822 Cream, label; milk glass; 2″ 1.00-2.00

6823 Cream, label; tan; 2″ 2.00-3.00

6824   6825   6826   6827   6828   6829   6830

6831   6832   6833   6834   6838   6840   6841   6842

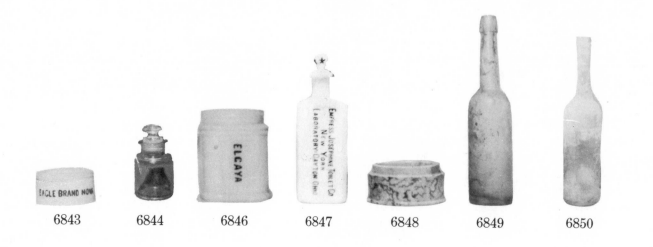

6843   6844   6846   6847   6848   6849   6850

6852	6854	6855	6856	6857	6859	6861

6824   Cream, label; milk glass; 2″ 2.00-3.00

6825   Cream, label; milk glass; 2½″ 1.00-3.00

6826   Cream, label; tan; 2¾″ 2.00-3.00

6827   Cream, label; milk glass; 2½″ 2.00-3.00

6828   Cream, label; milk glass; 2¾″ 1.00-3.00

6829   Cream, label; milk glass; 1¾″ 2.00-3.00

6830   Cream, label; tan; 3¼″ 1.00-2.00

6831   Cream, label; milk glass; 2¾″ 1.00-2.00

6832   CREME SIMON; *J.S. 80* under bottom; milk glass; sheared top; 2½″ 2.00-4.00

6833   THE CROWN PERFUMERY CO.; amber; 2½″ 2.00-6.00

6834   CRUSELLASH; wood marks; aqua; 11½″ 10.00-15.00

6835   CUTEX; rectangular; frosted; 1½″ x 1¾″ x 2½″ 2.00-3.00

6836   DAGGETT & RAMSDELL; *Perfect Cold Cream, Trade Mark Made in U.S.A.* on base; round; screw top; clear; 2¾″ 1.00-2.00

6837   DAYBROOKS DETROIT PERFUMERS on top in a round design; *3* on bottom; clear or amethyst; 6″ 3.00-6.00

6838   DEPAS PERFUME; clear; 4″ 15.00-20.00

6839   DERWILLO on the front panel; *For The Complexion* on the back; tapered to shoulders; square; clear; 3¾″ 1.00-2.00

6840   DE VRY'S DANDERO-OFF HAIR TONIC, label; clear; 6½″ 8.00-10.00

6841   DOLL figural; perfume; clear; 2½″   2.00-4.00

6842   DRYDEN & PALMER; *D&P* under bottom; clear; 7½″ 4.00-6.00

6843   EAGLE BRAND NOVA; milk glass; 1½″ 2.00-3.00

6844   MARIE EARLE, PARIS under bottom; clear; 2¾″ 6.00-8.00

6845   EAU DENTIFRICE DU DOCTEUR, JEAU-PARIS in four lines; clear or amethyst; 3″ 2.00-3.00

6846   ELCAYA; milk glass 2.00-3.00

6847   EMPRESS JOSEPHINE TOILET CO.; milk glass; 6¼″ 10.00-15.00

6848   Face cream, label; cream and black; 1½″ 2.00-3.00

6849   FLORIDA WATER, label; clear; *568* on bottom; 7¼″ 2.00-4.00

6850   FLORIDA WATER, label; pontil; aqua; 8″ 8.00-10.00

6851   FRANCO AMERICAN HYGIENIC CO, CHICAGO on front panel; *Toilet Requisites* on left side; *Franco-American* on the right side; rectangular; amethyst; 6″ 2.00-4.00

6852   FRANCO AMERICAN HYGIENIC CO.; other side *Franco American Toilet Requisites*; clear; 7″ tall, 1½″ x 1½″ base 2.00-6.00

6853   FROSTILLA on front panel; *Elmira N.Y., U.S.A.* on side; *Fragrant Lotion* on other side; clear; 4½″ 4.00-6.00

6854   German enamelled bottle; on front, painted on panels: a girl drinking from a glass; in back: five lines in German script; on each side on a panel: flowers; seven panels in all; pontil; small crude neck; around 1650; blue green; 5½″ .. 100.00+

6855   German enamelled bottle; hand painted; pontil; around 1650; blue green; 5½″ .... 85.00+

6856   GOURAUD'S ORIENTAL CREAM; *New York* on side; *London* other side; machine made; 4¼″ 1.00-2.00

6857   L.L.E. GRAND; *P.L.* on bottom; clear; 3½″ 3.00-6.00

6858   GRIMAULT & CIE PARIS; reverse side *PHARMACIE, DY*; pontil; clear; 4″ 4.00-8.00

6859   GUERLAIN PARIS; *Depose* in back; clear; 6¾″ 4.00-8.00

6860   GURRLAIN; *Eau Lustrale LUS* other side; broken pontil; raspberry; 6¼″ 4.00-6.00

6861   HAGANS MAGNOLIA BALM in three lines on front; beveled corners; ring top; milk glass; 5″ 8.00-12.00

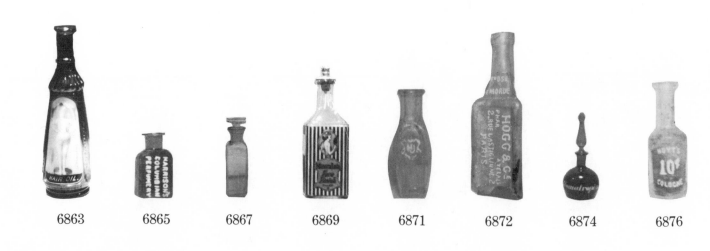

6863   6865   6867   6869   6871   6872   6874   6876

6882   6883   6884   6886   6893   6894   6897   6898

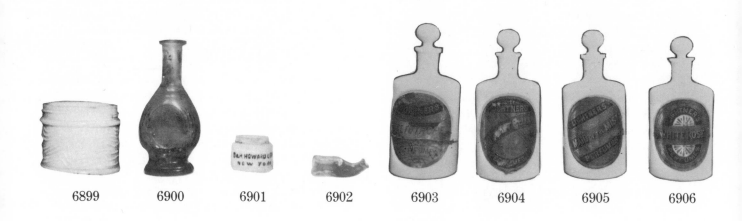

6899   6900   6901   6902   6903   6904   6905   6906

6862 same as above except turned-under top; 4½" 8.00-12.00

6863 HAIR OIL; label on back; amber; 10¼" 35.00-45.00

6864 HARMONY OF BOSTON on bottom; cold cream; eight panels; screw top; amethyst; 2½" 2.00-3.00

6865 HARRISON'S COLUMBIAN PERFUMERY; clear; 2¾" 4.00-8.00

6866 J. HAUEL; reverse *Philadelphia*; on side *Perfumer*; square; flared lip; open pontil; aqua; 3" 12.00-18.00

6867 H.B. & H. N.Y. on shoulder; clear; 3½" 4.00-6.00

6868 C. HEEMSTREET & CO., TROY N.Y.; eight panels; ring top; pontil; blue; 7" ...... 75.00+

6869 HESSIG-ELLIS CHEMIST, MEMPHIS TENN; *Q Ban For The Hair* on back; clear; 6½" 4.00-6.00

6870 HILBERT'S DELUXE PERFUMERY; flattened heart shape with long neck; clear; 3¼" 4.00-8.00

6871 H.J., perfume label; 2¼" 2.00-4.00

6872 HOGG & CO.; three-cornered bottle; 8" 8.00-12.00

6873 HOLT'S NICKEL COLOGNE in a sunken front panel; round; amethyst or clear; 2⅞" 2.00-4.00

6874 HOMATROPIN; perfume dropper; blue; 2" 8.00-12.00

6875 F HOYT & CO. PERFUMERS, PHILA. in sunken panel; round; amethyst; 3" ... 2.00-3.00

6876 HOYT'S; clear; 3¼" 2.00-4.00

6877 HUBBARD, HARRIET, AYER N.Y. in a square with monogram; *3¾ ounces* on the trunk; square; screw top; clear; 4¼" 1.00-2.00

6878 HUBBARD, HARRIET, AYER N.Y.; cosmetic jar; milk glass; square; screw top; 1½" or 2½" 1.00-2.00

6879 RICHARD HUDNUT, N.Y., monogram; *4 fl. Ozs. Net*; rectangular; clear; 5¾" 1.00-3.00

6880 RICHARD HUDNUT, N.Y. U.S.A. with eagle and monogram; tapered neck; round; clear; 5¾" 1.00-3.00

6881 RICHARD HUDNUT PERFUMER N.Y.; square; amethyst; 3" or 3½" 2.00-4.00

6882 RICHARD HUDNUT; clear or amethyst; 3" 3.00-5.00

6883 RICHARD HUDNUT; machine made; clear; 4" 2.00-3.00

6884 C. W. HUTCHINS PERFUMER, NEW YORK; clear; 3¼" 2.00-4.00

6885 HYACINTHIA TOILET HAIR DRESSING; crude applied lip; open pontil; rectangular; aqua; 6" 10.00-20.00

6886 IMPERIAL CROWN PERFUMERY & CO.; clear; 5" 4.00-6.00

6887 INGRAMS MILKWEED CREAM on shoulder; screw top; milk glass jar; white; 2¼" 1.00-2.00

6888 INGRAMS SHAVING CREAM on shoulder; screw top; round; cobalt; 2¼" 1.00-3.00

6889 JEAN MARIE FARINA COLOGNE; six-sided; pontil; clear; 4⅝" 25.00-35.00

6890 JEWELETTE LABORATORIES, PERFUMERS, CHICAGO; clear; 8" 6.00-10.00

6891 JUILLET 1827, 28, 29, 30; perfume; shaped like a harp with a rooster at base; improved pontil; double coated with a turquoise milk glass effect on the outside and a brilliant ultramarine effect on the inside; 5¼" .... 200.00+

6892 D. KERKOFF, PARIS; tapered; footed; rectangular; amethyst; 3¼" 1.00-2.00

6893 KERKOFF; clear or amethyst; 5¼" 2.00-4.00

6894 KIKEN ST. LOUIS under bottom; label; clear or amethyst; 8¼" 4.00-8.00

6895 DR. KOCH'S TOILET ARTICLES, WINONA MINN.; ring top; clear or amethyst; 5¼" 4.00-6.00

6896 KRANKS COLD CREAM; jar; milk glass; round; screw top; 2¾" 1.00-2.00

6897 G. W. LAIRD; milk glass; 4¾" 8.00-15.00

6898 LARKIN CO.; dark green; 3" tall, 1½" x 1¼" base 2.00-6.00

6899 LARKIN CO. under bottom; milk glass; 2" 2.00-4.00

6900 L B under bottom; clear or amethyst; 4" 4.00-6.00

6901 DR. H. HOWARD LEVY; milk glass; 1" 2.00-3.00

6902 L. H. on bottom; shape of a slipper; perfume; improved pontil; flared lip; clear; 3½" long 25.00-35.00

6903 LIGHTNER'S HELIOTROPE PERFUMES; lightning on back; in center, hollow letters *L.E.N. & Co. Detroit Mich.*; milk glass; 6½" 20.00-30.00

6904 LIGHTNER'S JOCKEY CLUB PERFUMES; lightning on back; in center, hollow letters *L.E.N. & Co. Detroit Mich.*; milk glass; 6½" 20.00-30.00

6905 LIGHTNER'S MAID OF THE MIST; lightning on back; in center, hollow letters *L.E.N. & Co. Detroit Mich.*; milk glass; 6½" 20.00-30.00

6906 LIGHTNER'S WHITE ROSE PERFUMES; lightning on back; in center, hollow letters *L.E.N. & Co. Detroit Mich.*; milk glass; 6½" 20.00-30.00

| 6907 | 6908 | 6909 | 6911 | 6912 | 6915 | 6918 | 6921 |

| 6922 | 6926 | 6927 | 6928 | 6929 | 6934 | 6935 | 6936 |

| 6939 | 6941 | 6942 | 6943 | 6944 | 6945 | 6946 | 6947 |

6948   6949   6950   6951

6907   LIT. PIVER PARIS under bottom; clear or amethyst; 3″ 1.00-2.00

6908   LUBIN; clear; 3¼″ tall, 1½″ diam. . . 2.00-4.00

6909   LUBIN PARFUMERS PARIS; pontil; clear; 3½″............................. 6.00-8.00

6910   MACK'S FLORIDA WATER; tapered top; aqua; 8½″ 4.00-6.00

6911   MELBA, label; machine made; clear; 4¾″ 2.00-4.00

6912   MINERALAVA FACE FINISH N.Y.; *Scotts Face Finish* on back; clear; 5¼″..... 4.00-6.00

6913   MONELL'S TEETHING CORDIAL, N.Y. on three of eight panels; aqua; 5″ tall, 1⅛″ round 3.00-6.00

6914   MORTON, CARPENTER CO., COLONITE BOSTON, MASS.; square; amethyst or clear; 4″ 2.00-4.00

6915   MURRAY & LANMAN; machine made; aqua 2.00-4.00

6916   MURRAY & LANMAN, AGUA DE FLORIDA, NEW YORK; 6″ or 9″ . . . 3.00-6.00

6917   MURRAY & LANMAN, AGUA DE FLORIDA, NO. 69 WATER ST. N.Y.; pontil; aqua; 9″ .... 25.00+

6918   MURRAY & LANMAN DRUGGISTS, FLORIDA WATER, NEW YORK in four vertical lines; aqua; 5½″ body, 3¾″ neck . . . 4.00-6.00

6919   same as above except smaller bottle . . 4.00-6.00

6920   NEWTON, LONDON; shape of a schoolhouse; flared lip; milk glass; 2⅝″ .... 40.00+

6921   THEO NOEL; aqua; 4½″ 2.00-6.00

6922   NUIT DE MONE around top; black glass; 3¾″ 4.00-6.00

6923   OBOL under bottom in sunken panel; front and back 1¼″ panels, plain; on each side three panels; three-part mold with short round neck facing out; ½″ open on one side; milk glass; 4¼″ tall, 2⅛″ x ¾″ 6.00-12.00

6924   same as above except no writing; flat bottom; 2″ 6.00-12.00

6925   ORIENTAL CREAM on side; *Gourauds, New York*; square bottle with short neck; clear or amethyst; 5¼″ 2.00-3.00

6926   ORIZA-OIL L. LEGRAND PARIS; *Modele Exclush Depose* on back; clear; 5¼″.... 2.00-4.00

6927   PALANGIE; *BL 2874* under bottom; clear; 5¾″ 2.00-4.00

6928   PALMER in script, vertically on flat sides; some round bottles; emerald green; 4½″... 4.00-8.00

6929   PALMER; metal crown, with *Salon Palmer Perfumer* and two stars; fancy shape; ribbed shoulders; emerald green; 5¾″..... 8.00-12.00

6930   same as above except with rings instead of ribs; glass stopper; *Salon Palmer Perfumer* on shoulder; 4½″..................... 8.00-12.00

6931   PALMER in script in center of bottle; ring top; 2″ round, 4½″ body, 2″ neck 6.00-10.00

6932   same as above except oval; 7¼″.... 6.00-10.00

6933   PALMER; clear or amethyst; 3¼″ .. 2.00-4.00

6934   PALMER; clear; 2½″.............. 2.00-4.00

6935   PALMER; flat front, round back; blue green; 4¾″........................ 4.00-6.00

6936   PALMER; *C2* under bottom; oval shape; blue green; 5″.................... 6.00-10.00

6937   PARIS PERFUME CO., JERSEY CITY, N.J. GUARANTEED FULL 2 OZ.; ring top; clear or amethyst; 6″ 2.00-4.00

6938   L. PAUTAUBERGE PHARMACIEU, PARIS in three lines; on bottom *R 6, 5862*; beveled corners; cobalt; 2¼″ square base, 6″ body, 2″ neck 10.00-12.00

6939   P.D. on base; aqua; 4¾″......... 30.00-40.00

6940   Perfume; fancy shape; four sides; round ribs on three sides; one plain ring; ring top; ring vase type body; 3¼″ tall, 2″ neck 7.00-10.00

6941   Perfume; fancy shape; clear; 3″..... 2.00-4.00

6942   Perfume, label; aqua; 6½″........ 8.00-12.00

6943   Perfume, label; clear or amethyst; 6¼″ 2.00-4.00

6944   Perfume, label; blue; 2¾″ 2.00-4.00

6945   Perfume, label; fancy shape; clear; 3¼″ 2.00-4.00

6946   Perfume, label; clear; 6½″......... 3.00-6.00

6947   Perfume, label; clear; 5½″......... 2.00-4.00

6948   Perfume, label; clear or amethyst; 3″ 2.00-4.00

6949   Perfume, label; clear; 2¾″......... 2.00-6.00

6950   Perfume, label; various colored stripes around bottle; 2″ 6.00-8.00

6951   Perfume, label; clear or amethyst; 3″ 2.00-3.00

6952 6953 6954 6955 6956 6957 6958 6959

6960 6961 6962 6963 6964 6965 6966 6967

6968 6969 6970 6971 6972 6973 6974 6975

6976   6985   6986   6987   6988   6989   6992   6993

6952	Perfume, label; aqua; 6"	3.00-6.00
6953	Perfume, label; clear; sheared top; 2½"	8.00-10.00
6954	Perfume, label; pontil; clear or amethyst; 4"	3.00-7.00
6955	Perfume, label; aqua; 7½"	4.00-6.00
6956	Perfume, label; clear or amethyst; 4¾"	2.00-6.00
6957	Perfume, label; eight panels; clear or amethyst; 1¾"	2.00-4.00
6958	Perfume, label; pontil; aqua; 3¾"	10.00-20.00
6959	Perfume, label; clear; 5¼"	2.00-6.00
6960	Perfume, label; clear or amethyst; 5½"	10.00-15.00
6961	Perfume, label; pinch bottle; pontil; green; 6"	6.00-8.00
6962	Perfume, label; golf frame around bottle with marble on each corner; aqua; 4"	6.00-10.00
6963	Perfume, label; flat front, round back; clear; 6½"	2.00-6.00
6964	Perfume, label; pontil; clear; 12¼"	10.00-15.00
6965	Perfume, label; clear; 6½"	15.00-20.00
6966	Perfume, label; cut glass flower satin glass; sheared top; 5"	8.00-10.00
6967	Perfume, label; clear; 4"	2.00-4.00
6968	Perfume, label; clear; 6½"	8.00-10.00
6969	Perfume, label; pontil; cobalt; 5"	35.00-45.00
6970	Perfume, label; snail design; machine made; satin, clear; 7½"	4.00-8.00
6971	Perfume, label; flowers around bottle; square; milk glass; pontil; 5"	15.00+
6972	Perfume, label; cobalt; 5½"	10.00-15.00
6973	Perfume, label; fancy shape; clear or amethyst; 3¼"	2.00-5.00
6974	Perfume, label; fancy shape; clear or amethyst; 3¼"	4.00-6.00
6975	Perfume, label; clear or amethyst; 3¾"	6.00-8.00

6976	Perfume; ½ bell shaped; clear or amethyst; 3"	5.00-10.00
6977	Perfume; eight vertical panels; ring collar; glass stopper; improved pontil; clear; 3⅛"	8.00-12.00
6978	Perfume; fancy hand-painted gold-leaf design; open pontil; deep purple appears black; 6½"	75.00+
6979	Perfume; very ornate; fancy scroll work around gothic letter M; reverse side has blank oval area for label; flared lip; open pontil; clear; 4"	35.00-45.00
6980	Perfume; shaped like a clam shell; still has partial paper label with round mirror glued to label; very crude; open pontil; clear; 3½"	65.00+
6981	Perfume; shaped like a woven basket with handles; small oval circle on front for paper label; open pontil; aqua; 2⅞"	25.00-35.00
6982	Perfume; figure of an Indian maiden sowing seeds on front; each side has a potted plant; fancy shape; fluted neck; clear; 4⅞"	15.00-25.00
6983	Perfume; violin or corset shaped; flared lip; open pontil; clear; 5⅜"	40.00-50.00
6984	Perfume; picture of an Indian holding a spear between gothic arches; open pontil; turquoise; 4"	30.00-40.00
6985	PERFUMERIE; clear; 3½"	2.00-4.00
6986	J. PICARD; clear; 3¼"	2.00-3.00
6987	ED PINAUD; clear or amethyst; 7"	4.00-6.00
6988	ED PINAUD; aqua; 6"	3.00-6.00
6989	ED PINAUD; clear; 3¾"	2.00-3.00
6990	Pinch bottle shaped; plain; light amber; 3½" body, 4½" neck	15.00+
6991	same as above except smaller	2.00-6.00
6992	POMPEIAN MASSAGE CREAM; clear or amethyst; 2¾"	3.00-4.00
6993	POMPEIAN MFG. CO.; machine made; clear or amethyst; 3¼"	2.00-4.00

6994 6995 6998 6999 7000 7002 7005 7006

7007 7008 7010 7013 7014 7016 7017 7018

7019 7020 7021 7022 7024 7025 7027 7028

This late 19th-century dresser or
toilet bottle most likely graced a lady's
vanity and could be conveniently refilled with any
perfume or other toiletry that the woman desired.

6994 POND'S; milk glass; 1¾" 1.00-3.00

6995 POND'S EXTRACT; *1846* on bottom; machine
made; clear; 5½" 2.00-4.00

6996 PREPARED BY N. SMITH PRENTISS,
ESPRIT DE _____,NEW YORK; perfume;
fancy shape; picture of young girl with an armful
of flowers on front; on reverse an embossed vase
and plant; open pontil; flared lip; aqua; 5½"
.... 40.00-50.00

6997 BY N. PRENTISS; reverse *28 John St. N. York;*
one side *Bearsoil;* other side *Perfumes;* square;
flared lip; open pontil; clear; 2¾"... 15.00-25.00

6998 Pumpkin seed; perfume; plain; clear or
amethyst; 3¼" 2.00-4.00

6999 Pumpkin seed, label; side strap; clear or
amethyst; 3½" 3.00-8.00

7000 QUENTIN; clear; 3" 1.00-3.00

7001 Q. T. on base; perfume; monument shaped with
round ball supported by eagles; flared lip; open
pontil; clear; 5" .... 50.00+

7002 RICKSECKER'S; clear; 3½" 3.00-6.00

7003 RIEGER'S CALIFORNIA PERFUMES;
crooked neck; clear; 3¼".......... 4.00-6.00

7004 R & M; shoe shaped; clear; 3½".... 10.00-30.00

7005 ROGER & GALLET; clear or amethyst; 4¾"
.... 2.00-4.00

7006 ROGER & GALLET PARIS on back; *8897 H.P.*
under bottom; clear or amethyst; 5½"   4.00-6.00

7007 ROGER & GALLET; clear or amethyst; 4¼"
.... 2.00-6.00

7008 J. ROIG; clear; 3¼".............. 2.00-4.00

7009 CHARLEY ROSS; picture of a boy; four sizes
.... 50.00+

7010 C.H. SELICK, PERFUMER N.Y.; ring top;
clear; 2⅝"........................ 4.00-6.00

7011 STIEGEL; perfume; teardrop shaped; sixteen
swirls to the left; improved pontil; clear; 3⅛"
.... 50.00+

7012 T; *oz.* on shoulder; square; cobalt; 2¾" 4.00-6.00

7013 TOILET WATER, on one panel of a six-paneled
bottle; roof type shoulder; lady's leg neck; barber bottle; milk glass; 3¼" body, neck and
shoulder 4½".................... 15.00-25.00

7014 Toilet water, label; amber; 7¼"...... 4.00-6.00

7015 T.P.S. & CO., NY on base; man's head figural;
three-part mold; metal cap; 7" .... 50.00+

7016 TREVILLE PARIS; green; 8¼"..... 4.00-8.00

7017 VAIL BROS; green; 3" 3.00-8.00

7018 VALENTINES; green; 2¾" 2.00-4.00

7019 VAN BUSKIRB'S; aqua; 5" 2.00-3.00

7020 VELVETINA; *Velvetina Skin Beautifier
Goodrich Drug Co. Omaha* on back; milk glass;
5¼"............................ 8.00-12.00

7021 VIN DE CHAPOTEAUT PARIS; clear or
amethyst; 10½" 2.00-4.00

7022 VIOLET DULCE VANISHING CREAM;
eight panels; 2½" 2.00-6.00

7023 VOGN in script; in two lines *Perfumery Co. New
York;* case type body; seam end at collar; clear;
7¾"............................ 3.00-6.00

7024 W.B. & CO. under bottom; aqua; 3½"   4.00-6.00

7025 W & H. WALKER; clear; 8¾"...... 3.00-6.00

7026 WHITE ROSE, label; second label picture of a
bird holding a note which reads *Faith and Love;*
cucumber shaped; turquoise green; 4⅜" long
.... 35.00+

7027 WITCH HAZEL; milk glass; 9¼".. 20.00-30.00

7028 ALFRED WRIGHT, PERFUMER,
ROCHESTER, N.Y.; cobalt or amber; 7½"
.... 6.00-8.00

7029 W.T. & CO.; V in center; *U.S.A.* under bottom;
beveled corners; ring top; milk glass; 5"
.... 6.00-10.00

Miscellaneous

A variety of necessities and luxuries have been and continue to be contained in glass. Everything from milk for nursing babies to fire extinguishing materials to candy has been put in bottles.

Charles M. Windship of Roxbury, Massachusetts, patented the first United States nursing bottle in 1841. Nipples in the nineteenth century were of the makeshift variety—rags, sponges and wood often serving the purpose until the rubber type replaced them in the early 1900's. Many nursing bottles of the late 1800's were made to lay flat and a few types were embossed with reminders such as "Feed the Baby." By 1945 there were over two hundred different kinds of nursing bottles in the United States.

Candy was popularly contained in figural glass bottles. One such container was in the shape of the Liberty Bell and was brought out at the Centennial Exposition in Philadelphia in 1876. Many from the last century were thought to be souvenir items since they bore the names of hotels and restaurants. Others were in the shape of railroad lanterns, horns, clocks, cars, planes, guns and battleships. Many converted into banks when empty.

Fire grenades—bulb-shaped bottles filled with carbon tetrachloride—were designed to be thrown and broken onto fires. Alanson Crane of Fortress Monroe, Virginia, was granted the first American patent for such an extinguisher in 1863. The most well-known maker of the product, the Harden Hand Fire Extinguisher Company of Chicago, was granted a patent on August 8, 1871, exactly two months before the Great Chicago Fire. Fire grenades were manufactured under various intriguing names including the Dash-Out, the Diamond, the Harkness Fire Destroyer, Hazelton's High Pressure Chemical Firekeg, Magic Fire and the Y-Burn Winner. The invention of the vaporized chemical fire extinguisher replaced them in 1905.

Intricate little bottles with likenesses of stars of the stage, favorite politicians or scenic pictures pasted on their surfaces and covered with glass were customarily given by barbers to their regular customers in the nineteenth century. Most of them were personalized with the

Representing some of the various types of 18th-century American nursing bottles are (left to right), a blown pale green bottle (#7243), a blown olive green bottle (#7117) made to lie flat, and a blown-molded aquamarine bottle (similar to #7052) with a bone nipple.

customer's name in gold lettering at the top. Brightly colored and found in a wide variety of surface patterns, these bottles contained such substances as witch hazel and perfumed alcohol. The majority of American bottles of this type were produced in Glassboro, New Jersey. Because of their beautiful nature, most are found in art collections today.

Samuel F. B. Morse received a patent for the telegraph in 1840. A means of insulating the telegraph wires was needed and inventor Ezra Cornell suggested using glass. He designed hollow glass bell-shaped caps to fit over the pegs on the telegraph poles. Louis A. Cauvet, a carpenter from New York, further improved on the insulator by designing caps with threads to secure the devices to the pegs in 1865. Most electric insulators used today are porcelain instead of glass but they have retained the bell shape.

Other types of interesting and collectable containers include bar bottles, shoe polish bottles, glue bottles, snuff bottles, blueing bottles, germicide bottles, cement bottles and oil bottles.

7030   7036   7038   7039   7040   7041   7043   7044

7045   7046   7048   7049   7054   7057   7058   7060

7062   7065   7066   7067   7069   7070   7077   7081

7030 A, MADE IN JAPAN; milk glass; 2½" 4.00-6.00

7031 Acid; plain; green; 6½" 2.00-3.00

7032 Acid; plain; green; 6½" 1.00-2.00

7033 Acid; plain; round; amber; 8" 1.00-2.00

7034 Acid; plain; round; gold; 12" 2.00-4.00

7035 Acid line; line around bottles; fire extinguisher; aqua or amethyst; 6" 1.00-2.00

7036 AGUA CARABANA; small kick-up; aqua; 9½" 2.00-4.00

7037 Airplane; figural candy container; clear; 4¼" long 10.00-15.00

7038 ALMA POLISH on shoulder; *M & Co.* under bottom; aqua; 5" 2.00-4.00

7039 AMES; clear; 1¾" 2.00-4.00

7040 AMMONIA; flask type; aqua; all sizes 1.00-4.00

7041 Apple bottle, label; machine made; clear frosted; 7" 2.00-6.00

7042 APPLEBY & HELMES, RAIL ROAD MILLS; reverse side *Snuff, 133 Waters, New York;* flared top; amber; 4¾" 6.00-12.00

7043 ARMERS TOP NOTCH BRAND; *Chicago* under bottom; clear or amethyst; 5½" 2.00-4.00

7044 ARNA'S 23 under bottom; amber; 8" 4.00-6.00

7045 E. ARNSTEIN, CHICAGO, ILL.; clear; 3¾" 2.00-4.00

7046 F.B. ASBURY, N.Y. under bottom; large plain shield on front; amber; 12" .... 20.00+

7047 AVERY LACTATE CO., BOSTON MASS., U.S.A. in center; picture of a woman with a bucket of milk on her head and a cow in back of her; two panels on each side; clear; 7" 8.00-12.00

7048 B under bottom; label; clear or amethyst; 7½" 2.00-4.00

7049 B & B under bottom; sheared top; amber; 3¾" 4.00-8.00

7050 Baby bottle; OUNCES on front; oval; ABM; clear; 5⅛" 2.00-6.00

7051 Baby bottle; OUNCES on front; cylindrical; ABM; clear; 6⅞" 2.00-4.00

7052 Baby bottle; flask; ABM; amethyst; 7" 2.00-5.00

7053 same as above except 4½" 2.00-4.00

7054 H. A. BARTLETT & CO., PHILADE; *Shoe Dressing* on bottom rim; aqua; 4½" .. 8.00-10.00

7055 BEECH NUT, CANAJOHARIE N.Y. on one line on shoulder; on bottom *23 N 51*; under bottom *B N P Co., A, 16*; machine made; aqua; 9½" 2.00-3.00

7056 BENTON HOLLADAY & CO.; shoe polish; aqua; 4½" 4.00-8.00

7057 B.F.B. CO. 2845 under bottom; aqua; 8" 2.00-4.00

7058 BILUK; aqua; 4" tall, 2¼" x 2¼" base 6.00-10.00

7059 BIXBY; shoe polish; aqua; 3¾" 3.00-4.00

7060 BIXBY under bottle; round bottle tapering to round shoulder; short neck; wide flared mouth; green; 4¼" tall, 2½" bottom 6.00-10.00

7061 same as above except clear 2.00-4.00

7062 BIXBY #15 on bottom; shoe polish; dark green; 4" 4.00-6.00

7063 BIXBY 6-83 on front; on bottom *patented mch*; shoe polish; conical; aqua; 3⅜" 3.00-4.00

7064 BIXBY, PATENTED MCH. 6, 83; bulbous shoulders; flared narrow collar; aqua; 4" 2.00-4.00

7065 S.M. BIXBY & CO.; aqua; 4¼" 4.00-6.00

7066 BIXBY'S FRENCH POLISH; fancy lettering; aqua; 3½" 4.00-6.00

7067 Bluing, label; different numbers on bottom; clear or amethyst; 4¾" 2.00-3.00

7068 THE BOYLE NEEDLE CO., CHICAGO; on side *3 oz. full measure;* machine made; clear; 6¼" 1.00-3.00

7069 BRAIN'S; *Cardiff* on back; *SAB* under bottom; inside screw top; machine made; amber; 10" 4.00-10.00

7070 BRAND BROS. CO. EIGENTHUMER ASETZLICH GESCHUTZT; three sides; fancy shape; amber; 5" 20.00-30.00

7071 BRYANT'S ROOT BEER, THIS BOTTLE MAKES FIVE GALLONS, MFG. BY WILLIAMS DAVIS BROOKS & CO. DETROIT, MICH.; amber; 4½" 4.00-8.00

7072 BULL DOG BRAND LIQUID GLUE around shoulder; crude ring collar; aqua; 3½" 2.00-4.00

7073 BURN OLNEY CANNING CORP.; catsup; clear; 8" 4.00-8.00

7074 CALA NURSER BABY BOTTLE embossed in circular slug plate; *ounces* on back; ring on neck; oval; ABM; clear; 7⅛" 2.00-6.00

7075 Candy bottles shaped as telephone, train, gun, phonograph or lantern; screw top; clear 8.00-10.00

7076 Car, figural; candy; clear; 4¾" 10.00-15.00

7077 CARBONA FIRE EXTINGUISHER, label; *Carbona* under bottom; amber; 11" 15.00-25.00

7078 CAULK; square; clear; 1¾" 1.00-2.00

7079 CHILD'S FIRE EXTINGUISHER, UTICA N.Y.; aqua; 6½" 10.00-15.00

7080 CHILD'S FIRE EXTINGUISHER, UTICA, N.Y., SULPHURIC ACID; 4 oz. line; aqua; 6¼" 8.00-15.00

7081 CHRISTO MFG. CO.; amber; 9½" ... 4.00-6.00

7082 CIRCLE A GINGERALE on bottom; round; aqua; 7⅜" or 9¼" 2.00-4.00

7083 CLEANFONT VENTED NURSING BOTTLE, FOX FULLY & WEBSTER, NEW YORK & BOSTON; *Patented Oct. 25, 1892* on bottom; ring top; Aladdin's lamp type; clear or amethyst; 5½" 10.00-20.00

7084   7085   7086   7087   7088   7089   7091

7093   7097   7098   7099   7102   7107   7109

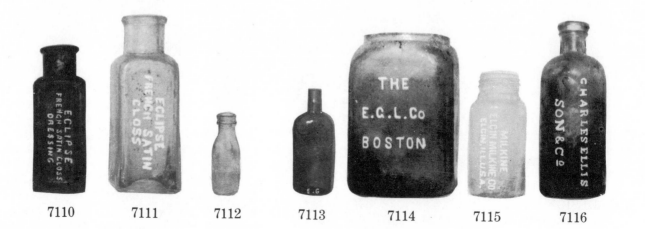

7110   7111   7112   7113   7114   7115   7116

7122   7124   7128

7084 C.L.G. CO. P under bottom; clear; 3½"
.... 2.00-4.00

7085 CLOROX; machine made; nine-part mold; amber; 8" 2.00-8.00

7086 CM under bottom; amber; 11½"...... 6.00-8.00

7087 COHEN COOK & CO., 229 WASHINGTON ST. NEW YORK; graphite pontil; aqua; 8¾"
.... 35.00+

7088 C 185 on bottom; label; amber; 3".... 2.00-3.00

7089 C 1637 on bottom; label; aqua; 5" 2.00-3.00

7090 COOK & BERNHEIMER CO.; *Full Quart, Refilling of This Bottle Prohibited*; under bottle *C&B Bottling* 8.00-10.00

7091 R. COTTER & CO., HOUSTON, TEX.; *I.X.L. Sarsaparilla & Iodide Potassium* on reverse side; aqua; 9½".................. 15.00-30.00

7092 COWDREY, E.T. CO. in center; twirl top and bottom; screw top and sheared top; 6¼"
.... 8.00-15.00

7093 CRIMAULT & CO.; clear; 6¼"...... 2.00-6.00

7094 CROWLEYS MILK CO. BEACON, N.Y. in circular slug plate; *Liquid One Quart*; large ring collar; ABM; clear; 9¾" 3.00-4.00

7095 C.W.&CO. under bottom; kick-up; dot in center; three-part mold; dark olive; 5" body, 2" blob neck, 3" bottom 8.00-12.00

7096 DAIRYMEN'S LEAGUE CO-OPERATIVE ASSOCIATION INC. REGISTERED; *Dairylea Reg. U.S. Pat. Off., One Quart Liquid* on back; large ring collar; ABM; clear; 9½"
.... 2.00-6.00

7097 Decanter; silver inlay; cobalt; 7"... 15.00-25.00

7098 Decanter; whiskey label; fancy sides; wine color; 10½".................... 8.00-15.00

7099 DEIMEL BROS. & CO. under bottom; clear or amethyst; 4¾" 2.00-8.00

7100 DESIGN PAT'D, FEB 16TH 1886 under bottom in sunken circle; five different sizes of rings on top of shoulder; one ¼" ring on bottom (trunk); clear; 12¼" 6.00-10.00

7101 DETROIT CREAMERY CO. DETROIT, MICH. REGISTERED; *DC CO. 12 OZ. LIQUID SEALED 48* on back; large ring collar; fourteen vertical ribs on shoulder; clear; pint; 5¼"
.... 3.00-6.00

7102 F. W. DEVOE & CO.; clear or amethyst; 3¼"
.... 2.00-4.00

7103 Dog, figural; candy; clear; 3¾" 5.00-10.00

7104 Dog, figural; beverage; clear; 10"... 4.00-8.00

7105 JOHN T. DOYLE & CO., NEW HAVEN, CONN., BOKASKA LAUNDRY SOAP; clear or aqua 4.00-8.00

7106 DUNKLEY'S GENUINE; bulge at shoulder; screw top; round; amethyst; 6"..... 1.00-2.00

7107 D.W. & CO. under bottom; aqua; 9½" 2.00-4.00

7108 DYSON NELSON, TRADE MARK; round; inside screw; aqua; 6¾" 2.00-6.00

7109 EASTMAN, ROCHESTER, N.Y.; clear; 5"
.... 2.00-4.00

7110 ECLIPSE; number on bottom; dark amber; 4½"
.... 3.00-4.00

7111 ECLIPSE; machine made; aqua; 4½" 2.00-3.00

7112 THOMAS A. EDISON in script; BATTERY OIL; clear; 4¼"................... 2.00-4.00

7113 E.G., label; *D* under bottom; aqua; 8" 2.00-4.00

7114 E.G.L. CO., BOSTON; *The Samson Battery No. 1* on one side; sheared top; aqua; 5¾" x 4" x 4"
.... 8.00-12.00

7115 ELGIN MILKINE CO.; sheared top; aqua; 5½"
.... 6.00-10.00

7116 CHARLES ELLIS & SON CO.; aqua; 7"
.... 4.00-6.00

7117 EMPIRE NURSING BOTTLE; *void* on one flat side; neck tapered; amethyst; 5¼"... 2.00-3.00

7118 CARLO ERBA on one panel; on back *Milano*; beveled corners; 1¾" square; 6"..... 4.00-8.00

7119 same as above except 7½" 4.00-8.00

7120 EVERETT & BARRON CO., SHOE POLISH, PROVIDENCE R.I.; oval; clear; 4¾" 1.00-2.00

7121 EVERLASTING BLACK DYE, BALTIMORE, MD.; ABM; cobalt; 4¾"............ 4.00-8.00

7122 E Z STOVE POLISH; *#14* on bottom; aqua; 6"
.... 2.00-8.00

7123 FAIR ACRES DAIRY, MOST MODERN DAIRY IN NEBRASKA, PHONE 511 in circular slug plate; large ring collar; ABM; clear; 5½"
.... 3.00-4.00

7124 FALK in sunken panel; IMPROVED FIRE EXT'R. in three panels; on shoulder *Pat. Appl'd. For*; green; 6½".................. 30.00-55.00

7125 FIRE EXTINGUISHER MFG. CO., BABCOCK HAND GRENADE on round panels; *S. Des Plaines St. Chicago; non freezing*; ball shaped; fourteen rings around bottle; clear; 7½"
.... 10.00-25.00

7126 THIS BOTTLE LOANED BY F.W. FITCH CO. on lower trunk; tapered neck; round; amethyst; 8".................... 2.00-4.00

7127 FIVE DROPS on one panel; *Chicago U.S.A.* on the other; rectangular; aqua; 5½"... 2.00-3.00

7128 W & J FLETT; aqua; 6¾" 15.00-20.00

7130   7131   7132   7134   7136   7137   7138   7139

7140   7143   7144   7145   7146   7149   7150   7156

7158   7159   7160   7161   7163   7164   7165   7166

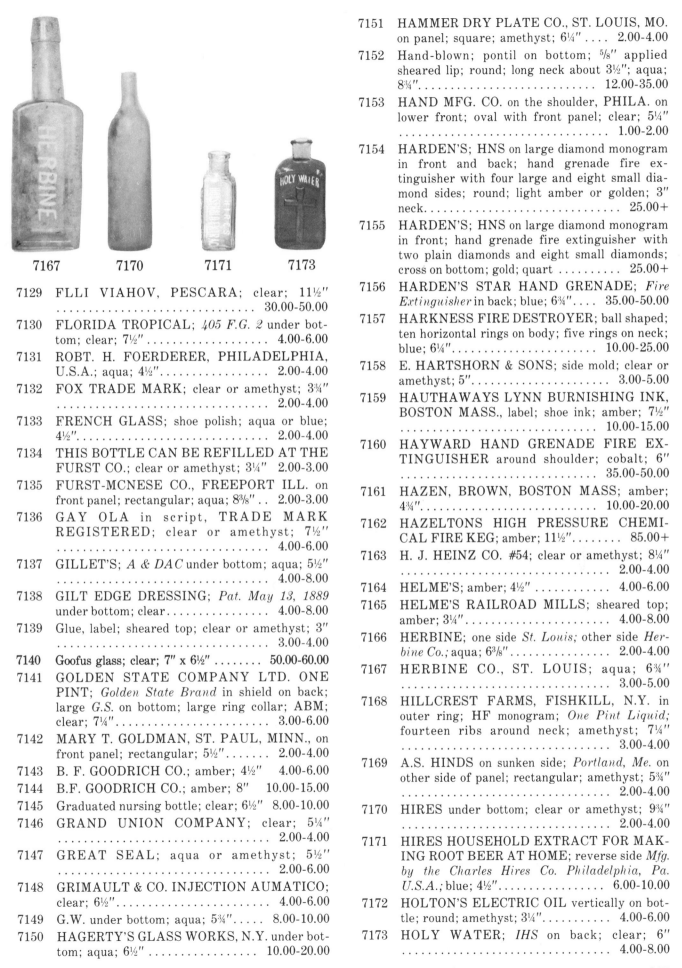

7167   7170   7171   7173

7129 FLLI VIAHOV, PESCARA; clear; 11½"
.... 30.00-50.00

7130 FLORIDA TROPICAL; *405 F.G. 2* under bottom; clear; 7½" 4.00-6.00

7131 ROBT. H. FOERDERER, PHILADELPHIA, U.S.A.; aqua; 4½" 2.00-4.00

7132 FOX TRADE MARK; clear or amethyst; 3¾"
.... 2.00-4.00

7133 FRENCH GLASS; shoe polish; aqua or blue; 4½" 2.00-4.00

7134 THIS BOTTLE CAN BE REFILLED AT THE FURST CO.; clear or amethyst; 3¼" 2.00-3.00

7135 FURST-MCNESE CO., FREEPORT ILL. on front panel; rectangular; aqua; 8⅜" .. 2.00-3.00

7136 GAY OLA in script, TRADE MARK REGISTERED; clear or amethyst; 7½"
.... 4.00-6.00

7137 GILLET'S; *A & DAC* under bottom; aqua; 5½"
.... 4.00-8.00

7138 GILT EDGE DRESSING; *Pat. May 13, 1889* under bottom; clear............... 4.00-8.00

7139 Glue, label; sheared top; clear or amethyst; 3"
.... 3.00-4.00

7140 Goofus glass; clear; 7" x 6½" 50.00-60.00

7141 GOLDEN STATE COMPANY LTD. ONE PINT; *Golden State Brand* in shield on back; large *G.S.* on bottom; large ring collar; ABM; clear; 7¼"............................. 3.00-6.00

7142 MARY T. GOLDMAN, ST. PAUL, MINN., on front panel; rectangular; 5½"....... 2.00-4.00

7143 B. F. GOODRICH CO.; amber; 4½" 4.00-6.00

7144 B.F. GOODRICH CO.; amber; 8" 10.00-15.00

7145 Graduated nursing bottle; clear; 6½" 8.00-10.00

7146 GRAND UNION COMPANY; clear; 5¼"
.... 2.00-4.00

7147 GREAT SEAL; aqua or amethyst; 5½"
.... 2.00-6.00

7148 GRIMAULT & CO. INJECTION AUMATICO; clear; 6½" 4.00-6.00

7149 G.W. under bottom; aqua; 5¾"..... 8.00-10.00

7150 HAGERTY'S GLASS WORKS, N.Y. under bottom; aqua; 6½" 10.00-20.00

7151 HAMMER DRY PLATE CO., ST. LOUIS, MO. on panel; square; amethyst; 6¼" 2.00-4.00

7152 Hand-blown; pontil on bottom; ⅝" applied sheared lip; round; long neck about 3½"; aqua; 8¾"............................. 12.00-35.00

7153 HAND MFG. CO. on the shoulder, PHILA. on lower front; oval with front panel; clear; 5¼"
.... 1.00-2.00

7154 HARDEN'S; HNS on large diamond monogram in front and back; hand grenade fire extinguisher with four large and eight small diamond sides; round; light amber or golden; 3" neck............................. 25.00+

7155 HARDEN'S; HNS on large diamond monogram in front; hand grenade fire extinguisher with two plain diamonds and eight small diamonds; cross on bottom; gold; quart .... 25.00+

7156 HARDEN'S STAR HAND GRENADE; *Fire Extinguisher* in back; blue; 6¾".... 35.00-50.00

7157 HARKNESS FIRE DESTROYER; ball shaped; ten horizontal rings on body; five rings on neck; blue; 6¼"............................. 10.00-25.00

7158 E. HARTSHORN & SONS; side mold; clear or amethyst; 5".................... 3.00-5.00

7159 HAUTHAWAYS LYNN BURNISHING INK, BOSTON MASS., label; shoe ink; amber; 7½"
.... 10.00-15.00

7160 HAYWARD HAND GRENADE FIRE EXTINGUISHER around shoulder; cobalt; 6"
.... 35.00-50.00

7161 HAZEN, BROWN, BOSTON MASS; amber; 4¾"............................. 10.00-20.00

7162 HAZELTONS HIGH PRESSURE CHEMICAL FIRE KEG; amber; 11½"....... 85.00+

7163 H. J. HEINZ CO. #54; clear or amethyst; 8¼"
.... 2.00-4.00

7164 HELME'S; amber; 4½" 4.00-6.00

7165 HELME'S RAILROAD MILLS; sheared top; amber; 3¼".................... 4.00-8.00

7166 HERBINE; one side *St. Louis;* other side *Herbine Co.;* aqua; 6⅜"............. 2.00-4.00

7167 HERBINE CO., ST. LOUIS; aqua; 6¾"
.... 3.00-5.00

7168 HILLCREST FARMS, FISHKILL, N.Y. in outer ring; HF monogram; *One Pint Liquid;* fourteen ribs around neck; amethyst; 7¼"
.... 3.00-4.00

7169 A.S. HINDS on sunken side; *Portland, Me.* on other side of panel; rectangular; amethyst; 5¾"
.... 2.00-4.00

7170 HIRES under bottom; clear or amethyst; 9¾"
.... 2.00-4.00

7171 HIRES HOUSEHOLD EXTRACT FOR MAKING ROOT BEER AT HOME; reverse side *Mfg. by the Charles Hires Co. Philadelphia, Pa. U.S.A.;* blue; 4½"................ 6.00-10.00

7172 HOLTON'S ELECTRIC OIL vertically on bottle; round; amethyst; 3¼".......... 4.00-6.00

7173 HOLY WATER; *IHS* on back; clear; 6"
.... 4.00-8.00

7174   7176   7178   7180   7181   7184   7189

7192   7194   7195   7199   7200   7201   7203

7204   7205   7210   7211   7212   7213   7214

7216 7217 7218

7174 Honey barrel; 5¼"............... 25.00-40.00

7175 HORLICK'S CORP. MALTED MILK, RACINE, WISC.; 5½"............. 4.00-6.00

7176 Horseshoe-shaped bottle; light amber; 4" 4.00-8.00

7177 J.F. HOWARD, HAVERHILL, MASS. around the lower part of trunk; round; fluted; clear; 7¼" 1.00-2.00

7178 HRRROL; green glass; painted black; 6¼" .... 10.00+

7179 HUBBARD'S VEGETABLE GERMICIDE, DISINFECTANT AND DEODORIZER, TRADE MARK J. HUBBARD & CO. BOSTON, MASS; clear; 4¾"................ 4.00-8.00

7180 HUNT MFG. CO.; machine made; clear; 2½" 2.00-4.00

7181 HUSBANDS; aqua; 4½".......... 3.00-6.00

7182 HYGIENIC NURSING BOTTLE, PREVENTS SICKNESS, PAT'D., EASILY CLEANED EASILY FILLED, GRADED MEASURE 1-8 OZ.; clear; 6½" 8.00-10.00

7183 HYNSON WESCOTT DUNNING; square; clear; 2" 1.00-2.00

7184 IMPERIAL POLISH CO., label; aqua; 7¼" 2.00-4.00

7185 INDIA CHOLAGOGUE; *N.Y.* on left; *Osgoods* on right; rectangular; aqua; 5¼".... 3.00-7.00

7186 same as above except *Norwich, Conn.* 3.00-7.00

7187 JENNINGS BLUING; blob top; aqua; 7" 4.00-6.00

7188 ALEXIS CODILLOT JEUNE on one curved panel; *Bordeaux* on one of four 1¼" x 1" curved tapered panels; curved corner panels; vase type blob neck; ring top; green; 9" tall, 1¾" mouth 7.00-12.00

7189 JOHNSTON & CO in horseshoe, under it PHILADA; in back, big monogram *J;* aqua 4.00-8.00

7190 JSP monogram in center of bottle; green; 9¼" 4.00-8.00

7191 KEEN KUTTER, ST. LOUIS, U.S.A., TRADE-MARK on front; *E.G. Simmons, Simmons Hardware Co.* on left; *Keen Kutter Oil* on right; rectangular; clear; 4"............. 2.00-4.00

7192 KELLER DETROIT under bottom; clear or amethyst; 2½" 3.00-4.00

7193 KELLERSTRASS DIS. CO.; *Reg. Dis, Kansas City, Mo.; U.S.A.* on bottle; round; tall ornate neck; amethyst; 12"............. 6.00-16.00

7194 Kerosene bottle; metal and glass; aqua; gallon 25.00-35.00

7195 WM. F. KIDDER; clear; 5¾"...... 3.00-6.00

7196 KILLINGER; square; aqua; 7⅞".... 3.00-4.00

7197 KNAPPS ROOT BEER EXTRACT, TRADE MARK; man holding glass with both hands; yellow green..................... 4.00-8.00

7198 KOKEN, ST. LOUIS, U.S.A., 10 FL. OZ.; round; clear; 7" 1.00-2.00

7199 KUTNOW'S POWDER; aqua; 4¾" 6.00-10.00

7200 KY. C.W. under bottom; aqua; 7".... 3.00-6.00

7201 KY GLASS WORKS under bottom; clear; 7" .... 8.00+

7202 LAKE CARMEL DAIRY, CARMEL, N.Y. in circular slug plate; *One Quart Liquid;* ABM; clear; 9½" 3.00-4.00

7203 LAKE SHORE SEED CO.; aqua; 5¾" 4.00-6.00

7204 LARKIN SOAP CO.; clear; 3½"..... 2.00-4.00

7205 LAROCHE; small kick-up; aqua 2.00-4.00

7206 REILLY LEAVY & CO, NEW YORK on panel; flat corner; roofed shoulder; amber; 2" neck, 2½" square, 9½" tall 6.00-10.00

7207 LEDYARD FARM, REG. N. READING T.M.C.T.; seal in circle on shoulder; clear; 7¼" 4.00-8.00

7208 P.C. LEIDIGH, ASLAND, PA.; P.C.L. monogram; blob top; aqua; 9¼"...... 4.00-8.00

7209 LINCOLN PENNY BANK; Lincoln figural; screw top; clear; 3½".............. 6.00-8.00

7210 LIQUID VENEER under bottom; clear or amethyst; 6¼" 2.00-6.00

7211 Loaf of bread figural; crude top; short neck; three-part mold; big pontil; green; 6½" tall, 10" long, 6" wide....................... 25.00+

7212 L S in a diamond shape under bottom; light amber; 6" 4.00-6.00

7213 MADE IN LYNCHBOR, NO. 44 (backwards) U.S.A.; insulator; green 5.00-10.00

7214 M.M. MACKIE SCOTT & CO.; row of dots on back; satin finish glass; 12½"...... 8.00-10.00

7215 K.H. MACY & CO. N.Y.; snuff; clear 10.00-20.00

7216 MAJOR'S CEMENT; *This is Major's Leather Cement* on back; aqua; 3".......... 3.00-4.00

7217 MAJOR'S CEMENT CO.; *N.Y. U.S.A., This Is Major's* and *Rubber Cement* on other sides; aqua; 4¼"................................ 6.00-8.00

7218 E. MALUWITZ; 3¾"............... 4.00-8.00

7219   7220   7221   7222   7223   7224   7226

7230   7231   7232   7233   7234   7235   7236

7237   7238   7240   7241   7244   7245   7246

7247	7248	7253	7255	7256	7258	7259

7219 THE MANOLA CO., label; machine made; amber; 9½".................... 2.00-4.00

7220 MARTIN & MARTIN; clear; 6".... 2.00-4.00

7221 W.E. MASTEN'S CAPITAL CITY FLA. WATER, ALBANY, N.Y.; aqua; 9" 8.00-10.00

7222 MAVIS under bottom; machine made; amber; 8".................... 2.00-4.00

7223 W. McCULLY & CO. under bottom; *Chicago* on back; olive; 10".................. 8.00-10.00

7224 McHENRY; amber; 10"......... 6.00-10.00

7225 LIBBY McNEIL, CHICAGO; clear; 8¼"............................ 30.00-50.00

7226 MELCHIOR BROS, CHICAGO; sunken panel in back for label; clear or amethyst; 8"............................ 2.00-6.00

7227 MILK 3c DEPOSIT around base; clear; 8½"............................ 8.00-10.00

7228 FRANK MILLER & SONS N.Y. PAT. DEC. 26, -76, NEWTONS; aqua; 5"...... 10.00-15.00

7229 FRANK MILLER'S CROWN DRESSING, N.Y. U.S.A.; *27* under bottom; aqua; 5"............................ 8.00-10.00

7230 MISSOURI LUMBER & MINING CO.; *Grandin Mo.* on label; clear; 5¾"....... 2.00-4.00

7231 MO; aqua; 2½" tall, 1½" x ¾"...... 2.00-4.00

7232 Monogram on bottom; aqua; 8¼".... 2.00-4.00

7233 MT. WASHINGTON GLASS CO.; 19th century; opaque glass encrusted with gold, roses and pastel flowers; 12¼"........... 300.00+

7234 T.H. MUSKOPF; sheared top; clear or amethyst; 5½".................... 4.00-8.00

7235 N under bottom in a small kick-up; aqua; 9½"............................ 2.00-4.00

7236 N & B CO. under bottom; amber; 7½" 2.00-4.00

7237 NELSON BAKER & CO.; amber; 12¾"............................ 8.00-12.00

7238 NEWBRO'S; clear or amethyst; 7".. 2.00-4.00

7239 NEWHOUSES RETAIL DEPARTMENT in fancy letters in two lines, with two flower designs; *Louisville, WT & CO* under bottom; emerald green; 5¼"................ 4.00-8.00

7240 NONPAREIL NURSER; aqua; 5½"............................ 12.00-18.00

7241 NOTOX, FEB. 14, 1922; #4 under bottom; inside screw top; amber; 7"......... 4.00-8.00

7242 NULINE PRODUCTS; almost all are machine made; reproduced from old molds such as *Cabin Bitters* and *Apple Bitters*........... 2.00-6.00

7243 Nursing bottle; in front, graduated scale of 1-8 ounces; under bottom *86*; triangle with *T* and *#1*; clear or amethyst; 6¼"......... 4.00-8.00

7244 WM. F. NYE OIL and a star under bottom; clear or amethyst; 2".................... 3.00-4.00

7245 OLD DR. J. TOWNSENDS; other side *Sarsaparilla 1860*; graphite pontil; blue green; 9½"............................ 85.00+

7246 C. OPPEL & CO. FRIEDRIGH SHALL under bottom; olive; 9"................. 6.00-8.00

7247 OXOLO; aqua; 8".................. 6.00-8.00

7248 PACKER 1870 WEST BROOK'S PAT. around base; amber; 8½".................. 55.00+

7249 Paste; plain; conical; aqua; 3¼"..... 2.00-6.00

7250 Paste; plain; twelve panels; conical; aqua; 3⅛"............................ 2.00-4.00

7251 GEO. R. PATTERSON, JEB-CITY; on back monogram *G.R.P.*; on each side *Trade Mark*; aqua; 7¼"............................ 2.00-4.00

7252 P.D. & CO.; under bottom *84*; round; short neck; green; 7½"............................ 4.00-6.00

7253 PEPPERMINT; pontil; clear; 6½" 8.00-12.00

7254 PERFECTION BOTTLE CO., WILKES BARRE, PA.; *Patd. March 3-97* on base; aqua; 8½"............................ 15.00-25.00

7255 Persian bottle; pontil; olive; 6¾"...... 30.00+

7256 Persian water bottle; saddle flask; label; pontil; green; 9"............................ 35.00+

7257 Pig figural; bank bottle; clear; 5½".. 4.00-8.00

7258 PILDEN CO., NEW LEBANON N.Y.; ST. LOUIS MO., label; clear; 8¼"...... 4.00-6.00

7259 P.L. under bottom; snuff; round corners; amber; 3" x 2¼" x 1½".................... 8.00-10.00

7260 P.L. CO. under bottom; snuff; beveled corners; amber........................ 8.00-15.00

7261   7262   7263   7265   7267   7268   7269   7270

7272   7274   7275   7276   7278   7279   7280   7281

7282   7283   7284   7285   7289   7290   7291   7292

| 7293 | 7294 | 7295 | 7296 | 7297 | 7298 | 7299 | 7300 |

7261 P.L. CO. under bottom; snuff; sheared top; amber; 4¼".......................... 4.00-6.00

7262 Pocket watch bottle, label; clear; 2½" 2.00-4.00

7263 Polish; plain; light green; 5"....... 1.00-2.00

7264 THE POTTER-PARLIN CO; under bottom *Cin*; ridge around bottom; vase type; sheared lip; clear........................ 3.00-6.00

7265 POTTER & MERWIN; plain back; on one side *St. Louis*; on other *Missouri*; beveled corner; roofed shoulder; tapered top; aqua; 5½" tall; 2½" x 1½"............................ 6.00-8.00

7266 same as above except pontil....... 8.00-12.00

7267 PRICES PATENT CANDLE COMPANY, TOPER LIMITED in five lines on front; square; in center *A.Y. 46* and *RD* with two lines under; cobalt blue........................ 25.00+

7268 THE PURDUE FREDERICK CO.; saddle side strap; clear or amethyst; 8"........ 3.00-4.00

7269 REED'S; *Reed's Patties Eugene O. Reed Co. Chicago* on back; cork top filler; clear; 11"
.... 4.00-8.00

7270 R G & CO.; clear; 4¾"............. 2.00-4.00

7271 RHUM VILEJOINT; embossed monogram and shield; emerald green; quart; 10" 10.00-20.00

7272 J. RIEGER & CO.; clear or amethyst; 4½"
.... 2.00-6.00

7273 WISDOM ROBERTINE in two vertical lines on front; cobalt; 5"................... 2.00-4.00

7274 ROCKFORD KALAMAZOO AUTOMATIC AND HAND FIRE EXTINGUISHER, PATENT APPLIED FOR; cobalt; 10¾" 25.00-35.00

7275 Roman bottle; tear drop; free-blown; pontil; aqua; 5"...................... 10.00-20.00

7276 E. ROOME, TROY NEW YORK; pontil; square; dark amber; 4½" corner panels; 4¼" tall
.... 35.00+

7277 L. ROSE & CO. LTD on shoulder; rose vine on bottle; pale green; 11¼" or 14"...... 6.00-8.00

7278 R & S 182 B under bottom; aqua; 9½" 2.00-6.00

7279 RUMFORD CHEMICAL WORKS; eight panels; blue green; 5¾".......... 4.00-8.00

7280 RUTARD 85 under bottom; clear or amethyst; 8½"........................... 10.00-12.00

7281 SAUER'S EXTRACT on each side in panels; clear or amethyst; 6".............. 2.00-4.00

7282 SAWYER'S; aqua; 5¾"........... 4.00-8.00

7283 CARL H. SCHULTZ, N.Y.; blue; 7½"
.... 15.00-20.00

7284 SCRUBBS; *Fluid* on back; *D & M Reg No 592584* under bottom; aqua; 8"..... 8.00-10.00

7285 S. & D. under bottom; amber; 2¾".. 2.00-4.00

7286 SEAMANS, POUGHKEEPSIE, N.Y. DAIRY; ONE QUART LIQUID in circular slug plate; large *S* on back in circular slug plate; large ring collar; ABM; clear; 9½".......... 3.00-4.00

7287 SEVILLE PACKING CO. N.Y.; preserves jar; green; 7"........................ 4.00-8.00

7288 SHAMROCK OIL; on one side *Cincinnati Ohio*; other side *C.B. Dodge*; aqua; 6½".... 6.00-8.00

7289 Shoe polish, label; aqua; 4¾"....... 2.00-3.00

7290 Shoe polish, label; *782 4* under bottom; 4¼"
.... 2.00-4.00

7291 Shoe polish, label; *4* under bottom; clear; 3¼"
.... 2.00-4.00

7292 Shoe polish, label; aqua; 3¼"....... 1.00-2.00

7293 Shoe polish, label; aqua; 4¼"....... 2.00-4.00

7294 SIMMONS HARDWARE CO. INC.; three-piece mold; clear or amethyst; 5¼".. 6.00-8.00

7295 JAMES P. SMITH & COMPANY; aqua; 4½"
.... 2.00-6.00

7296 JAMES P. SMITH N.Y. & CHICAGO; sheared top; clear; 5".................... 2.00-3.00

7297 JOHN J. SMITH; aqua; 6¾"....... 3.00-6.00

7298 Snuff, label; *#16* under bottom; beveled corners; amber; 4" x 2¼" x 2¼"............. 4.00-6.00

7299 Snuff, label; pontil; light olive; 5¾" 20.00-25.00

7300 Snuff, label; *#445* under bottom; beveled corners; amber; 4" x 2½" x 1"........ 4.00-6.00

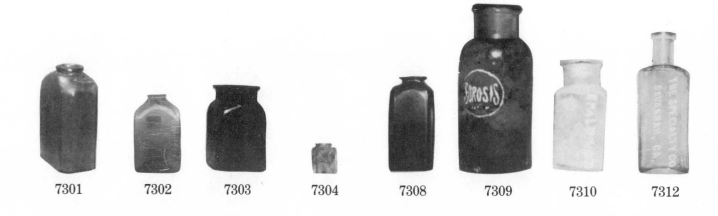

7301   7302   7303   7304   7308   7309   7310   7312

7313   7314   7315   7321   7323   7324   7325   7326

7327   7330   7332   7334   7335   7337   7338   7339

| 7340 | 7341 | 7344 | 7345 |

7301   Snuff, label; beveled corners; amber; 4¼″ x 1¼″ x 2¾″ 4.00-6.00

7302   Snuff, label; pontil; olive or amber; 4¼″ 25.00+

7303   Snuff, label; machine made; amber; 2½″ 1.00-2.00

7304   Snuff; plain; round sunken circle under bottom; ring neck; golden amber; 1⅞″ x 1¼″, 1⅜″ curved front and back 4.00-6.00

7305   Snuff; plain; beveled corners; crude top; golden amber; 2½″ square base, 4″ tall 6.00-12.00

7306   Snuff; plain; beveled corners; very short crude neck; pontil; amber; 2½″ square base, 4″ tall .... 25.00+

7307   Snuff; plain; beveled corners; sunken T under bottom; very short crude neck; olive; 2¾″ x 1¾″, 4¼″ tall .... 25.00+

7308   same as above except pontil; 6½″ tall ... 25.00+

7309   SOROSIS; aqua; 4″ 2.00-3.00

7310   SPALDING'S; *Glue* on back; aqua; 3¼″ tall, 1½″ diameter 2.00-6.00

7311   SPALDING'S; *Glue* on back; crude; aqua; 1½″ round bottom, 3¼″ tall 2.00-4.00

7312   THE SPECIALTY CO.; clear or amethyst; 5″ 1.00-2.00

7313   SPERM SEWING MACHINE OIL; *Will Not Gum* on one side; *Will Not Corrode* on other side; clear; 5½″ 2.00-4.00

7314   SPURR'S JAMAICA GINGER FLASK, BOSTON MASS, label; clear or amethyst; 4¾″ 8.00-10.00

7315   STANDARD OIL CO., label; *433* under bottom; clear; 6″ 4.00-6.00

7316   FREDERICK STEARNS & CO; *Detroit Mich* on side panel; three-cornered bottle; amber; 10¼″ 8.00-10.00

7317   same as above except machine made .. 2.00-4.00

7318   same as above except *F. Stearnes & Co.;* 6¼″ 8.00-10.00

7319   same as above except 4¾″ 8.00-10.00

7320   STICK WELL CO. on three panels; six panels in all; conical; aqua; 3″ 6.00-8.00

7321   STICK WELL & CO.; clear; 3″ .... 8.00+

7322   STODDARD SNUFF; beveled corners; open pontil; olive green; 4¾″ 10.00-20.00

7323   JOHN W. STOUT & CO in a half circle; in center big X, under it NEW YORK; globular body; tapered top; aqua; 4″ neck; 8¼″ tall 10.00-15.00

7324   STOVINK JOHNSONS LABORATORY WORCESTER MASS; clear; 4½″ ... 2.00-4.00

7325   TAPPAN; clear; 3¼″ 4.00-8.00

7326   TAPPAN'S; aqua; 5½″ 2.00-4.00

7327   TARRANT & CO.; clear; 2¼″ 2.00-3.00

7328   THOMPSON & TAYLOR, SHAKE THOROUGHLY, IT FOAMS; aqua or clear 4.00-6.00

7329   TRUE CEPHALICK SNUFF BY THE KINGS PATENT, 1848; pontil; 3½″ 30.00-50.00

7330   T.W.C. CO. U.S.A. on bottom; cobalt; 7½″ 8.00-12.00

7331   VAN DUZERS ESSENCE JAMAICA GINGER, NEW YORK; aqua; 6″ 4.00-8.00

7332   Vase; plain; green or clear; 8″ 2.00-6.00

7333   VENABLE & HEYMAN, 152 CHAMBERS ST. N.Y.; under bottom *Buckingham*; amber; 6″ 10.00-12.00

7334   VIRTRAY; green; 6¼″ 4.00-6.00

7335   VO2 under bottom; sheared top; clear; 6″ 2.00-6.00

7336   WARDLES, LONDON SUPERFINE; open pontil; clear or amethyst 10.00-20.00

7337   W. R. WARNER & CO.; *Phila.* on back; three-part mold; aqua; 8″ 2.00-6.00

7338   E. WATERS TROY N.Y.; *Leather Varnish,* label; 4¾″ .... 45.00+

7339   WEYMAN BRUTON CO. SNUFF, label; machine made; amber; 4¼″ 2.00-3.00

7340   WHARTON CHEMICAL CO.; clear; 6½″ 4.00-6.00

7341   R. WHITE; *R.B.R. 3213* on base; aqua; 8½″ 8.00-12.00

7342   WHITTEMORE, BOSTON, U.S.A. in sunken panel; ring top; aqua or clear; 5⅕″ tall, 1⁷⁄₁₆″ x 2¼″ 3.00-6.00

7343   WHITTEMORE, BOSTON, U.S.A. in a sunken panel; aqua; 5½″ 2.00-4.00

7344   WHYTE & MACKAY on back; M&M on front; three-part mold; aqua; 9¾″ 5.00-10.00

7345   EDWARD WILDER & CO., WHOLESALE DRUGGISTS, LOUISVILLE, KY.; reverse side *E.W. Sarasaparilla Potasil;* windows on panels; clear; 8½″ .... 75.00+

7346   W. WINTERSMITH, LOUISVILLE, KY. in two vertical lines in a slug plate; amber; 5½″ 2.00-6.00

7347
7349
7353

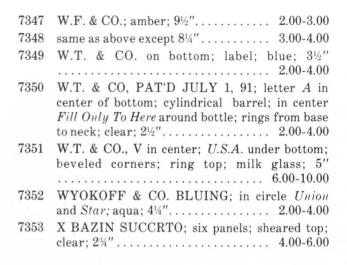

7347	W.F. & CO.; amber; 9½".	2.00-3.00
7348	same as above except 8¼".	3.00-4.00
7349	W.T. & CO. on bottom; label; blue; 3½"	2.00-4.00
7350	W.T. & CO, PAT'D JULY 1, 91; letter *A* in center of bottom; cylindrical barrel; in center *Fill Only To Here* around bottle; rings from base to neck; clear; 2½".	2.00-4.00
7351	W.T. & CO., V in center; *U.S.A.* under bottom; beveled corners; ring top; milk glass; 5"	6.00-10.00
7352	WYOKOFF & CO. BLUING; in circle *Union* and *Star;* aqua; 4¼".	2.00-4.00
7353	X BAZIN SUCCRTO; six panels; sheared top; clear; 2¾".	4.00-6.00

Above: These three containers are made of unrefined glass ranging in color from olive green to dark green or dark amber, referred to as "black glass." The left and middle containers are snuff jars (#7307) made shortly after 1814. The container on the right is a late 18th-century or early 19th-century American apothecary's beaker. Opposite: Manufactured between 1820 and 1850, this standard-size leather-blacking bottle still contains the original dauber.

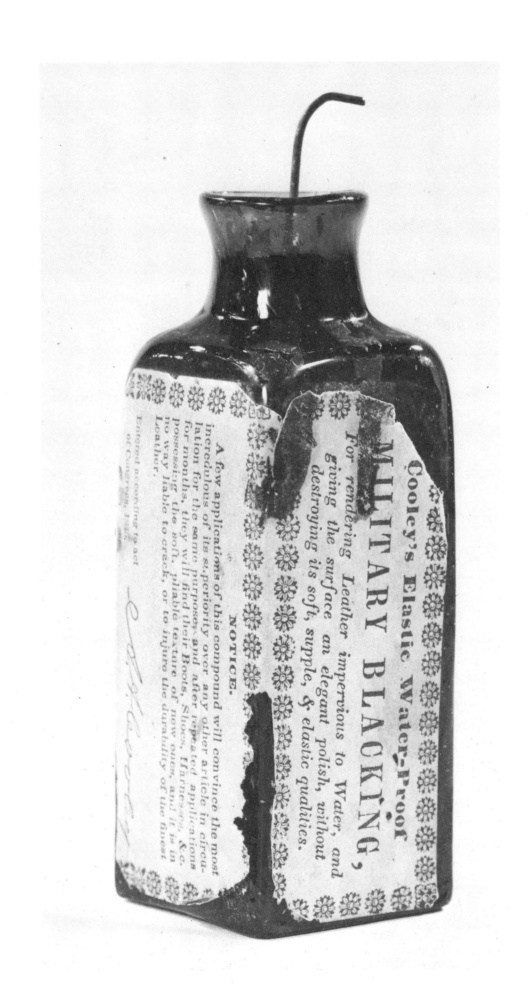

Cooley's Elastic Water-Proof
MILITARY BLACKING,
For rendering Leather impervious to Water, and
giving the surface an elegant polish, without
destroying its soft, supple, & elastic qualities.

NOTICE.

A few applications of this compound will convince the most
incredulous of its superiority over any other article in circu-
lation for the same purposes; and after repeated applications
for months, they will find their Boots, Shoes, Harnesses, &c.
possessing the soft, pliable texture of new ones, and it is in
no way liable to crack, or to injure the durability of the finest
Leather.

Entered according to act
of Congress, &c.

Embossed with the Past

Antique bottles, with both artistic and utilitarian qualities, are authentic expressions of individual craftsmen of times past

Above: This American snuff jar was used between 1797 and 1818. Snuff-taking in America began in earnest in the 18th century and fast developed into an art. A pinch of snuff or powder made from tobacco was taken from the container between thumb and forefinger and inhaled through a tube especially made for the purpose from a quill. Opposite: In most apothecary shops and later pharmacies, a few highly ornate bottles could be found filled with colored water and displayed in store windows. This drugstore showglobe dates back to the late 1800's. Left: This figural oil bottle, embossed "Independence Bell Oiler—1776-1876," was sold at the Centennial Exhibition held in Philadelphia in 1876.

409

In 1783 the Pitkin family of Connecticut made a finely swirled and
vertically ribbed pocket flask. Bottles with this pattern-molded decoration
soon came to be known by the generic term Pitkin, even though
they were produced by other glass works. This group of
Pitkin-type flasks dates back to circa 1800–1840.

Left: The exaggerated indentations in this 18th-century English molded-glass decanter are purely functional in that the indented body allows for an equal distribution of the liquid, thus facilitating the simultaneous cooling of the liquid.
Opposite: Though the label may be misleading, this actually is a gin or case bottle. Perhaps Samuel Tyler was trying to cut costs by bottling his product in a used or discarded container.
Below: Another example of a European case bottle (#3621-#3631), circa 1750, along with a Dutch squat wine bottle (#3660), circa 1700-1715, and a late 18th-century snuff container.

Above: *Though round bottles traveled better in shipments, spice containers such as this one usually had concave front and back panels. Opposite: The H. J. Heinz Company has been credited as one of the first companies to use clear glass strictly for the consumers' benefit. These bottles (#5301 to #5309) date back to 1869.*

This pleasant looking flowery crock (#6297) no doubt
added a touch of decor to the household kitchen in the early
1800's. Crocks were strictly utilitarian and were used as canning
crocks, pickle jars, butter crocks and pudding molds.

APPENDIX

WHAT TO TAKE ON A DIGGING TRIP

When you go digging, take a shovel, two potato rakes (three or four prong), a small short-handled scratcher (three prong garden type), a thin steel probe (rod), gloves, and a bayonet or hunting knife. If digging in woods take a bow-saw for cutting roots and hedge shears for cutting small roots. You will need insect repellent, a snake bite kit, drinking water and snacks. A deep wicker basket with handles is handy for carrying your finds.

RULES OF SAFETY

Never dig alone. Never tunnel into a wall, nor undercut or dig into a bank more than two feet high. Do not drink the contents of a bottle, no matter what the label says. Before reaching into tall grass or a bush, check for snakes.

HOW TO LOCATE BOTTLES

One of the methods of locating a suitable digging site is to find an older citizen in an area who can tell you where the trash was dumped many years ago. A dig in such a location will usually produce very old bottles of all types, but the digging may have to go as deep as 10-12 feet.

Do not overlook junk shops, trading posts, auctions, flea markets and in and around old houses or attics that have been undisturbed for many years. These areas may produce some very old bottles. A good metal detector is helpful in locating trash around old homesteads where bottles and trash are generally intermingled.

HOW TO CLEAN YOUR BOTTLES

Wash with a strong soap or detergent. Use a bottle brush or, in some stubborn cases, steel wool.
Soak in a weak acid for a day or two.
Soak in kerosene for two or three months in a stone jar.
Use baby oil to produce a shine on the bottle.
Some bottles that have become etched or cloudy with age will not come clean, but with plenty of elbow grease most bottles will clean up nicely.

HOW TO TURN CLEAR BOTTLES PURPLE (AMETHYST)

Only bottles that have manganese will turn purple. One method of turning clear bottles purple is by prolonged exposure to the direct rays of the sun. This can be accomplished by placing your bottles in a location where they are protected from damage but open to maximum sunlight. A sheet of aluminum foil placed on the flat surface of a roof with the bottles standing on it will hasten the purpling of the bottle.

Another method is by the use of artificial light. A G.E. G15T8 bulb can be attached to the inside lid of a fully enclosed box large enough to hold your bottle and room enough also for the bulb. Line the box with a reflecting material such as aluminum foil. By placing your bottles in the box and turning on the light the bottles will turn purple in approximately 48 hours. Warning: Be sure to follow printed warnings and instructions on bulb. *Never* turn the light on unless it is in the *closed* box. This light can damage your eyes.

WHERE TO SELL BOTTLES

The best way to sell your bottles is through an ad in a trade journal or magazine specializing in antiques. Be sure to thoroughly describe your bottle as to name, color, size, and so forth. If bottle is listed in this or any price guide, give the listing number. Be sure to state in the ad if the bottle is machine made or free-blown in mold. Also give the physical condition of the bottle—cracked, repaired, etc.

BOTTLE NEWSPAPERS & MAGAZINES

The American Collector, 3717 Mt. Diablo Boulevard, Lafayette, California 94549

Antique Monthly, P.O. Drawer 440, Tuscaloosa, Alabama 35401

Antique News, Box B, Marietta, Pennsylvania 17547

Antique Trader Weekly, P.O. Box 1050, Dubuque, Iowa 52001

Antiques Journal, P.O. Box 1046, Dubuque, Iowa 52001

The Antiquity, P.O. Box 307, Washington, New Jersey 07882

Bottle News, Box 1000, Kermit, Texas 79745

Collector's News, Box 156, Grundey Center, Iowa 50638

Collector's Weekly, Box 1119, Kermit, Texas 79745

Journal of the Federation of Historical Bottle Clubs, 10118 Schuessler, St. Louis, Missouri 63128

National Antiques Review, Box 619, Portland, Maine 04104

Old Bottle Magazine, Box 243, Bend, Oregon 97701

Pictorial Bottle Review, B & K Enterprises, Incorporated, Box 42558, Los Angeles, California 90050

Tri-State Trader, P.O. Box 90-DM, Knightstown, Indiana 46148

Western Antique Mart, Box 2171, Eugene, Oregon 97402

To contact your local bottle collecting club, write to:
Federation of Historical Bottle Clubs
c/o Gene Bradbury, President
4098 Faxon Avenue
Memphis, Tennessee 38122

Forced by a growing temperance movement and increasing liquor taxes, Americans began to consume more and more bitters in the 1860's in lieu of the hard stuff. From left to right, "Warner's" (#414), "Dr. J. Hostetter's" (#226), "Baker's" (#45) and "Goff's" (#178).

INDEX

Nyal's Emulsion 1653
Nyal's Liniment 1654
Wm. F. Nye Oil 7244
Oak Orchard Acid Spring 3468
Oakland Bottling Co. 3995
The Oakland Chemical Co. 1656, 1657
Oakland Pioneer Soda Work Co. 2943
Oakland Steam Soda Works, Inc. 2944
O. B. Co. 3996
Obol 6923, 6924
OC 5950
Occidental Bottle Works 2945
Oconto Brewing Co. 3997
Octagon Ink 6641
Od Chem. Co. 1658
Odiorne's 2946
Odoj 1659
John H. Oelkers 6299
Wm. G. Oesting 305
O'Hare Malt 4768
O'Hearn's Whiskey 4769
Ohio 4770
Ohio Quality Mason 5951
The Property of Ohlsson's Cape Brewery 3998
O. K. Bottling Co. 3469
O. K. Plantation 306, 1660
O. K. Soda Works 2949
O'Keefe Bros. Bottlers 2947, 2948
O'Keefe Bros. High Grade Mineral Water 3470
OL. Amygdal 1661
Ol. Camphor Forte 2241
Ol. Eucalypti 2242
Ol. Sinap. Aeth. 2243
Old Ashton 4771
The Old Bushmills Distilling Co. 4772
Old Charter Whiskey 4773
Old Continental Whiskey 6300–6302
Old Cutter Rye 6303
Old Dr. J. Townsends 7245
Old Dr. Townsend's Sarsaparilla 1662
Old Duffy's Apple Juice Vinegar 5389
Old Duffy's 1842 Apple Juice 4774
Old Edgemont Whiskey 4775, 4776
Old Family Wine Store 4777
Old Henry Rye 4778
Old Hickory Celebrated Stomach Bitters 307
Old Homestead Cabin Bitters 308
Old Homestead Wild Cherry Bitters 309–312
Old Hudson 4779
Old Irish Whiskey 4780, 4781
Old J. H. Cutter 4782
Old Joe Gideon Whiskey Bros. 4783
Old Jug Lager 6304
Old Kaintuck Bourbon 4784
The Old Kentucky 4785
Old Nectar Rye 6305
Old Port Haley Whiskey 4786
Old Prentice Whiskey 4787
Old Quaker 4788
Old Sachem Bitters 313–315
Old Servitor Distributing Co. 4789
The Old Spring Distilling Co. 4790
Old Spring Whiskey 4791
Old Taylor 6306
Old Time 4792
Oldridge Balm of Columbia 1663
O'Leary's 20th Century Bitters 316
Olive oil 5390–5405
J. M. Oliver & Sons 5406
The Oliver Typewriter 6642
W. Olmsted & Co. 3999
Olsen & Co. 2950
Olympia Water Co. 3471, 3472
Omega Oil Chemical Co. 1664–1668
One Minute Cough Cure 569, 570, 571
1 X L 6643
Opdyke 6644, 6645
Opdyke Bros. Ink 6646, 6647
Opium 1669, 1670
Opler Brothers Inc. 5952
C. Oppel & Co. 7246
Oppenheim 4793
Oregon Grape Root Bitters 317
The Orene Parker Co. 4794
Orge Monde 2244
Oriental Condensed Coffee 1671
Oriental Cream 1672, 6925
Original Calif. Mineral Water Co. 3473
The Original Copper Cure 572
Original Pocahontas Bitters 318
Oriza-Oil L. LeGrand 6926
Orizaba Bitters 319
D. L. Ormsby 2951, 6307
Osotite 5953
F. A. Osten's Pure Salad Oil 5407
Oswego Bitters 320
Otis Clapp & Son 1673
E. Otlenville, A. G. D. H. Co. 4795
E. Ottenville 2952, 2953
E. O. Ottenville 3474
Ottman Bros. & Co. 6308
Otto's Cure 573, 574
C. Owens 1674
Owl 1675
Owl Drug Co. 1676–1681, 2246, 2247
Owl Drug Store 1682
Owl Poison Ammonia 2245
Ox 1683
Oxien Pills 1684, 1685
Oxolo 7247
Oxygenated Bitters 321
Ozark Fruit Co. 2954, 2955
Ozo-Ola The Happy Drink 2956
Ozomulsion 1686
Ozon Antiseptic Dressing 1687
The Ozone Co. of Toronto 1688
The Liquid Ozone Co. 1689

Pablo & Co. Mineral Water 3475
Pabst Brewing Co. 4000–4002
J. Pabst & Son 7244
Pacific Bottling Works 2959
Pacific Congress Water 3476, 3477
Pacific Glass Works 5954
Pacific Mason 5955
Pacific & Puget Sound Soda Works 2958
Pacific S. F. Glass Works 5956
Pacific Soda Works 2960
Packer 1870 West Brook's 7248
B. Page Jr. & Co. 3478
Pain & Baylor 6310
Paines Celery Compound 1690, 1691
Palace Drug Store 1692, 1693
Palangie 6927
Palin Medicine bottle 1770–1772
The Palisade Mfg. Co. 1694, 1695
D. Palliser 2961–2966
Palmboom 3733
The Palmedo Brewing Co. 4003
Palmer 6648, 6928–6936
J. W. Palmer 6309
J. W. Palmer Whiskey 4796
Jas. Palmer & Co. 1696
Palmetto Bottling Works 2967
Palmolive Shampoo 1697
10 Panel 1698
Panknin's 322
Pa-Pay-Ans Bell 1699, 1700
Paragon, New 5957
Paraiso Mineral Water 3479
Paris Med. Co. 575
Paris Perfume Co. 6937
John D. Park, Dr. Cuysotts Sarsaparilla 1701
John D. Park, Dr. Wistars Balsam 1702
Parke Davis & Co. 1703–1706
Parker 1707, 2968, 6649, 6650
Parker Bros. 5408
Parker Rye 4797, 4798
Dr. Parker's Cough Cure 577
Parkers Hair Balsam 1708, 1709
Dr. Park's Indian Liniment 1710
Park's Sure Cure 576
E. Parmenter 2969, 2970
Parole 4799
Paskola's, Food Co. 5409
Paste 7249, 7250
Patent 4800
Patent Applied For 5958
Patented April 3d, 1900 4801
Patterson & Brazeau 3480
Geo. R. Patterson 7251
Patterson's Liquor Store 4802, 4803
Paul Jones 4804, 4810, 4814
Paul Jones Bourbon 4805
Paul Jones & Co. 4809, 4813
Paul Jones Gin 4815
Paul Jones Rye 4806, 4808, 4816
Paul Jones Whiskey 4807, 4811, 4812
Paul Westphal 1711
Paul's Inks 6651
Paul's Safety Bottle & Ink Co. 6652
Paul's Writing Fluid 6653
L. Pautauberge Pharmacieu 6938
Pavilion & United State Spring Co. 3481
Pawnee Bitters 323
Pawnee Indian Ta-Ha 1712
Pawnee Indian, Too-Ree 1713
P. B. Co. Ink 6654
P & C 3734
P. C. G. Co. 5959
P. D. 6939
P D & Co. 1714–1718, 7252
Richard Pearce 6311
The Pearl 5960
Ebenezer A. Pearl's Tincture of Life 1720
Pearl's White Glycerine 1719
Pearson Bros. 2971
Pearsons Pure Old Malt Whiskey 4817
Pearson's Soda Works 2972
Pease's Eye Water 1721
Pedro 4818
Prof. W. H. Peek's Remedy 1722
Peerless 5961, 6655
Dr. H. F. Peery's 1723, 1724
Wm. Pendleton 1725
Penn Mfg. Work 6657
The Penn 5962
J. W. Pennell 6656
Penns Bitters 324
Peoples Chemical Co. 1726
Peoria Pottery 5963
Peperazine Effervescente 1727
Peppermint 5410, 7253
Peppersauce 5411–5429
Pepsi-Cola 2973–2980
Pepsin Bitters 325
Pepsin Calisaya Bitters 326
Pepsine Chapoteaut 5430
Peptenzyme 1728
Peptenzyne 1729
Pepto-Mangan Gude 1730
Peptogenic Milk Powder 5431
Perfect Seal 5966, 5967
Perfection 5964
Perfection Bottle Co. 7254
The New Perfection 5965
Perfume 6940–6984
Perfumerie 6985
P. W. Perkins 2981
Perrins Apple Ginger 327
Perry & Co. 6658
Dr. D. S. Perry & Co. 328
Perry Mfg. Co., Inc. 2982
John A. Perry's, Dr. Warren's 329
Persian bottle 7255, 7256

Pet 5968, 5969
Peter Moller's Cod Liver Oil 1732
Dr. Peter's Kuriko 1731
J. J. Peters 3735
J. J. W. Peters 3736–3739
N. C. Peters 2983
M. Peterson Soda Works 2984
John V. Petritz 2985
H. W. Pettit 5970
Dr. J. Pettits Canker Balsam 1733
S. F. Petts & Co. 4819
Dr. Petzolds Cabin Bitters 330
Peychaud's American Aromatic 331
Henry Pfaff 2986, 2987
C. Pfeiffer Brewing Co. 4004
Pfeiffer Chemical Co. 1734
Geo. Pfeiffer, Jr. 2988
P. G. & Old Bristol 3740
P. H. Crystal Spring Water 3482
Phalon's Chemical Hair Invigorator 1735
Dr. O. Phelps 1736
John H. Phelps Pharmacist 1737
Philantrop 3741
C. H. Phillips 1739
Phillips Emulsion 1740–1742
Phillips Emulsion Cod Liver Oil 1738
Phillips Milk of Magnesia 1743
Phillipsburg Bottle Work 2989
Phoenix Bitters 332
Phoenix Bottling Works 2990
Phoenix Brand 5432
Phoenix Brewing Co. 4005
Phoenix Glass Work 2991
Pholon's Vitalia 1744
Phosphocyclo-fer 1745
J. Picard 6986
Pickle 5433–5482
Pickle or cherry 5483
Pickman's Chocolate 5484
Picnic flask 4820
Piel Bros. 4006–4009
R. V. Pierce, N.D. 1748, 2992
Dr. Pierces Anuric Tablets 1751
Dr. Pierces Anurid Tablets 2993
Dr. Pierce's Auguric Table 1749
Dr. Pierce's Favorite Prescription 1750
Dr. Pierce's Golden Med. Disc. 1747
Dr. Geo. Pierce's 1746
Dr. George Pierces Indian Bitters 333
The Goragas Pierie Co. 5971
B. Pietz 2994
Pig figural 7257
Pikes Peak flask 4181–4185
Pikes Peak Old Rye 4822
S. N. Pikes Magnolia 4821
Pikesville Rye 4823, 4824
Pilden Co. 7258
Pill Bottle 1752–1755
The Pillow Inhale Co. 1756
Pin Money 5486
E. D. Pinaud 5485
Ed Pinaud 6987–6989
Pinch bottle 6990, 6991
Pine Deluxe Jar 5972
Pine Mason 5973
Pine Tree Tar Cordial 1758, 1759
Pineapple Bottle 334, 335
Pineoleum for Cattarrhal 1757
Pinex 1760
Dr. Pinkham's 1761
Lydia E. Pinkham's 1762
Pinkston & Scruggs 1763
Pioneer Bottling Works 2995
Pioneer Soda Water Co. 2998
Pioneer Soda Works 2996, 2997, 2999
W. Pipe 3000
G. W. Piper 6312
Piperazine 1764
The Piso Company 1765
Piso's Cure 578, 579
Dr. S. Pitcher's 1766, 1767
Pitkin Ink Keene 6659
Pitkin Inkwell 6660
Pitkin type flask 4189
Dr. W. M. Pitt's 1768, 1769
Pittsburgh and eagle flask 4186–4188
Pittsburgh Brewing Co. 4010
P. L. 7259
P. L. Co. 7260, 7261
Dr. Planetts Bitters 336, 1773
Planks Chill Tonic Co. 1774
Joseph C. Plante & Co. 3001
Planter Mary Lou Rye 4826, 4827
Planter Rye 4825
Planters 5487, 5488, 5490
Planters Old Time Remedies 1775
Planters Salted Peanuts 5489, 5491
Platt's Chloride 1776
Plow's Sherry Bitters 337
Pluto Water 1777
P. M. F. S. & Co. 1778
Pocket watch bottle 7262
Poison 2248–2253, 2255–2275
Poison, Tincture Iodine 2234
Poland Water 3483
Polar Star Cough Cure 580, 581
Polish 7263
Pomeroy Ink 6661
Paul Pomeroy 3002
Pomlo Bitters Co. 338
Pompeian Brand Olive Oil 5496, 5497
Pompeian Mfg. Co. 6993
Pompeian Massage Cream 1779, 1780, 6992
Pond's 6994
Pond's Bitter Co. 339–341
Pond's Extract 1781, 6995
Pond's Extract Catarrh Remedy 1782

F. E. Suire & Co. 1955
J. P. Sullivan 3179
Sulpholythin 1956
Sultan Drug Co. 1957
Summer and winter flask 4237, 4238
Summers & Allen 3180
Summit Mineral Water 3509
Sumter Bitters 395
Sun 6064
Sunburst flask 4239-4244
Sunset Bottling Works 3182
Sunset Spring Water 3510
Superior Bottling Work 3182
Superior Ink 6720
Superior Soda Water 3183, 3184
Supreme Mason 6065
Sure Seal 6066
Sutherland Sisters Hair Grower 1958, 1960
The E. E. Sutherland Medicine Co. 1959
L. B. Sutton 1961
Swaim's 1962, 1963
E. Swasey & Co. 6336
Swayzee's Fruit Jar 6067
Swayzee's Improved Mason 6068, 6069
Dr. Sweet 396
Dr. Swett's Original Root Beer 6337
Swidler & Bernstein 3186
Swift & Pearson 6721
Swift's 1964
Swirled Pitkin 4245, 4246
Albert H. Sydney 3187
Dr. Sykes Specific 1965
Dr. Sykes Sure Cure 609, 610
Syphon Corp. of Florida 3188
Syr:Hypoph:Co. 2291
Syr:Fer:Iodid 2293
Syr:Fer:Pa:Co. 2292
Syr-Rhel Ink 6722
Syr:Rhoead 1966
Syrup of Thedford's 1967
T 7012
Tabasco 5540
Dr. Taft's 1968
Tamalon Safe Animal Cure 611
Tampa Bottling Works 3189
Tampa Cider & Vinegar Co. 3190
The Tampa Pepsi Cola Bottling Co. 3191
Tangin 1969
Tango-Cola 3192
Tappan 7325
Tappan's 7326
Tarrant & Co. 1970, 7327
B. F. Tatman 3193
Louis Taussig & Co. 4939, 4941
Taylor 3195
Brickett J. Taylor Ink 6723
C. Taylor 3196
Taylor & Co. 6070
E. B. Taylor 6338
Taylor & Ringgold 4247
Taylor Soda Water Mfg. Co. 3194
Taylor & Williams 4942-4945
Taylor & Wilson 3197
Taylor's Drug Store 1971, 1972
Taylor's Essence 1973
Taylor's Hospital Cure 612
T. C. C. R. 3765
Tea cup 4946
Tea Kettle Ink 6724-6730
Teaberry for the Teeth & Breath 1974
Teakettle Old Bourbon 4947
Tear drop 3198, 3199
Teikoku Beer 4049
Teinture de Cochenille 2294
Teinture D'Fotida 1975
Teissier Prevos A Paris 1976
Telephone Jar 6071, 6072
The Wide Mouth Telephone Jar 6073
Terre Haute Brewing Co. 4050
Texas 4948
A Texas Wonder 1977
Texas Mason 6074
T F 6075
Dr. Thacher's 1978, 1979, 1981, 1983, 1984
Dr. H. S. Thacher's 1980, 1982, 1985
Jas. Tharp's Sons 4949
Henry Thayer 1986
A. Theller 3766, 4950
Theodore Netter 4951
Thomas 6731
Thomas Electric Oil 1987
L. H. Thomas Co. 6732, 6733
L. H. Thomas Ink 6734-6736
Dr. S. N. Thomas Electric Oil 1988
W. Z. Thomas 3200
F. A. Thompson & Co. 2295
Thompson & Taylor 7328
Thompson's 1991
Dr. Thompson's 1990, 1992
Thompson's Herbal Compound 1989
Thompsons Premium Mineral Waters 3511
Thurston & Kingsbury 1993
Dr. Tichenor's 1994, 1995
Dr. G. H. Tichenor's 1996
Geo. A. Ticoulet 4051
Tight seal 6076
Tikheel 1997
Tilden 1998, 1999
Tillmann's 5539
Claes Tilly 2000
G. De Koning Tilly 2001
Tinct. Aconiti 2300, 2301
Tinct. Camph: Co. 2302
Tinct Celladon, Poison 2296
Tinct. Chlorof. et Morph. Co. 2303
Tinct. Conii Poison 2304
Tinct: Ergotae. Amm. 2305
Tincture Iodine 2297-2299

Tinct. Iodi. Mit. 2306
Tinct. Lobeliae Aeth. 2307
Tinct. Nux Vom 2308
Tinct. Opii 2309, 2310
Tincture: Senegae 2311
Tippecanoe 397, 398, 2002, 2003
LT & Co. 4940
Dr. Tobias 2004, 2005
W. B. Todd 6737
Todd's Bitters 399
Tode Bros. 6339
Toilet Water 7013, 7014
Toka 2006
TOKJ 4952
Toledo Brewing & Malting Co. 4052
Tolenas Soda Springs 3512
Tolle Bottling Works 3201
C. A. Tolle 3202
T. Tomlinson 2007
Toneco Bitter 400
Tonicio Oriental Para El Cabello 2008
To-Ni-Ta Lorents Med. Co. 2009
Tonopah Soda Works 3203
John Tons 4053
Tonsmeire & Craft 4953
R. E. Toombs, Jr. 2010
Tooth Powder 2011
S. A. Torino 4054, 4055
Tournades Kitchen Bouquet 5541
Towne's 3204
Dr. W. Towns 613
Old Dr. Townsend 401
Dr. Townsend Sarsaparilla 2012, 2013
T. P. S. & Co. 7015
The I. Trager Co. 4954-4958
Trappeys Tabasco 5542
A. Trasks 2014
Travel Ink 6738
Travelers Companion 4248-4250
M. Tregor Sons 2015
Treville Paris 7016
Trilets 2312, 2313
Triloids 2314
J. Triner 2016
Trinidad Bottling Works 3205
Tri-Seps 2315
Tri State Bottling Co. 3206
Trommer's Evergreen Br'y. 4056
Tropical Canners 6077
Triton Spouting Spring 3513
Trost Bros. 4959
Truax Rheumatic Remedy 2017
True Cephalick Snuff 7329
True Fruit 6078
True Seal 6079
Dr. Trues Elixir 2018, 2019
Try-Me Beverage Co. 3207
TS 3209
T. & S. Port Townsend Soda Works 3208
Tucker, Ala. 4960
H. A. Tucker, M. D. 2020
J. Tucker, Druggist 2021
Nathan Tucker, M. D. 2022
Tucson Bottling Works 3210
Tufts Angostura Bitters 402
F. G. Tulledge & Co. 4961
Turkish Foot Bath 2023
Turkish Liniment 2024
Robt. Turlington 2025-2027
Turner Brothers 2028
Turner Rothers 403
Turtle 6739-6741
Tuskaloosa Bottling Works 3211
Tuttle's Elixir Co. 2031
Dr. S. A. Tuttle's 2030
Dr. Tutt's 2029
T. & W. 3212
T. W. C. Co. 7330
Tweddles Celebrated Soda 3514
Twitchell 3213, 3215
G. S. Twitchell 3214
Two Fish Whiskey 4962
Tyler Bottling Works 3216
Tyler Union Bottling Works 3217
U. C. B. Co. 3218
U. D. O. 2316, 2317
Udolpho Wolfe's 2032-2037
Ullman & Co. 4963
Ulmar Mt. Ash Bitters 404
Dr. Ulrich 2038
Umbrella ink 6742-6753
Uncle Sam's 2039
Underwood 6754
John Underwood & Co. 6758
Underwood Inks 6755-6757
Underwood Spring 3515
Wm. Underwood & Co. 3219, 5543
Ungars Ofner Bitterwasser 3516, 3517
Union 4251, 4252, 6080
Union Beverage Co. 3220
Union Bottling Co. 3221
Union Bottling Work 3222
Union Brewing Co., Ltd. 4057
Union Fruit Jar 6081
Union Glass Works 3223, 3518
Union Ink Co. 6759-6761
Union Made C.B.B.A. 4964, 4965
Union Soda Water Co. 3224
Union Spring 3519
Union Square Company 4966
United Drug Co. 6082
United Glass Ltd. 6083
United States Brewing Co. 4058
U. S. A. Hospital Dept. 2041
U. S. Mail 4969
U. S. Marine Hospital 2040
U. S. Navy 5544
Universal 6083

Universal Bitters 405, 406
Universal L. F. & Co. 6084
Unka Bitters 407
Upham's Fresh Meat Cure 614
N. M. Uri & Co. 4967, 4968, 6340
A. Urmann 3226
Usaacson Seixas & Co. 408
Ute Chief of Mineral Water 3520
U2266 4253
Va. Brewing Co. 4059
Vacu-Top 6085
The Vacuum Seal 6086
Vail Bros. 7017
W. B. Vail 4970
Valentines 5545, 7018
Valley Park Bottling Works 3227
The Valve Jar Co. 6087, 6088
Van Antwerp's 2042
Van Buskirb's 7019
Van Duck's Genever 3773
Van Duzers 7331
S. Van Dyke 3774
H. Van Emden 3775
A. G. Van Nostrand 4060
Van Opsal & Co. 409
Van Scoy Chemical Co. 2043, 2044
Van Vleet & Co. 2046
The Vliet 6089
Dr. Van Werts 2047
Vancouver Soda Works 3228
Vandenburgh & Co. 3767-3770
J. Vandervalk & Co. 3771
Vanderveer's Medicated Gin 3772
J. H. Vangent 3776
A. Vanpraag & Co's 3777, 3778
Vanstans 2045
Vapo-Cresolene Co. 2318-2320
Varuna Mineral Water Wells 3521
Varwig & Son 4971
Vase 6341, 7332
Vaseline 2048, 2049
Vasogen 2050
C. J. Vath & Co. 4061
V. D. C. 5546
Vegetable Stomach Bitters 410
Velvetina 3522
Venable & Heyman 7333
L. Vereterra Oviedo 4972
Vermont Spring Saxe & Co. 3522
Vermont Stomach Bitters 411
The North Vernon Distilling Co. 4973
Vernon & O'Bryan 3229
Veronica Medicinal Spring Water 3523
Veronica Mineral Water 3524-3526
Veteran 6090
V. G. & C. 3779
VH & C 3780
Vhoytemaec 3781
V. H. P. 3782
VI 4974
Vichy Etat 3527
Vichy Water 3529
Vichy Water Cullums Spring 3528
John Vickery 3230
Vicks 2051
Vicksburg Steam Bottling Works 3231
The Victor 6091, 6092
Victoria Brewing Co. 4062, 4063
Victory 6093
Victory Hom-Pak Mason 6094
Victory Chemical Co. 2321
Vieux Cognac 4975
Vig-O 3232
VIII 3783
Vincent & Hathaway 3233
Vincent Hathaway & Co. 3234
Vin De Chapoteaut 7021
Vinegar 5547
Vinol 4976
Vin-Tone 2052
Violet Dulce 7022
Violin 4977-4981
Violin flask 4254
Virginia Fruit Juice Co. 3235, 5548
Virtray 7334
Daniel Visser & Zonen 3784
Viva Bottling Works 3236
Vogel Soda Water Co. 3238
The Charles A. Vogeler Co. 2053, 2054
Vogels Beverages 3237
VOGN 7023
Volgers Ink 6762
Albert Von Harten 3239, 3240
Von Harten & Grogan 3241
Dr. Von Hopf's 412
Voodoo face Jug 6342
VO2 7335
"W" 6096
W & Co. 6096
Wabash Bottling Works 3242
The Wacker & Birk Brewing Co. 4064
J. C. Wadleigh 2055
Wadsworth Liniment 615
Sidney O. Wagner 4065
Wagoner Bottling Works 3243
Wainscott's Distilled Waters 3244
Dr. R. B. Waites 2056, 2057
Wait's Wild Cherry Tonic 2058
Wakefields Berry Balsam 2059
Wakelee's Camelline 2060, 2061
Geo. E. Wales 6097
Walkdens Copying Ink 6343
The J. Walker Brewing Co. 4066
J. Walker Vinegar Bitters 413
Walkers Kilmarnook 4982
Walker's Tonic 2062
M. T. Wallace & Co. 5549
Wallaceburg Gem 6098

Walter's & Co. 4983
Walters Brothers & Co. 4984
Henry K. Wampole & Co. 2063–2068, 4067
Wan-eta Cocoa 6099, 6100
Samuel Ward & Co. 6763
Wardles 7336
Dr. Ward's 2069
Ward's Ink 6764
W. R. Warner & Co. 7337
Wm. R. Warner & Co. 2070–2075, 5550
Warner's Consumption Cure 623
Warners Imported 3785
Warner's Safe Animal Cure 616
Warners Safe Bitters 414
Warner's Safe Cure 617, 618
Warner's Safe Kidney & Liver Cure 619
Warner's Safe Nervine 622
Warners Safe Remedy 2077
Warner's Safe Rheumatic Cure 620, 621
Wm. Warners & Co. 2076
Warranted 4255, 4985–4988
Dr. Warren's 415
Warren's Mocking Bird Food 2078
Warsaw Pickle Co. 5551
The Warsaw Salt Co. 6101
H. S. Wartz & Co. 3245
Washington Brewing Co. 4068
G. Washington 4256
G. Washington & Albany 4257
G. Washington & A. Jackson 4258
G. Washington & T. Jefferson 4259
G. Washington & sheaf of wheat 4260
G. Washington & Z. Taylor 4261–4265
Washington Spring 3530, 3531
Washingtonian Sarsaparilla 2079
Waterlow & Sons 6344, 6765
L. E. Waterman Co. 6766
Waters Bros. Olive Oil 5552
E. Waters 6767, 7338
Waters Ink 6768
Watkins Chill Tonic 2080
Watkins Dandruff Remover 2081
The J. R. Watkins Co. 2083, 2084
J. R. Watkins Medical Co. 2085–2087
Watkins Trialmark 2082
Watson Bilton Park 3786
Watson's Pharmacy 2088
W. B. & Co. 7024
W. D. Co. 2093
W D S 5553
Weacle Vestry 3246
Wears Jar 6102
Webb & Riley 3247
Webbs 3248
Joseph Weber 3249
Louis Weber 4989
Web's A No. 1 2089
Webster Little 2090
R. B. Webster 3250
Weedon Drug Co. 2091
A. Wegener & Sons 3251
Weideman Boy Brand 6103
H. Weigel 3252
The Weir 6104
Weir Seal 6105
C Weisbecker 5554
Weiss Bier 3787
Edward Weiss 4990
J. W. Welch 3253
Wellcome Chemical Works 5555
Weller Bottling Works 3532
Geo. Weller 3254
The J. Weller Co. 5556
R. Weller 3255
Wells & Richardson Co. 5557
Wesson Oil 6345
Dr. T. West 2092
The West Electric Cure Co. 624
West End 4069
West End Old Timers Beer 4991
West End Wine & Spirits Co. 4992
Western 3257
Western Pride 6106
Western Stoneware Co. 6346
Westford Glass Co. 4267
Chas. Westerholm & Co. 3256
Ferdinand Westheimer & Sons 4993–4995
G. W. Weston & Co. 3533, 3534
Weyman Bruton Co. Snuff 7339
Weymans Snuff 6347, 6348
W. F. & Co. 7347, 7348
W. F. & G. P. 4070
W. F. & S. 3258, 4071–4073, 4996

W. & H. Walker 7025
Wharton Chemical Co. 7340
Wharton's Whiskey 4997
J. B. Wheatleys 2094
Wheaton 6107
H. Wheaton & Sons 3260
Hiram Wheaton & Sons 3259
Wheeler 6108
Wheeler Bros. 3261
Wheeler & Co. 3262
Dr. Wheeler's Tonic 416
Wheeler's Tissue Phosphates 2095
Wheeling, Va. 4266
Wheelock Finlay & Co. 2096
D. J. Whelan 3536
Whelan Troy 3535
C. T. Whipple Prop. 625
Whiskbroom 4268
Whiskey 4998–5080
Whiskey flask 4269
Whiskey, label 6349
J. M. Whitall 6769
Whitall's 6109, 6110
A. J. White 2097
A. J. White Curative 626
White & Co. 2098
White Crown Mason 6111
White-Hall 6351
N. A. White & Sons 6350
R. White 7341
R. White & Sons 3788
White Rose 7026
White Rye 5081
White Spring Co. 3263
White Sulphur Water 3537
W. P. White 3264
White Wine and Tar Syrup 2103
Whitehurst 2101, 2102
William Whiteley Leith 5082, 5083
White's Cream 2099
White's Liniment 2100
White's Quick Healing Cure 627
Whitewell's Temperence Bitters 417
Whitney Mason 6112, 6113
Whittemore 7342, 7343
Whittemore Bros. & Co. 6770
Whyte & Mackay 7344
H. Wickert 5558
Wiedemann 4074
J. T. Wiggins 418
Wilcox 6114
Wild Cherry Bitters 419
Edw. Wilder & Co. 420, 7345
Will you take a drink? 4271
Williams Bros. 3265
The Williams Bros. Co. 5559
Williams & Carleton 6771
George W. Williams & Co. 6772
Williams Magnetic Relief 2104
S. M. Williams 3266
Willington Glass Co. 4270
Willits Soda Works 3267
Wills & Co. 6115
Wilmerding & Co. 421
C. C. Wilson 3268
Wilson Fairbank & Co. 2105
J. H. Wilson 2106
The Wilson Laboratories 2107
Dr. Wilson's Herbine Bitters 422, 423
Winans Bros. 628
Winchester Crystal Cleaner 2108
J. Winchester 2109
Wine 5084–5112
Wing Lee Wai 6352
Wingfield 2110
Henry Winkle 3269
Winslow Jar 6116
Mrs. Winslow's Soothing Syrup 2111–2113
Winstead's 2114
Herman Winter 3270, 3271
Winter and Summer flask 4272, 4273
Wintergreen Cure 629
Wintersmith 2115, 2116
W. Wintersmith 7346
A. J. Wintle & Sons 3272, 5113
Jacob Wirth & Co., Inc. 3273
Wisconsin Select Beer 4075
Wiseola Bottling Co. 3274, 3275
L. Q. C. Wishart's 424
L. Q. C. Wishart's Cordial 2117
Dr. Wistar's Balsam 2118-2122
Dr. Wisters 425
Witch Hazel 7027

Witter Medical Springs Co. 3538, 3440
W. M. 5114
Woapollinaris-Brannen 6353
Wolfe's 2123
Wolfstirns Remedy 2124
The P. H. Wolters Brewing Co. 3276, 4076
That Wondrous Liniment 2125
Dr. Wonser's 426, 427
Wood Cooper Olive Oil 5560
Wood Great Peppermint Cure 630
N. Wood & Son 2127
Wood Pollard & Co. 5115
Woodard Clark & Co. 2128
Woodbury 6117, 6120
Woodbury Improved 6118, 6119
Woodbury's Bitters 428
Woodman's 3789
Woods Black Ink 6773
Wood's Pine Syrup 2126
Wood's Tonic 429
Woolridge Wonderful Cure Co. 631
Wootan Wells Co. 3277
Worcester 6121
Wormer Bros. 5116–5120
Worrell & Foster 6354
W. & P. Co. 3278
Alfred Wright 7028
Wright-Clarkson Merc. Co. 6774
Joshua Wright 6122
The Wright Rapid Relief Co. 2129
Wright & Taylor Distillers 5121, 5122
W. S. Wright 3279
Wrights 3280
Wright's Condensed Smoke 2130
Writewell & Co. Ink 6775
W. R. W. & Co. 2322
Wryghte's Bitters 430
W. S. S. Water 3541
W & T 2135
W. T. Co. 2131–2134, 3281
W. T. & Co. 7029, 7349–7351
W. T. U. D. Co. 2136
Wunder Bottling Co. 4077, 4078
W. & W. 3282
Wyeth 2137–2140
Wyeth & Bro. 2141–2143, 5123
John Wyeth 2144
John Wyeth & Bro. 2145–2152, 2324, 5124, 5125
John Wyeth & Co. 2323
Wyeth Poison 2325, 2326
WyKoop's 632
Dr. Wynkcops 2153
Wyokoff & Co. Bluing 7352
X 6355
X Bazin Sucerto 7353
X-Lalia 2154
XNOX 6123
XXX 3542
Y 4079
Yager's Sarsaparilla 2155
Yale 6776
Yale Bottling Co. 3283
Madame M. Yale Co. 2156
Yazoo Valley Bitters 431
Ye Old Mossroff Bourbon 5126
Yelone Jar 6124
Yeoman's Fruit Bottle 6125
Yerba Buena Bitters 432, 433
J. H. Yetter 3285
Yetter & Moore 3284
Yochim Bros. 434
Mrs. J. M. Yockers 6356
Yoerg Brewing Co. 4080
Adam W. Young 3543
Ben Lee Young 2157, 2158
Geo. Young California Pop Beer 4081
Philip Young & Co. 3286
Theo. Young 4082
Dr. Young's Wild Cherry Bitters 435
Yucatan Chill-Tonic 2159
Zanesville City Glass Works 4274, 4275
Zanesville, Ohio 4276
Zarembo Mineral Spring Co. 3544
Zeller Schwarze Katz 5127, 5128
Zemo Cures Eczemee 633
Mrs. B. Z. Zimmerman 3287
Zingari Bitters 436
Otto J. Zipperer 3288
Zipps 2160, 2161
Zoa-Phora 2162, 2163
Zoeler's Stomach Bitters 437
ZuZu Bitters 438
Zwack 5129